HELL AND ITS RIVALS

uenia ego spiciosus & mul
to misericors & pius sui
su puos. Dñs dix ad sco pau
lo; Cesto tibi dico. paren
tes tuos usqz ad nono ge
nuculo mis sus est came
los in euangtio uocatur
finis multas qui parentes
sci pauli. traxer deinfer
no; Serm Scti Aug epi :

Primu qui dem deca
nos audire iustitiam
di. dem de intellegere. p'
Intellegentiu fructum
red dere doctrinarum;
Quia nihil pdest audire

HELL AND ITS RIVALS

DEATH AND RETRIBUTION AMONG CHRISTIANS, JEWS, AND MUSLIMS IN THE EARLY MIDDLE AGES

ALAN E. BERNSTEIN

CORNELL UNIVERSITY PRESS

Ithaca and London

First published 2017 by Cornell University Press

Printed in the United States of America

Library of Congress Cataloging-in-Publication Data

Names: Bernstein, Alan E., author.
Title: Hell and its rivals : death and retribution among
    Christians, Jews, and Muslims in the early Middle
    Ages / Alan E. Bernstein.
Description: Ithaca : Cornell University Press, 2017. |
    Includes bibliographical references and index.
Identifiers: LCCN 2016051661 (print) | LCCN 2016052966
    (ebook) | ISBN 9781501707803 (cloth : alk. paper) |
    ISBN 9781501712487 (epub/mobi) |
    ISBN 9781501712494 (pdf)
Subjects: LCSH: Hell—Comparative studies. | Hell—
    Christianity—History of doctrines—Middle Ages,
    600–1500. | Hell—Islam—History of doctrines—
    Middle Ages, 600–1500. | Hell—Judaism—History of
    doctrines—Middle Ages, 600–1500.
Classification: LCC BL545 .B47 2017 (print) | LCC BL545
    (ebook) | DDC 202/.3—dc23
LC record available at https://lccn.loc.gov/2016051661

Cornell University Press strives to use environmentally responsible suppliers and materials to the fullest extent possible in the publishing of its books. Such materials include vegetable-based, low-VOC inks and acid-free papers that are recycled, totally chlorine-free, or partly composed of nonwood fibers. For further information, visit our website at www.cornellpress.cornell.edu.

CONTENTS

PREFACE

Hell is one of the most influential and vexing of religious ideas. For some it is a basic element of faith; for others it is a reason to reject religion altogether. In between, many wonder how divine justice and mercy can be reconciled. Whatever one's position, even hell's deniers know what it is. Hell became a fixture in European religion, social life, and political thought in the first centuries of the Common Era, yet the story of how it came to have this strategic position is not at all simple. Greco-Roman ideas and biblical Judaism together shaped the presentation of hell in the Christian Scriptures and the patristic period, a thesis I argued in an earlier work, *The Formation of Hell*. Here, I examine the next phase, from ca. 400 to ca. 800, when Jews, Christians, and Muslims explored various ideas of life, death, justice, and mercy to shape what became a common perception of the punitive afterlife.

Because Judaism, Christianity, and Islam (the "Abrahamic" religions) all adopted an eternal hell, their hells have more in common than the distinctive elements of their respective creeds. Further, each tradition had to meet similar challenges: the rivals to hell. Briefly put, hell's rivals are these: escape, periodic relief, and purification. All may be saved; hell exists but can be modified; hell exists, but individuals may be rescued from it or may be released through purification. Debates over these positions have lasted for centuries and, in some ways, still endure.

As long as I could, I resisted the conclusion that these religions shared similar eschatological ideas because they are monotheistic, yet that conclusion appears inescapable. Indeed, the teachings about postmortem punishment in Judaism, Christianity, and Islam derive from their monotheism. Without monotheism no one would ask whether God's justice is consistent with his mercy. Another indication of this homologous relationship is that each religion faced challenges to its views on hell from roughly the same directions. Supporting this statement requires close reading of many different texts, a task for the following chapters.

The authors we are about to examine communicate their ideas in various ways, as if on different levels. They teach the "highest," most abstract theology. They preach the gritty imagery of exemplary tales that draw the audience in and reinforce doctrinal conclusions. They report the visions of those "returned" from the land of the dead. They record the intentions of their charitable gifts. Because each source, and sometimes each sentence in a source, occupies its own position in this range of expression, it is necessary to consider each one as having its own point of view.

Given this range of levels, it follows that doctrinal declarations form only part of the story. Attending to theological conclusions alone would ignore the concern the authors invested in balancing fear of hell against love of God. This emotional side of the subject includes many associated issues that pure theology does not address. The thought of others involves not only their conclusions, but also their rationale. It is therefore vital to include data reported as directly seen (visionary literature) and oral traditions. One author to be examined below compares this range of levels to the different depths of flowing eloquence. This stream accommodates every hearer from the practiced expert who can dive below the surface to the beginner who only wades along the beach. For this reason, I investigate hell from the many different rhetorical levels we find in our sources: dogmatic, theological, philosophical, homiletic, visionary, and anecdotal. These levels of discourse and the different perspectives each one yields exist in Judaism and Islam as well as Christianity. Therefore I shall apply this method to hell belief in all three faiths and at all these levels.

In *Formation*, I emphasized how the idea of hell fit within an overarching judicial system. Here, I examine the infernal pains in detail and explore their links to social institutions. It is not my wish to reduce the idea of hell to a social function, but that is not to deny that it has one (or several). There is an understandable correspondence between the severest penalties in human criminal justice and in the universe ruled by a King of kings, a divine Lord. As opposed to the theology of hell, the history of hell cannot be understood without appreciating the interaction of religious and political patterns of thought.

Although the following chapters are not arranged chronologically, I have tried to maintain a rigorous respect for the meanings of words as they existed at the time the sources used them. Failure to respect the evolution of ideas over time can lead to fundamental misunderstandings. For instance, I have discovered a distinction between Hades and hell, two terms frequently treated as synonymous today. But the difference between Hades and hell is crucial, and coming to terms with it opens many doors. The same is true for the concepts to which words point. For instance, the fit between a crime and its punishment, the proportionality of penalty to offense, the understanding of severity as time served versus pain applied: these notions interacted in fascinating ways to produce what was much later called Purgatory. But if that term is carelessly applied to any antecedent notion that seems to anticipate it, the agony of debate about God and divine justice risks being lost.

Writing this book has also taught me that the study of a concept can benefit from the simultaneous examination of what it is not. Applying this method rejects any binary distinction between the concept and its opposite, between hell and "not-hell" or hell and heaven. Instead, important nuances appeared when I studied hell and its fringes, the darkness and its penumbra. Since hell is sometimes imagined as an abyss, one might say the trick is to study not just the chasm, but the geographical (and moral) inclinations that end there.

The same principle applies to the paths not taken. If the establishment of hell as a fixed concept in Western religious thought required a gradual evolution, then the threats to its survival must be identified and examined. The benefits of taking this more inclusive approach repay the effort because, as history tells us, hell is simply too important an idea to accept it unquestionably as a fixed essence. Not even its presence in Scripture gave it this status, because opponents could cite contrary proof texts in the Bible and raise other obstacles that had to be dealt with before hell could be clearly separated from the alternatives objectors presented.

For that reason this book examines how the three religions treat three key subjects: hell, its denial, and its mitigation. It proceeds in three stages. Part I, "Foundations," outlines the structural and conceptual background. Part II, "Alternatives to Hell," expounds the principal arguments against the absolute restriction of postmortem punishment to hell proper. Part III, "Hell in Abrahamic Religions," shows how hell's three rivals (no hell, mitigated hell, and an end to hell) are examined in Judaism, Eastern Christianity, and Islam.

Acknowledgments

During the years I have studied the history of belief in hell, institutions, scholars, and friends (and scholar-friends) have encouraged me in many different ways. Beginning with institutions, I thank the Department of History at the University of Arizona, my academic home for over twenty years. A welcome base for my teaching, the U of A also provided me with sabbaticals and a year's appointment as Research Professor. I have twice been a member at the Institute for Advanced Study, Princeton, and enjoyed its unparalleled resources and the stimulation of many colleagues. The School of Law at the University of California, Berkeley, has admitted me as a visiting scholar. I have received funding from the National Endowment for the Humanities.

Many persons have aided me with encouragement and particular insights whose impact will be visible here. Jacques Le Goff once welcomed me into postmortem studies when he shook my hand and said, "Very well, Mr. Bernstein, now we are neighbors in the other world." The late Donald Weinstein suggested the book's title, counseled me extensively on matters of style, and critiqued my ideas as I worked on them. Charles King taught me of the Roman manes. Oleg Grabar wryly observed that he could see why one might invent a heaven, but why hell?—a useful provocation. Peter Brown's suggestion that I consider melancholy in relation to hell aided the discovery of inner death. Anna Kartsonis indicated a fruitful path when she remarked, "There is no harrowing of hell!" Isabel Moreira was my sparring partner on Purgatory. Yohanan Friedmann and Mohammad Khalil have coached me in matters of Islam, J. Edward Wright on Judaism, and Jesse Torgerson on Greek terminology. Giles Constable mentored me during my visits to the Institute for Advanced Study, and Laurent Mayali at Berkeley.

Many colleagues and friends have encouraged me through their interest in the project. Within the academy I wish to thank Polly Aird, Jérôme Baschet, Jonathan Beck, Elizabeth A. R. Brown, Marcia Colish, Momodou Darboe, Richard Eaton, Edward English, A. J. Figueredo, Patrick Geary, Piotr Gorecki, Joscelin Hillgarth, Kathryn Jasper, Paul R. Katz, Geoffrey Koziol,

Richard Landes, Carol Lansing, Kathryn Larch, J. Hilary Martin, Elisabeth Mégier, Maureen Miller, Franco Morenzoni, Heiko Oberman, Elaine Pagels, Frederick Paxton, MuChou Poo, Nasser Rabat, Kevin Roddy, Guido Ruggiero, Jeffrey Burton Russell, Francesca Weinmann, and among ideal lay readers, Henry Berman, Howard Gitlin, and Beverly Parker.

In addition I feel indebted to some people with whom I have no personal relationship but upon whom I have come to depend for the utility and reliability of their work. They have been guides through the labor whose results are presented here: Marc Adriaen, Mary Boyce, Claude Carozzi, José Costa, Samuel J. Fox, Eileen Gardiner, Martha Himmelfarb, M. R. James, Hanna E. Kassis, Ramsay MacMullen, Theodore Silverstein, Jeffrey Trumbower, Adalbert de Vogüé. There are also many other editors, translators, librarians, authors of websites, compilers of databases, and other types of researchers and publishers whose labors greatly facilitated completion of this comparative history.

The greatest recognition of all goes to my wife and life's companion, JoAnne Gitlin Bernstein, a fine scholar herself, who has supported the vagaries of this investigation over many years. Her questions, suggestions, and editorial acumen all helped me endure the writing process and greatly improved the final product. To her I owe an indescribable debt, and thus I dedicate the book to her.

ABBREVIATIONS

AA	*Apocrypha Anecdota.* Ed. Montague Rhodes James. In *Texts and Studies*, ed. J. Armitage Robinson, vol. 2, no. 3. Cambridge: Cambridge University Press, 1893.
ANT	M. R. James. *The Apocryphal New Testament.* Oxford: Clarendon, 1924.
BT	*The Babylonian Talmud Translated into English.* Ed. Isidore Epstein. 34 vols. London: The Soncino Press, 1935–52.
Carozzi, *Le voyage*	Claude Carozzi. *Le voyage de l'âme dans l'au-delà d'après la littérature latine: Ve–XIIIe siècle.* Collection de l'École Française de Rome 189. Rome: École française de Rome; Paris: Boccard, 1994.
CCCM	Corpus Christianorum: Continuatio Mediaevalis. Turnhout, Belgium: Brepols, 1966–.
CCSL	Corpus Christianorum: Series Latina. Turnhout, Belgium: Brepols, 1953–.
CSEL	Corpus Scriptorum Ecclesiasticorum Latinorum. 1866–.
CTh	(Codex Theodosianus) *Les lois religieuses des empereurs romains de Constantin à Théodose II (312–438).* Vol. 1, *Code Théodosien, Livre XVI*, ed. Theodor Mommsen, trans. Jean Rougé, with Roland Delmaire and François Richard. SC 497. Paris: Éditions du Cerf, 2005. Vol. 2, *Code Théodosien, Livres I–XV*, ed. Theodor Mommsen, trans. Jean Rougé. SC 531. Paris: Éditions du Cerf, 2009. Original edition: *Theodosiani Libri XVI*, ed. Theodor Mommsen, Paul M. Meyer, and Jacques Sirmond (Berlin: Weidmann, 1905); English translation: *The Theodosian Code and Novels, and the Sirmondian Constitutions*, trans. Clyde Pharr (Princeton, NJ: Princeton University Press, 1952).
D	(Justinian's Digest, Digesta Justiniani) *The Digest of Justinian.* Ed. Theodor Mommsen with Paul Krueger, English

translation ed. Alan Watson. 4 vols. Philadelphia: University of Pennsylvania Press, 1985.

D-S   *Enchiridion symbolorum.* Ed. H. Denzinger and A. Schönmetzer. 34th ed. Barcelona: Herder, 1967.

DTC   *Dictionnaire de théologie catholique.* Paris: Letouzey et Ané, 1903–50.

EEC   *Encyclopedia of the Early Church.* Ed. Angelo di Berardina, trans. Adrian Walford. 2 vols. New York: Oxford University Press, 1992.

H-S   *New Testament Apocrypha.* Ed. Edgar Hennecke and Wilhelm Schneemelcher, trans. R. McL. Wilson. 2 vols. Philadelphia: Westminster, 1963–65.

LADR   José Costa. *L'au-delà et la résurrection dans la littérature rabbinique ancienne.* Paris and Louvain: Peeters, 2004.

LCL   Loeb Classical Library. Cambridge, MA: Harvard University Press.

MGH   Monumenta Historica Germaniae
 AA   Auctores Antiquissimi
 Capit.   Capitularia Regum Francorum. Legum Sectio II, Vol. 1, ed. Alfred Boretius. Hannover: Hahn, 1883. Vol. 2, ed. Alfred Boretius and Victor Krause. Hannover: Hahn, 1897.
 SS   Scriptores (in folio).
 SS RR MM   Scriptores Rerum Merovingicarum.

MRTS   Medieval and Renaissance Texts and Studies.

NPNF-1   *A Select Library of Nicene and Post-Nicene Fathers.* Series 1. Ed. Philip Schaff. 14 vols. New York: Scribner, 1898–1909.

NPNF-2   *A Select Library of Nicene and Post-Nicene Fathers.* Series 2. Ed. Philip Schaff and Henry Wace. 14 vols. New York: The Christian Literature Co., 1890–1900.

OCD   *The Oxford Classical Dictionary.* Ed. Simon Hornblower and Antony Spawforth. 3rd ed. Oxford: Oxford University Press, 1996.

ODCC   *The Oxford Dictionary of the Christian Church.* Ed. F. L. Cross and E. A. Livingstone. 3rd ed. Oxford: Oxford University Press, 1997.

PG   (Patrologia Graeca) Patrologiae Cursus Completus: Series Graeca. Ed. J.-P. Migne. 166 vols. Paris, 1857–66.

PL   (Patrologia Latina). Patrologiae Cursus Completus. Series Latina. Ed. J-P Migne. 221 vols. Paris, 1844–1902.

SC   Sources chrétiennes. Paris: Les Éditions du Cerf, 1942–.

HELL AND ITS RIVALS

Introduction

> Their own souls and their own conception did vex them
> when they reached the Bridge of the Judge, (there) to
> become guests in the House of Deceit forever.
>
> —*The Gāthās of Zarathustra*, Y 46:11

> Their worm shall not die, their fire shall not be
> quenched.
>
> —Isaiah 66:24

> It is better for you to enter the kingdom of God
> with one eye than with two eyes to be thrown into
> Gehenna where their worm does not die, and the fire
> is not quenched.
>
> —Mark 9:47–48

"A divinely sanctioned place of eternal torment for the wicked," hell emerged as a distinct concept from roots in the ancient cultures of Egypt, Persia, the classical thought of Greece and Rome, the Hebrew Bible, and the Christian Scriptures.[1] During the first millennium of the Common Era and well into the second, hell was a crucial element of religion, social life, and political thought in the Jewish, Christian, and Muslim worlds, but this development was far from linear. *Hell and Its Rivals* elucidates the debates concerning postmortem punishment in the three Abrahamic faiths—Judaism, Christianity, and Islam—during the formative period from ca. 400 to ca. 800 CE.

These three religions shared faith in many aspects of eschatology—the branch of theology that concerns the end (*eschaton*) of an individual's life and the end of time. Links between these eschatological beliefs take many forms. For example, the rabbis of this period advanced a very concrete hell they called Gehinnom, a term still used by Orthodox Jews. Muslims affirm the power of Jahannam, a transliteration of the Hebrew name for the same hell that Christians transliterate as Gehenna. As this book will show, the common

---

1. Definition from Alan E. Bernstein, *The Formation of Hell: Death and Retribution in the Ancient and Early Christian Worlds* (Ithaca, NY: Cornell University Press, 1993), 3.

features of eschatological faith transcend the etymology of any one term. Opposition to eternal punishment arose within each of these religions, and each entertained alternative beliefs about how wickedness in life might be punished in death.

Some believed divinely sanctioned torment could (by definition) only benefit those who experience it, and, as a result, the recipient would improve to the same level of goodness as at creation. There would be no need for further punishment; the soul would rejoin God. Others argued that escape was possible from hell as a result of prayers from pious kin or heavenly intercessors. Another idea held that on important occasions (the Sabbath, Sunday, Easter) within the religion rejected by the damned, relief from suffering would nonetheless be granted to them. Cure, escape, and periodic relief—not the other monotheistic religions—were the chief rivals to uniform and eternal perdition. Hell survived these threats, and, in the process of defending it, its advocates used the idea as a model of justice, a spur to right behavior, a guide to introspection, and a warning to neighbors in danger of damnation if they did not accept it and learn to respect the God whose sentence it executes.

Within the Abrahamic religions, at different times and in different ways, theological challenges and defenses by the most sophisticated thinkers mixed with other beliefs expressed at different levels of discourse. There arose a rich literature of visions, in which people "saw" into the afterlife and reported back on hell's torments. There was a remarkable sensitivity in visionary literature to the penumbra that surrounds hell itself. Far from envisioning a binary situation that divides the saved from the damned, heaven from hell, thinkers of this early period saw a gradual decline into sin and therefore into hell. Their visions largely avoided hell proper in favor of an abyss surrounded by a fringe or border area rife with potential for intermediate punishments and varied solutions to the problem of evil.

Hell was no abstraction for those we study here. It cannot be removed from broader questions of life and death, good and evil, intergenerational family ties, friends and enemies, order and chaos. Above all, hell involves the question of justice. Judaism, Christianity, and Islam shared many principles in approaching these questions of theodicy—the attempt to resolve the conflict between God's omnipotence and goodness on the one hand and the evil humans perceive on the other. Hell is important to theodicy because, to be just, it must punish genuine evil, but if God were omnipotent and good, there should be no evil. Within this theodicial context, the Abrahamic religions came to a common belief in a final judgment separating the just from the unjust and the everlasting punishment of the wicked. Remarkably, similar objections to eternal punishment arose in the three religions, but, more remarkable still, they each found similar ways to resist opposition within their particular belief systems. In the process, these communities affirmed a single place to discipline both the wayward of their own community temporarily and wicked "others" eternally.

Concepts of Death in the Ancient Mediterranean World

The religious idea of death fundamental to hell is one of several competing views found simultaneously in the ancient Mediterranean world. To understand this concept, which I call "moral death," it is best to contrast it to two other, competing ideas: "porous" and "neutral" death. Under porous death the boundary separating the living from the dead can be penetrated easily. The dead and the living interact. Spirits of the dead, parents, ancestors, return to guide the living or to make demands on them. The most famous example of this porosity in European literature is the ghost of Hamlet's father, who visits his living son to demand that the young prince avenge his murder. Far earlier, in the eleventh tablet of the *Epic of Gilgamesh*, the dead Enkidu explains the nature of the otherworld to his friend, the ruling king. In Homer's *Iliad*, the departed Patroclus prods Achilles to bury him (23.70–71). Sometimes the living prolong their bond with the dead to honor them and their principles. In his work *On the Republic*, Cicero has Scipio the African dream of the ghost of his grandfather, with whom he engages in dialogue about how civic obligations in the Roman Republic fit the structure of the universe, leading to eternal reward for patriots. In the Bible, a woman at Endor violates the law at the king's command and summons the ghost of Samuel for Saul. Samuel appears unwillingly and, with barely concealed anger at being "disturbed," foretells Saul's coming disgrace (1 Sam. 28:15).[2]

Eventually, as in the Near East during the third and second millennia BCE, the living wished to end these hauntings and gradually moved toward the idea of neutral death. They effectively banished their dead. In neutral death, the living imagine the dead surviving as shades or spirits confined in their own land of no return, ruled, in some systems, by the gods of the underworld, who prevent their escape. Here the fact of being dead defines their existence; how they lived their lives is of no importance. Death under this concept is neutral because the dead are not judged. The living were

---

2. An excellent historical overview of ghosts: R. C. Finucane, *Appearances of the Dead: A Cultural History of Ghosts* (Buffalo, NY: Prometheus Books, 1984). More specialized is D. Felton, *Haunted Greece and Rome: Ghost Stories from Classical Antiquity* (Austin: University of Texas Press, 1999). More comprehensive is MuChou Poo, ed., *Rethinking Ghosts in World Religions* (Leiden: Brill, 2009).

more concerned with putting their parents and ancestors at a distance than in evaluating them.

Neutral death did not exclude a moral code. Especially in certain books of the Hebrew Bible, it measured the moral quality of the living according to a covenant with God. In "covenant theology," or the "Deuteronomic code," obedience to the divine law provides prosperity and long life; spurning the commandments brings adversity and early death (Deut. 30:15–18; see also Deut. 11:26–28, and, in general, all of Deut. 11). Reward and punishment for one's adherence to the law (as revealed in the Torah) come in life. The sign of divine favor was prosperity and length of days (Deut. 30:20; Ps. 21:4; Prov. 3:2, 16). Early or ignominious death punishes impiety and disobedience. "Whoever has sinned against me, him will I blot out of my book" (Exod. 32:33).[3] With life conducted under these terms, death itself could, indeed, be neutral. There is no punishment for the dead; the end of life is itself a death sentence. However important the contrasts between them, these types of belief—porous, neutral, and moral death—are not historical periods; they are psychological states. Moral death may have arrived as an external influence and encountered some resistance before both ancient Greece and ancient Israel adopted it alongside their age-old views of porous and neutral death.[4] Once in place, these views of death came to exist simultaneously, blend, and compete.

Moral Death

The three faiths arrived at similar results in their eschatological reflections in part because they shared the idea of dividing the dead into good persons who receive rewards in the afterlife and evil persons who receive punishment—"moral death." The concept of moral death first divides the dead in ancient Egypt. Images from the *Book of Gates* show the afterlife fate of those who oppose the sun god, Re, as he progresses through the underworld at night to be resurrected at dawn each day. These were deniers of rebirth and enemies of Osiris, the god who is its symbol, bound and dispatched into immense ovens, whose flames consume them. The *Book of Gates* also shows a fire-breathing serpent annihilating human souls represented as prisoners, hands tied behind their backs. Texts inscribed on the inner walls of pyramids

---

3. See Bernstein, *Formation*, 133–53, esp. 146–51.

4. Shaul Shaked, "Iranian Influence on Judaism," in *The Cambridge History of Judaism* (Cambridge: Cambridge University Press, 1984), 1:308–25; Shaked, *Dualism in Transformation: Varieties of Religion in Sasanian Iran*, Jordan Lectures 1991 (University of London: School of Oriental and African Studies, 1994).

or tombs or on papyrus scrolls like the *Book of the Dead*, which began to circulate in the sixteenth century BCE, judged the deceased for their moral behavior. In one version of the *Book of the Dead*, the Papyrus of Ani, the soul of the deceased is symbolized by a heart in the pan to the viewer's left and weighed against a feather symbolizing *Ma'at*, the Egyptian concept of truth, justice, and order, in the pan to the right. If it balances properly, the soul will live on, if not, it is destroyed, sometimes horribly. Anubis regulates the balance, Thoth records the decision, and behind him, Ammit, the Devourer, a part-hippopotamus, part-leopard, crocodile-headed monster, waits to consume the hearts of those found wanting. Although in ancient Egypt the wayward are destroyed rather than punished forever, this judgment and division constitute moral death.

THE BRIDGE OF JUDGMENT: MORAL DEATH IN ZOROASTRIANISM

Equally poised to influence both ancient Israel and Greece was Zoroastrianism, another religious system that divided the dead into righteous and wicked. Zoroastrianism descends from its prophet Zoroaster (also called Zarathustra), who probably lived in the late second millennium BCE.[5] It was the dominant religion in Persia under the Achaemenid dynasty (559–331) until that regime fell to Alexander the Great. Later, Ardashir I, who founded the Sassanian or Sassanid dynasty in 226 CE, reestablished Zoroastrianism. After Islamic troops took over Persia in the seventh century CE, Zoroastrianism survived only in the Parsi communities of India. The Persians formed the great, rival power to the east of Greece in its classical age, and the Sassanids competed with imperial Rome for influence from Asia Minor to the Indus River.[6]

As presented in the Yasnas, traditionally ascribed to Zoroaster himself, Zoroastrianism proposes a distinctive view of the world as a conflict between two competing lords or spirits, one good and one evil, who oppose each other in thought, word, and action (Yasna 30:2–4). These opposing spirits are life and death, good and evil, truth and deceit. Each individual must chose between them. In the end, there will be a Great Retribution, when it will be

---

5. Mary Boyce estimates 1500–1200 BCE. Boyce, *A History of Zoroastrianism* (Leiden: Brill, 1975, 1982) 1:3–7 and 2:1–3. See also Peter Kingsley, "The Greek Origin of the Sixth-Century Dating of Zoroaster," *Bulletin of the School of Oriental and African Studies, University of London* 53.2 (1990): 245–65.

6. Mary Boyce, *Zoroastrians: Their Religious Beliefs and Practices* (London and Boston: Routledge & Kegan Paul, 1985).

seen that those who have chosen good have chosen correctly. Those who have chosen deceit will have the Worst Existence (resembling hell), but the truthful person will have the Best Thinking (resembling heaven).[7] This worldview is commonly called dualism, as it seems to posit a cosmos divided between opposed, eternal forces of good and evil. That is not a fully accurate characterization of Zoroastrianism because the Persian faith surrounds the epoch in which good and evil conflict (the present age) with an original period of pristine harmony and surpasses history with a new period of happiness under a single, Wise Lord after the destruction of all evil, including hell.

At the end of the conflict that marks our current world, good and evil forces separate. Truth divides itself from The Lie. The means of separation became one of the most influential images in the depiction of moral death. Zoroastrian judgment between the good and the wicked occurs on a Bridge of Judgment, the Cinvat Bridge, over which only the righteous can cross to an afterlife of bliss. Those who fail plunge to an eternity of unspeakable torments.[8] To be sure, the Egyptian *Book of the Dead* also presents a version of moral death, with judgment by the weighing of the heart. Yet the Egyptian judgment appears to have had few repercussions for several centuries. Conversely, the Zoroastrian expression, which arose prior to and geographically contiguous with the ancient Hebrews and Greeks, seems to have been an important stimulus to their eventual adoption of moral death together with, if not to the exclusion, of neutral death.

Yasna 46 condenses these basic ideas. Apparently in communication with the beneficent Lord, Zoroaster meditates about the different character and different fates of the good and the wicked. "That person is deceitful who is extremely good to the deceitful man, and that person is truthful for whom the truthful man is a friend" (Y 46:6). Zoroaster foretells how they will be separated. "I shall accompany in the glory of your kind—with all these I shall cross over the Bridge of the Judge" (Y 46:10). That is, Zoroaster himself will defend the friends of truth as they cross the Test Bridge. By contrast, the Test Bridge will reveal the evil nature of the friends of deceit. This is the essence of a structure that subsequently shaped Judaism, Christianity, and Islam: opposed forces will, at a climactic Judgment, be separated into good and evil and correspondingly receive reward or punishment. Zoroaster's rivals and the enemies of his people, he reveals, "yoked (us) with evil

---

7. *The Gāthās of Zarathustra*, trans. S. Insler, Acta Iranica 8 (Leiden: Brill, 1975), 33.

8. Michael Stausberg, "Hell in Zoroastrian History," *Numen* 56 (2009): 217–53, at 231. See also J. Gwynn Griffiths, *The Divine Verdict: A Study of Divine Judgement in the Ancient Religions*, Studies in the History of Religions (Supplements to *Numen*) 52 (Leiden: Brill, 1991), 242–51.

actions in order to destroy the world and mankind. But their own souls and their own conception did vex them when they reached the Bridge of the Judge, (there) to become guests in the House of Deceit forever" (Y 46:11). The "House of Deceit" is hell.[9] This is the earliest reference I know to this crucial eschatological image: the bridge as a measure, a rule, a gauge. By this technique, among others, the Good Lord will resolve the conflict of good and evil communities by distributing followers of either camp into separate fates in a new, eschatological time—a time of universal judgment according to moral character. Later, in the Sassanian period of the third to the seventh century CE, texts in Middle Persian (or Pahlavi) described the punishments to be endured by friends of deceit. In particular, the *Ardā Wirāz Nāmag* (The Vision of the Pious Viraf) provides excruciatingly detailed accounts of torments afflicting the wicked, but most notably offers an extended account of trial on the Bridge of Judgment, the Cinvat Bridge.[10]

From Hades to Tartarus: Moral Death in Ancient Greece

The division of the dead seen earlier in Egypt and Persia also came to Greece. In ancient Greece, Hesiod, who wrote around 700 BCE, describes how the Olympian gods divided the world when Zeus overthrew his father, Cronus, and his allies, the Titans. Zeus took the earth, Poseidon the sea, and Hades the underworld. Thus at death, a person passes to the house of Hades, not for punishment, but to live as a shade forever. The etymology of the term Hades is devoid of punitive connotations. Hades comes from *aeides* (invisible)— from *a-* (without) *eidos* (form, shape, appearance, that which is seen). Hades, then, rules over the invisible land, the land that conceals all its inhabitants, the shades. All humans are there, no matter how good or how evil. Their fate is eternal and miserable, but it is not punishment. They live on in a gray, dismal zone, yearning for life. Homer has the dead Hercules complain that he would rather be a slave pulling a plow for an impoverished owner than rule, in Hades' land, over all the dead. The comic Lucian jokes that all the wealth of Croesus and Mausolus was useless in the land of Hades. Each shade was alloted only one square foot: standing room only. Beautiful Helen of Troy is now a skeleton. These souls are not punished; they are just there, enduring a neutral death. The only one enriched by the dead is Hades under

---

9. *The Gāthās of Zarathustra*, 83 n. 11.

10. *Ardā Wirāz Nāmag: The Iranian "Divina Commedia,"* ed. Fereydun Vahman, Scandinavian Institute of Asian Studies Monograph Series 53 (London and Malmo: Curzon Press, 1986).

his other name, Pluto, which overlaps with the Greek for "wealth."[11] He is also rich with the grain entrusted to the earth and is thus wealthy in both seeds and souls.

Another dwelling existed in ancient Greece for the most serious miscreants. Tartarus was a prison as far beneath the realm of Hades as the earth is beneath Olympus. According to Hesiod, the Titans, those allies of Cronus who had resisted Zeus, were confined in Tartarus. Unlike the unbalanced in Egypt, who were destroyed, the Titans lived forever in the Tartarean dungeon. This is the first example of eternal punishment, but it applies only to superhuman offenders like the Titans, not to the general run of wicked humans. There is, then, a fundamental distinction between Hades, or more correctly the land or house of Hades, and Tartarus. The first is the neutral land of all the dead; the second is a prison, a place of punishment for rebels against the king of the gods and his Olympian clan. (See table 1 below.)

Around 380 BCE, Plato extended the potential welcome of Tartarus to the human race as a whole. Plato was concerned to show that the soul is immortal. It had to be, he reasoned, because if not, someone who sinned greatly in life and never got caught would remain unpunished forever. Therefore, the soul must survive life so that the individual's deeds can be judged, and, in the otherworld, the soul can endure the consequences of its actions on earth. A good soul would be promoted to time in the heavens with a view of the truth; a wicked soul would serve a full sentence beneath the earth. A *perfectly* good soul would remain forever in the heavens, and a perfectly wicked or *incurable* soul would remain forever in Tartarus. Thus, one's fate in the otherworld is determined by one's life on earth. In moral death, two outcomes are possible: reward and punishment.[12] In Plato's view, the souls of the dead return to earth to inhabit new bodies, after having been enlightened by what they learned in the otherworld. The dead are not segregated, but return with reminiscences of otherworldly truths. Plato's desire for justice, his unwillingness to let the wicked escape justice forever, drove this philosophical innovation.

Ancient Rome also knew this distinction between neutral death and moral death, though with significant differences. The general population of the dead inhabited Orcus or Erebus, also called generically the *inferi*, the "lands below," our "underworld," but the shades retained important links to the

---

11. Albert Henrichs, "Hades," *OCD*, 661b.
12. Thus moral death might also be called "dual" or "double issue" eschatology. See Eugene Tesselle and Daniel Patte, "Universalism," in *Cambridge Dictionary of Christianity*, ed. Tesselle and Patte (Cambridge: Cambridge University Press, 2010), 1278–79.

living and were regarded as *parentes*, "ancestors," venerated and considered divine.[13] Cicero reports that the perfectly good were distinguished by their citizenship and lived like stars in the heavens. In the *Aeneid*, Virgil relates how Aeneas peers down at the walls of Tartarus and hears the reverberating sounds of torture. Roman concepts preserve the distinction already developed in Greek sources.

FROM SHEOL TO GEHINNOM: MORAL DEATH IN JUDAISM

Moral death also arose to exist alongside neutral death in ancient Judaism. The oldest texts refer to a neutral underworld called Sheol. Like the house of Hades in Greek thought, Sheol contains all the dead, no matter how righteously or wickedly they lived.[14] As Jews spread around the Mediterranean and translated the Hebrew Bible into Greek, a version called the Septuagint, they rendered Sheol as Hades. But within the Jewish community some dissented from the idea that all the dead go, equally, to this neutral land, Sheol. Job confronts God with the injustice that consists of the good and the wicked sharing the same grave. "They lie down alike in the dust" (Job 21:26). This complaint is a call for a reconstruction of the otherworld. For Job, hell would have been a longed-for consolation. A cosmos perfect enough to have a hell was only a hope for him.[15]

Moral death came to Judaism, but it was a minority view in the Hebrew Bible. One sees an indication in Isaiah, when the prophet imagines a community of those who obey God drawn from all nations. They gather in Jerusalem, but rebels against God surround them. When the faithful leave their meeting, they find their enemies destroyed, their bodies rotting in heaps. "Their worm shall not die, their fire shall not be quenched" (Isa. 66:24a). Here is unending disgrace in the display of unburied carrion whose decomposition is "an abhorrence to all flesh" (66:24b). There is another scene in Ezekiel 32, which imagines "those who spread terror in the earth" moved

---

13. Charles King, "The Living and the Dead: Ancient Roman Conceptions of the Afterlife" (PhD diss., University of Chicago, 1998); King, "The Roman Manes: The Dead as Gods," in Poo, *Rethinking Ghosts*, 95–114; and King, "The Organization of Roman Religious Beliefs," *Classical Antiquity* 22.2 (2003): 275–312.

14. In the Hebrew Bible, Sheol sometimes appears to have punitive connotations and to be the fate of the ungodly, because death itself, especially early death, is punishment in the Deuteronomic system, a fact not considered by Philip S. Johnston, *Shades of Sheol: Death and Afterlife in the Old Testament* (Downers Grove, IL: InterVarsity Press, 2002), 80–82. In Isaiah 28:15 and 18, Sheol and Death (*Maveth*) are synonymous.

15. Bernstein, *Formation*, 154–62.

away from the honorable dead. "They do not lie with the fallen mighty men of old who went down [honorably] to Sheol" (32:27). Isaiah 14 taunts the king of Babylon, brought down not to Sheol, but to the depths of the Pit. Thus, with a distinction between Sheol in general and its depths, a pit reserved for the worst offenders, segregation occurs in the underworld—the possibility of a life after death spent in shame. Shame in death is the beginning of hell. To imagine that after death one's enemies endure a shame one could not force them to suffer on earth is to fantasize a comeuppance one is incapable of effecting oneself. To imagine eternal shame for one's enemies, whose wrongs one is powerless to prevent or punish, is to sublimate vengeance. This psychological phenomenon occurs in many religions, but it appears very starkly in the Jewish sources cited here. This is the hope that the afterlife perfects life.[16]

Moral death became more prominent in biblical Judaism as religious leaders imagined more places where the wicked dead might suffer. In addition to the Pit, another location appears in the Hebrew Bible to contain those who warrant horrible fates for worshipping false gods. The prophet Jeremiah designates Ge-Hinnom (literally, the valley of Hinnom, or sometimes Ge ben Hinnom, the valley of the son of Hinnom), a ravine outside of Jerusalem, as such a place.[17] Here, says the prophet, the dead lie unburied, their bones forever exposed to the sun and the stars which they wrongly worshipped. Their evil loyalties should be reflected in their evil fates, which should never end. As reference to a concept of endless suffering began to convey more meaning, the concrete, geographical label Ge-Hinnom evolved into a more abstract, metaphorical, theological Gehinnom. When Greek-speaking Jews translated the Hebrew Bible into the Greek version called the Septuagint, they transliterated Gehinnom as Gehenna, which became functionally equivalent to the Greek Tartarus. Gehinnom remained the term for Jewish writers in Hebrew. The translators who made the Septuagint rendered the contrast between the neutral Hebrew Sheol and the punitive Hebrew Ge-Hinnom into Greek as the neutral Hades and the punitive Gehenna, which now joined Tartarus as a place for the castigation of the wicked. (See table 1.) Both Gehinnom and Gehenna may be translated as "hell," but for analytical purposes it is better to retain the term used in the original language rather than its modern, English equivalent. Only in this way can the stages of the concept's evolution remain clear.

---

16. For this relationship between the afterlife and this world, see Timothy Brook, Jérôme Bourgon, and Gregory Blue, *Death by a Thousand Cuts* (Cambridge, MA, and London: Harvard University Press, 2008), 122–51.

17. Bernstein, *Formation*, 167–72.

The gradual introduction of moral death into ancient Jewish thought occurred during the time from the composition of Daniel, the Hebrew Bible's last book (ca. 165 BCE), and the Christian Scriptures (completed by ca. 100 CE). Moral death appears more clearly in Jewish apocryphal literature, writings that were not accepted as canonical by the editors of what became the Hebrew Bible, than in the Bible itself. Some of these texts were found in the Qumran Caves and are known as the Dead Sea Scrolls, and they present strong dualistic tendencies. A good example is "The Battle of the Sons of Light against the Sons of Darkness." More relevant for the history of punishment after death is the first "book of Enoch," called a "pseudepigraphal" text because its author (really, authors) ascribed it, falsely, to Enoch, a legendary ancestor of Noah. There are four books of Enoch, of various dates in various languages. 1 Enoch, in Ethiopic, diverges from the narrative of Genesis by presenting an independent theory for the origin of evil. There seems to be an allusion to this narrative in Genesis 6:1–4, but the full story, indeed five versions of it, are to be found in 1 Enoch. In brief, it was not the disobedience of Adam and Eve that brought evil into the world. Rather, evil originated in heaven when certain "sons of God," a phrase considered synonymous with "angels," beheld from afar the beauty of human females and abandoned the heavenly court to mate with them. This rebellion initiated sin. Further, as part of their courtship, these "watcher" angels brought to humankind various evil arts, from astrology to weaponry to deceit to cosmetics to jewelry to sex. Thereafter, human history became a struggle between angels and humans who remain faithful to God against those angels who "came into women" and the women who mated with them, and their offspring. 1 Enoch proposes horrible torments for these rebels and their vicious followers in distant valleys of fire and sulfur, where they will suffer forever.[18] The fate of the watcher angels and their progeny represents moral death in Jewish apocryphal writing.

Enoch's watcher angels provide an opportunity to refer again to the facility of communication and the frequent correspondence, even across religious boundaries, of important mythic themes. In 1 Enoch, heavenly beings abandon their posts to mate with human females and, after committing abominations, end up in subterranean prisons, subjected to fire and brimstone. In Greek mythology, after Zeus completed his generation's deposition of the tyrannical Cronus (Saturn), he imprisoned his father's allies, the Titans, beneath the earth in Tartarus. Similarly, Christian Scripture refers to

---

18. 1 Enoch 21–22, 27. James H. Charlesworth, ed., *The Old Testament Pseudepigrapha* (Garden City, NY: Doubleday, 1983), 1:24–25, 27. See Bernstein, *Formation*, 179–87.

the rebellion (see Luke 10:18–20; 2 Pet. 2:4; and Rev. 12:9) in which the most beautiful of the angels (Satan) leads a third of the other angels out of heaven, but they are eventually confined to hell, where, except during their forays on earth seeking to tempt humans into evil, they endure or will endure what Jesus, in Matthew 25:41, called "the eternal fire prepared for the devil and his angels." This archetypal theme of rebellion in heaven producing eternal, subterranean punishment is indispensable background in all three of these traditions. They interacted during the Hellenistic period.

FROM HADES TO GEHENNA: MORAL DEATH IN EARLY CHRISTIANITY

The formative distinction between Sheol and Gehinnom, between Hades and Gehenna or Tartarus, was crucial to Christians who lived before the New Testament was assembled, and who used the Septuagint as their Bible. As a result, the authors of the New Testament wrote in the light of both Greek and Hebrew traditions. They continued to separate Hades, which is neutral, from Gehenna and Tartarus, which are punitive. Gehenna became the term they employed to express the idea of eternal punishment. Still, a significant strain within Eastern Orthodox Christianity retained an affinity for Hades. As a result, various interpretations of postmortem punishment—not just one—seem consistent with the Christian Bible. Some passages suggest a divine force so attractive and potent that no evil can remain in the world. In 1 Corinthians 15:28, the apostle Paul looked forward to a time when God would "be all in all," a beneficent saturation so complete that the survival of an eternally suffering class of damned is impossible. From this and related texts arose universalism, the belief that all are saved. For example, Romans 11:32 indicates that God will "have mercy upon all." John 12:31 quotes Jesus as saying, "I . . . will draw all men to myself."[19] Some claim these texts remove the possibility of eternal damnation. Advocates of universalism still belong in the tradition of moral death, because they accept the need for postmortem punishment. In universalism, however, postmortem punishment is curative and removes the taint of sin; it is not eternal.

---

19. Other passages tending in the same direction are John 10:16: "And I have other sheep, that are not of this fold; I must bring them also, and they will heed my voice. So there shall be one flock, one shepherd"; Romans 11:32: "For God has consigned all men to disobedience, that he may have mercy upon all"; 1 Timothy 2:4–6: "[God] desires all men to be saved and to come to the knowledge of the truth. For there is one God, and there is one mediator between God and men, the man Christ Jesus, who gave himself as a ransom for all."

Using another approach, Paul distinguishes "those who belong to Christ" (1 Cor. 15:23) from those who will not "inherit the Kingdom of God," (1 Cor. 6:9–10), but he refrains from describing that exclusion any further. Romans 2:7–9 says God gives contrasting retribution to those who do good and those who do evil. To the good he gives "eternal life," to the wicked "wrath and fury, . . . tribulation and distress." Although this passage says the life for the good will be eternal, there is silence on the duration of suffering for the wicked.[20] In Galatians 6:8, Paul contrasts eternal life to "destruction." 2 Thessalonians 1:9 speaks of "*eternal* destruction," but the attribution of this letter to Paul is questionable. If 2 Thessalonians is by one of Paul's followers, the addition of "eternal" to "destruction" reflects an effort at synthesis by later writers concerned to harmonize Paul with the teachings of Jesus as reported, for example, by Matthew. Whether "destruction" is eternal or not, a reasonable inference from these passages might be that after the annihilation of the wicked nothing remains that does not cleave to God. In that sense, then, he is "all in all."

In contrast to Paul, other New Testament writers proclaim physical suffering for the wicked. Mark, the earliest, quotes Jesus advising resistance to physical temptation by amputating the offending hand or foot or eye, for it is better to enter the kingdom of God lacking a body part than with it "to be thrown into Gehenna where their worm does not die, and the fire is not quenched" (Mark 9:47–48). Mark's account names Jeremiah's Ge-Hinnom (Gehenna in the Septuagint) and defines it in terms of the fire and worm from Isaiah 66:24. Further, in Matthew 25:31–46 Jesus tells the apostles that when the Son of Man returns he will judge the nations, and he will say to the righteous: "Come O blessed of my Father, inherit the kingdom prepared for you from the foundation of the world." To the wicked he will say: "Depart from me you accursed ones to the eternal fire prepared for the Devil and his angels." This text anticipates Revelation's lake of fire and brimstone into which Satan and his followers will be cast "and the smoke of their torment goes up forever and ever" (14:11). Fire and sulfurous stench combine with darkness as the major torments of the damned in biblical texts. Thus Jesus contrasts those who "will sit with Abraham, Isaac, and Jacob in the kingdom of heaven" to those who "will be thrown into the outer darkness, [where] men will weep and gnash their teeth" (Matt. 8:11–12). Less well known, but extremely dramatic, is the possibility of bodily division, being cut into parts (Matt. 24:51; also Luke 12:46).

---

20. Bernstein, *Formation*, 205–27.

The Inauguration of Hell: Christ's Descent to the Underworld

An important Christian apocryphal text, the *Gospel of Nicodemus*, dramatizes the distinction between neutral and moral death in Christianity and shows that, even after the completion of the New Testament canon, further writings developed the idea. The focus of this narrative is Christ's descent to the underworld (also called the *Descensus ad inferos* or just the *Descensus*). In English, this event is often called, wrongly, the Harrowing of Hell—a misnomer. In Greek Christianity, it is called the Anastasis, which means "resurrection." The action involves Christ's descent, not to hell, but to the neutral underworld (Sheol/Hades) to resurrect those who languished, until that moment, under the control of death. The land to which Jesus descends has also been called limbo, the place where the righteous ancients awaited their redemption. They suffered no pain other than death itself (which is why it is Sheol/Hades). An important refinement distinguishes two aspects of limbo as a land where there is no direct vision of God—a psychological penalty without physical pain. The righteous Hebrews are in the limbo of the fathers; unbaptized children are in their own limbo.[21]

The setting is this: after the Crucifixion, Jesus was taken down from the cross and buried. During the time that his body lay in the grave, before his Resurrection, his spirit descended to the underworld, and, after defeating the angel Satan and the Greek god Hades, the guardians of that place, he rescued the dead; that is, he resurrected them and led them to heaven. This narrative is a principal frame of reference for all Christian eschatology. According to the accounts of Christ's Descent in the *Gospel of Nicodemus*, his Resurrection and that of the human race occur together. The texts vary on whether Christ transferred all or only some humans to heaven.

The *Gospel of Nicodemus* exists in a Greek version and two Latin ones, Latin A and Latin B.[22] The differences between them are differences in

---

21. Marcia Colish, "The Virtuous Pagan: Dante and the Christian Tradition," in *The Fathers and Beyond: Church Fathers between Ancient and Medieval Thought* (Aldershot, UK, and Burlington, VT: Ashgate, 2008), Essay VII, pp. 1–40; Jacques Le Goff, "Les limbes," *Nouvelle Revue de Psychoanalyse* 34 (1986): 151–73.

22. All three appear in Constantinus de Tischendorf, *Evangelia apocrypha* (Leipzig: Mendelssohn, 1876; repr., Hildesheim: G. Olms, 1966), 210–86 and 323–32 (Greek); 389–416 (Latin A); and 417–32 (Latin B). Of the English translations, the best, under the title *The Gospel of Nicodemus, or Acts of Pilate*, is in M. R. James, *ANT*, pp. 117–46, with important background at pp. 94–95. Unfortunately, in translating Latin A, James calls Inferus, the guardian of the underworld, Hell. Clearly, Inferus is the Latin name of Hades, who has that name in the Greek. Latin B does indeed call the guardian of the underworld Infernus, thus warranting James's rendering as Hell. See also Bernstein, *Formation*, 272–82.

infernalization, as will be explained. The Greek version says that after Christ's visit "not one dead man" is left in the underworld. Latin A calls Hades by the Latin term for the neutral underworld, Inferus, and explains that the cross undid the deeds of Eden, implying that *all* humans are now free and that, instead of Adam and his children, Satan will be in the power of Inferus forever. No humans appear to be damned; the underworld is empty except for Satan.[23] Latin B provides a fundamental example of infernalization; it calls the underworld official Infernus, or Hell, the name of the punitive underworld. Further, it divides Christ's action into two separate phases. First, he overcomes Satan and casts him, bound, into Tartarus, the eternal fire, the depths of the abyss. Then he surveys the underworld, and of those he found there, that is, the human dead, "he cast down part into Tartarus, and part he brought again with him on high."[24] In Latin B, some humans are unworthy of resurrection with Christ. When Christ casts wicked humans with Satan into Tartarus, hell begins to function as a recipient of the wicked.

These versions of the *Gospel of Nicodemus* underline trends described above. There is consistency in the view of neutral death in the Greek and in Latin A where Hades and Inferus oversee the neutral world of all the dead and the idea that Christ rescues all humans. In Latin B, the change in the official's name to Infernus coincides with a change in the action: here Christ sorts out the dead, takes only the blessed with him to heaven, and casts the rejects along with Satan into Tartarus. As compared to the Greek text and Latin A, Latin B is a clear example of infernalization. Further evidence will complement the impression gained here that the gates of Hades are more porous in Greek than in Latin Christianity.

Judging the Living and the Dead

The concept of moral death presupposes a moral judgment of the living after their death. Besides the difference between universalism and the possibility of damnation, there was still no unanimity, whether in Christianity or in the broader Greco-Roman world, on exactly what is judged or when the judgment takes place. In Plato's view, certain gods judge the soul, and judgment immediately follows the individual's death. For Daniel, all the dead lie buried for an unspecified time until resurrection. Only then, with their bodies restored, are some separated to experience either "everlasting life" or "shame and everlasting contempt" (Dan. 12:1–2). In Christian thought,

---

23. *Gospel of Nicodemus* 7 (27); ANT, p. 137.
24. *Gospel of Nicodemus* 9 (25); ANT, p. 139.

it is Christ and the idea of resurrection that synthesize these two different perspectives.

Christians believe an intersection of eternity with time took place with Christ's incarnation. In Christianity, the divinity, in the form of the Word, becomes flesh (John 1:14) and remains fully divine even while living as a human being. This God-Man, Jesus, through his suffering and death, redeems the human race from the consequences of sin, potentially all sin from the transgression of Adam and Eve until the end of time. But the life of Jesus can be analyzed further because, as a human, he lived in time. Many Christian festivals mark the stages of his earthly career: the Nativity, the Circumcision, the Crucifixion, the Resurrection. The Second Coming (or Parousia) will be the occasion of the Last Judgment. Those alive at the time of the Parousia will be judged directly, but those who have already died will not be spared scrutiny. All the dead will be resurrected. (This is the General Resurrection as opposed to Christ's Resurrection, which anticipates it.) The bodies of the resurrected dead will be reunited with their souls, judged for their thoughts and deeds, and dispatched to heaven or hell. As these sentences are pronounced, history ends; only eternity remains. The damned are in eternal suffering; the blessed in eternal bliss. Time now fades into eternity.

Between Death and Judgment: The Interim in Christian Eschatology

Belief in a distinction between the fates of good and evil people in eternity brought about important refinements in thinking about their fates in time. These refinements concern our individual deaths and the delay between them and the Second Coming, a period technically called the interim. As time passed between the prophecies about the coming General Resurrection and Last Judgment, it became increasingly necessary to understand how those who had died before the Second Coming would fare while asleep in the earth. John 3:18 provides the premises for reflection on this question: "He who believes in him is not condemned (Greek *krinetai*, "judged," and Latin *iudicatur*, "judged"); he who does not believe is condemned already" (Greek *ēdē kekritai*, "judged," and Latin *iam iudicatus*, "judged"). Here, faith is the criterion for judgment. The idea that some could be "judged already" implies an individual judgment that precedes the General Resurrection and the Last Judgment.

Variation in the fates of the good and the wicked during the interim leaves unanswered many questions that animated debate for centuries. If some can be judged already (like the rich man of Luke 16:19–31), do they go immediately to hell? That question was not dogmatically answered in the affirmative, until 1274.[25] Those assumed to go immediately to heaven, because they are not judged, are figures such as the martyrs and the good thief of Luke 23:42–43. When those whose fates are decided at their deaths are taken together with those judged at the end of time, such as in the parable of the sheep and the goats (Matt. 25:31–46), an implicit grid appears.[26] There are two times of judgment, at death and at the General Resurrection. At both times there are both saved and damned. Questions about such matters as prayers for the dead and the possibility of purgatory then arise about the condition of souls awaiting the Resurrection.

Once resurrection becomes a point on the timeline, there is an interim period between the moment an individual dies and the moment he or she is resurrected, judged, and either promoted to heaven or condemned to hell. Thus, *interim* becomes a technical term. If death is defined as the separation of the soul from the body, then, at that point, the body is buried in the grave, and the separated soul seems to be somewhere else, because it leaves the body. With this difference between death as the end of the individual's earthly life and the Last Judgment as the end of time, scholars have come to distinguish between two eschatologies, a personal and a general, an individual and a collective, a micro- and a macro-eschatology.[27] As in an optical illusion, one's perception depends upon the point of focus. A person's death and the universal Last Judgment each evoke different associations. The greatest difference between the time after one's death and after the Resurrection and Last Judgment is the presence of the resurrected body. In discussing the condition of the soul during this interim period, it is the soul as a spiritual entity, free of its body, that is the focus. The condition of the soul during the interim became the subject of mystical experience, the object of speculation, debate, and much later, partly because of Protestant denial of purgatory, war. For all the theological debate, many early medieval sources such as vision literature depict the separated soul in the interim as if it had a body. The tendency to

25. D-S no. 858, p. 276.

26. Two major discussions address this grid. One is in Augustine's *Enchiridion* 29.109–10; CCSL 46 (1946): 108–9 (as observed by Jacques Le Goff, *La naissance du purgatoire* [Paris: Gallimard, 1981], 106; Le Goff, *The Birth of Purgatory*, trans. Arthur Goldhammer [Chicago: University of Chicago Press, 1984], 74). The other is Pope Gregory I's *Moralia* 26.27.50–51; CCSL 143B: 1304–6, cited by Marina Smyth, "The Origins of Purgatory through the Lens of Seventh-Century Irish Eschatology," *Traditio* 58 (2003): 91–132, at 92–93. See Aron Gurevich, "The 'Divine Comedy,' before Dante," in *Medieval Popular Culture*, trans. János Bak and Paul A. Hollingsworth (Cambridge and Paris: Cambridge University Press and Maison des Sciences de l'Homme, 1988), 119.

27. Aron Gurevich, "The Individual and the Hereafter," chapter 5 in *Historical Anthropology of the Middle Ages* (Chicago: University of Chicago Press, 1992), 77; Gurevich, "The Divine Comedy before Dante," chapter 4 in *Medieval Popular Culture*, 137–44.

imagine the soul as if it were a body continues through the time of Dante (d. 1321), whose *Divine Comedy* was clearly meant to take place in the present time, prior to the Resurrection, when the souls Dante encounters have bodies, endure physical pains, and exist in a real landscape.

It is not only in Christianity that the interim offered a fertile field for speculation. The interim is the principal screen on which the living generally imagined their dead. This time after death is the base of operations for the unburied, the unavenged, the living dead, or any souls with unfinished business. Judaism and Islam also considered the interim key to their view of death and the proper relationship between children, parents, and ancestors. Folk beliefs and some religious doctrines bear on the activities of the dead coming, as in porous death, to request errands of the living: acquit a debt, avenge an offense, perform a pious deed left undone, or simple veneration. The demands of the dead elicit emotions ranging from fear to piety to hope. These attitudes toward the dead and this range of beliefs about the needs of the dead shape theology, funeral rites, and familial devotion in ways that are fundamental to the history of belief in hell.

Augustine on the Interim

A good point of departure for understanding the condition of the soul in the interim is a discussion by Augustine of Hippo (d. 430) in the *Enchiridion*, an overview of the Christian faith he composed at the request of a friend. The context of his discussion is the devotion the pious living show their predecessors. In particular, he examines whether these devotions (prayers, masses, charity), technically called suffrages, actually aid the dead. For Augustine, between death and the final Resurrection, the dead are held in three hidden receptacles (*in abditis receptaculis*).[28] They contain (1) those whose lives were so good they have no need of help, (2) those whose lives were so wicked they are beyond help, and (3) those in the middle, who can be helped by suffrages to the extent that their prior lives merited it. Augustine separated those in the middle receptacle into two parts, turning a tripartite into a quadripartite division. In the morally better portion are those who were not so good as to merit blessedness immediately, but still good enough to qualify eventually for a full remission of penalties. For souls in the morally inferior portion suffrages can produce improved conditions, a *tolerabilior damnatio*, literally "a more tolerable damnation."[29] The suffrages of the living and of the saints can aid the worst

---

28. Augustine, *Enchiridion* 29.109; CCSL 46:108; trans. J. F. Shaw (South Bend, IN: Regnery/Gateway, 1961), 127. See Bernstein, *Formation*, 322–24.

29. Augustine, *Enchiridion* 29.110; CCSL 46:108–9.

part of the middle group, the wicked but not very wicked, *in* their punishment, but not *from* it. Augustine's discussion served as the standard theological position on the interim, yet from the fifth through the eighth century (and indeed much longer) very few writers believed that Augustine's hidden receptacles actually confined souls. Death remained far more porous than Augustine's categories would appear to acknowledge.

One reason the interim became such a battleground is that as time passed and Christ did not return, the interim lasted much longer than originally expected. Christian Scripture offers differing views on when the Parousia or Second Coming will occur. Mark 9:1 says it will be within the lifetime of some of the apostles. As Christian history developed, it became clear that the Last Judgment and its consequent heaven or hell would only begin at some indefinite time in the future. The fate of the soul immediately after death therefore became increasingly urgent. The interim also figures prominently in the religious thinking of medieval Jews and Muslims. In the medieval imagination, the dead visit the living with information about the afterlife. It may well be the otherworld from which these revenants visited on temporary leave, but it was not eternity. If it were eternity, there would be no one living to receive their testimony. Conversely, percipients of near-death experiences visit the otherworld in the interim, not the eternal destinations of those with resurrected bodies.

Infernalization: Latin Translators Make Sheol/Hades Hell

To grasp the theological elaborations of the concept of hell within Judaism, Christianity, and Islam that is the subject of the rest of this book, it is necessary to understand the historical origins of the words used by the three faiths to name the places of postmortem punishment. The terminology transmitted from the Hebrew Bible to the Septuagint and from the Septuagint to the Greek New Testament preserves the fundamental distinction between the neutral land of all the dead, Sheol and Hades, over against the punitive land for the wicked, Gehinnom (Gehenna) and Tartarus. The situation is different in translations from Hebrew and Greek into Latin. Although the ancient Romans recognized a distinction between neutral and moral death analogous to that of the Jews and the Greeks, the Latin terminology requires further attention.

In classical Latin, *infernus* is an adjective describing "that which lies beneath the earth," as in the sequence "supernal," "terrestrial," "infernal." Classical Latin also has the term *inferus*, basically a synonym for *infernus*. We would translate both as "infernal," a term that, in English as in Latin, has negative connotations because what lies beneath the earth is concealed, a mystery, and therefore threatening. (The Greek Hades has the same overtones.) Moreover, as neutral death emerges alongside porous death, the land of no return holds its residents in place; it resembles a prison and so has negative associations, especially when early death is considered a punishment as in the Deuteronomic view. In neutral death, the dead are "merely" dead and not convicts. All the dead are there. That was the problem that evoked moral death.

Latin authors devised their own nomenclature for the dead. In Latin, a dead person, a shade or a spirit, is a *manes*, and all the dead are, collectively, the *manes*.[30] Honored as ancestors and venerated in the annual festival of the Parentalia, these spirits were considered divine and called the "divine manes," the *di manes*. These shades were "the inhabitants of the infernal regions, the dead," the *inferi*, "those below."[31] In classical Latin, the *inferi* were the neutral dead, like the residents of Sheol/Hades. In Christian times, translators of the Greek Bible, believers in a religion previously unknown, and assuming a concept of moral death, had to adapt classical Latin to their own needs and make decisions in rendering the Greek Hades. Over the centuries, a distinction emerged between the *inferi* (the dead) or *inferus* (the neutral underworld where they resided) and the proper noun Infernus (Hell), the punitive land for the wicked dead.[32] Consensus on this distinction had not crystallized completely by the time Jerome and his circle created the Vulgate Bible.[33] Table 1 delineates these distinctions.

With these distinctions set forth, it is now possible to recognize the terms most fundamental to the history of belief in hell. When I refer to Sheol/ Hades, I include the adjective *inferus* (the "under" world) and the noun *inferi* (the dead who continue to exist down there), and I refer to this area where all the dead live on as "the underworld." These terms designate the neutral land of all the dead. I will treat Gehinnom, Gehenna, Tartarus, and *infernus* as synonyms for hell; they designate the condition of eternal punishment. I base this nomenclature on the terminology chosen by the translators of scriptural

---

30. On these uses of *manes*, see King, "The Living and the Dead," 72; and King, "The Roman Manes," 104–5.

31. King, "The Ancient Roman Afterlife" (unpublished manuscript), 110.

32. For a good appreciation of this distinction, but in a different context, see Martin F. Connell, "*Descensus Christi ad Inferos*: Christ's Descent to the Dead," *Theological Studies* 62 (2001): 262–82, esp. 266–67.

33. For an excellent account of the layers of construction of the Vulgate text, see Catherine Brown Tkacz, "*Labor Tam Utilis*: The Creation of the Vulgate," *Vigiliae Christianae* 50 (1996): 42–72. For the text of the Vulgate, I have consulted *Biblia sacra iuxta Vulgatam versionem*, ed. Robert Weber, 4th ed., R. Gryson (Stuttgart: Deutsche Bibelgesellschaft, 1994).

Table 1   Underworld versus Hell

SOURCE	NEUTRAL LAND OF ALL DEAD	LAND OF WICKED DEAD
Greek literature	Hades	Tartarus
Hebrew Bible	Sheol	Ge-Hinnom
Septuagint	Hades	Gehenna
Greek New Testament	Hades	Gehenna[a]
Roman literature	Orcus, Inferi	Tartarus
Vulgate Old Testament	Infernus[b]	Vallis filii Ennom
Vulgate New Testament	Infernus (sometimes inferus)[c]	Gehenna, Tartarus, Infernus
RSV Old Testament	Sheol	Valley of the sons of Hinnom
RSV New Testament	Hades	Hell[d]

[a] One exception, 2 Peter 2:4, is discussed below, where the term refers to Tartarus.
[b] For exceptions, see table 2.
[c] *Inferus* occurs at Matthew 16:19 (18), *portae inferi*, and Revelation 6:8; 20:13; 20:14.
[d] The RSV complements the translation "Hell" with a footnote indicating that the Greek term is Gehenna.

texts from Hebrew and from Greek into Latin. A case-by-case examination of these translators' decisions shows that, in the process of rendering the Septuagint (the Hebrew Scriptures in Greek) and the Greek New Testament into Latin, they tended to interpret the Hebrew and Greek terms for the neutral underworld of all the dead as the punitive hell reserved only for the wicked.

The tendency to shade Hades into hell had precedent in Luke 16:19–31, the parable of the rich man and Lazarus, where Jesus tells how a selfish rich man denies charity to the sick Lazarus, who begs for a crumb from his table. The poor man dies and is transported to "the Bosom of Abraham," a dwelling for the innocent in the otherworld. The rich man also dies and is buried. Without saying how, the Greek text says he is then "in Hades," and the Latin Vulgate says he is "in inferno," where he burns in fire (verse 22). Still, he can see Lazarus in Abraham's bosom and appeals to Abraham to send Lazarus to him with a drop of water, because "I am suffering in this fire" (verse 24). Although they are within hailing distance, the two are separated by a great chasm. Here, then, Hades, the otherworld, divides into a place of comfort for the innocent and a place of torment for the wicked. Although the Greek Hades usually refers to the neutral land of all the dead, here it refers only to the punitive territory on the fiery side of the chasm, which Latin translators, with near unanimity, called *Infernus*.[34] This division of Hades by an abyss in

---

34. Joachim Jeremias, "Hades," in *Theological Dictionary of the New Testament*, ed. Gerhard Kittel (Grand Rapids, MI: Eerdmans, 1964), 1:146–49, explains the distinctions between Sheol and Gehinnom, Hades and Gehenna, but does not consider the Latin terminology. He speaks of a double meaning of Hades. "In some cases the term denotes the place of all the souls of the dead until the Resurrection (Acts 2:27–31 [which, N.B., quotes Psalm 16:8–11]), whereas in others it denotes the place of the souls of only the ungodly (Luke 16:23) or non-Christians (Rev. 20:13–14)." *Inferus*

Luke 16:26, where only the tortuous portion is called Hades, constitutes the sole association of Hades with punishment in the Greek New Testament. Despite its exceptional terminology, this is one of the most vivid depictions of postmortem retribution in the Christian Scriptures, and it provides scriptural authority for the tendency to infernalize Hades, first in the Latin church and then, to a much lesser extent, in Greek Orthodox thought.

The trend among Latin translators of the New Testament and the patristic interpreters of the following centuries was to designate the punitive afterlife increasingly as *infernus*, "hell," rather than the *inferi*, even when the Greek original is Hades or the Hebrew original is Sheol. Indeed, when the composers of the Old Latin version of the Bible rendered the Septuagint (Greek) book of Psalms into Latin, they translated Hades as *infernus* fifteen times, and *inferus* once. Similarly, when Jerome translated the Psalms from Origen's *Hexapla* (Greek) edition in 386–392 CE, and from Hebrew between 390 and 394 CE, he rendered Hades and Sheol as *infernus* fourteen times but *inferus* once and *silentium* once, as table 2 makes clear.[35]

This choice of words is all the more remarkable considering that the book of Psalms expresses religious ideas of the Jewish people, who, in biblical days, had only a modest notion of postmortem punishment, and the term that only indirectly expressed that idea, Ge-Hinnom, does not occur in Psalms at all. Nonetheless, in making the Vulgate, Jerome chose the punitive term, *infernus*.[36] In this he followed his predecessors who had created the Old Latin version. In rendering these verses that refer to the Jewish, neutral underworld, the Christian translators imposed on the term Sheol, their own, Christian idea of moral death. Another, dramatic example occurs in Psalm

---

usually translates Hades in the first sense, *infernus* in the other two. The use of *infernus* to translate Hades in the first sense (as in Acts 2:27–31) constitutes infernalization. Jeremias refers to "the sharp distinction" in the Greek New Testament between Hades and Gehenna. Hades receives the wicked only for the interim between death and resurrection, whereas Gehenna punishes them from the Last Judgment on, that is, forever. Moreover, Hades retains souls separated from their bodies (as it functions prior to the Resurrection) and Gehenna punishes them after the reunion of body and soul, that is, after the Resurrection and Last Judgment for all eternity. Joachim Jeremias, "Gehenna," ibid., 1:657–58.

35. For the dates, see Tkacz, "*Labor Tam Utilis*," 49–50.

36. For the Septuagint, the Vetus Latina, and the Clementine Vulgate in parallel columns, see *Bibliorum Sacrorum Latinae versiones antiquae: seu vetus Italica, et caeterae quaecunque in codicibus mss. & antiquorum libris reperiri potuerunt quae cum Vulgata Latina & cum textu Graeco comparantur . . .* , ed. P. Sabatier (1751; Turnhout, Belgium: Brepols, 1981). Improvements over Sabatier's edition are as follows. For the Old Latin, there are two publications: *Itala: Das Neue Testament in altlateinischer Überlieferung*, 4 vols. (Berlin: Walter de Gruyter, 1938); *Vetus latina: Die Reste der altlateinischen Bibel nach Petrus Sabatier neu gesammelt und herausgegeben von der Erzabtei Beuron* (Freiburg: Herder, 1956–2000), vols. 26/1 and 26/2. Beginning in 2002, this project was moved online. See the *Vetus Latina Database*, edited by Brepols (Turnhout, Belgium).

93:17, where Jerome translated *dumah*, Hebrew for "silence," as *infernus*. This is infernalization.

The same phenomenon also occurs in the New Testament. As table 3 shows, where Greek authors used Hades, the Vulgate's translators used *inferus* four times and *infernus* nine times.

Table 2   Latin translations of Sheol/Hades in Psalms using the Stuttgart Vulgate

PSALM	HEBREW	GREEK	RSV	VULGATE (GREEK) WEBER	JEROME (HEBREW) WEBER
6:6	Sheol	Hades	In Sheol who can give thee praise?	In inferno autem, quis confitebitur tibi?	In inferno quis confitebitur tibi?
9:18	Sheol	Hades	The wicked shall depart to Sheol.	Convertantur peccatores in infernum.	Convertantur impii in infernum.
15:10 (Acts 2:27)	Sheol	Hades	For thou dost not give me up to Sheol.	Non derelinques animam meam in inferno.	Non enim derelinques animam meam in inferno.
17:6ᵃ	Sheol	Hades	The cords of Sheol entangled me, the snare of death confronted me.	Dolores inferni circumdederunt me praeoccupaverunt me laquei mortis.	Funes **inferi** circumdederunt me praevenerunt me laquei mortis.ᵇ
29:4	Sheol	Hades	Thou has brought up my soul from Sheol.	Eduxisti ab inferno animam meam.	Eduxisti de inferno animam meam.
30:18	Sheol	Hades	Let the wicked be put to shame, let them go dumbfounded to Sheol.	Erubescant impii et deducantur in infernum.	Confundantur impii taceant in inferno.
48:15a	Sheol	Hades	Like sheep they are appointed for Sheol; death shall be their shepherd.	Sicut oves in inferno positi sunt: mors depascet eos.	Quasi grex in inferno positi sunt mors pascet eos.
48:15b	Sheol	Hades	Straight to the grave they descend, and their form shall waste away; Sheol shall be their home	auxilium eorum veterescet in inferno a gloria eorum.	Et figura eorum conteretur in inferno post habitaculum suum.
48:16b	Sheol	Hades	But God will ransom my soul from the power of Sheol.	Redimet animam meam de manu **inferi.**	Redimet animam meam de manu **inferi.**
54:16	Sheol	Hades	Let death come upon them; let them go down to Sheol alive.	Veniat mors super illos et descendant in infernum viventes.	Veniant mors super eos descendant in infernum viventes.
85:13	Sheol	Hades	Thou hast delivered my soul from the depths (tachtiyah, katōtatou) of Sheol.	Eruisti animam meam ex inferno inferiori.	Eruisti animam meam de inferno extremo.
87:4	Sheol	Hades	My life draws near to Sheol.	Vita mea in inferno adpropinquavit.	Vita mea ad infernum descendit.
93:17	**Dumah**	Hades	My soul would soon have dwelt in the land of silence.	Habitavit in inferno anima mea.	Habitasset in inferno anima mea.

(Continued)

Table 2   Continued

PSALM	HEBREW	GREEK	RSV	VULGATE (GREEK) WEBER	JEROME (HEBREW) WEBER
113:17ᶜ	**Dumah**ᵈ	Hades	The dead do not praise the Lord nor do any that go down into silence.	Non mortui laudabunt te . . . neque omnes qui descendunt in infernum.	Non mortui laudabunt Dominum, nec omnes qui descendunt in **silentium**.
114:3	Sheol	Hades	The snares of death encompassed me; the pangs of Sheol laid hold on me.	Circumdederunt me dolores mortis: pericula inferni invenerunt me.	cd. me funes mortis et munitiones inferni invenerunt me.
138:8	Sheol	Hades	If I make my bed in Sheol, thou art there!	Si descendero ad infernum, ades!	Si iacuero in inferno ades.
140:7	Sheol	Hades	So shall their bones be strewn at the mouth of Sheol.	Dissipata sunt ossa nostra secus infernum.	Sic dissipata sunt ossa nostra in ore **inferi.**

Source: Biblia sacra iuxta Vulgatam versionem, ed. R. Weber, 4th ed., R. Gryson (Stuttgart: Deutsche Bibelgesellschaft, 1994).

ᵃ Psalm numbers from 9 to 146 do not match in all versions. Non-Vulgate versions divide Psalm 9 at verse 21, considering verses 22–38 to be Psalm 10. Thereafter the non-Vulgate Psalm numbers are one higher than in Vulgate Bibles until the Vulgate combines Psalms 146 and 147 to equal non-Vulgate 147, when the versions number together. Verses may also vary, usually only by one.

ᵇ Boldface indicates exceptions to the claim that Latin translators rendered Sheol/Hades as *infernus*.

ᶜ In the Septuagint, Psalm 113:17=113:25.

ᵈ Dumah: "stillness, land of death."

The Latin translators preferred *inferus* when they regarded Hades as a synonym for *death* or as a personification. Three such examples are in the book of Revelation: "Its rider's name was Death, and Hades followed him" (Apoc. 6:8); "Death and Hades gave up the dead in them" (Apoc. 20:13); "Then Death and Hades were thrown into the lake of fire" (Apoc. 20:14). The occurrence of Hades in Matthew 16:18 ("The gates of Hades [in Latin: *portae inferi*] shall not prevail against [my church]") is more complex. It seems the translators emphasized their understanding of the future life by implying "the gates that enclose the dead shall not prevent the Resurrection."

A review of each occurrence shows how systematically Latin translators of the New Testament rendered Hades as *infernus*. Matthew 11:23 reads: "And you Capernaum, will you be exalted to heaven? You shall be brought down to Hades (*infernus*)." Luke 10:15 parallels Matthew 11:23 concerning Capernaum and its end in Hades (*infernus*). Acts 2:27 (quoting Ps. 16:10, where the term is Sheol) reads: "For thou wilt not abandon my soul to Hades (*infernus*). Acts 2:31 parallels Acts 2:27. Apoc. 1:18 reads: "I am alive for evermore, and I have the keys of Death and Hades (*infernus*)." The keys make Hades resemble a locked holding-place where all the dead await resurrection. The reference to keys recalls Matthew 16:18, "the gates of Hades." Matthew's use of Hades

Table 3   *Infernus* in the Vulgate New Testament

PASSAGE	GREEK	CLEMENTINE VULGATE	W-W VULGATE	EARLY COMMENTATORS
Matt. 11:23	eōs Hadou	in infernum	in infernum[a]	Iren. *Haer.* 4.36: "ad **inferos**"[b]
Matt. 16:18	pylai Hadou	portae **inferi**	portae **inferi**[c]	
Luke 10:15	eōs Hadou	ad infernum	ad infernum[d]	W-W cite Vercelli, Vienna, and Dublin MSS: "**inferos.**"
Luke 16:22	kai etaphē. En tō Hadē	et sepultus est in inferno	et sepultus est in inferno[e]	Among W-W's variants are (1) Vienna: "et sepultus est aput **inferos**[. I]n **inferno**"; (2) Vercelli: "et sepultus est apud **inferos**[. E]t de **inferno.**"
Acts 2:24	tas hōdinas tou thanatou	doloribus inferni	doloribus inferni[f]	Sabatier cites Iren. *Haer.* 3.12: "doloribus **inferorum**"; W-W add Bede: "mortis."
Acts 2:27	eis Hadou	in inferno	in inferno[g]	Sabatier cites a Cambridge MS with "apud inferos." W-W cite Beza Codex: "aput **inferos.**" [These are the same MSS; see W-W, 1:xxxi.] Acts 2:27 here quotes Psalm 16:10, where the Vetus Latina gives "apud **inferos.**"
Acts 2:31	eis Hadou	in inferno	in inferno[h]	Sabatier cites Iren. *Haer.* 3.12: "apud **inferos**"; W-W cite Beza: "aput **inferos.**"
2 Pet. 2:4	sairais zophou tartarōsas paredōken	rudentibus inferni detractos in tartarum tradidit	rudentibus inferni detractos in tartarum tradidit[i]	Sabatier cites "Auctor l. de promiss. Dimid. Temp" (Sabatier 959b). (Pseudo-)Prosper of Aquitaine is Quodvultdeus (d. ca. 453), *Liber promissionum et praedictorum Dei*, chap. 3, line 13 in CCSL 60, ed. R. Braun (1976): "carceribus caliginis **inferi** retrudens tradidit." W-W cite Fulgentius, Cassiodorus, and Bede using **inferi.**
Apoc. 1:18	tas kleis tou hadou	claves inferni	claves inferni[j]	Sabatier cites Iren. *Haer.* 4.20: claves inferorum. Cyp. l.2 Test.: claves **inferorum.** Victor [of Cartenna] *Contra Arium* 3.17: claves **inferi.** W-W add **inferorum** in Firmicus-Maternus, Tyconius (once), Capreolus, Primasius, Bede, and Beatus. (Bede also uses infernorum.)
Apoc. 6:8	ho Hadēs	Infernus	**inferus**[k]	W-W: MSS divide between **inferus** and **infernus.**
Apoc. 20:13	ho Hadēs	Infernus	**inferus**[l]	W-W cite six major MSS with Tyconius, Augustine, Pseudo-Prosper, Bede, and Beatus for **infernus.** Iren. *Haer.* 5.35, Ambrose, and Bede: **inferus**

(Continued)

Table 3   Continued

PASSAGE	GREEK	CLEMENTINE VULGATE	W-W VULGATE	EARLY COMMENTATORS
Apoc. 20:14	ho Hadēs	Infernus	**inferus**[m]	W-W cite same six MSS for infernus and only Iren. *Haer.* 5.35 for **inferi**.

Source: Based on Wordsworth-White Vulgate [W-W].

[a] Fate for Capernaum, not to be exalted to Heaven, but brought down to Hades.

[b] Boldface indicates exceptions to the claim that Latin translators rendered Sheol/Hades as *infernus*.

[c] "On this rock I will build my church, and the powers of death shall not prevail against it" (Greek: the gates of Hades).

[d] Fate for Capernaum, not to be exalted to Heaven, but brought down to Hades.

[e] Having refused charity to Lazarus the beggar, the rich man "died and was buried; and in Hades, being in torment . . . 'I am in anguish in this flame'."

[f] Of Jesus: "God raised him up, having loosed the pangs of death, because it was not possible for him to be held by it" (cf. Ps. 17:5–6).

[g] "For thou wilt not abandon my soul to Hades" (quoting Ps. 16:10).

[h] Same as for Acts 2:27. These are essentially the same entry, and count as only one occurrence.

[i] "[God] . . . cast them into hell [Tartarus] and committed them to pits of nether gloom."

[j] "I am alive for evermore, and I have the keys of Death and Hades."

[k] ". . . a pale horse, and its rider's name was Death, and Hades followed him."

[l] "Death and Hades gave up the dead in them."

[m] "Then Death and Hades were thrown into the lake of fire. This is the second death, the lake of fire." In the last three cases W-W differ from the commonly edited Vulgates (the Clementine), in prefering *inferus* to *infernus*. This is the reading accepted by Weber in the Vulgate published by the Deutsche Bibelgesellschaft in Stuttgart. I have checked the readings in Matthew and Luke against the Vetus Latina (*Itala: Das Neue Testament in altlateinischer Überlieferung* [Berlin: Walter de Gruyter, 1938]), and although it improves the system of sigla, the readings do not vary from those given in W-W.

leads into the promise to give Peter the "keys to the kingdom of heaven," where the contrast is not between heaven and hell, but between heaven and earth. In this case the keys serve to open heaven, not to confine in hell.

Translators of the New Testament also used *infernus* for Greek words other than Hades, such as *thanatos* (death) and Tartarus. In Acts 2:24, the Greek term is *thanatos*. One would expect *mors* or *inferus* to translate mere death,[37] but most translators chose *infernus*—not neutral death, but the punitive hell. In 2 Peter 2:4, the only reference in the New Testament to Tartarus, the Greek author made a verb out of the proper noun Tartarus, referring to an action that might be translated as "entartered" but is usually translated "cast into Tartarus." In English 2 Peter 2:4 says: "For if God did not spare the sinning angels, but drew them down into the roaring of hell and consigned them to Tartarus, to await judgment in torment. . . ." The references to chains, darkness, confinement, and the term Tartarus itself clearly make this action punitive. The accompanying, explanatory phrase, "committed them to pits of nether gloom," reads, literally, in the Vulgate "the roaring

---

37. A minority of versions of the Vetus Latina translate *thanatos* as *mors*, rather than *inferi* or *infernus*. See the *Vetus Latina Database*.

of infernus."[38] The plight of the sinning angels lasts only until the judgment, thus they are enchained in Tartarus from their fall to the end of time. If the judgment has not yet occurred, the interim is intended, and here, as in Luke 16 (the rich man and Lazarus), the interim acquires a punitive function for the sinning angels—a clear example of infernalization. What in the Hebrew Bible had been morally neutral, mere death, has become punitive in the New Testament. The Latin translations of Sheol and Hades carry out this development almost uniformly.

There is another dramatic example of infernalization in Augustine of Hippo's *Narrative Analysis of Psalms*. Psalm 85:13 says: "You have delivered my soul from the lower hell (*ex inferno inferiore* in the Vulgate)." Augustine regards this as a very difficult expression and continues cautiously: "We understand on this basis that there are, as it were, two hells, an upper one and a lower one: for how can there be a lower hell, unless there is also an upper?"[39] Prompted by the expression "lower hell" in the Latin Psalm 85 and by the need to separate Abraham and Lazarus from the rich man in Luke 16, Augustine suggests: "Therefore, perhaps there are two hells, in one of which the souls of the just find peace, in the other the souls of the wicked are tortured."[40]

Infernalization, that is, the use of *infernus* to displace *inferus*, impacted readers and hearers emotionally and carried major implications over the long term. The different connotations of Hades, the *inferi*, and *Infernus* imply shifts in belief. Preserved or even extended over time, they become historical changes and in some cases lead to divisions in the original faith community. These shadings indicate important differences between Latin and Greek Christianity. When Augustine proposed dividing Hades, translated in Latin as Infernus, into a higher section for repose and a lower section for punishment, he was on new ground, and he admitted he was unsure.

All three of the monotheistic religions developed the idea of hell. Around the Mediterranean and in Western Europe believers in the convictions already mentioned would spread, mix, and come into conflict. Their ideas

---

38. "Si enim Deus angelis peccantibus non pepercit sed rudentibus inferni detractos in tartarum tradidit in iudicium cruciatos reservari. . . ." This passage is only the first part of a very complex sentence with many parallel clauses.

39. Aug. *Enarrat. Ps.* 85.13.17, lines 9–13: "Incerta sunt haec. . . . [I]ntellegimus tamquam duo inferna esse, superius et inferius; nam unde infernum inferius, nisi quia est infernum superius?" CCSL 39, ed. E. Dekkers and J. Fraipont (1956), p. 1190.

40. "Ergo inter ista duo fortasse inferna, quorum in uno quieuerunt animae iustorum, in altero torquentur animae impiorum." Aug. *Enarrat. Ps.* 85.13.18, lines 36–38; CCSL 39:1191.

would interact not only on the conceptual level, but also as aspects of family structure, political groupings, and religious communities. Beneath these great historical themes resided personal and collective anxieties and the psychological motifs of a person's confrontation with death, with the past, and with the possibility of postmortem consequences for his or her thoughts and deeds. These ideas also affect the relationship between humans and their predecessors that influences their psychology and behavior in ways that surpass the succession of doctrines taught about that relationship. Beliefs about the interim between death and resurrection have profound implications for family structure, the distribution of wealth, the organization of piety, and the authority of the formal religious elite, whether priestly, ascetic, or either of these in some combination with civic power. This rich mixture of themes—religious, psychological, sociological, political—forms the backdrop for the history that follows.

To understand the course of this development it seems wise to begin with Pope Gregory I's magisterial statement of how this system fits the providence of a monotheistic God, how it accords with Scripture, and how it can be understood by the many. Gregory's power as a writer operated simultaneously on several levels: he wrote biblical commentary, he offered guidance in contemplation and introspection, he compiled edifying tales for use in sermons or for instructing novices in religion. In expounding his idea of inner death, he channeled perceptions that had spread with the rise of monasticism and articulated a particular view unknown to classical authors. At the same time, he displayed religious perspectives that were not completely abstract and drew from aspects of the social settings in which they developed. Frequently employing metaphor and figurative speech, he and other Christian leaders drew parallels from the world around them not only to explain what justice is and how it might be administered but also for help in imagining what pains might constitute punishments for what kinds of offenses. To this end they adapted the laws of ancient Mediterranean societies and, in particular, the institution of slavery as a primary frame of reference for thinking through the judicial system that informed their eschatology. In working out what hell might be, slavery was their model.

The resultant synthesis produced a rigor that was, for many, shocking in its absoluteness. Consequently, contemplatives, questioners, dissenters, saw possibly inhumane aspects of the proposed eschatology—aspects sometimes deemed contradictory to the very divine model according to whose standards humans were to be judged at the end of time. Objections were raised regarding an alleged disproportionality of the punishment to the offense, loyalties between living people and their deceased family, and the outstanding negative examples that seemed unrelated to less extreme cases. Even if a special fate must be conceived for Judas or for the selfish rich man of Luke 16, must every sinner be classified with these archetypal figures? These reservations stimulated a vast literature.

As hell became the solution to evil in the three Abrahamic religions each had to defend the hell it developed against the same sorts of objections. Proposed alternatives were restful interruptions of infernal torments, the possibility of complete escape from them, and a purgatorial rise out of apparently hellish tortures. There was also a large body of literature describing the perceptions of visionaries whose senses were heightened by special circumstances such as dreams, apparitions, illness, or near-death experiences. Freed from the rigors of logic as from their bodies, these souls viewed the otherworld in terms that suggested individual resolutions of the tensions between hell proper as an abstract, absolute, doctrine of damnation, and the personal cases of individual sinners who were not entirely wicked. Many of these issues arose among the rabbis who composed the Babylonian Talmud between the first and sixth centuries CE, whose debates strongly resemble the discussions of Christian theorists. These, in turn, tended to select more allegorical options in the Greek-speaking East and more literal options in the Latin-speaking West. To this variety of viewpoints the Islamic community added its perspectives in the seventh century and thereafter. As the following chapters will show, for all their differences, the three religions espoused similar eschatological doctrines and similarly rejected similar objections to the consensus positions.

PART I

Foundations

CHAPTER 1

Gregory the Great

Order in Chaos

Things are images through which we consider the
nature of their causes.

—*Dialogues* 4.38.3

The wicked end their iniquities [only] because they
end their lives.

—*Moralia in Job* 34.19.36

Then through the fire they writhe in the body and
through grief they burn in the mind.

—*Moralia in Job* 15.29.35

Considering the multitude and complexity of
the themes whose interaction shapes the history of belief in hell during
late antiquity and the early Middle Ages, it is a good idea to start with a
clear description of the literal hell. Explicit insistence on the uniform and
eternal nature of hell arose early in the Latin patristic tradition. Minucius
Felix (very late second or early third century) wrote in his *Octavius* concerning those in hell: "For their torments, there would be neither limit nor end.
There the intelligent fire reduces and yet reforms limbs, consumes and yet
restores them. Just as lightning bolts strike bodies but do not waste them,
just as the fires of Mount Aetna and Mount Vesuvius and wherever else
burn without exhaustion, even so, that punishing fire does not diminish by
the hurts it inflicts on those burning, but fuels itself from its inexhaustible
plunder of their bodies."[1] Discussing the postmortem fate of the persecutors of the Christian martyrs, in a letter of ca. 252 to Demetrianus, Cyprian
of Carthage agreed: "Burning Gehenna will always burn its inmates and
a ravenous punishment will burn them with living flames; nor will there

---

1. Minucius Felix, *Octavius* 35.4, trans. Gerald H. Rendall, LCL (London: William Heinemann,
1931), 422.

ever be a means by which the torments can either relax or come to an end. Their souls together with their bodies [will] endure an infinite wracking for their grief." Nor will any pleas be heard on their behalf: "There will then be a sorrow at the punishment without any benefit from the repentance; all weeping will be useless and prayer fruitless. . . . Too late do those believe in eternal punishment who did not wish to believe in eternal life."[2]

For all their force, these descriptions lack the systematic exposition that can alone provide a baseline from which to evaluate other statements. The writer best situated to offer this overview is Gregory the Great (d. 604), son of a senator, prefect of Rome, diplomat, monk, theologian, preacher, and pope. Gregory's account of postmortem punishment reveals how as pope he declares dogma, as a scholar he expounds theology, and as a preacher he tells exemplary tales. In each of these offices he employs a different register or level of discourse. Each is aimed at different parts of the larger community he ruled. A full appreciation of Gregory's thought requires understanding the relationship between these levels, but for the moment it is sufficient to cover the fundamental assertions on which he based his doctrine of hell.

Hell is eternal. Its fire and its worms torment the body physically and the soul psychologically. The body burns without ever being completely consumed. The soul burns with the passions that led it astray, and the residue of those fatal vices rots the mind and compounds hell's darkness. Blind and confused, the damned do not understand the justice that structures their punishment even though it is exquisitely ordered. As they sinned unceasingly in life, so they should be punished unceasingly in death. The saved are in eternal heaven; the damned are in eternal hell: as the glory, so the pain.

The fire of hell is material; it burns like the fire we know on earth. This is more than a simple resemblance; earthly fire foreshadows, symbolizes, signifies, the infernal blaze. Because the material fire of hell will burn the devil and his angels, whose bodies are entirely spiritual, it can also burn the separated human soul, which is also entirely spiritual. Portals to hell may be found in the volcanoes of Sicily, which expand as time passes and more souls are added to them. Swelling volcanoes indicate, symbolize, predict, signify, the infernal fires they contain so as to warn humans of the fate that threatens the impenitent. When correctly interpreted, these signs can improve human behavior. Hell is subterranean but divided into upper and lower spaces. The living may have some knowledge of hell through Scripture, through the observation of nature, or through the accounts of people

---

2. Cyprianus Carthaginensis, *Ad Demetrianum* 24, lines 466–91; ed. M. Simonetti, CCSL 3A (1976): 49–50.

who had near-death experiences or visions. These perceptions of the afterlife are now becoming clearer because the end time is approaching.[3]

The Fire and the Worm

These basic positions cover Gregory's teaching on hell, but they do not convey the force of his language or the character of his analysis. Since the inextinguishable fire and the undying worm from Isaiah 66:24 that Mark applied to Gehenna (9:47–48) informs much of Gregory's exposition, his discussion of these details provides a good example of his method. Gregory builds his analysis on the relationships between earthly and infernal reality, between objects on earth and aspects of hell, between the vices of sinners and the psychological suffering of the damned. The fire of hell is like the fire of earth because it is material, but the fire of hell is also figurative because it torments the soul as a continuation of the burning desire that drives a sinner to sin. Symbolic relationships between the literal and the figurative, the material and the spiritual, lifetime sin and future torment, simultaneously structure his exposition even as it rationalizes infernal punishment.

Although the fire of hell is corporeal, and corporeal fire requires fuel, the fire of Gehenna burns corporeally without need of fuel, ignition, or stoking. It is fueled by *ardor*.[4] Here Gregory's fuel requires a play on words by using "ardor" as both a noun and a verb (*ardeo*). This fire, then, is the burning of desire, the glowing with ardor, the ardent love that afflicts the wicked as they pant after the wrong things in this world. The ardor of that misdirected love then burns them eternally in the next. Moreover, God foreknew the fate of those with misdirected love: "The justice of the Almighty, foreknowing the future from the beginning of the world, created the fire of Gehenna, which, once it began to punish the reprobate, developed its own ardor (*ardor suum*), one that would never end, even without fuel."[5] The sinner's ardor for sin finds its match in hell's ardor for punishment. Here Gregory comes close to giving hell a personality with character traits similar to the sinners' vices.

---

3. These positions will be examined more fully below.

4. "Gehennae ignis cum sit corporeus, et in se missos reprobos corporaliter exurat, nec studio humano succenditur nec lignis nutritur, sed creatus semel durat inexstinguibilis, et succensione non indiget, et ardore non caret." Greg. *Mor.* 15.29.35, lines 6–10; p. 770. All references to Gregory's *Moralia in Job* are to the edition by Marc Adriaen, CCSL vols. 143, 143a, 143b (1979–85). Throughout this book, all translations are my own unless otherwise indicated. Because the pages are numbered consecutively through the three volumes, I omit the volume numbers. For "ardor" again, see below at line 14: "ardorem suum etiam sine lignis numquam finiret."

5. *Mor.* 15.29.34, lines 12–13; p. 770.

Beyond hellfire's punishment of the flesh is its attack on the soul, but Gregory attains the soul through the body. "Because," Gregory says, the reprobate "sinned here in the soul and the flesh at the same time, let them be punished there, *likewise*, in the soul and the flesh together."[6] After the wicked receive their flesh in the Resurrection, it will burn (*ardebit*) in the fire of Gehenna. They will long to escape from it, and only "then will the impious wish to avoid what [in life] they loved."[7] Gregory explicitly drives home the reversal. "And so as an increase in the punishment, both here (on earth at the time of death) will one be led unwillingly *out of* the body and there (in Gehenna) one will be held unwillingly *in* the body against one's will."[8] And this is just. "Because he put his flesh before God, when that God judges him, it will be arranged so that he will be punished in the fire all the more through that same flesh."[9] That is, he will be punished through that which he preferred to God. The justice of that reversal will then also begin to dawn even on the sinner: "For every sinner who was foolish in sin will be wise in punishment."[10] This posthumous recognition is not a full understanding of damnation; it is only the regret of the damned at finding themselves in their current circumstances. "Then through the fire they writhe in the body and through grief they burn in the mind."[11]

With the fire comes the worm. In this life, worms are the ambitions that gnaw away, always hungry for more. Those who seek prosperity now are guilty of loving the world, whether their anxiety comes from fear of losing what they have or impatience to gain what they lack. "The worms cover them together: either this one who would have what he lusts after or that one lest he lose what he has; carnal thoughts oppress them both."[12] But the worms do not cover the righteous, for those who are not perturbed by these anxieties "are not gnawed by thoughts of external loss, are not covered by the worms of the heart."[13] Here, the torment of worms joins the blindness and the fire. They are among the tortures of hell that can afflict the soul of the

---

6. "Quia ex anima simul et carne peccauerunt, illic in anima *pariter* et carne cruciantur." Greg. *Mor.* 15.29.35, lines 15–16; p.770; my emphasis.

7. "tunc incipit uelle uitare quod amauit." Greg. *Mor.* 15.30.36, lines 15–16; p. 771.

8. "Ad augmentum itaque tormenti et hic de corpore nolens educitur, et illic in corpore tenetur inuitus." Ibid., lines 20–21; p. 771; my emphasis.

9. Greg. *Mor.* 15.30.16, lines 16–17; p. 771.

10. Ibid., 15.53.60, lines 8–9; p. 787.

11. "[P]er ignem crucientur in corpore et per dolorem ardeant in mente." Greg. *Mor.* 15.29.35, lines 23–24; p. 770. In this connection Gregory offers an innovation beyond Augustine's discussion. What Augustine (*De civitate Dei* 21.3, line 30; CCSL 48, ed. B. Dombart and A. Kalb [1955], p. 760) considers a mysterious contrast—that the flesh will acquire the immortality of the spirit and therefore be able to endure eternal pain—Gregory considers a paradox that constitutes one of hell's torments.

12. Greg. *Mor.* 15.66.65, lines 55–56; p. 791.

13. Ibid., lines 59–61; p. 791.

living, on earth. The same gnawing the ambitious soul suffers now will turn to a corporeal worm after death and resurrection. Indeed, Gregory states as an axiom: "That sin is directed to the underworld which is not emended by correction and repentance before the end of the present life."[14] Applying the axiom specifically to the torment of the worm, Gregory develops a complex food chain. The same flesh served by those who love the world becomes food for worms in the afterlife. The worms prey not on healthy, but on decaying flesh. Therefore, worms symbolize decaying flesh. "The illicit desire of flesh leads to decay."[15] Again, "he who boils with the desire for carnal corruption, pants after the stench of decay."[16] Now, like the ardor for illicit things that fuels the fire, the unwavering ambition that brought worms to the hearts of the greedy in this world will intensify after death and, as in the grave, the rotting of the flesh will continue and be steadily renewed. What we know of how worms feed on decay on earth suggests how they feed, in hell, on the moral corruption that sank the sinner to that sewer.

The fire that burns and illumines on earth, but obscures the sinners in hell, can nonetheless allow them to see—not to console, but rather to augment suffering.[17] Their punishment will increase because they will be surrounded by their peers: like with like and rebels with their leaders. These groupings produce a social or political dimension to infernal punishment. Through that fire, the damned will be able to see those with whom they sinned, whose love they preferred to that of the Creator. Since Luke 16 shows that the rich man was grieved at the thought that his kin might later undergo his present torment, actually seeing them there will increase his suffering. "The fire that wracks in darkness should be believed to conserve enough light to punish."[18] Whereas the flame of Gehenna yields no light to console the damned, it does shine to punish them, that is, by showing them how the objects of their affection are also tormented.[19] They will also join the devil, since he is the first of the leaders to have a deviant will and the one whose will his followers preferred to God's.[20] The connections between the rich man and his brothers, and between sinners who followed the devil, are social bonds. They form a fundamental aspect of Gregory's hell. Hell's perverse society inverts the heavenly court. Structured by justice, it is a perfect alliance of the unjust.

---

14. Ibid., 16.68.82, lines 2–4; p. 847.
15. Ibid., 16.69.83, lines 23–24; p. 848.
16. Ibid., lines 25–26; pp. 848–49.
17. Ibid., 9.66.101, lines 32–33; p. 528.
18. Ibid., lines 54–55; p. 529.
19. Paraphrase of Greg. *Mor.* 9.66.102, lines 58–71; p. 529.
20. Greg. *Mor.* 9.66.102, lines 76–78; pp. 529–30.

Gregory's Levels of Discourse

One important aspect of Gregory's articulation of hell's nature is how often he uses material objects visible in the here and now to symbolize conditions after death. The fire may burn with misplaced ardor, the worms may feed on rot, but fire and worms are real things that his readers and his hearers know from everyday life. The relationship Gregory proposed between material things and the abstract statements of theology applies not only to his eschatology, but to all fields of religious knowledge from creation to the Incarnation to prophecy to the sacraments and redemption. This is his theory of signification, in which physical objects become signs of their causes and their relationship to a grander whole; as he said, "Things are images through which we consider the nature of their causes" (*ex rerum . . . imaginibus pensamus merita causarum*).[21]

Understanding reality to be stratified in this way, Gregory adjusted the rhetoric he employed to reach the different audiences that formed the community he ruled. In the *Cura pastoralis* (*On the Care of Souls*), a handbook for pastors, Gregory counseled priests to consider the unity of their parishes. In their teaching, priests should not shock the naive to impress the sophisticated or bore initiates to reach beginners. "The discourse of the learned ought to be formed according to the quality of the hearers so that it is adapted to the special needs of individuals without deviating from the goal of collective edification (*communis aedificationis arte*)."[22] He catalogued a series of character differences that the effective counselor would take into account. When discussing the contrast between the wise and the simple, he observed, "The former are for the most part converted by arguments based on reason; the latter are often converted better by examples." Retelling the tales of the martyrs may prove more inspirational than peppering people with scriptural passages. The types of language he used to address each level could be considered individual genres, each with its own conventions or styles or tones of voice. I call these "levels of discourse," though other expressions might also work. "Levels of discourse" has the disadvantage of seeming hierarchical and linear, yet that same feature underlines Gregory's hope of penetrating a community over which he asserted a doctrinal authority. Gregory's ability to shift levels of discourse was not only a matter of style; it was also a technique of governance.

---

21. Grégoire le Grand, *Dialogues*, 4.38.3, ed. and trans. A. de Vogüé, SC 265 (Paris: Éditions du Cerf, 1980), p. 136. All references to the *Dialogues* here are to book 4.

22. PL 77:49. Same expression also in Greg. *Mor.* 30.3.12, lines 99–100; p. 1499.

Gregory himself advocated accommodating language to circumstances. To preface his theological masterpiece, the *Moral Interpretation of Job* (the *Moralia in Job*, henceforth the *Moralia*), Gregory wrote a dedicatory letter to Bishop Leander of Seville that evokes the various techniques of human speech.[23] He distinguishes between the learned (*prudentes*) and unlettered (*simplices*), between public and private occasions, between experts in religion and beginners. "For just as the divine word fortifies those already trained in the mysteries, so it often leaves the uneducated lukewarm. In public it has the ability to nourish the little ones, but in private to lift minds in wonder at the highest of things."[24] Or again, Gregory compares sacred speech to a river that must follow the landscape on its way to the valley. Now it cascades in a torrent of enthusiasm; now it pauses, still, in a pool, to refresh those new to its ideas. The stream accommodates at different depths either a swimming elephant or a wading lamb.[25] Gregory's use of various levels of discourse also necessitates our using them to understand the variety in the sources. Each one incorporates a different rhetorical approach and sheds light in its particular way. Therefore, I shall adopt this strategy not only to interpret Gregory, but throughout this book to comprehend as much as possible the various ways different authors writing under different circumstances and for different audiences in different religious faiths brought different aspects of human experience, emotion, and aspiration into play as they wrestled with hell and its related issues.

The levels may be distinguished as follows. *Dogma* is that which must be believed on pain of exclusion from the community. *Theology* is the systematic exposition of the community's doctrines in the most abstract terms. It defines and explains doctrine and refutes opposing contentions. Theology might be considered the explanation of dogma as supported by Scripture and reason. *Preaching* communicates theology's conclusions to the populace at large. Preaching itself is multilayered. Preachers quote Scripture and invoke authoritative statements. Preachers also include illustrative tales (sermon stories, anecdotes, examples, edifying stories) to attract and retain the listeners' attention. (Excluded from this list are ritual and the visual arts, which combine these levels in different ways.)

The "lowest" level is *folklore*, a term that has recently been applied to the familiar knowledge shared by all members of a society, including the least

---

23. Greg. *Mor.*, *Epistola ad Leandrum*, §2, line 65; p. 3: "humani eloquii distinguere modos."
24. Ibid., §4, lines 173–77; p. 6.
25. "Quasi . . . est fluuius, . . . planus et altus, in quo et agnus ambulet et elephas natet." Greg. *Mor.*, *Epistola ad Leandrum*, §4, line 178; p. 6.

literate. An example would be the debate over the chicken and the egg. Folklore would include the elemental ideas of indigenous people, the target of conversion efforts by outsiders. The idea that dogma is higher than folklore is purely arbitrary except for the fact that once a religion acquires political backing, as Christianity did, its dogma can be enforced by the social organization, the powers that be, an advantage that confers an obvious superiority. Therefore, it makes sense to view the levels of discourse from the top down. Nonetheless, there are many instances of religious ideas pervading a society through the downtrodden and gradually attracting its higher echelons. Some consider Christianity such a case. According to this account, the populace converted first. Within local communities, bishops emerged who eventually reached the imperial court and attracted the emperor Constantine himself. Whether beginning with the grass roots or the palace, there is a creative tension between theology and folklore that will be a theme throughout this book. One need only consider how fire and worms can be used to teach religion.

As it happens, Gregory developed his ideas about hell in two separate works that illustrate his ability to use different levels of discourse. In his *Moralia*, Gregory used the formal conundrum to shape theological statements. In his *Dialogues*, he balanced edifying narrative tales, exempla, with doctrinal lessons. For him and many in his audience through the centuries, his works typify the practice of putting abstract truths into narrative, comprehensible, almost tangible form. This, in fact, is the combination of teaching and preaching, which in Gregory's eyes imitated the use Jesus made of parables.[26] Gregory's *Dialogues* present an imaginary conversation between Gregory and a student, the deacon Peter, who asks the questions Gregory expects of a well-intentioned, slightly skeptical beginner. Peter's questions represent their own level of discourse. Gregory's answers can combine a scriptural proof-text, theological inferences from it, an exemplary tale, and the moral he draws.[27] We see this method in action as Peter wonders about

---

26. For this ritual aspect of the sermon story, see Alan Bernstein, "The *Exemplum* as 'Incorporation' of Abstract Truth in the Thought of Humbert of Romans and Stephen of Bourbon." in *The Two Laws: Studies in Medieval Legal History Dedicated to Stephan Kuttner*, ed. L. Mayali and S. Jefferis-Tibbetts (Washington, DC: Catholic University of America Press, 1990), 82–96.

27. The authenticity of the *Dialogues* has been denied by Francis Clark, *The Pseudo-Gregorian Dialogues*, 2 vols. (Leiden: Brill, 1987). Marilyn Dunn, "Gregory the Great, the Vision of Fursey, and the Origins of Purgatory," *Peritia* 14 (2000): 238–54, provides a bibliography on both sides of the debate (239 n. 5). Clark's thesis has been convincingly dismissed by Carole Straw in terms akin to the question of levels of discourse: "Need we deny Gregory the privilege of varying his material to suit his purposes as a preacher and teacher?" Straw, review of *The Pseudo-Gregorian Dialogues*, by Francis Clark, *Speculum* 64 (1989): 397–99, at 397. She rightly decries "Clark's failure to make allowance for

the condition of the soul during the interim.[28] (Before the resurrection of the flesh that comes at the end of time, the souls of humans are incorporeal—or spiritual, as their flesh is the body in the grave. The flesh will not be returned to the soul until the General Resurrection at the end of time.) If some of these souls are believed to be in hell already, Peter asks, how can material fire (that is, the fire of hell) torment the spiritual soul (the soul outside the body of a dead person)?

Gregory begins by mentioning Jesus's parable concerning the rich man and Lazarus, in which the soul of the rich man, clearly only a spirit, says that he is suffering in the flames (Luke 16:24). Beyond this scriptural example, Gregory supplies one from his own experience.[29] He tells how he had heard about the death of Reparatus, "a prominent man" in the time of the Goths. Before he actually died, Reparatus lay apparently lifeless for a long time and then recovered. He related to the amazed bystanders that he had been in "the places of punishment" (loca poenarum). There, he saw two pyres of wood. One awaited a "dissolute and sensual" priest named Tiburtius, who was placed on the pyre and burned. After he recovered, Reparatus sent for information about Tiburtius, who lived not far away. Continuing his account of what he had seen, Reparatus reported, beyond this first pyre, another, immense one that seemed to reach to the sky. As he related this, a voice proclaimed whose pyre this was, and Reparatus himself died on the spot. Witnesses to the death of Reparatus then learned that the messenger had found Tiburtius dead. We are to infer, therefore, that events Reparatus saw in the otherworld corresponded to those he narrated during his brief return to life. They include his view of his own fate after death. Here, the momentary recovery of Reparatus helps Gregory explain what goes on in hell.

From this example it is clear how, in his replies to the novice Peter, Gregory moves from level to level as he shifts from anecdotes to explanations. Funeral pyres need little explanation. Reparatus dies as the voice assigning him to this pyre resounds in both worlds at once. From this dramatic coincidence Gregory shifts from the literal to the doctrinal, authoritative level

---

genre" (399). Patricia Deleeuw states that Gregory's sermons were the most frequent surviving homiliary in all Carolingian libraries, including those by contemporary Carolingian authors. Deleeuw, "Gregory the Great's 'Homilies on the Gospels' in the Early Middle Ages," Studi Mediaevali, ser. 3, 26.1 (1986): 868. The authorship of the homilies is uncontested, and they contain many of the same types of "superstitious" sermon stories that Clark thinks expose the Dialogues as inauthentic. See also Alan Bernstein, "Named Others and Named Places: Stigmatization in the Early Medieval Afterlife," in Hell and Its Afterlife: Historical and Contemporary Perspectives, ed. Isabel Moreira and Margaret Toscano (Farnham, UK, and Burlington, VT: Ashgate, 2010), 53–71, at 60 n. 32.

28. Greg. Di. 4.30.1–5; pp. 100–102.
29. Ibid., 4.32.1–5; pp. 106–8.

of discourse. Souls like those of Tiburtius and Reparatus burn in hell as if they were bodies on a funeral pyre on earth. Just as the material body holds the spirit prisoner in life, hell's material fires hold it after death. Further, Matthew 25:41 states that the devil and his angels will be consigned to eternal fire, and these beings—the devil and his angels—are incorporeal. The human soul will suffer similarly.[30] With this statement, Gregory moves to yet another level of discourse, higher than the doctrinal declaration. It gives the scriptural text and an analogy behind it. Further, the example is given in the course of a discussion of how the immaterial soul, separated from the body after the individual's death but before the General Resurrection, can suffer in material fire. Through categorization, the tale supports an even broader doctrinal lesson, while, simultaneously, the doctrinal abstraction embraces the tale as an example. Thus Gregory rationalizes the folkloric technique of portraying the soul as a body, something that can be consumed on a funeral pyre. Gregory's account of Reparatus illustrates how this pope deliberately combined various levels of discourse to establish his doctrinal lesson.

As the narrative of Reparatus and other cases to appear throughout this book show, a frequent figure in folkloric sources is the soul separated from its body, which nevertheless behaves like a body. It has full sense perception (sometimes enhanced), limbs, hair, and sex. It has a fixed identity and is marked by the merits or demerits acquired in life, though, at this level, that life is not always fully over. Thus the soul's lifetime deeds appear materialized and localized. Localized, because, in accordance with the Wisdom of Solomon 11:16, one is punished in the member with which one sinned. Finally, narrative and analysis at the folkloric level portray life from a worldly perspective: love and hatred, justice and mercy, power and helplessness, are presented in human terms.

By contrast, the theological level discusses hell abstractly and universally. Souls are far less like bodies. Indeed, there are few if any individual souls. Instead, one talks of "the just" or "the unjust" as categories. The damned are called "unbelievers" and "the impious," and not named as individuals. Their specific sins are not explained. The grouping of souls involves punishing like with like: adulterers, thieves, hypocrites, each together, within a single class. Other categories are those outlined by Augustine in the *Enchiridion*: the perfect, the good-but-not-perfect, the bad-but-not-completely-wicked, and the altogether-wicked.[31] At the theological level, hell is completely removed from earth. It is eternal and unchanging. It is an inversion of heaven. Just

---

30. Ibid., 4.30.5; p. 102.
31. *Enchiridion* 110.9–13; CCSL 46 (1969): 109.

as the saints are with God, the damned are absolutely excluded. No escape, not even the slightest contact, is possible. Theology describes hell from a heavenly perspective, as God might see it, that is, with the divine attributes of mercy and justice in perfect harmony.

The folkloric and doctrinal levels can operate independently of each other, but usually, and certainly in Gregory's *Dialogues*, a hegemonic action intervenes to co-opt the folklore, when the narrator shifts from tale-teller to interpreter. Then, the tale becomes bait for the doctrinal lesson. To that end, Gregory employed several techniques. Most evident is his use of the dialogue between master and pupil, Gregory and Peter, but in exempla the narrator can interrupt the story to explain its significance. In a vision, in which a soul is said to see the otherworld, the narrative can include a figure of authority, such as the psychopomp or guide, who explains to the visionary the significance of events. The best evidence for the hegemonic character of the exemplum comes in how the expositor projects the assumption that since these things are so, those who now understand them will amend their lives. These are behavioral goals, such as paying tithes, restoring appropriated ecclesiastical property, confessing one's sins, praying for the dead, endowing masses, converting to religion, making restitution of ill-gotten gains, or just plain mending one's ways. The history of belief in hell cannot be told without reference to these rhetorical devices. The doctrinal conclusion links the concrete detail (the funeral pyre) to the abstract lesson (separated souls suffer in material fire). It is this technique of exemplification, this symbolism, that links the many phenomena to be examined in this book. Gregory's view of hell and his method of expounding it authorize, exemplify, and aid in narrating this history. We shall also see how both the doctrinal conclusions *and* the symbols often migrate from religion to religion.

Symbolism Bridges the Narrative and Doctrinal Levels

It is in the *Dialogues* that Gregory evokes most frequently the physical pains of hell, yet even in this text, with its emphasis on the vivid and dramatic, he rarely mentions an external torment without its psychological counterpart. In the *Moralia*, Gregory explains these hurts at great length, and external, bodily pains appear to be symbols of inner, psychological ones. Given this connection of corporeal pain to inner anguish and to the sin that brought them on, the whole becomes an example of theodicy, of divine justice. Thus, for Gregory, no torment of hell fails to be an example of a predetermined order, an order that, by its nature, praises its creator and embellishes his creation.

Indeed, in the *Dialogues*, Gregory devotes much attention to a bridge—a prominent feature in the underworld, according to his informants and ancient tradition.[32] It seems he invites us to regard the bridge as a case study in connecting the various levels of reality and discourse. Focusing on the bridge makes it possible to move beyond Reparatus's glimpse into hell and understand better how Gregory explained his eschatological views to a broader audience and how, within the circle of his most literate correspondents, he gave more sophisticated expression to these theodicial associations.

In the *Dialogues*, Gregory compares the consequences of two men's near-death experiences. The first, Peter of Iberia, saw the fires of hell and the prominent men hanging on the gallows there. He returned to life and mended his ways.[33] The second, a ranking senator named Stephen, went to Constantinople, fell sick, died, and went to hell. When the superintendent of the punishments realized that this was Stephen the senator, and he had called for Stephen the blacksmith, he sent him back as a case of mistaken identity. Gregory treats this almost comic incident as a confirmation of these types of visions. Stephen the blacksmith died as soon as the senator came back to life. Says Gregory: "Thus it is proven that the words which he heard were true, for this is the import of the death [of the other] Stephen [the blacksmith]."[34] Nonetheless, while in hell, Stephen confirmed with his own eyes all he had previously heard about the place without believing. When Stephen finally did die, his condition was seen by a soldier who had a near-death experience at the same time and returned to tell what he had seen.

The soldier saw a bridge passing over a river of filth that produced a cloud of stench. Only those free of guilt (*quibus culpa non obsisteret*) can pass over the bridge and escape the river.[35] On the other side of the bridge was a meadow dotted with dwellings of gold and bathed in a sweet aroma, except near the banks, which were partially befogged by the river's stench. The soldier saw a prelate of the church held by heavy iron chains in a repulsive place by the river. When he asked how the man had deserved this fate, he was told that the official had abused his office and administered punishment cruelly. Conversely, a humble cleric traversed the bridge with as much assurance as he had purity of life. This anonymous answer in reply to the soldier's question injects a more authoritative view into the soldier's report. Among those whom the soldier saw attempt to cross the bridge was Stephen, this time

---

32. On bridges, see Carol Zaleski, *Otherworld Journeys: Accounts of Near-Death Experience in Medieval and Modern Times* (New York: Oxford University Press, 1987), 65–66.

33. Greg. *Di.* 4.30.5; p. 102.

34. Ibid., 4.37.6; p.128.

35. Ibid., 4.37.10; p. 130. What the soldier saw on the bridge is told in 4.37.8–13; pp. 130–132.

definitely dead. Stephen had slipped and fallen in such a way that the lower half of his body dangled from the bridge, and hideous men who had come up out of the river tried to pull him down. Meanwhile some brilliant and beautiful men, presumably from the meadow, began to draw him upward by his arms. The result of this drama is not known, because the soldier's spirit was recalled to his body before he could witness the outcome of the struggle.

So far, Gregory has used folkloric techniques to set the scene. He contrasts the river's stench to the meadow's delights, with the polluted banks as a transitional zone. Nothing could be more concrete than the chains confining the overzealous prelate. The narrative explains how the bridge detects the guilt of those who attempt to cross it. Stephen's body (actually, his soul represented as a body) is the prize in a tug-of-war between agents of the river and rescuers from the meadow. All this information comes from souls prematurely departed from their bodies, who see familiar, readily comprehensible objects. The listener, presumably, empathizes with Stephen.

With the suspense established, Gregory exploits the moment and introduces authoritative declarations from a higher level of discourse. He prefaces his explanations with clear-cut, dogmatic formulas that contrast suddenly with the narrative: "It may clearly be understood . . ." (*Aperte datur intellegi*) or, immediately below, "From which it is gathered . . ." (*Qua ex re colligitur*).[36] Elsewhere he says bluntly, "One must think . . ." (*Pensandum est*).[37] After the introduction of these phrases, Gregory interprets the vision univocally, imposing a single meaning on the folkloric data. The bridge, he says, represents the narrow way that leads to life (Matt. 7:14). The river stinks "because the flow of putrid vices of the flesh drain daily toward the abyss."[38] Stephen's body appeared suspended athwart the bridge because "in him the evils of the flesh struggled against his performance of alms." As Gregory put it, "He was pulled downward by his hips and upward by his arms" because, although "he loved to perform alms, he had not perfectly resisted the vices of the flesh, which drew him downward."[39] Then, returning to the consideration of the two men's near-death experiences, which structures chapter 37, Gregory contrasts the value of each. "For those [like Peter] who see them and understand the evils they must avoid, they are helpful; for those [like Stephen] who do not wish to avoid [these dangers] even after they have seen and known them, they serve to raise the stakes, so that those who ignore them

36. Greg. *Di.* 4.37.16; p. 134.
37. Ibid., 4.60.1; p. 200.
38. Ibid., 4.38.3; p. 136.
39. Ibid., 4.37.13; p. 132.

may be punished even more severely (*amplius*)."[40] The narrative of the bridge and the explanation of Stephen's fate (left in suspense) links on its own the dramatic level of the exemplum, the illustrative anecdote and the doctrinal lesson. The two co-exist like two liquids emulsified: narrative and exposition so intimately suspended as to make a single lesson from two essentially different styles. Simultaneously, the fundamental dichotomies of rhetorical antithesis unify the lesson in the oppositions of hands and loins, charity and sexuality, angels and demons, verdure and stench, and deeds in life versus the fate beyond.

These correspondences between the plot structure and religious meaning of the illustrative dramas in the *Dialogues* show again how Gregory explains the overarching principle informing his symbolic system and the difference between levels of discourse: "Things are images through which we consider the nature of their causes."[41] According to this scheme, our perceptions are images, provoked by realities, which in turn have causes that exist on a higher level. Dreams or the mystical experiences of charismatic figures, or the experiences of revenants, therefore, are links to or signs of higher truths attained by contemplation or divulged by revelation. Moreover, Gregory adds, disclosing a strong sense of apocalyptic expectation, "As the present world approaches its end, the future world becomes almost tangible in its proximity, and its signs are read that much more clearly."[42]

Gregory's first illustration of the relationship between "things" and the meaning of their causes is of vital importance to the history of belief in hell. Immediately following his interpretation of the stinking river that runs beneath the test bridge, he turns to the destruction of Sodom and Gomorrah. "'The Lord rained fire and sulphur on the Sodomites' (Genesis 19:24) so that both the fire would burn them and the stench of sulphur would destroy them. Because they burned with an illicit love of the corruptible flesh, they perished from a fire and a stench simultaneously, so that from their punishment they would be aware that they had relegated themselves to eternal death by the delight they took in their own stench."[43] The example of Sodom and Gomorrah had provided a precedent on which to base prophecies of horrible fates for other cities and peoples from the time of the Hebrew prophets (Isa. 13:19; Jer. 49:18, 50:40; Zeph. 2:9). Matthew 10:15 attributes the same strategy to Jesus: "It shall be more tolerable on the day of judgment for

---

40. Ibid., 4.37.14; p. 134.
41. Ibid., 4.38.3; p. 136.
42. Ibid., 4.43.2; p. 154.
43. Ibid., 4.38.6–4.39.1; pp. 136–38.

the land of Sodom and Gomorrah than for that town." Three references in Revelation (19:20; 20:10; 21:8) evoke the same model in referring to the lake of fire and sulfur. For this reason, it is worth reexamining Gregory's phrasing so as to emphasize the parallels he establishes between fire and burning and between carnal love, flesh, and stench. This close analysis of this one sentence is particularly important because it builds a bridge of signification from historical meaning, the destruction of Sodom and Gomorrah, to the higher, theological purpose, and establishes the method he uses also in the *Moralia*. More significantly, it illustrates how Gregory himself applies the slogan "Things are images through which we consider the nature of their causes."

The fire and the stench are separate punishments for different, but related sins. Gregory's verb, "to burn" (*ardeo*), puns on the noun for burning, "ardor." Thus the fire burns them because of the ardor of their love for the flesh. The sulfur punishes them because the love was illicit and its object was flesh, which is corruptible, and so is liable to rot and stench. Fire is to ardor as stench is to flesh. Ardor for corruptible flesh produces a combination of fire and stench (that of sulfur) to punish the Sodomites for the delight they took in their carnal pleasures. Note that Gregory does not name or describe the Sodomites' sin, except to say that it was carnal. Thus, Gregory uses the biblical fate of Sodom and Gomorrah as a generic model for the torments of hell and all suffering consequent on misdirected love, that is, love for any object lower than God. Such love leads to fire and brimstone, as the precedent of Sodom and Gomorrah, the warning of prophets, the threat of Jesus, and the Revelation to John all show. Thus do events, through their significations, cause us to reflect on the meaning of their causes.

There is an interesting parallel on the individual level to the method Gregory has just applied on the apocalyptic, global level. "It should be known (*sciendum est!*) that sometimes souls still located in their bodies see something of the punishments in the spirit world (*poenale aliquid de spiritalibus*), which usually edifies either that soul or the souls of those who hear the vision."[44] Before his death, the greedy and licentious Chrysaurius saw black and hideous spirits surround his bed. He begged them for a reprieve, but they wrenched his spirit away to the prisons of hell.[45] Another monk, one who had ostensibly fasted, reveals on his deathbed that all along he had eaten secretly. As his brothers surround his deathbed, he tells how a dragon has wrapped

---

44. Ibid., 4.40.1; p. 138.
45. Ibid., 4.40.6–9; pp. 142–44.

his tail around his legs to devour him. With his head down the monk's throat, the dragon sucks out his life force, leaving him no time to repent.[46]

If demons can act as heralds of hell, nature itself provides other hints of postmortem realities. On Lipari, a small island off the northern shore of Sicily, a holy man saw the death of Theodoric, the king of the Ostrogoths. The hermit who had seen the event related to visitors who believed the king still alive that he had witnessed Pope John and the patrician Symmachus toss the king into a neighboring volcano. And Gregory interprets: "Because [Theodoric] had killed Pope John with the hardships of imprisonment and had executed the patrician Symmachus with the sword, it seems very proper that the vision should show these two men hurling Theodoric into the fire, since he had condemned both of them unjustly."[47] The significance of the event transcends this one occurrence, for "in the islands of that region [Sicily], more than elsewhere, open craters belch forth the fire of the torments. Those who know say that each day their sides grow higher and they become larger. The end of the world is approaching and, the more damned persons there are to burn, the more the places of torment must expand. Almighty God wished to make them visible for the correction of those who live in the world. Thus the minds of unbelievers, who deny the existence of infernal torments, *see* the places of torments that they refused to accept when they were only *spoken of*."[48] So the volcanoes of Sicily provide physical evidence for infernal punishments. Even though souls of the dead are separated from their bodies until the General Resurrection, the volcanic islands of the Tyrrhenian Sea expand to accommodate the increasing numbers condemned to their torments.

Two Hells Must Be Accepted (*Credenda sunt*)

In the *Dialogues*, Peter the deacon asks his teacher where hell is. Gregory finds a clue in Psalm 85 (86):13 "You have delivered my soul from the depths of Sheol," which in the Vulgate reads "eruisti animam meam ex inferno inferiori" or, literally, "Thou has drawn my soul from the lower hell." If there is a lower hell, there must also be an upper hell. Gregory therefore infers that there are two hells, but he does not press the issue. Instead, he pursues the lower hell as a way of locating it. "If by 'hell' (*infernus*), we mean 'that which is inferior' (*inferius*), then hell must be to the earth what the earth is

---

46. Ibid., 4.40.11; p. 146.
47. Ibid., 4.31.4; p. 106.
48. Ibid., 4.36.12; p. 122; my emphasis.

to heaven"; and therefore, it would be subterranean. Indeed, Gregory concludes, "I see no objection to believing that hell is beneath the earth."[49] In order to stress its location beneath the earth, Gregory blends his upper and lower hells back into one subterranean location.

In the *Moralia*, the distinction between the two hells takes a much different turn. Gregory again refers to a superior hell, but consistent with his task of writing a commentary, he examines Job's lament (Job 17:16), asking whether all his expectations "descend into the deepest hell" (*in profundissimum infernum*). Gregory then makes two points. Because Job lived before the coming of Christ, even if he had to descend into hell, it could not have been the deepest hell.[50] But, Gregory is forced to admit, this observation itself raises another question. "Could Job refer to the higher places of the underworld (*inferi*) as 'the deepest hell' (*inferni*)?"[51] Drawing on the doctrinal lesson to be inferred from the version of the Descent of Christ known as Latin B, Gregory now feels obliged to extricate Job from referring to the deepest hell before Christ created it, at the time of his Descent, by abolishing Sheol/Hades, the neutral land of the dead.[52]

His solution is a remarkable display of ingenuity. In essence, he refers to a stratified model of the universe, moving from the heavens to the air to the earth to the upper hell. Given Job's perspective, Gregory argues, the upper hell may be considered the deepest hell, because it is below the earth, even though it is still above the lower hell. He says: "In comparison to the level of this same earth, those places of the underworld (*inferi*), which are above those other receptacles of hell (*inferni*), may not incongruously be signified by the name 'the deepest hell' (*profundissimus infernus*), because what the air is to heaven and the earth is to the air this higher region of the hells (*infernorum*) is to the earth."[53] Noteworthy in this explanation is Gregory's use of

---

49. "[Q]uid obstet non uideo ut sub terra esse infernus credatur." Greg. *Di.* 4.44.1; pp. 158–60. In this discussion, Gregory also advances Rev 5:1 and 5:5 to establish a similar inference from the expression "neither in heaven, nor on earth, nor beneath the earth."

50. Gregory might have said that these words of Job were a prophecy of a truth to be understood only later, but he did not do so here.

51. Greg. *Mor.* 13.48.53, lines 8–9; p. 696: "An ipsa superiora loca inferi profundissimum infernum uocat?"

52. For the knowledge of the Descent in the early Middle Ages, see Zbigniew Izydorczyk, ed., *The Medieval Gospel of Nicodemus: Texts, Intertexts, and Contexts in Western Europe* (Tempe, AZ: MRTS, 1997). For the place of Latin A in this literature, see Rémi Gounelle, "L'enfer selon l'évangile de Nicodème," *Revue d'Histoire et de Philosophie Religieuses* 86.3 (July–September 2006): 313–33.

53. "Quantum uero ad eiusdem terrae altitudinem et illa loca inferi quae superiora sunt aliis receptaculis inferni, hoc loco non incongrue inferni profundissimi appellatione signantur, quia quod aer ad caelum, terra ad aerem, hoc ille est superior infernorum sinus ad terram." Greg. *Mor.* 13.48.53, lines 18–20; p. 697.

Augustine's term "receptacles" and his preservation, almost in spite of himself, of the distinction between the underworld (*inferus*) and hell (*infernus*). It is clear, then, that when not qualified by the terms "superior" and "inferior" or their equivalents, the older distinction endures. Gregory confirms this inference when he again contrasts the two receptacles. "In the underworld (*apud inferos*) the just are not in places of punishment, but are held in the higher bosom of tranquility."[54]

Gregory also proclaims the upper hell in commenting on Job's almost despairing sigh (Job 14:13): "Oh that thou wouldest hide me in Sheol (*inferno*) . . . until thy wrath be past." The significance of Gregory's assertion becomes clearer in contrast to the tentative tone of Augustine's musings on "You have delivered my soul from the lower hell." Abandoning Augustine's caution, Gregory innovated: "One ought to believe (*credenda sunt*) that there are upper parts of hell and other, lower parts, such that in the higher parts, the just experience peace and in the lower, the unjust are wracked."[55] "One ought to believe"! Clearly we are in the realm of dogma from the pen of a pope. In addition to noting the difference between the authority apparent in Gregory's assertion as compared to Augustine's, it is also important to observe that Gregory worked out this discussion in the *Moralia*. In the *Dialogues*, Gregory's distinction between an upper and lower hell is fleeting; it collapses immediately into one subterranean receptacle. In a theological work like the *Moralia*, Gregory provides the scriptural basis, the theological reasoning, and finally the dogmatic assertion that there are two hells, one above the other.

The crucial difference between the upper hell (Sheol/Hades and the Bosom of Abraham) and the lower (Tartarus) emerged at the time of Christ's Descent (especially in Latin B). For "in returning from hell (*ab inferno rediens*), the Lord did not draw out both the elect and the reprobate, but he bore from there [only] those whom he had foreknown would cleave to him."[56] The hell that Christ visited in his Descent, however, is clearly Sheol/Hades, the place where the ancient blessed, those whom Christ knew would be faithful, awaited their redemption. Therefore, Gregory is applying the term "hell" (*infernus*) to the waiting place of the righteous ancients. Nonetheless, those who were not among his followers, he cast beneath, into the lower hell,

---

54. "[A]pud inferos iusti non in locis poenalibus, sed in superiori quietis sinu tenerentur." Greg. *Mor.* 13.48.53, lines 2–3; p. 696.

55. "Sed esse superiora inferni loca, esse alia inferiora credenda sunt, ut et in superioribus iusti requiescerent et in inferioribus iniusti cruciarentur." Greg. *Mor.* 12.9.13; p. 636.

56. "Non enim ab inferno rediens Dominus electos simul et reprobos traxit, sed illa exinde omnia sustulit quae sibi inhaesisse praesciuit." Greg. *Mor.* 12.11.15, lines 10–12; p. 637.

which the *Gospel of Nicodemus*, Latin B, calls Tartarus, the term the Greeks used to distinguish the place of punishment from the neutral land of all the dead.[57]

Gregory's distinction of the upper hell from the lower hell is a development of the greatest importance. He has aligned the upper hell (*infernus superior*) with the underworld (*inferus*) and the Bosom of Abraham. He reserved the lower hell (*infernus inferior*) for the worst cases. It is the eternal fire, the deepest hell, Tartarus, Gehenna. Isidore of Seville, the younger brother of Gregory's friend Leander, confirmed this conclusion in his *De differentiis verborum*, when he wrote: "The upper part of hell (*inferni*) is the underworld (*inferus*), where the souls of the just reposed, while awaiting the arrival of Christ."[58] Gregory's dogmatic assertion of the two hells reaffirmed the practice, which had been in effect since the Vetus Latina, of making the term "hell" (*infernus*) a synonym, a functional equivalent, of Sheol/Hades, the neutral land of all the dead, the *inferi*. Gregory's naming of the upper hell created a new epoch in the history of hell. The development, over centuries, of beliefs about the upper hell will be a major theme of this book.

Postmortem Purgation

Because the upper hell or *inferus* functions like the Bosom of Abraham in Luke 16 and the place of quiet where the ancient just awaited the coming of Christ, it has a temporal dimension. It is here the blessed wait for the full vision of God. This delay, Gregory says, Job called "darkness," and it consists in *taedium*. Consequently, whatever faults cause one delay in enjoying the vision of God, they occasion only tedium, which may still be putting it too strongly, for, as we have seen, those who are blessed but still in need of some discipline enjoy the higher bosom of tranquillity. Still, the verb "to hold" (*tenere*) expresses the idea of constraint and gives this time of delay a technical name, *dilatio*.[59] The question of a possible confusion between this place of delay and what came to be called purgatory arises in dramatic fashion in other sources to be considered in subsequent chapters.

---

57. See Alan E. Bernstein, *The Formation of Hell: Death and Retribution in the Ancient and Early Christian Worlds* (Ithaca, NY: Cornell University Press, 1993), 281–82; and table 1 in the introduction to this book.

58. "Pars superior inferni inferus est, ubi quieverunt ante adventum Christi animae iustorum." Isidorus Hispalensis, *Libri duo differentiarum, Liber primus De differentiis verborum, De littera "I"*; PL 83:39C.

59. Greg. *Mor.* 13.47.52, lines 5 and 23; p. 696.

In the *Dialogues*, Peter the deacon asks whether there is a purgatorial fire after death.[60] Gregory replies in the affirmative, citing among other biblical texts Matthew 12:31–32, which enumerates sins that can be forgiven, contrasting them to blasphemy against the Holy Spirit, which "will not be forgiven, either in this age or in the age to come." Gregory infers that although this one sin can never be exonerated, even in the age to come, others can. He stipulates, therefore, "It must be believed that there is a purifying fire for slight faults before the Judgment."[61] Such sins must be tiny, but they will not be negligible, because "faults not atoned for in life can still burden a soul after death."[62] In isolated passages, he gives examples of how this can happen. For nearly perfect souls, no place as coarse as upper hell or even a nameable physical location such as the Bosom of Abraham can be thought. It is enough to say that the delay occurs outside of heaven. "We cannot affirm or deny [that] all the elect [are already in blessedness], for there are certain souls of the just, who are still delayed in certain dwellings outside of the heavenly kingdom. And what could the delay imposed on them indicate except that they are still lacking in perfect justice?"[63] Perfect souls, however, attain heaven "as soon as they leave the body."[64] In pronouncing the existence of the upper hell, Gregory affirmed the peace the just experience in the bosom of tranquility. Yet in the *Dialogues*, he dramatizes these notions with a more tangible imagery, whether the dwellings (*mansiones*), where the nearly perfect are delayed, or the service rooms beneath the Roman baths, where minor subordinates perform manual labor. In the *Dialogues* Gregory provides two examples of ghosts performing expiation through manual labor or menial service on earth.

The late Paschasius, who erred by favoring the wrong candidate in a recent papal schism, works off his guilt laboring in the ovens that heat the water in the Roman baths at Città Sant'Angelo, near Pescara.[65] Momentarily free, by the way, of Augustine's "receptacles," this ghost requests prayers to speed his release.[66] The possibility of release supposes that Paschasius is one of the just, whom Gregory said in the *Moralia* are not tormented after death. Further, Gregory specifies that Paschasius had not sinned out of malice, did

---

60. Greg. *Di.* 4.40.13–4.43.5; pp. 146–56.

61. "de quibusdam leuibus culpis esse ante iudicium purgatorius ignis credendus est." Greg. *Di.* 4.41.3; p. 148.

62. "Quae cuncta etiam post mortem grauant, si adhuc in hac uita positis minime fuerint relaxata." Greg. *Di.* 4.41.4; p. 148.

63. Greg. *Di.* 4.26.1; p. 84.

64. Ibid.

65. The difficult place-name "Angulus" identified by the editor, de Vogüé.

66. Greg. *Di.* 4.42.3; p. 152.

not know that his action was a sin, and therefore did not repent of it. His wrong, therefore, is very slight—just the category in question. Nonetheless, Gregory's hegemonic, univocal intervention teaches that because "fault may not be released without punishment" (*neque . . . sine ultione laxaretur culpa*), it was precisely that minimal residue of guilt that required expiation by labor in the baths.[67]

A second exemplum has a similar setting. Bishop Felix occasionally went to the baths, where a servant distinguished himself for the meticulous service he rendered him. On one occasion, to show his appreciation, Felix offered the attendant two loaves of bread. Surprisingly, the attendant made a counterproposal: "Formerly, I was the lord of this place, but for my faults I have been assigned to serve here. If you wish to benefit me, intercede on account of my sins with the almighty God by offering this bread for me. You will know whether your prayers have been heard if, when you return to take the waters, you see me here no more."[68] Because the man refers to his faults in the plural, he appears to be worse off than Paschasius. Thus Gregory has provided a range of postmortem possibilities for those with differing degrees of minor faults. The place of their confinement varies from laboring beneath the baths to simply waiting "outside of heaven." Although Gregory gives no specific location for the purgatorial fire, he clearly asserts the possibility of postmortem purification leading eventually to the heavenly kingdom. These souls have clearly avoided the lower hell. It seems, therefore, that the upper hell goes from its lower boundary as far as heaven itself.

Paradox in the *Moralia*

It is already clear how the *Dialogues*, with their many exempla, differ from the *Moralia*. Whereas in the *Dialogues*, Gregory uses vivid images such as the measuring bridge across the stinking river, in the *Moralia* he uses theology. Rather than literal images, Gregory deploys a series of paradoxes to describe the eternity of infernal suffering. He dedicated the *Moralia* to Leander, his friend from Constantinople, who became bishop of Seville. It is addressed to specialists, readers whose training matches Gregory's own. Because the *Moralia* is a commentary on a biblical book rather than a systematic exposition of his ideas on punishment after death, one must reconstruct Gregory's view of hell from the many but scattered references to it. In the original, biblical text Job asks why the wicked prosper in life and never pay the price

---

67. Ibid., 4.43.4; p. 156.
68. Ibid., 4.57.6; p. 186.

for their wickedness, while the righteous obey God faithfully yet suffer from injustice. In its longing for a moral division of the dead, the book of Job voiced a novel and radical aspiration;[69] by the time of Gregory, the separation of the damned from the blessed had become a fundamental doctrine in Christianity.

Gregory's starting point is Job 10:22, where Job refers to "a land of misery and darkness, where the shadow of death dwells; where there is no order, but everlasting horror." In expounding these terms, Gregory defines "misery" (miseria) as external, physical grief, and "darkness" (tenebrae) as internal blindness.[70] Each damned person is inflamed by fire outside, but devoured inside by the fire of blindness, and placed in grief, confounded externally and internally, so that he might be tormented worse by confusion. For the damned, therefore, hell will have no order.[71] Conversely, attempting to present damnation theologically, as an aspect of divine will and divine justice, or put more concisely, from God's point of view, Gregory undertakes to show that despite its impact on the damned and the uninitiated, hell's apparent chaos can be explained rationally. For example, hell is orderly in the sense that in hell like is punished with like.[72] Further, eternity extinguishes time. Thus, in hell the difference between dread and pain vanishes. The damned experience simultaneously the pain they dread and the dread of that pain. Both these effects work externally and internally at once. The external fear (timor) is realized in physical pain (dolor), but internal anxiety (metus) is realized in spiritual suffering (poena).[73] Gregory's use of paradox, his ability to fuse verbal contraries to explicate existential truths, is typical of his theology. It means that these conditions are seen as chaos and confusion for the damned; to believers, it is sublime paradox.

Now Gregory concludes: "There will be death without death, and end without end, a weakening without weakening. Because the death lives, the end is always beginning, and the weakening will be unable to weaken."[74] This statement is the only one from the long discussion of damnation in the Moralia included in the Dialogues. There, the conclusion from a theological discussion stands alone and bears all the weight of authority when inserted in a dialogue between master and student. This observation recalls an important distinction between levels of discourse. Whereas theology proper displays

---

69. On Job, see Bernstein, Formation, 155–62.
70. Greg. Mor. 9.64.96, lines 1–2; p. 524.
71. Ibid., 9.65.99, lines 77–79; p. 527.
72. Ibid., 9.65.98, lines 48–49; p. 526.
73. Ibid., 9.66.100, lines 4–8; p. 527.
74. Ibid., lines 25–26; p. 528; Di. 4.47.2; p. 166.

the whole reasoning process necessary to establish points of doctrine, the lower levels of discourse contain only their *conclusions*.

Theodicy: Continuity of the Will's Perversion

The wicked do not understand adversity here as punishment for evil desires, and so they do not turn from them. Consequently, they get the rest of their evil portion after death.[75] Whether one experiences evil in death depends on whether one loved evil in life. Gregory's answer to Job, therefore, is that adversity is a warning of punishment to come. If one accepts adversity as chastisement and amends one's life, the experience is beneficial. If one refuses correction, that refusal itself justifies the suffering. Moreover, since the refusal was never reversed, the adversity is still deserved, and the punishment should continue. The driving assertion in Gregory the Great's *Moralia* is how continuity of the will's perversion entails continuous, and therefore unending, punishment. This principle undergirds Gregory's most famous statement on the justice of eternal punishment: The sinner would have continued to sin if he had not died, therefore the sinner sins in *his* eternity, but endures the penalty in *God's* eternity. As Gregory put it,

> The wicked end their iniquities because they end their lives. Indeed they would have wished to live without end so that they would have been able to persist in their iniquities. For they prefer to sin more than to live and therefore they desire to live here forever so that they would never leave off sinning as long as they live. It pertains to the justice of the strict and just Judge that no one whose mind ever wished to lack sin in this life should ever lack punishment, and that no end of vengeance is given to the wicked person, because, for as long as he was able, he did not wish to have an end to crime.[76]

Medieval writers for centuries would compete to paraphrase this idea in more and more pungent articulations.

Order through Time: Hell and the Course of Life

Given that the wicked wish no end to life because they wish no end to sin, the relationship between death and the life that precedes it is crucial. Thus it is the contemplation of one's death that should provide a key to self-reformation.

---

75. Greg. *Mor.* 15.45.50, lines 31–33; p. 784.
76. Ibid., 34.19.36, lines 41–49; p. 1759.

The context is a commentary on Job 10:20–21.

(20b) Therefore leave me,
     so that I may bewail my grief a little
(21) Before I go, not to return,
     to the land of darkness
     covered with the gloom of death.

For Job, these lines refer to the Hebrew Sheol, the neutral land of the dead, whose grouping of the just with the wicked Job lamented. Christianity and moral death gave Gregory another perspective. What Job considered the fate of all the dead, Gregory considered the fate of only the damned. What else could the land of darkness be but the "foul dungeon of Tartarus"? It is darkness, because the damned are unendingly separated there from the light, and it is a land because it holds its captives fast. And the dark dungeons of hell do not torture their prisoners with transitory or imaginary punishment, but they maintain a solid revenge of perpetual damnation.[77]

Job requests the time to lament his grief (verse 20b), but Gregory says reflection alone will not suffice. One needs to understand the pattern of *poena praesens*—adversity in life. The pains endured in life can only be life giving in the otherworld if received here in the right spirit.[78] Consciousness of pain is beneficial if seen as a stage in spiritual growth. Awareness of one's own responsibility (*reatus*, 9.62.93, line 12) in bringing on the suffering is crucial to the "full conversion" that follows, when, with God's grace, that happens. Thus we overcome the habits of the flesh, cultivate repentance in our minds, criticize ourselves, and freely come to despise what is blameworthy within us. To do this properly we must focus on the waiting pains of hell. "For we only truly accept responsibility for our actions when we anticipate with intense fear that dark retribution of hell for what we have done."[79] Fear of hell is an aspect of grace.

Hell and repentance, then, are intimately related. Reflection on the eternal punishment to be expected for evil becomes a spur to an inner revolt against bad habits (*consuetudines pravae*). Thoughts of hell, indeed, intense focus upon how it threatens us directly, are means by which God helps us overcome the obstacles to penance, such as the weight of earthly occupations,

---

77. Ibid., 9.63.95, lines 10–12; p. 524.
78. Ibid., 15.49.55, lines 23–25; p. 783.
79. "Sed tunc veraciter reatus nostri dolor plangitur, cum tenebrosa illa inferni retributio intento timore praeuidetur." Greg. *Mor.* 9.62.94, lines 39–41; p. 523.

patterns of life, and carnal desires. A single shiver, inspired by a Heaven-sent fear of hell, Gregory implies, dispels complacency. Then "our mind raises itself erect" and we "willingly combat that which we rightly condemn in ourselves."[80] Again considering these stages of growth, Gregory examines the word "before" from verse 21a. "Before" means before one dies, before the assignment of one's soul to its place in the otherworld. This examination of one's grief must be conducted in life because there is no repentance after death. Job calls the land of darkness a place from which he will not return (verse 21a), because, Gregory explains, after death there is no further mercy.[81]

Darkness, Chaos, and Inner Death Resolved through Paradox

Having considered the temporal aspect of verse 21, concerning life before consignment to the land of darkness, Gregory now moves to verse 22, which, he holds, describes its effects on the damned. This is one of the most quoted statements from the *Moralia*. The theology here is more complex than usual and requires treatment in two stages: first a technical exposition very close to Gregory's own language, then a recapitulation. The text of Job 10:22 is this:

> A land of misery and darkness
> where the shadow of death dwells
> where there is no order, but everlasting horror.[82]

Misery refers to external, physical grief *(dolor)*, darkness to the internal blindness.[83] So there is a distinction between the inner and outer suffering. Outside, physical pain *(dolor)* wracks those whom, inside, blindness *(caecitas)* obscures from the true light."[84] The difference between "misery" and

---

80. Greg. *Mor.* 9.62.93, lines 17–18, lines 16–19; 9.62.94.

81. "Nequaquam ultra misericordia parcentis liberat quos semel in locis poenalibus iustitia iudicantis damnat." Greg. *Mor.* 9.63.95, lines 24–26; p. 524. Cf. lines 19–21; p. 524: "Sanctus autem uir . . . dimitti se postulat, antequam uadit; non quia ad terram tenebrosam qui culpam deflet iturus est sed quia ad hanc procul dubio qui plangere neglegit uadit."

82. Job 10:22b has been rendered with great latitude. The Vulgate, which I translate here, offers a more clearly paradoxical description. After the key Hebrew phrase "lo s'dareem" ("nullus ordo" = "chaos" RSV), the Hebrew provides an example: "where the light is like darkness." Jerome took a different course. Eschewing reference to the confusion of light and darkness, he drew on its emotional impact: "sed sempiternus horror." He contrasted "ordo" to "horror," thus using a near rhyme to enhance a near antithesis. Because of the authority of the Vulgate, the opposition "ordo"-"horror" informed subsequent medieval discussions of hell.

83. "Miseria ad dolorem pertinet, tenebrae ad caecitatem." Greg. *Mor.* 9.64.96, lines 1–2; p. 524.

84. "Foris dolor cruciat quos diuisos a uero lumine intus caecitas obscurat. Greg. *Mor.* 9.64.96, lines 4–5; p. 524.

"darkness" (verse 22) is the difference between external and internal suffering. Crucial to this passage, therefore, is that elemental contrariety between inner and outer. So basic is it here that it leads Gregory to coin a new phrase, one that is fundamental to the history of belief in hell from the early Middle Ages on. Gregory distinguishes outer death, the extinction of physical life, from inner death, the extinction of the soul's relationship with God:

> Just as outer death divides the flesh from the soul, so inner death separates the soul from God. Therefore "the shadow of death" (verse 22b) is the darkness of division, because, when each damned person burns with eternal fire, he is blocked off from the internal light. For the nature of fire is that it illumines and burns. But the flame of hell, which avenges vices that have been acted upon, burns but sheds no light. . . . Thus the grief of burning will torment them on the outside and the punishment of blindness will obscure them on the inside. It is fitting that the fire should punish them in two ways, on both the outside and the inside, since those who have abandoned their creator in body and heart should be punished together in both body and heart. And those who, while they lived, pursued their depraved delights with both body and heart will feel the punishments in both ways.[85]

If defined as that which separates the soul from God, "inner death" is a synonym for the "second death" of Revelation 20:14 and 21:8, but Gregory distinguishes them by defining inner death as a fate in life. The inner torment of the damned, a death after death, is the blindness or confusion that prevents them from understanding the justice of their punishment. Further, continuing from Job to the New Testament lens through which Gregory views him, Job's reference to darkness becomes a prophecy or allegorical sign of the threatened outer darkness, as in Matthew 8:12, 22:13, and 25:30. Gregory implies that if sinners had understood the justice of eternal punishment, they would have drawn back from their sins, and would have avoided hell. However, since they continued to sin with body and soul, so they are

---

85. "Sicut mors exterior ab anima diuidit carnem, ita mors interior a Deo separat animam. Vmbra ergo mortis est obscuritas diuisionis, quia damnatus quisque cum aeterno igne succenditur, ab interno lumine tenebratur. Natura uero ignis est, ut ex se ipso et lucem exhibeat, et concremationem; sed transactorum illa ultrix flamma uitiorum concremationem habet et lumen non habet. . . . [U]t et foras eos dolor combustionis cruciet et intus poena caecitatis obscuret; quatenus qui auctori suo corpore et corde deliquerunt, simul corpore et corde puniantur. Et utrobique poenas sentiant, qui dum hic uiuerent pravis suis delectationibus ex utrobique seruiebant." Greg. *Mor.* 9.65.97, lines 3–20; p. 525. Another passage that contrasts hell's effects on the outside and inside of the damned is Greg. *Mor.* 6.30.47, lines 18–19; p. 318: "intus per desiderium ardet conscientia, et foris carnem cruciat gehenna." Cf. Greg. *Mor.* 7.32.47, lines 7–9; p. 370.

punished physically and psychologically, externally and internally, with both corporeal pain and mental anguish. Inner death consists in the link between the blindness of the damned in hell and the same blindness that prevented them, when alive, from understanding divine justice. In that it is the same blindness that afflicts the damned in hell and the stubborn on earth, it may be said that the pain of hell attacks the living. The blindness or stubbornness that prevents respect for divine directives or repentance for violating them in life, is *a future hell pain already suffered here*. Hell then grasps the living person's heart and thereby begins to separate the soul from God and introduces hell's torments during one's life. Hell's foothold in the living person's soul is inner death. Chapter 2 is devoted to exploring this theme further.

After considering the darkness Job said pervades the underworld, Gregory now examines Job's claim that the land where the shadow of death dwells is one with "no order" (verse 22c). But Gregory objects. Several aspects of hell are clearly ordered. Like are punished with like (*pares paribus*), those polluted by the same fault endure the same punishment, and, for all, the same pride is overturned and its victims punished beneath the same oppression.[86] There are also differences. Using the theological description of hell by means of a reverse analogy with heaven, Gregory states that just as in the house of my father there are many mansions (cf. John 14:2) to accommodate the diversity in virtue, so difference in crimes subjects the damned to different punishments in the fires of Gehenna.[87]

These differences also increase the confusion of the damned. In varying the punishments to suit each type of sinner appropriately, many of the elements that punish them take on, or appear to take on, properties different from those they have on earth.[88] That will happen when both the physical qualities of hell (e.g., the fire and other elements) and the psychological qualities of horror (e.g., the simultaneous experience of dread and pain) vary from what they are on earth (where dread and pain are distinct). This deviation from essential qualities allows fire to burn while it blinds (whereas on earth it burns and illumines), to mirror, as it were, the offense of the sinners, who themselves departed from the goodness that was potentially theirs. The sinners' inability to penetrate the seeming deviation (chaos) in the relation between punishment and sin reflects the error of their original deviation

---

86. Greg. *Mor.* 9.65.98, lines 48–55; p. 526.

87. Ibid., 9.65.98.

88. "Vel certe abesse ordo suppliciis dicitur, quia quibuslibet rebus in poenam surgentibus propria qualitas non seruatur." Greg. *Mor.* 9.65.99, lines 77–79; p. 527.

from the will of God, which is the essence of sin. Because of this confusion, the punishments will intensify, diversify, and multiply.

Employing one of his formulas based on antithesis, Gregory sums up this idea. "*Then* let grief completely absorb those who *now*, subject to their own delights, completely oppose the justice of the Just Judge."[89] This formula offers both continuity and contrast. The continuity consists of the two totalities: that of sinners' opposition to God's laws and that of their subjection to his punishments. The contrast opposes the two times (*nunc* and *tunc*): *now*, when the sinners chase their depraved delights, and *then*, when their active rebellion becomes the passive reception of physical pain and mental turmoil.

Yet, again, this diversity is limited in two ways. Those who indulged the same vice are punished together, and those who followed another into sin are punished with their tempter. Implicitly, the model is the punishment of the fallen angels, who followed Satan into rebellion.[90] This principle was key to a political application of hell, where sinners are compared to vassals of Satan or satraps or followers of any sort. They belong to his company, they are part of his body. In a theological inversion of the community of the saved, the church, which is the body of Christ (Eph. 5:23), they form the body of Satan. They are his members. This notion appeared in Revelation 2:9 and 3:9, where the Jews are described as forming "the synagogue of Satan." The idea of the wicked as followers of Satan remains prominent throughout the Middle Ages, and attaches not only to Satan but also to the Antichrist, another important, related development. The idea is also very prominent in the Qur'ān, where this designation, "followers of Satan," characterizes not only the present-day wicked, but also the ancestors who resisted the reforms of the Prophet, and their descendants, who, in blind allegiance to clan traditions, remained or remain faithful to the polytheism of the old religion.

The synthesis of Job's "order" and "horror" makes paradox essential to damnation. Indeed, Gregory itemizes a series of paradoxes to describe the condition of the damned. The tortures (*supplicia*) wrack (*cruciant*) their victims beyond their powers, yet they keep them alive. The torture always weakens the damned but never extinguishes them.[91] As Gregory put it, "For

---

89. "[U]t tunc eos undique dolor absorbeat, qui nunc suis delectationibus subditi, undique contra iustitiam iuste iudicantis pugnant." Greg. *Mor.* 9.65.97, lines 28–30; p. 526; my emphasis.

90. "Reprobates who, moved by whatever vice, execute the will of the cunning persuader in the here and now will reach the torments of their leader in the end. And although the nature of the angels is far from that of men, nonetheless one punishment entangles those whom one guilt binds in crime." Greg. *Mor.* 9.66.102–3, lines 76–82; pp. 529–30.

91. "Quae tamen supplicia in se demersos et ultra uires cruciant, et in eis uitae subsidium exstinguentes seruant, ut sic uitam terminus puniat; quatenus semper sine termino cruciatus uiuat quia et ad finem per tormenta properat, et sine fine deficiens durat." Greg. *Mor.* 9.66.100, lines 20–24;

those miserable ones, therefore, let there be a death without death, an end without end, a weakening without weakening, because simultaneously death lives and the end always begins and the weakening is unable to weaken."[92] Here Gregory gives a near-mathematical description of what in colloquial language today we refer to as "rotting in hell." Taking a more analytical approach, it might be possible to consider hell's paradox an asymptotic relationship with death. Its sufferers increasingly approach death without ever reaching it, yet the process is always reversed, and the nonexistent end point is also, forever, its starting point. Thus, what was weak becomes strong and what was strong becomes weak, but never to the point of extinction. Both contradictory processes continue simultaneously forever.

Turning Hell to the Good

If the evil the righteous suffer in life strengthens their faith in an evil-free afterlife, then God turns human afflictions into a blessing. Gregory asserts that not even the devil (or his symbols Behemoth or Leviathan) can pry the righteous from their proper end. However unintentionally, Leviathan serves God, for the divine artisan uses the devil like an anvil! Satan's temptations shape us to the form God desires.[93] As both the source of the temptations by which the virtuous prove their goodness and the nadir of all evil, the devil, together with his companions in damnation, embellishes the universe. One of the devil's temptations is the belief that hell is not eternal.[94] Those who perceive the error of the satanic claim persevere; those who succumb writhe in pain before the eyes of the just.[95]

> And while the just behold these torments, they grow in their praise of God, because they perceive in themselves the good by which they are

---

p. 528. The word *deficiens* causes problems here. A nominative singular present active participle, it modifies *cruciatus*, which is also singular, as we learn from "cruciatus uiuat." Literally, *deficiens* must connote a weakening of the torment, which will nonetheless not die. Nothing, however, prepares us for (or ever reinforces) the notion that the torment would diminish, weaken itself, or ever end. We must understand that *deficiens* alludes to the effect of the torment on the sufferers, who may in some way be deadened to repetition or continuation of the same punishment. The resultant atrophy of the sense organs or flesh or spirit will not weaken the effect of the punishment. This interpretation is borne out in the next sentence, which specifies that there will be "a weakening without weakening" (*defectus sine defectu*) and that "the weakening will be unable to weaken" (*deficiere defectus nescit*).

92. Greg. *Mor.* 9.66.100, lines 24–26; p. 528.

93. Ibid., 34.6.11, lines 14–15; p. 1741: "Recte ergo Leuiathan iste incudi comparatus est, quia nos illo persequente componimur."

94. Greg. *Mor.* 34.19.35, lines 6–9; p. 1758.

95. In *Di.* 4.34.4, p. 114, Gregory uses Luke 16:23–26 to show that, in their tortures, the wicked can see the blessed and vice versa.

rewarded, and in those others [the damned] they consider the punishment that they have escaped. Then will the whole world be beautiful, as Gehenna justly wracks the impious and eternal happiness justly rewards the pious.[96]

In a sermon Gregory devoted to the parable of Lazarus and the rich man in Luke 16, he extended the force of this narrative to dogmatic heights, not just emphasizing the contrast between the two men, but dogmatically defining the consciousness that the righteous have of the wicked, and vice versa, first until the Last Judgment, and then forever.

> For [when he looked up, the rich man] recognized Lazarus, whom he had despised, and he remembered his brothers whom he had predeceased. Indeed, vengeance would not have been perfect for the poor man [Lazarus] if [the rich man] had not, as part of his punishment, recognized him. And the punishment would not have been perfect [even] in the fire if he himself had not experienced anxiety about his own kin. Therefore, in order that sinners may be punished in greater torment, they should be tortured both by seeing the glory of those whom they scorned and the punishment of those whom they loved to no purpose.[97]

The dogmatic applications follow. Here are further specifics about what the damned can see in the fire and darkness:

> Therefore one must believe (*credendum est*) that before the retribution of the Last Judgment, the unjust see the peace of certain of the just so that, in seeing their joy, they may be wracked not only from their own torture, but even from the benefits of those they see. Conversely the just are always permitted to see the unjust, so that *their joy may thereby grow* because they perceive the evil that they have mercifully escaped; as much to be able to return thanks to the one who removed them as to see in the others what they themselves would have endured had they

---

96. Greg. *Mor.* 33.14.29, lines 41–45; p. 1698: "Quos scilicet cruciatus dum iusti conspiciunt, in Dei laudibus crescunt, quia et in se cernunt bonum quo remunerati sunt, et in illis inspiciunt supplicium quod euaserunt. Ita enim tunc pulchra erit uniuersitas, dum et gehenna iuste cruciat impios, et aeterna felicitas iuste remunerat pios." Cf. *Mor.* 34.19. 37; p. 1760; and Greg. *Homiliae in euangelia* 2.40.8, lines 288–307; CCSL 141, ed. Raymond Etaix (1999), 405.

97. "Cognoscit enim Lazarum quem despexit, fratrum quoque suorum meminit quos reliquit. Perfecta quippe ei ultio de paupere non esset, si hunc in retributione non recognosceret. Et perfecta poena in igne non esset, si non hoc quod ipse patitur etiam in suis timeret. Ut ergo peccatores in supplicio amplius puniantur, et eorum uident gloriam quos contempserunt, de de illorum etiam poena torquentur quos inutiliter amauerunt." Greg. *Homiliae in euangelia* 2.40.8, line 288; p. 405.

been abandoned. Nor will the experience of having viewed the punishment of the damned sully the clarity of such great beatitude in the souls of the just, because where compassion for misery never resided, it certainly cannot diminish the happiness of the blessed.[98]

The beauty of the cosmos consists in the downtrodden receiving perfect vengeance, and the persecutors perfect punishment. As a corollary to this conception, the saved increase in their joy from seeing the pains of the damned, which, as Gregory puts it, they have mercifully escaped.[99]

Behavioral Reform

Scripture informs us about the torments of damnation so that we may escape them, Gregory says. We must therefore cultivate a concern for living well (*bene vivendi studio*) so that we may flee the avenging torments in store for the wicked.[100] The phrase *bene vivendi* is an old one, a favorite of Cicero. It means not "living well," but "living right." Augustine knew the phrase and called Christ an example of living right,[101] but also insisted that living right does not suffice for salvation, which also requires divine grace.[102] Gregory refers to right living throughout the *Moralia* in several contexts. It describes the way of life of one

---

98. "Credendum uero est quod ante retributionem extremi iudicii injusti in requiem quosdam iustos conspiciunt, ut eos uidentes in gaudio non solum de suo supplicio, sed etiam de illorum bono crucientur. Iusti uero in tormentis semper intuentur iniustos, *ut hinc eorum gaudium crescat*, quia malum conspiciunt quod misericorditer euaserunt; tanto que maiores ereptori suo gratias referunt, quanto uident in aliis quid ipsi perpeti, si essent relicti, potuerunt. Nec illam tantae beatitudinis claritatem apud iustorum animum fuscat aspecta poena reproborum, quia ubi iam compassio miseriae non erit, minuere procul dubio beatorum laetitiam non ualebit." Greg. *Homiliae in euangelia* 2.40.8, lines 291–98; p. 405; my emphasis.

99. The idea that the joy of the blessed increases from their view of the damned in torment was first called "the abominable fancy" by F. W. Farrar and effectively dramatized by Alice K. Turner and Anne L. Stainton, "The Golden Age of Hell," *Art & Antiques*, January 1991, 53, but without reference. D. P. Walker identifies the doctrine and credits Farrar with naming it in Walker, *The Decline of Hell: Seventeenth-Century Discussions of Eternal Torment* (Chicago: University of Chicago Press, 1964), 31. In this published edition of his own sermon, Farrar includes useful references and quotations back to Tertullian; Farrar.*Eternal Hope: Five Sermons Preached in Westminster Abbey, November and December, 1877* (New York: E.P. Dutton, 1878). Alix Cavanaugh follows the idea up to Nietzsche; Cavanaugh, "The Abominable Fancy," *Venia Legendi* (blog), accessed January 8, 2008, http://venialegendi.blogspot.com/2007/08/abominable-fancy.html. The idea illustrates how vengeance colors the idea of hell. Rather than calling the belief "abominable," it may be enough to underline how it considers the pains of the damned a joy to the blessed.

100. Greg. *Mor.* 9.66.104, lines 100–101; p. 530: "Tota ergo intentione curandum est ut, cum uacationis tempus accipimus, bene uiuendi studio, malorum ultricia tormenta fugiamus."

101. Augustine, *Epistulae* 188.3, line 19; CSEL 57 (1898): 128.

102. Ibid., 235.2, line 3; CSEL 57:523.

who has successfully undergone moral transformation.[103] Perhaps the most he grants it is the highest human conception of what one can achieve on one's own, when he speaks of a person who desires to attain the peak of right living (*celsitudinem bene uiuendi*).[104] For all this, in the *Moralia*, right living remains an abstraction, as Gregory recommends no steps. In the *Dialogues*, by contrast, his advice is very specific. Given that the afterlife is as he has explained in book 4, the consequences of living wrong can be dire. There are actions that can benefit the soul after death, but they must be performed by the living. Thus, "the good that one wishes might be done for one after death by others, one ought to do for oneself while alive."[105] The greatest boon for the soul in life and after death is Mass. Of five exempla to demonstrate this point, two stand out.

The first exemplum, one examined above, illustrates the utility of Mass for one in an uncomfortable and degrading condition but certainly not in torture. The unnamed attendant in the baths, the man who refused Bishop Felix's offer of two loaves because he was a soul performing purgatorial service on earth, requested, instead, that Masses be said to aid his soul.[106] The second exemplum shows the efficacy of Mass for one threatened much more directly with damnation. Just before his death, the monk Justus confessed to his own brother, Copiosus, a member of the same monastery, that he had concealed three pieces of gold in his cell. When Gregory, who was the abbot of this monastery, learned of this, he resolved to take a dramatic action that would benefit both the delinquent monk and the other brothers, lest they, too, should be tempted to violate the rule of communal property. Gregory ordered all the monks to withhold all moral support from Justus as his end approached. Gregory's hope was to inspire a dramatic anxiety (*anxietas*) and remorse (*amaritudo*) (two technical terms to be discussed in the next chapter) in Justus, whose force would intensify the cleansing of his guilt. In fact, as the end approached, the brothers told Justus that they considered him *abominatus*, an outcast. "At once, he sighed vehemently for his guilt and exited his body in extreme sadness (*tristitia*)."[107] Instead of burying him in the communal cemetery, Gregory laid him in a depression in the dung heap, onto which Gregory cast the three pieces of gold, using the words that the apostle Peter hurled at Simon Magus in Acts 8:20, "May your money be with you in perdition." Then Gregory began to pity Justus and wished to improve his situation. Sig-

---

103. Greg. *Mor.* 31.46.92, lines 22–24; p. 1613.

104. Ibid., 29.33.77, line 30; p. 1490.

105. "[B]onum quod quisque post mortem suam sperat agi per alios, agat dum uiuit ipse pro se." Greg. *Di.* 4.60.1; p. 200.

106. Greg. *Di.* 4.57.3–7; pp. 184–86. Cf. Paschasius, in Greg. *Di.* 4.42.

107. "Qui protinus de reatu suo uehementer ingemuit, atque in ipsa tristitia e corpore exiuit." Greg. *Di.* 4.57.13; pp. 192–93.

nificantly, he referred to Justus as being "wracked in the fire" (*igne cruciatur*), as if Gregory knew he were in hell or some purgatorial fire. He then ordered the prior to say Mass daily for the deceased monk. At the end of a month, Justus appeared to his brother in a dream and informed him: "Up until now, I have done badly, but now I am doing well, because today I have received communion."[108] The monk's release from the fire was accomplished partly by the intensity of his own contrition. He died a penitent. It is nonetheless clear from Gregory's apparent curse (borrowed from Peter), the dung heap, and Gregory's premise that Justus was suffering in fire, that in order to edify the other brothers, Gregory affected to assume no hope of release and behaved as if the offense were more powerful than the repentance. He exaggerated the threat to heighten the sanction. Combined, the contrition and the Masses rendered Justus's greed pardonable. It is important to see, however, how clearly Gregory structures the story to contrast the confession Justus made to his brother very late in life and the Masses said for his soul after his death. The story of Justus, then, illustrates both ends of Gregory's contention: the soul may be helped after death, Mass is effective in this way, but it is better to take your own initiatives before you die.

Mass, therefore, is Gregory's preferred behavioral recommendation in light of the nature of the afterlife and the consequences of wrong living. Yet Gregory's advice in the *Dialogues* must clearly accord with the principles and interpretations offered in the *Moralia*. A passage from the end of book 9 of the *Moralia* offers a very detailed analysis of damnation. Here Gregory charts the contrarieties that can lead the soul astray, but in a more positive light. These oppositions are not the dimensions of hell's pains; they are the tendencies of the mind. If handled right, Gregory states, they can be steered away from infernal shipwreck. Thus he concludes:

> We must always consider with careful focus what we do in action and what we consider in the heart, lest either become enmeshed in terrestrial cares, by entangling the mind outside, or, perhaps, believing in its own moderation, exalt itself inside. Thus, when we fear the divine judgments with wariness of the future, we may evade the tortures of unending horror.[109]

---

108. "Nunc usque male fui, sed iam modo bene sum, quia hodie communionem recepi." Greg. *Di.* 4.57.15; p. 192.

109. "Unde sollerti semper custodiae intentione pensandum est uel quid opere agimus, uel quid corde uersamus, ne aut mentem praepediens, foras se terrena cura multiplicet, aut saltim de eius moderamine intus se cogitatio exaltet; ut cum diuina iudicia temporali circumspectione metuimus, sempiterni supplicia horroris euadamus." Greg. *Mor.* 9.66.106, lines 166–72; pp. 532–33.

The Bridge of Meaning

Gregory's contribution to the career of hell was immense. Gregory first defined upper hell as dogma. Gregory asserted inner death. His flair for paradox allowed him to pursue difficult analyses by combining opposed pairs to explain, for example, how the pains of hell could confound the damned and gratify the saints. He was able to combine dogmatic declarations illustrated by exemplary narratives for the many with substantiation for the few. The bridge that tests souls as they migrate from life to death links more than this world and the next. It also links levels of discourse. If "things are images through which we consider the nature of their causes," then Gregory's statement articulates a cosmos in which a just Judge corrects all wrongs and rewards all righteousness. The balance he asserts between continuity and contrast in his punishments links the lives of sinners to their pains after death, still haunted by their old obsessions. The disorder in the desires of the damned distorts their perceptions of reality, but the confusion they suffer in hell can be understood outside. Through paradox, chaos becomes order.

CHAPTER 2

Inner Death

Hell in the Conscience

> For these people, [who avoid confronting their faults] there is a double damnation, a twin beating strikes them, because they experience both the beginning of their torments here and the culmination of their punishments there [i.e., in hell].
>
> —Isidore of Seville, *Synonyma* 1.31

The patristic view of damnation, especially as articulated by Gregory I, included not just the physical Gehenna that torments the flesh, but also an inner wracking of the spirit. Inner death occurs when the suffering associated with hell occupies a living person. If not corrected, this torment becomes eternal. The locus of this perturbation is the conscience. (The terms "heart," "mind," "soul," "breast," and "conscience" were functionally equivalent in this context.) These infernal attacks in the conscience constitute, for monks and nuns, an early warning system.[1]

The monastic environment was the incubator for this new psychology as men and women obeyed a call to place moral rectitude above physical comfort and other temptations of society such as urban life or family ties or political ambitions. This impulse preceded Christianity as the Buddha became an example of the solitary contemplative in much of Asia, and as the Essenes in Judaism and John the Baptist clearly show. Stoics, too, had their sages, known for repudiating the temptations of career, family, and wealth. Within the growing Christian movement, at first a trickle of holy

---

1. On this subject, see Alan E. Bernstein, *"Tristitia* and the Fear of Hell in Monastic Reflection from John Cassian to Hildemar of Corbie," in *Continuity and Change: The Harvest of Late-Medieval and Reformation History; Essays Presented to Heiko A. Oberman on His 70th Birthday*, ed. Robert J. Bast and Andrew C. Gow (Leiden: Brill, 2000), 183–205.

men and women such as Saint Anthony retreated in solitude to outposts in the wilderness. Gradually disciples followed them, setting up communities dedicated to the pursuit of a pure life under the guidance of these "desert fathers." Starting in the fourth century, a cenobitic or communal form of monasticism began to eclipse this heremetical or solitary type. The head could be an abbot like Pachomius (d. 346–47) or a bishop like Augustine of Hippo, a city near ancient Carthage. Cenobitic monasticism was the most common form in the West and had both male and female heads. Bishop Caesarius of Arles wrote a rule for nuns and set up his sister Caesaria over a woman's community. Queens of the Frankish royal line, the Merovingians, such as Radegunda established houses for women. Mixed establishments also developed in which nuns and monks living in different buildings were nonetheless united under an abbess but received spiritual instruction from male priests who alone were permitted to administer the sacraments. Isolation was not the only motive for a monastic foundation. Book 2 of Gregory the Great's *Dialogues*, which relates the life of Saint Benedict, tells how he founded Monte Cassino on the site of a temple to Apollo and thereby rededicated this long-venerated High Place. It would have been at Monte Cassino that Benedict, if he is indeed the author, wrote his *Rule for Monks*, to be examined below.

Monastic communities required material support in many forms. The land on which monks or nuns lived, the fields they cultivated, the buildings and sacramental vessels they needed for churches, dormitories, meeting houses, kitchens, all required major capital outlays. Sometimes, as in the case of Cassiodorus (d. ca. 580), a member of the wealthy landowning class would devote an estate to religious purposes and become abbot or abbess of a monastic house. Relatives of monks or nuns would give or bequeath further lands, whose revenues, called prebends, supported the ascetics. These same families provided personnel in the form of (usually) younger sons or daughters who became monks or nuns, sometimes unknowingly, as oblates, while still children. The monasteries or convents often became the kernels of future economic development as artisans and markets attached themselves to the new, but increasingly prosperous foundations. At the other extreme were some houses established in isolated sites, such as mountain fasts, exposed shores of tiny islands, and the barren moors of heath-covered wastes. Monastic houses in all their variety became the think tanks where outstanding intellectuals articulated their version of the principles of an ideal Christian life. Their view of repentance, pursuit of humility, fear of hell, and longing for God inspired a psychology that institutionalized the concept of inner death for the first time.

Proof of the existence of inner death comes from examining the interpretation of the fire and the worm that Mark 9:47–48 takes from Isaiah 66:24 to describe the fate of those who prefer the integrity of their sin-prone body to that of their soul: "It is better to enter the kingdom of God with one eye [or foot or hand, if it leads you to sin] than with two eyes to be thrown into Gehenna, where their worm does not die, and the fire is not quenched." In the spiritual reflection of the period, monastic theorists sought to understand the import of Mark's fire and worm and Matthew's outer darkness (8:12; 22:13; 25:30) and related them to the suffering of hell. Significantly, they also applied the terms to the suffering of the guilty soul while alive. Introspective ascetics themselves, they knew the experience of ferreting out guilt, of examining their own thoughts, of beating down pride to seek humility. They used various terms for this condition: sadness (*tristitia*), bitterness (*amaritudo*), grief of spirit (*dolor animi*), affliction (*afflictio*), and anxiety (*anxietas*); but they knew it was painful. Monks or nuns stricken with this dejection (the generic term I shall use when convenient) knew well the exertion and discipline required to escape it.[2] This struggle, which takes place in the conscience, they considered indispensable to salvation. To evade the challenge was to fall. Thus, one must engage this pain as a corrective now or suffer it involuntarily and greatly increased later. This link between the fire and the worm in hell and in the conscience of the living person was not just a slippery slope down which the unwary might slide; it could go both ways. In one direction the slothful sink into hell from lack of discipline. In the other direction, hell attacks. When you are prey to tribulation, Augustine says, "the grief of hell finds you."[3] The result is that in allowing their concept of hell to shape their analysis of conscience, the monastic theorists of this period developed a language that in turn colored their perception of hell.

Inner death derives from some fundamental Christian principles, but, as far as I know, scholars have not identified it as a concept. If Christ's resurrection ended Death's hold on humankind, then physical death could no longer be the dividing line it once was. Christ's rescue of the dead from the underworld, the raid against Hades, inaccurately called the Harrowing of *Hell*, defeats Death and opens new possibilities. Physical death may then become the pathway to eternal life. It is only for the wicked that physical death initiates endless suffering. In Revelation 20:14 and 21:8, therefore, damnation is

---

2. Monastic dejection certainly resembles modern depression, but the institutional framework and the religious associations are so different that applying the same term to both would be misleading.

3. "Inuenit te dolor inferni." Aug. *Enarrat. Ps.* 136.5, lines 16 and 20–21; CCSL 40, ed. E. Dekkers and J. Fraipont (1956), p. 1966.

referred to as "the second death." Augustine elaborated on this phrase: "The first death expels the unwilling soul from the body, the second death holds the unwilling soul in the body."[4] In the first, mere death, the righteous soul welcomes escape from the body's temptations, and this separation liberates. In the second death, damnation, the wicked soul vainly desires escape from the body because it suffers physical pain in hell. Gregory I made the distinction even more basic: "Just as true death is that by which the soul is separated from God, so the shadow of death is that which separates the flesh from the soul."[5] The end of physical life is only the shadow of death; damnation, which separates the soul from God, is *true* death. Or, more tellingly: "Just as exterior death divides the flesh from the soul, so inner death separates the soul from God."[6] With real life now placed after physical death, the criterion for acceptance in the afterlife becomes how one lived in this life; and the best guide is to keep the future judgment always in mind. Thus Gregory advises: "The perfect life is the imitation of death."[7] Monks of the period practiced self-*mortification*, which derives from a verb that means literally to make oneself dead. Those who rejected this discipline fell prey to sin and died an internal death.[8] Thus Augustine could say, "With death in the heart, one is sent to Gehenna."[9]

If physical death leads the righteous to eternal life, then hell itself would seem to become less menacing. Yet a humble contemplative considers

---

4. Aug. *De civitate Dei* 21.3, line 30; CCSL 48, ed. B. Dombart and A. Kalb (1955), p. 760.

5. Greg. *Mor.* 4.16.30; p. 183.

6. "Sicut mors exterior ab anima dividit carnem, ita mors interior a deo separat animam." Greg. *Mor.* 9.65.97, lines 1–3; p. 525.

7. "Perfecta vita est imitatio mortis." Greg. *Mor.* 13.29.34, lines 7–8; p. 687.

8. Other works that consider views of death in late antiquity and the early Middle Ages include Peter Brown's two lectures under the collective title "The End of the Ancient Other World": Lecture I, "Gloriosus Obitus: Death and Afterlife, 400–700 A.D."; Lecture II, "The Decline of the Empire of God: From Amnesty to Purgatory," in *The Tanner Lectures on Human Values* 20 (Salt Lake City: University of Utah Press, 1999), 21–50 and 51–85. The second of Brown's lectures has also been published with modifications as Peter Brown, "The Decline of the Empire of God: Amnesty, Penance, and the Afterlife from Late Antiquity to the Middle Ages," in *Last Things: Death and the Apocalypse in the Middle Ages*, ed. Caroline Walker Bynum and Paul Freedman (Philadelphia: University of Pennsylvania Press, 2000), 41–59. See also Frederick S. Paxton, *Christianizing Death: The Creation of a Ritual Process in Early Medieval Europe* (Ithaca, NY: Cornell University Press, 1990); Arno Borst, "Three Studies of Death in the Middle Ages," in *Medieval Worlds: Barbarians, Heretics, and Artists in the Middle Ages*, trans. Eric Hansen (Chicago: University of Chicago Press, 1992), 215–43; Éric Rebillard, *In Hora Mortis: Évolution de la pastorale chrétienne de la mort aux IVᵉ et Vᵉ siècles*, Bibliothèque des Écoles Françaises d'Athènes et de Rome 283 (Paris: Boccard, 1994); Patrick Geary, "Exchange and Interaction between the Living and the Dead in Early Medieval Society," in *Living with the Dead in the Middle Ages* (Ithaca, NY: Cornell University Press, 1994), 77–92.

9. "Morte cordi mittatur in Gehennam." Aug. *Contra adversarium legis et prophetarum* 1, line 665; CCSL 49, ed. Klaus D. Daur (1985), p. 57.

himself or herself unworthy of heaven, indeed worthy only of hell. Thus, hell becomes more aggressive, capable of invading the living person through the conscience. Medieval writers did not call hell aggressive, but, as this book's cover shows, they used a voracious mouth to represent it; fire, which can easily spread, to characterize it; and, in the words of Augustine quoted above, attributed to it the ability to seek one out and afflict one with grief. When hell may be said to "find" living victims, it has become aggressive. A logical inference leads from an aggressive hell to the notion of inner death.

The channel between hell and the soul of a living person is the conscience. Romans 2:15 says the conscience (*syneidesis*) acts as a witness before the tribunal of Christ when the judge hears testimony about an individual's life. This person need not be Christian, for even the Gentiles "show that what the law requires is written on their hearts, while their conscience also bears witness and their conflicting thoughts accuse or perhaps excuse them on that day." Here the conscience is a faithful observer of one's life. In Romans 13:5, the conscience takes its place beneath God and his earthly establishment, "the powers that be," whose ordinances function as God's. Below the political powers are individuals, who are ruled, it is implied, by a conscience ideally in harmony with those higher powers. "Therefore one must be subject, not only because of wrath but also because of conscience." Conscience is therefore that personal mental faculty, attuned to the divine will and the political order, that evaluates the goodness or evil of an individual's thoughts and actions. The following review of leading monastic thinkers will show how the connection between hell and the conscience transcended personal introspection to inform whole institutions and color a European way of life for centuries.

Jerome's Dream and Fire in the Conscience

Jerome of Stridon (Sdrin in Croatia), Saint Jerome, whose translations from Greek and Hebrew formed the basis of the Latin Vulgate Bible strengthened the connection between hell and the conscience considerably. In a famous letter to Eustochium (*Epist.* 22.30), as he confides to her how he experienced the guilt he felt over his enthusiasm for Cicero's Latin, he explains how his pangs of conscience resembled an experience in hell. His account sketches a multilayered universe composed of hell, earth, and heaven, with the conscience serving as a channel between them. Once, he relates, when he was sick and hovering near death, visitors were called in to stand around his bed. He was taken in the spirit to the divine tribunal. When asked to state his identity, he replied that he was a Christian, but the Judge said: "You lie. You are not a Christian, but a Ciceronian, for 'where your treasure is, there also is your heart (*cor*) (Matt. 6:21)'." "And then," continues Jerome, "I was silent and among the blows—for he had ordered that I be beaten, I was tortured more by the fire of conscience (than by the lashes) as I considered in my mind the verse (Psalm 6:5) 'in hell (*inferno*) who will acknowledge you'." During the beating he begged for mercy and the onlookers fell to their knees, interceding with the judge. They attributed Jerome's excesses to his youth and sought that "he be given the opportunity to repent for his error on the condition that he would undergo wracking (*cruciatus*) in the future if he should ever read pagan works again." Jerome so swears. After making this commitment "I returned to the upper world" (*revertor ad superos*).[10]

Though Jerome does not state, theologically, that the judge could see his inner thoughts at the time of the beating, the judge ascertained the penchant of his heart. At this moment, Jerome sees within himself three levels of the universe: in heaven, the God of justice; on earth, the fire of conscience, with its obvious connection to the third, the *infernus* of Psalm 6:5. The moment, therefore, is pivotal: having sensed the fire of hell in his conscience, he abandons Cicero for Christ, escapes from the underworld to his sickbed, and recovers.

Jerome refers specifically to the guilty conscience and its continued existence after death in his commentary on Ezekiel 32:20–32. The prophet sees discrimination in Sheol for those who brought terror to the land of the living. These violent rulers are denied burial in the traditional tombs of their people and, instead, are placed in a separate area called "the uttermost parts of the Pit" (*yarch'tey bor*). These kings and their armies, who brought terror to the land of the living, will be brought down trembling to Sheol and segregated from the average dead to live on, stigmatized, in the underworld.[11] Ezekiel says these violent ones "bear their shame with those who go down to the Pit" (32:30). Jerome interprets their fate like this: "They go down to the lower world (*ad inferos*) full of fear, relying on their former strength; but there they sleep unclean and they will bear their confusion—or torment—as the unending penitence of having a guilty conscience, such that their fire will not be extinguished and their worm will not die."[12] Their evil consciences (*malae conscientiae*) come from their original malice (*malitiam pristinam*).

---

10. Jacqueline Amat says that Jerome imagines himself already in hell. Amat, *Songes et visions: L'au-delà dans la littérature latine tardive* (Paris: Éditions augustiniennes, 1985), 220.

11. Alan E. Bernstein, *The Formation of Hell: Death and Retribution in the Ancient and Early Christian Worlds* (Ithaca, NY: Cornell University Press, 1993), 164–66.

12. Hieronymus, *Commentarii in Ezechielem* 10.32, lines 978–83; CCSL 75, ed. F. Glorie (1964), p. 465.

When Pharaoh, too, descends to this shameful zone, Jerome says he will be consoled to see his companions in aggression already suffering there, "confounded in their tortures and terrors" and "proceeding on to everlasting tortures."[13] Jerome, then, says the foul conscience not only characterizes aggressors but also continues to torment them as they live on forever in disgrace.

For Jerome, this passage of Ezekiel identifies a shameful area in the land of the dead existing, really, outside the minds of the individuals punished. His conviction came dramatically to the fore when Jerome turned his attention to Origen of Alexandria, whose works Rufinus had just translated into Latin. Origen, who died in 254, believed postmortem punishment to be finite, depending on the individual's degree of guilt. The sinner sins by neglecting God, a neglect punished after death until the suffering produces a new devotion, which, after many reincarnations and sufficient retribution, results in an eventual restoration of the individual's pristine relationship with God. The biblical authority on which Origen relied most heavily is Isaiah 50:11: "Walk by the light of your fire and by the brands which you have kindled." The internal, we would say subjective, quality of this system Origen highlighted explicitly when he explained, "The fire by which each person is punished is proper to that person."[14] It is precisely this subjective, internalized, self-contained view of postmortem suffering that Jerome abhorred. Even in his dream he specifies that the fire his conscience inflicted on him, harsher than the blows imposed by the judge, had its source in the lower world, from which he ascended only after promising to forgo Ciceronian sonorities. Jerome could not be clearer on this point in his criticism of Origen. He puts it thus in a letter to Avitus concerning Rufinus's translations:

And the fire and the torments of Gehenna, which Holy Scripture uses to threaten the sinners, he [Origen] does not put in the torments, but in the conscience of sinners when, by the power and virtue of God, all memory of the evils done is placed before our eyes. Left in the soul, like certain seeds, the whole crop of vices grows up, and whatever we may do in life, whether evil or impious, it is portrayed as an image for

---

13. Ibid., 465–66.
14. "Unusquisque peccatorum flammam sibi ipse proprii ignis accendat." Origen, De principiis 2.10.4; ed. Paul Koetschau, vol. 5 of Origenes Werke, Die griechischen christlichen Schriftsteller der ersten drei Jahrhunderte 22 (Leipzig: Hinrichs, 1913). G. W. Butterworth has translated Koetschau's edition as Origen, On First Principles (New York: Harper and Row, 1966). See Bernstein, Formation, 308–13.

us and, perceiving past pleasures, the mind is punished by the burning of the conscience and stabbed by the pricks of repentance.[15]

For Origen, this condition constitutes the extent of postmortem suffering, and it ends when the accumulated guilt has been expiated over repeated reincarnations. For Jerome, this condition continues into the otherworld, and so forever.

Jerome builds here on the interpretation Mark 9:47–48 gives Isaiah 66:24. Whereas Isaiah referred to unending fire and undying worms in heaps of carrion, Mark placed those terrors in "Gehenna, where the worm does not die and the fire is not extinguished," and thereby enshrined Isaiah's prophecy in Christian Scripture. As aspects of hell, the fire and the worm became subjects of extended reflection. One interpretation, dating probably from before the early seventh century and wrongly attributed to Jerome, joins the fire and the worm in infernal industry and leads to a narrowly conceived allegorical interpretation that endured at least as late as Thomas Aquinas and Bonaventure in the thirteenth century. These early commentators distinguished the labor of the worm from that of the fire. "The worm is the procrastinating conscience, the fire is the punishment that continues its work."[16] The distinction appears to be temporal: the worm refers to the past and punishes the conscience for not ruling the soul better during the life of the sinner; the fire represents an eternal future of pain. The same anonymous commentator also associates Isaiah 50:11 ("Walk by the light of your fire"), on which Origen relied so heavily, with Mark 9:47 (on the Gehenna of fire), thus asserting that these sufferings of the conscience are not limited to the life of the living guilty, or that they are purely internal; rather, the fires exist in Gehenna, where the worm does not die, and the fire will not be extinguished. Then, and only then, in hell, must sinners "walk by the light of [their] fire and in the flames which [they] have kindled."[17]

Having considered this division of labor between the fire and the worm, it is worth digressing a moment to recover the early medieval understanding of what a worm is. According to Isidore of Seville's *Book of Etymologies*, the biblical worm was not just the common earthworm, or even the maggot that attacks dead flesh, but an assortment of beasts that swim, fly, and crawl. How different they are from modern expectations becomes clear from Isidore's

---

15. Hieronymus, *Epist.* 124, ad Auitum; CSEL 56, ed. Isidorus Hilbert (1918), p. 104.

16. "Uermis est conscientia sera; ignis, poena inconsummata." [Jerome,] *Expositio Evangelii secundum Marcum*, CCSL 82, ed. Michael Cahill (1997), pp. 43–44. On authorship, see Cahill's introduction at pp. 118*–19* and the Library of Latin Texts under the lines just quoted.

17. [Jerome,] *Expositio Evangelii secundum Marcum*, CCSL 82:43–44.

assertion that they are generated without sexual intercourse, although some, like the scorpion, hatch from eggs (12.5.1). The spider, he says, lives in the air; in the water lives the leech, (12.5.3); on the ground the scorpion crawls. The moth lives in cloth. In Latin it is called the *tinea* because it is tenacious, totally consuming the clothing it feeds on. Thus the fire and worm give Gehenna a more complex arsenal than just the two elements mentioned by Isaiah and Mark. Another association of the worm with rot derives from the appearance of manna in Exodus 16:20. When, against express instructions, some of the fleeing Hebrews took more than one day's ration, they found, on the next day, the remainder was putrid and teeming with worms. Job associated this scene with the grave: "To the rot I have said 'you are my father,' to the worms 'you are my mother and my sister'" (Job 17:14). Christian commentators, who confused the neutral grave of Job (Sheol) with hell, considered worms and rot as a postmortem punishment for disobedience. Similarly, Isaiah looks forward to the day when a persecuting king will fall from the heights of his throne to the underworld, and the other dead will taunt him: "Maggots (*tinea*) are the bed beneath you and worms (*vermes*) are your covering" (Isa. 14:11). These worms of the underworld are the punishment for pride.

As much as the conscience is liable to infernal torment both in life and after death, it also has a connection to the divine and shares in its regulatory function. This point emerges as early as Jerome's interpretation of Ezekiel 1:6–8, where the prophet sets forth his vision of four beings each having four faces: those of an ox, a human being, a lion, and an eagle. Jerome correlates the four animals with the four faculties of the soul: the rational, the irascible, the concupiscent, and the conscience. Jerome defines this fourth faculty, which the Greeks call *syneidesis*, as the spark of conscience that was not extinguished even in the breast of Cain after he was ejected from paradise and by which we know that we sin. They rightly (*proprie*) attribute this to the eagle, which does not mix with the other three but corrects them when they err, and which we read is sometimes called the Spirit, which "intercedes for us with sighs too deep for words" (Rom 8:26). Therefore, God now directs this *quadriga* (four-horse chariot) as a charioteer, and shapes the gait from uncontrolled steps, makes it docile, and forces it to obey his command.

Here Jerome establishes an analogy. Just as God rules the universe and a charioteer directs a team, even so the *syneidesis* or conscience, symbolized first by the high-flying eagle and then by the charioteer, regulates the other (rational, irascible, and concupiscent) aspects of the human mind. The overall image is one of contained conflict, a correct ordering of interactive parts, under the control of a single power, the charioteer-like, eagle-like, God-like, conscience, which knows when we err and pulls us back on course. Not even in the breast of Cain is the conscience extinguished—"extinguished" because God's punishment of Cain forces him to suffer indefinitely, "tortured by the fire of your conscience."[18] This is the fire that Jerome had felt in his own conscience, and since Jerome moved from his fit of guilt back *ad superos*, he established a clear link between hell, the moralized underworld, and the conscience of the living sinner.

Cassian: *Tristitia* and *Amaritudo*

The intricate relationship that grew up between the fire and the worm, between hell and the conscience, would continue to evolve over the ensuing centuries. One important figure in this evolution was Jerome's younger contemporary, the desert father John Cassian (ca. 360–435). In his *Institutes*, where he discusses the spiritual life of monks, Cassian considers the vice of sadness (*tristitia*), which, like sloth or *acedia* (listlessness), is dangerous because it can lead to spiritual paralysis. The risk of both sadness and listlessness is that they bring on despair. *Acedia* deprives the stricken monk of his resolve, makes him feel he has mistaken his calling and achieved no spiritual benefits from his ascetic discipline. Either his cell disgusts him, and now he yearns to leave it to socialize with the other monks or he retreats into constant sleep (hence "sloth" for this inactivity; however, clearly, the English term understates this complex disturbance).[19] Thus undermotivated, he becomes a distraction or, worse, a bad influence on his fellows. Attacks by such enemies against a monk vulnerable to them will only multiply. Since the monastic vocation campaigns against the devil, *acedia* is a retreat by the troops, flight from battle. "And so the warrior of Christ is made a fugitive and a deserter from the campaign."[20] Mental disquiet becomes insubordination, even treason, and the melancholy monk is to be shunned, disciplined, even discharged like a runaway or a traitor. That is why the true "athlete of Christ" must extirpate this disease from the inner recesses of his heart and renew his zeal in the battle for perfection.[21]

Just as the monk suffering from *acedia* is a threat to the community, so one immobilized by *tristitia* is of no more value than worm-ridden lumber,

---

18. "[C]onscientiae tuae igne torqueberis." Hieronymus, *Epist.* 36.2; CSEL 54:271.

19. Jean Cassien, *Institutions cénobitiques* 10.2; ed. and trans. Jean-Claude Guy, SC 109 (1965), pp. 384–87.

20. "[I]ta militiae suae fugitiuus ac desertor Christi miles effectus." Cassian, *Inst.* 10.3, lines 15–16; pp. 388–91.

21. Cassian, *Inst.* 10.5; pp. 390–91.

fit only for the fire.[22] No one could miss this recurrence of worms and fire. These spiritual illnesses render the monk useless, like the worthless (*inutilem*) servant in the parable of the talents, sent to the outer darkness (Matt. 25:14–30), or the tree that bears no fruit consigned to the fire (Matt. 3:10 and 7:19). The path that leads from *acedia* and *tristitia* to damnation is therefore clear. That clarity, however, makes one form of sadness *useful*, since it causes ascetics to examine their lives and to correct what is wrong.[23] From Cassian on, monastic reflection saw *tristitia* as a challenge. If confronted positively, it spurs repentance and launches an amended spiritual life; if neglected, its uncorrected psychological conflicts lead to hell, where they continue, like worms in rot, to attack the tormented soul.

The crucial aid in the struggle against *tristitia* and *acedia* is humility. Cassian's prescribed path to this virtue was to have immense influence. Both the *Rule of the Master* and the *Benedictine Rule* would adapt it. The starting point he offers is the fear of God, which in turn provokes the cleansing of vices and the cultivation of virtues.[24] To encourage humility further, Cassian provides some "guides to thought."[25] These principles emphasize two interrelated themes: meek acceptance of hardship, which Cassian calls *vilitas*, and self-humbling.[26] One, "Present yourself like an evil and useless worker," is particularly important because it recalls the fate of the useless servant and the barren tree cast into the fire. For those who succeed, however, Cassian describes this advantage:

Once [humility] is truly attained, it will immediately guide you across its highest step to the charity which has no fear, through which all that you considered previously not without the pain of fearfulness, you will begin to regard without any labor, as if naturally, not out of the contemplation of punishment or out of any fear, but out of the love of the good itself and delight in the virtues.[27]

---

22. Ibid., 9.3, line 4; pp. 370–71.

23. "Hence, in one way only *tristitia* ought to be considered useful for us, namely when we conceive it either enflamed by a repentance for our wrongs or by a desire for perfection or through the contemplation of future blessedness." Cassian, *Inst.* 9.10; p. 376. Note also the positive connotations of *tristitia* in 2 Cor. 7:10.

24. Cassian, *Inst.* 4.39.1–3; pp. 178–81.

25. "cogitationum principia"; Cassian, *Inst.* 4.37.10; p. 178.

26. Cassian, *Inst.* 4.39.2; pp. 180–81.

27. "Quae cum fuerit in ueritate possessa, confestim te ad caritatem, quae timorem non habet, gradu excelsiore perducet, per quam uniuersa, quae prius non sine poena formidinis obseruabas, absque ullo labore uelut naturaliter incipies custodire non iam contemplatione supplicii uel timoris ullius, sed amore ipsius boni et delectatione uirtutum." Cassian, *Inst.* 4.39.3, lines 27–33; p. 180.

What had been done from the "pain of fearfulness" is now done from charity. Cassian does not explain the source of that fear. An inkling comes, however, when he evokes the consequences of the ascetic's inner loyalties. We have within us, he says,

> friendship with either the vices or the virtues, through which we prepare either the kingdom of Christ or of the devil. . . . Consequently, if the kingdom of God is inside us, and the kingdom of God consists of justice and peace and joy, whoever abides in these qualities is doubtless in the kingdom of God, whereas those who occupy themselves in injustice and discord and sadness (*tristitia*) are established in the kingdom of the devil and in hell and in death (*in regno diaboli et in inferno ac morte*).[28]

The parallel arrangement of the final sentence is instructive. One who abides in the virtues is in the kingdom of God; those who practice injustice or tolerate *tristitia* are in hell. Our present attitudes do not merely foretell our fates; they link us to them now. Heaven already rewards the living righteous; the devil, hell, and death already punish the living wicked.

The *Rule of the Master* and the *Rule of Benedict*: Humility from Fear

Cassian's special attention to the hermit's frame of mind informed the monastic movement from early on. Without sacrificing the spiritual aims of individual contemplatives, leaders in the West gradually added a more institutional approach. They addressed the monastic community's government, the powers of the abbot, and the monks' duty of obedience. Cassian already saw hell as the destination of insubordinates, deserters, and all who tolerate vice, but Gehenna and fear of its torments appeared much more prominently in the anonymous *Rule of the Master* (RM) of about 520 and the *Rule of Benedict* (RB), the most famous of all, probably composed in the middle third of the sixth century.[29] In his Prologue, the Master sets forth two alternatives. If

---

28. John Cassian, *Conlationes xxiiii*, 1.13, line 15; CSEL 13, ed. Michael Petschenig (Vienna: Gerold, 1886), p. 15.

29. To survey the other monastic rules for men and women that circulated in the West, see Timothy Fry, *The Rule of St. Benedict in Latin and English with Notes* (Collegeville, MN: Liturgical Press, 1980), 42–65; Rosamond McKitterick, *The Frankish Kingdoms under the Carolingians* (London and New York: Longman, 1983), 109–24; C. H. Lawrence, *Medieval Monasticism*, 2nd ed. (1984; London and New York: Longman, 1989), 1–85. For the relationship of the *Rule of the Master* to the *Benedictine Rule*, see Fry's synthesis, 69–90, and in particular, *La Règle de Saint Benoît*, ed. Adalbert de Vogüé and Jean Neufville, SC 181 (1971–72), 1:245–314.

one obeys his *Rule,* one attains "eternal glory with the saints."[30] Conversely, should one not fulfill the precepts he offers, one finishes "in the eternal fire of Gehenna with the devil" (RM Prol. 22). Benedict also emphasizes hell in his Prologue, as he recommends submission to monastic discipline for all who "flee the pains of Gehenna and wish to attain eternal life."[31] Both the Master and Benedict surpass Cassian in explicit references to Gehenna. Following the lead of Cassian, the RM lists principles of good living, a Holy Craft (*ars sancta*), among which we find number 51, which advises: "Cultivate a horror of Gehenna" (*Gehennam expavescere;* RM 3.51). Benedict also provides Tools of Good Works (*instrumenta bonorum operum*), which include the same principle (RB 4.45).

The most important image in these two monastic rules is the famous Ladder of Humility. RM 10.7 states how ascent occurs by self-humbling (*humilitate*), and descent occurs by self-exaltation (*exaltatione*), and Benedict adopts the same ladder (RB 7). This strategy of reversal has a strong foundation in Scripture. Psalm 9:15 exults that the nations have fallen into a pit of their own digging, their foot caught in the net they set for others. Isaiah announces: "The lofty will be brought low" (Isa. 10:33). The New Testament also delights in turning the tables. Luke provides a cyclical paradox: "Everyone who exalts himself will be humbled, and he who humbles himself will be exalted" (Luke 14:11 and 18:14).[32] Again in Luke (16:25), Abraham explains how the conditions of Lazarus and the rich man have been reversed. In other passages the first become the last (Matt. 19:30, 20:16; Mark 10:31; Luke 13:30). Passages where the haughty are humbled draw their rhetorical force from antithesis, not from quantification. What differs in the RM and the RB is precisely the effort to calibrate the degrees of humility, to show at what rung one stands in progressing downward through pride or upward through humility.[33]

According to the RM (10.11), "The disciple scales the first step of humility on the ladder to heaven if, always placing the fear of God before his eyes so that he may ever flee complacency and always be mindful of all that God has commanded, he always turns over in his mind how Gehenna burns those who despise the Lord by their sins and that which eternal life has prepared for those who fear God." Benedict's variations are minor (RB 7.11). Then, if

---

30. *La Règle du Maître,* Prologue, 20, ed. Adalbert de Vogüé, SC 105 (1964).

31. "[F]ugientes Gehennae poenas, ad vitam volumus pervenire perpetuam." RB Prol. 42; Fry, p. 164, line 42.

32. Other examples: Ps. 87:16; Job 22:29; Matt. 23:12; James 4:10; 1 Peter 5:6. See Bernstein, *Formation,* 235–38, for reflections on proportionality in punishment.

33. Peter Brown correctly attributes calibration to Gregory the Great. Brown, Lecture I, "Gloriosus Obitus," 37.

the monk also renounces his own will and perverse thoughts, he will be a "useful brother" (*utilis frater*, RM 10.19; RB 7.18). The association of these ideas combines another echo of Matthew 25:30 and the "outer darkness" for the useless brother. It forms another unambiguous reference to Gehenna. External discipline, particularly obedience to the abbot, for which "fear of Gehenna" is a prominent reason (RM 7.3; cf. RB 5.3), furthers the monk's internal, spiritual ascent.

On the twelfth step, the Master and Benedict urge that even here, at the pinnacle, the monk should "consider himself guilty of his sins at all times and picture himself already present at the terrible judgment" that is to come (RM 10.84; RB 7.64). The twelfth step does not threaten damnation, but the immanence of judgment opposes any self-satisfaction in the monk's humility.

In concluding the discussion of humility, the RM and the RB sum up the spiritual progress accomplished via the twelve steps with a statement that resembles Cassian's, but which is more specific about the nature of the fear. First, the RM:

> Therefore, when the disciple has ascended all these steps of humility, he will be well advanced up the ladder of this life in the fear of God, and will soon attain that perfect love of the Lord which expels the fear through which all that he had previously obeyed not without dread he will begin to accomplish without any effort, as if naturally, out of long training, no longer through the fear of Gehenna, but through the love of that good training itself and delight in the virtues.[34]

Benedict varies the language slightly:

> Therefore, when the monk has ascended all these steps of humility, he will soon attain that perfect love of God which expels the fear through which all he had previously obeyed not without dread he will begin to accomplish without any effort, as if naturally, out of long training, no longer from the fear of Gehenna, but from the love of Christ, and from that good training itself and from delight in the virtues.[35]

The core of this analysis is Cassian's, but the Master and Benedict explicitly name Gehenna as the source of the fear without which one might not turn to Christ. As in Cassian, the formulation "not without dread" implies that an important part (but not all) of the progress comes from the removal of a

---

34. RM 10.87–90.
35. RB 7.67–69; Fry, 200–202. This and other translations, which are based on Fry's bilingual edition, are my own.

negative motivation. Whereas there is no fear in perfect love, not everything was done from dread even prior to attaining that state.

In the Ladder of Humility put forward by the *Rule of the Master* and adopted by Benedict, then, hell appears positively, as a stimulus *nearly* indispensable to undertaking monastic discipline because the fear of God, along with fear of Gehenna, is the first rung on the Ladder of Humility. Ninth-century commentators on the *Benedictine Rule*, such as Smaragdus of St. Mihiel and Hildemar of Corbie, will further expand this positive function of hell.

Fear of God and of Gehenna is only the first step. Reaching pure love is a long process. The vices are certainly obstacles, particularly *acedia* and *tristitia*. Whereas the Master and Benedict are virtually interchangeable on the substitution of *caritas* for fear, Benedict is far more attuned than the Master to the dangers of *tristitia*. His sensitivity emerges particularly in the chapters concerning excommunication.

In the RM, an insubordinate disciple threatens the house's order. He is a demonic tool. The Master prescribes a formal denunciation followed by an intimidating tirade. The offender is a rebel, another Judas. The abbot is to evoke an image of the culprit's future, cowering before the awe-inspiring divine judgment and recoiling from the ridicule the blessed will heap upon him as he departs with the goats to damnation (RM 13.15). Then the wayward monk will be exiled from the common table and sentenced to menial work in isolation, where no brother will offer any comfort. Guilt will be his only consolation (RM 13.49). When an excommunicated monk seeks to return, the repentant brother is to prostrate himself and, from the floor, deliver a long prescribed speech in which, among other things, he beseeches the abbot to behave like the shepherd who left ninety-nine sheep to find one wanderer (after Matt. 18:12–13; cf. Luke 15:4) and forgive him. The abbot then reproaches the monk for his fault. Finally the brothers pray for him. The monk then prays to God directly and, finding evidence of divine mercy in Scripture, begs forgiveness. At last, by the ceremony of washing the hands of his brothers, he is reintegrated into the community (RM 14).

In his discussion of excommunication (RB 23–27), Benedict mostly follows the order of topics of the RM, but condenses the treatment considerably. What differs most is the tone. It is not the suppliant excommunicant who begs the abbot to show mercy, but Benedict as author of the *Rule* who stipulates that he must. The abbot, in particular, is to counsel the backslider wisely and energetically, lest he lose one of his sheep. Senior monks are to comfort the wavering brother in private and urge him to make satisfaction by returning to humility and "to console him lest he be caught up in even deeper sadness (*tristitia*)," soothingly paraphrasing 2 Corinthians 2:7 rather than some harsher texts (RB 27.3).[36] The RM has no counterpart to this gentleness with regard to excommunicates.

Another contrast will help elucidate this difference in approach. In describing the abbot, both the Master and Benedict say that he occupies in the monastery the place of Christ and that his name, *abba*, means "father" (RM 2.2–3; RB 2.2–3). Unlike the Master, however, Benedict continues by encouraging monks to take up the commitment to the religious life, so that they may be spared divine justice, a force Benedict compares to two dangers: an angry father who would disinherit his sons, and a dread lord who would condemn his evil servants (or slaves) to eternal punishment (RB Prol. 6–7). This series of authority figures—Christ, abbot, father, and lord—is the key to *tristitia*'s profound ramifications in RB 27. When the monk is out of alignment with these authorities, his sadness could be aggravated by undue harshness from the abbot.[37] Thus he urges the abbot not to worsen a bad situation.[38] Benedict (and not the Master) makes avoidance of *tristitia* into something more than an individual battle against vice, but rather like Cassian's discussion of *acedia*'s dangers, he regards it as an institutional necessity because *tristitia* threatens collective morale. Given the danger of sadness to the psychological fabric of the monastery, it is not difficult to see why it would enter speculation about the otherworld.

Gregory I Names Inner Death

In his magisterial commentary on Job, Gregory the Great crystallized the expression "inner death" in a new form. There is no doubt that, at the Last Judgment, "the guilty soul clouds over and the conscience attacks itself with darts from its own memory."[39] But, according to Gregory, the cares in our hearts even now are worms. "From [our] corruptible nature and perverse custom we are driven and vexed, as if by worms, and so we are wearied by uneasy cogitations in the mind. . . . Because they generate innumerable cares of infirmity in our hearts, the worms are well called 'mother' and 'sister'.

---

36. Marian Larmann, "*Contristare* and *Tristitia* in the RB: Indications of Community and Morale," *American Benedictine Review* 30 (1979): 167.

37. Confirmation occurs in Benedict's Prologue, which describes those enrolled in the monastery as taking up arms to fight under Christ the king (another image of authority, RB Prol. 3), whom the monks do not wish to distress (*contristari*) by their evil actions (RB Prol. 5).

38. RM gives *tristitia* little attention; See Larmann, "*Contristare* and *Tristitia*," 168–69. RM 5 is a list of vices. Neither *tristitia* nor *acedia* appears. They are replaced by *pigritia*, "laziness." The vices come from the devil, and those who fail to uproot them will receive the "Gehenna of perpetual fire."

39. "Animum reatus obnubilat et recordationis suae iaculis ipsa se conscientia impugnat." Greg. *Mor.* 8.53.90, lines 8–10; p. 453.

They consume the spirit when the cares disturb it."[40] As already appears from our troubles in this world, the psychological fate of the damned is to be consumed internally, in the conscience, by the same vain cares that pursued them in life. "Inside, the conscience burns with desire, while outside Gehenna wracks the flesh."[41] The gnawing and the burning that are to torment the conscience in hell recall Jerome's dream and the affliction of his conscience while he was still alive and Cassian's rooting of the wicked, already, in hell. The term that Gregory highlighted, inner death, therefore identified a concept previously established in Jerome, Cassian, Augustine, the RM, and the RB, but without the label. His readers, among Europe's most literate, would develop the theme further.

Isidore of Seville: Twofold Torture

Cassian had explained that *acedia* and *tristitia* would lead to hell, but Isidore of Seville (560–636) declared them, along with their related disorders, such as bitterness (*amaritudo*), characteristic of hell itself. Younger brother of Leander, who was his predecessor in the see of Seville and who corresponded with Gregory I, Isidore wrote histories, reference tools (the *Etymologies* and a kind of dictionary, *Differences*), meditations (the *Soliloquies* or *Synonyms*), and theological synthesis (the *Sentences*). As bishop, Isidore presided along with the Visigothic kings over important councils in Seville and Toledo that shaped jurisprudence for all of Spain. His output earned him immense influence throughout the medieval period.

In his *Sentences*, Isidore develops Cassian's notion that *tristitia* has a positive side, which is "tempered and reasonable, arising from repentance over wrongs done."[42] He recounts struggles within the mind as it laments past sins, fears future punishment, and hopes for eternal reward. He says the penitent "blushes internally" in an introspection that "already punishes" the contemplative "by means of his own judgment in repenting."[43] Cassian had referred to this phenomenon as the good form of *tristitia*; Isidore calls it *amaritudo*. "Bitterness causes the soul to repent, to examine its deeds more carefully, and to remember, in weeping, the gifts of God that it has spurned. Indeed, there is nothing worse than to perceive one's guilt without

---

40. Greg. *Mor.* 13.46.50 (on Job 17:14); p. 695.

41. "Intus per desiderium ardet conscientia, et foris carnem cruciat Gehenna." Greg. *Mor.* 6.30.47; p. 318.

42. "[T]ristitia, . . . temperata et rationabilis, de delictorum poenitudine veniens." Isidorus Hispalensis, *De differentiis rerum siue Differentiae theologicae uel spiritales* 2.40.166; PL 83:96D.

43. Isidore, *Sent.* 2.12.5; CCSL 111, ed. Pierre Cazier (1998), p. 119.

weeping."[44] Isidore says, "To scorn repentance and to remain in guilt, is to descend into hell after death."[45] Sidestepping *amaritudo* becomes contempt and entails damnation. What you avoid now, you endure later.

The suffering of the conscience foreshadows the suffering of hell. "Even before it suffers the punishments of Gehenna, it already suffers the punishments of the conscience through the disordered longing of the soul."[46] One's guilt pursues one, through the conscience, from life to death and beyond. "Therefore a double judgment occurs in that person: here he is punished by the guilt (*reatus*) of his conscience, and there he is damned by perpetual punishment."[47] "This is the meaning of [Psalm 41.8 Vulg = 42.7 RSV] 'the abyss calls to the abyss in the roar of the rapids.' For the abyss to call to the abyss is to go from the judgment of one's own conscience to the judgment of perpetual damnation."[48] Unless it can unload its burden of guilt, the conscience cascades from this world into hell. In hell, it suffers the same penalty it paid in this world. "The punishment of the damned in Gehenna is twofold: *tristitia* burns the mind, and fire burns the body."[49] He concludes with an incendiary image: "Nor is it surprising that those who did not in the least dampen the flame of cupidity when they were alive should be consigned to the fires of hell when they die."[50]

In his *Book of Synonyms* or *of Soliloquies*, Isidore examines how that theory might play itself out in the mind of a penitent individual.[51] His inner

---

44. Ibid., 2.13.4; p. 120.

45. "[C]ontemnere paenitentiam, et permanere in culpa, descendere in infernum post mortem est." Isidore, *Sent.* 2. 14.2; p. 124.

46. Isidore, *Sent.* 2.26.1; p. 144.

47. "Duplex fit ergo in eo iudicium, quia et hic suae conscientiae reatu punitur, et illuc perpetuali poena damnatur." Isidore, *Sent.* 2.26.3; p. 145.

48. Isidore, *Sent.* 2.26.4; p. 145.

49. "Duplex damnatorum poena est in Gehenna, quorum et mentem urit tristitia, et corpus flamma." Isidore, *Sent.* 1.28.1; p. 86. Note that this quotation continues: "in alternation, so that those who treated in the mind what they carried out with the body should be punished simultaneously, body and soul." Isidore's debt to Gregory (see above, note 44) is evident.

50. Isidore, *Sent.* 2.41.9; p. 182. This idea goes back to Origen and through him to Isaiah 50:11: "Walk by the light of your fire and by the brands which you have kindled." There is similar language in the eighth-century *Vision of Fursey*: "uniuscujusque cupiditas in hoc igne ardebit." See below, chapter 6.

51. I cite the edition of this work by Jacques Elfassi, CCSL 111B (2009). See also Elfassi's articles: "Les *Synonyma* d'Isidore de Séville: Un manuel de grammaire ou de morale?," *Revue d'Études Augustiniennes et Patristiques* 52 (2006), 167–98; "Les deux recensions des *Synonyma*," in *L'édition critique des oeuvres d'Isidore de Séville*, ed. Maria Adelaida Andrés Sanz, Jacques Elfassi, and José Carlos Martín (Paris: Institut d'Études Augustiniennes, 2008), 153–84; "Genèse et originalité du style synonymique dans les *Synonyma* d'Isidore de Séville," *Revue des Études Latines* 83 (2006): 226–45; "Los dentones de los *Synonyma* de Isidoro de Sevilla," in *IV Congresso Internacional de Latin Medieval Hispânico*, ed. Aires A. Nascimeto and Paulo F. Alberto (Lisbon: Centro de Estudos Clássicos, 2006), 393–401.

debate, his soliloquy, is a dialogue between a soul in despair and Reason, who appears to him and tries to encourage the guilty sufferer to renounce evil behavior, take the path of penance, and trust in divine mercy. A collection of equivalent aphorisms, the *Book of Synonyms* is a rhetorical exercise using different, but basically synonymous, language with each restatement. The overall effect is especially powerful in the passages where the soul bemoans its guilt, doubts whether it deserves divine attention, and, close to declaring itself incapable of salvation, nearly enters formal despair. Though the term *tristitia* is not used in its technical meaning (in this work it means only "regret"), this drama employs precisely the constructive dejection that produces self-examination and eventual repentance in a soul that will return to health.

In the *Soliloquies* Isidore states: "No pain is more grievous than that of the conscience."[52] Therefore, it is imperative to perceive the first hints of guilt in the conscience and so turn this spiritual affliction (*angustia, dolor et tristitia*) to advantage.[53] When done properly, the result is a strengthened spirit (*confirmatus animus*).[54] But when the soul resists the first sparks of guilt, there is a direct connection between these pains and hell's. Using the repetitive style demanded by the use of synonymous expressions, Isidore declares: "For these people there is a double damnation, a twin beating strikes them, because they experience both the beginning of their torments here and the culmination of their punishments there [i.e., in hell]."[55] Thus he advises, "Let your heart speak to you."[56] "Acknowledge your faults at least once they have attacked you!"[57]

Adversity can be constructive because knowing the progression from the suffering conscience to the torture of damnation makes it easier to avoid sin. Focus on the fires of Gehenna averts the fires of lust.[58] Sensuality, that constant distraction, can best be avoided not merely by thinking of how hell penalizes one's faults, but by circumventing the senses altogether. In a statement that rhymes (*morientis uocatio tua sit emendatio*) Isidore exhorts, "Let the profession of dying be the theme of your vying."[59] His slogan recalls Gregory's: "The perfect life is the imitation of death."

---

52. "Nulla poena grauior conscientiae." Isidore, *Syn.* 2.61, line 636; p. 112.

53. Isidore, *Syn.* 1.26, lines 230–31; p. 21.

54. Ibid., 1.27, line 241; p. 22.

55. "His duplex damnatio est, gemina his percussio est, quia et hic habent initium tormentorum, et illuc perfectionem poenarum." Isidore, *Syn.* 1.31, lines 291–93; pp. 26–27.

56. Isidore, *Syn.* 1.34, line 317; p. 29.

57. Ibid., 1.38, line 366; p. 32.

58. "Recordatio ardoris gehennae ardorem excludat luxuriae." Isidore, *Syn.* 1.46, line 440; p. 38.

59. Isidore, *Syn.* 1.50, lines 483–84; p. 41.

This desire for change following internal experience is real contrition;[60] thus the benefits of dejection are clear. Gehenna plays a crucial role in how they are expressed. Isidore's human begins a lamentation on the extent of his guilt and on divine mercy. He reiterates this theme three times: (1) "Tartarus hardly suffices for my wrongs";[61] (2) "The punishment of my damnation is lighter than my sin";[62] (3) "Lighter is my wound than the weight of my sins."[63] And yet, the evil committed brings on a guilt that surpasses all torture, a dread of the coming judgment, by which the guilty soul expects damnation. Here again is the theme of continuity, from present sin, certified by final judgment, to future punishment. "I dread the torments of Gehenna on the basis of my guilt. Already the present punishment lacerates me, but the one to come disturbs me more."[64] Isidore works the divine scrutiny of the conscience into the continuous flow from sin to guilt (and suffering through the guilty conscience) to judgment to hell. These thoughts provoke a plea for grace in the form of correction (1.75, 2.82). The tone recalls the supplications in Psalms, but it goes further, pleading not for the postponement of death, but escape from a hell barely imagined in Psalms.[65] "Help me, my God, before I die," before the flames, the darkness, Tartarus, overtake me, "before the fires of Gehenna devour me, before I am wracked without end."[66]

Broadening out, Isidore shows how the different vices ensnare different segments of society, especially those in command: princes, lords, judges (2.30, but esp. 2.82–94). Reason explains how each vice damns. For example, "libido sinks one into hell, it sends one to the Tartarean torments, it leads to the punishments of Tartarus,"[67] The cure for this conspiracy of the vices is the one advanced by Cassian, the *Rule of the Master*, and by Benedict: Be humble (2.20); descend to ascend (2.21). Remember that even God came humble (as a human infant) into the world. Therefore, "accept harsh conditions, abjection, scorn. Displease yourself, inspire disdain of yourself within yourself."[68] Be grateful for these feelings. "Do not be saddened by your infirmities; thank

---

60. "[C]ontritio prius intus agitur, ut post extrinsecus ostendatur." Greg. *Mor.* 25.8, line 51. Cf. Greg. *Mor.* 25.8, line 71: "Ista ergo contritio prius serpit in mente, ut postmodum procedat in opere."

61. Isidore, *Syn.* 1.58, line 587; p. 48.

62. Ibid., 1.59, line 596; p. 48.

63. Ibid., 1.60, line 601; p. 49.

64. Ibid., 1.62, lines 616–17; p. 50.

65. Two potential exceptions are Psalms 49 and 73. See Bernstein, *Formation*, 155, 161–62.

66. Isidore, *Syn.* 1.63, lines 620–25; cf. *Syn.* 1.72.

67. Ibid., 2.10, lines 94–94; p. 70.

68. "Existe uilis, existe abiectus, existe dispectus. Displice tibi, despectus esto apud temetipsum." Isidore, *Syn.* 2.22, lines 203–4; p. 79.

God for your woes."[69] The cure for all the vices and temptations is a focus on our common end, death itself. Therefore hold death always before your eyes and live as one who is already dead and buried (*tanquam mortuus, sicut sepultus, tanquam defunctus*).[70] These counsels are familiar from Cassian, the *Rule of the Master*, and the *Benedictine Rule*. The human soul promises to compensate Reason for this good advice by following her precepts and acknowledges that these should be the rules for living (*vivendi regula*, 2.102). Thus, Isidore endorses monastic principles for the secular elite. Whether addressing contemplatives or lay leaders, Isidore shows the link between the conscience and hell. By bitterness (*amaritudo*), he refers to the pain on earth that should provoke confrontation with one's faults. Infernal bitterness results from not confronting the sin in one's own mind. The discipline denied in life dominates death.

Smaragdus: Hell the Springboard

This function of dejection was important also to Smaragdus of St. Mihiel, a comparatively little-known figure active in the circle of Benedict of Aniane and at the courts of Charlemagne and Louis the Pious. He was made abbot of Castellion in 800 and of Saint-Mihiel on the Meuse in 814 and lived until past 826.[71] In 817, in conjunction with the reforming synods of Aachen, he wrote what is considered to be the earliest surviving commentary on the *Benedictine Rule*.[72]

Smaragdus blended his understanding of *amaritudo* into *afflictio* (affliction), a condition of the mind in repentance and a condition of the damned in hell. Following Isidore, Smaragdus calls the mental anguish that arises from opposing evil thoughts *amaritudo*. When the affliction of the guilty soul brings repentance, "it does not advance to wracking (*cruciatus*), but [instead] the affliction in thought cleanses the mind as quickly as mental iniquity

---

69. Isidore, *Syn.* 2.26, lines 254–55; p. 82.

70. Ibid., 2.95, lines 1038–41.

71. Smaragdus's commentary, the *Expositio in Regulam S. Benedicti*, appears in PL 102:689–932; and in Corpus Consuetudinum Monasticarum [CCM], ed. A. Spannagel and P. Engelbert (Siegeburg, Germany: F. Schmitt, 1974). There is an English translation by David Barry, *Commentary on the Rule of Saint Benedict*, Cistercian Studies Series 212 (Kalamazoo, MI: Cistercian Publications, 2007). The citations of Smaragdus below refer to the Spannagel-Engelbert edition.

72. The commentary attributed to Paul the Deacon would be earlier, but it is actually by Hildemar of Corbie, whom I discuss below. It dates from 845–50. See Wolfgang Hafner, *Der Basiliuskommentar zur Regula S. Benedicti: ein Beitrag zur Autorenfrage karolingischer Regelkommentare*, Beiträge zur Geschichte des alten Mönchtums und des Benediktinerordens 23 (Münster: Aschendorf, 1959), 97. For the activity of Benedict of Aniane and the synods of Aachen, see C. H. Lawrence, *Medieval Monasticism*, 2nd ed. (London and New York: Longman, 1989), 76–82.

pollutes it."[73] Those who spurn affliction now will suffer *cruciatus* forever. This consequence of the failure to engage dejection is by now familiar. Smaragdus encourages his reader to undertake *amaritudo* or *afflictio* with a call to humility. "The more precious one is to oneself, the baser he is to God; the baser he is to himself on account of God, the more precious he is to God."[74]

Considering Rung Six of the Ladder of Humility, which urges the monk to identify himself with the evil and unworthy laborer headed for the outer darkness (Matt. 25:14–30), Smaragdus writes: "For we do our work externally, but internally we do not know how the work may be received by the Lord. Therefore, [the monk] should consider himself unworthy . . . because however good our work is, it is not worthy of acquiring the eternal glory or rewards."[75] The point of this apparent self-deprecation emerges when Smaragdus comes to Rung Seven and the worm of Psalm 21:7 ("But I am a worm, and no man"). As the first shall be last, so the vile worm feeds on the wood and becomes pure. In this context, "feeding on wood" alludes to the wood of the Cross. Thus, "the worm seems to be more humble and more vile than all the beasts. But the worm feeds on a Wood that proves to be purer the frailer it is. To this the monk may be compared, for the more he is despised and considered weak and vile, the holier and purer he is before God."[76] In the pursuit of humility, one must consider oneself not only liable to damnation, like the evil and unworthy laborer or the worm, but virtually damned. Thus, the monk approaches the lip of hell. Augustine called this ability to face up to the possibility of being damned a "constructive fear" (*terror utilis*).[77] It also appears in Isidore's *Soliloquies*.

Just as one senses that the contemplative has reached bottom, Smaragdus begins to shift from an emphasis on one's own worthlessness to

---

73. Smaragdus, *Expositio* 4.50; p. 131, lines 3–10, quoting Gregorius Magnus, *Regula pastoralis* 3.29; PL 77:109C.

74. "Tanto ergo fit quisque vilior deo, quanto pretiosior sibi; tanto pretiosior deo, quanto propter [ed.: per] eum vilior sibi." Smaragdus, *Expositio* 7.4; p. 163, lines 22–24.

75. "Ideo monachus operarium iudicat se malum, quia quomodo opus eius recipiatur necscit a domino. Operamur enim nos exterius, sed quomodo opus a domino recipiatur nescimus interius. Ideo indignum se iudicat, quia sicut 'non sunt condignae passiones huius saeculi ad futuram gloriam quae revelabitur in nobis,' ita non sunt digna quamvis sint bona opera nostra ad conquirendam gloriam vel praemia sempiterna." Smaragdus, *Expositio* 7.49; p. 184, line 29–p. 185, line 3.

76. "Vermis enim humilior cunctis animantibus esse videtur et vilior. Nutritus enim vermis ex ligno quanto fragilior, tanto esse probatur et purior. Cui comparatur monachus, qui quanto in hoc saeculo fuerit dispectior, infirmus et vilior, tanto apud deum sanctior invenitur et mundior." Smaragdus, *Expositio* 7.52; p. 186, lines 8–12. Smaragdus's taste for these biblical paradoxes is apparent, as he paraphrases 1 Cor. 1:25, 1:27, and 3:19 at ibid., 7.50; p. 185, lines 6–7: "Apud saeculum enim istum se iustus cognoscit stultum, ut inveniatur sapiens apud deum."

77. Augustine, *Contra adversarium legis et prophetarum* 1, line 665; CCSL 49, ed. Klaus D. Daur (1985), p. 57.

humility as a source of strength.[78] "Humility, that glorious culmination, attains Jerusalem."[79] Or again: "Whereas pride thrusts one down to Tartarus, humility raises one to Heaven."[80] The nadir and the zenith interact and nearly correspond. The perfect acceptance of guilt, self-humbling, and worthlessness becomes not a low point, but a foundation or even a springboard that gives access to the pinnacle of heaven. The culmination of humility, which includes the admission that one is fit only for hell, identity with the useless servant bound for the outer darkness, is also the culmination of hope—the achievement of one's nearly abandoned desires. Pursuit of humility through the pit of self-abasement becomes, paradoxically, not a dead end, but an entrance to the desired realm, one whose price of admission was, precisely, despair of ever reaching it. It is at the moment of recognizing one's fitness for damnation that one attains humility and heaven opens up. As Smaragdus put it, "Let us humble ourselves for glory" (*Humiliemur ad gloriam*).[81] The descent of humility into apparent baseness and abjection switches back and ascends. The theme of reversal, so important in connection with making the last first and other forms of status inversion, instead of an ironic turning of the tables, becomes a deliberate strategy of spiritual advancement.

Hildemar of Corbie: On Pure and Servile Fear

Hildemar was a monk of Corbie from 821 or 826 until 841, when he went to northern Italy to reform a house in Brescia, and then to Civate (near Lecco). He wrote his *Commentary on the Benedictine Rule* probably in the last five years before he died ca. 850.[82] Hildemar builds on the statement found in Cassian, the RM, and the RB: what had formerly been achieved only through

---

78. See Francis F. Seeburger, "Humility, Maturity, and the Fear of God: Reflections on RB 7," *American Benedictine Review* 46.2 (1995): 149–68, esp. 160, where he compares this Benedictine view of humility to the way an alcoholic reverses direction after "bottoming out."

79. Smaragdus, *Expositio* 7.54; p. 187, line 5.

80. "Nam sicut superbia mergit ad tartarum, ita ista tollit ad caelum." Smaragdus, *Expositio* 7.54; p. 187, line 6.

81. "[H]umiliemur ad gloriam." Smaragdus, *Expositio* 7.65; p. 191, line 8. In his commentary on Luke 18:14, Bede uses this same phrase. In contrast to those who promote themselves to ruin, "let us," he says, "humble ourselves to glory." In *Lucae Euangelium expositio* 5.18, line 1179; CCSL 120, ed. D. Hurst (1960), p. 325.

82. For Hildemar, see Louis Gaillard, "Hildemar," *Dictionnaire de spiritualité*, vol. 7, pt. 1 (1969): 521–22; G. Bernt, "Hildemar v. Corbie," in *Lexikon des Mittelalters* 5 (1990): 15–16; Klaus Zelzer, "Überlegungen zu einer Gesamtedition des frühnachkarolingischen Kommentars zur Regula S. Benedicti aus der Tradition des Hildemar von Corbie," *Revue Bénédictine* 91.3–4 (1981): 373–82; Zelzer, "Von Benedikt zu Hildemar: Die Regula Benedicti auf dem Weg zur Alleingeltung im Blickfeld der Textgeschichte," *Regulae Benedicti Studia* 16 (1987): 1–22; Zelzer, "Von Benedikt zu Hildemar: Zu Textgestalt und Textgeschichte der Regula Benedicti auf ihrem Weg zur Alleingeltung," *Frühmittelalterliche*

fear of punishment the humble contemplative, approaching perfection, can now achieve easily through acquired discipline. Assumed as axiomatic is the statement in 1 John 4:18, "There is no fear in love, but perfect love casts out fear." Traditionally, there were considered to be two types of fear. Servile fear (*timor servilis*) is base; it comes from fear of punishment and the pain that follows. Pure fear (*timor castus*), sometimes called filial fear, is the respect one attains from understanding the justice that comes from castigation. It fades into love for perfect authority. One might regard the Ladder of Humility as a progression from servile to pure fear, as if an ascent along a straight line, but Hildemar's idea is more subtle. The progression up the ladder no longer seems linear, but circular: at the pinnacle, servile and pure fear are side by side, interacting. From his vantage point atop the twelfth rung, Hildemar asks two rhetorical questions that juxtapose the first step with the twelfth. Why did Benedict say that the first stage of humility is the fear of God? And why in describing the twelfth rung, the consummation of perfect love (*caritas*), did Benedict admonish: "One must consider oneself guilty (*reum*) of one's sins *at all times*" (*reum se* omni hora *aestimet de peccatis suis*)? Hildemar answers by adding a complication not present in Benedict. Though surely Benedict hoped to avoid complacency on the twelfth rung, Hildemar elaborates: "Benedict knew that a man can fall even from the height of perfection, if, before becoming completely confirmed (*solidatus*) in divine charity, that is, in pure fear, he should take pride in himself."[83] Here Hildemar emphasizes the evocation of the first step implicit in the term "guilty" (*reum*) and the allusion to the Last Judgment by stating: "[Benedict] therefore mentions fear in this very twelfth step, because servile fear is necessary to protect virtue precisely when the person applying [that virtue], is passing into pure fear."[84]

Although on the twelfth rung one may eventually experience pure fear alone and reach perfect charity, Hildemar insists that the two fears are mixed, at least temporarily, even there, until the transition is completed:

Before [attaining perfect charity] the monk may [occasionally] possess pure fear, but not completely, because he is accustomed to be overcome by servile fear. And from this, one may know that sometimes

Studien 23 (1989): 112–30; Mayke de Jong, "Growing Up in a Carolingian Monastery: Magister Hildemar and His Oblates," *Journal of Medieval History* 9 (1983): 99–128.

83. "[P]osse cadere hominem etiam de summa perfectione, si, antequam solidatus fuerit in caritate divina, i.e. in casto timore, superbierit." Hildemar, *Expositio Regulae ab Hildemaro tradita*, ed. P. Rupertus Mittermüller (Ratisbon, NY, and Cincinnati: Frederick Pustet, 1880), 266.

84. "[I]deo etiam in isto gradu duodecimo mentionem timoris fecit, quia timor servilis adeo est necessarius, ut tegat virtutem, quam operatur quis, donec transeat in castum timorem." Hildemar, *Expositio* 266.

servile fear and sometimes pure fear leads to the good, because sometimes this happens by the love of God and sometimes by the fear of
Gehenna, that is, through tears and all the rest.[85]

Tears, contrition, repentance, are left behind no more than servile fear. One
senses in Hildemar how many reverses impede the contemplative striving
for humility.

Thus, for Hildemar, Gehenna and the fear of hell are so crucial to the
monk's progress that he includes interaction between servile fear and pure
fear even on the twelfth rung, at the last instant before pure fear dissolves
into perfect charity. This blend of the meanest and the noblest forms of fear
constitutes a structural parallel to the interaction that Smaragdus had sensed
between the consciousness of guilt and liability to hell at the extreme of
humility (at once a nadir and a zenith) and, at the other extreme, attainment
of the culmination, the *fastigium*, of the Heavenly Jerusalem.

The two fears encompass a ladder that guides the religious, but even its
lowest rung is above the reach of some souls. When, following Cassian, the
Benedictine Rule enjoins moderation in dealing with an excommunicated
monk "lest he be absorbed in a greater *tristitia*," Hildemar adduces the
example of Judas: "For when he ought to have repented for the evil he committed, Judas lost his bearings (*oblitus est sui*) and was sucked in. He hanged
himself in a noose through excessive sadness."[86] This obsession with sadness,
or despair, should not befall wayward monks lest, like Judas, they perish eternally.[87] For Hildemar, it was *tristitia* as despair that blocked Judas's path to
repentance. In such a situation, even *timor servilis* is a step up. When *tristitia*
prevents access to even the most basic fear of God, damnation results.

John the Scot Erigena: Twofold Torture by Wrong Desires

John the Scot was one of the rare thinkers in Western Europe who knew
Greek and was perhaps the outstanding Latin-writing philosopher between

---

85. "[A]nte monachus habeat castum timorem, sed tamen non perfecte, quia superabatur a
timore servili; nam in hoc potest cognoscere, quod aliquando timore servili aliquando timore casto,
quia aliquando amore dei, aliquando timore Gehennae agit bonum, i. e. lacrimas et reliq[ua]." Hildemar, *Expositio* 269.

86. "Ne abundantiori tristitia absorbeatur: sicuti Judas absorptus est; ille enim cum debuerat
agere poenitentiam de malo, quod fecit, oblitus est sui et absorptus est, prae nimia tristitia laqueo se
suspendit." Hildemar, *Expositio* 357.

87. "Hanc vero absorptionem, i.e. desperationem voluit cavere S. Benedictus, . . . ne frater prae
nimia tristitia desperet et sibi aliquid mali, sicut Judas fecit, inferat et in aeternum pereat." Hildemar,
Expositio 357.

Augustine and the twelfth century. He translated and commented on the works of Dionysus the pseudo-Areopagite, a major Christian mystic and Neoplatonist of the late fifth or early sixth century. Moreover, he was not a bishop or an abbot, but an adviser to King Charles the Bald and lived as a court intellectual.[88] He died around 877 or 880. In his masterpiece, *On the Division of Nature*, a philosophical examination of all creation including time itself, John the Scot pursues the logical extreme of inner death. For him hell exists only in the conscience. Whereas Cassian expressed the danger of *acedia* and *tristitia* as potentially leading to hell, and Isidore of Seville had considered dejection (he called it *amaritudo*) characteristic of both the guilty conscience and of hell, John the Scot viewed it (*tristitia* is his word) as the essence of hell. For John, Hades, hell, and *tristitia* are synonymous. Since this view is similar to Origen's, the position that attracted Jerome's ire, it suggests that these thinkers have completed a circle, but John's conclusions differ significantly from Origen's.

Understanding John and his departure from Origen requires a brief digression on Neoplatonism. This philosophical system proposes different levels of being arranged in a cycle of emanation and return. At the top of this hierarchy is God's absolute existence. As sole cause, God freely confers existence on lower levels such as humans, other animals, and, finally, inanimate, unformed matter. Because this hierarchy is a cycle of emanation and return, all existing things return to their cause. In religion, this means a return to God. Origen of Alexandria had used these premises to propose a system whereby the suffering of wicked souls would enhance consciousness of their existence and hence their source. This recovered awareness of the God they had wrongly neglected, this consciousness of their origin, is curative. Thus, once cleansed, there would be no reason to punish them further, and the chastened humans or angels could regain their original image-likeness to God. Thus the end would resemble the beginning, and all would be united in God. In Origen's thinking, it might require many reincarnations for a single soul to neglect God and then experience the punishment, illumination, and recovery before a full return to God. This process would apply to every rational soul, whether human or angelic; hence all would eventually be saved. Origen's ideas were opposed in both the Eastern and Western churches and condemned twice in the East by the emperor Justinian in 543 and 553, but because of their affinity with Neoplatonism, they retained an important attraction.

---

88. *ODCC*, 558a–559a.

One challenge in analyzing John the Scot is to acknowledge his debt to Neoplatonism and Origen and still explain how he avoids the transmigration of souls and universal salvation. John derives his understanding of damnation from his definition of evil. In Neoplatonism, evil has no existence because God himself and all creation are good by definition. Since God created every existing thing, if evil were an existing thing, God would have created it. Since God is perfectly good, he did not create evil.[89] Rather, evil consists in a person's use of the will's freedom to seek false goods, like wealth, physical pleasure, or political power, rather than what is truly good, like the health of the soul, the love of God, and God himself. Since any other perceived good is inferior, the preference for an inferior good is an evil turn of the will, an evil choice, and this turn, rather than the chooser or the thing chosen, is evil.[90] Hell therefore is not physical punishment in some place, but psychological torment by the images of the false goods already freely chosen by the sinner. These deceptive goods are unattainable, but they plague the mind forever. That frustration, that absurdity, that vanity, present only in the distorted wills of sinners, constitutes their damnation. In contrast, the blessed, through the process of deification or *theōsis*, reach the plane occupied by God. What is crucial in studying John the Scot is to understand how he used these Neoplatonic premises of emanation and return without adopting reincarnation, and thus avoided Origen's universalism, the idea that all are saved.[91]

Sin does not destroy human nature, created in the image and likeness of God, yet evil, the free choice of inferior goods, haunts damned souls forever. For John, that unfulfilled desire of false goods produces *tristitia*, which becomes the essence of hell. John states that *infernus* (hell) is the

89. Johannes Scotus, *De divisione naturae*, PL 122:925D, where this position is stated in somewhat different terms: "The divine spirit knows no evil and no malice. For if it did, [evil] woud exist as a substance, and would not lack a cause."

I base this sketch of John's theories on book 5 of his *Periphyseon: De divisione naturae*. Its Latin text is in PL 122:439–1022. Edward A. Jeauneau published the last volume of his edition of this work CCCM 145 (2003). Jeauneau organized his edition to take five different stages of the text's execution into account. He published the last four stages in parallel columns. In order to coordinate all five redactions he shows the equivalent column numbers from vol. 122 of Migne's Patrologia Latina. Consequently, these constitute adequate references, though it is necessary to check all five of the versions Jeauneau published. The Latin I use is from the first of his versions. For full information on the versions, see the introduction to book 1 in CCCM 161 (1996), lxxxi–xc. A partial English translation of the *Periphyseon* has been edited and translated by Myra L. Uhlfelder, with the untranslated gaps filled in by the summaries of Jean A. Potter (Indianapolis: Bobbs-Merrill, 1976).

90. For the unreality of all that is perceived by the senses and all that changes in place and over time, see *De divisione*, PL 122:914A. These are transitory images, like shadows or echoes.

91. On Origen, see Bernstein, *Formation*, 305–13; Wolf-Friedrich Schäufele, "Die Höllen der Alexandriner: Negative Jenseitsvorstellungen im frühchristlichen Ägypten," *Zeitschrift für Kirchengeschichte* 117.2 (2006): 197–210.

Latin translation for the Greek "Hades," which he derives etymologically from *a-* (without) and *ēdus* (pleasure), that is, sadness (*tristitia*).[92] Because the suffering occurs internally, the torments exist in no place, but rather in the evil will. "Those who diligently examine the nature of visible and invisible things are not able to find the place of tortures except in the poverty of the lustful will of evil humans and angels, and from the defect and privation of the things which they loved intemperately, from which arises *tristitia*."[93] John puts much more emphasis on *tristitia* as a characteristic of the afterlife than earlier monastic theorists; nonetheless it is clear that his view of the condition is consistent with the idea of inner death, since it can afflict the individual conscience now, in life, and after death become an eternal fate. He continues: "It is from [the *tristitia* that arises from this defect and privation] that the irrational desires of rational souls torture them either in this life or the next."[94] John insists that "the conscience of the impious is punished within itself,"[95] and that "each one of us, in our own particular conscience, will either receive rewards or pay penalties inside the self."[96]

Because the torment arises from the sinner's conscience, it is not God who punishes the soul, but the sinner's own inordinate desires. Thus, the torments are psychological, not physical. Pursuing his analysis of the Greek approach and the etymology of Hades, he continues:

> It [Hades] is called *"lype"* or "pain," whose translation is "tristitia" or "mourning" or "grief." And it is accustomed to be called *"Haxos"* [ache], that is, the gravity of a desperation that covers the submerged and concealed evil lusts, the craving for temporal things that they intemperately coveted in this life, [and these seekers after wrong are] afflicted as if in some extremely deep abyss where they are wracked by the mists of vain fantasies of sensuous things and irreversibly despised

---

92. "Infernus itaque, qui a graecis 'Hade,' hoc est tristitia uel deliciarum priuatio." *De divisione*, PL 122:954C. Just below he states again, "Haden (ut diximus), hoc est tristitiam, apellauerunt infernum" (955A). In his *Etymologies* (14.9.6), Isidore of Seville had linked *tristitia* with the Styx, one of hell's underground rivers. "Styx *apo tou stygeros*, id est a tristitia, dicta, eo quod tristes faciat vel quod tristitiam gignat." Jeauneau illustrates the breakdown of Hades into *a* + *ēdus* clearly at *Periphyseon, Liber quintus* (2003), ix.

93. "Naturam siquidem rerum uisibilium et inuisibilium diligenter rimantes, locum suppliciis inuenire non potuerunt, nisi in libidinosae uoluntatis malorum hominum et angelorum egestate rerumque (quas intemperanter amauerant) defectu et priuatione. Ex quibus tristitia nascitur" *De divisione*, PL 122:955A.

94. *De divisione*, PL 122:955A.

95. "Impiorum conscientia intra semetipsam punitur." *De divisione*, PL 122:955B.

96. "Vnusquisque itaque in sua conscientia intra semet ipsum aut praemia recipiet aut poenas luet." *De divisione*, PL 122:978B.

and perpetually trampled by the weight of an incommutable divine sentence.[97]

The lack of one's desires is only one side of a double *tristitia*.[98] Even as the damned suffer from the failure to attain their illicit longings, their obsessions loom up before them, not like the fruit before Tantalus, but like hideous beings that terrify them forever:

There is another type of punishment common to all the impious: all the vices perpetrated in this life [return] . . . in fierce and horrible forms, such as, for example, those of wild beasts, to the increase of their torments, so that what they wickedly favored here among the living, will appear frightening, there, in a most just manner of punishing.[99]

Images of distorted earthly desires themselves become distorted and in this monstrous form plague the wicked forever.

The resultant horror from perpetual attraction to unobtainable desires that themselves become terrifying—this distortion—is itself part of a providential plan, a cause that is also a goal, to which everything returns. Their perception of this order—this retaliatory disorder of the damned—gives satisfaction to the righteous. "The blessedness of the just extracts glory from the sufferings of the impious and joy from the *tristitia* of the perverse."[100] The pains of damnation "are neither torture, nor miserable, nor ugly, nor dishonorable, nor evil. Indeed, whatever is ordained by the rulings of divine providence is good and beautiful and just."[101] The pain of the wicked is a good for the good, and its beauty increases providentially.

It is easier to see the function of hell by considering its place in emanation and return. There are three aspects to John's Neoplatonic return.[102] The first is a general return of all nature. The second is a general return for rational beings: angels and humans. The third is a special return limited to the blessed, those who persevered in righteousness. It is the second and third returns that are relevant here. The second, or general, return concerns sinners, who, despite their sin, recover their original image-likeness to God.

---

97. *De divisione*, PL 122:971B.

98. Ibid., 950D.

99. "Est etiam alia forma poenarum omnibus impiis communis, quae omnia uitia in hac uita perpetrata . . . in trucibus horribilibusque ueluti ferocium bestiarum speciebus ad cumulum tormentorum administrat, ut quae hic delectabiliter impie uiuentibus arrident, illic terribiliter appareant justissimo puniendi modo." *De divisione*, PL 122:977B–C.

100. *De divisione*, PL 122:954A.

101. Ibid.

102. "Reditus triplex." *De divisione*, PL 122:1020A.

The general return occurs "in such a way that no man should be deprived of the natural goods in which he was created, whether he lived well or evilly in this life."[103] This consequence follows from John's use of freedom in his definition of evil. Since the choice of evil is impossible without freedom, that freedom, however abused by sinners, was part of their image-likeness to God. Even sinners retain that aspect of their creation, their freedom being essential to their sin. If evil does not exist, and sin consists of the illicit desire for lesser goods, then not even these wrongs sully the basic human nature that sinners, like all free beings, originally received. Still, those possessed by their base desires do not escape the consequences, for these same longings remain (as we have seen) to taunt their wills forever. The painful yearning for inexistent things causes suffering, but "what emanates from the supreme good is a punishment for no one."[104] Since these desires come from free wills, God does not cause their suffering, their obsessions do. That frustration, that *tristitia*, that hell, is not divine punishment, but self-inflicted pain.

The third, or special return, is deification, promotion to the exquisite level of God's own existence. The difference between the second and third aspects of return is this: "[a] it is one thing for the same human nature to be *restored* to the dignity of the divine image which, through its own freedom, it lost by sinning, and [b] it is another for one's own conscience in the good merits of each of the elect, by which in this life they served their God in everything, to be *deified* above all power of humanity, and in the same way always and blessedly to live and to be exalted above all that is."[105] Restoration returns the former *to* their pristine human nature in their original image-likeness to God. Deification promotes the latter *above* their human nature to a supernatural or superessential being.

The distinction between restoration and deification is the key to John the Scot's eschatology. All souls are restored to the human nature they had when formed in God's image and likeness according to Genesis 1:26. Extremely virtuous souls attain not just a return to a pristine human nature, but elevation to divine nature, *theōsis*, "deification," where they reach what John calls

---

103. "ita ut nemo hominum naturalibus bonis, in quibus conditus est, priuetur, siue bene siue male in hac uita uixerit." *De divisione*, PL 122:1020B.

104. "dum in nullo punitur quod a summo bono manat." *De divisione*, PL 122:1020 B–C. Though I have revised it, Myra Uhlfelder's translation is particularly helpful in this passage. I also wish to thank Donald Weinstein and Kathryn Jasper for their help with difficult Latin passages.

105. "[A]liud est eandem humanam naturam in suam gratiam quam peccando perdiderat (divinae videlicet imaginis dignitatem) restitui, aliud uniuscuiusque electorum propriam in bonis meritis conscientiam, qua in hac uita deo suo in omnibus seruierunt, super omnem humanitatis uirtutem deificari, eoque modo semper ac beate uiuere et super omnia quae sunt exaltari." *De divisione*, PL 122:948D–949A.

a superessential existence together with God. Because these destinies result from an individual's own life, there is no need for reincarnation as Origen maintained. Because the wicked suffer from the promptings of their own wills, their *tristitia* attacks their own conscience, within, and there is no need for a physical hell, although, indeed, damnation is their fate. *Tristitia* in the individual conscience is John the Scot's escape from a physical hell; the distinction between the second and third returns (restoration as opposed to deification) is his escape from universalism, and the adequacy of one life's illicit desires for an eternity of suffering is his escape from Origen's theory of reincarnation: one life is enough. John's theory of hell accounts for the evil desires of freely chosen deviation from the divine will. From John's point of view, that would include fidelity to a religious faith he considers erroneous. The delusion of nonbelievers and their ultimate disappointment rank among the vain human desires that are frustrated.[106]

Deliberate Fear

The concept of inner death was an invention of the early Middle Ages. Augustine called it "death in the heart"; Gregory used the actual term "inner death" (*mors interior*). "The perfect life is an imitation of death," said Gregory, suggesting that inner death is a voluntary model for life. It embraces the idea of mortification: being dead to the world. These expressions go back to Paul and have certain affinities with the apathy of the Stoic sage and Essene renunciation in Judaism, but it was in the lives of the hermits that the notion of inner death became enshrined. It became institutionalized in monastic writings, including Cassian's *Institutes* and *Conferences* and, later, the *Rule of the Master*, the *Benedictine Rule*, and Benedict's subsequent commentators. Fear of hell is an aspect of inner death that practitioners cultivated as a deliberate, self-imposed discipline precisely to keep them *from* hell. Inner death with its concomitant fear accepts one's liability to hell and acts on the belief that engaging one's offenses and their postmortem consequences in this world would forestall them in the next, absent pride. Humility, the proper strategy, requires focusing on one's shortcomings in order to spring from the intimation of one's damnation to the culmination of Jerusalem.

For these ascetic theorists, the pangs of the guilty conscience foreshadowed the pains of hell. They differed on whether the only real suffering after death was in the conscience or whether the guilty soul, reconnected with its

---

106. *De divisione*, PL 122:949 C–D.

body after the Resurrection, could also be the site of postmortem suffering. Isidore of Seville gave equal weight to spirit and flesh: "The punishment of the damned in Gehenna is twofold: *tristitia* burns the mind, and fire burns the body." Yet medieval writers continued to weigh the theological and psychological benefits of a focus on the conscience. Jerome had attacked Origen on precisely this point. Hell cannot exist solely in the conscience. Nonetheless, Cassian and Smaragdus approach, and John the Scot advocates, an exclusively psychological torment.

Still, not even John the Scot completes the cycle back to Origen. John does not restore the sinners unqualifiedly to union with God. By distinguishing between the restored and the deified rational souls, human and angelic, he avoids the universalism that made Origen's theory of restoration incompatible with Christian eschatology. He spurns reincarnation and thus retains the linearity of Western eschatological thinking. One's death remains the last chance to change one's fate. Those who do not change remain eternally frustrated by their failure to attain their desires.

Monastic reflection indicates one path to an understanding of hell, a path that fits the institutional circumstances of the monastic experience. But there were other paths: that of the public, which often retained beliefs from Germanic or Celtic myth, and that of the lay nobility, including the princes. Justinian learned to use hell as a sanction that could reinforce his own imperial view of the cosmos and its political order. Because of its ideological utility, the material hell could not be sacrificed and was not. Augustine retained it, as did Gregory and Justinian. Still, the internal hell of Cassian, Smaragdus, and John the Scot complemented the physical one. For those who explored inner death, who benefited from its connection to the conscience, it encouraged an examination of the self even in an environment that taught monks to deny their own personal value, their self. Reflexive verbal constructions rather than any substantive did the work of our term "self," without which we cannot even translate their language. Whereas medievalists traditionally claim that the history of Western individualism began primarily in the twelfth century, there is ample evidence in these texts from late antiquity and the early Middle Ages to warrant a modification of that chronology. The individual was active indeed in the early Middle Ages. That these contemplative individuals shared common goals is an important condition of their existence, but to deny them a lively sense of their own internal lives is a serious distortion.

CHAPTER 3

The Punishments

Slavery, Torture, and Hell

> Anyone who commits sin is a slave to sin.
>
> —John 8:34

The first teachers of the Christian message sought to reach their listeners in terms they could understand. The parables of Jesus draw their moral lessons from common social situations: the tasks of shepherds (finding lost sheep, dividing sheep from goats), farming (sowing and reaping, separating wheat from chaff, burning weeds), assignment of tasks to slaves (the parable of the talents), child rearing (the prodigal son), or ethical dilemmas (the good Samaritan, the rich man and Lazarus). Paul said: "I am speaking in human terms, because of your natural limitations" (Rom. 6:19). We have seen how Gregory I explained the connection between the literal and spiritual levels of religious ideas. Given how these techniques informed communication in the early centuries of Christianity, historians may today work in reverse and look from doctrine back to social institutions and physical experience for keys to symbolic expression. This approach makes it easier to understand our ancient sources as their audiences understood them. In this way, we help *our* contemporaries understand how these distant "others" are relevant to "us." This method informs the thesis I argue here: the discipline of slaves framed the conception of hell.

To be sure, law was not the only social factor that colored depiction of the damned. Some punishments derive from antecedents in the Hebrew Bible, such as the fire and sulfur that rained down on Sodom and Gomorrah (Gen. 19:24). Others were inspired by dramatic scenes in mythological literature, such as the stories of Tantalus or Prometheus, or the vengeance Odysseus wrought on the servants who betrayed him.[1] The nature of the crime itself modeled other punishments. In retaliation, the punishment imitates the crime.[2] Even so, there is an additional factor. Because the criminal has abandoned the norms of society, its retributive power falls upon an outsider, one who has made himself "other." In ancient society, the chief other, besides the criminal, was the slave. Thus the otherness of criminality links the criminal to the slave because the Romans would not enslave their own citizens, and the monotheistic religions generally prohibited the enslavement of their own adherents. Both the Roman state and the monotheistic communities subjected only noncitizens or nonbelievers—"others"—to slavery. The religions further taught that deviants in faith receive hell's torments. The ancient discipline of slaves also provides important clues to understanding the punishment of the dead because, like the damned the visionaries saw in hell, slaves were categorically subject to unending physical torment.

Postmortem Punishments

To evaluate this connection between slave discipline and infernal torment, it is best to review first the tortures reported in the earliest Christian visions of hell. For all their horrors, the postmortem punishments of the New Testament occur mostly in isolation. Some fates differ markedly from others. Mark 9:48 mentions unquenchable or eternal fire together with undying worms.[3] Matthew 22:13 and 25:30 bind sinners hand and foot and cast them into outer darkness where there is weeping and gnashing of teeth,[4] but there is no fire or worm. In Matthew 24:51 and Luke 12:46, the sinner is cut into pieces (*dichotomēsei*). Fire reappears in Luke 16:24–26, where the rich man suffers thirst in a blazing area confined by an abyss. Revelation 14:10–11 and 20:10 plunge the damned endlessly into a lake of fire and sulfur, where an angel bearing a key and a chain (Rev. 20:1) encloses them. Later vision

---

1. Eva Cantarella, *I supplizi capitali in Graecia e a Roma* (Milan: Rizzoli, 1991), 19–40; and Istvan Czachesz, "The Grotesque Body in the *Apocalypse of Peter*," in *The Apocalypse of Peter: Studies on Early Christian Apocrypha* (Leuven: Peeters, 2003), 108–26.

2. In the seventh century, Isidore of Seville put this nicely: "Talio est similitudo vindictae, ut taliter quis patiatur ut fecit." (Retaliation is the similarity of the punishment to the crime such that the perpetrator suffers similarly to what he has done.) The core of his definition is the etymological link he imagines between *talio* and *taliter*. *Isidori Hispalensis episcopi Etymologiarum sive Originum libri XX*, ed. W. M. Lindsay (1911; Oxford: Clarendon Press, 1971) 5.27.24. For many related nuances, see William Ian Miller, *Eye for an Eye* (Cambridge: Cambridge University Press, 2006), esp. 58–88.

3. Mark thus identifies the torments of Isaiah 66:24 with Gehenna—and Matthew 25:41.

4. The second reference to outer darkness omits bound hands and feet.

literature and sermons combine these elements dramatically. Taken individually, though, the torments consist of burning, gnawing, dismemberment, and imprisonment bound or chained in darkness.

The fire and worms come from Isaiah 66:24, from the experience of death itself, and the possibility of cremation or putrefaction later. Genesis 19:24 tells how fire and sulfur rained down on Sodom. Gog met a similar fate in Ezekiel 38:22. Fire and sulfur also form part of volcanic action in the ancient view.[5] Darkness could be a reference to the state of the world before creation (Gen. 1:2) or simply a contrast to light, as often in Paul. Least familiar is the dismemberment or tearing asunder (*dikotomezein*) of Matthew 24:51 (and Luke 12:46). These fates appear frequently as the tradition develops.

The *Apocalypse of Peter*

After the completion of the New Testament canon, two apocryphal texts, the *Apocalypse of Peter* and the *Apocalypse of Paul* complement the biblical punishments to establish a large proportion of the standard tortures of the Christian hell until the twelfth century. The first major exploration of the punitive afterlife in a Christian context after the New Testament occurred in the *Apocalypse of Peter*.[6] The most recent studies date it late in the first half of the second century, that is, ca. 140. Surviving versions are fragmentary: one, more complete and closer to the Greek original but in Ethiopic; the other a Greek version discovered in Akhmim (the ancient Panapolis) in Egypt.[7] When the apostles met Christ on the Mount of Olives, as the text narrates, Jesus showed them in his upraised palm a vision of the otherworld and its torments for the wicked. Not the account of a human visionary, this narrative is framed as a direct piercing of the boundary between life and death, between the present and the future, a gracious revelation to a privileged few.

---

5. Sulfur: Ps. 10:7; Isa. 30:33; Luke 17:29 (on Lot).

6. Martha Himmelfarb, *Tours of Hell: An Apocalyptic Form in Jewish and Christian Literature* (1983; Philadelphia: Fortress Press, 1985). Albrecht Dieterich, *Nekyia: Beiträge zur Erklärung der Neuentdeckten Petrusapokalypse* (Leipzig: Teubner, 1893); Dimitris J. Kyrtatas, "The Origins of Christian Hell," *Numen* 56.2–3 (2009): 282–97; Jeffrey A. Trumbower, *Rescue for the Dead: The Posthumous Salvation of Non-Christians in Early Christianity*, Oxford Studies in Historical Theology (Oxford: Oxford University Press, 2001).

7. For this background, see Jan Bremmer, "Christian Hell: From the *Apocalypse of Peter* to the *Apocalypse of Paul*," *Numen* 56 (2009): 298–325, at 299. See also Christian Maurer's general introduction to Hugo Duensing's translation in H-S 2:663–68; for the text itself, see 668–83. This edition presents the two versions in parallel columns on the same page. I cite first the Ethiopic, then the Akmim (Greek) version (separated by a slash), then the page number. I have also analyzed the *Apocalypse of Peter* in *The Formation of Hell: Death and Retribution in the Ancient and Early Christian Worlds* (Ithaca, NY: Cornell University Press, 1993), 282–91.

The offenses mentioned show how early in the history of Christianity the *Apocalypse of Peter* was written. *Peter* mentions no institutional office in the church and no identifiable doctrine. It condemns those who persecuted Christians or betrayed them to authorities (9/27, 675; 9/29, 678), and hypocrites who preach a morality they violate themselves (12, 678). Religious offenses are vague and not clearly distinguishable from those punished by Jews: manufacture of idols (10/33, 677); blasphemy (7/23, 672); denial of righteousness (7/23, 672–73); challenging the righteous (9/28, 676). The text censures deeds many other communities would also condemn: adultery (7/24, 673); surrender of virginity before marriage (11, 678); abortion (8/26, 674); sorcery (12, 678). Although it condemns usury (10/31, 676), it does not mention bribery or the falsification of weights, measures, or coins. It strongly faults the violation of household loyalties such as neglect of widows and orphans (9/30, 676), neglect of parents (11, 678), disobedience to parents or elders (11, 678), and a slave's disobedience to master or mistress (11, 678). The absence of any mention of doctrinal error or of church officials' hypocrisy shows that the *Apocalypse of Peter* appeared very early in the church's history. Nonetheless, the pseudonymous author of *Peter* supported New Testament injunctions against unruly slaves with specific postmortem sanctions.[8]

These offenses generate a panoply of penalties. As the apostles view the torments revealed through Christ's palm, they see the consequences of the Last Judgment—the cataracts of fire that sweep the damned away. (Even the seas turn into coals of fire.) Within this conflagration individual tortures emerge: burning, hanging, falling (being cast down, precipitation), and immersion. Each of these torments has subdivisions or variations. One hangs by the tongue for blasphemy, by the genitalia for fornication, and, for enticing men into this sin, women who adorned themselves seductively hang by their hair over boiling mire. Sorcerers whirl about, turned by spinning wheels of fire, perhaps because necromancers summon spirits into circles. Birds peck at the suspended bodies of children who morcellated their

---

8. For a review of the biblical imperatives, see Keith Bradley, *Slavery and Society at Rome* (Cambridge: Cambridge University Press, 1994). At p. 150 he cites Eph. 6:5 ("Slaves [*douloi*], obey . . . your earthly masters [*kurios*] . . . as serving the Lord [*kuriōi*]"); Col. 3:22–23 ("Slaves, obey in everything those who are your earthy masters, not with eyeservice, as men-pleasers, but in singleness of heart, fearing the Lord"); 1 Tim. 6:1 ("Let all who are under the yoke of slavery [*douloi*] regard their masters [*despotas*] as worthy of all honor"); 1 Peter 2.18 ("Servants [*oiketai*], be submissive to your masters [*despotais*] with all respect, not only to the kind and gentle but also to the overbearing"). Bradley also cites 1 Cor. 7:21, but if extended to verse 24, its message is more nuanced than the previous examples and ill fits this list. It begins: "Were you a slave [*doulos*] when called? Never mind." Bradley then goes further: "With the argument that obedience was to be given to them 'as unto Christ', Christian slaveowners gave themselves a stronger grip on their slaves than they had ever had before" (151).

parents' authority. If one suffers in the member through which one offended, that member allows the punishments by hanging. Punishing angels execute by precipitation. They cast sinners down "into fear," into fire, onto sharp rocks (or onto pointed pillars that impale them), into a lake of filth, or into a recipe of combined torments such as a "fiery gorge full of venomous beasts and clouds of worms" (7/25, 673). Immersion can be in mire, blood, coals, fire, darkness, or a cacophony of wailing. Crammed into every section of hell, the damned suffocate each other by their very abundance.

Not only the population density, but varied external agents also torment the damned. These tormentors can be beasts (gnawing worms) or birds or punishing angels, who hang their victims on wheels of fire, and beat them with red-hot rods, fiery chains, blades, or stones sharp as swords. The angel Ezrael torments idol makers with blazing chains made of metal remolded from the idols themselves (10/33, 677). Hell's helpmates attack the offending body parts: voluptuous hair, gluttonous gullets, lying lips, tongues, and mouths. Women who exposed or killed their own children suffer milk to flow from their breasts, to congeal and rot. This putrid mess breeds flesh-eating beasts who devour the women and their men (8, 674–75). Sometimes the damned even torment each other: men and women smite each other with glowing rods (10/33, 677). Other deviants are "burned and turned" in the fire, as on a spit (10/34, 677). In their anguish, the sufferers attack themselves. They chew their own tongues—a sign of remorse delayed (a visual pun on *mordeo*, "to bite").

From the outside, too, comes eternal scorn. Earlier victims turn the tables on their offenders, who suffer in shame beneath their disapproval. Sometimes, this takes the form of segregation by clothing that indicates the sin. Hypocrites who gave charity and professed righteousness but did not strive for it must pack themselves together, fall on hot coals, as they are struck blind and dumb and dressed ostentatiously in white clothes—the color symbolizing the purity they themselves undermined (12, 678). There are men and women in a high place who make a false step and "roll down to where the fear is" and fire flows in a process repeated forever. This is the punishment of those who neglected their fathers and mothers. To increase the shame from such abasement, angels bring children to witness it (11, 678). Men and women in filthy garments are cast or rolled down onto stones (or pillars) sharp as swords, and therefore impaled, because they ignored the commandment to care for widows and orphans (9/30, 676). Those who "defiled their bodies," men who behaved with each other as with women, "and the women with them, . . . who behaved with one another as men with a woman," repeatedly cast themselves down from great heights (10/32, 676–77). Murderers are cast into a fiery gorge full of venomous beasts and clouds of worms. Their victims look on and praise the justice of God (7/25, 673). Most of the punishments in the *Apocalypse of Peter* are explicitly said to apply to men *and* women. In one case it is "maidens" who are clad in "darkness" while their flesh is torn in punishment for losing their virginity before marriage, but their seducers apparently go unpunished (11, 678). The darkness of their garb represents, perhaps, the secrecy of the offending act, while the willful but illicit penetration of the flesh is punished in the flesh. Shame also attends other sexual crimes. Women who procured abortion are confined in a pit of waste—presumably the fluids attendant on this operation—while, on the banks above them, are the unborn from whose eyes go forth fiery rays into the eyes of the women (8/26, 674).[9] In this interpretation, these accusing looks from their victims shame for eternity the women who sought abortion.

Sometimes torments are combined. Viewers see men and women with their lips cut off while the fire entering their mouths penetrates their entrails. These are the false witnesses, whose lying slew (or blasphemed) the martyrs (9/26, 676). Murderers, as we have seen, suffer simultaneously from fire, poisonous beasts, worms, and the shaming, active attention of their victims. Just as "burning" is not always as simple as burning at the stake, so "hanging" can sometimes be varied and complex. At the bottom of a fiery place to which offenders roll down, those who reject parental authority are hung up to be "punished with pain" and "with many wounds which flesh-eating birds inflict," and angels bring children and maidens to view this torment (11, 678).

In the *Apocalypse of Peter*, Jesus concludes the vision he has granted his disciples by reassuring them of eternal life for "my elect and righteous." Among the boons granted the blessed is that " 'They shall see their desire on those who hated' them, when he punishes them" (13, 679). Jesus promises to effectuate a vengeance promised in the Hebrew Bible (Ps. 54 and 59:10). Through him, he says, victims will be able to turn the tables on their former persecutors. The realization of this powerful wish becomes a fundamental element in the structure of infernal torments. To the cries for mercy that will emerge from hell, the angel in charge of the punishments, Tartarouchos (Tatirokos), whose name derives from the classical Greek term Tartarus, will reply that the time for repentance has passed. The damned will then acknowledge the justice of God

---

9. For a thorough examination of abortion and the condition of procurers and victims of abortion, see Danuta Shanzer, "Voices and Bodies: The Afterlife of the Unborn," *Numen* 56 (2009): 326–65. These punishments figure prominently in Callie Callon, "Sorcery, Wheels, and Mirror Punishment in the *Apocalypse of Peter*," *Journal of Early Christian Studies* 18.1 (Spring 2010): 29–49.

and that they are punished according to their deeds.[10] Having learned these things, Peter must now spread this word to the world. Christ now promises his "elect and righteous" a place with him "in the field Akrōsjā (=Acherusia), which is called Anēslaslejā (=Elysium)" (14, 679).

Another fragment of the *Apocalypse of Peter*, preserved in the Rainer Collection in Vienna, provides additional details on the blessings of the elect. According to the Rainer fragment, Christ says to Peter, "Then will I grant to my called and chosen whomsoever they shall ask me for out of torment and I will give them a precious baptism unto salvation from the Acherusian lake, which men say is situated in the Elysian field, the portion of the righteous with my holy ones."[11] This statement gives the saved a chance to rescue from the torments of hell some named souls, who would then inhabit the Elysian fields along with Christ and his holy ones. Another example of discontent with an absolute, irreversible damnation occurs in the *Apocalypse of Paul*. The implications of these challenges to the idea of hell belong in a subsequent chapter. It is the catalogue of punishments that interests us here, and we turn now to the second major apocryphal description of the afterlife, the *Apocalypse of Paul*.

The *Apocalypse of Paul*

This apocryphal work had its greatest impact in its "long Latin" version composed some time at the end of the fourth or early fifth century.[12] The preface that now introduces the long Latin version states that it was found in a manuscript "discovered" under Paul's house in Tarsus when Theodosius and a certain Cynegius were co-consuls, that is, in 388.[13] This date could be

---

10. Punishments that the victims desire to inflict on their previous tormentors may differ from punishment according to their deeds. There are many distinctions to be made on this subject. For one suggestion, see Callon, "Sorcery, Wheels, and Mirror Punishment," 31–32.

11. H-S 2:679 n. 3. For the argument (unconvincing, in my view) that this portion of the *Apocalypse of Peter* constitutes its original core, rather than an interpolation, and that it represents the original Christian message, see Dimitris J. Kyrtatas, "The Origins of Christian Hell," *Numen* 56 (2009): 282–97.

12. I cite the long Latin version of the *Apocalypse of Paul* in M. R. James, *Visio Pauli*, in *AA*. I use the section numbers followed by the page and line number of that edition. I have subdivided some of James's very long sections by adding the letters a, b, c, etc. for each paragraph. For an English translation, see Hugo Duensing in H-S 2:755–98; and M. R. James in *ANT*, pp. 525–55. See also Bernstein, *Formation*, 292–305.

13. It has been claimed that Origen (d. ca 254) mentions this work, but Pierluigi Piovanelli has convincingly refuted this. Piovanelli, "Les origines de l'*Apocalypse de Paul* reconsidérées," *Apocrypha* 4 (1993): 25–64 summarized in Piovanelli, "Le texte originel de l'*Apocalypse de Paul*: Problèmes de datation," *Bulletin de l'AELAC* (Association pour l'Étude de la Littérature Apocryphe Chrétienne) 3 (1993): 25–27. Following this new chronology is Bremmer, "Christian Hell," 303–7. Theodore Silverstein and

a later fabrication, but the core of the text was certainly written before 416, when Augustine, in his *Treatise on John*, denounced "a contrived *Apocalypse of Paul* full of I know not what fables and rejected by the wholesome Church."[14] Augustine objected to the passage in *Paul* where Christ is said to grant the damned a regular period of relief from torment either every Sunday or every Easter or some variation of these ideas depending on the version of the text. Since Prudentius wrote his *Cathemerinon*, which opts for annual relief in hell, before 402, it may indicate the existence of the *Apocalypse of Paul* even before that date.[15]

The *Apocalypse of Paul* elaborates on 2 Corinthians 12:2, which refers to a man taken up to the third heaven. In this vision the rapt soul ascends to the divine court and witnesses the trial of the recently deceased. There an angel is assigned to give him a tour of heaven, a tour of the punishments, which are divided into two levels, and a return to heaven. Many subsequent, shorter versions eliminate the trial and the two scenes in heaven to focus on the voyage through hell. The shorter versions, in their many redactions, are

Anthony Hilhorst, eds., *Apocalypse of Paul: A New Critical Edition of Three Long Latin Versions with 54 plates* (Geneva: Cramer, 1997), p. 19 n. 3, agree with Piovanelli: the only Theodosius who was ever consul together with a Cynegius became Theodosius I. The Cynegius with whom he served his second consulship died in 388. The text was known to Augustine, who argues against its import around 416 in his *Treatise on John* (98.8) and in the *Enchiridion* of ca. 420 (29.112–13; CCSL 46:109–10), where he ridicules tenderhearted souls who would deny eternal punishment for the wicked, cited in R. P. Casey, "The *Apocalypse of Paul*," *Journal of Theological Studies* 34 (1933): 1–32, at 29.

14. "quidam apocalypsim pauli, quam sana non recipit ecclesia, nescio quibus fabulis plenam." Augustine, *In Iohannis euangelium tractatus* 98:8; CCSL 36, ed. R. Willems (1954), p. 581.

15. A Coptic translation is the best witness to a now-lost Greek original, also from that period, according to Casey, "*Apocalypse of Paul*," 18, 27–28. For an overview of the dating issue, see Theodore Silverstein, "The Date of the 'Apocalypse of Paul'," *Mediaeval Studies* 24 (1962): 335–48. Silverstein (347) endorses Casey's inference about the Coptic text. The most detailed analysis is in Lenka Jiroušková, *Die Visio Pauli: Wege und Wandlungen einer orientalischen Apokryphe im lateinischen Mittelalter* (Leiden: Brill, 2006). This work applies the title *Apocalypse of Paul* to the longer versions, which include prefatory and concluding scenes in heaven, as opposed to the title "Vision of Paul," for versions that shorten the work to focus only on the punishments (5–11). More importantly, Jiroušková separates the Latin redactions from one another and explores translations into German and Czech. Her analysis includes a line-by-line commentary that embraces the various Latin versions, long and short. A facsimile edition of the long Latin version can be found in Silverstein and Hilhorst, *Apocalypse of Paul*. Claude Carozzi regards the *Apocalypse of Paul* as so fundamental that he almost completely omitted it from his magisterial *Le voyage de l'âme dans l'au-delà* in order to focus on it in *Eschatologie et au-delà: Recherches sur l'Apocalypse de Paul* (Aix-en-Provence: Publications de l'Université de Provence, 1994), 12–14. For an overview of the vernacular adaptations and translations in the later Middle Ages, see H. R. Patch, *The Other World, According to Descriptions in Medieval Literature* (Cambridge, MA: Harvard University Press, 1950); D. D. R. Owen, *The Vision of Hell* (Edinburgh and London: Scottish Academic Press, 1970), passim; Jérôme Baschet, *Les justices de l'au-delà* (Rome: Bibliothèque de l'École française de Rome, 1993); and, for the Latin, English, Anglo-Norman, and French traditions, H. Braet, "La réception médiévale de l'Apocalypse paulinienne: Une réécriture de l'au-delà," in *Miscellanea di studi romanzi offerta a G. Gasca Quierazza* (Alexandria: Edizioni dell'Orso, 1988), 75–89.

called the *Vision of Paul*. As he follows his angel and crosses the upper plain, Paul sees a river of fire with different sinners immersed to different heights. There are deep pits filled with blood or pitch. Within them souls moan and sigh. Some cannot speak, call out, or plead for mercy; others cannot see. Some agonize like Tantalus, in front of fruit trees they cannot reach. These souls suffer for their wrong behavior. When Paul sighs from compassion, the angel remarks that these are not even the worst torments. He takes Paul to a well whose lid is sealed with seven seals. Opened, the lid releases a woeful stench, but then the angel guides Paul through this cylindrical passageway to the lower zone. Below the well the punishments are seven times worse than above. These inmates are in oblivion, outside the consciousness of any other being. They have sinned by denying key Christian doctrines. Thus, offenses against correct belief are more severe than offenses against correct behavior. In the basement level of *Paul*, fire is everywhere except a frigid zone where an immense two-headed worm presides as sinners gnash their teeth. Again, Paul sighs from compassion. Sensing his discomfort, the court of heaven descends to this lowest level of hell. Out of friendship for Paul, Christ grants the damned a suspension of punishment every Sunday forever. Like the *Apocalypse of Peter*, *Paul* presents a wide range of hell's torments in extremely vivid terms, yet it, too, hopes—in even more dramatic terms—for a potential modification of hell's absolute, unchanging damnation.

As compared to the *Apocalypse of Peter*, *Paul* stresses the overall darkness of the place, but finds rivers of fire within it. "There was no light in that place, but darkness and sadness and gloom" (§31; p. 28, lines 23–24). In the rivers of fire, sinners are immersed to the appropriate parts of their bodies: knees, navel, lips, brows. The differences in these levels are a measure of guilt, absent from *Peter*. Unlike *Peter*, in *Paul* the pits are located in particular directions, and their depth is measured, though in terms borrowed from Greek mythology. Hesiod's *Theogony* echoes in the statement that it takes a soul fifty years to reach the bottom of the pit![16] As noted before, the *Apocalypse of Paul* displays a considerably more institutionalized church than the *Apocalypse of Peter*. Among its offenders are readers, deacons, priests, bishops, and false monastics. Church buildings and prayer services are mentioned. Those in *Paul's* lower hell denied that Christ came in the flesh, that the Virgin Mary bore him, that the bread and the chalice of the eucharistic benediction is the body and blood of Christ, that Christ was resurrected from the dead, and that his flesh (meaning, I think, the rest of humanity) is resurrected

---

16. *Theogony* 722–25. Tartarus is as far beneath the earth as the earth is beneath the sky. It would take an anvil of bronze ten days to fall that distance.

(§§41–42; p. 34, line 14–p. 35, line 4). *Peter* lacks such institutional and doctrinal specificity.

One place where *Paul's* revision of *Peter* is most apparent is in the treatment of parents' crimes against their children. In *Paul*, the sin condemned is not abortion but the exposure of children. "I looked and I saw other men and women upon a fiery obelisk [*sic*] and beasts tore them apart and they were not permitted to plead to the Lord for mercy" (§40b; p. 32, lines 22–25). This literal translation implies several possibilities. The bodies of these offenders may be piled up and set upon by beasts. They may be tied to a pointed stake and burned (hence, a fiery obelisk), but then the beasts would have trouble eating them. Since this punishment is for exposing one's children, punishment by exposure to ravenous predators seems fitting. The "obelisk" may refer to a pile of bodies so high that it comes to a point at the top. M. R. James translates: "men and women upon a spit of fire, and beasts tearing them" (*ANT* 545); Hugo Duensing gives: "men and women on a fiery pyramid and wild animals were tearing them to pieces (H-S 2:784). A pyramidal stack of bodies set upon by beasts, or bodies tied to stakes and attacked by wild animals, evokes the execution of Christian martyrs in the Roman arenas.[17]

When asked to identify those so tormented, the angel replied, "These are women who stained the image of God, who bore infants from their wombs, and these are the men who lay with them." Although there has been no mention of the children, we now learn, "But their children implored the Lord God and the angels who were in charge of the punishments, saying 'Accursed now are our parents, for they have stained the image of God. They assumed the name of God, but did not observe his precepts. Instead they gave us to be eaten by dogs and trampled by pigs. Others they threw into the river'." This author assumes the scene in the *Apocalypse of Peter*, where procurers of abortion are punished in reeking pools while their victims pierce them with accusing looks. In the *Apocalypse of Paul*, the voices of the exposed (not aborted) children cry out. The children do not suffer with their criminal parents. "But then these children were given over by the angels of Tartarus who were in charge of the punishments so that they might lead them to a spacious place of mercy." The parents enjoy no such exit. "Their fathers and mothers, however, were to be strangled in perpetual punishment" (§40b;

---

17. Jan Bremmer discusses the torture of martyrs as a source for the fantasies of infernal torments in "Christian Hell," 315–16. To this valuable insight one should add the consideration that, in many cases, the martyrs are examples of citizens treated like slaves, that is, deprived of the immunity from physical punishment considered a privilege of the free. The loss of this advantage emerges more clearly below.

p. 32, line 32–p. 33, line 6).[18] The sanctions mentioned or implied include burning, mangling by beasts, imposed silence, receiving curses (or at least public accusation), and strangulation.

The *Apocalypse of Paul* presents one group of victims without any parallel in the earlier work. Christian ascetics suffer in *Paul* because they assumed the garb of their calling but ignored the discipline to which they appeared dedicated, thus misleading the faithful. "And after this I saw men and women clothed in clothing imbued with pitch and burning sulfur and there were dragons draped about their necks and arms and legs and angels having flaming horns confined them and struck them and closed their nostrils (§40c; p. 33, lines 7–10). Seneca spoke of refined tortures that forced victims to put on clothing saturated with oil and then burned.[19] Virgil's *Aeneid* relates how two giant sea serpents killed the Trojan priest Laocoön and his two sons. In his *Commentary on the Aeneid*, Servius specifies that the priest had profaned the sacred statue by making love with his wife in its precinct.[20] *Paul*'s composite image, then, appears to derive from Latin literature and, indeed, the practice of torture, if Seneca reports it accurately.

Like the *Apocalypse of Peter*, *Paul* stresses the intense crowding of the damned, impelled by river currents, confined in pits. The sense of enclosure is extreme in the lower hell, covered by a lid and sealed with seven seals. No consciousness of those within reaches the outside. They are in oblivion. Their dwelling is a place of cold and gnashing of teeth and permeated with a horrendous stench. Above the well, however, pits also confine the damned in pools of noxious substances: fire, blood, cold, stench, darkness, dust, pitch, noise from wailing and complaining, and the rotting body's own worms. Between the many pits runs a river full of worms that eat a multitude of men and women. These are usurers, consumed just as the interest they demanded consumed their debtors (§37; p. 30, lines 32–34). In such deep pits souls have the sensation of falling, but they can also sink into the rivers of fire. Unlike *Peter*, there is no mire, filth, or waste. Sinners bear external marks of their shame on their blackened faces, or they wear rags, black clothes, or ironic white.

In addition to suffering from feelings of remorse, scorn from victims, the harsh environment, the damned also suffer attacks from external agents. The Angels of Tartarus herd and prod them; the beasts to whom sinners exposed

---

18. Shanzer, "Voices and Bodies."

19. Seneca, *Ad Lucilium epistulae morales* 14.5, ed. and trans. Richard M. Gummere, LCL (1917), 1:86; cited by Ramsay MacMullen, "Judicial Savagery in the Roman Empire," *Chiron* 16 (1986): 147–66, at 151.

20. Herbert Jennings Rose and Karim W. Arafat, "Laocoön," *OCD*, 814b.

their children, the two-headed worm, dragons, a hail of stones, all afflict the damned. The *Apocalypse of Peter* also exposes the damned to beasts, but in the later work *imaginary* creatures such as the two-headed giant worm and dragons appear. The Angels of Tartarus wield implements—flaming razors, daggers, pitchforks, and chains. These weapons produce lesions that gape and rot. Voracious animals tear the flesh, leaving victims wounded and partly consumed. Only blades could have produced the bodies with severed limbs that lie naked and bleeding on the ice and snow, the fate of those who harmed orphans, widows, and paupers (§39b; p. 31, lines 32–34). Sometimes no external agent is needed. The damned may consume themselves, gnawing on their hands in anxiety or macerating their own tongues. Some limbs become targets, because they are the organs that committed the sins. Self-indulgent, vain, openly voluptuous, or lecherous women hang by their hair, a symbol of their vices. Eyebrows, intestines, lips, tongue, faces, necks, hands, and feet also endure attack.

Retribution focused on specific body parts involves retaliation, the punitive strategy that covers many, but not all, of the punishments in the *Apocalypses of Peter* and *Paul*. Retaliation imitates the crime but also limits the punishment, as in "an eye for an eye" (Deut. 19:21).[21] In the Deuteronomic example, justice demands a compensatory matching loss (an eye, a hand, a foot, a tooth, even a life) to avert prolonging or expanding a conflict. In punishment by the offending limb, the limb is not removed, but rather receives the punishment. The best statement of this general principle—also the oldest I have found—is in the Wisdom of Solomon (11:17): "Let one be wracked through that by which one sins." (*Per quae peccat quis per haec et torquetur.*)[22] Jerome of Stridon put it like this: "One should be punished in that member through which one has sinned."[23] In the *Apocalypses of Peter* and *Paul* and related literature, as Martha Himmelfarb rightly observes, this principle finds

---

21. For the importance of *talion* as a limitation of punishment, see Callon, "Sorcery, Wheels, and Mirror Punishment," 29–49; Miller, *Eye for an Eye*, chaps 5–6; pp. 58–88.

22. Martha Himmelfarb has traced the principle through numerous Jewish apocrypha in the intertestamental period and later. She finds it (*Tours of Hell*, 85) embedded in the Elijah fragment as quoted in the Epistle of Titus in this form: "By the limb with which each man sinned, by the same limb will he be punished." I find it as "The Pseudo-Titus Epistle" (trans. A. de Dantos Otero), in H-S 2:141–66, at 158, in this form: "The multiplicity of the torments answers to the diversity of the sins of each." This is an excellent rendering of "Per ipsa uero uaria supplicia ostenditur uniuscuiusque actus" in Donatien de Bruyne, "Epistula Titi, Discipuli Pauli, De dispositione sanctimonii," *Revue Bénédictine* 37 (1925): 47–72, at 58.

23. "In quo peccauit, in ipso puniatur." Jerome on Malachi 2:16, which says "operiet autem iniquitas vestimentum eius." The implication is that since the sin occurred in the clothing of the flesh, the flesh should not escape punishment. Hieronymus, *Commentarii in prophetas minores*, CCSL 76A, ed. M. Adriaen (1969–70), *In Malachiam* 2, line 474, p. 925. See Yael Shemesh, "Punishment of

dramatic expression in punishments by hanging. To pick the most obvious example, if one has sinned via the genitals one is punished via the genitals: gender specificity does not change the principle. Retaliation is extremely prominent in Scripture and visionary literature, but also in ancient Mediterranean legal traditions. A look at the choice of punishments in the ancient world will inform any conclusions about the influence of law on religion or vice versa.[24]

Worldly Punishments

In order to examine the punitive repertory around the Mediterranean it is necessary to identify key assumptions in these early legislative traditions. A review of Babylonian,[25] Egyptian,[26] and Jewish[27] law codes of the pre-Christian eras shows that, despite differences in spirit, these traditions have much in common as concerns actual punishments applied to particular crimes. Capital punishment occurs in all three societies, though in Mesopotamia, they not only drown capital criminals but also hang, burn, and impale them. In Egypt they chiefly impale capital criminals but also drown and possibly decapitate and burn them, and in Israel and Judah, they chiefly stone these offenders but also burn, decapitate, or strangle them. In noncapital cases, Babylonia and Judah employ retaliation to moderate the severity of justice, and in Egypt penalties are set according to fixed ratios of harm to

the Offending Organ," *Novum Testamentum* 55.3 (July 2005): 343–65. Further interesting reflections in Himmelfarb, *Tours of Hell*, 69–92, where she discusses "measure-for-measure punishments."

24. A very short apocalypse appears in the apocryphal *Acts of Thomas* (trans. G. Bornkamm, H-S 2:425–531), where the vision proper occurs as part of the Sixth Act, §55, pp. 473–75. Preaching in India, Thomas used the horrors of hell to persuade his audience.

25. Raymond Westbrook, *A History of Ancient Near Eastern Law* (Leiden: Brill, 2003), 8 and 361–430; for the Code of Hammurabi, see *The Babylonian Laws*, ed. with tr. and com. D. R. Driver and John C. Miles, 2 vols. (Oxford: Clarendon Press, 1955); see also Russ VerSteeg, *Early Mesopotamian Law* (Durham, NC: Carolina Academic Press, 2000), 126–28.

26. David Lorton, "The Treatment of Criminals in Ancient Egypt: Through the New Kingdom," *Journal of the Economic and Social History of the Orient* 20.1 (1977): 2–64, at 12, 52. Cf. Richard Jasnow, "New Kingdom," in *History of Ancient Near Eastern Law*, ed. Raymond Westbrook (Boston: Brill, 2003), 289–360, at 342–46.

27. Gunther H. Wittenberg, "Legislating for Justice: The Social Legislation of the Covenant Code and Deuteronomy," *Scriptura* 54 (1995): 215–28; T. C. Vriezen and A. S. van der Woude, *Ancient Israelite and Early Jewish Literature*, trans. Brian Doyle (2000; Leiden: Brill, 2005), 119–23, 225–40, and 252–64; Raymond Westbrook, "What Is the Covenant Code?," in *Theory and Method in Biblical and Cuneiform Law*, ed. Bernard M. Levinson (Sheffield, UK: Sheffield Academic Press, 1994), 15–36; for the death penalty in biblical and rabbinic Judaism, see Haim Hermann Cohn, Louis Isaac Rabinowitz, and Menachem Elon, "Capital Punishment," in *Encyclopaedia Judaica*, ed. Michael Berenbaum and Fred Skolnik, 2nd ed. (Detroit: Macmillan, 2007), 4:445–51. See also the cross-references there to flogging, cremation (burning), impalement, detention, *karet* (premature death), and imprisonment.

punishment. All three societies employ penal slavery, particularly for debt, although the Hebrews limited the term of forced labor for Hebrew slaves and mitigated the fate of other slaves under particular circumstances. The threat of horrible punishments may frequently have encouraged suspects to speak quickly in the hope of avoiding them, but torture was not part of the readily visible legal procedure. Because Deuteronomy requires two witnesses to establish guilt, not even the suspect could condemn himself, thus excluding confession and, by the same token, torture from Jewish trials in biblical and rabbinic times.[28] In principle only slaves, never citizens, endure torture. Slavery appears in these laws but not nearly as pervasively as in ancient Athens and Rome. Slavery was so obviously indispensable in the regions dominated by these cities that they may be considered history's first slave societies.[29] Therefore, the treatment of slaves in the criminal law of Athens and Rome is central to the thesis we examine here.

Ancient Athens

One candidate for correspondence between Athenian practice and early Christian visionary literature is the technique of intentionally shaming criminals by casting their bodies down into quarries. In Athens, some executed corpses were dumped in the Orugma, a quarry adjacent to the city walls. Farther away, there was the Barathron, for disposal outside of Attica, the surrounding jurisdiction. Other ancient Greek city-states cast criminals' bodies over a cliff.[30] In Sparta it was called the Kaiadas (Caeadas). In Delphi, critics of the sacred treasure in the Temple of Apollo are "thrown down the precipice" (*katakrēmnizetai*).[31] Memories of a mythic past would recall how Zeus cast the Titans into Tartarus for eternal confinement.[32] In Luke 4:29, "those in the synagogue" threatened Jesus with the same fate (*katakrēmnizo*). 2 Peter 2:4, which refers to the rebel angels, creates a new term, *tartaroō*, meaning "to entartar" (from the word Tartarus)—which refers specifically to casting down into hell.[33]

---

28. Haim Hermann Cohn, "Confession," in *Encyclopaedia Judaica*, 5:147.

29. Keith Bradley, *The Cambridge World History of Slavery*, vol. 1, *The Ancient Mediterranean World*, ed. Keith Bradley and Paul Cartledge (Cambridge: Cambridge University Press, 2011), 1.

30. See the list in Louis Gernet, "Sur l'exécution capitale," in *Droit et institutions en Grèce antique* (Paris: Flammarion, 1983), 174–211, at 185 n. 32.

31. Demosthenes 19.327, cited by Danielle S. Allen, *World of Prometheus: The Politics of Punishing in Democratic Athens* (Princeton, NJ: Princeton University Press, 2000), 219.

32. Observation of Allen, *World of Prometheus*, 205; Hesiod, *Theogony* 674–744 for the Titans; 720–24 for the great drop from Olympus to Tartarus. *Hesiod, the Homeric Hymns, and Homerica*, trans. H. G. Evelyn-White, LCL (Cambridge, MA: Harvard University Press, 1982).

33. See Bernstein, *Formation*, 251.

SLAVERY AND TORTURE IN ATHENS

These parallels are indicative, but to go farther we must understand how differently the law treated citizens and slaves. Athenian justice exhibited comparative mildness to citizens. Because citizens were not to suffer in their bodies for noncapital offenses, the most common punishment was the payment of a fine. The Decree of Scamandrius said only slaves could be tortured, not citizens.[34] What the citizen paid in coins, the slave paid in lashes.[35] Demosthenes put it another way: citizens pay with their purse, slaves with their person.[36] In the plays of Aristophanes and Menander, slave owners strike, beat, brand, bond, or starve their slaves.

Athenian law also offered eloquent testimony to the slave's availability for torture. A procedure called the *basanos* allowed a citizen litigant to back up the truth of his story by offering one of his slaves for torture. Whether this ever happened or was simply a trial lawyer's ploy, it means that there existed a credible threat, or at least a right, to torture a slave for deeds witnessed rather than committed or alleged. The term *basanos* extends further to any ordeal or painful experience. Two examples appear in the Christian Scriptures. The term applies to the jailers, *basanistēs*, who appear in Matthew 18:34 to hold the uncharitable slave until he pays his debt.[37] More poignantly, in Luke 16:23, it describes the fate of the rich man in Hades, who suffers in the torments (*en basanois*).[38] *Basanos* is a good example of how a legal procedure or the discipline of slaves could be transferred to the biblical description of hell.

The worst fate for a slave was confinement in the mill: a separate room, an outbuilding, or a kind of jail in a slave-owning household where slaves were isolated to labor. They could be chained there sometimes wearing special collars (*pausikakē*) to prevent them from eating any of the grain they processed.[39] The horror the mill represented appears in a speech by Lysias whose client testifies that he offered his slave girl a choice either to tell the truth in a certain matter and thus receive pardon or "to be whipped and thrown

---

34. The Decree of Scamandrius could be suspended by a vote of the Assembly. Virginia J. Hunter, *Policing Athens: Social Control in the Attic Lawsuits, 420–320 B.C.* (Princeton, NJ: Princeton University Press, 1994), 173–74.

35. Hunter, *Policing Athens*, 155.

36. Demosthenes 22.55. Hunter qualifies this formula in *Policing Athens*, 155–56.

37. Hunter, *Policing Athens*, 92–93, 134, 168; Gerhard Thür, "Reply to D. C. Mirhady: Torture and Rhetoric in Athens," *Journal of Hellenic Studies* 116 (1996): 132–43, at 133. See also Michael Gagarin, "The Torture of Slaves in Athenian Law," *Classical Philology* 91.1 (January 1996): 1–18.

38. For a review of this parable's roots in different Mediterranean traditions (Egyptian, Jewish, Greek), see Richard Bauckham, "The Rich Man and Lazarus: The Parable and the Parallels," *New Testament Studies* 37 (1991): 225–46.

39. Liddell and Scott, *Greek-English Lexicon*, 1350a, s.v. pausikakos.

into a mill (*mulōna empesein*), and consigned to never ceasing evils" (*mēdepote pausasthai kakois*)—in a place, that is, like hell.[40] The slave's unending liability to physical punishment and, in the worst case, to segregation in the mill, has analogues in some of the punishments the New Testament threatened for the damned. Moreover, because slave status was hereditary, descending through the mother, the condition of the slave did not end with death.[41]

Ancient Rome

In contrast to Athenian law, where only fragments of legislation survive, where political oratory allows inferences about some legal practices, and highlights from literature hint at what audiences expected or tolerated, Roman law has survived in codes. True, the earliest, the Twelve Tables of 450 BCE can be reconstructed only indirectly,[42] and the latest, Justinian's *Digest* of the mid-sixth century CE, mostly combines selected remnants and interpretations of older law; however, this legal library provides a wealth of information.[43] Moreover, some provisions in the Twelve Tables pervaded Roman law down to Justinian's time. One commentator whose opinion is preserved in the *Digest* restates an important principle from the Twelve Tables: "In every punishment, our ancestors penalized slaves more severely than free men and men with tainted reputations more than those with a clear record."[44] Under the Republic, the Senate had the ability to legislate, each act being a "Senatusconsultum," and the edicts of praetors had legal force. Commenting on

40. Lysias, *On the Murder of Eratosthenes*, 1.18; ed and trans. W. R. M. Lamb, LCL (1930), cited by Hunter, *Policing Athens*, 171.

41. *Cambridge World History of Slavery*, 1:ix: "Chattel status is a heritable condition passed down through the mother." Leonhard Schumacher, *Sklaverei in der Antike* (Munich: Beck, 2001), 25, 265: children generally inherit the condition of their mother. Catherine Hezser, *Jewish Slavery in Antiquity* (Oxford: Oxford University Press, 2006), 22: "Children borne by slave mothers would automatically obtain slave status." Although not stated so bluntly, the criterion of the mother's unfree status appears significant in Dio Chrysostom 15; "Slavery and Freedom, Discourse II," LCL (1939) and http://penelope.uchicago.edu/Thayer/E/Roman/Texts/Dio_Chrysostom/Discourses/15*.html; quoted in Thomas Wiedemann, *Greek and Roman Slavery* (London: Taylor and Francis, 1981), no. 235, pp. 215–23. In addition, Dio Chrysostom considers as slavery the experience of the Athenian prisoners in the *latomiae* of Syracusa, Sicily.

42. The website Bibliotheca Augustana gives a Latin text: http://www.hs-augsburg.de/~harsch/Chronologia/Lsante05/LegesXII/leg_intr.html. I have also consulted an English translation at the website http://www.constitution.org/sps/sps01_1.htm, which numbers the Twelve Tables and provisions differently and takes many liberties with the text.

43. For Justinian's legislation online in Latin, see http://webu2.upmf-grenoble.fr/Haiti/Cours/Ak/. This site has a link to an English translation of many of these sources, but it is inadequate.

44. "Maiores nostri in omni supplicio seuerius seruos quam liberos, famosos quam integrae famae homines punierunt." D 48.19.28.16. See, for example, in the Latin, Table 8, Law 14; in the English, Table 2, Law 5.

these institutions, the mid-first century BCE philosopher Lucretius used the harshness of penal justice as the basis of his theory, which is also the thesis I am arguing: contemporary Roman judicial practices shaped the fear of postmortem retribution.

Roman ingenuity found many ways to end a criminal's life. This variety of punishments appears as early as the Twelve Tables, which, as reconstructed, assigns these penalties: hanging (8.9; 8.24a); beating and burning (8.10); casting down from the [Tarpeian] Rock (8.14, 8.23); and expelling the convict as an outlaw, who can then be killed with impunity (8.21). Later, the Roman Republic also devised other methods. Officials could attach a criminal's body to the trunk or hang it from the limb of a barren tree. Some executions occurred in stages. A convict could be forced to carry a yoke (*furca*) on his shoulder along an assigned path while citizens beside the way would ritually beat him. This flogging would continue until he reached the place of execution, where the executioner would administer a final stroke. The instrument for this blow was, in the early days, an ax borne along the procession route wrapped in a bundle of twigs collectively called the *fasces*, but later, decapitation by the sword was considered more honorable. Some criminals would be drowned in a leather sack. Others were enclosed. The Vestal Virgin who took a lover died immured; the lover died bearing the *furca*, through the beating, to his decapitation.[45] The body of an executed criminal could be abused by denial of burial. This would be the fate of anyone drowned in a sack, cast over a precipice, or dragged with hooks down the Stair of Sighs and cast into the Tiber. In addition to recognizing that anyone denied proper burial might be compromised in the hereafter, a belief shared widely throughout the Mediterranean world, there are other parallels to be drawn from this list of early punishments. The Carcer and Tullianum were two subterranean prisons beneath the Capitoline Hill, which overlooks the Forum.[46] Release from the Carcer was possible, but many were demoted, through a hole in its floor, into the Tullianum, where they were strangled. Since the Tullianum's greater security suggests it received more serious offenders, it parallels the lower hell in the *Apocalypse of Paul*, where graver sins receive punishments

---

45. Cantarella, *I supplizi capitali*, 136–40, 262; for the man, 211–13.

46. Michel Humbert, "La peine en droit romain," in *La peine/Punishment*, pt. 1, Antiquity, Transactions of the Jean Bodin Society for Comparative Institutional History 55 (Brussels: DeBoeck Université, 1991), 133–83, at 177; and Jean-Michel David, "Du Comitium à la roche Tarpéienne," in *Du châtiment dans la cité: Supplices corporels et peine de mort dans le monde antique*, ed. Yan Thomas, Collection de l'École Française de Rome 79 (Rome: École française de Rome, 1984), 131–75; Nicole Loraux, "Le corps étranglé," ibid., 195–224; Dominique Briquel, "Formes de mise à mort dans la Rome primitive: Quelques remarques sur une approche comparative du problème," ibid., 225–40.

seven times more severe than those above. The *Apocalypse of Peter* also presents a dramatic glimpse of afterlife torments, as sinners hang from trees with their bodies drawn by the currents of rivers of fire.

It is tempting to take these one-to-one correlations at face value, but some ambiguities intrude. For example, a capital punishment may be distinct from the shaming ritual that preceded it or from the torture that may have been considered a part of the execution. A rack called the *eculeus* stretched the body by attaching weights to pull limbs in opposite directions. If left unchecked, this method could end in dismemberment and death. Is it torture or execution? Would it count as Matthew's and Luke's "tearing asunder" (*dikotomēsei*)? Conversely, some torments that end in death can be used either for temporary punishment or for torture. In ancient Athens, there were two different kinds of stocks: the *apotumpanismos*, which retained and exposed a criminal until death, and the *poddokakē*, which was "merely" temporary and shameful and traditionally limited to five days and five nights. The Romans used the wooden instrument already mentioned called the *furca*. When curved, it served as a yoke; when forked, as a gallows. From a labor-saving device (for balancing loads), and hence a mark of shame, to an implement of torture or execution, the *furca* could be imposed by a master on his slave, a magistrate on a condemned man, or a military commander on his captives. (Captives were "subjugated," from *jugum*, another term for "yoke." They were also likely to be enslaved.) The same would apply to fire: burning condemned criminals is hardly fire's only function. Indeed, fire's very commonness increased the shame of subjection to it. Whatever the literal correspondence between the elements and implements of torture in hell and execution on earth, there is a crucial difference. Unlike hell, execution brings an end to suffering. In hell there is no coup de grâce. Capital punishments seem relevant to hell because, in most circumstances, they were painful for the convict, and, from the legal perspective, they were the most severe sanctions available. In ancient Rome, one synonym for the death penalty was *summum supplicium*, "the ultimate suffering." Yet, because hell's torments never end and capital punishment does, the parallel fails.

The human institution of exile is a different situation. Augustine of Hippo (d. 430) ranked eternal exile from the presence of God as a worse consequence of damnation than hell's physical tortures, and certainly worse than temporal exile on earth, which he considered life's equivalent of unending punishment.[47] But the legal institution of exile was complex. Like stoning, it

---

47. Augustine, *Enchiridion de fide et spe et caritate* 29.112; CCSL 46, ed. M. Evans (1969), 110; trans. J. F. Shaw (South Bend, IN: Regnery/Gateway, 1961), 131.

has overtones of collective execution. Two old forms of exile in early Rome involved a kind of banishment. By denying water and fire (*interdictio acquae et ignis*) to a convict, the community forces him to leave the territory in order to survive. A further provision was the curse *Sacer esto* (Be you holy), which drew on the assumption that the survival of a criminal angers the gods, and that anyone who kills him restores divine favor to the community.[48] Presented as a curse to initiate exile, it was in fact a death sentence. Anyone who kills a person bearing this curse kills with impunity.

Exile was not always for life. In "relegation" a convict was excluded from a province (and thus had considerable leeway outside it) or confined on an island (and so was restricted to a comparatively small place). Relegation could be for a period of time or permanent. "Deportation" was permanent. A relegated exile would return to society, but with limited rights—a penalty on its own, called *infamia*. The Roman jurists understood the postmortem disgrace of people who died deported or relegated to an island. The criminal's families were not permitted to recover their bodies because "the punishment endures even after death."[49] The physical separation of the convict from the rest of society was deemed a stigma worth preserving beyond the end of the exile's life. Segregation and endlessness are important features of exile that both earthly and afterlife punishments share.

Another form of noncapital punishment that segregated convicts from the general population was forced labor in the mines, quarries, or factories. Prisoners condemned *ad metallum* wore heavier chains than those condemned *in opus metalli*. Condemnation *ad metallum* involved loss of freedom. Women so condemned did not perform heavy labor, but supported the men who did, either for a time or permanently; if permanently, they lost their freedom.[50] Reduction to slavery, another degrading punishment, also created a stigma that surpassed an individual's life. Indeed, all unfree status carries this implication of endlessness, because slavery is hereditary; it descends through the mother.

SLAVERY AND TORTURE IN ROME

In Rome the difference in the punishment of slaves and free men and women was apparent as early as the Twelve Tables. The free were punished for open

---

48. Jörg Rüpke, "You Shall Not Kill: Hierarchies of Norms in Ancient Rome," *Numen* 39.1 (1992): 58–79, at 67; Harold Bennett, "Sacer Esto," in *Transactions and Proceedings of the American Philological Association* 61 (1930): 5–18.

49. D 48.24.2. Marcianus says the emperors Severus and Antoninus granted waivers to "many."

50. D 48.19.8.4–8.

theft by enslavement, but slaves were to be beaten and cast from the Tarpeian Rock (8.14). (A convicted free man caught a second time, as a penal slave, would be put to death, but a slave would only have to be apprehended once to pay the ultimate penalty.) Owners could confine slaves in the *ergastula* or mill and force them to grind grain. In large establishments, the best torturer might be the one who could discipline slaves without impairing their productivity for too long. There were even independent contractors called *tortores* who could be hired by the day to administer this discipline.[51] The Greek New Testament refers to such a specialist as a *basanistēs*. Roman slaves who fled or rebelled could be crucified, as were the 6,000 who joined Spartacus in 73 BCE. Runaways recaptured but not crucified could be forced to wear an iron collar bearing their return address on a small metal tablet. Christian owners did not significantly alter this treatment. Paul converted the runaway slave Onesimus when they were together in prison, but sent him back to his owner, Philemon, himself a Christian. Ephesians 6:5 urges slaves to "be obedient to their masters . . . as to Christ."[52] The parables of Jesus also assume the existence of slavery. In the parable of the talents (Matt. 25:14–30), the master sends the offending slaves to an "outer darkness" reminiscent of the mill on a Roman estate. In the parable of the unmerciful slave (Matt. 18:23–35), when a king returns and discovers the misdeed of the slave to whom he had shown much kindness, "his lord delivered him to the torturers" (Greek, *basanistais*; Latin, *tortoribus*). Again, in the parable of the wicked servant (Matt. 24:45–51; also Luke 12:42–46), when the lord returns and finds his administrative slave, one who is in charge of other slaves, abusing his position of authority and taking advantage of the lord's absence, "he will cut him into pieces (*dikotomēsei*) and place his portion among the hypocrites."[53]

Can this "cutting into pieces" be intended literally? A softer translation of the Latin *dividere* or the Greek *dikotomeō* would make the term mean "divide him off," "separate him out," from the good, and set him with the hypocrites. This action would then resemble the separation of the sheep from the goats in Matthew 25:31–46. It would recall the various punishments by segregation. Still, the literal interpretation seems unavoidable. *Dikotomeō* is the term used in geometry for dividing a line, in logic for a dichotomy, and in Plutarch's *Life of Pyrrhus* for the sword stroke that slices an enemy in two,

---

51. Hunter, *Policing Athens*, 172. More specifically for Rome, see Bradley, *Slavery and Society at Rome*, 166; Schumacher, *Sklaverei*, 276–84.

52. Bradley, *Slavery and Society at Rome*, 148.

53. Jennifer A. Glancy, "Slaves and Slavery in the Matthean Parables," *Journal of Biblical Literature* 119.1 (Spring 2000): 67–90. See also her monograph *Slavery in Early Christianity* (Oxford: Oxford University Press, 2002).

causing either half of his body to fall on opposite sides of the horse (sōmatos dixotomēthentos).[54] Before relegating the issue of bodily division to the category of rich ambiguity, it is useful to recall that the idea occurs in connection with torture. Seneca has provided important examples in describing the eculeus rack and other "machines."[55] According to the surviving fragments of the Twelve Tables, if someone is in debt to several lenders, and the usual delays have been exhausted, the creditors are permitted to divide the person's body.[56]

The division of persons also appears, but somewhat differently, in the Senatusconsultum Silanianum of 10 CE, which sheds much light on slaves' liability to torture and on division in punishment. The assumption behind this legislation is that any slave who lives "under the same roof" as his master is obliged to give up his life in defense of his owner. If the master is murdered and the slave alive, the slave must be "put to the question," that is, subjected to torture, in order to determine his or her involvement in the murder. A male or female slave can be put to the question even if the owner has committed suicide (D 29.5.1.22). A slave girl in the same room as her mistress will also be executed for failing to call for help (D 29.5.1.28). If a slave has several owners, and they are all attacked, and he could have helped them all but helped only some, he must be executed (supplicio adficiendum, D 29.5.3.4). Here, the use of torture as part of the questioning blends into torture as part of capital punishment.[57]

Because the Senatusconsultum Silanianum affected slaves who lived under the same roof with their masters and mistresses, it excluded slaves who were enclosed and chained (clausi and vincti) elsewhere and were consequently unable to aid their owners (D 29.5.3.6). This provision implies the existence of separate quarters within a family's compound where slaves would be unaware of events in the main house. It seems to be an indirect reference to the mill and, if so, supplies the information that those so enclosed might commonly be held in chains. It also sheds a metaphorical light on the matter of division. The slave of a murdered master must be put to the question even if the victim was only a joint owner of the slave (D 29.5.1.6; cf. 29.5.6.2).

---

54. Plutarch, Pyrrhus 24.3; Plutarch's Lives, ed. and trans. Bernadotte Perrin, LCL (Cambridge MA: Harvard University Press, 1959), 9:426–27.

55. Seneca, Ad Lucilium epistulae morales 14.5; 24.14; 67.3; 78.19.

56. Twelve Tables 3.6 (Latin); 3.10 (English). Cf. Aulus Gellius, Noctes Atticae 20.1.48–52.

57. A dramatic example occurs in Plutarch's Life of Artaxerxes [II] 16.3 (trans. Perrin, 11:162–65), where the horrible "torture of the boats" (skapheuthēnta) lasted seventeen days. Bruce Lincoln asserts that this tortuous execution reflects torments in the Zoroastrian hell. Lincoln, Religion, Empire, and Torture (Chicago: University of Chicago Press, 2010), 85–90.

Thus the slave can be tortured to elicit testimony about the crime, or for suspicion of violence against one's part owner. Liability to torture for questioning on the fate of one's partial owner is a metaphorical form of division, but it echoes the very concrete provision in the Twelve Tables that creditors could divide a person in debt to several of them.

The Senatusconsultum Silanianum shows that the distinction between torture and execution dissolved before citizens lost their protection from torture. Torture could deliberately, exquisitely,[58] bring about death from the first century on, and Constantine later endorsed the procedure, but torture remained, in principle at least, the mark of the slave. Even as this distinction faded, another mark of slavery paralleled the fate of the damned. The slaves' liability to torture was unending in that it could be passed on between the generations, from a slave mother to her children.[59]

Christian Changes?

Christianity did not spread smoothly through the Roman world. Imperial persecution produced startling and dramatic injustices. Martyrs appeared in all parts of the empire. With the emperor Constantine and his Edict of Toleration in 313, things slowly began to change. Indeed, the fourth century saw the gradual increase of an officially sponsored Christianity. This period of conversion may be said to have closed between 380, when the coemperors Gratian, Valentinian, and Theodosius I declared all religion but Catholic Christianity heresy and infamy (CTh 16.1.2), and 395, when the same Theodosius made participation in pagan rituals treason, and therefore a capital crime (CTh 16.10.13). For example, an act of 386 assimilated dissenters from the First Council of Constantinople to "authors of sedition . . . who should pay with head and blood the punishment for treason."[60] The question arises whether this implementation of a Christian framework affected the imperial administration of justice. Ramsay MacMullen sees a steady decline in judicial standards through the whole imperial period with no particular improvement after the acceptance of Christianity.[61] The

---

58. "exquisitis . . . suppliciis," CTh 1.22.1; cited by MacMullen, "Judicial Savagery," 157.

59. D 1.5.5.1, "On the Status of Persons"; quoted in Wiedemann, *Greek and Roman Slavery*, no. 4, p. 20. Sandra Joshel, *Slavery in the Roman World* (Cambridge: Cambridge University Press, 2010), 125: "The owner of a slave mother also owned her children." Yan Thomas presents important nuances, rightly combining the issue of freedom with the issue of legitimate birth. Thomas, "The Division of the Sexes in Roman Law," in *A History of Women in the West* (Cambridge, MA, and London: The Belknap Press of Harvard University Press, 1992), 83–137, at 122–23.

60. CTh 16.1.4.

61. Ramsay MacMullen, "Judicial Savagery," 147–66.

expansion of empire, the resultant independence of far-flung governors, and ethnic "distance" between the governors serving as judges and the people whose cases they tried often made sentences arbitrary and harsh. Though acknowledging many exceptions, Jill Harries attributes important differences in the administration of justice to the introduction of Christians, mostly as bishops, into imperial councils. Bishops dared to correct emperors. To the early imperial goal of retribution and deterrence, she observes, Christians added reform and penance; hence they regarded the death penalty differently.[62] Bishops preferred repentance to quick execution of criminals.[63] Yet mercy could occur on either side of the religious divide. Ambrose, bishop of Milan, knew some pagan governors were proud of never inflicting the death penalty during their administrations, even though it was within their authority. In writing to his friend Studius, Ambrose exerted the pressure of a bishop and imperial counselor: "If pagans do this, what should Christians do?"[64]

Some of Constantine's decisions tended to make imperial justice more merciful and resulted clearly from religious inspiration. He eliminated execution by exposure to beasts in the arena.[65] He made the *furca* supplant crucifixion. Because Constantine said the human face reflects the divine image, he forbade branding on the forehead and instead punished with the *furca*. But Constantine did not consistently lighten penalties; he classified some thirteen new crimes as capital.[66] He was severe against government corruption; officials convicted of greed should have their hands severed.[67] A judge who denied the rights of a female head of household (*materfamilias*) whose reputation was untarnished (*quae non inhoneste vixit*) "should be beyond any indulgence and struck with capital punishment or, rather, [pushed] with refined tortures to the point of death."[68] Here, Constantine condones a change in the purpose of torture. Instead of limiting torture to the discovery of truth in criminal investigations like the jurist Ulpian (d. 223), who urged that torture

---

62. Jill Harries, *Law and Empire in Late Antiquity* (Cambridge: Cambridge University Press, 1999), 147–49.

63. Ibid., 136.

64. Ambrose, letter 25.3; cited by Peter Brown, "Saint Augustine's Attitude to Religious Coercion," *Journal of Roman Studies* 54.1–2 (1964): 107–16, at 115. For the Latin: Ambrosius Mediolanensis, *Epistulae*, Book 7, letter 50, par. 3; CSEL 82, pt. 2, ed. M. Zelzer (1990), p. 57, line 24.

65. Harries, *Law and Empire*, 138; Cantarella, *I supplizi capitali*, 198.

66. MacMullen, "Judicial Savagery," 157 n. 32.

67. CTh 1.16.7.

68. "Citra ullam indulgentiam capitali poena vel exquisitis potius exitii suppliciis plectetur." CTh 1.22.1; cited by MacMullen, "Judicial Savagery," 157. For the definition of a materfamilias, see Ulpian, D 50.16.46.1, in conjunction with 50.16.195.2 and 3.

should not be a means of execution,[69] Constantine allowed it to become part of the punishment. In one remarkable punishment Constantine prescribed pouring molten lead down the throats of those who contributed to the seduction or rape of girls. These nursemaids are false counselors (as Dante called similar sinners in canto 26 of the *Inferno*), guilty of breaking the implicit pact between the nurse and the girl herself by relating vicious fables (classical literature?) or otherwise offering false encouragement to wickedness. These elders guilty of misleading the young should have their mouths and throats filled with molten lead.[70] Apparently this was retaliation in the case of those who had abused their vocal chords to lead the innocent astray.

As in Athens, slaves in the Roman Republic could be tortured at any time, and only slaves could be tortured. No citizen, whatever the crime, should ever endure such discipline.[71] Crucifixion was also unique to slaves. But gradually, and especially in the fourth century, the treatment of slaves encroached on the treatment of the free, and not just plebeians. It had been assumed that the higher one's social rank, the greater one's immunity from the empire's most degrading punishments.[72] Constantine had used the traditional considerations of rank to determine differences in judicial penalties. He acted against counterfeiters with different punishments for each social level. The decurion he banished to any municipality, the plebeian he struck with perpetual punishment and the forfeit of his property, the slave he punished with the supreme penalty.[73] By 384, however, this gradation of penalties yielded to one: death. The Theodosian Code of 438 clearly shows that from Constantine on, through the fourth century, punishments of remarkable severity and ingenuity fell on people who, earlier, would have been exempt. One example is an act of 358 by which the coemperors Constantius and Julian explicitly overrode any exception based on rank. They decreed the use of magic[74] so grave an evil that anyone caught practicing those arts "should not escape wracking and torment by invocation of rank," but "should be given over to the rack (*eculeus*) and have his sides perforated by [hooks called] 'the cutting claws' as worthy punishments for this special outrage."[75] By around 400 CE,

---

69. "Nec ea quidem poena damnari quem oportet, ut uerberibus necetur uel uirgis interematur, nec tormentis." D 48.19.8.3 quoting Ulpian's *Duties of a Proconsul*, book 9.

70. CTh 9.24.1; MacMullen, "Judicial Savagery," 157; Harries, *Law and Empire*, 140.

71. Consider Paul before the Roman tribune in Jerusalem, Acts 22:24–29.

72. A. N. Sherwin-White and A. H. M. Jones, "Decuriones," *OCD*, 437–38.

73. CTh 9.21.1; Harries, *Law and Empire*, 140; MacMullen, "Judicial Savagery," 157 n. 32.

74. "Magic" included the use of potions, salves, incantations, necrology, divination, and curses. Under the Christian empire, magic appeared to compete with divine power.

75. "praesidio dignitatis cruciatus et tormenta non fugiat. Si convictus ad proprium facinus detegentibus repugnaverit pernegando, sit eculeo deditus ungulisque sulcantibus latera perferat poenas

the exemption from torture for the free no longer held. From the point of view of penal justice, all were liable to torture; all were potentially treated as slaves.

Also beginning with Constantine and continuing, with some interruptions, through the fourth century was the effort to repress religious challenges to orthodox Christianity, itself an idea in the course of self-definition. These challenges included faiths such as Judaism, many varieties of what the laws denounced as paganism, and heretical variations of Christianity. One of the new capital punishments Constantine introduced was death by fire for Christian heretics, specifically Arians. In 333 he decreed, "If anyone should be caught and be found to possess or to have concealed a work composed by Arius he should be given over at once for burning."[76] Christians were not the only protagonists in the conflict of religions, and Constantine's approach was not one-sided. Any Jewish elder who stoned converts to Christianity should be immediately consigned to the flames together with his accomplices.[77] The stoning of Stephen in Acts 7:58–8:1 comes to mind in this connection. Perhaps this reference spread as a literary commonplace from that incident. Still, Constantine also protected Jews who had done no wrong; they were not to be persecuted for remaining Jews.[78]

The emperors who followed Constantine (except Julian, himself a pagan) continued the campaign to extirpate paganism. In the 340s and 350s they targeted rites such as entering temples, conducting sacrifices, or venerating idols. They expanded the list over the decades to include the inspection of animal entrails for good omens (CTh 16.10.9). They threatened offenders with decapitation by the sword (*gladio ultore sternatur*, CTh 16.10.4 and 16.10.6). Identical penalties awaited local officials who failed to punish these evils. In 385, the coemperors Gratian, Valentinian, and Theodosius threatened those who violated these provisions with "the wracking of even stronger tortures" (*acerbioris supplicii cruciatus*, CTh 16.10.9). A logical culmination to the establishment of Christianity appeared in 395 when Arcadius and

---

proprio dignas facinore." CTh 9.16.6; MacMullen, "Judicial Savagery," 162.

76. "Si quispiam ab Arrio confectum opusculum habere fuerit deprehensus vel absconditum minime tradiderit exurendum." Hans-Georg Opitz, *Urkunden zur Geschichte des arianischen Streites*, in *Athanasius Werke* 3.1 (Berlin: De Gruyter, 1935), no. 33, pp. 66–68; cited by MacMullen, "Judicial Savagery," 157 n. 32 end. Burning appears as a penalty in Constantine's legislation from 320–29 in CTh 9.16.1; 7.1.1; 10.4.1; 9.24.1; 9.9.1. This list compiled by Roland Delmaire in Jean Rougé, *Les lois religieuses des empereurs romans de Constantine à Théodose II (312–438)*, vol. 1, *Code Théodosien, Livre XVI*, SC 497 (Paris: Éditions du Cerf, 2005), p. 369 n. 4. The text from outside the Theodosian Code cited by MacMullen extends the dates of Constantine's use of burning to 333.

77. CTh 16.8.1.

78. CTh 16.8.21.

Honorius equated Christian heresy with paganism as an offense worthy of severe penalties (CTh 16.10.13), which henceforth were to be administered even more energetically (*nunc acrius exsequendum*).

That Christian emperors should impose the death sentence for religious deviance constitutes a monumental policy of retaliation. Even though the techniques of execution were less violent (decapitation rather than expo-sure to beasts in the arena), the imperial program begun by Constantine and extended by his Christian successors reversed an earlier abuse, the persecution of Christians: what you found to be a capital offense in us, we now find in you. This judicial inversion of religious policy reflected the recent rise to domi-nance of the new faith. Christian rulers threatened opponents of their religion with corporal penalties previously reserved for slaves, but they themselves had previously suffered the same abasement. In 203, the Roman procurator of Carthage sentenced Vibia Perpetua to die exposed to beasts in the arena. She was the daughter of a pagan father of distinguished lineage. If the *honestiores* were exempt from corporal punishment, certainly that privilege should have applied to her. But her crime was her Christian faith and the resultant insub-ordination to her father and the Roman procurator of Carthage brought her exposure to the beasts in the arena. We would miss an important element in the judicial reflections circulating in the Mediterranean world at this time were we not to hear the anger of early leaders such as Tertullian, possibly the editor of Perpetua's autobiographical account of her trial, imprisonment, and execution. Indeed, for Tertullian, as for Dante centuries later, the ranked seats of the arena suggested something of the heavenly hierarchy, and, look-ing down, Tertullian saw the torments of the damned as a delicious turning of the tables: What you imposed you now endure! In hell, he said in paraphrase, the persecutors will suffer in even fiercer flames than those to which they con-demn the Christian martyrs. This spectacle will provide more pleasure to the inhabitants of heaven than the gladiatorial games gave to the pagan masses.[79]

One can only speculate why torture spread throughout the empire from the slaves up through the privileged classes—how citizens lost their immu-nity. Perhaps the common practice of torturing slaves brought about an insensitivity to pain (that is, when inflicted on others), a notion that pain was a fact of life and could be employed positively. The Senatusconsultum Silanianum of 10 CE had found new grounds for making slaves liable to tor-ture. In this way, the mistreatment of slaves in the smallest establishments spread upward to meet the downward contagion of imperial despotism.

---

79. Tertullian, *De spectaculis* 30; trans. T. R. Glover (London: Heinemann, 1931), 296–301.

Amnesty

Though acts of imperial clemency were not unique to Christian emperors, the Easter amnesty surely was. Beginning in 367 and reissued until 386, these provisions granted amnesty at Easter to certain criminals. The emperors give the official reasons for these actions in prefaces to each annual renewal. A typical explanation comes from a decree of 386 by the coemperors Valentinian, Theodosius, and Arcadius. From the time of their ancestors, they state, Easter provided an occasion to manifest the indulgence of imperial compassion by freeing almost all persons now under punishment according to the laws. Then they list the convicts they wish to spare: those in chains, in the mines, in exile, and those under orders of deportation. Nonetheless, they reason, if absolutely all criminals were to be pardoned—regardless of their crimes—their victims would rebel.[80] The emperors therefore exclude from the pardon homicides and persons guilty of adultery, along with astrologers, poisoners, magicians, and, first included in 381, counterfeiters.[81] Also excluded from the Easter amnesty were traitors, a category that, as we have seen, included participants in pagan rituals and heretical Christians. The final Easter amnesty corresponded in time to imperial provisions that tended more and more to establish Christianity. As Christianity permeated governmental thinking, so did the conviction that some offenses were beyond pardon. The gravity of these crimes outweighed the legal exemptions of the social elite in the calculations of imperial jurists. Put differently, Roman social distinctions collapsed as all became liable to torture. When the categories of unpardonable offenses expanded, the death penalty became more common, and physical punishment, previously the burden only of the unfree, potentially threatened all. Therefore, law and eschatology influenced one another.

By the end of the fourth century, torture, previously a punishment limited to slaves, hung over all, and just as slavery, a hereditary condition, was endless, so slavery seemed increasingly a lens through which to understand damnation.[82] We recall the frequent reference to darkness in connection with hell in both biblical and visionary sources. Infernal darkness, often taken

---

80. This rhetoric appears clearly in the *Constitutiones Sirmondianae*, no. 8, an act of Valentinianus, Theodosius, and Arcadius of 386, which complements vague expressions in CTh 9.38.8 of 385.

81. Michael F. Hendy, *Studies in the Byzantine Monetary Economy, c. 300–1450* (Cambridge: Cambridge University Press, 1985), 323.

82. Isabel Moreira correctly connects the condition of slaves to the damned. See Moreira, *Heaven's Purge* (Oxford: Oxford University Press, 2010), 43–62; "In hell all sinners were slave bodies to be tortured" (49) or, again, "Slaves and the damned were outcasts alike, their fate to endure the misery of corporeality" (63). By contrast, consider the incorporeality of shades in classical antiquity (*Odyssey* 11.202–22; *Aeneid* 6.700–702).

figuratively, receives a different interpretation in the research of Virginia Hunter on Athens and Jennifer Glancy on Rome. They refer the darkness tentatively to a public prison but more specifically to "the mill," that specific place of forced labor in the slaveholding compound.[83] While the Bible's "outer darkness" is possibly a reference to exile, "darkness" alone may refer to the prison or the mill. Darkness was the first thing Perpetua noticed as she entered her prison to await the murderous games.

Hell and Torture Overlap

The torments of slaves, the punishments of some criminals, and the fate of the damned resemble one another. This "fit" between Roman slaveholding practices and the overtones of the New Testament, and especially some of its parables, becomes even clearer after reflection on the terminology involved. For example, the parable of the unmerciful slave, Matthew 18:23–35, applies not only to one dishonest slave and one particular master. It orients the relationship of all slaves in obedience to their masters, and, more important, conversely, the relationship of all superiors to all subordinates. The king, a slave owner, threatens to sell his *doulos* (slave, not servant—one doesn't *sell* servants) for failure to pay a large debt, but then pardons the debt. Meeting a fellow slave in debt to him, however, the unmerciful slave denies a reprieve and puts the subordinate slave in prison.[84] When the king learns of this injustice, he upbraids the unmerciful slave: "Should you not have mercy on your fellow slave as I had mercy on you?" He then turns the first slave over to the torturers (*basanistais*) until he pays the previously forgiven debt.

This parable has important ramifications for ancient, Christian, and medieval political thought. These become clearer when one notes that classicists translate the Greek terms *kurios* and *doulos*, and the Latin terms *dominus* and *servus*, as "master" and "slave." In most English translations of the Bible, they are rendered as "master" and "servant." This convention in translation conceals the ancient institution of slavery and undermines the rhetorical strategy of the parables themselves, which depend on making abstract truths accessible through reference to what is familiar. Medievalists dealing with the postpatristic, early Middle Ages have typically translated these same terms as "lord" and "serf." In the Christian liturgy, however,

---

83. Glancy, "Slaves and Slavery in the Matthean Parables," 67–90; Glancy, *Slavery in Early Christianity* (Oxford: Oxford University Press, 2002); Hunter, *Policing Athens*, 171.

84. The term given here, *eis phulakēn*, differs from the term that usually describes the mill as prison.

kurios is "lord," and it applies as much to the Lord God as to any slave-owner.[85] In Greek, two other terms for "lord" and "slave" are *despotēs* and *oiketēs*.[86] Both *kurios* and *despotēs* can refer to God or Christ as Lord, but what is remarkable is the durability of *doulos* as "slave," and its migration up the social and political ladder to refer to high members of the aristocracy and court. Justinian and Theodora insisted on being called *Despotēs* and *Despoina* (Lord and Lady), but called even their chief officials "slaves."[87] Every Christian was considered a slave of God, a *Theodoulos*, and in the West, the pope was *servus servorum Dei*.[88] Obviously, social realities evolve. The continuity in the language underscores a fundamental social relationship between owner and slave that this parable and several others assume as normal and familiar.[89]

To be sure, the prevalence of slavery as an institution sometimes encouraged the figurative use of the term "slave." Biblical authors propose an antithesis between slavery to opposed lords, one good and one evil. Romans 6:16 states that slavery to sin leads to death (meaning damnation) whereas slavery through obedience to God leads to righteousness.[90] In order to set up these contrasts, Paul makes the literal and obvious point that "if you yield yourselves to any one as obedient slave, you are slave of the one whom you obey." Then, after further contrasts between slavery and freedom, sin and

---

85. In the Septuagint, "the Lord your God" is *kurios ho theos sou* (Exod. 20:2). In neo-Babylonian documents in Akkadian, from the sixth to fifth century BCE, "*ardu* [a term for "slave"] denotes a subordinate relationship, such as that between a subject and the king, or between the king and a deity." H.D. Baker, "Degrees of Freedom: Slavery in Mid-First Millennium BC Babylonia," *World Archaeology* 33.1 (June 2001): 18–26, at 20. William Fitzgerald also notes the ambiguity in translating *doulos* as "servant" rather than "slave" in *Slavery and the Roman Literary Imagination* (Cambridge: Cambridge University Press, 2000), 112–13. He continues to explore the metaphor of the slave in the earthly career of Jesus and the subsequent interpretation of his life (113–15).

86. These terms also appear in the Christian Scriptures. See above, note 8. For more on this terminology in its social and legal context, see Peter Sarris, "Social Relations and the Land: The Early Period," in *The Social History of Byzantium*, ed. John Haldon (Chichester, UK: Wiley-Blackwell, 2009), 92–111. I thank Jesse Torgerson for help on this point. Note that *kurios* refers also to the owner of an animal.

87. Paul Magdalino, "Court Society and Aristocracy," in Haldon, *The Social History of Byzantium*, 212–32, at 222, quoting Procopius, *Anecdota* 30.12–31.

88. Michael McCormick, *Origins of the European Economy* (Cambridge: Cambridge University Press, 2001), 734–35.

89. Glancy, *Slavery in Early Christianity*, 122–23: "Jesus himself relied on the figure of the slave in his teachings. . . . [He] drew his metaphors from the culture in which he lived, and he lived in a slaveholding culture." What is the difference between a slave and a serf? Jean-Pierre Devroey gives a convenient entrance to the question in "Men and Women in Early Medieval Serfdom: The Ninth-Century North Frankish Evidence," *Past & Present* 166 (February 2000): 3–30.

90. "The Christian owes Christ the unconditional obedience and unquestioning loyalty of a slave." Dale B. Martin, *Slavery as Salvation: The Metaphor of Slavery in Pauline Christianity* (New Haven, CT, and London: Yale University Press, 1990), 60–61.

righteousness, he explains, "I am speaking in human terms, because of your natural limitations" (Rom. 6:19). It is as if Paul felt that in order to explain the relationship between sin and righteousness he had to draw on "everyone's" common understanding of the relationship between a slave and a master. Just as an appreciation of freedom is essential to understanding the New Testament, so is slavery; as heaven, so hell. The polarity informs antitheses that shape the biblical message.

Given this context, it seems that the goal of the parable is to model mercy as the basic rule of conduct between superiors and subordinates: lords and slaves, kings and subjects, and, at the highest level, God and humans. Rejecting this ideal model of the divine hierarchy or its human replica, the political order, is insubordination or, as Roman jurists called it, "contumacy."[91] In Roman law, before the end of the fourth century, the punishment for contumacy was loss of the case[92] or aggravation of the sentence.[93] In the late fourth to early fifth century, after the experiment with the Easter amnesty, when the legislation against pagan practices was becoming more pronounced, and as monasticism was beginning to spread from east to west, the penalty became expulsion from the community. In his *Institutes of the Life of Monks*, a work of the 420s, John Cassian lists examples of disobedience demanding correction. Resistance to that discipline he calls "contumacy," and it should be met first by spiritual sanctions, then physical punishments, and finally, expulsion.[94] Orosius, the student and collaborator of Augustine, in his *Histories* of 416 and 417, extended this expulsion to the otherworld. He said, "In the beginning, the human race was created and established to this end, that, living peacefully under religion, by the fruit of obedience rather than of toil, we might gain (*promerere*) eternity, but we abused the goodness of the creator

---

91. As far back as the Hebrew Bible these basic principles were clear. See Joshua 2:12: "As I have dealt kindly with you, you also will deal kindly with my father's house" (said by a prostitute in Jericho to Joshua's spies); 2 Sam 22:26; the same term, "trust" (*haseed*), expresses this idea in Ps. 18:25. What one offers, one receives back. Parents must also overturn the fractiousness of a stubborn and rebellious son. They must denounce him to the town elders, who will stone him to death at the city gate (Deut. 21:19–20).

92. "Let the judge punish anyone who knowingly fails to appear for the trial with [the threatened] punishment." (Eum, qui sciens iudicio adesse neglexerit, ut contumacem iudex poena multabit.) CTh 2.18.2 of 322.

93. "Contumacy augments the punishment." (Contumacia . . . cumulat poenam.) Marcianus, quoted in D 48.19.4.

94. "Si superflue, si durius, si contumacius responderit, . . . non illa increpatione, quam diximus, spiritali, sed vel plagis emendantur, vel expulsione purgantur." *De coenobiorum institutis* 4.16; PL 49:172A–174A. In the *Rule of Benedict* 71, this provision is shortened to "Si contumax fuerit, de monasterio expellatur." *The Rule of St. Benedict*, ed. Timothy Fry, (Collegeville, MN: Liturgical Press, 1981), 292.

and turned from liberty to license and contumacy, and from contempt we sank into oblivion."[95] For Orosius, contumacy brings damnation.

Then, no longer in the recesses of the monastery or the study of an intellectual, but in the imperial chancery, Justinian, perhaps in 538, decreed execution (*ultimis suppliciis*) for contumacy, that is, continued disregard of an imperial prohibition.[96] As imperial subjects became liable to life-ending tortures, as privilege exempted fewer and fewer, monarchy assumed ever greater powers over the bodies of subjects in their liability to capital punishment and physical pain. In the vision literature from this period and continuing ever after, the postmortem punishments applied to the damned paralleled the tortures imposed on slaves. A decree of Constantine from 319 is a good example of how the state sanctioned the physical discipline of slaves. It defends slave owners who might accidentally kill a slave when administering discipline.

If a master beat a slave with a rod or whip or put him in chains to guard him, and the slave dies, the master need to have no fear of prosecution. . . . He should, of course, not use his right immoderately, but he will be charged with murder only if he killed the slave intentionally, by a blow from the fist or a stone, or, by using a weapon, he inflicted a lethal wound, or ordered him to be hanged by a noose, or by a wicked order instructed that he be thrown from a high place, or administered the virus of a poison, or tore his body by public punishment, that is, by tearing through his sides with the claws of wild beasts [that is, metal implements curved like claws, for tearing the flesh], or by burning him with fire applied to his limbs, or if, with this savagery of monstrous barbarians, he forced the slave to leave his life almost in the tortures themselves, with the destroyed limbs flowing with black blood.[97]

The normal discipline of a slave, beating with rod or whip or chains (in the mill?), cannot incriminate an owner. The owner is liable only if he inflicts

95. Paulus Orosius, *Historiae adversum paganos* 7.1, CSEL 5, ed. C. Zangemeister (Vienna: Gerold, 1889), from the website http://www.attalus.org/latin/orosius7A.html, accessed February 13, 2011. Cf. PL 31:1060B.

96. Although the decree specifically prohibits acts against nature, and illicit sensuality, the language more generally threatens anyone who persists in forbidden behavior. Officials who fail to act against these misdeeds are condemned not only by the emperor, but also by God. "Si enim et post hanc nostram suasionem quidam tales invenientes hos subtercelaverint, similiter a domino deo condemnabuntur." *Corpus Iuris Civilis*, vol. 3, *Novellae* 77.1.1–2, ed. R. Schoell and G. Kroll, 6th ed. (Berlin: Weidmann, 1954), 382–83.

97. CTh 9.12.1; trans. Alan Watson in *Roman Slave Law* (Baltimore: Johns Hopkins University Press, 1987), 124–25.

death intentionally. Some of these killing methods come from the state's own discipline of criminals. New in this list are poison and the deliberate laceration of the flesh. Poison, like hemlock, is an import from Greece; fire is related to burning at the stake and may also be related to the hot metal plates and pitch mentioned by Lucretius and Seneca. More important are the pains that occur both here and in the religious literature. Common to the discipline of slaves and either the *Apocalypse of Peter* or the *Apocalypse of Paul* we find hanging, casting down, (no poison in the religious texts,) tearing of the body, and burning. The last two clauses in Constantine's decree are ambiguous. They suggest, on the one hand, a death from abandonment in the stocks, like the *apotumpanismos*, or the *furca* (forcing "the slave to leave his life . . . in the tortures themselves") or, on the other hand, the dismemberment of the severed limbs, bleeding in the snow of the *Apocalypse of Paul* (§39b; p. 31, lines 32–34). These are extensions of the normal cutting inflicted with "the claws." Constantine's decree distinguishes between those treatments regarded as normal and unlikely to cause death and others that only an enraged owner would indulge when carried away by anger or unusual cruelty, thereby intentionally causing the death of a slave. In the first category are the rod, the whip, or the chains reminiscent of the mill and its darkness. In the second category are the other methods that correspond to the techniques of capital punishment found around the ancient Mediterranean, but which the emperor considered abusive in connection with the discipline of slaves. The infernal scenes reported in the *Apocalypse of Peter* and the *Apocalypse of Paul* incorporate pains from both these public and private torments.

The liability of slaves to physical punishment corresponds also to their otherness in religion. Just as wrong belief determined one's liability to torture in the afterlife, it also determined one's liability to slavery here and now. The torture of slaves largely focused on ethnic and religious others because Judaism, Christianity, and Islam forbade the enslavement of their fellow believers. Thus religious differences came to provide a rationale for damnation, the ultimate othering.[98] In addition, lifetime suffering, including torture, imposed on slaves strongly influenced images of postmortem retribution. Therefore, wrong religion made one liable to both enslavement here on earth and damnation in the otherworld.

---

98. See Orlando Patterson, *Slavery and Social Death* (Cambridge, MA: Harvard University Press, 1982), 43–44; cited in Benjamin Braude and Marie-Pierre Gaviano, "Race, esclavage et exégèse entre islam, judaïsme et christianisme," in *Annales: Histoire, Sciences Sociales* 57.1 (2002): 93–125, at 113.

None of the three rival, monotheistic religions opposed slavery, though each sought to prevent believers from enslaving their coreligionists or selling them as slaves to members of another group.[99] These statements assimilate the nonbeliever and the slave. If each religion protected its own from slavery, then only nonbelievers could be slaves. Jews could own fellow Jews, but that servitude was limited to six years (Exod. 21:2 and Deut. 15:12). Observance of this restraint was worse than spotty, however, as the prophet Jeremiah excoriates the Jews of his day for not following the law.[100] In Leviticus 25:39–55 the prohibition is even more stringent. No Jew may enslave another Jew: "The people of Israel" are slaves of God. They are his! (verse 55; cf. verse 42). Christians were not supposed to enslave Christians nor were Muslims to enslave Muslims.[101] Legislators did not permit others to own members of their own group. Constantine prohibited Jews from owning Christian slaves.[102] Muslims also regulated ownership of Jewish or Christian slaves. They embraced Jews and Christians as members of their own group but with a diminished status. Because Muslims regarded Jews and Christians as earlier recipients of the prophecy that culminated in Muhammad's recitation, they did not consider them outright nonbelievers. They called them Children of the Book, and offered them a special protection (dhimma). In return for this protection, a dhimmi paid a special tax called the jizya. One consequence of dhimmi status was that these people could not, in principle, be enslaved by Muslims.[103]

All three religions included reasons for, or examples of, merciful behavior toward slaves. Traditions concerning Muhammad show him both obtaining

---

99. Toni Oelsner and Henry Wasserman, "Slave Trade," in Enyclopaedia Judaica, 18:670–71. Hezser, Jewish Slavery in Antiquity, 10, 22, going beyond the religious classification, observes that the Romans, too, saw slavery as incompatible with Roman citizenship.

100. Jeremiah 34:8–16; cited by Haim Hermann Cohn, "Slavery," in Encyclopaedia Judaica, 18:667–70, at 668. See also the even more absolute prohibition in Lev. 25:39–46, which nonetheless allows Jews to enslave non-Jews at verse 45.

101. For Christians, see the secular legislation cited in McCormick, Origins, 740 n. 57, and, for papal alarm over frequent violation, 748 n. 79. It is clear that Christian merchants sold Christians outside the political boundaries of Christian lands, that is, to Muslims, and, using Jewish intermediaries, they sell Christian slaves to other Christians (that is, Venetians, for eventual transfer to Muslim owners) (766). For Muslims, see Elizabeth Savage, A Gateway to Hell, a Gateway to Paradise: The North African Response to the Arab Conquest, Studies in Late Antiquity and Early Islam 7 (Princeton, NJ: Darwin Press, 1997), 67–87, at 75.

102. CTh 16.9.1; but cf. 16.9.2, also 3, 4, and 5.

103. For the incentives to expand the status of dhimmi, see Yohanan Friedmann, "Classification of Unbelievers in Sunnī Muslim Law and Tradition," Jerusalem Studies in Arabic and Islam 22 (1998): 163–95, at 167.

and releasing slaves.[104] The parables of Jesus endorse charitable treatment of the least fortunate in the community. In addition to the parable about the unmerciful slave, there is the statement in the parable of the sheep and the goats, in which Jesus sums up the criteria for assignment to either eternal punishment or eternal life on behalf of "the least" of his brethren (Matt. 25:40, 45, 46). The philosopher Maimonides, writing at the turn of the thirteenth century, epitomized a Jewish perspective on the same issue by quoting Job's thoughts on the master's relationship to the slave (Job 31:13). It should be modeled on the relationship the pious person hopes to have with God: "If I did despise the cause of my man-servant or maid-servant when they contended with me, what then shall I do when God riseth up? And when He remembereth what shall I answer?'"[105] In other words: treat your servant the way you wish your Lord to treat you.

In principle, then, slavery was permissible if structured according to the believer's own relationship to God, according to one's own religious law. It was the Muslim relationship to the tradition of prophets from Moses through Jesus and including Job that protected the *dhimmis*. Despite the qualification of the *dhimmis*, however, the statement holds: all three of the Abrahamic religions prohibited enslavement of their own people, but allowed ownership of slaves taken from outside their own communities. These communities were defined by religious identity. Therefore, the same people who were liable to damnation for nonbelief were also liable to enslavement for the same reason.

---

104. For example, under "manumission of slaves" in Sahih Bukhari at ahadith.co.uk (especially hadith 703) and www.searchtruth.com (hadith 693) both accessed Dec. 16, 2016. See also Irene Schneider, "Freedom and Slavery in Early Islamic Times (1st/7th and 2nd/8th centuries)," *Al-Qanṭara* 28.2 (July–December 2007): 353–82, at 355. Schneider observes important limits to the extent of slavery in Islam. One is not enslaved for debt or for crime. For an overview of slavery in Islam, see Jonathan E. Brockopp, "Slaves and Slavery," in *Encyclopaedia of the Qur'ān*, ed. Jane Dammen McAuliffe, Brill Online, accessed May 14, 2011; Brockopp, "Slaves and Slavery," in *Encyclopaedia of the Qur'ān*, ed. McAuliffe (Leiden: Brill, 2001–6), 5:56b-60b. See also Antoine Fattal, *Le statut légal des non-musulmans en pays d'Islam* (Beirut: Imprimerie Catholique, 1958), 149–50; and the website http://www.jewish virtuallibrary.org/jsource/History/legislation300_800.html, accessed May 13, 2011, which correctly omits the provision that Fattal attributes to Charlemagne. Adel Khoury, *Toleranz im Islam* (Kaiser: Grünewald, 1980), 167–68.

105. As quoted by Cohn, "Slavery," 670. The modular quality of the analogy between the slave master and God emerges in the discussion by Hezser, *Jewish Slavery in Antiquity*, 23 and 346–50. In addition to the contributions of the book of Exodus and the Hebrews' escape from Egyptian slavery in shaping Jewish identity, Hezser points to the "slave parables" in rabbinic literature and midrashic texts, where a king will stand in for God (as in the parables in the *Tanna debe Eliyyahu*, below, chapter 7). Job 31:13 may be compared to Prov. 21:13 and Luke 16:19–31. For an even broader study, see Ignaz Ziegler, *Die Königsgleichnisse des Midrasch beleuchtet durch die römische Kaiserzeit* (Breslau: Schottlaender, 1903).

Besides the doctrines of Gregory I and monastic inner death, examined in chapters 1 and 2, slavery is the third pillar of this book's part I on the foundations of belief in hell.

The physical torment that threatens both slaves and the damned is present in the Bible, but it is brought to a poignant culmination in the visionary literature. The Bible often opposes the freedom of the righteous to the slavery of the sinner. Romans 6:16 contrasts the "slaves of . . . sin, which leads to death" to the "[slaves] of obedience, which leads to righteousness"; John 8:34 quotes Jesus: "Anyone who commits sin is a slave to sin." Tautologically, the slave to justice would obey every one of its dictates. Conversely, sin would entail the punishments the secular law meted out for disobedience, rebellion, or contumacy. These punishments and many of the physical torments in ancient criminal law applied to insubordination at all levels: on the smallest scale, in the household as defiance of father or master; on the political scale, as disobedience to the king; and, on the cosmic level, as scorn of God. This common parallel between the slave owner as lord (*kurios, dominus*), the secular ruler as lord, and God as Lord creates a modular analogy that standardizes relationships within the household (*familia*), the city, the royal or imperial regime and God's cosmic rule that represses all rebellion as contumacy requiring endless punishment.[106] If criminal executions cannot be regarded as the source of infernal punishments because the death penalty puts an end to suffering, they nonetheless apply in one important regard: execution resubordinates the condemned criminal. The convicts' lives are subject to the authority that ends them. A greater authority, such as that of a slave owner over a slave, is that which can impose any physical pain at any time on any body. This subjection is greater because it is arbitrary and endless. The slave's liability to torture lasts not only for his or her lifetime, but beyond, because the child of a slave mother inherits her status. In this sense, the slave's liability to torture becomes hereditary and, therefore, interminable.

---

106. Keith Bradley puts it like this: "The absolute authority commanded by the object of worship over the worshipper was precisely the same as that commanded by the earthly slaveowner over the slave, while the powerless subjection of the worshipper before God was exactly the same as that characterising the earthly slave's relationship to his owner." Bradley, *Slavery and Society at Rome*, 151. A related and functionally similar modular relationship emerges from the very different metaphor by which Pliny referred to the relationship between the slaves and their owners, in the household, as a *res publica*, an image of a city within a city: "The household provides slaves with a country and a sort of citizenship" (*servis res publica quaedam et quasi civitas domus est*). Pliny, *Letters* 8.16.1–3, trans. B. Radice, LCL; cited in Joshel, *Slavery in the Roman World*, 112, 128. On this theme, see William Fitzgerald, "The Continuum of (Servile) Relationships," in *Slavery and the Roman Literary Imagination* (Cambridge: Cambridge University Press, 2000), 69–86.

As Augustine observed, it is not religion that innovated in creating endless punishment. Even he invoked human institutions in defense of divine declarations. Paul also explained his own frame of reference in terms of the relationship between "human terms" (Rom. 6:19) and higher truths. Therefore, it is no historian's distortion to say that the torments of hell put forward in religious texts incorporate suffering that blends with the penal institutions of the surrounding culture. More particularly, the legal model for the condition of the damned is not the experience of execution for a capital crime but the perpetual liability to torture of antiquity's most despised others, the slaves.

PART II

Alternatives to Hell

CHAPTER 4

Exceptions to Hell

Relief and Escape

> Then I understood that he had been transferred out
> of the punishment.
>
> —*Passion of Perpetua*
>
> The refreshment of this one day is more valuable to
> us than all the time of our lives, when we were on
> earth.
>
> —*Apocalypse of Paul*

If hell's torments even subliminally evoked the
torture of slaves—the first revealed or inferred from Scripture, the second
witnessed directly—it is small wonder that some, mindful of equity in law and
mercy in religion, should propose alternative scenarios. Gregory I attempted
to devise explanations that could permeate the church from the top down and
create a single orthodoxy for all Catholics. Despite his efforts, a wide range
of thinkers expressed profound ambivalence regarding the idea of eternal
damnation and devised alternatives that survived for centuries in the Latin
church. These are the subject of part II of this book. Recovering underground
currents within the Christian tradition requires some versatility in discovering
and interpreting different types of sources. Unlike the extensive and explicit
expositions of Augustine in the *City of God* and Gregory in his *Dialogues* or
his commentary on Job,[1] authoritative authors whose major works are well
represented in manuscript traditions, the ideas that demonstrate ambivalence
about hell are rarer, more dispersed, and differ more from one another. The
excavation required to uncover ambivalence about or opposition to hell is
no indication of the significance of those ideas. The visions, miracle stories,

---

1. See Augustine, *The City of God*, book 21; and Alan E. Bernstein, *The Formation of Hell: Death
and Retribution in the Ancient and Early Christian Worlds* (Ithaca, NY: Cornell University Press, 1993),
314–33; for Gregory, see above, chapter 1.

saints' lives, letters, and anecdotes gathered here fully warrant collection, reflection, and synthesis to reconstruct an unofficial history.

Of these countercurrents, the first is mitigation: the torments of hell can be interrupted, and periodic relief given to the damned. This idea occurred in Jewish speculation as well as Christian and derives ultimately from Genesis 2:2–3, God's rest on the seventh day.[2] The reasoning is that if God rests, he does not punish. The Qur'ān also presents examples of softening hell's torments. Periodically, then, the punishment of the damned may be lightened or suspended. Second is an end to hell. Hell can end if sinners are rescued from it—not from Hades as in Christ's Descent, but from hell, the place of eternal torment. The underground current favoring the mitigation of hell existed for generations before Augustine derided its proponents as "soft-hearted," and its variations continued long after him.[3] Another end to hell appears in a related, third strand that combines Matthew 12:31–32 and 1 Corinthians 3:13–15, and presents the idea of forgiveness in the otherworld for some sins, but not the very worst, and explicitly not for blasphemy against the Holy Spirit. This is the option of therapeutic suffering, specifically through a fire that gradually purifies and then releases its sufferers to join the community of the saints. It was only in 1254 that Pope Innocent IV declared dogmatically that this curative fire occurred in a specific place to be called purgatory. These options differ markedly from the eternity and uniformity postulated in Latin theological writing, and strongly contradict the aggressive hell of inner death. In a pungent phrase, Jérôme Baschet calls this "a counterattack of mercy."[4] I postpone study of the calibrated, purgatorial fire to the next chapter. For now, it is sufficient to consider the first two types of resistance in order: the idea that there is periodic relief from torment within hell, and the idea that rescue is possible from hell.

Relief in Hell

One major challenge to the idea of hell attacked not its duration or the solidity of its walls, but the uniformity of its punishments. From an early period,

---

2. For the Jewish sources, see below, chapter 7.

3. Augustine, *Enchiridion de fide et spe et caritate* 29.112–13; CCSL 46 (1969): 108; *The Enchiridion on Faith, Hope, and Love*, trans. J. F. Shaw (South Bend, IN: Regnery/Gateway, 1961), 130–31. See Bernstein, *Formation*, 324–25.

4. Baschet's context is the later Middle Ages, but the insight is nonetheless valid. Jérôme Baschet, *Les justices de l'au-delà: Les représentations de l'enfer en France et en Italie (XIIe–XVe siècles)*, Bibliothèque des Écoles Françaises d'Athènes et de Rome 279 (Rome: École française de Rome, 1993), 547: "La miséricorde pousse plus loin encore son pouvoir."

evidence survives of an undercurrent favoring momentary relief within hell. The infernal holiday or sabbatical rest is one of the major cross-cultural themes to appear in late antiquity and the early Middle Ages. Continuing belief in a periodic interruption of hell's punishments reflects a widespread wish for a less harsh damnation. The comparatively small number of surviving instances of this theme known to me is far outweighed by its psychological power. Augustine knew of this current and ridiculed it in his *Tractates on the Gospel of John* (98:8), in the *City of God* (21.16–17), and in the *Enchiridion* (chapters 112–13). He considered it, as it were, "only *human*." In the end, this desire for relief from hell helped shape what would become the doctrine of purgatory, but that required a very gradual evolution. The recurrent manifestations of these emotions indicate a centuries-long protest against an absolute hell.

The *Apocalypse of Paul*

Although many texts testify to a hope that relief may be provided for the damned, the idea of a periodic reprieve in hell was most pervasively disseminated in one particular text, the *Apocalypse of Paul*. We have already examined this text to analyze its many detailed torments; here we consider the rest Christ grants the damned. The angel who guides Paul through the two levels of hell leads him from heaven across the ocean to "the souls of the wicked and the sinners" so that he might "know what *the place* is like."[5] The punishments here endure forever. After guiding Paul through a plain filled with torments described in detail, the angel promises he will show him tortures that are "seven times worse."[6] The sinners' double-tiered prison is not called "hell" but "the place" or "the punishments." Only when challenged at the covered entrance to the well that leads to the lower level does the angel insist that Paul is "to see all the punishments of *hell*" (ut uideat omnes penas *inferni*).[7] This is the only use of *infernus* to name "the place." Inside the well are Christians whose belief is not entirely orthodox, not those entirely independent of Christianity such as Jews or pagans, whose presence can only be inferred.[8] The fate of the inmates in this lower region moves Paul to sigh and weep. When the damned see this display of compassion, they pray directly to

---

5. "Veni et sequere me, et ostendam tibi animas impiorum et peccatorum, ut cognoscas qualis sit *locus.*" *Visio Pauli* §31; ed. Montague Rhodes James, in *AA*, p. 28; my emphasis. The text is translated by James in *ANT*, pp. 525–55, at 538–39; my emphasis. See Bernstein, *Formation*, 292–305, at 300.

6. *Visio Pauli* §40; *AA*, p. 33, line 35; *ANT*, p. 546.

7. Ibid. §41; *AA*, p. 34, lines 3–4; *ANT*, p. 546; my emphasis.

8. Jan Bremmer, "Christian Hell: From the *Apocalypse of Peter* to the *Apocalypse of Paul*," *Numen* 56 (2009): 298–325, at 314.

God for mercy. The heavens open, and the archangel Michael and the heavenly host descend into this lower level of hell where Paul stands among the damned. Michael scolds the prisoners and says he has been praying for them all along. The inmates give their excuses for ignoring God and refusing ever to repent. Together, Michael, all the angels, and Paul then pray that Christ pity humankind, his own image. Suddenly, accompanied by the twenty-four elders and the four beasts, the Son appears among the damned. The damned again pray, this time face-to-face with Christ.

These souls, already damned, who resisted religion and repentance all their lives, now, in hell, learn to pray. Neither their death nor their damnation prevents their change of heart. Even though it was primarily the harshness of the infernal prison that brought it about, so also did the nearness of the God they had spurned. At first, Christ rebuffs them; he rehearses the sins and impenitence of those "throughout the punishments."[9] But then, Christ grants the damned relief from their punishments! Both the long and the short versions include this dramatic scene, but different manuscript traditions divide over whether the pause in torment occurs weekly on Sunday or annually on Easter.

The Coptic text, as translated by R. P. Casey, reads, "I will give unto you rest upon the Lord's Day every week and during the fifty (*sic*) days which follow the [day of the] Resurrection, whereon I rose from the dead."[10] The long Latin text says, "On the very day on which I rose from the dead I grant to all of you who are in the punishments a day and night of rest for ever."[11] The Coptic text gives every Sunday *and* the fifty days from Easter on as periods of rest; the long Latin text leaves it ambiguous whether the *single* day is every Sunday or every Easter. Either possibility could be understood as the day Christ rose from the dead. This effort at clarification indicates a chronological span. Texts with ambiguity predate texts that choose either the weekly or the annual reprieve.

This technical point in no way obscures the psychological force of popular pressure for relief of the damned evident in the *Apocalypse of Paul*. But

---

9. *Visio Pauli* §44; *AA*, p. 36, lines 5–13; *ANT*, p. 548; H-S 2:788.

10. R. P. Casey, "The Apocalypse of Paul," *Journal of Theological Studies* 34 (1933): 1–32, at 18. The (*sic*) is Casey's. It is occasioned by the text's confusion of Ascension with Pentecost, which was generally considered to have been resolved by the late fourth century. By then, Ascension was celebrated on the fortieth day after Easter; Pentecost on the fiftieth. *EEC* 2:669 s.v. "Pentecost"; *ODCC*, 112–13, 1253, 1738, s.vv. "Ascension," "Pentecost," and "Whitsunday." Liturgists may find here a clue for dating the *Apocalypse of Paul*.

11. "The day on which I rose from the dead" is ambiguous and could mean either Sunday or Easter. Later, however, the malign angels complain that the damned have just received "magnam gratiam nocte et die dominice refrigerium" (this great grace, even refreshment for the night and day of the Lord's day), which indicates Sunday. *Visio Pauli* §44; *AA*, p. 36; *ANT*, p. 549.

there is a corollary: this periodic relief in hell resulted from prayers for the damned, beginning with Paul's sigh, including a crescendo added by the heavenly hosts, and remarkably including the pleas of the damned on their own behalf. In the long Latin version, Christ offers reasons for this great boon. He does this "out of love for Paul . . . and for those of your brothers who remain on earth and make their offerings (*oblaciones*) and, more, because of my own goodness."[12] These reasons are crucial: Christ's own goodness, Paul's intercession, and the living on earth who "make their offerings." The prayers of survivors on behalf of the dead, even though damned, are added to the explicitly mentioned prayers of the damned themselves, to become factors in this remarkable act of grace. After hearing Christ's words on the floor of hell, the damned declare in unison: "The refreshment of this one day is more valuable to us than all the time of our lives, when we were on earth."[13] By cataloguing the infernal torments and narrating this remarkable solution, the *Apocalypse of Paul* simultaneously publicized hell's terrors and the hope of temporary relief. This and other factors came to make prayers to ease afterlife pain a major theme in the history that follows.

Prudentius in the *Cathemerinon*

Another example of aspiration for the annual reprieve in hell occurs in the *Cathemerinon*, hymns 4 and 5, by the Spanish poet Prudentius (348–ca. 410). Prudentius praises God for his rescue of the Hebrews out of Egypt, the three boys from the fiery furnace, and Daniel from the lion's den, and then alludes to the liberation of humankind from death. In reference to the Descent as an aspect of the Resurrection, Prudentius suggests that in so great an inversion of life over death, even those still bound in Tartarus enjoy a weakening of its torments at Easter:

> On that night when holy God returned from the swamps of Acheron to the heavenly regions, there is a season of rest beneath the Styx from the punishments the often hurting spirits endure. . . . The regions of Tartarus grow weak, their torments soften, and the people of the shadows, free of the fires, taunt their useless prison as the rivers of brimstone lose their accustomed rage.[14]

---

12. *Visio Pauli* §44; *AA*, p. 36, lines 15–18; *ANT*, p. 548.
13. Ibid., lines 22–24; *ANT*, p. 549.
14. "Sunt et spiritibus saepe nocentibus/ poenarum celebres sub Styge feriae / illa nocte sacer qua rediit deus / stagnis ad superos ex Acherunticis. . . . Marcent supliciis tartara mitibus / exsultatque sui carceris otio / umbrarum populus liber ab ignibus / nec feruent solito flumina sulp[h]ure.

These lines by Prudentius made their way into some liturgical books and were recited as prayers for the mitigation of hell's pains. A Paris manuscript (BNF Lat. 12048, ff. 249v–250v) that contains the Sacramentary of Gellone, from which many copies and variations derive, dates from the second half of the eighth century. It includes a mass sung for "those whose soul is in doubt." The text refers to the underworld (*inferi*) rather than hell proper, but the prayers ask that the soul's torments be made more tolerable, borrowing the language from Augustine's *Enchiridion*.[15] Despite the use of *inferi*, it is clear that if the dead are suffering torments, the place is no longer the neutral underworld, but hell itself. These prayers would therefore aim to benefit those in hell.

The *Voyage of St. Brendan*

A combination of weekly and annual respites also appears in the *Voyage of St. Brendan*, an Irish tale whose text can be traced back to the tenth century, but which relates intervening legends surrounding a sixth-century personage.[16] In this tale, the intrepid monk and his companions undertake a grueling sea voyage of a type traditional in Irish literature, called the *imram*. They brave various adventures in sailing from island to island. One of these contains many forges whose blacksmiths throw gobs of slag at the monks, who seem to be driven there fatally by the wind. As they escape, all the forges seem to come together and produce a single, huge ball of fire that causes the surrounding water to boil. Even from a great distance the rowing monks hear the sounds of hammers on anvils and smell the stench. "Now we are near the mouth of hell," says Brendan to his men—a very aggressive hell, too.[17] At another stop, demons kidnap one of Brendan's monks, who is aflame even before he reaches his destination. Then the island-mountain

---

Cathemerinon 5.125–36; *Aurelii Prudentii Clementis Carmina*, ed. Mauricius Cunningham, CCSL 126 (1966), p. 27. The core of this story informs the vision of Odo and Peter Damian's account of the birds of Pozzuoli, below. See also Carozzi, *Le voyage*, 422.

15. A. Cabassut, "La mitigation des peines de l'enfer d'après les livres liturgiques," *Revue d'Histoire Ecclésiastique* 33 (1927): 65–70.

16. My analysis is based on the oldest surviving Latin version published as the *Vita et navigatio Sancti Brendani*, ed. W. W. Heist, in *Vitae sanctorum Hiberniae*, Subsidia Hagiographia 28 (Brussels: Société des Bollandistes, 1965). A convenient translation is found in Eileen Gardiner, *Visions of Heaven & Hell before Dante* (New York: Italica Press, 1989), 81–127. See also D. D. R. Owen, *The Vision of Hell* (Edinburgh and London, 1970), 22–24. For much of the relevant scholarship and a comprehensive examination of the crisscross of folkloric motifs and literary themes, see Dominik Pietrzik, *Die Brandan-Legende*, Bremmer Beiträge zur Literatur- und Ideengeschichte 26 (Frankfurt: Peter Lang, 1999); for Judas, see Pietrzik, 155–62.

17. *Vita et navigatio S. Brendani* §41, p. 71.

erupts like a pyre (or a volcano). Having left the island hell and its aggressive demons safely to the north, the monks encounter one of its notorious inmates.

In the midst of a dense fog, they see a man sitting on a rock beaten by the waves. In front of him a cloth that beats his face in the wind is suspended on two iron rods. When questioned by Brendan, the man identifies himself as Judas Iscariot, enjoying the cool of this storm, which seems to him a paradise compared to the cauldron of molten lead in the core of the undersea mountain, where he is usually confined along with Herod, Pilate, Annas, and Caiaphas. The image of a volcano is implicit here, an echo of the boat's previous adventure. Judas relates that the pit of his island is the dwelling of Leviathan, who, together with his satellites, rejoiced at the fate of the sailor kidnapped by the demons and sent forth huge flames of delight as he always does when he devours the souls of the wicked. (The voyage of Brendan shares this theme of hell as a devouring beast with some dramatic verses of the Qur'ān, notably 25:12 and 67:7–8.) Because of the mercy of Christ and in honor of his resurrection, Judas is allowed up on the wind-tossed, wave-battered surface of the rock during the periods from Christmas to Epiphany and from Easter to Pentecost, on all the feasts honoring Mary, and every week from Saturday evening until Sunday evening. At the request of the infamous betrayer, Brendan and his companions pray and obtain a further respite for Judas that lasts until Monday morning.[18]

Beyond divine mercy, there is a specific rationale for Judas's condition. Every aspect corresponds to one of his rare good deeds. The rock on which he sits is one he once moved into a gap in a Roman road, thus easing traffic. The cloth he once gave to a leper, but since it was not his to give, it acts to his detriment, by repeatedly striking him. The two iron rods he once gave to priests to support a kettle. This reappearance in the otherworld of implements, props, once used in this life is a theodicial theme I call "radical continuity." The *Voyage of St. Brendan* adds an important new element to the development of periodic reprieve. In addition to the rest on Christmas, Easter, and Sundays, based on the life of Jesus, Brendan's encounter with Judas teaches that the feasts of Mary also have their reverberations in the otherworld. That link becomes even more apparent in the next text, where it is Mary herself whose voyage to hell occasions the temporary remission of punishment for the damned.

---

18. Ibid., §43, p. 73.

The *Apocalypse of Mary*

A Middle Byzantine text of the period between the ninth century and the beginning of the eleventh purports to record what Mary saw when guided on a tour of the otherworld.[19] Famous for its extremely detailed descriptions of the torments, the text also stands out for portraying Mary's appeal to Jesus for mercy on the damned. Jesus grants this favor to his mother, but different versions express his accord differently. In the Greek manuscripts, Christ says that on behalf of his mother and the saints, he "grants you to have rest on the [fifty] days of the Pentecost to glorify the Father, the Son, and the Holy Spirit."[20] In an Ethiopic version, it is Jesus himself who acts as guide. After showing his mother the heavens and the beginnings of hell, he causes the doorkeepers of Gehenna to expose what is inside. The souls within, recognizing the visitor, praise her, and Mary, in turn, intercedes for them. "My son responded and said, 'I will have mercy [on them] for you from the evening of the sixth day of the week until the morning of the second day of the week.' And when I heard these words I gave thanks to my son, and the damned celebrated him with praise."[21] The release from punishment in this version would be from Saturday evening until Monday morning, thus framing the nights on either side of Sunday, or the equivalent of two days each week.

Besides offering a weekly rather than an annual reprieve, the Ethiopic version raises another point of interest. When Mary sees some who are horribly punished, she learns that they are nuns who conceived children after taking the veil and who destroyed them either before or after birth. After

---

19. Jane Baun entitles the text the *Apocalypse of the Holy Theotokos* and dates it to the eleventh century because its earliest witnesses are two eleventh-century manuscripts, which each offer a long recension. This must be the earliest version, she reasons, because later manuscripts progressively condense the text. Baun, *Tales from Another Byzantium: Celestial Journey and Local Community in the Medieval Greek Apocrypha* (Cambridge: Cambridge University Press, 2007), 386–400, at 387. See pp. 366–85 for Baun's suggestion that the text emerges from a less-than-elite type of confraternal, lay piety, specifically not monastic, and specifically addressing the "parochial," pastoral concerns of a popular audience. Martha Himmelfarb considers the punishments in detail in *Tours of Hell: An Apocalyptic Form in Jewish and Christian Literature* (1983; Philadelphia: Fortress Press, 1985), 100–104, 119–26, 178–79, and passim.

20. *Apocalypsis Mariae Virginis*, ed. James, in *AA*, pp. 109–26, at 126. In my analysis, section numbers and key terms are from James's Greek; the English translation is from Baun, *Tales from Another Byzantium*, 386–400. There are minor variations in Hubert Pernot, "La Descente de la Vierge aux enfers d'après les manuscrits grecs de Paris," *Revue des Études Grecques* 13 (1900): 233–57, at 237, 256.

21. Translated into Latin, the Ethiopic version reads: "[A] vesperis feriae sextae usque ad matutinum feriae secundae." *Apocalypsis seu Visio Mariae Virginis*, trans. Marius Chaîne, in *Apocrypha de B. Maria Virgine*, Corpus Scriptorum Christianorum Orientalium: Scriptores Aethiopici, 1.7 (Rome: Karolus de Luisi, 1909), 43–68, at 67–68. The connection of this text to the *Apocalypse of Paul* is so intimate that R. P Casey ("The Apocalypse of Paul," 4) considers it an adaptation of *Paul* §§13–44.

Jesus explains this cause of eternal punishment for the nun-mothers and the fathers, Mary asks whether he would pardon them. Christ will forgive them, he says, "if they atone in penance with trusting hearts."[22] These potential penitents are already dead and in hell. The same is true of those who, when they saw Mary examining their torments, praise her and then praise Christ for granting the intermission. As in *Paul*, the damned can repent, praise Mary, and praise Christ. A tradition existed, therefore, in which the damned could "find religion." They could express sentiments they had denied or repressed all their lives. The theological justification for this occurrence belongs in the context of Greek Orthodox Christianity, to be treated below; for now it is sufficient to observe how the damned can discover their piety posthumously.

The *Apocalypse of Mary* belongs in any discussion of pressure to diminish the pains of hell, but important qualifications apply. First, hell has different regions for those of different religions and those who committed particular sins. In a boiling black river, Mary sees Jews (the Ethiopic text singles out Muslims) and others (pagans) who refuse baptism. There also are those who abuse the ties of godparenthood for sexual exploitation, those who commit incest, women who kill babies, those who use the sword to kill, and sorcerers.[23] Later, Mary is taken to see a different part of hell where Christians are punished, for Christians can also commit these serious sins. Further, in the Greek manuscripts, Jesus does not accede to his mother's request without some bargaining. In the process, Mary allows that she does not seek mercy for all the damned, such as "unbelieving Jews," but only for Christians. It is possible that all Christians remain together, for those among the damned are "those who were baptized and swore allegiance to Christ in word, but did the deeds of the devil."[24] For these, too, Mary intercedes, reminding her Son that these are his people. "I will not forsake" those who have called on your name, he replies. It is assumed that this provision covers many (§§25–26). Seeking a broader commitment, Mary urges other saints to join in her plea. In terms reminiscent of Abraham's reply to the rich man in Luke 16, Christ rejoins that the Christians should have believed and followed the Scriptures. The debate continues. Christ says he will hear her plea for anyone who did not return evil for evil (§28). After Gabriel adds his voice (§28), Christ leaves his throne, descends to "those who were in the punishments," and, after

---

22. "Si cum corde confidente poenitentiam egerint, condonabo eis." Chaîne, *Apoc. Mariae*, 65; James, *ANT*, p. 564.

23. Baun, *The Apocalypse of the Holy Theotokos* §23; pp. 397–98.

24. Ibid., §24; p. 398.

itemizing all the wrongs they have done him, nonetheless concedes to all Christians an annual reprieve for the days (*tas hemeras*) of Pentecost (§29).

The *Apocalypse of Mary* derives from the *Apocalypse of Paul*, even though it attributes the deeds of Paul to Mary. In the process of transfer, the reprieve lengthened. One is tempted to remark that pressures against the absolute, unvarying hell continued to mount and can be measured in the number of days per year on which the damned receive exemption from punishment. So linear and quantified an approach would be wrong. Still, the differences in methods of counting and the varieties in the textual record themselves testify to the strength of a yearning for mitigation and the breadth of the oral tradition.

The Bird-Souls of Pozzuoli

Additional testimony concerning regular reprieve for the damned comes from the influential abbot and reformer Peter Damian (d. 1072), eventually a cardinal, who records a remarkable report he heard from Archbishop Humbert (of Silva Candida, also a future cardinal, d. 1061). When Humbert had been in Puteoli (now Pozzuoli), local people told him of a curious phenomenon in the region. Nearby, as Humbert informed Peter, there is a black lake, whose waters seem to exhale a fetid air beneath craggy, overhanging cliffs. At the time of vespers on Friday until sunrise on Monday, ugly little birds with human features ascend from the lake, extend their wings, plume their feathers, and disport themselves without restraint. Unlike others, these birds are never seen caught in birdlime or trapped in nets, no matter how cleverly set up. As Monday morning begins to dawn, a great crow resembling a vulture caws and herds them back below, and they are not seen again until the following Friday evening, when "they emerge again from the depths of the sulfurous lake."[25] On this basis, "some maintain that they are souls assigned to the avenging tortures of Gehenna, who are wracked for all the rest of the week. But to honor the glory of the Lord's resurrection, they get relief for the Lord's day and the day and night on either side."[26] Damian observes that these strange occurrences accord vaguely with the periodic relief in hell as explained by the poet Prudentius. When he mentioned Humbert's appar-

---

25. Peter Damian, Letter 72, in *Die Briefe des Petrus Damiani*, ed. Kurt Reindel, Die Briefe der deutschen Kaiserzeit, pt. 4 (Munich: MGH, 1993), vol. 2, p. 335, line 10.

26. "Unde nonnulli perhibent eas hominum esse animas ultricibus gehennae suppliciis deputatas. Quae nimirum reliquo totius ebdomadae tempore crutiantur, dominico autem die cum adiacentibus ultro citroque noctibus pro dominicae resurrectionis gloria refrigerio potiuntur." Letter 72, p. 335, lines 10–14.

ent confirmation of Prudentius, Desiderius, the abbot of Monte Cassino, replied he believed none of it. Later, when Damian was together with both the skeptical abbot and Cardinal Humbert, his source, they compared notes, and Humbert said, "I do not in fact defend the evidence for this allegation. Indeed, I only related what I have heard from the residents of that place."[27]

Humbert, then, learned this story from the locals. The area adjacent to Pozzuoli includes Cuma, once believed to be the home of the Cumean Sybil, important in Greek and Roman mythology. Between Cuma and Pozzuoli is Lake Averno, famous in Virgil's *Aeneid* (6.239–42). The groves on its banks concealed the Golden Bough, which served Aeneas as ticket to the underworld. The waters of this lake emit so great a stench that birds can not fly across it. Hence, Virgil says, the Greeks called it Aornum (Without Birds).[28] The mouth of the Cumean Sibyl's cave was the starting point, as she guided Aeneas through the underworld to meet his father. On her altar, Aeneas, the Trojan emigrant, founder of Rome, invoked Hecate, infernal Juno, and Pluto (Dis), king of the Styx. The local lore that Humbert told Peter Damian concerning the weekly release of souls from hell, up through Lake Avernus, is not just a random invention. Its location and its cultic associations evoke ancient memories. Beyond that, its mention of a reprieve from hell shows that this belief spread across the Mediterranean and endured until at least the mid-eleventh century. What Humbert learns from local informants in Pozzuoli, that birds escape the depths of a nearby lake connected to the underworld, in honor of the Resurrection, is a Christian overlay on a very ancient myth. Whether in Humbert's oral report or Peter's written account, the influence of Virgil is manifest, but whether it is competition with pagan culture in its highest literary expression or residual folk belief, the ability of condemned souls to escape the inky water in honor of the Resurrection and fly about in freedom wins out over an absolutely uniform damnation. The biblical hell takes a back seat to a periodic relief for lost souls. Some damned souls periodically escape hell's torments!

Escape from Hell

In addition to the idea that the pains of the damned could abate at certain intervals, there was also a durable undercurrent of belief in the possibility

27. "Ego quidem huius allegationis testimonium non defendo, verumtamen hoc simpliciter retuli, quod ab accolis loci illius audivi." Letter 72, p. 336, lines 3–5.

28. See the commentary on the sixth book of Virgil's *Aeneid* by R. G. Austin (Oxford: Clarendon Press, 1977), 109 (on lines 239ff.). For Virgil and the history of belief in hell, see Bernstein, *Formation*, 61–73.

of escape from hell. The prayers of others were the primary means of gaining release from the infernal prison.[29] The first example of a pious person praying another from punishment may predate the quotation from Minucius Felix that opens chapter 1 and does precede that of Cyprian.

Perpetua's Prayer for Her Unbaptized Brother

The passion narrative of Vibia Perpetua (martyred 203) relates, mostly in her own words, the experience of a young Roman woman pregnant and imprisoned together with a group of other catechumens for failure to make a sacrifice according to imperial orders. While in prison she has a pair of visions in which she sees her brother Dinocrates, who had died at age seven from an illness that left his face covered with gangrene. She sees him exit from a "dark place."[30] Showing his scabby face, he approaches a font full of water whose rim was above his reach. As the parable of the rich man and Lazarus presents an abyss between those in shelter and those in torment, so here a gap separates Dinocrates from his sister, and he is denied access to the refreshing water. In the time following this apparition, Perpetua prays for Dinocrates and eventually sees him appear again in the same landscape, but he is clean, a scar replaces his wound, the rim of the font is lowered, and a golden bowl placed on the rim allows him to drink. Perpetua interprets the second apparition as proof that Dinocrates has been released from punishment: "Then I understood that he had been transferred out of the punishment."[31] Perpetua is still alive when she prays for her brother, so her story illustrates the efficacy of prayer by the living for the dead and, particularly, their ability to end afterlife punishment. When, as a martyr, she becomes a saint, she retains that power. Because Perpetua was the first in her family to adopt Christianity, Dinocrates died without baptism.[32] The text does not call the "dark place" of the unbaptized, hell, but her ability to move him to the fountain suggests that she not only ended his punishment, but also opened to him the benefits of accepting her faith.

---

29. For this topic, see Marcia Colish, "The Virtuous Pagan: Dante and the Christian Tradition," in *The Unbounded Community: Conversations across Times and Disciplines*, ed. Duncan Fisher and William Caferro (New York: Garland, 1996), 43–91. Colish discusses Thecla, Perpetua, Brendan, and, because he ends up in Dante's *Paradiso*, Trajan.

30. "De loco tenebroso ubi et conplures erant." *Passio Perpetuae* 7.4; ed. H. Musurillo, *The Acts of the Christian Martyrs* (Oxford: Clarendon Press, 1972), 106–30, at 114–15; English translation in Elizabeth Alvilda Petroff, ed., *Medieval Women's Visionary Literature* (New York and Oxford: Oxford University Press, 1986), 70–77.

31. *Passio Perpetuae* 8.4, pp. 116–17.

32. The saintly can pray non-Christians out of hell. See Jeffrey A. Trumbower, *Rescue for the Dead: The Posthumous Salvation of Non-Christians in Early Christianity*, Oxford Studies in Historical Theology (Oxford: Oxford University Press, 2001). Dinocrates was a "dead pagan." See Trumbower, 76, 84.

Thecla and the Beasts

A similar case, also stressing the power of a woman at prayer over hell, is less explicit. In Seleucia, near the southern coast of present-day Turkey, Paul's convert and close companion Thecla is condemned to the beasts, but the prominent matron Tryphaena, whose own daughter Falconilla has just died, befriends her. In a dream, Falconilla asks her mother to accept Thecla in her place so "that she may pray for me and I be translated to the place of the just." Tryphaena asks Thecla to pray for Falconilla so "that she may live." Thecla prays that "her daughter Falconilla may live for ever." Before entering the arena, Thecla again prays that God "reward Tryphaena" for her compassion. After Thecla remains impervious to the beasts' attacks, she explains her faith to the governor in charge of the games. "Whoever does not believe in him shall not live, but die for ever": this last phrase counterbalances the boon Thecla requested for Falconilla, namely, that she live forever. Yielding to the pressure of Tryphaena and the women in the arena seats, whose growing support for Thecla is a major factor in the narrative, the governor releases Thecla. Hearing the news, Tryphaena greets Thecla and declares, "Now I believe that the dead are raised up! Now I believe that my child lives!" To be sure, the narrator is in complete sympathy with Tryphaena, yet the text makes no claim outside the charitable pagan matron's declaration of belief that her daughter has been transferred from eternal death to eternal life.[33] By contrast, Perpetua makes that claim for Dinocrates via her own dream narrated by herself.

The *Apocalypse of Peter*

In these two examples, named persons renowned for their piety, have achieved remarkable rescues through prayer. The belief was actually broader. Some believed unnamed saints, people among the ordinary saved, have the ability to rescue people of their choosing from damnation. As we have seen, the *Apocalypse of Peter* is a second-century text famous for its detailed catalogue of sins and the corresponding infernal torments. In this text, after Christ shows the apostles the nature of the postmortem punishment that will afflict the wicked, he turns to the rewards of the saved. One boon associated with salvation is the ability to bring about the rescue of specific people in the torments. A single Greek fragment of the *Apocalypse of Peter* preserved in

---

33. The narrative is from the "Acts of Paul and Thecla," in H-S 2:353–64. For analysis, see the introduction to that text, H-S 2:322–51; and Trumbower, *Rescue for the Dead*, 66–70. One conclusion the story teaches, concludes Trumbower (70): "Thecla has the power to rescue even a dead polytheist like Falconilla."

the Rainer collection in Vienna reads, "Then I shall give unto my called and my chosen whomsoever they shall ask me for, out of torment, and will give them a fair baptism in (or unto) salvation from the Acherusian Lake which men [say is] in the Elysian Field, (even) a portion of righteousness with the holy ones."[34] Though this statement has only been located in this one fragment, there is a parallel in the *Second Sibylline Oracle*, which reads, "To these pious ones the imperishable God, the universal ruler, will also give another thing. Whenever they ask the imperishable God to save men from the raging fire and deathless gnashing he will grant it, and he will do this. For he will pick them out again from the undying fire and set them elsewhere and send them on account of his own people to another eternal life with the immortals in the Elysian plain where he has the long waves of the deep perennial Acherusian lake."[35]

These two texts differ in that the Sibylline text distinguishes two separate dwellings for those originally saved and those brought out through their intervention, but Jeffrey Trumbower rightly observes an essential similarity. As in the accounts of Perpetua's prayers for Dinocrates and Thecla's for Falconilla, individual saved persons are able to intercede and end the damnation of people for whom they request it. In these texts, one's eternal fate is not sealed at death; intercession by saints is able to extract certain of the wicked from their initial damnation even after judgment would seem to have been made. Moreover, the beneficiaries of these prayerful intercessions are not Christians; they are pagans, polytheists, and lack Christian faith altogether.[36]

The *Vision of Paul*, R 6

These beliefs continued into the late eighth or early ninth century, at least.[37] We have seen how the *Vision of Paul* claims temporary but regular relief for the damned in the lowest portion of hell. But the complex manuscript tradition of this text preserves a particular turn in one version of the tale, known

---

34. Trumbower, *Rescue for the Dead*, 50–51, cites the Rainer fragment of the *Apocalypse of Peter*, in H-S 2:679 n. 3. The original Latin is in M. R. James, "The Rainer Fragment of the Apocalypse of Peter," *Journal of Theological Studies* 32 (1931): 270–79. For the *Sibylline Oracle*, see H-S 2:718–19.

35. The translation is by J. J. Collins, "The Development of the Sibylline Tradition," in *Aufstieg und Niedergang der römischen Welt* 2.20.1, ed. Wolfgang Haase (1987), 442; cited by Trumbower, *Rescue for the Dead*, 52; H-S 2:718.

36. Trumbower, *Rescue for the Dead*, 50–52, 85.

37. See Dimitris J. Kyrtatas, "The Origins of Christian Hell," *Numen* 56.2–3 (2009): 282–97, who takes these references as the original Christian belief. He makes no reference to Redaction 6.

as Redaction 6 (or R 6, for short).[38] Aside from the two oldest manuscripts of the *Apocalypse of Paul*, which date from the ninth and tenth centuries,[39] there are summaries that Theodore Silverstein, the pioneer in this research, identified as falling into nine classes of "Redactions" (R 1–9). As condensations of *Paul*, they preserve only the infernal tour and omit Paul's own ascension, the two trials in heaven, and Paul's return there. Some scholars distinguish between the *Apocalypse of Paul*, which preserves the whole, and the *Vision of Paul*, which presents only the journey to hell. There are three versions of the long Latin text, and only two of its manuscripts date from the ninth century. The surviving manuscripts of the nine redactions date from the twelfth century or later. Only R 6 dates from our period.[40] The best surviving manuscript of R 6, at the monastic library of Saint Gall in Switzerland, nonetheless presents a corrupt and lacunary text possibly because it was copied from an earlier exemplar in a script unfamiliar to the scribe (see the frontispiece to this book).[41] The surviving manuscript was executed in the early or mid-ninth century, but affinities between the sins punished in this hell and offenses condemned in contemporary ecclesiastical legislation suggest to Claude Carozzi a date for the redaction itself closer to 745 or 750.[42]

As presented in R 6, Paul's tour of hell has a very different ending from that in the full *Apocalypse of Paul* or the other condensations that make up the *Vision of Paul*. Instead of sighing about the fate of the worst of the damned, Paul asks, "Where are my parents?" As is clear from the story of Paul's own conversion in Acts 9, his parents were Jews. Raphael, who is his guardian

---

38. Theodore Silverstein, *Visio Sancti Pauli: The History of the Apocalypse in Latin together with Nine Texts*, Studies and Documents 4 (1935; London: Christophers, 1955); henceforth HAL 9. Silverstein introduces the text at 58–59, interprets it at 82–90, and edits it at 214–18. See also Lenka Jiroušková, *Die Visio Pauli: Wege und Wandlungen einer orientalischen Apokryphe im lateinischen Mittelalter* (Leiden: Brill, 2006), 918–24. For analysis, see Carozzi, *Le voyage*, 263–79; Isabel Moreira, *Heaven's Purge: Purgatory in Late Antiquity* (Oxford: Oxford University Press, 2010), 132–34 and notes on 256. See also Theodore Silverstein, "The Vision of Saint Paul: New Links and Patterns in the Western Traditions," *Archives d'Histoire Doctrinale et Litteraire du Moyen Age* 26 (1959): 199–248; henceforth NLP.

39. Paris, NAL 1631, ff. 2vb–25vb (ninth c.); Saint Gall, MS 317, ff. 56–68 (ninth c.); Escorial, Codex a.II.3, ff. 154ra–157rb (tenth c.). See Theodore Silverstein and Anthony Hilhorst, *Apocalypse of Paul: A New Critical Edition of Three Long Latin Versions* (Geneva: Patrick Cramer, 1997), 23–31. Claude Carozzi in consultation with Jean Vézin dates Paris, NAL 1631 (which Carozzi calls "Fleury" after the monastery that was its original home) as perhaps late tenth or early eleventh century. Carozzi, *Eschatologie et au-delà: Recherches sur l'Apocalypse de Paul* (Aix-en Provence: Université de Provence, 1994), 181.

40. Silverstein, HAL 9, 41–59, estimates the dates of the MSS containing the nine redactions and dates two MSS (one only a fragment containing the beginning) of R 6 as ninth century. See also the dates assigned to the relevant MSS in Jiroušková, *Die Viso Pauli*, 29–35.

41. The manuscript is visible online at http://www.e-codices.unifr.ch/en/csg/0682/; pp. 193–204.

42. Carozzi, *Le voyage*, 270.

angel in this version, answers, "They are paying interest in hell" (*in infernum usurantur*).[43] When Paul hears that his parents are in hell he weeps and prays: "May the merciful God permit me to enter hell (*intrare in inferno*) on account of my parents." He throws himself upon it (*super inferno*), or perhaps on a door in its roof or, as in the long Latin version, on the lid of the well that permits entrance, so that he might pass through and visit his parents. The area he would enter is the lower hell. The term "hell" (*infernus*) is not used in R 6 before this point, but here, with five uses in one paragraph, the text refers to the hell that punishes wrong belief. In the *Vision of Paul* tradition, the place where errors of belief are punished is below the well, in the lower hell. Seldom have these visions or tours of hell referred, even indirectly, to Jews or other non-Christians. R 6 is exceptional in this respect.

In reply to Paul's plea, God said, "Let them receive grace. I am open (*spatiosus*) and greatly merciful, and I have been merciful to you." The climactic sentence that follows conceals a lacuna because it begins with Christ speaking in the first person to Paul and ends in a third-person account that describes the action. Broken down into its mangled parts, it seems to read as follows: "The Lord said to Saint Paul, 'your parents [that is, those related to you] up to the ninth degree [of consanguinity] have been sent for to the farthest borders,'" . . . then a garbled phrase . . . ,[44] then a recapitulation in the third person: "who drew the parents of Saint Paul from hell" (*qui parentes sancti Pauli traxerunt de inferno*). The gist of this passage seems to be that Christ sent messengers to gather Paul's family and extract them from hell, even from its farthest corners. With this conclusion, R 6 departs markedly from the long Latin version. The general population of hell receives no relief. Christ grants no weekly reprieve for the worst of the damned and removes only Paul's family from hell.[45] The idea that someone who is saved can name people to be rescued from the punishments occurs in only one line of a fragmentary version of the *Apocalypse of Peter* and a poetic paraphrase of

---

43. Carozzi, *Le voyage*, 267, says *urantur* is meant. There is no reason why *usurare*, a verb based on the idea of usury, cannot parallel *dare* (as in "quomodo hoc enim *dant*") to indicate the payment one makes for one's sins, as in retribution. Silverstein, HAL 9, 89, connects usury (from *usurare*) to wealth and the statement "It is easier for a camel to pass through the eye of a needle than for a rich man to enter the kingdom of God" (Matt. 19:24; Mark 10:25; Luke 18:25).

44. Here there occurs a lacuna or mangled phrase involving the camels referred to in the Gospel. The sentence survives as follows: "Certo tibi dico. parentes tuos usque ad nono genuculo missus est camelos in euangelio uocatur finis multis qui parentes sancti pauli. traxerunt de inferno." For *nono genuculo*, the camels, and other difficulties with this passage, see Carozzi, *Le voyage*, 268–69. By some folkloric metamorphosis these camels might be available for errands in hell. The gist of this mangled sentence is that some unnamed agents "extracted the family of Saint Paul from hell."

45. Carozzi, *Le voyage*, 268–69.

that text, the *Sibylline Oracle* 2:330–39.[46] These two isolated sentences have a common origin in the hope that salvation carries with it benefits for the saint's kindred or other loved ones.

This aspiration for release was not confined to escapes from hell in the Roman Mediterranean. The institution of slavery provided one context where the possibility existed of a higher authority graciously according liberation to chosen individuals. A further example of this psychology, already examined in the preceding chapter, occurred in the later fourth century when the Christian emperors, citing their imperial clemency, evoked a parallel between the prisons that confine criminals and the underworld where death had confined all humanity before Christ's coming. Drawing on the model of Christ's Descent into the underworld, they issued a limited amnesty, and ordered the release of low-level prisoners at Easter each year.

Clement in Germany

Could even more be rescued? The *Apocalypse of Peter* asserted the power of the ordinary saved to designate others for salvation, but ordinary believers might also hope for this kind of liberation. Evidence for this belief emerges from the correspondence of Boniface, the eighth-century Anglo-Saxon missionary. Born ca. 672–75 as Winfrid (or Wynfrid), at about age forty he began his missionary activities on the Continent where he attracted the attention of Charles Martel and his son, Pepin III (the Short), the Frankish Mayors of the Palace, and then of Pope Gregory II, who made him bishop. After studying and serving as a diplomat in Rome, he adopted the more latinate name of Boniface. Pope Gregory III made him archbishop of Mainz in 732. He founded the abbey of Fulda in 744. Boniface was famous for challenging the pagan rituals of the Saxons. According to his biographies, he felled with one stroke the great oak sacred to Thunor at Geismar and built a chapel with planks cut from its trunk. When opponents of his preaching killed him as he traveled through the salty marshes of Frisia, a freshwater spring arose on the spot where he expired. Some of his letters deplore the influence of a possibly Irish priest named Clement who insisted that at the time of Christ's Descent into the underworld (*ad inferos*), he liberated everyone, believers and unbelievers alike, whom hell's prison (*inferni carcer*) had held there. In response, Pope Zachary and his council in Rome condemned in 745 what must have seemed to them a purposeful exploitation of ambiguity in the

---

46. Trumbower, *Rescue for the Dead*, presents other occurrences of this theme (e.g., the cases of Perpetua and Thecla). He does not mention Redaction 6 of the *Vision of Paul*.

tradition about the Descent into Hades. Papal and missionary anxiety about this vagueness suggests considerable variation in popular belief as well as fear that Clement's teaching could gain widespread acceptance.[47] If Clement did preach that Christ freed all souls, righteous and unrighteous, believers and nonbelievers, from the lower hell, this would be a rare instance of universalism in the Latin West.[48] The different versions of the *Gospel of Nicodemus* indicate more interpretive leeway on this point than Boniface and Pope Zachary admitted.

Saint Patrick in Ireland

It may be questionable whether the wandering preacher Clement was Irish, but the connection to Ireland of another figure credited with liberating souls from hell is much clearer. Saint Patrick was born in Britain of a Christian father who was also a minor Roman official. He was kidnapped as a teen by pirates and taken to Ireland as a slave. After escaping some six years later, he received more formal Christian education in Gaul but returned to Ireland where he became bishop of Armagh. For the conversions he effected, he is considered the apostle of the Irish. The former slave Patrick had a particular interest in the otherworld—not only a saint's desire for heaven and the salvation of his fellows, but a particularly aggressive attitude toward hell. Earlier biographies are silent on this subject, but the *Tripartite Life of Patrick*, dated variously late ninth–early tenth century or late tenth–early eleventh century, attributes to him a hunger strike of forty days and forty nights when he bargained with an angel to win spiritual benefits for the Irish. Among the boons he obtained was that seven people should be removed out of hell every Thursday and twelve every Saturday.[49]

---

47. D-S no. 587. In Bonifatius and Lull, *Epistolae*, ed. Michael Tangl, MGH, Ep. Sel. 1 (Berlin: Weidmann, 1916), p. 112, lines 19–25; but cf. p. 118, lines 14–20; Boniface, *Letters*, trans. Ephraim Emerton Columbia University Records of Civilization (1940; New York: Norton, 1976), 96–106; for a brief analysis, see also Emerton's introduction, 14. For a particularly sensitive appreciation of the case, see Peter Brown, *Rise of Western Christendom*, 2nd ed. (Oxford: Blackwell, 2003), 421–22.

48. Boniface's letter characterizes Clement's teaching differently in two different passages. On p. 112, lines 19–25, he claims Clement preached that "in descending to the lower world, he liberated all whom the prison of hell (*inferni carcer*) confined, believers and unbelievers, those who worship God together with those who adore idols." Later in the same letter, at p. 118, lines 14–20, according to Boniface, Clement taught that "in descending to the underworld (*ad inferos*), he extracted all, whether believers or impious." Moreira notices the contradiction and observes the implication that Christ would then have liberated all from the *lower* hell. Moreira, *Heaven's Purge*, 189 and 274 n. 41.

49. On the ranges of dates estimated for the *Tripartite Life*, see Dagmar Bronner, "Codeswitching in Medieval Ireland: The Case of the *Vita Tripartita Sancti Patricii*," *Journal of Celtic Linguistics* 9 (2005): 1–12; Kenneth Jackson, "The Date of the Tripartite Life of St. Patrick," *Zeitschrift für celtische*

Trajan and Gregory

The most famous of all the liberated damned is the emperor Trajan, who ruled from 97 to 117. This celebrity comes from the fact that in Dante's *Divine Comedy*, the emperor is found in the constellation of the imperial eagle (*Paradiso* 20.106–7). Yet Trajan died a pagan, unbaptized and, one would think, destined for hell. Evidence for belief in his release comes in the first *Life* of Gregory I by an anonymous, early eighth-century monk of Whitby. Known and debated throughout the Middle Ages, versions of this story differ over whether Gregory actually prayed for the soul of the damned Trajan or whether he simply wept, and God, understanding the holy man's wish, deigned to grant it. According to the tale, Trajan was hastening out of Rome at the head of a military expedition when a widow stepped into the road in front of the troops and demanded that he render justice in the wrongful death of her son. Trajan excused himself and tried to avoid the issue, explaining the urgency of his mission. When the woman insisted on her right to be heard, and observed that Trajan could die in battle leaving this wrong uncorrected, he dismounted, tried the case, and found on her behalf.[50]

Centuries later, when Pope Gregory was walking through the Forum of Trajan, he regretted that so ardent a lover of justice should die a pagan. Remembering Trajan in his prayers at the Basilica of St. Peter, he heard that Trajan's soul had been spared the wracking of hell (*Trajani animam ab inferni cruciatibus liberatam*).[51] The second biographer of Gregory, John the Deacon, a late ninth-century monk, who wrote at the request of Pope John VIII,[52] observes that one does not read that the soul of Trajan was liberated from hell (*ab inferno*) at the prayers of Gregory and repositioned in paradise, but that Trajan's soul "was liberated only from the wracking (*cruciatibus*) of hell. . . . For the soul is able to exist in hell and, through the mercy of

---

Philologie 41 (1986): 5–45. For Irish eschatology, see Benjamin Hudson, "Time Is Short: The Eschatology of the Early Gaelic Church," in *Last Things: Death and the Apocalypse in the Middle Ages*, ed. Caroline Walker Bynum and Paul Freedman (Philadelphia: University of Pennsylvania Press, 2000), 101–23 and notes on 301–6.

50. *The Earliest Life of Gregory the Great by an Anonymous Monk of Whitby*, text, trans., and notes by Bertram Colgrave (Lawrence: University of Kansas Press, 1968), chap. 29, 127–29. See also Gordon Whatley, "The Uses of Hagiography: The Legend of Pope Gregory and the Emperor Trajan in the Middle Ages," *Viator* 15 (1984): 25–63.

51. John the Deacon, *Life of Gregory I*, PL 75:105B-C. Note that the earlier version, by the Monk of Whitby, says only that he prayed and wept "until he gained at last by divine revelation the assurance that his prayers were answered, seeing that he had never presumed to ask this for any other pagan" (trans. Colgrave).

52. Whatley, "Uses," 28.

God, not feel its wracking."[53] In his own *Dialogues*, Gregory himself explicitly opposes praying for the damned on the grounds that such prayers will have no merit in the eyes of God. The premise is that those in hell can no longer be changed. The prayers would be useless, and so, offensive to God.[54] Central to the uncertainty about the mechanics of sparing Trajan from the fate of pagans are questions about hell's holding power and the efficacy of prayers for the dead and, particularly, those presumably damned for unbelief. The different versions of the Trajan story support the notion that religious leaders can provide release from hell or relief within it for named beneficiaries. In the case of Trajan, to use Trumbower's phrase, this release is for "a dead pagan."

Wiborada

The story of Trajan gave shape to other tales of rescue from awkward connections between the world of the living and of the dead. For all the ambiguities of Trajan's situation as an unbaptized pagan, he at least lived as a man of probity. In the next source, the soul involved is that of an unbaptized infant, presumably innocent, but compromised (it was thought) by his parents. Saint Wiborada (Viborada) lived as a recluse adjacent to the monastery of St. Gall and was martyred during a raid by invading Magyars in 926. The first *Life* written ca. 960–970 by Hartmann omits this incident, but the second one of 1075 by Hepidannus includes it.[55] As the story makes clear, Wiborada's prestige allowed her to act as an arbiter among the townspeople in a way that cloistered religious could not. On one occasion she intervened in the case of a certain woman who bore a boy after committing adultery and, "adding sin to sin," drowned the child in a pond. To provide her with an opportunity for repentance, the people of the area tied her naked to a stake for public penance and, on feast days, allowed her to display herself as a penitent until, after a year, the blessed Wiborada called her and indicated that the curb (i.e., her punishment) had already been lifted, and pronounced the boy to be in a place of refreshment (*in refrigerium*). In later parlance, and if Wiborada had been male and a priest, she would have declared the woman absolved, as do the editors of the text. What is equally interesting is the ambiguous fate of the infant, who clearly had not been baptized, yet can be known to Wiborada as being *in refrigerium*. This phrase frequently describes those removed from hell or purgatory to a place of peace as opposed to punishment.

---

53. "Ab inferno solummodo cruciatibus liberata. . . . Valeat anima in inferno existere, et inferni cruciatus per Dei misericordiam non sentire." PL 75:105–6; Whatley, "Uses," 29 n. 14.

54. *Di.* 4.46.6–7. Cf. Augustine (*Civ. Dei* 21.18), who also responds to a rhetorical question about the saints praying for their enemies.

55. See Johannes Duft, ed., *Die Abtei St. Gallen*, vol. 2, *Beiträge zur Kenntnis ihrer Persönlichkeiten* (Sigmaringen: Jan Thorbecke, 1991), 175–81.

The narrative leaves the boy's condition open until the end. Immediately after reporting Wiborada's judgment, Hepidannus comments that what Wiborada did for the boy is "not dissimilar" to what Gregory I did for Trajan. He then proceeds to interpret the Trajan story in the manner of John the Deacon. Trajan was not liberated from hell proper, but from its wracking: "For a soul is able both to be in hell and, by God's mercy, not feel its pains."[56] Hepidannus implies that Wiborada similarly sheltered the murdered infant, who nonetheless remains in hell. Augustine had insisted on the damnation of unbaptized infants, but considered their damnation "the mildest of all." It would be wrong, he continued, to argue that they are not damned.[57] Moreover, in 418, the Council of Carthage anathematized anyone who would use John 14:2 ("In my Father's house are many rooms") to argue that heaven might include some special place of blessedness for infants who died without baptism, which alone can wash away original sin.[58] The narrative of Hepidannus assumes this position. Further discussion of this issue led to the doctrine of limbo only in the Scholastic period.[59] It is worth noting, however, that Augustine's concession that children who die without baptism, although damned, suffer only the slightest of punishments implies a gradation in postmortem penalties, a theme that will become more important as we proceed.

Martin of Tours Rescues Warrior Priests

Variations on the idea of rescues from hell seem to have accelerated between the time when Hartmann omitted the story of Wiborada in the late tenth century and Hepidannus included it in the late eleventh. The following incident can be dated with comparative precision after the Basilica of St. Martin at Tours had burned down in 988 and was reconstructed and reconsecrated in 1014. On this occasion, a holy man in Tours claimed to have overheard authorization

56. *Alia vita auctore Hepidanno Wiboradae martyris* 1.26, in *Acta Sanctorum*, May 2 (Antwerp, 1680), vol. 1, cols. 301D–302C. Arturo Graf, *Miti, leggende e superstizioni del medio evo* (1892–93; Milan: Mondadori, 1984), 163, compares this rescue to the one Perpetua accomplished for Dinocrates. Whatley, "Uses," does not mention this application of John the Deacon's interpretation.

57. Augustine, *De peccatorum meritis et remissione, et de baptismo parvulorum* 1.16.21, line 20; CSEL 60, ed. Karl Franz Urba and Joseph Zycha (Vienna: Tempsky, 1913), pp. 3–151, at 20; PL 44:120. Jacques Le Goff, "Les limbes," *Nouvelle Revue de Psychoanalyse* 34 (1986): 151–73, at 161, observes that "the mildest" (*mitissima*) also describes the pains of the children in Augustine's *Enchiridion* 23.93, lines 133–37; CCSL 46, ed. E. Evans (1969), p. 99.

58. D-S no. 224, p. 83.

59. For more on limbo, see A. Gaudel, "Les limbes," *Dictionnaire de théologie catholique* 9 (Paris, 1926), 760–71; George J. Dyer, *Limbo: Unsettled Question* (New York: Sheed and Ward, 1964); Elke Pahud de Mortanges, "Der versperrte Himmel: Das Phänomen der *sanctuaires à répit* aus theologiegeschichtlicher Perspektive," *Schweizerische Zeitschrift für Religions- und Kulturgeschichte* 98 (2004): 31–47.

from on high for Saint Martin, patron saint of that city, to name those he wishes to have removed from hell's torments. This is the theme encountered above in the *Apocalypse of Peter* and in Redaction 6 of the *Vision of Paul*. Ralph Glaber, the monk of Cluny who wrote a chronicle covering events almost until his death in 1046 or 1047, explains the circumstances under which this report of otherworld procedures reached him, but his contemporary Hugh, the archdeacon of Tours, put it in a more explicit eschatological perspective.

Ralph praises the activity of a certain Hervé, the son of a prominent military family of the region, who, despite the aspirations of his parents, wished to become a monk in the house of St. Martin in Tours. After much negotiation between the monks, his father, and Hervé himself, King Robert of France made him treasurer of that church, but he lived outside, walled up in a cell nearby, where he practiced great austerities. It was the talented Hervé who supervised the basilica's repair. As the day for its reconsecration approached, there was much expectation that the saint would perform a miracle to mark the occasion. Hervé himself petitioned the saint for such a sign, but Martin appeared in a vision to chide him gently, saying he *constantly* intercedes with the Lord for *all*, and particularly for faithful servants of the church at Tours, that is, the clergy. But then: "Certain of these have become more involved than is proper in the business of this world, and while serving the arms of war they have fallen victim to them in battle. I do not wish to conceal from you that it was only with difficulty that I won from the clemency of Christ that, snatched from the servants of the shadows, they should dwell in places of refreshment and light (*ut erepti de ministris tenebrarum locis refrigerii ac lucis sistere mererentur*)."[60] In other words: the saint intercedes regularly for the clergy of Tours, but these particular churchmen, active as warriors and recently cut down in battle (*trucidati in prelio*), presented unusual problems. Only with difficulty did the saint receive the result he desired from his petitions. Ralph's story fits in the context of a growing contemporary protest movement against clerical participation in warfare.[61] It is only in spite of their military activities, Martin explains, that the saint was able to obtain the transfer of these warrior priests' souls from the darkness to refreshment and light.

---

60. Glaber, *Histories* 3.4.15; *Rodulfus Glaber Opera*, ed. John France, Neithard Bulst, and Paul Reynolds, trans. John France, Oxford Medieval Texts (Oxford: Clarendon Press, 1989), 120.

61. As far back as the Concilium Germanicum held under Carloman in 742, the Carolingians forbade priests from bearing arms. The scruples engendered by Christ's order "Put up thy sword" (John 18:11) go back even farther than that. For an overview of this issue, see Katherine Allen Smith, *War and the Making of Medieval Monastic Culture* (Woodbridge, UK: Boydell Press, 2011), esp. 44 and n. 20; Carl Erdmann, *The Origin of the Idea of Crusade*, trans. Marshall W. Baldwin and Walter Goffart (1935; Princeton, NJ: Princeton University Press, 1977), 76–80; John Damon, *Soldier Saints and Holy Warriors: Warfare and Sanctity in the Literature of Early England* (Burlington, VT: Ashgate, 2003).

Another witness to Hervé's account of this apparition from Saint Martin was the church's archdeacon, Hugh, who described it in a short literary dialogue addressed to a certain Fulbert, perhaps the famous bishop of Chartres. Hugh's account changes the perspective of the encounter.[62] He makes no mention of warrior priests and makes the archdeacon's words not a criticism of the ascetic treasurer, but of the impatient crowd. Hervé chastises the people for their ingratitude toward Martin. How could they have forgotten that Martin had healed so many of the sick as to constitute "a new raid against hell" (*nova spoliatione inferni*)?[63] He insists Martin was able to remove many thousands of captive souls from the underworld to the heavenly Jerusalem (*ab inferis ad supernam Hierusalem*) after the example of the Redeemer—an imitation of the Descent.[64] According to Hugh, Hervé revealed he had seen Martin petitioning before the divine judge, who said to him:

> If it is your prayer, my beloved, for those languishing who are in your care, it is right that you not doubt concerning those for whom you plead. For your great faith merits similarly great things in return. Deliverance is granted to any for whom you make the request.[65]

In Hugh's account of Hervé's words, Martin's "new harrowing" fits in the tradition of the Latin B version of the *Gospel of Nicodemus*, in which Christ slides those not qualified for salvation at the time of his own Resurrection, into Tartarus with the devil. In the narrowest sense, Hervé refers only to Martin's ability to heal the sick, but in his vision of Martin pleading before Christ, the saint is granted the acceptance of any petition on behalf of "any" of those in his spiritual care, which would include the priests Ralph mentioned, who died bearing arms. For a new raid against hell to take place in this tradition, it would be a liberation not from death or purgatorial punishment, but from hell. Given how different Ralph's account is from Hugh's, his stress on the taint of military service and death while bearing arms—presumably sudden and violent and quite possibly without prior confession or penance—would suggest damnation, though this interpretation can only be

---

62. Archdeacon Hugh's dialogue with Fulbert, the "Dialogus ad Fulbertum amicum suum de quodam miraculo, quod contigit in translatione Sancti Martini," in Jean Mabillon, *Vetera analecta*, vol. 1 (1675–1676), 349–74; and the nova editio (Paris: Montalant, 1723), 213–17; cited in *Glaber Opera*, li and 116–17 n. 3. I have used the 1723 edition. In their introduction (p. li), John France and Paul Reynolds state Ralph's interpretation: "those freed from hell by the saint were brethren who had indulged in warfare."

63. "Dialogus ad Fulbertum," 215b.

64. Ibid. The application of imagery from the Descent to the intercessory power of Martin of Tours and of the saints in general comes out forcefully in Moreira, *Heaven's Purge*, 63–80 and in the references on 229–38.

65. "Dialogus ad Fulbertum," 215b.

speculative. Ralph's evident disapproval of fighting priests argues for this view, though he is writing a chronicle, not canon law. Combining the salient points of each account indicates an early eleventh-century belief that Martin of Tours had the ability to rescue souls from hell, an ability so comprehensive that he could rescue even priests who died in battle.

The Vision of Odo

The story about Saint Martin's powers might have given rise to some overly optimistic speculation about potential escape from hell. One sign of this fear is another story recounted by the same Ralph Glaber. As before, his is only one version of the event, but the statement of his contemporary also sees diabolical overtones insinuating an exaggerated confidence in rescues from hell. The most explicit surviving version, traditionally attributed to a certain Ansellus Scholasticus, is really a record made by Ansellus of a vision dictated to him by Odo, abbot (1032–52) of Saint-Germain of Auxerre.[66] Ralph Glaber lived at Saint-Germain of Auxerre during two stages of his life, from his earliest time as a monk, ending sometime after 1010, and again from 1036 or 1037 to his death around 1046.[67] Odo was abbot during this second stay. This story advances the idea of an annual cleansing of the worthy from hell at Easter. It is hard to determine how widespread this extension of the report by Hervé of Tours might have been. The late fourth–early fifth-century poet Prudentius depicted demons complaining that Easter brings an annual diminution of infernal pains, but relief is not escape. When an exaggerated version of this literary theme combined somehow with the story of Saint Martin, Abbot Odo undercut it by putting it in the mouth of a devil. The story occurs in two versions, one in prose and one in verse, so this is not an isolated reference. Ralph Glaber offers an account of his own, which has added interest because he knew Odo and his secretary Ansellus.

Here, then, in the mouth of the devil who guided Odo's soul through hell, is the complaint that monastic prayer, even from unworthy monks, deprives the demons of their prey and demolishes the walls of hell so that, each Easter, those to whom these prayers have been dedicated and whose lives were worthy can escape hell.

---

66. Carozzi, *Le voyage*, 412–26. See also Baschet, *Les justices de l'au-delà*, 538–40; Michel Aubrun, "Caractères et portée religieuse et sociale des 'Visiones'," *Cahiers de Civilisation Médiévale* 23.2 (1980): 109–30, at 119.

67. *Glaber Opera*, xxxii–xxxiii. This story is at *Histories* 5.1.1; pp. 216–19.

The prose account follows.

Pontifices sacrilegi et abbates indisciplinati, prespiterique nequissimi, sacerdotes diaconique mendacissimi, moniales meretrices cum clericellis parvulis, seu monachi invidi turbidique murmurantes, instantes precibus nocturnis sive diurnis iugiter per annum, garrulitate sua istum nobis inferunt luctum.

Sacrilegious pontiffs, and undisciplined abbots, evil presbyters, priests and deacons who lie, nuns who sin with their little clerics, and envious and riotous monks who complain, [nonetheless] by the urgent nightly or daily prayers that they offer constantly through the year, by their garrulousness, impose this grief on us.

Sed et cupidissimi ac tenacissimi laboratores helemosinis suis, quibus egenos recreant, ita ut cernis nostra castra spoliant.

The very greedy and tenacious laborers (i.e. the monks) destroy our fortresses (in hell) as you see, using the alms with which they relieve the needy.

Quicumque ergo a pasca usque ad pascam ita a penis redimi ab amicis potuerit, salvabitur. Nemo autem a nobis exiet, nisi prius Deo placita opera fecerit, quibus bona merita acquiruntur.

Therefore, from Paschal season to Paschal season, whoever shall have been able to be redeemed in this way by friends will be saved. But no one goes out from among us unless he has previously performed deeds pleasing to God, by which good merits may be acquired.

Nam homicide, iracundi, luxuriosi, adulteri, raptores, contra naturam peccantes, periuri, qui cuncta Deo semper contraria agunt omnino nostri sunt et in perpetuum nobiscum condempnati.

For the murderers, the wrathful, the vain, the adulterers, the robbers, the sinners against nature, the perjurers, who always do everything against God are wholly ours and are condemned to live with us forever.[68]

---

68. J. Leclercq, "Une rédaction en prose de la 'Visio Anselli' dans un manuscrit de Subiaco," *Benedictina* 16 (1969): 188–95, at 193–94.

The version in verse goes like this.

Postquam surgens a mortuis	Afterwards, when he was rising
Heu! Proh dolor! nos superans	from the dead, Alas, O grief, in
Imperium comminuit	overcoming us, he weakened our
Nostrumque decus abstulit.	control and took away our glory.
Dum redeunt Paschalia	At every return of Easter tide—
Vobis grata solemnia,	a festival welcome to you but
Nobis semper sed timida;	always threatening to us—the One
Sic consuevit facere	we did not revere was accustomed
Non veritus nos vincere.	thus to conquer us.[69]

Ralph may be concealing Odo's identity when he says that a demon spoke to a *monk* of his acquaintance and claimed that there is no need for monastic discipline. With diabolical logic, the deceitful counselor advised the monk against superfluous austerities because all reach "the same peace (*eandem requiem*) in the end. For it is known that every year, on the day on which Christ, rising from among the dead, repaired the life of the human race, all that Tartarus holds was stolen from it, and those who belonged to him (*suos*) were led back above, for which reason you have nothing to be afraid of."[70] The key word is *suos*, all of "his" people. The ambiguity is intentional: if "all Christ's people" means the whole human race, then on Easter, all who died in the intervening year are saved. If it means only the faithful, that would presumably not include anyone persuaded by this little devil or any unrepentant sinner. Even in the more restricted sense, in this account, it is Tartarus, not purgatory or the purgatorial fires that Christ scans on Easter for his followers in order to reenact the Descent as part of the feast day's commemoration of his own Resurrection. Monks and nuns therefore waste their efforts in spiritual discipline because, once in hell, they need only await the annual Easter rescue.

The ramifications of the devil's suggestion go farther than would at first appear because among the disciplines in question are surely the monks' prayers on behalf of the dead, those that convey suffrages or aid to souls in the otherworld. More will be said about this intercessory system, but it is important to recognize that in the belief system of the time, prayers for the dead were a

---

69. PL 151:649–50.

70. "Nam constat omnibus annis, die qua Christus resurgens ex mortuis uitam reparauit humani generis, ab eodem uniuersa spoliari tartara, et suos quoque reduci ad supera; pro qua re nil uobis pertimescendum." Glaber, *Histories* 5.1.1; p. 216.

fundamental aspect of the rationale for both monastic prayer and economic support of monastic institutions. Should monks yield to demonic promptings the decrease in aid would prolong the pains of souls in postmortem expiation.

Monks Pray a Brother from the Devil's Presence in Tartarus

Peter Damian, whose correspondence with Cardinal Humbert of Silva Candida has proven instructive above, also relates a tale about a monk who died in the monastery of St. Sylvester in Urbino at cockcrow and lay dead until the second hour after sunrise. His brothers attend his body and sing psalms and masses. Amazingly, he returns to life, but having recovered, he spews out insults and curses. Why? Because "I have descended into the depths of the flaming Tartarus. It was there my master and lord Lucifer assigned me irrevocably. He placed on my head his copper crown that always burns with inextinguishable force."[71] And "he draped me in a metal mantle, of the same type he wears himself. It was so long that it reached my heels and so hot that molten metal dripped from it."[72] Even when it was clear what danger he had been in and what risks his anger still entails, so furious was the monk's rebellion and despair that he rejects all his brothers' pleas to confess sins he had not yet acknowledged. Undeterred, the monks strip away his clothes, assault his body, fast, pray, and weep until, like a drowning man returning to the surface, he praises God, renounces the devil's deceits, adores the cross, and abases himself in repentance. In this way, "prayer wrenched this victim from the very bowels of Gehenna" and placed him in the heavenly Jerusalem.[73]

Ambiguous Cases of Relief and Rescue

Such transfers as these, it would seem, can only be read one way: the escape is total. Other stories are more ambiguous. The reasons to hesitate in classifying the following examples are apparent, but the examples are valuable because they indicate a tendency to favor rescue.

The *Deeds of Dagobert*

The case of Dagobert I, king of the Franks, who ruled 623–639, registers a near miss, but his story displays some important principles in the relationship

---

71. Peter Damian, Letter 72, p. 339, lines 15–17.
72. Ibid., lines 18–21.
73. Ibid., p. 340, lines 14–15. There are other stories of similar import in Damian's Letter 72.

between the lay patronage of churches and the saints' protection. The *Deeds of Dagobert*, a compilation from chronicles, saints' lives, and charters, put together around 830, probably at Saint Denis, records that King Dagobert bequeathed all his property, including many gems and gold pieces, to the monastery and provided decoration for the interior and exterior of the church.[74] When he began to feel death approaching, he summoned his counselor, his wife, and his son and required them to swear to respect the gifts he had made so that no one would presume to modify his arrangements and thus incur the ire of God and Saint Denis. Louis signed a document confirming his father's order. When he died, Dagobert was buried to the right of the altar with due honor.[75]

Afterward, though, things did not go as the pious king or his saintly protectors expected. On the day that Dagobert died, his spirit was seen being maltreated by ugly demons who were conducting him in a rapid boat toward one of the seismically active volcanic islands of the Aeolian archipelago off the north coast of Sicily. The Frankish emissary, Ansoald of Poitiers, and his delegation, who were on a mission nearby, came ashore to meet a famous recluse, who informed them of this news. He told them that he had seen the king being drawn toward an active volcano. One need only recall the similar story told in Gregory I's *Dialogues* (4.31), about another hermit on Lipari, who saw Theodoric dumped into a volcano, the mouth of hell, in order to understand the threat to the Frankish king's soul. But, says the hermit, the king called out to Saints Denis, Maurice, and Martin with insistent appeals for his release. The saintly team intervened to transfer Dagobert to the Bosom of Abraham. The account ends with a reference to the king's gifts to churches, which "he enriched far and wide." The presence of Saint Denis as recipient of endowments and a member of the rescue squad is no accident. Nor is it an accident that the Church of St. Denis retained a copy of Dagobert's will and compiled this biography of the king. Whatever the

---

74. For other testimentary provisions, see *Gesta Dagoberti I regis francorum*, cap. 39; ed. Bruno Krusch, MGH, SS RR MM 2:416–19. Krusch identifies components of the *Gesta* from as late as the ninth century. Régine Le Jan provides the date 830 in "La sacralité de la royauté mérovingienne," *Annales: Histoire, Sciences Sociales* 58 (2003): 1217–41, at 1225 n. 41. Laurent Morelle considers Abbot Hilduin of Saint Denis to have directed a collaborative authorship around 835. One member of the team may have been the young Hincmar. Morelle, "La mise en oeuvre des actes diplomatiques: L'*auctoritas* des chartes chez quelques historiographes monastiques (IXe–XIe siècle)," in *Auctor et auctoritas: Invention et conformisme dans l'écriture médiévale*, ed. Michel Zimmermann (Paris: École des chartes, 2001), 73–96, at 83. Baschet, *Les justices de l'au-delà*, 549–52. On Dagobert and the legends about him, see Laurent Theis, *Dagobert: Un roi pour un peuple* (Paris: Fayard, 1982), 38–39.

75. *Gesta Dagoberti*, pp. 419–21.

social, political, and economic context, Dagobert can be counted as one said to be saved, if not out of hell, certainly from the rim of its crater.[76]

The Girl in Toulouse

The difficulty in interpreting the following tale depends on differences in the versions that preserve it. In the days when the Arian Visigothic king Alaric II ruled from Toulouse (485–507) a young girl was believed possessed by demons if not by the devil himself until Saint Remigius (d. 533) saved her. Two lives of Saint Remigius and one reference by Gregory of Tours preserve the story.[77] It was Remigius who baptized Clovis, the Frankish king, the first Germanic ruler to become a Catholic (as opposed to an Arian), and the man reputed to have killed Alaric II at the Battle of Vouillé, thus ending the reign of Arianism over much of Southern France. Remigius, along with Saint Denis, was a patron saint of the Frankish kings. The earlier, sixth-century biography, at first attributed to the poet Venantius Fortunatus, considers her return to health a defeat of death; the other, by Hincmar of Reims (d. 882), a rescue from hell. As Hincmar was archbishop of Reims, a city that took its name from Saint Remigius, he had an obvious interest in promoting the reputation of his illustrious predecessor, even after a lapse of 350 years.

According to the early version, the girl had been "held captive in the siege of evil spirits" (*vesani spiritus tenebatur obsidione captiva*). Her pious parents, close relatives of the king, took her to the tomb of Saint Peter in Rome where a certain unnamed religious leader (called a *servus dei*) attempted an exorcism unsuccessful in every regard except that, from within the girl, the Ancient Enemy announced that only Saint Remigius could dislodge him. Thus King Alaric and the girl's parents and the religious leader now named as "Benedict himself" invited Remigius to Toulouse.[78] When he arrived, he urged that the people of Toulouse pray for the girl, which they did. The evil spirit exited the girl's mouth with a revolting stench (*obsceno fetore*), but then she died. Her bier was placed in the Church of St. John the Baptist, where Saint Remigius prostrated himself on the floor, wept, prayed, and urged the

---

76. Ibid., pp. 421–22. Baschet, *Les justices de l'au-delà*, 549: "It is no exaggeration to say that Dagobert was liberated from hell."

77. Gregory of Tours alludes to this tale in his *Glory of the Confessors* §78, trans. Raymond van Dam (Liverpool: Liverpool University Press, 1988), 81.

78. It would be interesting to know whether this Benedict is Benedict of Nursia. In the *Life of Benedict* that forms book 2 of Gregory's *Dialogues*, similar cures are attributed to Benedict in chaps. 16, 23, 30, 31, and 38.

others to do the same. As a result, "he revived the dead girl whom he had healed earlier when she was sick."[79]

Hincmar's version appropriates most of the earlier account's exact words, including all those quoted here. However, he adds this line, as if to explain more fully the exact nature of the girl's revival: "Immediately, she rose in the fullness of health, as she afterwards acknowledged, from the very prisons of hell (*ab ipsis inferni claustris*)."[80] It is possible that Hincmar's reference to hell is an infernalized interpretation of the land of the dead, Hades, the *inferi*. Still, in defense of Hincmar, one must observe that the girl is consistently referred to as a prisoner (*obsidione captiva*) of her demons or of the Ancient Enemy, that is, Satan, which suggests that the narrator believes her spirit to have been not merely in the underworld, but, precisely, in hell. If that is the case, the saint would have released the girl from the clutches of the devil and the snares of hell. Because of the contrast in the two versions, I consider this only a qualified liberation from hell.

Hell as Agenda

Notwithstanding the efforts of theologians and religious authorities to present a systematized otherworld that would correspond to theological doctrine and ecclesiastical institutions, there remains considerable evidence of alternative beliefs. Although references to these beliefs are scattered, they are persistent enough from the third to the eleventh century to show that many took exception to the doctrine of eternal damnation. Though total escape is more spectacular than temporary relief, both ideas persisted. The *Apocalypse of Peter* gave hope that the saved could rescue persons of their choosing from hell. A tradition to this effect can be traced. Especially saintly persons (Perpetua, Gregory I, Paul) can obtain the total release of some named individuals (Dinocrates, Trajan), or even Paul's family, a designated kin group, from hell. The *Apocalypse* or *Vision of Paul* fed a long tradition in which Christ himself appears in the lowest hell and personally grants all the damned a weekly (or annual) rest from its pains. From this, numerous sources imply that the damned may enjoy periodic relief from their torments even as they remain captives in hell. Whether protest or folkore or minority religious beliefs, these themes acquired a certain coherence from Ireland to Germany

---

79. [Venantius Fortunatus,] *Vita Remedii (Remigii)* 9.16–27; ed. Bruno Krusch, MGH, AA 4.2 (1885), 64–67.

80. *Vita Remigii auctore Hincmaro* (Hincmar's Life of Saint Remy) §9; MGH, SS RR MM 3:239–349, at 286, lines 12–14.

to Sicily. Popular religion is not the sole explanation for the continuity of these traditions. Byzantine theology is supremely sophisticated, and it, too, preserved beliefs in these "exceptions to hell" that contradicted Western, Latin theological contentions.

Nonetheless, Western thinkers pursued themes central to these exceptions and explored the idea that the disciplinary consequences of hell's torments are cleansing so that when chastisement is complete, no more punishment is due. Since God would not exact undue punishment, the discipline ends, and the purified sinner would advance to the divine presence. This strand articulates not eternal but temporary punishment. Although this possibility was sketched by some leading thinkers, its impact on conceptions of postmortem discipline remained unclear for a long time, as the next chapter will show.

CHAPTER 5

Calibrated Justice and Purgatorial Fire

We will spend as long in that purgatorial fire as necessary to consume these minute sins like wood, hay, and straw.

—Caesarius of Arles

What is accomplished in the reprobate by variation in the punishments will be accomplished in those who are to be saved through fire by the measurement of time.

—Julian of Toledo

Either they are made clean from the filth of their vices by the fire's long examination until the day of judgment, or perhaps they may be released from punishment and arrive at the peace of the saints earlier by means of the prayers, alms, fasts, tears, or offerings of the salutary host from their faithful friends.

—Bede

The idea of eternal damnation long had critics, such as Clement of Alexandria and his student Origen. In Origen's view, no one experiences eternal death, but only temporary, medicinal suffering. Such suffering may require many reincarnations to be completed, but eventually it cures and restores all to unity with God. Adherents of this view saw invariable, eternal punishment as incompatible with the goodness and effectiveness of the divine Redeemer, whose sacrifice, itself achieved through suffering, produced salvation. If suffering can save, why would postmortem punishment be any different? In part II, which comprises chapters 4–6, we see how this and other questions challenged belief in hell and changed perceptions of it.

A temporary, therapeutic system of punishment after death that progressively cleanses sinners and thereby permits them to enter heaven did not come to be called purgatory for many centuries. According to Jacques Le Goff, there were two dramatically different phases in this development. First, he says, is a perception that suffering for those who die with only slight sins will cleanse them through punishments that are "purgatorial." The adjective "purgatorial" describes certain pains (such as purgatorial fire) that remove the last imperfections from a saved soul needing only slight amendment before admission to heaven. Then, around 1170, in the urban environment of the embryonic University of Paris, thinkers began to conceive of purgatory as a place, considered as a proper noun (in technical terms, a "substantive"), with a name of its own, *purgatorium* in Latin, occupying a demarcated, physical space between hell and heaven.[1] Only in 1254 did Pope Innocent IV declare belief in purgatory necessary for Catholics. He was concerned because authorities within the Eastern Orthodox or Greek church taught many similar ideas, but adhered to no fixed formula. There is, Innocent acknowledged, a shared doctrinal core, in the East and the West, to the effect "that the souls of those who die having undertaken penance, but without completing it, or who die without mortal sin, but with venial and tiny ones, are purged after death and are able to be aided by the suffrages of the Church." His concern, he said, was to provide a proper name for the place where that function occurs: "because they say that the place of this purgation has not been indicated by a certain and proper name (noun) by their [theological] doctors we, according to the traditions and authorities of the holy fathers, wish to name it 'Purgatory' and wish that from now on they, too, call it by that same name." That fire, he continued, purges not unatoned major sins, but tiny ones that still weigh down the soul after death even if they have been loosed in life. Returning to major sins, he declared that anyone who dies in mortal sin without penance goes to "eternal Gehenna."[2]

---

1. Jacques Le Goff, *La naissance du purgatoire* (Paris: Gallimard, 1981), translated by Arthur Goldhammer as *The Birth of Purgatory* (Chicago: University of Chicago Press, 1984). Among the many reviews of Le Goff's book, the following counterarguments may be noted in particular. Elisabeth Mégier names Otto of Friesing and Odericus Vitalis as two exceptions to Le Goff's dating (ca. 1170), localization (the University of Paris), and profession (theologians) in "Deux exemples de 'prépurgatoire' chez les historiens," *Cahiers de Civilisation Médiévale* 28.1 (1985): 45–62. Barbara Newman notes another outstanding exception in "Hildegard of Bingen and the 'Birth of Purgatory'," *Mystics Quarterly* 19.3 (1993): 90–97. Richard W. Southern strongly attacks Le Goff's insistence on the terminology of purgatory as place and proper noun. He also moves the new prominence of purgatory earlier, to the mid-eleventh century. Southern regards as crucial the introduction of tithing and the creation of new parishes that greatly decreased the average donation. The rest of his theory is implicit, but it suggests that as these far more numerous, much smaller offerings in coin replaced aristocratic bequests of large landed estates, contributors had higher expectations of otherworldly benefits. Because, during the interim, heaven is immediately open only to the perfect, purgatory treats all but the worst sinners, thus expanding hope for these marginal contributors. Southern, "Between Heaven and Hell," *Times Literary Supplement*, no. 4133 (June 18, 1982), 651–52.

2. Latin text: D-S nos. 838–39, pp. 271–72. Jacques-Guy Bougerol, "Autour de 'la Naissance du Purgatoire'," AHDLMA 50 (1983): 7–59, cites and comments on unpublished passages by lesser Parisian theological writers not treated by LeGoff. Aron Gurevich is skeptical of the need for Le Goff's strict periodization. He writes, "Purgatory is present in concept in this literature [i.e., visionary literature] from the very beginning, even if it is not so called and not outlined as a separate realm."

Repentance remains the decisive factor between the purgatorial and the eternal fires. For now, the issue is whether Le Goff's claim is accurate. Is there a fundamental difference between claiming a cleansing function for a purgatorial discipline somewhere in the otherworld and claiming a separate place called purgatory for that function but distinct from heaven and hell? Is this difference so dramatic that, in discussing eschatology in the period before theologians themselves used the term, we today should refrain from calling the purgatorial fire purgatory? In the past, I have implied that the concept of purgatory existed before it was given an actual name and located in a defined place, and therefore this technical lack should not prevent us from calling it purgatory.[3] What once appeared to me as a commonsense approach now seems a costly shortcut. Telescoping the development of terminology applied to the otherworld deprives thinkers and visionaries of their voice, obliterates sincere hesitations, and crushes the confusions that, in their own way, provoked the very expressions we seek to understand. If death were so readily comprehensible and the landmarks in the otherworld so clear, the world might have only one religion, or none! Indeed, to insist on calling the first intimations of postmortem purgatorial functions by the term *purgatory* when those who expressed them referred to "places of punishment" or "purgatorial fire" or "trial," would be to impose the same authoritative dominance on them as Innocent IV sought to impose on the Eastern Orthodox Catholics. I will therefore attempt to respect all the seemingly circuitous expressions tested by the writers of late antiquity and the early Middle Ages and use their own phrases even when they seem to be circumlocutions. However tedious it might be to refer to "what would become purgatory" or "the eventual purgatory," anything else is anachronistic. We cannot let the present bully the past.

Biblical Authority

As the acceptance of purgatory has been contested for centuries within the Christian community, between Orthodox Greek believers and the Roman

---

Gurevich, *Medieval Popular Culture: Problems of Belief and Perception*, trans. János Bak and Paul A. Hollingsworth (Cambridge and Paris: Cambridge University Press and Maison des Sciences de l'Homme, 1988), 148. Again: "Although the word *purgatorium* appears rather late, I am not inclined to attach too much significance to the long absence of the term"; and in the relevant note: "Ultimately Bede's expression 'locus in quo examinandae et castigandae sunt animae' (HE v.2 [that is: 5,12, the Vision of Drythelm] 'the place in which souls are to be examined and castigated') communicates the essence of purgatory just as well as the term *purgatorium*"; ibid., 143 and 247. Observe that here Bede refers to what Gurevich calls "the essence of purgatory" as a place (*locus*).

3. Review of *La naissance du purgatoire*, by Jacques Le Goff, *Speculum* 59 (1984): 179–83. The reference to Damian I criticize in the review may be found in Le Goff, *Naissance*, 243–45; Le Goff, *Birth*, 178–80: "It is clear that the places of punishment (*loca poenalia*) and instruments of torture (*lora poenalia*) . . . belong to what would later be called Purgatory, since no one returns from Hell."

church, and between Protestants and Catholics, it is wise to begin by considering the biblical basis claimed by its defenders. The first formal, papal definition of purgatory, Innocent IV's letter "Sub catholicae professione," begins by quoting two lines of Scripture.

The first is 1 Corinthians 3:13–15, which refers to one "saved as if by fire." It reads as follows:

> Each man's work will become manifest; for the Day will disclose it, because it will be revealed with fire, and the fire will test what sort of work each one has done. If the work which any man has built on the foundation survives, he will receive a reward. If any man's work is burned up, he will suffer loss, though he himself will be saved, but only as through fire. (RSV)

This crucial passage begins with a metaphor representing a person's life as a construction made of various materials ranging from straw to gold. Using these materials, one "builds" on the foundation of Christ. At the end, on "the Day," comes a probative fire that tests what has been built. What remains is the best in one's character. If enough remains firmly based on the foundation, that person receives a reward. If a person's work is burned up, that person suffers but is still saved as if by the fire. It is important to note the force of the term "as" (Latin: "sic tamen *quasi* per ignem"), because it underlines the metaphorical import of the passage. In the history of the reflections that eventually led to the doctrine of purgatory, including the visions described in the next chapter, this probative fire was not reserved for the last day. It comes immediately at death and tries the souls of the deceased as they exit the body. Seen from this perspective, the image of "fire now" is a variation on the fire in the conscience and the invasion of the end time—eschatological testing brought into the minds of living persons—seen in inner death.

The most pungent, direct, concise expression of a potential purgatorial path to salvation comes from Matthew 12:31–32, concerning the gravity of blasphemy against the Holy Spirit, which in the theology of the Trinity, is divine. Matthew quotes Jesus as saying:

> Every sin and blasphemy will be forgiven men, but the blasphemy against the Spirit will not be forgiven. And whoever says a word against the Son of man will be forgiven; but whoever speaks against the Holy Spirit will not be forgiven, either in this age or in the age to come.[4]

---

4. This saying of Jesus interestingly matches a description of Gehenna (Gehinnom) in the Talmud. The idea that blasphemy against the Holy Spirit will not be forgiven in this world or in the world to come (Matt. 12:31–32) corresponds to the presentation of Gehinnom in rabbinic Judaism. See below, chapter 7.

From the point of view of the evolution of purgatory, the key phrase is the last because it implies the possibility of forgiveness in the age to come. This passage also implies the gradation of sins by identifying blasphemy against the Holy Spirit as the worst and unforgivable. Still, the hierarchy of deeds or elements of character in 1 Corinthians 3:13–15, ranging from gold, silver, and precious stones down to wood, hay, and straw, when combined with Matthew 12:31–32, fills in this gap. There is biblical warrant for a ranking of sins and a divine tendency to forgive all but the worst by a process akin to purifying metal or burning a house.

This idea of gradation in postmortem punishment requires an important qualification. The major scriptural supports for hell itself do not indicate any variation in punishments. In Luke 16:19–31, the rich man is in fire, below Lazarus and across a chasm in a fiery area that is not further described. In Matthew 25:31–46, the Son of Man consigns those who refuse to perform the deeds of charity to eternal fire with Satan and his angels: no levels, circles, or distinctions. In Revelation's lake of fire, there are no islands, sandbars, or beaches: one either adored the Beast or the Lamb; the situation is binary. The discrimination of fates in hell is a further, theologizing development, one that combines biblical passages not originally connected. For example, in the mid-fourth century, Zeno of Verona used Psalm 1 to outline the degrees of virtue ranging from the wicked to the simple sinner to the just, suggesting (as we shall see) different fates for each. Likewise, in his *Dialogues*, Gregory the Great used Matthew 13:30 and 13:40 (weeds bound in bundles to be burned) to claim that the damned are grouped by their sins and punished similarly for similar sins: the greedy with the greedy, the lustful with the lustful. These distinctions subdivide the otherworld conceptually if not geographically and provoke speculation as to the criteria for discipline in either temporary or eternal pains.

A third text cited by Catholic authorities in favor of purgatory strongly indicates postmortem forgiveness but has no bearing on the question of gradation. It occurs in a work considered apocryphal by Protestants, namely, the book of 2 Maccabees. It was written ca. 163 BCE, long before the first two proof texts.[5] In this narrative of the Jewish rebellion against Syrian oppressors, after a battle in which Jewish soldiers were slain, as the survivors proceeded to the burial, commanders found prohibited amulets, idolatrous tokens, concealed on the fallen warriors. In an effort to avert the direst of postmortem consequences, Judah Maccabee led the army in prayer pleading for divine mercy on behalf of the soldiers' souls in the otherworld and took

---

5. Neil J. McEleney, "1–2 Maccabees," in *The New Jerome Bible Commentary* (Englewood Cliffs, NJ: Prentice-Hall, 1990), 421–46, at 423 and 446.

up a collection so as to send cash to Jerusalem for a sin offering (2 Macc. 12:39–46). If successful, this would be an example of release from death obtained by the prayers of the pious. Thanks to this intervention, the fallen soldiers would recover, in the Jewish phrase, their "portion in the world to come." The text observes at the end, "If he were not expecting that those who had fallen would rise again, it would have been superfluous and foolish to pray for the dead" (12:44).

In addition to these Jewish and Christian passages, there are also notable antecedents in classical literature. For example, Virgil's Aeneas passes the fork in the road that separates the wicked from the virtuous: those headed to Tartarus from those headed for Elysium. From the shade of his father, Aeneas learns how some elemental, physical drives, still rooted in the dead, require expiation in the afterlife by dangling in the wind (air) or immersion in deep currents (water) or refining flames (fire). "Each shade (*manes*) suffers for its own faults." This doctrine has deep roots in pagan literature related to important themes in Orphism and Platonism—for example, in Plato's "Myth of Er" at the end of the *Republic*. In the *City of God*, Augustine explicitly criticized the Platonists on this point, because, he said, they consider these forms of purgation, preparatory to reincarnation, as the only type of punishment in the afterlife. Not knowing the *Republic*, Augustine feared they had no separate punishment for the incurably wicked.[6]

Postbiblical Testimony

Purgation for light sins, compared in 1 Corinthians 3:13–15 to mere wood, hay, or straw, which cannot affect the architecture of virtue and faith, would seem to require comparatively fleeting efforts at refinement in order to attain purity. In one subtle but telling image, the punishment is no more than delay in entering the city of God. The image comes in the same long version of the *Apocalypse of Paul* mentioned above in connection with the sabbatical repose in hell. After his tour of hell, Paul visits the territory of the blessed. There, he comes to the walls of the city of Christ. Outside this beautiful city (69.20), stranded in the boughs of fruitless trees, are certain souls, forcefully abased as the wind blows the branches down. These are religious persons, monks or virgins, who must wait in these trees and watch

---

6. *Civ. Dei* 21.13; CCSL 48, ed. Bernard Dombart and Alphonse Kalb (1955), pp. 778–80; *The City of God*, trans. Marcus Dods (New York: The Modern Library, 1950), 783–84; cf. *Civ. Dei* 6.12. See R. G. Austin, *P. Vergili Maronis Aeneidos Liber sextus, Commentary* (Oxford: Clarendon Press, 1977), 226; Plato, *The Republic* 614b–621d. See also Alan E. Bernstein, *The Formation of Hell: Death and Retribution in the Ancient and Early Christian Worlds* (Ithaca, NY: Cornell University Press, 1993), 52–61, 68–73.

other, more blessed souls enter the city, but wait for their own entrance until the Parousia. They experience this fate because they wrongly took pride in their discipline (69.28–70.12) and failed ever to repent of this unwarranted self-magnification.[7] Now they are delayed in these trees, bowed down (at last!) by the wind, enduring a temporary punishment.

In more explicitly theological terms, Augustine interprets the passage on wood, hay, and straw in his little handbook, the *Enchiridion*. On the one hand, he explains, there are actions that may be licit in themselves, but represent attachment to worldly things (the wood, hay, and straw). In times of adversity, these worldly things may be destroyed, thus causing grief. On the other hand, if one's heart is rooted in Christ, the loss of those worldly things, however painful, will not eradicate one's faith or overturn the foundation. "If the man, though burning with grief, is yet more willing to lose the things he loves so much than to lose Christ—he is saved by fire." Another man, who prefers worldly things to Christ, will have no foundation left and be lost. Augustine stressed that the passage states "the fire shall try every man's work," so that not even the just are spared this test.[8] In the *City of God*, Augustine incorporates this trial of the heart into his theory of history. In so doing, he includes all adversities, not just the probative, postmortem fire. He includes the Sack of Rome in 410 as an outstanding example, but he means all the difficulties life presents. Further, he sees all human history as a consequence of Adam and Eve's disobedience. Thus, all history is punitive. Life itself is probative. In the *City of God*, he says, "Even in this life some punishments are purgatorial," provided that one uses those reversals to amend one's life (21.13):

> All other punishments, whether temporal or eternal, inflicted as they are on every one by divine providence, are sent either on account of past sins, or of sins presently allowed in the life, or to exercise and reveal a man's graces. . . . Temporary punishments are suffered by some in this life only, by others after death, by others both now and then; but all of them before that last and strictest judgment. But of those who suffer temporary punishments after death, all are not doomed to those everlasting pains which are to follow that judgment; for to some, as we have already said, what is not remitted in this world is remitted in the next, that is, they are not punished with the eternal punishment of the world to come.[9]

---

7. *Visio Pauli* §24, ed. Montague Rhodes James, in *AA*, pp. 24–25. The text is translated by James in *ANT*, pp. 525–55, at 538–39.

8. Augustine, *Enchiridion de fide et spe et caritate* 68; CCSL 46, ed. E. Evans (1969), pp. 86–87; *The Enchiridion on Faith, Hope, and Love*, trans. J. F. Shaw (South Bend, IN: Regnery/Gateway, 1961), 80–81.

9. Augustine, *The City of God* 21.13; p. 784; cf. 21.26, pp. 800–802.

As long as one retains one's foundation and withstands adversity by accepting it patiently as providential chastisement, as temporary punishment, the suffering it causes is curative, purgatorial, therapeutic, and, whether it endures after death or not, it leads to an escape from eternal punishment, and hence, to salvation.[10] But, Augustine warns, no one should be fooled into confusing a postmortem discipline that ends at the Last Judgment or before with the fate of those damned at that judgment to eternal punishment (*Civ. Dei* 21.16).

Still, even though hell's fire has no end, "the eternal fire will be proportioned to the deserts of the wicked, so that to some it will be more, and to others less painful, whether this result be accomplished by a variation in the temperature of the fire itself, graduated according to everyone's merit, or whether it be that the heat remains the same, but that all do not feel it with equal intensity of torment."[11] This conviction that hell's punishments are graded or calibrated according to the severity of individual guilt leads into Augustine's notion of a more tolerable damnation in chapter 110 of the *Enchiridion*. The idea that postmortem punishment can improve those who endure it further suggests purgatorial suffering. If some mortal sins deserve less intense suffering than others, is it not reasonable that lighter, minor offenses deserve special treatment and, surely, something less than eternal punishment? But how much lighter than what deserves damnation can it be? In the history of thought about purgation, the question of where to draw that line became crucial. In Matthew 12:31–32, the boundary seems to be quite close to hell, because in that passage, all but the very worst offense, blasphemy against the Holy Spirit, can be forgiven in the otherworld. Augustine's model, however, would move the border closer to heaven, because he divides his middle category more nearly in the middle. It will become clear in other documents that very grave sins indeed can also be expiated short of damnation. The corollary will be that the more serious the sins that can be forgiven, the more hellish the punishments must be in the interim. Le Goff referred to this perception as the infernalization of purgatory.[12]

---

10. For more on Augustine's theory of postmortem punishment, see Bernstein, *Formation*, chap. 13, 314–33; and, specifically on purgation, Jacques Le Goff, *Birth* 61–85.

11. Augustine of Hippo, *The City of God* 21.16; 787–88.

12. Discussing Bonaventure, Le Goff considers various options in locating purgatory nearer to paradise or nearer to hell. Le Goff, *Birth*, 252; Le Goff, *Naissance*, 339; and referring to Arturo Graf with no citation.

Picking up on the implications of gradations in postmortem punishments was Caesarius, bishop of Arles (d. 543), author of rules for monastic communities, one for men, one for women. In his Sermon 179, devoted entirely to the purgatorial fire, Caesarius opposes the danger of complacency among those who misread the lesson of 1 Corinthians 3:13–15: "What is the difference," he paraphrases the slackers, "if I must suffer temporarily as long as I am saved?" Hence, he assures them, the pains of purgatorial fire are worse than any that can be known or imagined on earth. Care must be taken of all sin, he says, because it is not only capital crimes (*capitalia crimina*) that are punished after death, but even minute sins (*minuta peccata*). Thus, if in life we do not expiate our slight faults by performing good works or by patiently accepting adversity in this world, then "we will spend as long in that purgatorial fire as necessary to consume these minute sins like wood, hay, and straw."[13] Moreover, even these minor sins "can accumulate and, in the end, become overwhelming."[14] Although in principle these minor sins do not kill the soul, they deform it. If left unattended, a sufficient mass accumulates and, as is the case for one who did not repent of major sin, "it will not be possible to be purged in that transitory fire of which the Apostle spoke, and one will suffer in the eternal flame without any remedy."[15] Those guilty of capital crimes, mortal sins, however, do not even attain the fire that purges. Rather, they receive the dire sentence to eternal punishment. What is significant here is the explicit quantification. One's term in the purgatorial fire is determined by the quantity of one's minor sins. One may qualify for the purgatorial fire provided one's guilt has not reached a critical mass too great to be purged in the transitory fire and so, necessarily, still remaining for the eternal fire. Caesarius, therefore, implies a single distribution in the interim across a graded scale, where the severity of the punishment varies according to the severity of the sin, whether in the purgatorial fire or in hell. It is crucial to observe, however, that Caesarius makes no distinction as to place, only as to sentence. Flexibility in the length of the sentence introduces a fluidity in reckoning punishments, though only on the virtuous side of mortal sin.

It might seem that hell recedes as the steps toward its fringes come to be quantified, but for Caesarius, the purgatorial fire is in hell, not separate from it. There is no evidence that the purgatorial pains are outside hell or that they are different in nature from the punishments that afflict the damned, except

---

13. Caesarius Arelatensis, Sermon 179, cap. 4, lines 22–23; CCSL 103–4, ed. G. Morin (1953), p. 726.

14. Ibid., cap. 4, line 3; p. 726.

15. Ibid., cap. 2, lines 33–34; p. 725.

in duration. His view becomes clearer in the light of the difference between citizens and mere visitors, legal resident aliens, within a city, as understood in Roman law. Citizenship is an honor, and hellfire a punishment, but the parallel holds. Those assigned to the eternal fire are its citizens; those assigned to the transitory fire are merely residents enjoying (or in this case suffering) the "benefits" of the city provisionally. This is the difference between citizens (*cives*) and residents (*incolae*).[16] The city or the fiery punishment affects all, but the citizens have an essential bond to it; the residents, an incidental bond. Those to be saved after enduring purifying fire are *in* it, but not *of* it. They are citizens elsewhere (heaven, eventually), and the toxic environment of the city where they reside affects them, but does not accord with their inner nature. Only the damned are *of* hell. This fluidity between the experience of those in the fire temporarily and those who are in it eternally would continue to influence conceptions of postmortem discipline for centuries. It is particularly characteristic of the otherworld visions to be examined in the next chapter.

It is not coincidental that Caesarius should draw on a conceptual framework related to citizenship, since Augustine, in his historical masterpiece, the *City of God*, had done so a century before. When speaking of the division in history between the two types of people, good and evil, Augustine considers them as members of the heavenly and earthly *cities*.[17] He divided people who subordinated themselves to the divine will from those who did not. The bonds among those in each group he compared to citizenship in either one or the other city, that of earth and that of heaven. In the *Enchiridion* he reiterates this distinction: "There will be two cities, one of Christ, the other of the devil, one of the good, the other of the wicked."[18] What Caesarius of Arles achieves, therefore, is to blend his teachings on those in the purgatorial fire, those in the middle category, into the binary division in Augustine's metaphor of citizenship.

The purgatorial fire was also of deep concern to Gregory I, as we have seen. Curiously, it is only in book 4 of his *Dialogues* that he explains his views on the subject. Gregory does not seem to have discussed these notions in his commentary the *Moralia on Job*, where he analyzes hell so subtly. Some use

---

16. Yan Thomas, "Citoyens et résidents dans les cités de l'Empire romain: Essai sur le droit d'origine," in *Identité et droit de l'autre*, ed. Laurent Mayali, Studies in Comparative Legal History (Berkeley: The Robbins Religious and Civil Law Collection, 1994), 1–56. I thank Laurent Mayali for this reference.

17. *The City of God* 11.1, 19.1; for the cities of Christ and of the devil, 17.20 and 20.11.

18. Aug. *Ench.* 29.111, lines 33–35, p. 109; *The Enchiridion on Faith, Hope, and Love*, trans. J. F. Shaw, ed. H. Paolucci (South Bend, IN: Regnery/Gateway, 1961), 129.

this as an argument for the inauthenticity of Gregory's *Dialogues*, claiming that they are a later compilation.[19] But the doctrinal differences between the *Moralia* and the *Dialogues* are not as great as some critics claim. Both works apply the axiom *pares paribus*, like are punished with like (*Mor.* 9.65.98; *Di.* 4.36.14). In the *Moralia*, the gradation of fates is a crucial aspect of the order that Gregory says underlies the chaos of hell. He uses the parable of the sower from Matthew 13:30, where the landowner commands his workers to gather the weeds into bundles for burning. There is sorting in judgment and punishment. Thus, Gregory introduces qualitative differences to distinguish fates in the afterlife. "The retribution of vengeance pursues the damned according to the manner of the crime."[20] Or again, "the punishment varies according to the type of guilt."[21] In the *Dialogues* 4.36.13, referring to heaven, he assures that "various qualities of retribution . . . result from different works,"[22] and in the *Moralia* he says, "Dissimilarity in the crimes subjects the damned to different tortures in the fires of Gehenna. For although Gehenna is one for all, not all burn with one and the same quality [of burning]."[23] It is there in Gehenna as it is here under the sun, for "here not all react to the sun by burning in the same way. What different conditions of bodies did here, different degrees of merit exhibit there."[24] He introduces qualitative measures to distinguish levels of punishment because "one is wracked according to the nature of one's own guilt."[25]

Because of these qualitative differences, it might follow that a hierarchy of punishments can imply some sins too light to deserve eternal punishment. Gregory does not develop this implication in the *Moralia*, but he does in the *Dialogues*, where he asserts that the existence of a purifying fire for those dying with unexpurgated slight faults "must be believed" (*credendum est*). Such souls experience a delay before entering heaven, a delay proportioned

---

19. Francis Clark, *The Pseudo-Gregorian Dialogues*, 2 vols. (Leiden: Brill, 1987). See above, chapter 1, note 26. See also Giorgio Cracco, "Uomini di Dio e uomini di Chiesa nell'Alto Medioevo (per una reinterpretazione dei *Dialogi* di Gregorio Magno," in *Ricerche di Storia Sociale e Religiosa*, n.s. 12 (1977): 163–202. In another work, Cracco points to Byzantine notions of the afterlife, where the land of the dead is still called Hades. That otherworld is, as we shall see, extremely flexible and could indeed foster speculation on the purification of the soul after death. Cracco, "Gregorio e l'oltretomba," in *Grégoire le Grand*, Colloques Internationaux du CNRS (Paris: Éditions du CNRS, 1986), 255–56.

20. Greg. *Mor.* 9.65.98; p. 526.

21. Ibid.

22. Grégoire le Grand, *Dialogues* 4.36.13; ed. and trans. A de Vogüé (Paris: Éditions du Cerf, 1978–80), 4:124–25.

23. Greg. *Mor.* 9.65.98; pp. 526–27.

24. Ibid., p. 527.

25. "[I]uxta modum culpae cruciatur." Greg. *Mor.* 9.65.98; p. 527.

to the tenacity of the soul's superficial blemishes.[26] Because the *Dialogues* are didactically pitched to his interlocutor, Peter, a novice, Gregory illustrates his doctrinal declaration with the exemplary tales concerning Pachasius laboring in the baths after his death and concerning the unnamed bath attendant who impressed Bishop Felix. From these exempla we know theirs were minute sins, not capital crimes. However binary the *Moralia*, primarily concerned with conditions in eternity, Gregory introduces qualitative considerations into both hell and heaven, grading fates to levels of blame or merit. In the *Dialogues*, when he has his interlocutor introduce the purgatorial fire, the master presents a consistent proportionality, with delay measured according to guilt. Gregory therefore applies to the interim considerations similar to those mentioned by Caesarius of Arles. The severity of one's minor faults determines how long one spends in the purgatorial fire. More importantly, Gregory thus endorses the implication that derives from Caesarius's sermon. There is a single scale of proportionality, whether for the blameless who go to heaven immediately, for those bearing slight guilt into the purgatorial fire, and even in hell. No single statement makes this declaration, but the leading thinkers cited so far seem to be piecing together the elements of such a doctrine. Gregory's discussion in the *Dialogues* differs from that of Caesarius, however, in that the two exempla he provides show the guilty working off their purgatorial punishments on earth, in the baths. Moreover the proportionality of punishments is, in his tales, offset by two critical factors: each guilty man admits his guilt, and, in each case, the penitent offers suffrages (prayers in one case, loaves of bread as alms in the other) and asks for intercession. These explanatory stories do not have the normative force of theological declarations, but they were intended to be indicative of doctrine. What emerges from this contrast between Gregory and Caesarius is that Caesarius sought to discourage his hearers from assuming laxity in the otherworld and Gregory stressed the power of intercessory actions, especially masses, which speed one through postmortem discipline.

Another thinker who postulated a difference between gradations of suffering in the purgatorial fire and those in hell was Julian of Toledo (642–90). Julian was a Christian whose parents had converted from Judaism.[27] In 688–89, Julian wrote his *Forecast of the Future World* (*Prognosticon futuri saeculi*), an unusual work because it deals exclusively with the afterlife.[28] Like Augus-

---

26. Greg. *Di.* 4.26.1; pp. 84–85.

27. M. Diaz y Diaz, "Julian of Toledo," in *EEC* 1:458–59.

28. For his Jewish parentage and the date of composition, see Joscelin Hillgarth, "St. Julian of Toledo in the Middle Ages," *Journal of the Warburg and Courtauld Institutes*, 21.1–2 (1958): 7–26.

tine, he distinguishes the two fires: "The one is that future fire concerning which the Lord, after he has completed the judgment, will say: 'Depart from me, you accursed ones, into the eternal fire,' and the other is the one that is properly called purgatorial because of those who will be saved through it."[29] In the way he writes of "those who are believed to be saved through the fire," Julian has given the purgatorial fire and its clients a certain reality, an almost institutional stability. More important, Julian takes farther than anyone so far the implications of having a calibrated hell alongside a calibrated purgatorial fire. Here is his advanced analogy:

> Just as not all the reprobate who will be plunged into eternal fire are to be condemned to one and the same type of torment, so all those who are believed to be saved through purgatorial punishment will not sustain wracking of the spirit in one and the same duration of time (*spatio*); similarly, what is accomplished in the reprobate by variation in the punishments will be accomplished in those who are to be saved through fire by [differences in] the measurement of time.[30]

The gist of this passage is that *time* is to those being cleansed what *diversity* is to those in hell. It comes very close to saying that these are two separate places, but the distinction is one of function, not location. Diversity of punishments afflicts those in the *eternal* fire; time punishes those in *purgatorial* fire. It is clearly implied, though, that these functions are sufficiently distinct that it would be hard for them to share the same location. A progression that begins "not one and the same punishment," "not one and the same duration," could easily be assumed to continue "not one and the same location." Still, Julian refrains from calling these separate places. Julian's retention of two functions in one place parallels the position taken in Hebrew sources attributable to the School of Shammai, one of the major traditions in the Talmud. The juxtaposition of one fire that punishes the wicked eternally and another that purifies the righteous is remarkable. These two functions in postmortem punishment seem to delineate a distinct specialization for the purgatorial fire. For Julian of Toledo, at least, this fire has acquired the function of purgatory even if it has not yet received that name.

Hillgarth also attests to the dissemination of Julian's work throughout the areas influenced by Celtic and Anglo-Saxon monastic expansion.

29. Julian, *Prognosticon futuri saeculi* 2.20; CCSL 115, ed. Joscelin Hillgarth (1976), pp. 56–57.

30. "Sicut non omnes reprobi, qui in aeterno igne mersuri sunt, una eademque supplicii qualitate damnandi sunt, sic omnes qui per purgatorias poenas salui esse creduntur, non uno eodemque spatio cruciatus spirituum sustinebunt, ut quod in reprobis agitur discretione poenarum, hoc in istis qui per ignem saluandi sunt, mensura temporis agitetur." Julian, *Prognosticon futuri saeculi* 2.22; p. 59.

However distinct the purgatorial from the eternal fires, the fact that both are calibrated according to the nature of the fault tends to imply that small differences in merit or charitable activity or religious behavior impact one's fate after death. Julian of Toledo does not speak explicitly of suffrages, but includes the conviction that the blessed dead pray for the salvation of their loved ones still on earth. If even the wicked rich man of Luke 16 prayed from the fire for his sons, how could it be thought that more pious souls would fail their relations? Such a belief surely aids the cult of saints and the dedication of prayers to the pious dead. Drawing further on recognition of suffrages in practice without naming them, Julian reasons from what he says was common practice in the church. "The faith of the living would not request [aid in the future world] from those passing over if they believed certainly that in no way were they able to help them after death."[31] Besides, the disposition of the blessed to such intercession is all the more credible because these saintly souls are no longer trammeled by their bodies, and so they are freer to remember those they left behind on earth.[32] In short, then, Julian logically combines these elements of the doctrine of purgatory: graded punishment in the interim, intercession on behalf of souls in the punishments, imprecations from the living for that intercession. In sum, Julian implies a separate place for purification, though he gives it no name. Less important, but still significant, Julian alludes to prayers as pleas to the saintly dead for intercession, but he ignores alms or other good works done on their behalf; his focus is on prayers, not deeds.

The clarity of this distinct function for the purgatorial fire receives further support in a passage by the Anglo-Saxon Bede (d. 735), chronicler, hagiographer, biblical commentator, and monk first at Wearmouth, then at Jarrow. Bede almost takes for granted the existence of a fire capable of purifying intermediate souls. What he adds is a more specific sense of the circumstances in which that function is achieved. Bede supplies a tantalizing possibility of a separate location for the purgatorial fire. In a sermon for the first Monday of Advent, after referring to the hope of the pious to see God as soon as they die, he notes that there are others who will still see him, but after a delay:

Some of those preordained because of their good works to enjoy the fate of the elect, nonetheless, exit the body tainted because of some evil deeds. These persons may, by means of a severe process of castigation,

---

31. Julian, *Prognosticon futuri saeculi* 2.26; p. 63.
32. Ibid.

be drawn out from the flames of the purgatorial fire. Either they are made clean from the filth of their vices by the fire's long examination until the day of judgment, or perhaps they may be released from punishment and arrive at the peace of the saints *earlier* by means of the prayers, alms, fasts, tears, or offerings of the salutary host from their faithful friends.[33]

The soul of a person saved although tainted by sin progresses through the purgatorial fire by the examination of the fire alone, by suffrages alone, or by the two working in concert. The key to this statement is "earlier," the idea that external aids from devoted friends within the faith speed the exit of the slightly guilty soul from the severe castigation of the purgatorial fire. This flexibility in time of exit expands the role of temporary punishment. Those destined to be saved despite their minor faults, mere sinners in the purgatorial fire, seem to receive new visibility as compared to the wicked in hell. Bede's reference to "the flames of the purgatorial fire" (*flammis ignis purgatorii*) is also translatable as "the flames of the fire of purgatory." Because the matter is formally ambiguous, I momentarily postpone discussion of whether this is a reference to purgatory proper. This ambiguity leads to the reflection that it is one thing to propose a purifying fire in the interim, and another to explain which types of souls qualify for which fates during that time. Who goes immediately to heaven, who to hell, and whose fate is known but not yet realized because of slight but residual guilt?

Mere Sinners and the Truly Wicked

Bede attempted to answer by addressing the purgatorial fire again in his *Commentary on the Book of Proverbs*, which in chapter 11 presents a reversal of fates between the righteous and the wicked. Verse 8 says, "When the wicked man (*impius*) dies, there is no further hope for him, and his expectation that anyone may be solicitous will perish." Perhaps no one will be solicitous of the

---

33. My emphasis. "At uero non nulli propter bona quidem opera ad electorum sortem praeordinati sed propter mala aliqua quibus polluti de corpore exierunt post mortem severe castigandi excipiuntur flammis ignis purgatorii et uel usque ad diem iudicii longa huius examinatione a uitiorum sorde mundantur uel certe *prius* amicorum fidelium precibus elemosinis ieiuniis fletibus et hostiae salutaris oblationibus absoluti a poenis et ipsi ad beatorum perueniunt requiem." Bede, *Homeliarum evangelii libri II*, 1.2, *In Adventu*, lines 212–20; CCSL 122, ed. D. Hurst (1955), p. 13; cited in Henry G. J. Beck, "A Ninth-Century Canonist on Purgatory," *American Ecclesiastical Review* 111.4 (1944): 250–56, who attributes this quotation to Hincmar of Reims. M. Thomas Aquinas Carroll, "An Eighth-Century Exegete on Purgatory," *American Ecclesiastical Review* 112.1 (1945): 261–63, correctly observes that Hincmar was quoting Bede. I thank Isabel Moreira for these references.

wicked, who, Bede would say, are in oblivion, but what of those who have
some faults, but are not entirely wicked? Bede turned for clues to the book
of Psalms and to earlier Christian commentators. Psalm 1:1 says, "Blessed is
the man who walks not in the counsel of the wicked, nor stands in the way
of sinners." The parallel construction of this verse raises the question of
whether the wicked (*impii*) and sinners (*peccatores*) are synonymous.[34] Zeno
of Verona (d. before 380) said, "There is as much difference between a wicked
person (*impius*) and a sinner (*peccator*) as there is between a sinner and a just
person (*iustus*)." And the differences between them are expressed "gradually,
through their merits" (*gradatim pro meritis*).[35] He saw all souls spread across
a spectrum, separated by degrees of moral character. The damned surpass
a certain degree of sin. Zeno considered mere sinners, intermediate souls,
liable to judgment, but not by probatory fire, rather by a personal judge. The
just receive their crown, the wicked eternal punishment, but the sinners are
mercifully either pardoned or chastised.[36] The gradual progression between
these degrees of difference comes at the expense of hell because it sets up a
boundary between the damned and other sinners. For Jerome (d. 420), the
difference is this: "The wicked person denies God, the sinner acknowledges
[him] but sins."[37] Augustine (d. 430) conceded that "sinners are understood
as wicked" and "every wicked person is a sinner, but not every sinner is
wicked."[38] Thus he preserved the distinction proposed by Zeno and Jerome
between the wicked and the sinners. In the *Enchiridion*, Augustine put those
who were so wicked as to be beyond the reach of suffrages, and saints, for
whom suffrages are superfluous, at opposite poles. But in between he posited
intermediate souls who could benefit from suffrages in varying degrees.[39]
Gregory I agreed with Augustine: "Every wicked person is a sinner, but not
every sinner is wicked"; he added, however: "The sinner who remains in faith

34. The two terms in Greek are *asebōn* and *hamartōlōn*; Hebrew: *rshoim* (wicked) and *chtaim* (sinful). The separation of the "wicked" (*impium*) from the "righteous" (*iustum*) also occurs in Malachi 3:17–4:6, divides those who serve God from those who do not, on a great Day of Reckoning. *Impius* can also mean "godless," especially when equated with *infideles* or contrasted to *fideles*. Thus, Gregory I says the *impii* are *infideles*, whereas the *peccatores* belong to the church in faith but not in action. *Mor.* 25.10, lines 9–13: "Impios uero scriptura sacra proprie infideles apppellat. . . . Impius uero proprie dicitur qui a religionis pietate separatur"; CCSL 143B, ed. M. Adriaen (1985), p. 1250. Cf. Taio of Zaragossa, *Sentences* 5.17: "Quid differt inter peccatores et impios"; PL 80:973A–B.

35. Zeno of Verona, *Tractatus* 1.35, lines 23–26; CCSL 22, ed. B. Löfstedt (1971), p. 89.

36. Ibid., lines 78–80; p. 91.

37. Hieronimus, *Tractatus lix in Psalmos*, Psalm 1, line 190; CCSL 78, ed. G. Morin (1958), p. 9.

38. Augustine, *Enarrat. Ps.* 1.5, lines 7–8; CCSL 38, ed. E. Dekkers (1956), p. 3.

39. Augustine, *Enchiridion* 29.110; CCSL 46, ed. E. Evans (1969), pp. 108–9; trans. Shaw, p. 127; Bernstein, *Formation*, 316–19.

is pious [despite his sin]."[40] In Julian of Toledo's eyes, "It must therefore be believed that all will be resurrected at the same time, but the wicked to their torture, sinners to that Last Judgment, and all the saints to their reward."[41] The intermediate (sinners) must undergo the final reckoning, but the fates of the wicked and the saints are already known.

With these ideas of his intellectual predecessors at his disposal, Bede had before him a middle population of souls in the interim who were neither very evil nor very pure. Bede considers the possibility of cleansing the middle group but only in the context of suffrages—a context that goes back to Augustine's discussion of the aid the living can render the dead. Bede's exposition goes in two directions. First, he explains and rejects Origen's theory of postmortem rehabilitation. Then, he substitutes a system of his own that incorporates the aid of a community of prayer supporting a deceased person's progress through the purgatorial fire.

Bede's statement is best understood one part at a time, as a medieval commentator might approach it. "When the wicked man (*impius*) dies, his hope perishes" (Prov. 11:8); Bede goes beyond stating that there is no hope for a wicked man. By excluding hope from the wicked, he reserves it for the sinner. Bede goes on to challenge Origen's theory that allowed for the eventual restoration of all the dead through postmortem refinement over many reincarnations, ending in heavenly unity: "This statement involves Origen, who believed that after the last and universal judgment life should be given to all the wicked (*impiis*) and the sinners (*peccatoribus*)."[42] Bede's objection is that Origen's restoration would include all who are less than perfect, no matter how grave their sin. In order to show differences between those whom Origen would indiscriminately promote to heaven, Bede distinguishes the *impii* (wicked), who are damned, from the *peccatores* (sinners), who can be cured. At the virtuous extreme, the *iusti* (the just), such as martyrs, are immediately saved. These terms change from author to author through the Middle Ages, but the three categories remain fundamental to reflection about postmortem purification. In Bede's briefly sketched system, the wicked are truly lost, but there is hope for those who die with lighter sins:

> It should be noted, however, that even if there is no hope of mercy for the wicked after death, there are nonetheless those who died while still tainted by lighter sins, who are able to be absolved or made chaste again through punishments, or cleansed through the prayers, alms,

40. Greg. *Mor.* 25.10, lines 7–8; CCSL 143B:1250.

41. Julian, *Prognosticon* 3.19, lines 12–15; pp. 93–94.

42. Bede, *In prouerbia Salomonis libri iii* 2.11, line 19; CCSL 119B, ed. D. Hurst (1983), p. 70.

and the celebrations of masses performed by their people (*suorum*). No matter who performs these [charitable actions], they are done both before the judgment and on behalf of those who have erred only in comparatively slight ways.[43]

This passage is noteworthy in two regards. First, it provides further evidence about those who perform suffrages. In the Advent sermon, Bede called them "faithful friends," and here they are "their people." The earlier phrase suggests one's monastic brothers or sisters; the latter phrase suggests one's blood relatives and, to a lesser extent, political and economic dependents. In the emerging application of suffrages for aid in the purgatorial fire, the two types of helpers blend together and constitute an overlap between one's religious and one's social support group.[44]

Second, the passage modifies the idea of Caesarius of Arles, who implied that all evil deeds range across a single distribution, whether in the temporary or the eternal fire. The former may be expiated with greater or lesser difficulty; the latter may be punished (but never expiated) with greater or lesser severity, according to the gravity of the sin. Bede limits the effectiveness of suffrages to those paying for very slight sins. Thus, Bede coordinates the postmortem condition of the nearly perfect with the help of their associates in religion and society. Bede's formulation retains the term "sinners" for all those in the middle category. Alcuin of York, we shall see, will modify this term so that the connotations accord more with the slightness of the offenses that can be pardoned by suffrages, but Bede has succeeded in opposing Origen's idea that the wicked and the sinners—together, all of them—can still attain heaven.

To the best of my knowledge, the importance of Bede's reference to Origen in connection with suffrages was first observed in a paper by Isabel Moreira.[45] Bede's theory, Moreira reasons, is "not a reaction against hell, but a response to Origen." I would interpret Moreira's insight as follows. The function of purgatorial fire moves Origen's therapeutic afterlife in two direc-

---

43. "Notandum autem quod, etsi impiis post mortem spes ueniae non est, sunt tamen qui de leuioribus peccatis quibus obligati defuncti sunt post mortem possunt absolui uel poenis uidelicet castigati uel suorum precibus, elemosinis, missarum celebrationibus absoluti. Sed haec quibuscumque fiunt et ante iudicium et de leuioribus fiunt erratis." Bede, *In prouerbia Salomonis* 2.11, lines 22–27; p. 70.

44. On this "friendship," see Isabel Moreira, *Heaven's Purge: Purgatory in Late Antiquity* (Oxford: Oxford University Press, 2010), 166–73.

45. Isabel Moreira, "Hell, Purgatory, and the Negotiation of Salvation" (paper presented at the conference "Hell and its Afterlife," Salt Lake City, Tuesday, October 24, 2006); Moreira has expanded the paper in *Heaven's Purge*, 162–65.

tions. First, it adapts the ancient, cyclical afterlife to the (Jewish, Christian, and Muslim) linear interim of late antiquity and the early Middle Ages. Second, instead of allowing progress to all sinners, as Origen does, it limits hope to the nearly perfect, those guilty of only light sins. Bede's purgatorial fire appropriates Origen's therapeutic afterlife but adds entry requirements that exclude the incurably wicked.

The social pressures that encouraged belief in suffrages among Christians of late antiquity and the early Middle Ages were much broader than the theological debate over Origen. Suffrages involve popular, emotional reactions to death at the level of the family and kin group; they evoke memories of parents and predecessors. In Bede's day, the church was only implicitly and sporadically the type of hierarchical institution that could define ideas at the top and disseminate orthodoxy down through the population. As Bede's *History of the English Church and People* makes clear, the population itself was far from homogeneous; many who called themselves Christian were recently and imperfectly converted from their previous Germanic or Celtic ideas.[46] Members of the literate elite recorded efforts to shape some of these currents into cohesive narratives of lived experiences in the form of visions. Bede himself knew and recorded for posterity visions of souls near death. The vision literature will help compensate for the fragmentary nature of the often scattered and heterogeneous evidence indicative of what would become purgatory. Bede's two references to the purgatorial fire lack context. It is as if they were appositional afterthoughts, a later definition of terms. Unlike the statements in Julian of Toledo's *Prognosticon*, it is not clear why Bede's references appear in their particular work.

Bede's contribution to the idea of purgatorial fire was to propose a potential improvement in the afterlife for certain kinds of people (sinners, but not the wicked), and to connect this possibility to the suffrages that speed passage through the purgatorial pains. Some historians, however, argue that Bede did much more. They contend that Bede first offered "the substantive use of Purgatory" and "synthesized" the teachings of the councils of Lyon II and Trent on purgatory, a place with a name of its own.[47] To evaluate

---

46. For these worldviews, see, as a quick introduction, Richard Abels, "What Has Weland to Do with Christ? The Franks Casket and the Acculturation of Christianity in Early Anglo-Saxon England," *Speculum* 84.3 (July 2009): 549–81, esp. at 567–72. A vast literature has been devoted to this subject. For the early Anglo-Saxon period one might consider the literature devoted to the finds at Sutton-Hoo or the background to *Beowulf*.

47. Beck, "Ninth-Century Canonist," 250, attributes the phrase to Hincmar of Reims. Carroll, "Eighth-Century Exegete," 261–63, correctly identifies the crucial phrase as coming from Bede, though she acknowledges that Bede also uses *purgatorius* as an adjective. Still, she calls the passage identified by Beck as a "pithy and correct statement of doctrine on Purgatory" (261). Beck (250)

this assertion it is necessary to return to the statement that persons dying with slight sins "may be drawn out from the flames of the purgatorial fire" (*excipiuntur flammis ignis purgatorii*). Henry G. J. Beck, who first discovered the phrase in the writings of Hincmar of Reims, calls this the earliest known reference to purgatory used as a proper noun. Considering *ignis purgatorii* an appositional genitive, he translates it as "the fires of Purgatory."[48] Although Sister M. Thomas Aquinas Carroll correctly shows that Hincmar was quoting Bede, thus giving the phrase an even longer lineage, she agrees with Beck's translation.[49] Beck himself concedes, "It may be, of course, that here 'purgatorii' is still an adjective modfying 'ignis,' but [continues Beck] I do not think that we can dismiss the possibility that it has already begun to be used as a noun. Neither the context nor the actual form of the word itself make untenable the view that 'purgatorii' is here an appositional genitive."[50] So momentous an event should be more firmly established than a possibility not to be dismissed and by evidence better than not untenable.

I consider it much more likely that, by the time Bede wrote this passage, the purgatorial fire had, implicitly, become a compound, such as *latifundia* (extensive estate) or *paterfamilias* (head of clan) in Latin, or *moonlight, earthquake, afterlife*, or *otherworld* in English.[51] Another example of how early medieval usage can develop into something more precise is the term Francia, the name given by early medieval writers to the land dominated by the tribe or people of the Franks.[52] In the early Middle Ages, Francia sometimes straddled the Rhine and sometimes the Seine. Sometimes it stretched south to incorporate what was then called Burgundy, itself a very flexible designation (today the Auvergne and Languedoc). How remarkable that a term sometimes rendered today as France could include part of Germany and sometimes lack the lands south of the Loire! Only Francia can resolve this dilemma.[53] The purgatorial fire is to purgatory as early medieval Francia is to France. Even though the idea of the purgatorial fire became an emotional force by about 700, the authoritative pronouncement that defined purgatory did not come until 1254. If, in this early period, *purgatorium* had been a

erroneously attributes the first "use of the term *Purgatory* in its form as a *noun*" to Hildebert of Le Mans (1055–1143). The sermon to which he points is actually by Peter Comestor, also called Petrus Manducator. See Le Goff, *Birth*, 155 and 392 n. 4.

48. Beck, "Ninth-Century Canonist," 250 and 256.

49. Carroll, "Eighth-Century Exegete," 261.

50. Allen and Greenough, *New Latin Grammar*, §343d (1888; Boston: Ginn, 1931), 212.

51. See examples at http://bit.ly/1h9GfRP, accessed Feb 11, 2014.

52. The ethnic composition of the Franks is also open to question. Patrick J. Geary, *Before France and Germany* (New York: Oxford University Press, 1988), 77–79, 95–96.

53. Paul Fouracre, *The Age of Charles Martel* (Harlow, UK: Longman, 2000), 4–5.

noun, it would have occurred alone, yet it never appears without *ignis* until the examples cited by Le Goff with the exceptions noted in Bede. It only became "purgatory" when "fire" could be omitted. The evidence does not yet support the idea of an independently conceived purgatory; calling it that is a backreading from later dogmatic definitions.

For its part, the concept represented by the compound "purgatorial fire" very definitely existed. Julian of Toledo saw in the purgatorial fire a separate function and a separate time but not yet a separate place. Bede adds suffrages as what might be considered a special currency that speeds souls through their correction. As will become clear in the next chapter, the *Vision of Drythelm* (or *Drychthelm*), and maybe even the slightly earlier *Vision of Fursey*, present the concept of a purgatorial function. Significantly, however, both visions imagine that function operating in radically different ways and in radically different places. This function, existing vaguely in some kind of space, where the fire purifies but does not imprison eternally, and where sentences vary in duration, existed most clearly as a compound noun, the "purgatorial fire."

Bede provided a nomenclature for souls according to the fates they would experience after death. Consistent with the centuries-long effort to mitigate the stark, binary division of the dead into saved and damned, came another development at the turn from the eighth to the ninth century in the thought of Alcuin of York. Alcuin expressed his views on the purgatorial fire in his summary of Catholic teaching, *On the Faith* (*De fide*), which he offered his royal patron, Charlemagne, in 802.[54] Whereas Bede, following Zeno of Verona, called the middle category "sinners" (*peccatores*), Alcuin, who followed him by two generations, called them "the righteous" (*iusti*), the term Bede had used for those who go to heaven immediately at death. By promoting the middle group from "sinners" (*peccatores*) to "righteous" (*iusti*), Alcuin emphasizes the slightness of their faults and their position among the saved. As he turns to his eschatological lesson on the reward for the just and the punishment of sinners, Alcuin begins with 1 Corinthians 3:13, which he immediately identifies as the purgatorial fire. He momentarily ignores the difference between probative fire in the interim and eternal fire after the Last Judgment and imagines a single fire on a continuous timeline.

There can be no doubt that he [the apostle Paul in 1 Cor. 3:13] spoke here of the purgatorial fire, which affects the *wicked* differently, the

---

54. Donald A. Bullough, *Alcuin: Achievement and Reputation: Being Part of the Ford Lectures Delivered in Oxford in Hilary Term 1980* (Leiden and Boston: Brill, 2004), 18 n. 38.

saints differently, and the *righteous* differently. Now indeed, from the wracking of this fire, the *wicked* are drawn down to the flames of the perpetual fire. The *saints*, who are without any stain of sin, will be resurrected together with their bodies, because they built gold, silver, and precious stones on the foundation, which is Christ, and they will triumph over that fire with as much ease as they had integrity of faith and love of Christ and respect for his commandments in this world.[55]

The saints will emerge unscathed, like the boys from the furnace in Babylon. The *righteous*, who die still tainted by minor sins, will endure some pain:

> There are still certain people, the *righteous*, obligated [merely] for certain minute sins because they built on the foundation that is Christ, wood, hay, and straw, which are purged by the ardor of that fire, by which, once they are cleansed, they are made worthy by the glory of eternal felicity.[56]

All this, so far, is the function of the fire referred to in 1 Corinthians 3:13, considered to burn in the interim. Alcuin connects it directly to the Last Judgment, which takes over and completes the separation, thus distinguishing the saved from the damned. He achieves this by turning his discussion of the transitory, probative fire from 1 Corinthians 3:13 into an allusion to Augustine's two cities, here called congregations, from the *City of God*, but in words he takes from the *Enchiridion*, chapter 111:

> Once that transitory fire has done its work and the whole judgment of the Last Day has been completed, two congregations will be divided: one of the saints and one of the wicked; [and, as Augustine says in the *Enchiridion*,] 'one of Christ, the other of the devil; one of the good, the other of the wicked, whether they be angels or humans. Neither the will of the former, nor the power of the latter will be able to achieve any sin, nor will there be any way to die. The former will live truly and happily in eternal life, the latter will endure miserably an undying torment that lasts forever.'[57]

Pursuing the fate of the damned, he explains to the emperor in terms reminiscent of Gregory I's qualitative refinements for punishments in hell (itself a gloss on the same chapter of the *Enchiridion*), but not in his exact words,

---

55. Alcuin, *De fide sanctae et individuae Trinitatis . . . Libri tres* 3.21: "De justorum praemio et poena peccatorum"; PL 101:53B.
56. Ibid., PL 101:53B–C.
57. Ibid., 53C.

"according to the quality of the sins, those who are weighed down by a lighter weight of misdeeds will be tortured more mildly." Conversely, "the saints, too, have various merits, and each will receive the reward of blessedness according to the magnitude of their merits."[58]

What is important here about the roots of what would become purgatory is how Alcuin fused the acquired observations of Augustine, Gregory, and Bede to make not just another interpretation of 1 Corinthians 3:13, but to present a unified doctrine of purgatorial fire before and eternal fire after the Last Judgment. Alcuin takes the old distinction between "capital crimes" and "minute sins" and, building on terms associated by Bede, filters it through a second separation of human moral natures: the wicked (*impii*), the righteous (*iusti*), and the saints (*sancti*).

This threefold division became a conceptual model in its own right. Indeed, this tripartition of souls in the interim gives purgatorial fire its function. Alcuin's shift of the righteous into the middle position reflects the progress of the purgatorial fire and the increased optimism about those who died repentant of their sins. It moves the boundary (never clearly fixed) between purgatorial and eternal punishment at the expense of hell. Like Bede, who stressed the ability of one's fellow monks or one's kin to devote suffrages to the deceased, Alcuin locates the purgatorial fire farther from hell and closer to heaven—just suffrages away! What this means is that in the interim, the same fire, *called* purgatorial, simultaneously punishes both those to be cleansed and those to be damned, as Julian of Toledo and (as we shall see, in Jewish circles) the School of Shammai had taught. This simultaneity is another reason why the purgatorial fire is not yet purgatory: during the interim it doubles as punishment for the damned.

These two perspectives begin to work together. On the one hand, only the righteous can benefit from purgation. The wicked retain their sin, which remains incurable either through its excessive quantity or its criminal nature. The burden of their sin survives the transitory and must endure the eternal fire. The ambiguity of such expressions as "the places of punishment," "the punishments," the *loca poenalia*, springs from this double function of the purgatorial fire, which, during the interim, torments both the righteous to be cleansed eventually and the damned who will never escape. This apparent reticence in naming the punitive locations during the early Middle Ages, despite the distinctions between sins (major and minor) and persons (wicked, righteous, saints), is only a difficulty if we expect earlier documents to present the clarity of later doctrinal distinctions.

---

58. Ibid., 53A–D.

One senses that Alcuin's understanding of Bede, Julian, Gregory, Caesarius, and Augustine incorporated a cumulative doctrinal sense, a matter of one insight provoking another. Afterward, the passages on which Alcuin relied, and he in turn supplied, produced a series of doctrinal units, commonplaces, that could be linked in modular fashion as needed, like steps in the proof of a theorem or precedents in support of a judicial decision. In the Carolingian period, monastic scriptoria began to collect these patristic and early medieval quotations, called *sententia*, and classify them according to context to achieve a certain standardization whereby these "proof texts" could be filed, combined, and recombined as needed. Thus arrayed, they could be invoked on behalf of any given doctrine. Those combined by Alcuin became standard supports for the exposition of the purgatorial fire. One example of how Carolingian scriptoria employed this technique appears in Archbishop Hincmar's *Life of Remigius*, which we have already encountered in the story of the resurrection of the little girl of Toulouse. Immediately after relating the story of the wondrous cure of the girl, Hincmar expands on the nature of death itself. First, he affirms the existence of purgatorial fire. He starts by quoting Bede's statements from the *Commentary on the Book of Proverbs* and his Advent sermon: "There are some who are destined for the fate of the elect, but who, because of certain minor faults, still require some cleansing."[59] He then quotes Alcuin's distinction between the saints, the righteous, and the wicked. Now Hincmar quotes Alcuin quoting Augustine's *Enchiridion* on how Judgment Day will separate all into two communities. Then Alcuin again: each person will either be damned or crowned according to the nature of their merits.[60] Fixed associations of *sententia* could acquire near-authoritative force. As Hincmar's treatment shows, Alcuin's teaching on the purgatorial fire is set, at least as a cliché in theology, until further notice.

How Did Purgatorial Fire Spread?

We have examined the many alternatives proposed to mitigate the idea of an eternal hell. Yet Alcuin's explanation of the purgatorial fire reflects the

---

59. On this quotation, see Beck, "Ninth-Century Canonist," 250–56; Beck regards it as the first reference to purgatory as a place. In the next issue of the same journal, however, Carroll, "Eighth-Century Exegete," 261–63, found the same statement in Bede. I have examined both in this chapter. In the clause that both authors regard as the first use of *purgatorium* as a substantive, "severe castigandi . . . flammis ignis purgatorii," I see no reason to regard it as such. The phrase reads perfectly well as "the flames of purgatorial fire," which is more consistent with the patristic use to which both Bede and Hincmar were deeply indebted.

60. Hincmar Remensis, *Vita Remigii Episcopi Remensis 9*, ed. Bruno Krusch, MGH, SS RR MM 3 (1896; Hannover: Hahn, 1977), 285–90, at 287–88.

standardization that contemporary ecclesiastics and educators in the early part of Charlemagne's reign sought throughout his lands—a movement called the Carolingian Renaissance. Alcuin's statement remained more or less fixed until the changes Le Goff identified in the 1170s. If this is the culmination of a development that we have traced from 1 Corinthians through Zeno of Verona and Caesarius of Arles to Alcuin, how may we understand its staying power?

Despite the data provided by canonical texts and empirical evidence, ideas about the otherworld were not confined to a spiritual vacuum. The accounts of calibration and proportionality so fundamental to the theological speculations traced above were not imported only from Scripture. They were also shaped by societal influences, such as the institution of slavery, military discipline, imperial administration, patterns of monarchy, territorial disputes, and copious legal texts, whether the Hebrew Bible (seen as a guide to monarchical rule), Roman law, or the burgeoning canon law of the developing church. Politics also affected thought about death as reflections on royal jurisdiction, imperial power, and divine rule competed to provide conceptual models for understanding society and the cosmos. Monastic introspection concerning the debts one owes for moral offenses brought hell into the conscience of the pious. Despite Augustine's insistence that the dead are confined in "hidden receptacles," popular belief favored a free exchange within a long-lived gray area between visionaries, who travel from this world to the next, and ghosts, who appear from beyond. As a result, there emerged a pattern whereby perceptions of this world and the otherworld mutually affected each other.

Records of late ancient and early medieval politics represent many events on the ground as interactions between humans and their supernatural opponents or protectors. When Benedict of Nursia established Monte Cassino, he selected a hilltop that had previously been sacred to Apollo. He drove out "demons" to prepare the way.[61] When two Merovingian kings competed for possession of Paris, saints were invoked to enforce the terms of negotiations that had been sworn to in their names.[62] Kings could turn a previously pagan (or Arian) people Catholic with a single command to be baptized.[63]

---

61. Gregorius Magnus, Dialogorum libri IV, 2.8.10, lines 97–102; ed. A. de Vogüé, SC 260 (1979), p. 168. Cf. the translation by Myra L. Uhlfelder: Gregory the Great, Dialogues, Book II: Saint Benedict, The Library of Liberal Arts (Indianapolis: Bobbs-Merrill, 1967), 18.

62. Gregorius Turonensis, Libri historiarum decem 7.6; MGH, SS RR MM 1 (1885), p. 294; Gregory of Tours, The History of the Franks, trans. Lewis Thorpe (Harmondsworth, UK: Penguin, 1974), 391–92.

63. Numerous examples can be found in Gregory of Tours (see note 61) and Bede: Historia ecclesiastica gentis Anglorum, ed. Charles Plummer, 2 vols. (Oxford: Clarendon Press, 1896); A History

In Roman law, citizens and visiting aliens share the same environment. In this period of intense military, political, ethnic, and religious interaction, the merely wayward could mingle with the cruelest of criminals in the punitive fires. The patterns of these relationships were as complex in the otherworld as they were on the ground, and each affected perception of the other.

This view of the confluence between earthly and heavenly narratives receives support from the research of Friedrich Prinz on the early history of monasticism in Frankish territory. Prinz has shown how, when the Frankish aristocratic clans began to rule Late Roman Gaul and penetrate the major aristocratic houses of the empire, they established monasteries as an expression of their status as local rulers and thereby enhanced their prominence. In essence, kings or great lords, their daughters, wives, or widows established monastic foundations from family lands. Thus, they became the patron saints of these houses, were buried there, and their graves became pilgrimage sites, their bones relics. The monasteries or convents (or double monasteries, that is, joint foundations housing both sexes) they had endowed lived from revenues deriving from the original family estate, which served as its endowment. These initial foundations became self-perpetuating and conferred prestige on the family descended from the saintly ancestor. Over time, founders' descendants, when they became monks or nuns, received livings called prebends or shares of the revenue streams from the initial endowments, while, at the same time the family enjoyed enhanced standing from this ancestral charisma celebrated in locally produced saints' *Lives*. This type of self-glorification recalls, at least in function, the funeral processions Polybius analyzed among the ancient Romans of the second century BCE.[64] Unlike these ceremonies of ancient Rome, the religious foundations of the early Frankish aristocracy were intensely local, thus fostering greater diversity in the associated cults of individual saints.[65]

---

of the English Church and People, trans. Leo Shirley-Price, rev. R. E. Latham (Harmondsworth, UK: Penguin, 1955).

64. Friedrich Prinz calls the process "self-justification" if not "self-sanctification" (*Selbstheiligung*) and "self-sanctioning" (*Selbstsanktionierung*). *Frühes Mönchtum im Frankenreich* (Vienna: Oldenberg, 1965), 489, 502.

For a different evaluation of the founders' social function, see Jamie Kreiner, *The Social Life of Hagiography in the Merovingian Kingdom*, Cambridge Studies in Medieval Life and Thought (Cambridge: Cambridge University Press, 2014). See also Polybius, *Histories* 6.53–54, trans. W. R. Paton, *Polybius*, vol. 3, LCL (Cambridge, MA: Harvard University Press, 1979), 389–93; and Bernstein, *Formation*, 109–11.

65. For the specific application of this pattern to Ireland, see Peter Brown, "The Decline of the Empire of God: Amnesty, Penance, and the Afterlife from Late Antiquity to the Middle Ages," in *Last Things: Death and the Apocalypse in the Middle Ages*, ed. Caroline Walker Bynum and Paul Freedman (Philadelphia: University of Pennsylvania Press, 2000), 41–59, at 52.

In short, as religious faith described unseen powers in the otherworld it also reflected and modeled the earthly realities of early medieval society. Augustine himself built on the assumed parallel between worldly and otherworldly realities when he described damnation as exile from the presence of God (*Enchiridion* 29.112) and called all suffering purgatorial (*City of God* 21.13), because, if accepted piously, it reveals the virtue of the tested soul. In the same way, intercession in real life carried over into the afterlife and vice versa. The gradations in power so crucial to each hierarchy, worldly and otherworldly, fostered a durable belief that the evaluation of merits and demerits, charitable acts and sins, could also be calibrated. This perception that the otherworld hierarchy accurately reflects the structures of this one encouraged an approach to postmortem judgment and discipline to which the calibrated places of punishment, and particularly the purgatorial fire, were especially well adapted. The visionary accounts of the otherworld to be examined in the next chapter will illustrate this point dramatically.

Suffrages

The fragmentation of political power and of cult moved hand in hand with the calibration of hierarchies and carried important consequences for every soul and every religious house. Because the donations of local patrons allowed devotees of the saints whose bones were buried beneath their altars to venerate their hallowed ancestors and moral models, the saints, the gifts were acts of piety that did not go unrewarded. Chief among the rewards were the prayers of these saints for the souls of the donors. The living members of the communities (monasteries or cathedrals) that had custody of the graves joined their entreaties to the intercession of the saints, already in heaven. This complex of gifts, whether in the form of land, cash (there was very little cash), veneration, or prestige, permeated the system, whose goal was to request help from holy, ancestral patrons, the saints. If one regards the saints as the community of those in heaven capable of interceding on behalf of living devotees, then loyalty to these select dead could arise from allegiance to one's own clan or the clan of the locally dominant family (thus blending family ties into political allegiance). The liturgy of monks or nuns who prayed on behalf of contributors then joined social bonds to piety.

All these forms of aid—donations to the establishments that supported religious specialists, prayers from the living, intercession from the saints—were called by the generic term *suffragia* (suffrages). In the late Roman imperial government, *suffragia* were payments made to the treasury prior to the award of a government office, that is, bribes.[66] Justinian prohibited payment of suffrages in his *Novella* 8 in 535 CE,[67] but in the ecclesiastical context, *suffragium* (payment for offices) becomes a metaphor. The pious make "payments" in the form of prayers, alms, or masses, and the "offices" are the religious services, masses, offerings, prayers, or intercession by religious specialists to the saints, or by the saints to yet higher authorities, Mary or Christ. These prayers were offered on behalf of deceased family members or oneself in the future. Expressions of this purpose sometimes form the preamble to charters documenting pious donations made to monasteries and preserved within their chartularies. The stated motivation appears in the record of a gift made on August 20, 762, to the monastery of St. Gall, near Lake Constance, in the foothills of the Swiss Alps:

I [and the name of the donor], considering the purview of God and divine retribution, and wishing that I may become worthy of meriting mercy for my sins, do therefore give on this day a gift that I intend to be perpetual to the monastery of Saint Gall, where he himself rests in his body, over which place bishop John presides, together with his monks. [The donor describes the property to be transferred.] [I give] so that they might possess it perpetually and have the power to do with it whatever they wish. But if, indeed, anyone, either myself or some one of my heirs or any other person, however farfetched this fear may be, should obstruct or wish to break this donation, which I have asked in good will to be done for the salvation of my soul, especially if [the offender] be unwilling to make amends, let [the offender] incur the wrath of God [and] of all the saints and greatly fear to undergo the penalties of hell and be excluded from every church and above all be forced to pay five pounds of gold [and] ten weights of silver to the treasury (of the church).[68]

---

66. A. H. M. Jones, *The Later Roman Empire* (Baltimore: Johns Hopkins University Press, 1986), 1:230, 279, 306–7, and passim. C. du Fresne du Cange, *Glossarium mediae et infimae latinitatis*, 10 vols. in 5 (1883–87; Graz: Akademische Druck, 1954), 7:650b–651a, gives "suffragium: pecuniae, quae suffragii titulo ab Imperatoribus accipiebantur, cum honores deferebant" at 650b under "suffragium, 1." For a breathtaking survey of bribery as a cultural phenomenon, and *suffragium* (payment for office) in particular, see John T. Noonan, *Bribes* (New York: Macmillan, 1984), 119–20.

67. As Du Cange observes (see note 66), suffrages occupy Title 8 of Justinian's *Novellae. Corpus Juris Civilis*, vol. 3, ed. R. Schoell and G. Kroll (Berlin: Weidmann, 1928), 64–78. The emperor wishes officials to be content with their wages. See Charles Pazdernik, "'The Trembling of Cain': Religious Power and Institutional Culture in Justinianic Oath-Making," in *The Power of Religion in Late Antiquity*, ed. Andrew Cain and Noel Lenski (Farnham, UK: Ashgate, 2009), 143–54, at 149.

68. *Urkundenbuch der Abtei Sanct Gallen*, pt. I, *700–840*, ed. Hermann Wartmann (Zurich, 1863), no. 26, p. 30.

This document is not just a real estate contract; the charter places the gift in a supernatural context. It first mentions divine providence, future judgment, an awareness of the donor's own sins, and a perceived need for mercy in their evaluation. The donor expressly indicates that the gift is made to the monastery where the saint is buried, his tomb tended by a given abbot (or in this case an abbot who is also a bishop) and his monks, who cultivate the grave of the patron saint, the founder. The gift is to last forever, that is, until the Second Coming. It is understood that the monks, aided by the saint beneath the floor of their church, are to pray for the soul of the donor. The permanence of the gift is crucial to its effectiveness. Nothing may interrupt the monks' prayers and the intercession of the saint. Should any person interfere with these regularly instituted prayers, either the donor changing his mind, or any of his heirs, or any outsider, severe penalties are to follow: consciousness of liability to hell's pains, exclusion from churches (some contemporary documents add denial of communion), and payment of a monetary fine.[69] It is worth emphasizing the connotations of the expression I have translated as "greatly fear to undergo the penalties of hell" (penas inferni experire pertimescat) because it seems closely related to the idea of inner death.[70] The document does not call for the violator's damnation; it evokes an anxiety about being in a bad status prior to judgment and hence, being concerned about suffering hell's pains. It does not say, "May you go to hell," but only "May you live in fear of hell," another severe threat.

No single document can comprise all the relevant variations of these clauses. Often the donors express the desire to have intercession for the souls of their parents as well as their own. Sometimes in the preamble the donor invokes not the fear of damnation, but desire for heaven, or, more vaguely, expresses a hope "for the benefit of my soul." Some of the other options among clauses of intention follow. Between 716 and 720 a father and his sons give because "we have considered the purview of God and the divine

---

69. The measure of gold mentioned in these clauses is the "libra," which must have weighed approximately 300–400 grams. It is obvious that sums of this amount, even if paid in smaller coins adding up to these notional values, could not possibly figure as a practical deterrent to grabbing land from monasteries. Harald Witthöft, "Die Rechnung und Zahlung mit Gold und Silber nach Zeugnissen des 6. bis 9. und 13./14. Jahrhunderts," Hamburger Beiträge zur Numismatik 32 (1978): 9–36, at 24. For background and broader perspectives, see Adriaan Verhulst, The Carolingian Economy (Cambridge: Cambridge University Press, 2002), 117–23; Simon Coupland, "The Early Coinage of Charles the Bald," Numismatic Chronicle 151 (1991): 121–58 and pls. 21–24; Philip Grierson, "Coinage in the Feudal Era," in Il feudalesimo nell'alto medioevo, Settimane di Studio 47 (Spoleto: Centro italiano di studi sull'alto Medioevo, 2000), 949–63.

70. The same clause occurs in Urkundenbuch der Abtei Sanct Gallen, no. 7, p. 7, dated November 19, 741: "iram Dei et poenas inferni experire pertimiscat."

retribution and [give] so that we might merit grace for our sins."[71] In 735 a single individual gives with the same phrase referring to "his" rather than "our" sins.[72] To the wish for mercy, a donor in 731 or 736 adds, "so that in the future, good rewards may arise for me and grow."[73] In 745 Landbert, son of Landoald and Beata, gives, "considering the purview of God and the remedy of my soul and for eternal reward and, for my substance, because I wish to have while I am alive what I give to that church [at my death]," and later adds, "for the salvation of my soul and the remedy of [the souls of] my mother and my father and, as we have said above, while I am alive, for my substance, which is a necessity for me."[74] In Landbert's case, the gift only takes full effect at his death; in the meantime, he enjoys usufruct, the revenues, from his land. This transaction was known as the *precarium*, because the gift is temporarily granted back to the donor at his request (*prex, precis*). Thus, as Landbert makes clear, bequeathing land to the local monastery can also be good business while one is alive.[75]

The sanction clauses also vary, as the following examples show: "May he incur the wrath of God and pay double as compensation";[76] "May he incur the judgment of God and pay two pounds of gold";[77] "May he incur the wrath of God and be excluded from the communion of the body [of Christ] and from the priests."[78] Some sanction clauses include only fines, but donors clearly considered otherworld penalties an additional guarantee of a contract's execution, especially when its terms stipulated adherence in perpetuity. The perpetual validity of a contract is a human imitation of eternity.

The desired afterlife benefits of gifting to churches is clear in the expressed intentions of donors and recipients. The charter evidence shows how individual believers or married couples hoped each parcel of land would forecast a favorable review in the passage from life to death if not a similarly choice lot in the otherworld. Earthly considerations were also a factor. Gifts of property assured good relations with monasteries, the abbots and their monks; convents, the abbesses and their nuns; cathedrals, the bishops and their canons. Such gift giving conformed to the pattern of other, local

71. *Urkundenbuch der Abtei Sanct Gallen*, no. 3, p. 3.
72. Ibid., no. 5, p. 5.
73. Ibid., no. 6, p. 6.
74. Ibid., no. 12, p. 14.
75. Similar terms endure in the documents of Saint Gall as late as 905 (906). See *Urkundenbuch der Abtei Sanct Gallen*, no. 747, pp. 349–50, where the gift is made "pro remedio animę meę parentumque meorum."
76. *Urkundenbuch der Abtei Sanct Gallen*, no. 2, p. 2.
77. Ibid., no. 3, p. 3.
78. Ibid., no. 4, p. 4.

landholders and political figures, who were sometimes the kin of both the donors and the recipients.[79] These gifts provided for the inclusion of the donors in the prayers of the religious community through the year's liturgy and on the anniversary of the donor's death. Looking, then, from the grass roots up toward the local abbot or abbess, toward the cathedral with prebend-endowed canons and politically prominent bishops, the intervention of spiritual superiors was a necessity.[80] From the other perspective, the religious establishments had patron saints, potential advocates for their religious communities and their individual donors in the court of heaven. Gifts made to religious foundations in perpetuity fit the system of property disposition and estate planning of early medieval land tenure and family organization. Looking toward the future, endowments assured property rights for one's descendants and prayers to aid one's own soul; looking toward the past, they expanded the reputations of saintly ancestors, and, as suffrages, they aided one's predecessors in expiation of their minor faults or confessed major sins. Indicating another parallel between worldly actions and otherworldly aspirations, earthly gifts given in perpetuity, it was hoped, gained favor in eternity. The ability of the donor to make a gift on earth for a benefit hereafter assumes an understanding of the otherworld reinforced by a body of visionary literature to which we now turn. The visions to be examined in chapter 6 will show how eschatological expectations could be predicated on an otherworld presented in images familiar from the features of geography, the discipline of slavery, and the calibrations of the earthly and heavenly hierarchies.

---

79. Lay society also had a strong intercessory component. See Geoffrey Koziol, *Begging Pardon and Favor* (Ithaca, NY: Cornell University Press, 1992); and, in a more specialized vein, Koziol, *The Politics of Memory and Identity in Carolingian Royal Diplomas*, Utrecht Studies in Medieval Literacy 28 (Turnhout, Belgium: Brepols, 2011), 68–69 and passim.

80. Moreira, *Heaven's Purge*, 166–73.

CHAPTER 6

Visions

Rights to Souls

This man is no sharer in your perdition.

—*Vision of Fursey*

He is not your friend but ours.

—*Vision of Barontus*

You have no rights to the soul you have seized.

—*Vision of the Monk of Wenlock*

This is not the hell that you think.

—*Vision of Drythelm*

In the visionary otherworld of the early Middle
Ages the damned can improve or even be saved, the living can see death, the
dead can return. In these visions the percipients and their audience were
negotiating the conventions for exchanging merits and demerits, sentiments
of contrition for past deeds or wicked thoughts, and the comprehension of
otherworld realities. Set forth as narratives, the visions do not relay fixed
doctrines but competing ideas about the relationship of life to death and
sin to its postmortem penalties. The variation in early medieval visions
shows even more clearly than the inconsistencies in contemporary theology that the later distinction between purgatory and hell did not obtain. In
fact, these two zones had never been fully distinct. Peter Dinzelbacher has
put it dramatically: "In the Middle Ages hell and purgatory became increasingly interchangeable."[1] This absence of precision is not a lack; it proves the

---

1. "[M]an denn im Mittelalter Hölle und Fegefeuer immer wieder verwechselte." Peter Dinzelbacher, *Vision und Visionsliteratur im Mittelalter* (Stuttgart: Anton Hiersemann, 1981), 103. Claude
Carozzi also states "There is no clean break between a provisional hell and a definitive hell." Carozzi, *Le voyage*, 375. So complex is the overlap between eternal and temporary hell that Carozzi
devotes twenty pages to the evolution of a purgatorial hell ("l'Enfer-Purgatoire"), 253–79. Maria Pia

dynamism of a centuries-long negotiation by which Europeans sought a collective understanding of death.[2] Given the broader tapestry against which this tournament of values was fought, there is no more anachronistic response than to say: "Because these torments end, this is not hell!" The juxtaposition of purgatorial discipline and eternal pain in "the punishments" is too intimate for that. The *Vision of Paul* alone shows that "the punishments" included hell, in a basement, for deniers of basic Christian doctrines, and other punishments for other faults. Where later commentators and historians expect to find a distinct hell and a distinct purgatory, contemporaries found what they called "the places of punishment" (*loca poenalia*), sometimes just "the punishments" (*poena*), and sometimes just "the place" (*locus*). Purgatory and hell share a gray area known to the literature of late antiquity from the *nekyia* of ancient Greece and Rome and, as we shall see, from the debates of rabbinic sages. In the West, precision spreads systematically through the schools only in the 1170s, as Jacques Le Goff points out, although earlier examples occasionally occur.

The flexibility with which this earlier age viewed the otherworld appears in Gregory I's revision of Augustine on the difference between the lower and upper hells. If the major theologians disagreed in such attempts at definition, it seems unreasonable to expect consistency between visions. To insist on a firm distinction between the lower and upper hells would be to miss altogether the tremendous deterrent effect of this not-quite-hell. In the visions of Barontus and of the monk of Wenlock, two examples to be examined below, the fact of the soul's trial alone is a deterrent that competes in force with hell itself. Moreover, in the visions, the souls, separated from their bodies, still seem to be bodies, and suffer as if they were, even though the resurrection by which the body rejoins the soul has not yet taken place. A theologian might attempt to reconcile these discrepancies; in the visions they are irrelevant. Worse, the visions would lose much of their impact if they respected these theological distinctions. The visions should not be taken as part of the history of doctrine, but as the psychological history of individuals

---

Ciccarese refers to "the still fluid state of the conception of purgatory" in the late ninth century. Ciccarese, "Le più antiche rappresentazioni del purgatorio, dalla *Passio Perpetuae* alla fine del IX sec.," *Romanobarbarica* 7 (1982–83): 33–76, at 71.

2. Jacques Le Goff, *The Birth of Purgatory*, trans. Arthur Goldhammer (1981; Chicago: University of Chicago Press, 1984), 9–116, acknowledges the value of these discussions from the early Middle Ages, even though overall he characterizes them as "stagnant" (96). The thrust of his book puts the emphasis on the twelfth-century "innovation." Jérôme Baschet, whose focus is on the period after 1100, similarly stresses the earlier literature's common features over its tensions. Baschet, *Les justices de l'au-delà: Les représentations de l'enfer en France et en Italie* (XIIᵉ–XIVᵉ siècle), Bibliothèque des Écoles Françaises d'Athènes et de Rome 279 (Rome: École française de Rome, 1993), 87–99.

living in the Middle Ages under the religious framework of a Catholicism competing with residual, indeed resistant, Germanic and Roman paganisms. Visions are personal efforts to work out how the religious system does or does not function, or, better, how the competing religious systems (learned and popular, pagan and Christian) interact. Herbert Vorgrimler suggests that the visions replaced theology, but the relationship between visions and theology was much more complex and dynamic: in the visions sometimes untrained people (who told what they saw to members of the literate elite) combined visceral fears, archetypal themes, key scriptural terms, theological givens, with their own perceptions in groping, approximate, undogmatic, religious forms.[3] If there is theology in the visions it comes from the angels who guide the souls through their troubles. Although the guardian angels offer "correct" theology to the visionary, they also represent one important mitigation of infernal discipline in that they provide providential aid at the personal level and represent a merciful aspect of the system.

In this chapter are six visionary narratives recorded from the mid-seventh to the mid-eighth century. They represent the experiences of living persons in the land of the dead. I will stress the narrative and the visual aspects of visions. In the narrative, the soul moves from one scene to the next. Some areas they visit have names (but not purgatory), others physical descriptions. As a visual experience, the soul sees the victims suffering and the environments or agents (with their implements) that inflict it. Once this review of the visions is laid out, I shall consolidate the findings by grouping the torments as aspects of hell belief in the early Middle Ages. It is not enough to present the vision- ary texts. It is also necessary to regroup key aspects of the whole dossier to understand century-long trends. Besides, details of these reports replicated themselves in later centuries. Cultivation of the visionary genre catalyzed the European imagination and made it easier for other visions to appear.

Fursey and the Fiery Globe: Refinement and Retention

One of the best examples of the flexibility of perceptions of the other- world—how visions range from announcing theological principles to explor- ing personal anxiety—is the *Vision of Fursey* (or *Furseus* or *Fursa*), which occurs in a *Life* datable to 656 or 657.[4] This Latin text is the basis for the

---

3. Herbert Vorgrimler, *Geschichte der Hölle* (Munich: Wilhelm Fink Verlag, 1993), entitles his chapter 9 (132–74) on medieval visions before Dante "Visionen statt Theologie."

4. The *Vision* comes from a *Life of Fursey*, but the *Vision* alone appears in Bede's *History*. Carozzi, *Le voyage*, 99–102; Carozzi's excellent edition of the *Vision* (extracted from the *Life*) is at 679–92. My

account Bede abbreviates in his *History of the English Church and People* (3.19).[5] Fursey was Irish and studied religion in Ireland; then he founded a monastery there. In the early 630s he moved to England to do further missionary work. He attracted the patronage of King Sigbert (or Sigeberht) of the Anglo-Saxon kingdom of East Anglia, who granted him the land on which to build a monastery. Later, when eastern England became subject to military or political unrest, he went to France and established ties with King Clovis II and his adviser Erchinoald, who helped him found a monastery at Lagny, east of Paris.[6] Thus Fursey was one of the Irish missionaries whose efforts comprised both Anglo-Saxon England and Continental Europe.

Fursey's two visions occurred during his time in Ireland, when he fell ill. In the first incident, three angels lifted him from the darkness that surrounded him to an aerial region where he could see little because of the great brightness, but he heard many hymns.[7] His soul then returned to his body. The second out-of-body experience was far more developed and frightening. Accompanied by the same angels, his soul again left his body. He traversed a huge, dark cloud, where demonic voices grated. A formation of black, ugly demons attacked the holy man with fiery arrows and hurled accusations against him, but a shield-bearing angel forced them aside. "This man is no sharer in your perdition," the angel taunted the devils.[8]

At a great height above the earth, which seemed a dark valley far below, the angels and their charge encountered four fires. Mimicking the way sin accumulates sin, the four great globes of fire united into a huge sphere that engulfed Fursey. Devils tormented the souls inside the flame, but angels intervened to defend the innocent. Fursey was afraid of the "threatening fire," but he need have no fear, his angel explained, because the fire "scrutinizes each individual according to the merit of their deeds, and the passions of each

references to this edition are marked "C" followed by the paragraph number, the line, and the page. For the *Life of Fursey* in its entirety, see W. W. Heist, *Vitae Sanctorum Hiberniae*, Subsidia Hagiographica 28 (Brussels: Société des Bollandistes, 1965), 37–55. I refer to Heist's edition as "H" followed by paragraph number, page, and lines.

    5. *Historia ecclesiastica gentis Anglorum* 3.19; ed. Charles Plummer (Oxford: Clarendon Press, 1896), 1:163–68; *A History of the English Church and People*, trans. Leo Shirley-Price (Harmondsworth, UK: Penguin, 1955), 171–75.

    6. For the complexities, see Paul Fouracre and Richard Gerberding, *Late Merovingian France* (Manchester and New York: Manchester University Press, 1996), 99–106.

    7. The soul's experience in an aerial postmortem trial and subsequent punishment have roots in non-Christian literature easily recognizable in Plutarch, *On the Delays of the Divine Vengeance*, in his *Moralia*, trans. Phillip H. De Lacy and Benedict Einarson, LCL 405, (1959). See Alan E. Bernstein, *The Formation of Hell: Death and Retribution in the Ancient and Early Christian Worlds* (Ithaca, NY: Cornell University Press, 1993), 73–83.

    8. "[H]ic homo non est particeps perditionis uestrae." C §6, line 16, p. 681; H §9, p. 40, line 16.

one will burn in this fire. For just as the body burns with illicit pleasure, so will the soul burn with the punishment it deserves.[9] The converse is also true: "What you have not lit will not burn within you."[10] Here the principles behind inner death inform the narrative of a lived experience. The flames Fursey saw attacking sinners's bodies on the outside had their counterparts consuming their souls inside. Within the flames, the devil or his demons cited flaws in Fursey's conduct and quoted harsh lines of the New Testament against him, but his guardian angel defended him with softer lines generally having to do with intention in the commission of the alleged wrong or the idea that contrition begun works as atonement completed. Thus, "Whenever one hopes for penance, divine mercy obliges";[11] then, against demonic nit-picking: "No one perishes for tiny flaws."[12]

Trial by fire is familiar from 1 Corinthians 3:13–14: "The fire will test what sort of work each one has done. If the work which any man has built on the foundations survives, he will receive a reward." Trial by fire functions like the Book of Life, the bridge in Gregory's *Dialogues*, and the Zoroastrian Cinvat Bridge. Caesarius of Arles (d. 543) had also imagined a fire that meted out punishment: "We will spend as long in that purgatorial fire as necessary." Fursey's fire, therefore, is not hell's fire, but a test fire.[13] In itself, the trial imposed by this ordeal has a deterrent force like hell's, but it is logically prior.

Even as Fursey followed the path that the angel cleared for him through the fire, the trial continued amid much ambiguity. The prosecutorial team of evil voices indicted Fursey and divine justice: "If God is just, this man will not enter the kingdom of heaven," or conversely, "If God is not evil, this man will not be free of the punishments."[14] Note that the alternative to the kingdom of heaven is not "hell," but "the punishments," a term loose enough to cover both Gehenna and the purgatorial fire. The implication seems to be that this airborne globe of fire, floating in the sky, where it intercepts souls

---

9. C §8, lines 16–19, p. 683; H §9bis, p. 41, lines 17–20. Proportion in the relationship of guilt to flame has an ancient history. See Isid., *Sent.* 2.41.9; CCSL 111:182. The idea goes back to Origen's *On First Principles* 2.10.3; trans. G. W. Butterworth (New York: Harper and Row, 1966), 141. Origen cites Isaiah 50:11: "Walk by the light of your fire and by the brands which you have kindled." See Bernstein, *Formation*, 311.

10. "Quod non accendisti, non ardebit in te." C §8, lines 15–16, p. 683; H §9 bis, p. 41, lines 15–16.

11. C §9, lines 19–20, p. 684; H §11, p. 42, lines 6–7.

12. C §7, line 4, p. 682; H §9, p. 40, lines 25–26.

13. In *The City of God*, 21.26 Augustine deliberately distinguishes the fire that will try "every man" from 1 Cor. 3:13, that is, the probative fire, from the eternal fire of Matthew 25:34 and 41. In the same place, Augustine also assimilates the trying fire of 1 Cor. 3:13 to that in Ecclesiasticus (Sirach) 27:5.

14. C §7, lines 11–12, p. 682; H §9, p. 30, lines 35–36. Cf. C §10, lines 2–3, p. 685; H §12; p. 42, lines 21–22.

as they leave their bodies, puts the punishments not beneath the earth, but in the air. Because the angel answered all the demons' charges, this fire would be purgatorial for Fursey, but others, deeper in the fire, would not escape. (The idea that one fire can have two functions also occurred in earlier, rabbinic literature, as we shall see, but this is the first time I know where it appears in a vision.) One of the demons' allegations reveals much about the logic behind the vision itself. The narrative states that the angels successfully rebutted all the demons' accusations, but it seems he had failed to encourage penance adequately.

The victorious angels guided Fursey closer to heaven, and with "their wings like an immense gleaming brightness surrounding him, he casts aside all fear of the fire and terror of the demons."[15] In heaven, Fursey met two Irish holy men, his countrymen and predecessors, Bishops Beoanus and Meldanus, who told him that he must return to his body and preach according to their instructions. He must announce "to all that the rod [of vengeance] is near."[16] Bede omits this whole encounter in heaven, but the vision as recounted in the *Life of Fursey* gives it a lengthier treatment than the very dramatic confrontations with fire and devils.

Beoanus and Meldanus provided Fursey a heaven-crafted model sermon—the only example I know. Beoanus particularly attacked the vices where they take root, in the heart. The sermon's last line excoriates the corrupt clergy who preach to secure human favor rather than to advance virtue. This toleration of society's sins, a sin of omission, is one that the devil launched at Fursey during his ascent through the fire. The model sermon accords with the angels' words to Fursey during his soul's first ascent: "What we announce by our labors, demonic forces dissipate by corrupting human hearts (*corda*)."[17] The battleground, then, is not in the air, but in human hearts. The aerial fire burns inside.

Or does it? As the three angels guided Fursey back to earth, they passed again near the fiery globe. The demons took one of their victims from the fire and hurled him at Fursey. The flaming body struck him on the cheek and shoulder, causing scars that remained with him even after his soul reentered his body. Fursey's relationship to this man and the question of whether the sins of the one should mark the body of other are central to the vision. It appears that as this man lay dying, he had made a deathbed restitution of a cloak that he had wrongly acquired. Instead of giving it to the poor, Fursey

---

15. C §11, lines 2–4, p. 686; H §13; p. 43, lines 7–9.

16. C §2, lines 5–6, p. 687; H §15, p. 44, lines 1–2.

17. C §11, lines 23–24, p. 687; H §14, p. 43, lines 31–32.

himself kept it. Since the man was a sinner, the devil insinuated that the coat was tainted, and Fursey should have refused it. This time the angel agreed: "Whoever renounces all his former iniquities should distribute alms copiously to the poor. . . . What you have kindled, burns within you. If you had not taken up the clothing of this man when he died in his sins, his punishments would not burn in your body."[18]

Fursey's experience in the outer fringes of the fire as he ascended purged him, but he was still singed by the sinner the demons hurled at him as he descended back to earth. The angel's message to Fursey stresses the beneficial aspect of monastic bitterness, and the heart as the site of introspection. In the outer fringes of the fire, Fursey reviewed all aspects of his inner life; the thief in the fire's core did not. In Fursey's case, there is an external consequence: the scar remained visible. The angel's explanation for why the miscreant's hurtling body burned Fursey has an authoritative status akin to the sermon Beoanus and Meldanus dictated in heaven, but its visual immediacy is greater.

Fursey's narrative of his out-of-body experience recapitulated itself as the angels guided him back to his inert body, still laid out on what had appeared to be his deathbed. Fearing that his body might contaminate his spirit if it reanimated what looked like his corpse, Fursey needed reassurance that it would not. The angel said: "Fear not. . . . You have overcome unlawful lusts through this tribulation so that your old urgings no longer prevail against you."[19] Fursey's experience in the fringes of the fire purified him to the point where his spirit would escape contamination from his body. Still, even after reinvigorating his body, "he felt the fire that he had assumed from the evil man between his shoulders and it appeared on his face. And so what the soul alone sustained became visible, in a wondrous way, on his flesh."[20]

Fursey related the crisis (*tribulatio*) he endured when his sins seemed certain to doom him. Over against his anxieties, expressed as the legalistic accusations of his demons, he heard the voice of his guardian angel, who deployed more equitable interpretations on his behalf. Fursey's burden, his one sin of commission, appeared before him to mark his memory and his face. As will appear in the case of Barontus, there is no sign earlier in the narrative of a crisis of conscience. In *Fursey*, fear of the fire as a venue for judgment seems to outweigh, or at least precede, the fear of hell. This attack of

18. C §16, lines 12–19, pp. 691–92; H §22, p. 47, lines 27–36.

19. "Noli timere. . . . Concupiscentias enim inlicitas in hac tribulatione superasti, ut uetera contra te non preualeant." C §17, lines 7–8, p. 692; H §23, p. 48, lines 5–7.

20. C §17, lines 17–18, p. 692; H §23, p. 48, lines 16–18.

monastic *amaritudo* had two high points: first, when the demons made their accusations against him and he saw all his sins personified, and second, when the body from the fiery globe struck him. For all this vision's debt to monastic inner death, Fursey's scar makes liability to "the punishments" more than an affair of conscience. The scar is the mark of a contrite sinner made new. In the airborne fire, symbol of his heart, Fursey has completed his penance. The *Vision of Fursey* explains that probative fire burns no one beyond what is fair ("What you have not lit will not burn within you"); it does not teach, as purgatory will, that all who undergo it will be saved and that only those who qualify experience that treatment. The three-dimensional space implied in the contrast between Fursey's purgatorial experience on the fringes of the fire and the condition of the sinner propelled from its depths deserves special comment. It is the first Christian image to combine purgatorial and infernal functions in one space. We have seen this near fusion, what Claude Carozzi has called "hell-purgatory,"[21] in the writing of Caesarius of Arles (d. 543)[22] and Julian of Toledo (d. 690).[23] Both texts follow, possibly by centuries, a similar conception already expressed by the School of Shammai in a key passage of the Babylonian Talmud's Tractate Rosh Hashana, which will come under review in the next chapter.

Barontus and the Tug-of-War

Another aerial battle between angels and demons over the fate of a soul appears in the *Vision of Barontus.*[24] The percipient was a nobleman who became a monk at the house of St. Peter in Longoret.[25] When he awakened after appearing to have died, in 675, with his son Aglioaldo and a fellow monk watching at his bedside, he recounted what he had seen. After angels

---

21. Carozzi, *Le voyage,* 265. Carozzi entitles this section of his book "From Purgatorial Fire to Hell-Purgatory" (253–79) and explains, "Purgatorial fire has become a temporary hell devoted to the purgation of souls." My differences from this interpretation are clear, since I have shown that hell (infernal fire) itself provides the purgatorial function, but the term "hell-purgatory" is suggestive and useful.

22. Caesarius Arelatensis, Sermon 179, cap. 4, lines 22–23; CCSL 103–4, ed. G. Morin (1953), pp. 725–26.

23. Julian of Toledo, *Prognosticon futuri saeculi* 2.20; CCSL 115, ed. Joscelin Hillgarth (1976), pp. 56–63.

24. For the *Vision of Barontus,* I provide the section, page, and line numbers of the Latin edition, *Visio Baronti Monachi Longoretensis,* ed. W. Levison, MGH, SS RR MM 5 (Hannover and Leipzig, 1910), 368–94; trans. Jocelyn Hilgarth in *Christianity and Paganism, 350–750* (Philadelphia: University of Pennsylvania Press, 1986), 195–204.

25. For the character of his life, see §12; p. 386, lines 11–14. For Longoret or Lonrey, see Carozzi, *Le voyage,* 140 n. 4. The house was later called Saint-Cyran.

and demons wrestled over his soul, he briefly saw the outer gates of heaven. Then, Saint Peter required him to visit hell. After seeing what he could of hell, his spirit reentered his body, whereupon Barontus recovered and narrated his out-of-body experience. His account shares with the *Apocalypse of Paul* and the later *Visio Anselli* the motif of a heaven-ordered tour of hell. Far from observing a "taboo" against entering hell, Barontus learned enough, as he put it, to "frighten" his fellow monks. He also saw a certain mitigation within the infernal torments, an extension of the theme already noted in the *Apocalypse of Paul*. Damned souls who have done at least one good deed receive heavenly consolation. Thus, the *Vision of Barontus* combines two important themes. It dramatizes the conflict between good and evil forces as angels and demons perform aerial combat to possess a soul, and in hell itself it reports a measure of relief for some hellmates who in their lives had done some good, however little.

The battle for the soul of Barontus began as he suffered from his disease, even before he died. Two ugly demons seized his soul and tried to drag him down to hell, but the archangel Raphael (also here called Saint Raphael) intervened (§3; p. 379, line 20). At Raphael's touch Barontus's soul left his body. It felt light and fluffy to him, like a newly hatched chick. He had his sight and his other senses, but he was unable to speak as the struggle (*contentio*) for possession of the soul took place on his chest (§4; p. 380, line 16). It was, in effect, a jurisdictional dispute. Raphael wished to take Barontus's soul to the divine court, but the demons would not let him go until the angel surrendered any hope for the body's recovery (§3; p. 380, line 6). As the tug-of-war proceeded, Saint Raphael suppported Barontus's right side and tried to lift him up, while one demon pulled hard on his left side, and a second, kicking from behind, angrily threatened him: "I have had you in my power before and I have hurt you greatly, but now you will be wracked eternally in hell" (§4; p. 381, lines 1–2). This was Barontus's old, personal demon, a bad influence on him all his life, now coming to collect his reward, the damnation of his victim.

At this point an important aspect of this vision came into play: the correspondence of the prayers by the monks, explained via the liturgical hours as tolled by the church bells, with eventual victory in the struggle for the soul of Barontus. Precisely at vespers (§2; p. 378, line 16), when the brothers began to chant lauds, the airborne battlers heard the bells and Raphael taunted the demons: you can no longer harm this soul, because of his brothers' prayers (§5; p. 381, lines 5–7). Though Barontus had "died" only an instant before, suffrages had already begun to take effect. The battle progressed through the air, eventually hovering over the monastery of Millebeccus (or Meobecque), where the prayers of yet another house aided the beleaguered soul. At one point, demons dragged Barontus so close to hell (*iuxta inferno*) that "we saw the guardians of the infernal regions (*custodes infernorum*)" (§7; p. 383, line 4). Now the struggle approached the first gate of paradise, where Barontus met some deceased brothers of his own monastery awaiting the Day of Judgment to enter into eternal joy. When they saw him beset by so many demons they said this had never before happened to one of theirs, and Barontus, employing one of the most important motifs in vision literature, avowed his own guilt: "I do not deny that all that I suffer results from my own faults and wrongs."[26] Since the airborne battle brought both heaven and hell into view, Barontus, under considerable duress, made his confession. The relationship of his self-examination to inner death is evident.

As the conflict moved past the gates of heaven, the converted noble met Betolenus, a former monk of Longoret now, from heaven, charged with lighting all the world's churches. He observed to Barontus that his own monastery does not provide adequate illumination. Having just seen what the prayers of heaven dwellers can do for his soul, Barontus now learns that there are ritual responsibilities that encourage them. Indeed, the *luminaria* represent a constant expense, the need for candles to light the churches. The donation of candles was a pious contribution and could, as suffrages, provide aid to departed souls. This reminder was part of the message that Barontus brought back from his near-death experience.[27]

Raphael then sent for Saint Peter, patron of Longoret, who challenged the demons to specify the charges against Barontus. They said he had committed all the principal vices. "He had three wives, which were not permitted to him, and he committed other adulteries and many other faults that we tempted him into."[28] Barontus admitted: "And those which I had been accustomed to commit from my infancy, and which I had never considered since, they recalled one by one" (§12; p. 386, lines 11–14). Barontus conceded the truth of these charges, but Peter defended him. "Even if he has committed some wrongs (*aliquid contrarium*) he has given alms, and alms liberate from death [cf. Tobit 12:9]. He has confessed his sins to priests and has done penitence for those sins and beyond that he has deposited the hair from his head

---

26. *Visio Baronti* §8; p. 383, lines 19–20.

27. *Visio Baronti* §11; p. 385, line 19–p. 387, line 1. Note that the earliest document preserved in the Chartulary of the Abbey of Saint Gall is a gift to provide *luminaria*, that is, to assure the lighting of the church. *Urkundenbuch der Abtei Sanct Gallen*, pt. I, *700–840*, ed. Hermann Wartmann (Zurich, 1863), no. 1, ca. 700, p. 1.

28. For "resource polygyny" and its importance for the Frankish church and society, see David Herlihy, *Medieval Households* (Cambridge, MA: Harvard University Press, 1985); and Suzanne Fonay Wemple, *Women in Frankish Society: Marriage and the Cloister, 500–900* (Philadelphia: University of Pennsylvania Press, 1981).

[i.e., taken the tonsure], in my monastery. He has abandoned all for God and given himself over into the service of Christ" (§12; p. 386, lines 16–19). Invoking a quantitative standard, Peter claimed, "These good deeds outweigh the evil ones you reported. Now you are unable to take him from me. Admit it, he is not your friend (*socius*) but ours" (§12; p. 386, lines 19–21). *Socius* is a key term here. It implies not possession but membership in a group—here the group of monks, saints, and angels. This statement is therefore the functional equivalent of the angels' claim against the demons in the *Vision of Fursey*, "He is no sharer (*particeps*) in your perdition." The demons asserted that only God can loose Barontus from their grip. At this challenge to his jurisdiction, Peter indignantly raised three keys as if to strike the demons, but they fled through the air (§12; p. 386, line 20–p. 387, line 9). Having warded off the demons, Peter turned to Barontus and brought up two new sins. When Barontus had first entered the monastery, he had confessed only partially and withheld some property. Now, Peter required him to give directly into the hands of the recipients a solidus a month for twelve months to pilgrims or the poor, all under the supervision of his abbot. Should Barontus withhold anything this time or revert to any other behavior characteristic of his earlier life, Peter said, "you will greatly regret the ruin of your soul, and its condition will be worse than before" (§13; p. 388, lines 8–9). However, if Barontus fulfills this penance, "his burdens will immediately be removed from him" (*statim ei dimittuntur facinora sua*, §13; p. 388, lines 12–13).

Beyond the compensatory charity, Saint Peter ordered Barontus on a tour of hell (*infernus*) "so that I might see and understand all the torments of sinners."[29] He arranged for Framnoaldus, a former monk at Longoret, to guide the noble and gave him a wax seal to use as a talisman against "malign spirits" who would try to keep them in the dark. As further protection, a monk, Ebbo, advised Barontus of the apotropaic formula password "Glory to you, God" that would ward off demons. On their voyage, they encountered Father Abraham, who shelters some souls between heaven and hell (*inter paradysum et infernum*) in his bosom.[30] "Then, pursuing our voyage, we arrived at hell, but we did not see what was going on inside because of the darkness and the smoke. I will recount as much as God permitted me to see through the defenses that the demons maintained."[31]

---

29. *Visio Baronti* §13; p. 388, lines 15–19.

30. Ibid., §16; p. 390, line 18. Jérôme Baschet has written extensively on Abraham and the Bosom of Abraham. See, for example, Baschet, *Le sein du père: Abraham et la paternité dans l'Occident médiéval* (Paris: Gallimard, 2000).

31. *Visio Baronti* §17; p. 390, line 24–p. 391, line 2.

Despite his disclaimer, Barontus saw enough to inspire fear in those to whom he dictated his experience and all who would hear it thereafter. "I saw there," he recounted, "innumerable thousands of men tied and harshly constrained by a great many demons and [heard] the bitterness of a moaning similar to the buzzing of bees returning to their hive. Thus, the demons dragged the souls enmeshed in sins to the torments of hell and commanded them to sit in a circle on seats of lead" (§17; p. 391, lines 2–7). Sitting in a circle would allow them to see each other. Barontus saw the sinners classed together according to sins and order. These are the "ranks of the wicked in their associations" (*ordines malorum et societates eorum*). The choice of words is vague, as these terms sometimes had legal connotations, but this "order" accords with what Gregory says in his *Dialogues* (4.38) when he quotes Matthew 13:30, "They bound them in bundles to be burned." Like are bound with like.[32] "There are held the proud with the proud, the sensuous with the sensuous, perjurers with perjurers, murderers with murderers, the envious with the envious, detractors with detractors, liars with liars; but they [all] moaned together" (§17; p. 391, lines 7–9). Mentioned separately were the innumerable "deceived clerics," all males, who "had violated their oaths," and "wailed loudly, vexed by the torments." The addition of "deceived" introduces an element of gender. Though it does not pry the priests from the grip of hell, that term disproportionately blames the women for their liaisons and partially exculpates the men who "stained themselves" with allegedly deceitful sexual partners.[33]

Barontus named specific individuals, though not much is known about them. Earlier visions name people seen in heaven, but none in hell. The flaming body who burned Fursey was not identified. But Barontus saw Bishop Vulfoleodus (of Berry, d. before 672), exhausted, damned by deception (and so guilty of fornication?) or by the deceptions he committed, since he sat there in filthy clothes like a beggar. Also in hell was Bishop Dido (of Poitiers), whom Ansoaldus succeeded in 677.[34] Barontus admitted taints on his own family tree, as he recognized some of his own relations there.[35] And there were the foolish virgins, who had done no good works (cf. Matt. 25:3).

32. Ibid., p. 391, lines 2–10.

33. Ibid., lines 11–13.

34. Levison, *Visio Baronti*, p. 391 nn. 3 and 4. For Dido, see See Isabel Moreira, *Dreams, Visions, and Spiritual Authority in Merovingian Gaul* (Ithaca, NY, and London: Cornell University Press, 2000), 163 n. 108. Dido helped send King Dagobert II into exile, but that need not be why he is depicted in hell. The original source is *Liber historiae Francorum*, cap. 43, ed. Bruno Krusch. MGH, SS RR MM (Hannover: Hahn, 1888), 238–328, at p. 316, line 3. See also Carozzi, *Le voyage*, 165.

35. *Visio Baronti* §17; p. 391, line 17.

The hell Barontus visited did not exclude all relief. There was a distinction between those damned who had done some good in the world and the self-recrimination of those who learned, too late, that the smallest service in life could be rewarded even in hell:

> And I saw there other matters to inspire great dread in sinners. All those who were held under the guardianship of the demons were tied up together in chains. [But] around the hour of sexts, those who had done anything even partly good in the world were offered manna brought from paradise which had the appearance of a cloud. And it was put before their noses and mouths, and they were refreshed by it. And those who offered it had the appearance of deacons, dressed in white vestments. And others, who had done nothing good in the world, to them nothing was offered; but moaning, they closed their eyes and beat their breasts and called out in a loud voice: "Woe to us pitiful ones, who did nothing good when we were able!"[36]

As in the broader society of the early Middle Ages, where new parties laid claims to old cultic sites and geopolitical boundaries on earth were established through the invocation of saints, the otherworld Barontus saw required similar negotiation. The absolute damnation advanced by Augustine and Gregory faded under these social pressures. Presumably after trials like that of Barontus himself, Bishops Vulfoleodus and Dido and some of Barontus's own (unnamed) relatives were condemned to hell. Yet, provided they had done any good in their lives, the manna softened their fate with the daily presentation at sexts of a refreshing heavenly substance that they could perceive but not eat. This kindly version of the punishment of Tantalus would be a relief from an eternal and unchanging torture. These souls were not in oblivion. This idea will have a long future. As we have seen in the *Voyage of St. Brendan*, it can apply even to Judas. The regular appearance of the manna-bearing deacons at the hour of sexts underlined the importance of monastic prayer, already evident in the aerial battle over the body of Barontus.

Barontus was certain his story would guide all but the *increduli*— "unbelievers": "For who has a mind so closed, I ask, dearest brothers, as not to be frightened by these tortures I have described, when the demons take away every sinner as quickly as he exits the body and drag him to hell?"[37] Here the sanction, at least immediately, is not hell, but, as in Fursey's experience in the

---

36. Ibid., p. 391, line 20–p. 392, line 5.
37. Ibid., §20; p. 393, lines 14–17.

fireball, which was also in the air, the terror of the trial, the demons' tactics, their flawless, literal record of one's life. Against the devils there are still angels and saints who advocate on one's behalf. This balance takes a visual, almost sinewy form in the contest above the forests of eastern France in the tug-of-war between angels and demons. The saints also have perfect memories, and Saint Peter at the gate of heaven can assign Barontus a harsh penance for his partial confession and the incomplete disclosure of his wealth when he entered the monastery. Saints and angels advocate for humans who offer candles to light their churches, alms to the poor, and prayers to God. In the aftermath of his trial, Barontus qualifies the hell he saw with the notion that when one's misdeeds outweigh one's merits, all good deeds, no matter how few, count in favor of the damned. Still, nothing in his experience assures Barontus of his salvation, which remains conditional on his satisfying the penitential acts assigned. However fleeting and obscure his glimpse into the smoky hell, Barontus saw that the damned are not, as Augustine had taught, in a hidden receptacle. Nor are they in oblivion, but within reach of heaven-sent deacons who reward selected sinners with manna for their few good deeds. Barontus's trip presents a hell closely linked both to heaven, from which the manna came on a daily basis, and to earth, from which Barontus could travel and to which he could return after seeing both of the afterlife's final destinations.

Drythelm: The Valley and the Hellmouth

In contrast to the two previous visions, where souls endure aerial scrutiny, the *Vision of Drythelm*, as related by Bede, features a clearly defined punitive landscape divided into two zones and surmounted to the right and eastward by two distinct spaces, one more pleasant than the other. A man named Drythelm, with a wife, children, and property, who lived around Cunningham (Ayrshire) near the west coast of Scotland, developed a sickness that steadily worsened until it appeared that he had died. The next morning he rose from his deathbed to tell of a vision he experienced while out of his body. He divided his property, giving one-third to his wife, one-third to his children, and one-third to the poor. Afterward he adopted a life of contrition and took up residence in the monastery of Melrose. The end of his vision states that King Aldfrid found his narrative edifying and that he used to come often to hear Drythelm tell it. Aldfrid's death in 705 provides the most convenient indication of a date for the vision.[38]

---

38. *Historia* 5.12; ed. Plummer, p. 294. Note 1 to 5.12 observes that the previous chapter of Bede includes the dates 692–96, and the *Anglo-Saxon Chronicle* dates it in its MSS D and E to 693. Aldfrid reigned 685–705. Carozzi, *Le voyage*, 227, also gives "pre-705."

As his illness appeared to remove him from life, a guide of brilliant coun-
tenance and splendid apparel led Drythelm through an otherworld landscape remarkably similar to the logical arrangement Augustine outlined in
his *Enchiridion*. First, Drythelm saw an infinitely long valley. On one side
was terrible fire; on the other, hail and blowing snow. Human souls jumped
back and forth, seeking at least momentary relief in the alternation between
the heat and cold. As the extent of this area was boundless and the torment
without interruption, it seemed to Drythelm that this must be hell, but his
guide, reading his thought, declared unbidden: "This is not the hell that you
think."[39] This phrasing may betray Bede's own belief in two hells, an upper
and a lower. But both sides of this valley were equally punishing. Each side
of the path was "no less intolerable" (*non minus intolerabile*) than the other,
no one could find any rest on either side (*neque ibi . . . requiei inuenire ualerent*),
and it seemed to be hell (*infernus*). It is also not either Augustine or Gregory's
upper hell, where the just experience peace. More information comes as the
trip progresses.

After the guide's declaration, the way grew dark. Echoing a phrase from
Virgil's account of Aeneas's descent into the underworld, he was no better
able to navigate than "by the shadows of the night"—another indication that
Bede's learning is coloring the layman Drythelm's simpler perceptions.[40] In
an echo of the exodus, like the manna in *Barontus*, Drythelm followed the
light that emanated from the raiment of his guide through the darkness of
adversity. Suddenly he distinguishes "dense globes of hideous flames" rising
out of a pit and falling back into it. At this horrifying moment, when Drythelm learns that there is a place worse than the valley he has just traversed,
his guide disappeared and "left me alone in the midst of the darkness and
horror of the vision."[41] A potent motif in visions, this moment of abandonment forces the visionary to draw on his own resources as supernatural help
apparently ceases. Still, Drythelm resented it greatly and complained that
his guide had "abandoned" (*reliquit*) him. It is not until the twelfth-century
Vision of Tundal that narrators develop the full potential of this moment in
visions, but it also appears in an anonymous, early eleventh-century vision
from Saint-Vaast.[42]

---

39. "Non enim hic infernus est ille, quem putas." Bede, *Historia* 3.5; Plummer, p. 305.
40. *Aeneid* 6.268.
41. Bede, *Historia* 5.12; Plummer, p. 305.
42. Hughes de Flavigny, *Chronicon*, II, ed. G. H. Pertz, MGH, SS 8 (Hannover, 1848), 380–91, at
p. 387, line 9–p. 388, line 16.

Without the guide's illumination, everything was murky, yet Drythelm was able to discern a pattern. He became aware that the fiery globes spread not light but darkness. An incomparable stench permeated the area. Within these dark clouds, as within flames, Drythelm perceived tiny bits like black sparks, which were in reality human souls carried by the convection of the smoky currents.[43] These dark sparks alternately burst up to the heights and fell back into the depths.

Immobile with fear, Drythelm hears behind him a crowd of demons taunting five sinners as they lead them into the pit. Among them was a tonsured cleric, a layman, and a woman, but they are not named. As they disappeared, it became impossible to distinguish the wails of the damned from the gleeful cheers of the evil spirits. Then devils came up out of the flame-emitting pit and surrounded Drythelm, jeering and mocking him, breathing their sulfurous breath in his face, glaring at him, and threatening him with tongs. Desperately looking about for help, Drythelm espied his guide, like a star in the darkness, drawing closer to rescue him.

The guide presently (*mox*) led Drythelm right and eastward to an infinite wall, which they somehow surmounted, reaching a vast, fragrant grassland that made Drythelm forget the stench of the dark furnace. Men and women (not called "souls" here) dressed in white rejoiced in the meadow. The light, the aroma, and the happiness of the inhabitants made Drythelm think " 'This may be the kingdom of the heavens about which I have very often heard in sermons,' but [the guide] answered his thought: 'No' said he, 'this is not the kingom of the heavens, as you assume'."[44] They traversed these dwellings of the blessed spirits until Drythelm saw a light, so much greater than before, heard voices singing so sweetly, and sensed aromas so fragrant that the pleasures of the meadow seemed slight in comparison. Just as Drythelm began to hope he could pass within, his guide declared it was necessary to go back. As they were returning through the joyful dwellings of the souls in white, the guide explained to Drythelm what he had seen.

1. The valley of flames and snow "is a place to appraise and punish the souls of those who delay to confess and expiate the wrongs they have

---

43. "[F]astigia flammarum plena esse spiritibus hominum, qui instar fauillarum cum fumo ascendentium, nunc ad sublimiora proicerentur, nunc retractis ignium uaporibus relaberentur in profunda." Bede, *Historia* 5.12; Plummer, pp. 305–6. Here is a dramatic parallel with Dante's *Inferno*, canto 26, line 42: "e ogne fiamma un peccatore invola." In the *Vision of the Monk of Wenlock*, to be treated below, human souls emerge from what seems to be a volcanic crater, in the form of black birds, and then fall back in.

44. Bede, *Historia* 5.12; Plummer, p. 307.

done, who, finally, at the very point of death, have recourse to penance and thus exit their bodies. And, because they undertook confession and penance even in death, all will attain the kingdom of heaven on the day of judgment."[45] It is "a place." In the meantime, "they are greatly aided by the prayers, alms and fasting of the living, and especially by masses, so that they may be liberated [from these torments] even before the day of judgment."[46]

2. The fiery and stinking pit is "the mouth of Gehenna, out of which no one who has once fallen in will ever be liberated."[47] The use of "liberated" in sentences about both the valley and the pit strengthens the contrast between the torments in both places. From the valley of snow and fire one may be liberated at various times by suffrages; from the mouth of Gehenna, one may never be liberated. The only difference between the two places appears to be confession. Nothing is said about the gravity of the misdeeds in either case.

3. The flowery grassland is "a place [another place!] . . . in which are received the souls of those who exit the body having done good works, but who are nonetheless not of such great perfection that they merit introduction into the kingdom of the heavens immediately. Still, they will all enter into the vision of Christ and the joy of the heavenly kingdom at the day of judgment."[48]

4. The perfect, however, are admitted immediately (*mox*) to the brilliant and harmonious place that Drythelm was able to approach but not enter.[49]

Having explained the layout of the otherworld, the guide tells Drythelm that when he returns to life he must direct his actions to righteousness and simplicity so that he may die again and rejoin "these joyful troops of blessed souls," that is, those in the meadow. It was to verify this possibility that his angel had left Drythelm during that lonely moment by the mouth of

---

45. Ibid., p. 308: "[I]pse est locus in quo examinandae et castigandae sunt animae illorum, qui differentes confiteri et emendare scelera, quae fecerunt, in ipso tandem mortis articulo ad paenitentiam confugiunt, et sic de corpore exeunt; qui tamen, quia confessionem et paenitentiam uel in morte habuerunt, omnes in die iudicii ad regnum caelorum perueniunt." Aron Gurevich considers this the expression in which "purgatory is present in concept." Gurevich, *Medieval Popular Culture* (Cambridge: Cambridge University Press, 1988), 148 and 247 n. 85.

46. Bede, *Historia* 5:12; Plummer, p. 308.

47. Ibid.: "os gehennae, in quo quicumque semel inciderit, numquam inde liberabitur in aeuum" (my emphasis).

48. Bede, *Historia* 5:12; Plummer, p. 308.

49. Ibid., pp. 308–9.

Gehenna. Drythelm did not want to return to his body, but did not ask questions. He awoke among living humans.

Aware that certain truths and certain manners of expressing them are better suited to some audiences than others, Drythelm only told these things to people who could benefit. Among these was an Irish monk and priest named Haemgil, whom Bede says told the story to him. Drythelm also related the events of his vision to King Aldfrid, who eventually became a monk at Melrose. When people visited Drythelm and remarked about the ascetic practices he had adopted, such as bathing in icy rivers, he would say: "I have seen greater cold, I have seen more austerity." The knowledge that Drythelm acquired through his out-of-body experience combined with these changes in how he lived is another instance of inner death. Bede knew as much. Introducing the tale, he remarked that it served "to rouse the living from the death of their souls."[50] It is also an example of how a vision can change the life of the visionary.

The dominant feature of this vision is its apparently clear-cut map of the otherworld. Obviously, there are four main divisions, a fact that immediately recalls the plan of Augustine's *Enchiridion*, where he postulated a middle category of sinners, some of whom could be aided by suffrages to full remission of their sins, and some of whom could receive only a more tolerable damnation (*tolerabilior damnatio*).[51] Those in the lower category of the middle group, the wicked but not very wicked, could be helped *in* their punishment, but not *from* it. The guide in the *Vision of Drythelm* says that they are helped if they have confessed. *Drythelm* makes confession the difference between the very wicked and the not very wicked, and it obliterates the more tolerable damnation as a fate, authorizing complete remission for both the not very good and the not very wicked. By modifying the fate of the not very wicked, *Drythelm* revises Augustine in the direction of greater leniency. Indeed, Augustine had even mocked his contemporaries who thought God should have made his world even more merciful, as if they could "soften" the divine will to "accommodate human emotion."[52] Moreover, in the *Vision of Drythelm*, the separated souls of the living in near-death experiences can find souls who Augustine said are concealed in "hidden receptacles"! In fact, it would appear that, provided one has confessed, complete remission is

50. Ibid., p. 303. Cf., at the end (p. 310), "multisque et uerbo et conuersatione saluti fuit." (Many were saved by both his words and his conduct.)

51. "abditis receptaculis." Augustine, *Enchiridion de fide et spe et caritate* 29.109; CCSL 46, ed. E. Evans (1969), p. 108; trans. J. F. Shaw (South Bend, IN: Regnery/Gateway, 1961), 127. See Bernstein, *Formation*, 322–24.

52. Augustine, *Enchiridion* 29.112; p. 109, line 43.

available no matter how grave the sin committed. This position is consistent with what Bede expounded in his Advent sermon and his *Commentary on the Book of Proverbs*. Bede's argument also appears in an important but hard-to-date pseudo-Augustinian treatise, *De vera et falsa poenitentia*, influential for centuries, which claims that confession makes mortal sins venial or, more literally "what was criminal in commission becomes venial in confession."[53] Were it not for the fact that Bede provides the only surviving account of this vision, the near-death experience of Drythelm, a married country man, might reflect doctrinal tensions between the formal theology of literati and a more popular current favoring an emphasis on divine mercy. Against that implication is the vision's studied symmetry, the text's overt biblical and even classical references, and the placement of its doctrinal significance in the mouth of the angelic guide, a heavenly voice, representing the same ostensible perspective as theology itself. It is also the angel's pronouncement that, when repeated as a part of the vision, broadcasts the doctrine that purgatorial suffering, conditioned on confession and repentance, leads to heaven. That is not the perspective of the sinners jumping back and forth between the snow and the fire, but it is perhaps the most significant moral of the story as declared doctrinally and unequivocally by the heavenly informant. Moreover, these two sides of the road, taken together, Bede calls a "place." It is clear from both the description of the scene and the use of this term that he intends a physical place. We are dealing here with "the place to appraise and punish the souls of those who delay to confess and expiate the wrongs they have done."[54] Bede also calls the verdant meadow for those who will eventually be saved a "place." In his conformity to the physical quality Augustine gave his "hidden receptacles," Bede is unusual. At the same time he allows more escape than Augustine did and accepts the idea that Drythelm has seen what Augustine said was hidden.

---

53. "[F]it enim per confessionem veniale, quod criminale erat in operatione." *De vera et falsa poenitentia* 10.25; PL 40:1122. Le Goff dates the treatise to the late eleventh or early twelfth century. Le Goff, *Birth*, 364–65; see also P. Glorieux, "Pour revaloriser Migne," *Mélanges de Science Religieuse* 9 (1952), cahier supplémentaire, p. 29, cites Portalié in *DTC*, s.v. "Augustin," vol. 1 (1903), col. 2310, who calls it eleventh century. In Gratian's *Decretum* we find the statement "fit enim veniale per confessionem quod criminale erat in operatione," *Corpus Iuris Canonici*, ed. E. Friedberg, pt. 1, *Decretum Magistri Gratiani, Tractatus de Penitentia*, distinctio 1, cap. 88 (1879; Graz: Akademische Druck, 1959), col. 1188; and Peter Lombard, in *Sententiae in 4 Libris Distinctae* 4.17.1.6 (Grottaferrata: Collegii, S. Bonaventuarae ad Claras Aqua, Grottaferrata, 1981), vol. 2, p. 344, quotes Ambrose, *De paradiso* 14, n. 7l (PL 14:310D; CSEL 32, II, p. 321): "Non potest quisquam iustificari a peccato, nisi fuerit peccatum ante confessus." Gratian (ibid. c. 74) and Lombard (ibid. n. 8) again quote Ambrose (ibid.): "Venialis est culpa, quam sequitur professio delictorum."

54. Quoted above, note 45.

The *Vision of Paul*, R 6: Rustlers Ride Their Mounts

Some decades after Bede recounted the afterlife visions in his *History* another document emerged that also calls attention to the criteria for escape from hell. Even though the *Apocalypse of Paul* introduced the idea of periodic relief within hell, that text also preserved extremely vivid, physical torments of hell itself. We have seen that Redaction 6 of *Paul* relates how the apostle obtained the astonishing liberation of his Jewish forebears from the far-flung corners of hell. But R 6 is a much more fully developed vision than that one detail would suggest, and continues the catalogue of sins and punishments so dramatically presented in the *Vision of Paul*.

The complete version of R 6 is contained in only one manuscript, and much in its interpretation depends on understanding the process by which that manuscript was compiled and preserved. Although the script was executed in the early or mid-ninth century, it seems that this version of the vision itself was conceived around 745 or 750. A major reform in handwriting took place in the interim, and possibly the original text was in a script unfamiliar to the ninth-century scribe.[55] Although the text was written in a dark brown ink, a rubricator added a heading in red ink that says: "Here begins 'Saint Paul's Reproof of Human Sinners Who Sin and Improve'."[56] Later, a sixteenth-century librarian compiled a table of contents for the entire manuscript with its assorted texts and entitled this portion as follows: "The Vision of Saint Paul Concerning the Improvement of Sinners."[57] A close examination of the punishments in R 6 shows how these titles misrepresent the text as a whole.

In R 6, the narrative relates a dialogue between Paul and the archangel Raphael as they move from scene to scene: "And he came to another place"; "And he saw men [or men and women, or girls—it varies] in punishment," and Paul asked, "How have these sinned, lord?"; "And the angel answered him, 'these are the ones who. . . . And because they did neither public nor private penance, they each have their own punishment'." This formulaic structure creates a logical grid, whose sections can be numbered. In each section the punishments can be described alongside Raphael's explanations. Despite the liberties this redaction takes with the *Apocalypse of Paul*, one constant remains: the underworld is divided into two levels variously called "the punishments" and "hell." Indeed, if this work had a title before a later writer

---

55. Carozzi, *Le voyage*, 270.

56. "Incipit castigatio sanctae paule de hominis peccatoris, qui peccant et emendant." St. Gall, MS 682, p. 193.

57. "Visio B. Pauli de peccantium emendatione." St. Gall, MS 682, p. V1.

added the rubric, it would have been the text's opening line: "Saint Paul is led into the kingdom of God so that he may see the works of the just and the punishments of the sinners."[58] Paul is not shown a named place, but the sinners and "the punishments."

Omitting the formulas, these are the sins and their punishments. Devils drag men and women in chains through fire because they sinned against their father or mother (§2).[59] Men and women have their tongues pulled out and their cheeks transfixed by nails while boiling pitch, lead, coal, and sulfur are poured into their eyes because they bore false witness (§3).[60] In a fire under boiling streams of tar, sulfur, and pitch stand those impenitent men and women who abused their position as godfathers or godmothers (§4). Paul sees men boiling in molten lead and tar. The text specifies "men" because these are impenitent bishops and priests. They abandoned chastity, fasting, and alms, committed perjury, oppressed orphans and the poor, and accepted bribes (§5). Next Paul saw a deacon and other clerics standing in varying depths of molten lead. They violated their chastity, vomited the host (because of drunkenness and gluttony), perjured themselves, committed theft and robbery, and never repented (§6).

At this point, the narrative formula breaks down briefly. In section 7, instead of asking how the sufferers offended, Paul names the sin and asks what the penalty is: "These are those who offended chastity. How do they pay for that?"[61] Given the angel's repeated insistence that those Paul has seen so far in R 6 have died impenitent, it is not hard to imagine Paul asking what might have happened had one done penance. The angel answers, "Had he done penance while he lived, the Lord would pardon him his sin."[62] Again Paul: "Suppose a priest or a deacon or subdeacon or virgin or bride of Christ should commit a sin, how would they pay for that?" After prescribing a difficult physical penance and assuming the previous condition (contrition while alive), the angel answers, "The Lord will pardon him his sin."[63] Since section 7 specifically

---

58. Theodore Silverstein, *Visio Sancti Pauli: The History of the Apocalypse in Latin together with Nine Texts*, Studies and Documents 4 (1935; London: Christophers, 1955), p. 215, § 1, line 1; henceforth HAL 9.

59. References to sections are those in Silverstein HAL 9, pp. 214–18.

60. Silverstein, HAL 9, pp. 82–83, notes the influence of the *Apocalypse of Peter* on this punishment. See James, *ANT*, p. 509, §§28–29; pp. 515–16.

61. See Isabel Moreira, *Heaven's Purge: Purgatory in Late Antiquity* (Oxford: Oxford University Press, 2010), 134, for this difficult Latin. She correctly suggests that Carozzi has unneccessarily corrected the manuscript, though in most places his emendations are indispensable.

62. HAL 9, §7, p. 216: "Agat paenitentiam dum aduixerit parcet ei dominus peccatum suum."

63. The penance is this: "You should do four years directly on the ground, [and / or] two on stone, and during those very years the unjust should reconcile, fasting on bread and salt and water." (Annos

conditions divine pardon on penance performed by living penitents, it is not grounds for considering this a purgatorial section of the punishments.

The tour of hell resumes in the next place, where men and women who (used magic to) rouse up storms or burned their neighbors' crops and never did penance burn in fire (§8).[64] In another place Paul sees men riding flaming horses and mules and other quadrupeds made of bronze—red-hot instruments of torture in the form of the animals these sinners stole (§9). In yet another place, men and women who stole farm implements and never repented receive those very tools like blades in their eyes (§10). In still another place the punishment is not clear. It seems to be raining coins and the offense involves betrayal, perhaps selling people into slavery or, for a reward, revealing the hiding place of a refugee (§11). These punishments, from sections 2 through 11, except for 7, are for wrong action. The sinners receive hell for impenitence. Their sins are typical of those punished above the well in the long Latin version.

Although these first eleven sections of R 6 conform in spirit to the *Vision of Paul*, the final section deviates from it severely. When Paul asks about the condition of his ancestors, Raphael tells him that they are in hell. Paul prays for their release, and God grants it (§12). This incident puts R 6 in the category of exceptions to hell discussed in chapter 4. Paul's successful petition for the release of his forebears from hell taken together with section 7, which speaks of penance and its fruits, may have induced the rubricator to compose the overly optimistic title given to the whole of R 6.

Despite its title, there is nothing in R 6 concerning the postmortem improvement of dead sinners except for the family of Paul, whose special status is self-explanatory.[65] Paul's relatives do not improve; their salvation results from Paul's request. Redaction 6 describes not purgatory but hell. All the sinners

---

quatuor iaceas a terra pura duas super lapide et ipsos annos iniusto paciant famem apud panem et sale et aqua.) HAL 9, §7, pp. 216–17. Cf. Carozzi, *Le voyage*, 274; Moreira, *Heaven's Purge*, 133–34.

64. Carozzi, *Le voyage*, 271–72, interprets the offenses.

65. The best that can be said for the title is that it exaggerates section 7, with the troublesome phrase "quomodo hoc enim dant." The rubricator changed "enim dant" to "emendant," and subsequent interpreters have been distracted by the rubric. Carozzi tries to interpret the rubric to make this voyage (changing *vita* Pauli to *via* Pauli) one through or into purgatory, but it is through "the punishments": the unnamed hell/purgatory. Putting all the stress on "emendare," Carozzi suggests that what Paul does for his parents, anyone can do for theirs (269–70). He calls this "a purgatorial hell" (*un enfer purgatoire*, 278) At the end of his discussion, Carozzi considers a major step taken here, from a purgatorial fire effective only for slight sins (such as those of monastics like Bede) to a purgatorial hell effective against major sins (279). But he omits the condition provided by section 7, namely, that penance must be performed while alive. Moreira, who solved the puzzle of "quomodo hoc enim dant," concludes (*Heaven's Purge*, 134), "the scribe who added the title in the ninth century understood the vision through the lens of purgatory."

punished are explicitly called impenitent. The two penances conceded to clerics who abandon their chastity must be performed while alive. In R 6, the boon granted Paul for his family is a privlege, not a precedent, whereas in the long Latin version, Christ says, "I give to *all* of you who are in the punishments a day and a night of relief forever."[66] If Paul obtained special privileges for his family, it was because of his exceptional sanctity and his desire to specify particular targets for the divine favor that resulted. His parents benefited from a special grace, as described in a single sentence of the much earlier (mid-second century) *Apocalypse of Peter*. Otherwise, as appears in Bede's *Vision of Drythelm*, "confession and penance" are the only way out.

The Monk of Wenlock's Volcano

The *Vision of the Monk of Wenlock*, which I shall call *Wenlock* for the sake of convenience, also relates a harrowing aerial scrutiny like that in *Fursey*. *Wenlock* survives among the letters of the great Anglo-Saxon missionary Boniface. We have already encountered this "Apostle to the Germans," who wrote to Pope Zachary in 745 about the priest Clement's preaching that Christ emptied the underworld of both the wicked and the blessed at the time of his Descent. The following account comes from the correspondence between the missionary and his friends in leadership positions in England's churches. Boniface wrote to Eadburg, abbess of Thanet,[67] in reply to her request for an account of a vision experienced by a monk of Wenlock who had died and returned to life (*redivivus*). The vision itself refers to the death of Ceolred of Mercia, which occurred in 716.

From above, the monk saw volcanic pits, whose eruptions lead him to a further perspective taking in a river crossed by a bridge of trials, which in turn progressed beyond and upward to the heavenly Jerusalem. Angels play an active role in *Wenlock*, carrying the monk from one perspective to another, but the visionary seems to have had no individual guardian angel. When a huge flame ascended toward him (as in the *Vision of Fursey*), an angel protected him. The monk of Wenlock said that he saw a huge crowd of good and wicked people mixed in with angels and demons, who conducted a

---

66. "Dono uobis *omnibus* qui estis in penis noctem et diem refrigerium in perpetuum" (my emphasis). Montague Rhodes James, in *AA*, p. 36.

67. Bonifatius and Lull, *Epistolae*, ed. Michael Tangl, MGH, Ep. Sel. 1 (Berlin: Weidmann, 1916), pp. 8–15. For an English translation, see *The Letters of Saint Boniface*, trans. Ephraim Emerton, Columbia Records of Civilization (New York: Norton, 1976), number II [10], pp. 25–31. I cite Wenlock from Tangl's edition. For analysis, see Carozzi, *Le voyage*, 195–225.

disputation (*disputationem habuisse*) over their lives; the demons accusing, the angels defending.[68] And he could hear himself confessing or learning that his deeds, from earliest childhood, were sins, and the deeds themselves spoke in accusation: "I am your greed . . ." and so on through the list.[69] He had once inflicted a wound on a man, and, open like a mouth, that wound itself testified even while still bleeding.[70] Devils cheerfully assented (p. 9, lines 16–21), but then the individual's virtues defended him (p. 10, line 24–p. 11, line 2).

He saw, as if in the interior of the earth, pits of fire emitting the spirits of men, in the form of black birds, who wailed as they were cast up and then fell back in. One of the angels said that this moment in the air, out of the pit, is a period of relief (*refrigerium*) indicating that, at the Last Judgment, these souls will know "eternal peace" (*requiem perpetuam*, p. 11, lines 10–13).[71] While these suffering souls are in the volcanic smoke, enjoying their periodic reprieve, they weep and howl and "bemoan their just deserts" (*lugentes propria merita*, p. 11, line 8). The groaning, therefore, is constructive, since it reflects personal acknowledgment of one's sins. Though the angel informed the monk that the souls who admit their wrongs will be saved at the Last Judgment, there is no evidence that the souls themselves were conscious of it. From beneath the pits "as if from the lower hell" (*quasi in inferno inferiori*)— the image suggests the magma pool beneath a volcano—there emerged the wailing of those souls who will never know any relief, whom God's mercy will never reach, but whom the eternal flame will wrack endlessly.[72]

The monk of Wenlock then saw a place of great delight that angels told him was paradise (p. 11, lines 21–27). From there he could no longer see any of the terrors, but from the pits extended a wooden bridge that crossed a Tartarean river (*Tartareum flumen*), a river of fire and boiling pitch, perhaps functioning like a stream of lava. This bridge conducts the worthy to the pleasant land, while the unworthy fall off into the flames and pitch, each to the appropriate level. Still, all exit from this "Tartarean" river on the other side more beautiful than when they fell in. An angel associated with one of these falling souls explained that they had incompletely atoned for their minor faults, thus needing some slight additional chastisement before they were ready to attain the distant shore.[73]

---

68. *Wenlock*, p. 9, lines 16–25.

69. Ibid., line 26–p. 10, line 9.

70. "[C]uius cruentatum et patens vulnus et sanguis ipse propria voce clamans." *Wenlock*, p. 10, lines 16–20.

71. *Wenlock*, p. 11, lines 11–13.

72. Ibid., lines 18–20.

73. Ibid., p. 11, line 28–p. 12, line 9.

There seem to be two purgatorial functions at work in this vision: the trial bridge over the river of fire and boiling pitch is for those with slight sins who can advance as soon as these have been cleansed, but the souls in the cycle of volcanic eruptions, experiencing momentary relief while in the air, must remain there until the Last Judgment.[74] Unlike the *Vision of Drythelm*, *Wenlock* distinguishes between souls with major and minor sins, with different punishments and different durations for each. The distinction between the ash cloud, the lava flow, and the magma pool presents three punitive functions from one source of fire.

In the air the monk saw angels defend an abbot from evil spirits (*quasi cum angelis contra daemones pugnam inirent*). An angel commanded, "Know this now, and understand, you have no rights to the soul you have seized. Now, most miserable of spirits, depart into the eternal fire."[75] The angel's command echoes the condemnation of the deniers of charity in Matthew 25:41. The demons obeyed, but, after a slight delay, they reemerged ready for combat. Soon they were again disputing the merits of souls (*de animarum meritis disputabant*) and their respective rights to each one.[76]

The different *merita* and *scelera* (deeds good and wicked) of people living on earth are known and recorded by their own personal, protective angels or persecuting demons who are the very ones who had been urging them all their lives in their respective directions toward good or evil.[77] The monk saw how angels and demons behaved toward some living and some dead persons. The demons rejoiced at the case of a living girl who stole a spindle. The visionary recognized the soul of a certain brother who had died recently and over whose obsequies the monk of Wenlock had presided. As his dying wish, the man asked the visionary to ask the dying man's brother to grant freedom to a serving woman, presumably a female serf, whom they owned jointly. The monk's selfish brother refused. Up there, the departed brother lamented greatly.[78] His grief implies that the deceased can benefit from acts of restitution the living make on their behalf. The monk of Wenlock also saw the trial of the still living Mercian king Ceolred. An angel attempted to shield the king against a demon who argued that Ceolred "should be enclosed in the straitest walls of the underworld and there be wracked with eternal torments as he deserves for his sins." But considering the evidence, the defending angel

---

74. For this interpretation, see Ciccarese, "Le più antiche rappresentazioni del purgatorio," 49.
75. *Wenlock*, p. 12, line 32–p. 13, line 1.
76. Ibid., p. 12, line 19–p. 13, line 6.
77. Ibid., p. 13, lines 7–21.
78. Ibid., lines 28–36.

withdrew his support. At once a crowd of rejoicing demons assailed him with manifold torments and wearied him beyond calculation.[79]

After he had seen these things, the angels directed the monk back to his body, but his own flesh disgusted him beyond everything but the demons and the fire. He resented the efforts of those who were attending what they thought was his corpse. The angels eased his return; they instructed that he should tell what he had seen to all sincere inquirers but not to scoffers.[80] To establish the truth of his experience, the angels advised him to question some living people about secret sins he learned about while in the air.[81] Even after he was *redivivus* in the body, he remained invisible for a week, and his eyes dripped blood. Afterward, the reports of those he warned, followed by the death of King Ceolred in 716, proved to all that what he had seen was true.[82]

Wenlock brings together many themes with which we are now familiar, but often with variations that require comment. For example, the vomiting pits the monk sees propel upward only those worthy of relief from unremitting torment. The vertical axis of this image would appear to reflect the distinction between the upper and the lower hells, and indeed the narrative does identify the area beneath these pits as the lower hell, but Gregory's upper hell is a place of rest. Perhaps *Wenlock* presents an interpretation of the more tolerable damnation. If so, these souls will eventually be liberated, unlike those so described in Augustine. It is clear that there is a muddling of categories here; different authors (or the visionaries whose perceptions they report and surely sometimes interpret) are working out their own understanding of these closely related functions. In the process, they exhibit their ideas of theodicy.

A similar example occurs in *Wenlock*'s cleansing river of flame and pitch, which Boniface considers "Tartarean." In antiquity, Tartarus inflicted eternal punishment as distinct from Hades, which held souls but did not punish them. In the New Testament, 2 Peter 2:4 turns the term "Tartarus" into a verb to describe the act of casting the rebel angels down and holding them "until the Judgment." This may suggest that they may not be held any longer than that, but eventual liberation for the rebel angels seems unlikely considering the nature of their offense and the authority against whom they revolted. Still, in the late sixth century, Gregory I used "Tartarus" in the classical sense in his *Moralia*. In his *Dialogues* (4.37.8), the black, stinking river into which

79. Ibid., p. 14, lines 1–19.

80. Ibid., lines 20–24.

81. For this understanding of the rationale for the subsequent orders, see Carozzi, *Le voyage*, 198.

82. *Wenlock*, p. 15, lines 3–18.

souls fall from the test bridge either *is* hell or leads irretrievably *to* hell. In *Wenlock* Boniface applies the term to a river that, although fetid, cleanses minor sins and prepares souls for paradise, even before the Last Judgment. *Wenlock* therefore bends the meaning of "Tartarean" to cover temporary punishments, and thereby weakens a distinction that had held from Hesiod's *Theogony* to Gregory the Great. Like the outer areas of Fursey's globe of fire, the fringes of hell are taking on a new, purgatorial function.

This more generic use of "Tartarus" cannot be attributed to provincialism or lack of sophistication. Boniface employs motifs that resonate with the broadest range of Mediterranean literature and religion. The sense that a veil has been removed from the monk's eyes employs a figure used in the Qur'ān where a veil is sometimes said to conceal the truth from people who do not deserve to see it until the proper time (7:46–53; 12:107; 18:102–6; 83:14–18). Another example occurs in the passage where the monk hears the accusatory calls from the personified sins of the souls in the fire: "I am your cupidity, . . . I am your vainglory, . . . I am the lie by which you have sinned." This rhetorical device occurs in the important Zoroastrian vision, the *Ardā Wirāz Nāmag* (Vison of the Pious Viraf), where the deceased is confronted by his or her soul in the form of a beautiful or hideous woman, whose appearance sums up the the person's moral state.[83] Similarly, in subsequent Islamic traditions, but not the Qur'ān itself, the body in the grave receives the visit of the person's good and evil deeds, which compliment or blame him or her for producing such creatures as they are.[84] I do not mean to imply that the monk of Wenlock or Boniface knew either the Qur'ān or the *Ardā Wirāz Nāmag*, only that certain metaphors have a cosmopolitan character, and their appearance here would preclude the isolation of Scotland or England or northern Germany as a reason why Boniface would have a paler notion of Tartarus or find Tartarus a less useful idea than in previous centuries.

Letter 115 after 757 CE: Naming Names and Bringing Shame

This fragmentary vision circulated as number 115 among the letters of Boniface, but it is not by him. It was written after the death of King

---

83. *Ardā Wirāz Nāmag: The Iranian 'Divina Commedia'* ed. Fereydun Vahman, Scandinavian Institute of Asian Studies Monograph Series 53 (London and Malmo, 1986), 9 (the girl of great beauty), 21 (the hideous whore).

84. Jane Idleman Smith and Yvonne Yazbeck Haddad, *Islamic Understanding of Death and Resurrection* (Albany: SUNY Press, 1981), 31–61; Al-Ghazali, *The Remembrance of Death and the Afterlife*, trans. and comm. T. J. Winter (Cambridge: Islamic Texts Society, 1989), 121–47; specifically, 136–37: in the grave, "I am your righteous deeds"; "I am your foul deeds."

Aethelbald of Murcia,[85] who was murdered in 757, while Boniface died in 755. Although a male may have written Letter 115, it appears that the visionary was a woman.[86] The fragment begins with lines describing various souls immersed to various degrees in a "torment from which arose a fire and inky darkness" (smoke). Among them are abbots, abbesses, counts, identified by profession, and "a multitude" of others "of both sexes." Here, too, pits are prepared for those still living, regardless of sex or rank, "according as their sins warrant."[87] Remarkably, "all the souls in pits are 'soluble,' that is, to be released sometime, either on Judgment Day or before."[88] The celebration of Mass can accelerate release for those to be freed before the Last Judgment. Punishment in these pits is purgatorial. This explicit reference to suffrages in the form of masses is exceptional in this set of visions (that is, from *Fursey* and *Barontus* to this fragment). Such appeals become typical of visions only after ca. 820.

The narrator tells how the visionary then turned her gaze from the demons' labors back to the very pits containing souls whose punishments are soluble, and who exit at the Last Judgment or before. The sinners first seen in the pits are explicitly said to get out, but the sinners are not named, and neither are their sins. We learn only that the offenders' sins have warranted these torments. But now she sees other souls in those pits. These sinners mentioned are named later, their punishments described in detail and published on earth. This difference between the two groups of souls in pits might seem to suggest that the pits are located in different places with different functions, one purgatorial, the other eternal. But the second set of sinners is introduced as being "in *the very same* (or *precisely those*) punishing pits" (*in ipsis poenalibus puteis*).[89] Both sets of sinners are therefore in the

---

85. Bonifatius et Lullus, *Epistolae*, ed. Michael Tangl, MGH, Ep. Sel. 1 (Berlin: Weidmann, 1916), no. 115, pp. 247–50, at p. 248, lines 4–5. I cite pages and lines from Tangl's edition of Letter 115. For an English translation, see *The Letters of Saint Boniface*, trans. Ephraim Emerton, Columbia University Records of Civilization (1940; New York: Norton, 1976), 189. See Carozzi, *Le voyage*, 258–65, for extensive analysis.

86. "Et antea hanc miseram vitam, dum ex superiore contemplatione *reversa* fuerat, vitiis superbie, invidiae, cupiditatis, detractionis ceterisquae quasi nigerrimo peplo *contectam* et sine lumine remansisse aeternae claritatis conspexisse se lugens protestabatur." Letter 115, p. 250, lines 8–10 (my emphasis). Dinzelbacher, *Vision und Visionsliteratur*, 14, says the visionary was a woman, but offers no evidence. Danuta Shanzer, citing "feminine participles at 249.29–30 and 250.8–10" in Tangl's edition, comes to the same conclusion. Shanzer, review of *Heaven's Purge*, by Isabel Moreira, *History of Religions* 53.4 (May 2014): 401–5, at 405 n. 15.

87. Letter 115, p. 248, line 3.

88. Ibid., lines 4–5: "Et omnes animas in puteis quandoque solubiles esse vel in die iudicii aut ante."

89. Letter 115, p. 248, line 30; my emphasis.

same type of "soluble" pits and suffer temporary punishments. There is no distinction between purgatorial and eternal torments in Letter 115. These pits are simply "the places of punishment" or "the punitive pits."

Far more important than the differences between the two sets of souls in the pits in Letter 115 is the fact that the visionary *names* four souls she saw in the second view. It has been almost a century since Barontus, a soul returning from the other world, ca. 675, named contemporaries. In the early Middle Ages, this important feature of vision literature was very rare. (True, in the *Voyage of St. Brendan*, Judas named Herod, Pilate, Annas, and Caiaphas, but these were archetypal evildoers, not contemporaries of Brendan and his monks. The monk of Wenlock also identified the Mercian king Ceolred, whose death soon after the vision predicted it is cited as proof of its validity, and he specifies three other individuals anecdotally, but without naming them.) In Letter 115, looking within the punitive pits, the visionary sees Queen Cuthburgh,[90] Queen Wiala, and Count Ceolla Snoding. The identity of Ceolla Snoding is uncertain.[91] Nothing is known of Queen Wiala. The *Anglo-Saxon Chronicle* has some information on Cuthburgh. In 718 "Cuthburh founded 'the life' at Wimborne; and she had been given to Aldfrith, king of Northumbria [this is the same Aldfrith of Drythelm's vision in Bede], and they separated during their lifetime."[92] Of their punishments, Letter 115 specifies: "In the punitive pits were plunged Cuthburgh and Wiala, once holders of queenly power." Each suffers a different punishment. Cuthburgh is sunk to her armpits, her head and shoulders free, her other limbs covered with blotches. Above the head of Wiala spread a flame that made her whole soul burn. "The servants in the punishments (*poenarum ministros*) threw the individual, carnal pleasures of these women in their faces like so much boiling filth, and she heard the screeching of their voices resound miserably as if through the whole world."[93] Whatever credit Cuthburgh earned for abandoning carnal marriage and founding a double monastery, it was diminished by notorious sins. To the best of my knowledge, Queens Cuthburgh and Wiala are the first women ever sighted and named in hell. This breakthrough

---

90. "Aldfrith, king of the Northumbrians, married Cuthburh, but they both renounced connubial intercourse before her death, for the love of God." *The Chronicle of Florence of Worcester* (London: H. G. Bohn, 1854), 38, AD 718.

91. According to Carozzi, *Le voyage*, 262 n. 488, Ceolla is a nickname for Ceolfrith. An abbot of Jarrow named Ceolfrith is mentioned by Bede in the *Ecclesiastical History* (4.18). He was a friend and spiritual father of Bede.

92. On Queen Cuthburgh or Cuthburh, see *The Anglo-Saxon Chronicle*, Winchester Manuscript A for the year 718, ed. and trans. M. J. Swanton (New York: Routledge, 1998), p. 42.

93. Letter 115, p. 248, line 35–p. 249, line 2.

does not require a female visionary, but the feminine participles that describe the percipient, who was "raised" (*reversa*) above the world to view it and "returned" (*reddita*) to her body, supports the supposition that the visionary was a woman.[94] Here too was King Aethelbald of Mercia, "the late royal tyrant."[95] The banished Count Ceolla Snoding was confined by iron rods that bound his limbs behind him. In the same region were crowds of weeping children who, under the irresponsible bishop Daniel, had died unbaptized. Alongside these departed souls suffering exemplary punishment belong "the knights Daniel and Bregulf and their peers."[96] As these worthies were still alive, Letter 115 not only warns what torments afflict which dead sinners, it also labels named offenders as bound for the same types of suffering when they die.

These identifications carry political punch. The depth of this stigmatization is clear because, according to the narrative, after the visionary returned to the flesh, she saw "an innumerable multitude of unclean spirits moaning disconsolately because they knew that the evil deeds they had done had been revealed to men as if through a divine favor."[97] The idea that the shame of those the visionary saw could be a divine gift is the psychology of the visions in Gregory I's *Dialogues*, where the pope wonders for whose benefit visions appear.[98] These "unclean spirits" now experience shame in the world because their secrets are out.[99]

In Hell or On Its Fringes?

The use of visions to stigmatize the living as bound for hell is unusual in this early period. Instead, during the century 657–757, visions more typically used intentionally ambiguous terminology, such as "the punishments" or "the punitive places," and so gave hell a fringe to accommodate hell-like punishments that cleanse and free. These visions include places of purgation, but painful purgation, that supplanted Gregory's "upper hell." Purely a hypothesis for Augustine, the upper hell resembles the Bosom of Abraham

---

94. Letter 115, p. 250, line 8 (*reversa*) and p. 249, line 23 (*reddita*).
95. Letter 115, p. 249, line 6. Aethelbald's murder in 757 provides the *terminus a quo* for this lettter.
96. Letter 115, p. 249, lines 13–15.
97. Ibid., lines 24–27.
98. Greg. *Di*. 4.32.5, pp. 108–9; 4.37.14, pp. 134–35.
99. For a discussion of stigmatization in otherworld visions, see my article "Named Others and Named Places: Stigmatization in the Early Medieval Afterlife," in *Hell and its Afterlife: Historical and Contemporary Perspectives*, ed. Isabel Moreira and Margaret Toscano (Farnham, UK, and Burlington, VT: Ashgate, 2010), 53–71.

for Gregory, who insists that it is a place of peace for the just. By contrast, in these seventh- and eighth-century visions, places of punishment like the valley in Drythelm's vision look like hell but are not. They are explicitly described as places of punishment that purify and end. In *Fursey*, the demons in the fire refer to "the punishments," but the drama of this vision occurs instead in the airborne globe of probative fire. Through his exposure to that fire Fursey conquers his lusts, whereas the man whose coat he accepted, once hurled out from its depths, returns and will presumably never surface again. That fire does double duty: its perimeter tries marginal souls, thereby purifying those qualified to pass through, while its core confines those destined never to leave. Barontus goes to hell (*infernus*), called by its own name, and describes what he is able to see. The daily delivery of manna retains a connection between hell and heaven; thus not all of hell is in oblivion. *Drythelm* keeps the valley of snow and fire apart from the mouth of Gehenna. From the valley, which Drythelm mistook for hell (*infernus*), victims receive promotion to heaven because they made confession, no matter how late. From the mouth of Gehenna damned souls erupt in the form of dark sparks, but they fall back in, perhaps to shoot upward again, perhaps not, but never to exit completely.

Although *Drythelm* clearly distinguishes the valley of snow and fire from Gehenna's mouth, that valley encapsulates an important change. In the *Enchiridion*, Augustine stated that those who were wicked but not too wicked do receive help from suffrages, yet, he insisted, they cannot be aided beyond, at most, "a more tolerable damnation." In *Drythelm*, all who have exited the body in penitence, even if only at the last moment, receive full remission. Particularly because Drythelm's otherworld geography seems to map the logic of the *Enchiridion* so closely, its adoption of temporary punishment is especially noteworthy. To vary Augustine by making all but the very worst souls (those so wicked as to be beyond the help of suffrages) qualify for not just a more tolerable damnation, but for salvation itself, is to unify Augustine's divided middle category into one and make confession the essential criterion for salvation. The *Vision of Drythelm* visualized the function of purgatory without giving it a name.

In R 6, as in the long Latin version of the *Apocalypse of Paul* itself, the general field of torments is called "the punishments of the sinners"; it is separate from a lower, enclosed chamber that the text calls "hell" five times. Therefore, the underworld of R 6 has two levels, both for eternal punishment. Those in the upper part sinned in behavior; those below, failed in faith. R 6 is devoted to the impenitent damned, and wrong believers are in the lowest of its sections yet, consistent with the remarkable arrangement mentioned in the *Apocalypse of Peter*, at Paul's request, divine agents drew his *parentes* (parents and ancestors) from its depths. The escape in R 6 is from its lowest level. *Wenlock* offers the complex image of the volcanic pits, from which souls in the form of black birds escape in a repeated cycle, rising temporarily into the air, but falling back into the fires. Via this constructive process, these air-borne souls admit their faults and eventually attain salvation. Beneath these flame-throwing pits, however, is "the lower hell," explicitly so called, which is described as endless wracking in oblivion, where neither mercy nor the per-cipient's gaze will ever penetrate. Still, the monk of Wenlock uses the term "Tartarean" to describe a river beneath the trial bridge from which souls fall for purification in fire and pitch. Even the classical Tartarus has become a place of purification! Both sets of pits in Letter 115 also lead to salvation. Because it is a fragment, we do not know whether it once included eternal punishments. These "upper hells" are not Gregory's place of rest for the just, but punitive spaces, practically indistinguishable from hell proper, except for their purgatorial function and the term put to their pains.

If these visions from the century between Fursey and Letter 115 assigned a purgatorial function to an ill-defined portion of the punitive places, does this mean that by the seventh and eighth centuries purgatory has stolen hell's fire? The answer is no. One crucial characteristic of these purgatorial experi-ences (or even purgatorial places, as in *Drythelm*) is that they strongly resem-ble what the living consider to be hell. His guide had to inform Drythelm that the valley was not hell. Without that similarity, these functions would lack their deterrent sting. Hell was an indispensable aid to the credibility of postmortem purgation. As in Caesarius of Arles, if one's sins were too great to be purged, one simply remained in the fires forever, but if the temporary punishments were not practically indistinguishable from hell, the purgatorial pains would be a far less effective threat.

The deterrent power of infernal punishment produced a widespread and persistent desire to temper the uniformity and eternity of hell, but the idea of purification merely extends an important aspect of hell that had been present in eschatological thought all along. As Gregory I put it, like are punished with like, and the punishments vary according to the severity of the sin. It follows that lighter sins would be punished with lighter penal-ties. What remained to be negotiated were the criteria for measuring the gravity of sins and the means of expiating them, whether in life or after. Most important was the beginning of the appearance of behavioral crite-ria for the difference between curable and incurable offenses. Signs appear that these are two: undertaking penance (beginning with confession) and performing suffrages such as donating land, paying for *luminaria* (candles

needed to light churches), attending Mass, preaching repentance, and praying for the dead. These behavioral indices become much clearer after ca.
820, but they can already be seen now. The literature reviewed here includes
these specific behavioral recommendations: preach repentance (*Fursey*), pray
(*Barontus*), give coins to the poor or pilgrims (*Barontus*), confess and do penance (*Drythelm,*) distribute property to the poor (*Drythelm*), pray for your
ancestors—such prayers are suffrages (R 6, §12), acknowledge your faults
(*Wenlock*), attend Mass (Letter 115). The calibrated view of sin and punishment breaches once more the boundary around hell. Some souls were guilty
of sins that did not seem to merit eternal punishment, or acknowledged
their fault when faced with the fire. The plight of these sinners attracted
the devotion of others. At this point the term Saint Peter used to defend
Barontus from the demons becomes crucial: "He is not your friend (*socius*),
but ours." As with alliances in the real world, loyalty pays. The lord (or Lord)
recognizes his faithful. The tug-of-war between allegiance to good or evil can
take place in the air, close to the heavenly Jerusalem, or within view of hell's
gates. What could be more natural in a society whose territorial boundaries
and legal systems were still open to modification by force, diplomacy, and,
as many believed, divine intervention?

The places and functions in this patchwork pattern were closely related
but not identical. Places of eternal punishment differ from purgatorial disciplines and from judicial venues like Fursey's fiery globe or the air above
Barontus's house at Longoret or *Wenlock*'s chaotic airspace. An educated
elite comprising writers like Gregory I, Isidore of Seville, Julian of Toledo,
or Bede sought to shape this confusion by organizing their eschatological
discussions topically and carefully defining technical terms, but their refinements remained esoteric. Only centuries later did they become standard.
The resultant leeway opens the question of whether there is not some more
inclusive term that more closely approximates the idea that shaped all these
concepts at once. In this connection, it is helpful to observe that the discussion over the locus and duration of postmortem punishment is not uniquely
Christian. Before ca. 500 CE at the latest, and possibly much earlier, the rabbis who compiled the Babylonian Talmud attributed both purgatorial and
eternal functions to the Hebrew Gehinnom. In Islamic sources of the next
few centuries, Muslim sinners must face the sight (if they do not enter it
briefly) of hell and therefore the threat of damnation—that is, they have
a slight infernal experience—before being removed to paradise through
the intercession of the Prophet. We shall examine both these provisions in
subsequent chapters. What emerges, I believe, is a remarkable community
of concern between contemporary Christian, Jewish, and Islamic thinkers.

Visions from late antiquity and the early Middle Ages, therefore, show that eternal and temporary punishments occur in one place, not hell, not purgatory, but somewhere vaguely called "the punishments." It is one place of punishment with two functions: temporary expiation and eternal damnation. In these sources, there are various torments suffered in the different areas of this broad zone, but different visions separate them differently. Even though there was no doctrinally defined physical boundary between hell and purgatory, the theological distinction between eternal and purificatory punishments was clear.

Characteristic Pains, Eternal and Temporary

The six visions reviewed above took place within a century, 657–757. They offer considerable dramatic power through a horrifying succession of scenes, but the individual torments transcend their respective narratives because they requite types of sins with specific types of torture. Chapter 2 has shown the relationship of these torments to the Romans' treatment of slaves, but the specific punishments take on a new emotional value when ascribed to postmortem discipline. The remainder of this chapter will examine those tortures in the light of their overall function. In both the seventh and eighth centuries, the *loca poenalia* or "places of punishment" contained both temporary and eternal tortures, but this mixture raises the question of whether certain torments came to be seen as typically temporary or typically eternal.[100] The answer is difficult because some symbols are multivalent and mean different things in different contexts, and some can have more than one meaning within a single occurrence. For example, when Fursey looks down at the earth, he sees that it is a dark valley. That darkness symbolizes the confusion consequent to the fall of Adam and Eve, not any subsequent, individual sin. That punishment is borne on earth, not in the otherworld, even though earthly darkness distorts moral choices, which in turn, absent penance, affect the afterlife. In the *Vision of the Monk of Wenlock*, "Tartarean" describes the river that cleanses and releases its captive souls. If even the distinction between Hades and Tartarus can shift with the passage of centuries, generic terms like "filth" or "darkness" are far more malleable.

This flexibility was also known to authors we have examined. Julian of Toledo said that *time* is to those being cleansed what *diversity of pains* is

---

100. Ciccarese, "Le più antiche rappresentazioni del purgatorio, 54 and nn. 42–44, proposes the simultaneous application of heat and cold as "constantly" infernal, a suggestion that prompted my own effort, here, to separate typically infernal from typically purgatorial punishments.

to those in hell.[101] The reduction in the variety of torments applied in the interim, as related in these visions, bears out Julian's pronouncement. All this makes one wonder whether institutional concerns over suffrages and the hope of eventual salvation, even after painful postmortem correction, put hell into a momentary eclipse. The most useful baseline to test this hypothesis is the long Latin version of the *Apocalypse of Paul* because it provides the most detailed description of hell.

In the *Apocalypse of Paul* sinners fall into hell, and gravity exacerbates the crowding there. The first torment Paul sees is a river of fire, and fire dominates the area above the well. Beneath the well it is cold. Hanging occurs frequently in *Paul*. In addition, Paul sees sinners in blood, worms from putrefaction, darkness, bodily filth, and pitch. The worms, rot, sores, and bodily decomposition are characteristic of death, and its undying worms are traceable to Gehenna in Mark 9:48 (quoting Isa. 66:24). Giant, two-headed worms immediately after the entrance to the well typify the idea of unending decay. The *Apocalypse of Paul* targets many specific body parts, including lips, tongue, neck, and intestines. Despite the dramatic announcement of periodic relief from punishment in hell that climaxes the *Vision of Paul*, all its punishments were otherwise eternal. Periodic relief is not escape. Similar considerations apply to the *Vision of Paul*'s R 6. In this account, demons drag sinners through fire in chains; they attack tongues and cheeks with nails. The damned suffer in molten tar, sulfur, pitch, or lead. Stolen or wrongfully obtained animals, tools, or coins become implements of torture. Despite the dramatic liberation of Paul's extended family from hell at the end of R 6, its punishments were varied and eternal. Escape for some named beneficiaries does not close down hell. These two texts nonetheless underscore, albeit differently, the enduring opposition to belief in a uniform, eternal, uninterrupted, and inescapable hell.

Fire

One of the most adaptable of all biblical symbols is fire. It can represent the divine presence, as in the burning bush through which God spoke to Moses or the pillar of fire that guided the Hebrews through the wilderness. Exodus 24:17 compares God's glory to a devouring fire. In the passages that approve burnt sacrifices, fire is the means of conveying human piety upward. It is the fury of God in Jeremiah 4:4 and 21:12. Fire presents

---

101. Julian of Toledo, *Prognosticon futuri saeculi* 2.22; CCSL 115:59.

the four creatures that appeared to Ezekiel (Ezek. 1:4), permitting him to prophesy. In Ezekiel 38 and 39, fire is the divine wrath that threatens Gog and Magog. Nehemiah calls it divine fury (Neh. 1:6). In Malachi 3:2, it is the irresistable "refiner's fire." Isaiah 66:24 pairs the unquenchable fire with the undying worm as symbols of unending punishment. As in Hebrew Scripture, so in Christian is fire a multiform symbol. There is a baptism of fire in Matthew 3:11. Paul calls God himself a consuming fire (Heb. 12:29). As a symbol of the presence of the Holy Spirit, tongues of fire appear over the heads of the apostles at Pentecost (Acts 2:3). Beings with eyes of fire appear in Revelation 1:14 and 19:12, and fire is a sign of God's power in Revelation 13:13 and 20:9.

Even punitive fire requires attention to nuance. It is explicitly called "eternal" in Matthew 25:41, "inextinguishable" in Mark 9:44, and in Revelation 20:10, it is the lake of fire and sulfur, whose torments are endless. The fire in Luke 16:23 that tormented the rich nan in the abyss of Hades attracted divergent interpretations among early Greek theologians, as we shall see. Macrina, the older sister of Gregory of Nyssa and Basil the Great, tended to see it figuratively. Paul's use of simile authorizes some allegorization when he says that postmortem purification can take place "as" (Greek: outōs . . . hōs; Latin: quasi) through fire (1 Cor. 3:15). The suffering that may cleanse a person after death, even to the point of salvation, may resemble burning in fire.

In the early medieval visions, the situation can also be ambiguous. There is the dark and eternal fire of Gehenna's vomiting pit in *Drythelm*; yet even there this fire is preceded by the alternating, transitory torments of fire and snow for those who have confessed and will be saved. In *Fursey*, the heat of the fire varies with the degree of guilt. Fire as a locus of judgment is not actually hell; it is the assurance of a just trial ("What you have not lit will not burn within you"). In *Wenlock* the souls who suffer beneath the pits in eternal fire as if in the lower hell will never know any relief. Here fire doubles with oblivion. Even so, Letter 115 in the same collection (though not by the same author) speaks of the "fire and inky darkness," which here refers to the temporary section of the punishments. Fire also burns the soul of Wiala in the same letter, another temporary punishment. The Byzantine *Apocalypse of Mary*, which derives from the *Apocalypse of Paul*, features numerous rivers of fire that burn sinners of all sorts eternally. In this text the lake of fire is only a part of hell not the whole of it, as it is in Revelation 20:10, 20:14, 20:15, and 21:8. There Mary obtains relief for Christians who died in sin but had called on her name during their lives (§§25–26). In sum, fire does not, in itself, indicate eternal punishment.

Being Suspended

Bearing in mind the interlaced connotations that enrich these images, it is still possible to identify certain recurrences among these early medieval visions that lend coherence to the genre. Being suspended in the air is dreaded as if it were a punishment in itself, but is well adapted to the interim because it represents a trial of the soul. It contrasts to hanging, which is more often associated with eternal punishment. Those who hang in hell suffer as bleak a future as those who hang on earth. While in midair, Barontus confesses and receives suffrages in the form of prayers from his brother monks, even though he did not request them. His aerial battle is more a part of his apparent death than a postmortem punishment. The monk of Wenlock sees angels and demons dispute over souls in their airborne flame. In the second scene of *Wenlock*, souls in the form of black birds gain relief from volcanic pits, but in the uprushing flames they acknowledge their sins. Whether it is this midair confession that achieves their pardon or whether what the monk sees indicates a prior confession, we readers of the visionary's narrative see the air as a place where borderline souls can be separated. This condition concerns the interim; the Last Judgment seems far off.

The Test Bridge

Though not suspended in midair, souls tried on the test bridge are high above the stench- or fire-filled stream that runs below. From Zoroastrian Scripture to Gregory I's *Dialogues* 4.37, and Islamic, postqur'ānic developments of the notion (cf. Sura 37:23–24), there is a bridge that runs over hell.[102] The bridge in the monk of Wenlock's vision allows progress, but those in need fall into the "Tartarean" river to receive further cleansing before reaching the pleasant shore. Although not, strictly speaking, punishments as much as trials, these bridges inspired considerable dread, and, for those with the greatest guilt, they were distinctly painful—making the ordeal itself the beginning of a punishment that, logically, should only follow. Whereas the height of the bridge dramatizes the fear of the trial (as one would fear a deep fall), the length of the span measures the soul's virtue, because the fall into hell occurs at the point where merits run out.

---

102. Yasna 46:10–11, in *The Gāthās of Zarathustra*, trans. S. Insler, Acta Iranica 8 (Leiden: Brill, 1975), 83. The bridge also occurs much later in the *Ardā Wirāz Nāmag* 8–10; 194–96. For Islam, beyond the suggestive allusion in the Qu'rān itself (37:23–24), there is Al-Ghazali, *Remembrance of Death and the Afterlife*, 206; E. Cerulli, *Il "Libro della Scala" e la questione delle fonti arabo-spagnole della divina commedia*, Studi e Testi 150 (Vatican City: Biblioteca Apostolica Vaticana, 1949), §§196–98, pp. 206–11.

Immersion

Varying the depth of immersion in rivers of fire or pits of other noxious substances was a common technique of apportioning the intensity of pain to the level of one's guilt. The convention goes back as far as the *Apocalypse of Peter* and the *Apocalypse of Paul*, where the punishments are clearly eternal. In early medieval examples, Cuthburgh resides in a punitive pit, sunk to her armpits. This measure of guilt may apply to temporary punishments as well. In Letter 115 (after 757), those sunk in rivers of fire and various pits are said to exit at the Last Judgment or before. If, as Julian of Toledo said, variation in eternal punishments translates into duration in temporary ones, these measurements of depth reflect the proportionality asserted for both purgatorial and infernal punishment.[103]

The Bathhouse

In Latin literature, use of the bathhouse as a scene for temporary, postmortem cleansing seems to be the invention of Pope Gregory I; it appears twice in his *Dialogues* (4.42 and 4.57). Gregory hears of two dead men guilty of slight sins who were seen working off the consequences of their errors as laborers in the Roman baths. Through their postmortem service here on earth they escaped worse punishment in hell. Other common Roman punishments, such as labor in the mines or exile for a determined time, might have served equally well, but they lack the association with cleansing, a fundamental aspect of the baths. Water as a cleansing element is the least ambiguous indicator of temporary punishment.

External Agents

Demons, serpents, and other external agents attack those in the punishments. Who could forget the airborne struggle over the soul of Barontus, with angels and demons pulling from either side? This balance in forces suggests a temporary situation. Only in the *Apocalypse of Peter* do exposed children and aborted fetuses help inflict pain on those who conceived them. In the *Apocalypse of Paul* exposed children call out for justice to be done, but do not administer it. The later texts omit this personal aspect of postmortem retaliation.[104] Instead, worms or snakes or monsters such as dragons or

---

103. Julian of Toledo, *Prognosticon futuri saeculi* 2.22; CCSL 115:59.
104. Danuta Shanzer, "Voices and Bodies: The Afterlife of the Unborn," *Numen* 56 (2009): 326–65.

demons (the most versatile tormentors) vex the sinners. In the *Apocalypse of Paul*, four major "angels of Tartarus" with names or titles derived from terms for Tartarus preside. It is an angel who guards the lid on the well. Other, unnamed, subordinate "evil" or "dreadful" angels, some with fiery horns, are indispensable as laborers in the punishments, whether purgatorial or infernal. These demons or evil, ugly spirits or devils accuse, taunt, herd, probe, pierce, burn, and breathe sulfuric breath at their victims. Lesser creatures also appear in hell. Worms infest the *Vision of Paul*, where two-headed worms live just below the lid of the well that separates the two divisions of the torments. In *Paul*, these are endless situations.

Handmade Objects

The demons are well equipped. The naming of particular handmade objects is characteristic of biblical and early medieval texts. Jude 1:6 states that the fallen angels will be bound or chained in darkness until the judgment, and chains confined prisoners in the imperial mines and slaves in the mills of ancient Roman estates. It is no surprise that these objects should reappear in early medieval visions. They are prominent in the *Vision of Paul*. Barontus sees the damned chained to their seats in the infernal amphitheater. Demons drag chained sinners through fire in R 6. In *Fursey* there are fiery arrows; tongs appear in *Drythelm*. The greatest number and variety of tools appear in R 6, where the damned endure nails, farm implements turned against them, and blazing bronze horses whose hot surfaces scorch the rustlers forced to ride them. In R 6, all the punishments are eternal.

Darkness

Because of its prominence in the New Testament (Matt. 8:12, 22:13, 25:30), where it is frequently made the antithesis of light (Rom. 13:12; 1 Thess. 5:5; John 3:19; Acts 26:18), darkness may have seemed inappropriate for repentant sinners in transition between extremes. The fundamental opposition of darkness to light also appears in the *Gospel of Nicodemus*. In both the Greek and Latin versions, Christ as light (echoing Isa. 9:2) penetrates the netherworld prior to freeing the dead, but in the Latin Version B, he casts those who remain in darkness even lower. Both the *Apocalypse of Peter* and the *Apocalypse of Paul* find darkness in the punishments, and that tradition continues. Demons would keep Barontus in the dark to prevent him from learning the nature of hell. Hell itself is dark, permitting only a clouded view. In *Fursey*, it is the earth beneath that is shrouded in darkness, but it represents ignorance, not punishment. In *Drythelm*, the penitents are in snow and ice, not darkness. Though it is surrounded by a dark area through which Drythelm must pass, it is Gehenna itself that emits a dark fire from beneath the surface. Fire and inky darkness in the fragmentary Letter 115 ends at the Last Judgment.

The Color Black

Darkness may sometimes be represented by the color black as a sign of eternal punishment. In the *Vision of Paul*, demons wear black clothes and have black faces. The demons who attack Fursey are black. Drythelm sees black sparks coming out of Gehenna. In Gregory I's *Dialogues* (4.37.8), it is a black, stinking river into which souls fall from the test bridge. For all their power as symbols of ignorance, evil, and oblivion, darkness and the color black also appear in temporary punishments. Black birds come out of pits in *Wenlock*, though these are the souls of those to be liberated at the Last Judgment. Smoke, pitch, and coal also indicate the fusion of blackness and darkness in the punishments. Because of their close association, darkness and black may also be penetrated by light, and this contrast can occur in situations where there is a potential for illumination. To the "after" of redemption, darkness and black represent "before."

Cold

Although it is nowhere stated, it seems to be assumed that the biblical outer darkness (Matt. 8:12, 22:13, 25:30) is cold. In the long Latin version of the *Apocalypse of Paul* there is cold and snow beneath the lid of the well. To the north, there is also snow. Above the well, too, there is a place of ice and snow where body parts bleed. Fursey traverses a cold, dark cloud, where black, ugly demons attack him, but he escapes. The snow and hail opposite the fire in the valley Drythelm traverses is certainly cold, but it alternates with extreme heat, and those in that valley have confessed and eventually progress. Cold appears to be neither exclusively eternal nor exclusively temporary.

Oblivion

Aside from the explicit use of the term "eternal," reference to oblivion is the most characteristic feature of hell. To paraphrase colloquially, the damned are "out of sight and out of mind." In theological terms, this expression attains exponential force because such souls are no longer present even to the mind of God. Still, that oblivion is not absolute. Oblivion would appear to be the condition of the souls beneath the well in the *Apocalypse of Paul*. That Christ bestows a periodic reprieve on precisely these sinners is part of the wonder of this vision. The dark sparks emitted from the Gehenna of *Drythelm* indicate other excluded sinners, because they fall back into it and never escape. Bede's account contains no hint that this momentary suspension above the mouth of hell confers any relief on these damned souls.[105] Drythelm himself experiences a taste of oblivion when he believes his angel has abandoned him, but his protector is in reality only obtaining permission to extend Drythelm's tour. This sense of isolation is one of the most powerful experiences in vision literature. It occurs to Tundal in the twelfth century and to Dante (not only in the dark wood, but also much later, in the *Purgatorio* (30.43–50), after the Pilgrim turns toward Virgil, his guide to that point, only to see that he is no longer there).[106] In the *Vision of the Monk of Wenlock*, beneath the pits that emit sinners' souls in the form of birds who confess in the air, there is an area from which emerge only the howls of those contained "as if in the lower hell." These are souls "who will never know any respite, whom God's mercy will never reach, but whom the eternal flame will endlessly wrack."[107] Beneath the volcanoes these souls are in oblivion. Oblivion and its associated symbols are the least ambiguous indicators of eternal punishment.

The Torments and Inner Death

It might be argued that the torments described in the visions have nothing to do with inner death because inner death is not one of hell's torments. Rather, it is Gregory's term for damnation itself. Therefore the torments described in the visions have everything to do with inner death. There is a paradox involved. Just as we cannot know the threat of oblivion unless someone tells us that souls are lost "there," so we cannot know the horrors of hell unless, in some way, we can experience them before we die. Certainly, revenants and visionaries can offer their testimony, but other introspective souls and penitents can even now sense their impending damnation and its consequences, torture by torture, as they contemplate their guilt. In this way, the pangs of conscience, the revulsion over evils done and the dread of evils to be endured in retaliation, characteristic of inner death, signify all the possible pains of hell and certainly those articulated in the visions.

---

105. Bede, *Historia* 5.12; Plummer, p. 305.

106. For Tundal, see Eileen Gardiner, *Visions of Heaven and Hell before Dante* (New York: Italica, 1989), 160; for the Latin, see *Visio Tnugdali*, ed. Albrecht Wagner (Erlangen: Deichert, 1882), p. 17, line 23.

107. *Wenlock*, p. 11, lines 14–20.

These considerations highlight the significance of inner death and make it hell's most pronounced advance against the alternatives to hell, the subject of part II. Hell's rivals did not prevail, but they affected perception of it and produced a fringe where modified forms of torment could be seen to take place. Both theology and vision literature explored this area and tested functional relationships between different aspects of postmortem discipline. The visions of the seventh and eighth centuries did not arrive at purgatory, but through participation in the psychology of inner death and the conventions of visionary literature, they blended these conflicting currents. With the advance of monasticism, theorists increasingly encouraged examination of the conscience, through which one could contemplate one's faults over against the afterlife consequences they might entail. The ability to address one's sins and the risk of hell came to be seen as a grace. Introspection followed. In visions, therefore, sins are personified, angels parry demonic accusations, wounds testify, souls fall off test bridges when their virtues run out. The pains of hell, or hell-purgatory, took on a penitential allure. By making the contemplation of hell into a penitential discipline, inner death connected temporary and eternal punishment and developed hell's fringes.

The broad spectrum of overlapping temporary and eternal postmortem tortures and the ambiguous terminology characteristic of these seventh- and eighth-century visions built the hope for hell's purgatorial functions on the deterrent power of hell itself, and survived in symbiosis with it. Still, these purgatorial-temporary and infernal-eternal pains reported in the visions were severe enough that any relief would be of great value. Suffrages therefore appear in these visions as a factor in "the punitive places," but curiously the souls encountered there do not request them. During this century, it was enough to map out a fringe area of "the punishments" where impure but penitent souls, people who were sinners but not fundamentally wicked, might expiate their faults in hell-like torments and eventually attain salvation. Suffrages are useful there, but they are only one aspect of the punishments, not the behavioral recommendation of the percipient's tour, which is what they become in later centuries. Similarly, the percipients name very few of the inmates they see. Vicious behavior and wrong belief are condemned, but the perpetrators belong to no named religious groups. In these places of punishment there are neither Jews nor Muslims. These punitive places contain errant Christians, backsliders, those who discredit the faith, but not those who will, in later centuries, be considered opponents of Christianity. In this period, inner death, self-discipline, introspection, are more important than the stigmatization of others.

Part III

Hell in Abrahamic Religions

CHAPTER 7

Rabbinic Judaism: One Fire, Two Fates

> Seven types of sinners receive perpetual torment;
> . . . these will go down to Gehinnom and be punished
> there *for all generations.*
>
> —Bab. Tal. Rosh Hash. 17a

> And their faces shall be black like the sides of a
> pot. . . . No matter how beautiful they were before,
> they shall be called 'sons of Gehinnom'.
>
> —Bab. Tal. Rosh Hash. 17a

> All Israel have a portion in the world to come.
>
> —Bab. Tal. San. 90a

> The righteous of all nations will have part in the
> world to come.
>
> —Tosefta, San. 13:2

The development of Christian literature was only part of a more general Mediterranean discussion about postmortem justice. Part III will put the Latin Christian developments in the context of the beliefs of their coreligionist Greek Orthodox Christians, Jews of the rabbinic period, and Muslims of the first Islamic centuries. This examination will show that, in matters of eschatology, these faiths shared similar convictions derived from their common monotheistic premises. The method of triangulating different levels of discourse, already applied to parts I and II, will inform the investigation. In the following chapters doctrinal declarations will be amplified by theological-philosophical expositions and traditional exemplary tales.

It is often said that Judaism has no belief in hell.[1] Supporters of this view cite God's covenant with the Jews as recorded in the book of Deuteronomy:

---

1. "Eternal punishment was never accepted as a doctrinal belief in rabbinic Judaism." Simcha Paull Raphael, *Jewish Views of the Afterlife* (1994; Lanham, MD: Rowman & Littlefield, 2004), 144. See his preliminary reflections, 11–40. Daniel Cohn-Sherbok has assembled a further list of denials

obey and prosper, disobey and perish.[2] These sanctions pertain to this life not the afterlife. Later books of the Hebrew Bible known collectively as the wisdom literature reflect considerable discomfort with this view.[3] For example, the book of Job confronts the apparent injustice that the innocent suffer while the wicked prosper in life, and yet in death "they lie down alike in the dust" (Job 21:26).[4] Other biblical passages evoke an unspecified time of retribution. As early as the first half of the fifth century BCE, Malachi spoke of a coming "day," that would reverse the fates of oppressors and oppressed. "All the arrogant and all evildoers will be stubble; the day that comes shall burn them up" completely. "But for you who fear my name the sun of righteousness shall rise, with healing in its wings. . . . And you shall tread down the wicked, for they will be ashes under the soles of your feet, on the day when I act, says the Lord of hosts" (Mal. 3:19–20 [4:1–2]). By 165 BCE the prophet Daniel added resurrection to this theme. "And many of those who sleep in the dust of the earth shall awake, some to everlasting life, and some to shame and everlasting contempt. And those who are wise shall shine like the brightness of the firmament; and those who turn many to righteousness, like the stars for ever and ever" (Dan. 12:2–4). Here is a vivid contrast of postmortem fates after resurrection: "everlasting life" versus "everlasting contempt."

About a generation after Daniel, there arose in the Jewish community a sect or school known as the Pharisees that advocated belief in resurrection, judgment, and reward or punishment after death.[5] Jewish thinkers came to consider the worthy dead as having a share or a portion in "the world to come." They believed the wicked suffer in Gehinnom. With the function of unending postmortem suffering established, it becomes possible to observe the evolution of the concept from Jeremiah and Malachi to the Pharisees and then on to the rabbis, fondly called "the sages," who composed the Talmud. Perennial debates over these beliefs occupied the schools of the Rabbis Hillel and Shammai, Akiba and Ishmael, during the rabbinic period.

from early twentieth-century experts in "The Jewish Doctrine of Hell," *Religion* 8 (1978): 196–209. "There is evidence of the reluctance on the part of the Rabbis to think of an endless punishment." A[braham] Cohen, *Everyman's Talmud* (1949; New York: Schocken, 1975), 377.

2. See, for example, Deut. 30:16–18.

3. For a classic survey, see Oliver Shaw Rankin, *Israel's Wisdom Literature* (1936; New York: Schocken, 1969).

4. For Job, see Alan E. Bernstein, *The Formation of Hell: Death and Retribution in the Ancient and Early Christian Worlds* (Ithaca, NY: Cornell University Press, 1993), 155–61. For some chronology of biblical composition, see Joseph Blenkinsopp, "Deuteronomy," in *The New Jerome Biblical Commentary* (London: Prentice-Hall, 1990), 94–95; Richard Elliott Friedmann, *Who Wrote the Bible?* (Englewood Cliffs, NJ: Prentice-Hall, 1987).

5. This is the opinion of the Jewish historian Josephus, who wrote in the the first century CE. See also Solomon Zeitlin, "The Origin of the Pharisees Reaffirmed," *Jewish Quarterly Review*, n.s., 59 (April 1969): 255–67.

Discussion of these subjects continued long after the talmudic canon was closed. In the ninth century Saadia Gaon presented a pioneering effort at a systematic theology of Jewish belief in which this eschatology played a major role. By that time also, a large compilation of Jewish interpretation and anecdotes known as *The Lore of the School of Elijah* (*Tanna debe Eliyyahu*) illustrated the range of talmudic opinion with apposite illustrations (*exempla*). Opinion was not unanimous, and rabbis differed on exactly how it functioned, but these sources affirm that eternal punishment exists for the most wicked persons.

Although many Jews today deny that Judaism embraces any afterlife at all, this chapter will show that postmortem sanctions attracted Jews for centuries.[6] In biblical times, postmortem punishment was a minority opinion, but hints of segregation in Sheol and postmortem shame for the wicked can be traced from the writings of Jeremiah on.[7] Then, early in the Common Era, even though the talmudic rabbis considered resurrection, the world to come, and Gehinnom as cornerstones of their religion, they held no unanimous view on any one subject.

The Pharisees maintained that, in addition to the *written* Torah revealed through Moses, there is a parallel *oral* Torah, consisting of scriptural interpretations elaborated over time. These teachings or opinions or traditions circulated among the rabbis of Judea and, increasingly, in areas of the diaspora, that is, areas to which Jews had migrated or, in the case of Babylonia, been forcibly removed. After the Romans sacked Jerusalem and destroyed the temple in 70 CE, scholars felt the need to preserve this oral tradition in writing. Their efforts culminated about 200 in a Hebrew codification called the Mishnah. Rabbis who taught in this period are called the Tannaim,[8] and they are identified as belonging to one of five generations, which are indicated by the designation T1 through T5. Because absolute dates are hard to determine, this convention makes it possible to approximate the chronological position of particular statements within the tradition.[9]

---

6. It is important not to exaggerate the modern Jewish rejection of the otherworld. Recent studies underline its importance. See the statement by the Orthodox Rabbinical Council of California, accessed July 28, 2007, http://bit.ly/1jDAWrU; Raphael, *Jewish Views*; Martha Himmelfarb, *Tours of Hell* (Philadelphia: University of Pennsylvania Press, 1983); Lavinia Cohn-Sherbok and Dan Cohn-Sherbok, *Judaism: A Short Introduction* (Oxford: Oneworld Press, 1999).

7. Bernstein, *Formation*, 178.

8. Daniel Sperber, "Tanna, Tannaim," in *Encyclopaedia Judaica*, ed. Fred Skolnik and Michael Berenbaum, 2nd ed. (Detroit: Macmillan, 2007), 19:505a–507b.

9. I follow the designations of José Costa, *L'au-delà et la résurrection dans la littérature rabbinique ancienne* (Paris and Louvain: Peeters, 2004), p. 621, complemented by Sperber ("Tanna, Tannaim"), who explains the debate about how to divide the generations. Jewish tradition favors a five-generation system that dates from the twelfth century. Some rabbis were active in two generations.

By the time the Mishnah was completed, major academies had emerged in Sura and Pumbedita on the Euphrates in addition to those in Judea (such as at Yavneh). After the Romans repressed the Bar Kokhba revolt of 135, conditions in Judea declined markedly. A new wave of scholars called Amoraim then commented and taught the Mishnah.[10] The resultant efforts produced the Jerusalem Talmud and the Babylonian Talmud. The tractates of the two Talmuds are organized similarly. Each chapter begins with a section of the Mishnah in Hebrew followed by a section in Aramaic called Gemara, which consists of explanations drawing on various Tannaitic opinions from other parts of the Mishnah or other Tannaitic writings, and interpretations by the Amoraim themselves. Thus, the Talmuds can be read in "layers" from the Mishnah with its generations of Tannaim to the Gemara with its generations of Amoraim. David Weiss Halivni has uncovered another layer of commentary and extends the final editing to ca. 600.[11] The Babylonian Talmud is better known by far, and it is the text I use for the first section of this chapter.[12] As in distinguishing between generations of the Tannaim, I will similarly identify Amoraim by their generation (A1 through A8) and their locality (Babylonia or Palestine, B or P), when this is known.[13]

Talmudic Positions on a Punitive Afterlife

The talmudic sources present four main positions. (1) Wicked people may be excluded from the world to come, but it is unclear whether they will be

---

10. Adin Steinsaltz, *The Essential Talmud* (New York: Bantam Books, 1976), 40.

11. For the geology of these compositional layers, see Jeffrey L. Rubenstein, introduction to David Weiss Halivni, *The Formation of the Babylonian Talmud* (Oxford: Oxford University Press, 2014), 1–6, for this overview. The background in Rubenstein's introduction is especially helpful.

12. I use the translations edited by Isidore Epstein, *The Babylonian Talmud*, 35 vols. (London: the Soncino Press, 1935–52). Epstein conforms to tradition and retains the numeration of the folios (double-sided pages) of the 1520 Bomberg edition of Venice as redone by the Rom family in Vilna around 1900 (Harry Gersh, *The Sacred Books of the Jews* [New York: Stein & Day, 1972], 112). Thus, I cite tractate, Vilna folio number, and Epstein's page number. The Soncino edition's translators are inconsistent in their practice of rendering Gehinnom as Gehenna or preserving the Hebrew. When I quote a translator from Hebrew who substitutes "Gehenna," I use parentheses to indicate that the original was "Gehinnom." In discussions of Christian thought, I call it Gehenna. Tractates translated under Epstein's supervision may be consulted online at dtorah.com and come-and-hear.com, but the scanning and transcriptions in both are spotty. An online topical index to the Talmud may be found at http://www.webshas.org/index.htm.

13. Thus A3 B designates an Amora of the third generation active in Babylonia. I will follow the generations as indicated by Costa and the locations and English transliterations of the names according to Alyssa M. Gray, "Amoraim," in *Encyclopaedia Judaica*, 2:89a–95b, and, where this leaves some doubt, Wilhelm Bacher, Jacob Zallel Lauterbach, Joseph Jacobs, and Louis Ginzberg, "Tannaim and Amoraim," in *The Jewish Encyclopedia* (New York: Funk and Wagnalls, 1906), 12:49–54. The generations are approximate and may overlap. Some rabbis were active in both Palestine and Babylonia. Some identifications are uncertain.

annihilated or punished. (2) There is an actual place for postmortem suffering called Gehinnom, which is the locus of eternal punishment for some, but purification for others. (3) Gehinnom truly exists; it has three gates and seven names, but there are ways to get out. (4) There is no physical Gehinnom; its functions are accomplished by other means.[14]

The Wicked Barred from the World to Come

Tractate Sanhedrin examines the question of capital punishment and, at the end, moves from the fate of executed criminals to the subject of death in general.[15] Here the Mishnah makes a remarkable declaration: "All Israel have a portion in the world to come" (San. 90a; p. 601). This manifesto does not mean that only Jews may enjoy this inheritance, but rather that even criminals executed by the local courts do. It must be assumed that their deaths purge them of their sins. Even though Jewish criminals who endure execution have a portion in the world to come, some other Jews do not: "The following have no portion therein: he who maintains the resurrection is not a biblical doctrine [or that] the Torah was not divinely revealed, and an [Epicurean]." The list of reasons for exclusion from the world to come increases when the passage continues: "Rabbi Akiba (T3) added: One who reads uncanonical books" and one who recites a magical charm to heal a wound, and, adds Abba Saul (T4), one who violates the prohibition against pronouncing the Divine Name as it is spelled (San. 90a; pp. 601–2).[16] Specified evildoers and wrong believers have no admittance to "the world to come."

The Mishnah reinforces the postmortem sanction by naming outstanding wrongdoers: "Three kings and four commoners have no portion in the world to come. The three kings are Jeroboam, Ahab, and Manasseh" (San. 90a; p. 602). Their offenses appear in the Bible. Jeroboam, king of Israel, sowed division with Judah and set up golden calves at Dan and Bethel (1 Kings 12:1–20). Ahab, an even more notorious king of Israel, married Jezebel, the daughter of Ethbal, king of Sidon, and tolerated her family's religion. After she framed the innocent Naboth, Ahab took his property, thus earning the condemnation of Elijah (1 Kings, chaps. 16, 18, 21–22). Manasseh, king of

---

14. Respect for these complexities is found in George Foot Moore, *Judaism* (Cambridge, MA: Harvard University Press, 1950), 2:389.

15. Costa, *LADR*, 120. Here the Mishnah examines four types of capital punishment to which the criminals of Israel would be subject.

16. Orthodox Jews avoid referring to the divinity by name and, instead, use a pious circumlocution such as "the Lord," "the Name," or "the Holy One." In English one finds the custom of writing "G-d." This mishnaic provision attacks those who flout this convention.

Judah, sponsored pagan practices and "led Judah into sin with his idols" (2 Kings 21:11). So vital is debate to the spirit of rabbinic composition, however, that, at the very mention of Manasseh, and before listing the commoners, the text inserts the objection of R. Judah (T4) that Manasseh should not be excluded, because, despite his evil deeds, after being taken as a captive to Babylon and held there in prison, he repented and was restored to his kingship (2 Kings 21:12–18; 2 Chron. 33:11–17). The Mishnah overrules Judah's point by referring to the consensus of the sages. Because of his repentance he was restored to his kingdom, they conclude, but not to his portion in the world to come.

The four wicked commoners are Balaam (a non-Jew, and three Jews), Doeg, Ahitophel, and Gehazi. Balaam disobeyed a divine order not to work for Balak, the king of the Moabites, who had paid Balaam to curse the Israelites. Balaam never did curse Israel; indeed he prophesied a victorious future for it, but he ignored the initial prohibition (Num. 22–24). Doeg helped divide David from Saul (1 Sam. 22:21). Ahitophel favored Absalom in his rebellion against David (2 Sam. 15–17). Gehazi, whom Elisha turned into a leper for lying, doubted the resurrection (2 Kings 5:19–27).

The Mishnah now moves from individuals distinguished by their wickedness to notorious groups (San. 107b–108a; pp. 737–39). These are "the generation of the flood" (Gen. 6:5–7, 11–12), "the generation of the dispersion" (Gen. 11:1–9, the Tower of Babel), "the men of Sodom" (Gen. 13:13), "the spies" (Num. 13–14, those who tried to discourage entry to the land of Canaan), "the generation of the wilderness" (Num. 14:35, the fainthearted, who urged return to Egypt), "the congregation of Korah" (Num. 16, who challenged the authority of Moses and Aaron).

A portion in the world to come is assumed to be a blessing, like an inheritance. The righteous receive their share, but not the wicked. Following these givens stated by the Mishnah, the Gemara interprets further. Thus an anonymous Tanna said of Gehazi, "Since he denied the resurrection of the dead, therefore he shall not share in that resurrection, for in all the measures [of punishment or reward] taken by the Holy One, blessed be He, the Divine act befits the [human] deed" (San 90a; p. 603). This is retaliation: as the human offends, so God punishes. One who denies the existence of the world to come is denied entrance to it.

If the statement "All Israel have a portion in the world to come" leads to exceptions—a list of those Jews who do not—what about those who are not part of Israel? The answer seems to hinge on the Gemara's commentary to the Mishnah's condemnation of the seven notorious sinners. The compilers of the Gemara focus on the non-Jew: "Only Balaam will not enter [the future world]." This time, the rabbis argue backward from the exception to the general principle. If all Gentiles are by definition excluded from the world to come, why specify that Balaam is barred? Because, as the Amoraim reason, "other [heathens] will enter (San. 105a; p. 715). In support, they cite a confrontation recorded not directly in the Talmud, but in the Tosefta, a Tannaitic compilation contemporary with and parallel to the Mishnah:

> R. Eliezer (T2) holds: None of the heathen has any share in the world to come, for it is written: "The wicked shall return to Sheol, all the heathen that forget God" (Ps. 9:17). "The wicked shall return to Sheol," these are the wicked in Israel; "All the heathen that forget God,"— these are the wicked among the heathen. R. [Joshua] (T2) said to him, "If Scripture had said: 'The wicked shall return to Sheol, *all* the heathen' and then said no more, I should have spoken according to thy words; but since Scripture says: 'who forget God,' behold there must be righteous men among the heathen who have a share in the world to come."[17]

R. Joshua insists that the verse (Ps. 9:17) refers only to those non-Jews who forget God, and not simply "all heathen." Given the context (whether all non-Jews are excluded), R. Joshua's conclusion must be a double negative (Some non-Jews are not excluded). Later writers have cast this line more positively: "The righteous of all nations will have part in the world to come."[18] These considerations lead to the conclusion that this section of the Babylonian Talmud completes a full cycle of questions concerning all Jews and all Gentiles. Hence, "all Israel have a portion in the world to come," except those excluded by name, by offense, or by generation. Conversely, those non-Jews excluded by name are barred from the world to come, and, provided they do not forget God, the others will attain it.[19] How, exactly, can non-Jews be mindful of (that is, not forget) God?

The answer appears in the Noachide laws, seven commandments set forth in the covenant between God and Noah after the flood, binding on "Noah and his sons," a phrase taken to mean all humankind (Gen. 9:1–17). In contrast to the Ten Commandments given to Moses on Mount Sinai and

---

17. *Tractate Sanhedrin: Mishnah and Tosefta*, trans. Herbert Danby (London and New York: Macmillan, 1919), Tosefta, San. 13:2, p. 122.

18. David Castelli, "The Future Life in Rabbinical Literature," *Jewish Quarterly Review* 1.4 (July 1889): 314–52, at 328.

19. Evan M. Zuesse, "Jacob Neusner and the Rabbinic Treatment of the 'Other'," *Review of Rabbinic Judaism* 7 (2004): 191–229; Zuesse insists on the universality of these claims at 223–24. See Jacob Neusner's reply, "Response to Evan M. Zuesse," *Review of Rabbinic Judaism* 7 (2004): 230–46.

forming the basis of the Torah (Exod. 20:1–17; Deut. 5:4–21), to which only the Hebrew people bound themselves, the Noachide laws define righteousness for all peoples. "Our Rabbis taught: seven precepts were the sons of Noah commanded: social laws; to refrain from blasphemy, idolatry; adultery, bloodshed, robbery; and eating flesh cut from a living animal" (San. 56a; pp. 381–82). The injunction to create "social laws" is the obligation to establish civil courts to enforce the other provisions or at least law and order.

R. Joshua's articulation of this precept was a resounding call for mutual understanding in the Roman-dominated Mediterranean world. In the midst of popular paganisms that varied in every locality, philosophical paganisms such as Stoicism and Neoplatonism that were tending toward an abstract monotheism, and mystery religions such as those of Mithra and the Great Mother, and coinciding with the early growth of Christianity, this is a remarkable declaration of a potential for harmony based on recognizable principles prohibiting cruelty even to animals. Still, there is some question about how universal these values could become. The Noachide laws prohibit blasphemy: one might wonder against whom? They prohibit idolatry; so worship of false gods is still a failure of righteousness. In the polytheistic context of late antiquity, not worshipping false gods becomes a creedal standard.[20] Despite these doubts, the outward-looking response of R. Joshua is the stance that the compiler of the Gemara preferred, but it did not then have an authoritative superiority beyond its placement as a contradiction of R. Eliezer's denial. The consequence of R. Joshua's declaration is that, for some schools of rabbinic thought, admission to the world to come requires adherence to no specific creed. Good conduct is sufficient.

The favorable representation of R. Joshua's position still constitutes an exception to the idea that a religion with a God who constitutes absolute truth must damn nonadherents. Nonetheless, to the best of my knowledge, within the Talmud and during the rabbinic period, the conclusion that R. Joshua proclaimed remains a single statement; it does not overturn a more

---

20. The sages distinguished different kinds of religious observance among non-Jews and different degrees of offense in these practices against their God. Eugene Korn, "Gentiles, the World to Come, and Judaism: The Odyssey of a Rabbinic Text," *Modern Judaism* 14 (1994): 265–287. Jacob Neusner has identified the same point—namely, that not forgetting God, avoiding idolatry and blasphemy, implies a certain level of recognition of Israel's God. The point at issue is whether Israel is or should be an ethnically closed, inward-looking community or an open one with ties to a cosmopolitan Roman world, even while insisting on the Noachide laws, defined moral standards, and a shared recognition of God, but divergent observances. Eliezer and Joshua differed on this question. Neusner, "Response to Evan M. Zuesse," 230.

established consensus. There are other theological positions, such as belief in resurrection, that are required of any who would be saved. Thus, with the exception of R. Joshua's statement, Judaism conforms to the rule that claims—in religions asserting absolute truth for their precepts—hell results from denying the religion's declarations of faith. The tendency represented by R. Joshua takes its place within the moderating influence found in the three Abrahamic traditions. In Christianity, there is a universalist trend, although it is a minority position. In Islam, allegorical interpretations of Scripture lighten the interpretation of Jahannam. In Judaism, the doctrine that the righteous of all nations have a place in the world to come redefines the stark dualist categories of some rabbinical opinions, such as R. Eliezer's. Each of the three monotheistic religions harbored a tendency toward universalism.

The difference between R. Joshua and R. Eliezer introduces debate as the characteristic method of talmudic exposition. The back-and-forth style of reasoning allows many contributions of many rabbis to remain, not with authoritative finality, but nonetheless with a secure place in tradition. Even as it affirms the resurrection of the flesh, Sanhedrin 90 preserves, challenges even, grand general principles such as "All Israel have a portion in the world to come." These debates also entail exceptions that ground fateful exclusions. R. Eliezer excluded all non-Jews. In addition to this talmudic statement, this punishment also exists in the Christian Bible, espoused in some places by Paul (1 Cor. 6:9: "will not inherit"; Gal. 5:21: "shall not inherit"; Rom. 11:22: "shall be cut off").[21]

However forbidding these exclusions, mishnaic disputation outlines other options. Seeking a more optimistic destiny, the same R. Eliezer (T2) who denies non-Jews the life to come points to the implications of resurrection: "'The Lord killeth and maketh alive: He bringeth down to the grave (Sheol) and bringeth up" (1 Sam. 2:6; San. 108a; p. 739). This passage provides one of the most powerful arguments in the Hebrew Bible for those who emphasize divine mercy and the possibility of attaining the world to come. In the following Gemara, however, R. Menahem son of R. Jose (T5 or 6) was far more negative, postulating not merely annihilation, but active punishment: "Even when the Holy One, blessed be He, restores the souls to the dead bodies, their souls shall grieve them in the Gehenna (Gehinnom), as it is written . . . 'your soul (ruach), as fire, shall devour you'." (Isa. 33:11; San. 108a; p. 739). In the Talmud, Tractate Rosh Hashanah specifies more clearly than Tractate

---

21. For this theme in Paul, see Bernstein, *Formation,* 207–17. For the more literal sense of being cut off (*apokopsontai*) from the community, see Galatians 5:12.

Sanhedrin that those denied a portion in the world to come endure postmortem punishment.

Eternal Punishment for the Thoroughly Wicked

Just as Latin translators of the New Testament moved from the term Hades to *infernus*, so the rabbis moved from Sheol to Gehinnom.[22] The rabbis turn Sheol into a place of punishment by blending into it references to Daniel 12:2, concerning everlasting shame, and Isaiah 66:24, concerning the worm that does not die and the fire that will not be extinguished. The Christian Scriptures also use Isaiah 66:24 to define Gehenna in Mark 9:43–48. Because Gehinnom replaced Sheol in the Talmud, there is infernalization also in Judaism.[23]

The rabbis differed on who is liable to Gehinnom, how long one suffers there, and on the nature of the place. No passage is more informative on this point than the discussion of divine punishment and mercy in Tractate Rosh Hashanah. Because of Rosh Hashanah's connection with repentance, the Talmud tractate devoted to that festival is a rich repository of reflections on divine justice, mercy, and the life of the soul.

God judges one's actions at the beginning of each year. The rabbis concentrate on two major but different metaphors of judgment. The first depicts judgment as inscription in one of three books: one for the thoroughly good, one for the thoroughly wicked, and one for the intermediate. After ten days of trial, the intermediate move to one of the other two books. These expressions acquire the force of technical terms, thus I italicize them at first for emphasis:

> Three books are opened [in heaven] on New Year, one for *the thoroughly wicked*, one for *the thoroughly righteous*, and one for *the intermediate*. The thoroughly righteous are forthwith inscribed definitively in the Book of Life; the thoroughly wicked are forthwith inscribed definitively in the Book of Death, the doom [judgment] of the intermediate is suspended from New Year till the Day of Atonement. If they deserve well,

---

22. The talmudic Tractate Erubin quotes R. Joshua ben Levi's observation that "Gehenna (*Gehinnom*) has seven names" of which Sheol is the first. In support he quotes Jonah 2:3, "Out of the belly of Sheol I cried." The substitution can also work the other way (see Costa, *LADR*, 260).

23. Laurentino Jose Afonso and Batya Kedar, "Netherworld," in *Encyclopaedia Judaica*, 15:110b–112b, at 111b: "The name Gehenna takes the place of the biblical Sheol as the abode of the dead."

they are inscribed in the Book of Life; if they do not deserve well, they are inscribed in the Book of Death. (Rosh Hash. 16b; p. 63)[24]

The fate of the intermediate therefore hangs in the balance during the critical ten-day period of self-examination between New Year's and the Day of Atonement. These judgments, however, concern only whether one will survive for another year. The rabbis next examine the even more consequential matter of how judgment is made concerning one's fate in the hereafter.

Here, the rabbis outline a traditional debate, dating back to the days of the rivalry between the followers of Hillel (ca. 70 BCE–ca. 10 CE) and the followers of Shammai (ca. 50 BCE–ca. 30 CE), who disagreed on the fate of the intermediate group. It does not necessarily follow that the school's founders taught positions attributed to their followers. Nonetheless, these opinions ascribed to the School of Hillel (also Bet Hillel) and the School of Shammai (also Bet Shammai) probably date from the first generation of teachers recorded in the Talmud. Their statements may be contemporaneous with, and may even precede, the composition of the New Testament Gospels. The followers of Shammai set up the issue like this: "There will be three groups at the Day of Judgment: one of the thoroughly righteous, one of the thoroughly wicked, and one of the intermediate. The thoroughly righteous will forthwith be inscribed definitively as entitled to everlasting life; the thoroughly wicked will forthwith be inscribed definitively as doomed to Gehinnom" (Rosh Hash. 16b; p. 64). Having delineated these options, the text cites Daniel 12:2, "And many of them that sleep in the dust of the earth shall awake, some to everlasting (*olam*) life and some to reproaches and everlasting (*olam*) abhorrence." Scripture here covers the two possible assignments to an eternal fate that begins immediately. The thoroughly righteous go to "everlasting life"; the thoroughly wicked go to "reproaches and everlasting abhorrence." Logically and theologically, the School of Shammai has now classified the thoroughly righteous and the thoroughly wicked.

The debate now focuses on the middle group. In favor of their belief that, after death, morally average persons experience only temporary punishment, the followers of Shammai adduce two texts. Zechariah 13:9 says, "And I will bring the third part through the fire, and will refine them as silver is refined, and will try them as gold is tried. They shall call on my name and I will answer them." Second, they cite 1 Samuel 2:6, "The Lord killeth

---

24. The figure of the book may be found in Exod. 32:32, Ps. 69:29, and Dan. 12:1, as well as in Rev. 3:5, 13:8, 17:8, and throughout Rev. chaps. 20 and 21.

and maketh alive, he bringeth down to the grave (*sheol*) and bringeth up."
Hence, they conclude that the intermediate would "go down to Gehinnom
and squeal [on account of their punishment] and then rise" (Rosh Hash. 17a;
p. 64). According to the School of Shammai, therefore, the punishment of
Gehinnom is temporary and purifying. It enables middle-category sinners to
suffer enough to call out ("they shall call on my name") and so expiate their
misdeeds and then rise, eventually gaining a portion in the world to come.
Christian Scripture (1 Cor. 3:13–15) also offers this option in the afterlife.
Persons guilty of light or intermediate sins who, despite their guilt, remain
faithful to the principles of their religion will suffer, as through fire, but in
the end be saved.[25]

The School of Hillel took a softer position and argued that the intermediate will not go to Gehinnom at all. They claimed that "he that abounds in
grace [cf. Exod. 34:6–7] inclines towards grace;" and cited Psalm 116, where
it is said:

(1) I love the Lord because He has heard my voice and my supplications. Because He inclined his ear to me, therefore I will call on Him
as long as I live. (2) The snares of death encompassed me; the pangs of
Sheol laid hold on me; I suffered distress and anguish. . . . (5) Gracious
is the Lord and righteous; our God is merciful. (6) The Lord preserves
the simple; when I was brought low, He saved me. (Rosh Hash. 17a;
p. 64)

Therefore, Hillel and his followers concluded that the Holy One exempts
all but "the thoroughly wicked" from postmortem punishment. Moreover
the authority, Psalm 116, refers to Sheol, not Gehinnom. Equally important,
even according to the strict position of the School of Shammai, Gehinnom
is purgatorial for the vast majority: those who are neither thoroughly wicked
nor thoroughly righteous.

The limitation of some postmortem punishment to twelve months is
one of the most controversial propositions in talmudic eschatology. Some
modern Jewish interpreters use it to deny a Jewish belief in hell—since here
Gehinnom is not eternal—and so consider Gehinnom a Jewish version of
purgatory. Also equating Gehinnom with hell, Christians later considered a
one-year sentence lax to the point of licentiousness.[26] It is evident, however,

---

25. John T. Townsend, "1 Corinthians 3:15 and the School of Shammai," *Harvard Theological
Review* 61.3 (July 1968): 500–504.

26. The idea that hell could last for only a year was one of the items specifically mentioned in
1240 and 1244 when the University of Paris condemned the Talmud under the supervision of the

that this position was embraced by the School of Shammai only. However influential, it was not unanimous. Nor would it remain intact.

Reflection on the twelve-month purification for the morally intermediate produced important distinctions not attributed to any specific author; hence they may come from R. Ashi (A6 B), the Babylonian Talmud's chief compiler, ca. 375–425.[27] There are "wrongdoers of Israel" and "wrongdoers of the Gentiles" who "sin with their body" (as opposed to other, so far unnamed sins). They all "go down to Gehinnom and are punished there for twelve months." This raises the question, "What is meant by 'wrongdoers of Israel who sin with their body'?" Rab (A1 B) answered: "This refers to the cranium which does not put on the phylactery," in other words, neglect of ceremonial dress, but as for "the wrongdoers of the Gentiles who sin with their body, . . . Rab said: this refers to [sexual] sin."[28] According to this text, an error in ritual will condemn a Jew to postmortem discipline, because Jews have bound themselves to the high standard of the Torah. As it is put elsewhere, Jews descend from the generation that heard the law pronounced from Mount Sinai, and replied, "We have heard and will obey" (Exod. 24:7). For a Gentile to receive the same fate would require one or more sexual sins. Polemic enters here by claiming a higher moral standard for Jews. They receive equal punishment with Gentiles but for far less serious sins.

There is a further, unattributed amendment to the idea of the twelve-month "purgatory." In contrast to the view of the School of Shammai, which would raise wrongdoers up after they call out from Gehinnom, this view evokes Malachi 3:21 [4:3] and condemns wrongdoers to annihilation: "After twelve months their body is consumed and their soul is burnt and the wind scatters them under the soles of the feet of the righteous" (Rosh Hash. 17a; p. 64). Seen in the light of this text, Gehinnom changes character. Unlike purgatory, and unlike amnesty after a year, Gehinnom leads not to the world to come, but to annihilation. The manner of annihilation, however, gratifies some desire for vengeance: the righteous tread on the ashes of the wicked.

There were other revisions of Bet Hillel's bypass and Bet Shammai's doctrine of purgation. Some challenged the breadth of a category for *all* the

---

king of France, Louis IX (Saint Louis), and the bishop of Paris, William of Auvergne. The classic studies are these: Isidore Loeb, "La controverse de 1240 sur le Talmud," *Revue des Études Juives* 1 (1880): 247–61; 2 (1881): 248–70; 3 (1882): 39–57; and Judah M. Rosenthal, "The Talmud on Trial: The Disputation at Paris in the Year 1240," *Jewish Quarterly Review* 47 (1956–57): 58–76, 145–69.

27. "R. Ashi himself is not mentioned in the Talmud as often as other sages, but the large quantity of material cited anonymously bears his individual hallmark." Steinsaltz, *Essential Talmud*, 47.

28. Cohen, *Everyman's Talmud*, 374.

intermediate sinners. They tried to narrow this middle group to claim that only the absolute equality of good and evil deeds attracts God's mercy:

There is no remedy for them when their iniquities are more numerous [than their good deeds]. We now speak of those whose iniquities and good deeds are evenly balanced, but whose iniquities include that which is committed by sinners of Israel with their body. In that case they cannot escape the doom of "I shall bring the third through the fire" but otherwise [in regard to them], "He that is abundant in grace inclines towards grace," and of them David said, "I love that the Lord should hear." (Rosh Hash. 17a; p. 66)

Whereas the Schools of Hillel and of Shammai had debated where to put *all* the middling sinners, this passage divides the intermediate category down the middle.[29] Those whose evil deeds outweigh their good deeds cannot escape the purgatorial twelve months in Gehinnom, but if the good deeds outweigh the bad deeds or if both kinds of deeds are numerically equal, and none of the bad deeds include a sin of the body, those intermediate offenders will escape Gehinnom altogether, as in the view of Hillel's school. The rest suffer twelve months of punishment, as Shammai's school had urged.

A countercurrent resisted undue mercy for the intermediate. Not all sins are merely physical. There are also the more serious sins of intention. Some sins committed by intermediate sinners, who have done some good, are so grave as to disqualify them from the twelve-month term. Here is the principle of the exception to the exception. Those in the intermediate category can have temporary (or even no) punishment in Gehinnom if their good and bad deeds are nearly equal in number or in weight. But none of the bad deeds—even if balanced in number or gravity by good deeds—can be among those that by their very nature condemn to eternal punishment. Thus, seven types of sinners receive perpetual torment: (1) heretics, (2) informers, (3) scoffers (those who treat the rabbis and the students of the Torah with disdain), (4) those who reject the Torah and deny the resurrection of the dead, (5) those who abandon the ways of the community, (6) those who "spread their terror in the land of the living" (cf. Ezek. 32:23), and (7) those who sinned and made the masses sin, like Jeroboam and his fellows[30]—these will

---

29. Augustine of Hippo also divides the intermediate according to their character. Augustine, *Enchiridion de fide et spe et caritate* 29.110; CCSL 46, ed. E. Evans (1969), pp. 108–9; *The Enchiridion on Faith, Hope, and Love*, trans. J. F. Shaw (South Bend, IN: Regnery/Gateway, 1961), 127.

30. For this theme, see those who "walked in the way of Jeroboam and made Israel to sin" in 1 and 2 Kings.

go down to Gehinnom and be punished there *for all generations*, as it says, "And they shall go forth and look upon the carcasses of the men that have rebelled against me. For their worm shall not die, their fire shall not be quenched, and they shall be an abhorrence to all flesh" (Isa. 66:24). The sages continue, "Gehinnom will be consumed but they will not be consumed, as it says, 'and their form shall wear away the nether world (*Sheol*)'" (Ps. 49.15). For "they that strive with the Lord shall be broken to pieces" (1 Sam. 2.10). The Amora R. Isaac b. Abin explained, "And their faces shall be black like the sides of a pot"; to which Rabba (A3 B) added that no matter how beautiful they were before, they "shall be called 'sons of Gehinnom'" (Rosh Hash. 17a; p. 65).

The naming of these seven types occurs in the midst of the discussion of the intermediate. Presumably, then, this parenthesis concerns people who are partly good and partly bad, but who lose their status as intermediate because their sins include one of these special offenses. This is the logic of the exception to the exception. Intermediate sinners suffer in Gehinnom only temporarily (the first exception) unless (the second exception), among their sins, there is one of these seven unforgivable types.[31] The principle of the exception to the exception has also appeared in Christian thought. It applies to the juxtaposition of Matthew 12:31–32 and 1 Corinthians 3:13–15, where those with minor sins can be saved as if through fire, provided none of their sins includes blasphemy against the Holy Spirit.[32] It informs the distinction made from Zeno of Verona through Augustine to Bede between sinners (the intermediary) and the (thoroughly) wicked.

Three things are especially noteworthy in this discussion of the fates of these seven types of sinners. First, there are the categories themselves.

---

31. Another tractate admirably sums up this situation with parallel exceptions. "R. Hanina (A1) said: All descend into Gehenna (*Gehinnom*), excepting three. 'All'—can you really think so! But say thus: All who descend into Gehenna (*Gehinnom*) [subsequently] reascend, excepting three, who descend but do not reascend: He who commits adultery with a married woman, publicly shames his neighbour, or fastens an evil epithet [nickname] upon his neighbour." BT Baba Metzia 58b; trans. H. Freedman (1935), p. 349. According to Matt. 5:21–30, Jesus of Nazareth considered and modified these provisions (adultery and insulting a neighbor) in the Sermon on the Mount. For Jesus, the penalty is "the hell [Gehenna] of fire."

In view of the concern of modern Jewish scholars to deny Jewish belief in eternal punishment, the note to this passage in Baba Metzia is illustrative. The translator H. Freedman fails to acknowledge the force of the exception to the exception. "It is noteworthy that apart from these three—which are obviously stated in a heightened form for the sake of emphasis—. . . the idea of endless Gehenna is rejected. Cf. Morris Joseph, *Judaism as Creed and Life* (London: Macmillan, 1903), pp. 145 seq. 'Nor do we believe in hell or in everlasting punishment. . . . If suffering there is to be, it is terminable. The idea of eternal punishment is repugnant to the genius of Judaism'."

32. It also appears, but much later, in the *Apocalypse of Mary*, where Christian sinners receive temporary relief in hell, unless they are guilty of particularly serious sins.

How can these be understood? Some are sins of doctrine, some of behavior. Heretics, scoffers, deniers of the Torah, and those who contradict belief in the resurrection of the dead are guilty of heterodoxy. Their sins attack the community by undermining the unity of its belief system. Repudiators of "the ways of the community" could be either self-exiles or nonconformists within it. Informers are self-explanatory when a minority lives at the mercy of a majority culture. The remaining types of sinners offend by a despotic abuse of authority. Singling out these sins seems to target people of influence, much as the prophets did, by evoking divine sanctions, to persuade them to maintain correct belief, correct behavior, and wise government. The list also applies to private individuals, but the prescriptive force of the religious teaching indicates an important political dimension. It recalls the seven sinners denied access to the world to come in Sanhedrin 90.

Second, these offenders receive endless punishment. How the form (*nephesh*) of these inmates can wear away the nether world (Sheol, from Ps. 49:15) and yet be prisoners of Gehinnom forever is not specified. It would seem that the status of alienation from God transcends the merely physical character of their prison or the merely conventional name (*Gehinnom*) of the place where they are said to be condemned. This is the idea of oblivion. "The sons of Gehinnom" obtain no reprieve, whether by promotion or destruction. They will remain "for all generations." This rabbinical opinion quotes two biblical passages implying the longest expressible sentence. Daniel 12:2, where the School of Shammai regards "the thoroughly wicked" as condemned to "everlasting (*olam*) contempt," and Isaiah 66:24, which specifies that the punishments will be unending: "Their worm will not die (*lo tamut*) and the fire will not be extinguished (*lo tikhbeh*)." For these seven types of sinners, punishment in Gehinnom is endless and undying (Rosh Hash. 17a; pp. 64–65).

Third, this passage exemplifies infernalization in the Talmud. The proof text (Ps. 49:15) for the long duration of punishment for the wicked refers to Sheol, whereas the rabbis' contention is that these sinners endure damnation in Gehinnom. At the very least, in this passage, one might say that Gehinnom here resembles the grave, because it is a physical place that could disintegrate. Still, this is not Sheol, the neutral grave, but Gehinnom, the place of eternal punishment. Because of infernalization, the terminology overlaps here, but eternal punishment is clear. The itemization of sins, the blackening of faces (from soot), the expression "for all generations," the consensus of the rabbis cited, the proof texts assembled, and the conclusion all point to eternal punishment and all contradict modern observers who claim Judaism has no hell. Even if the torments of the wicked outlast Gehinnom itself, their punishment, like the fire and the worm of Isaiah 66:24, does not end.[33]

This fact merits reflection. The difficulty in understanding this provision of Rosh Hashanah 17 comes from the fact that Gehinnom executes both expiatory and eternal punishment. As José Costa put it, "Gehenna contains simultaneously the wicked and the mediocre."[34] The rabbinic Gehinnom—one fire with two functions—strongly resembles that expressed by Caesarius of Arles and Julian of Toledo and evoked by the narrators of visions in Christian literature of the early Middle Ages, such as the *Vision of Fursey* and the *Vision of the Monk of Wenlock*. The Gehinnom of Rosh Hashanah 17 is the *locus poenalis* (the generic "punitive place") par excellence. It treats all but the perfectly good. It is the place where the middling sinners to be promoted expiate their sins for a time, and in that function it resembles the Christian purgatorial fire, but it is also the place where the thoroughly wicked and the intermediate sinners who have committed any of the seven unforgivable sins will suffer endlessly.[35]

Eternal suffering was an option that structured the sages' debate and clearly existed in their minds as punishment for the worst kinds of sins. For the thoroughly wicked it was a definitive outcome from the first century CE. Bet Hillel did not contest the fates of the extreme characters, only the intermediate. The implication is that Bet Hillel and Bet Shammai agreed on eternal punishment for the thoroughly wicked. Later rabbis modified Bet Shammai's position on the intermediate who descend to Gehinnom. Instead of letting them all out after a year, as Bet Shammai would have it, they named seven sins so serious that they ensnare the "sons of Gehinnom" and punish them "for all generations."

The sages believed it possible to spend numberless ages in Gehinnom, but they held out one possible escape. There is, in short, another exception. If *we* waive our right to exact punishment, God will waive *his*. The Talmud teaches: "He who forgoes his right is forgiven all his iniquities, as it says 'Forgiving iniquity and passing by transgression' [Micah 7.18]." And again, "Who is forgiven iniquity? One who passes by transgression (against himself)" (Rosh Hash. 17a; p. 67). This moral is very close to New Testament

---

33. I agree with the conclusion of Costa (*LADR*, 259): "Some [sinners], indeed, undergo eternal punishment. . . . Eternal punishment engulfs those whose sins transcend strictly individual offenses: those who challenge the principles of the religion, those who cause the whole community to sin, and those who attack the Land of Israel and the Temple."

34. Costa, *LADR*, 257.

35. On this correspondence, see David Castelli, "The Future Life in Rabbinical Literature," *Jewish Quarterly Review* 1 (1889): 314–52, at 351.

sayings that teach that one is judged in death by how one judged in life.[36] The lesson of this parable is that, of all the ways to gain favor in God's eyes (charity, repentance, prayer, and the study of Torah), the most important is overlooking offenses, because the latter practice can, in itself, result in forgiveness of one's own transgressions. That is precisely the recommended attitude for the penitential season of the High Holy Days ending in Yom Kippur, the Day of Atonement. The season for judging humans, inscribing them in the Book of Life or not, is a good time to cultivate the practice of overlooking transgressions.

The long discussion on repentance that concludes Rosh Hashanah 17 supports this impression. R. Huna (A2 B) points out that Psalm 145:17 says, "The Lord is righteous in all his ways" and "gracious in all his works." Dividing the verse, he reasons, "In the beginning he is only just, but in the end he is pious," that is, first he renders justice, and then he pardons. Possibly, then, appeals might be launched even from Gehinnom. In the other direction, a text limits effective repentance to the ten days of atonement between Rosh Hashanah and Yom Kippur: "He who repents [then] is forgiven, but if he does not repent . . . he is not pardoned." That would limit the effect of repentance to this world and to the proper season. Whatever the restrictions, the overall sentiment is that of R. Johanan (A2 P), who said, "Great is repentance, for it averts the (evil) decreed against a man" (Rosh Hash. 17b; p. 68). Other rabbis considered the study of Torah and the performance of charitable deeds as measures that can modify divine judgment (Rosh Hash. 18a; p. 71). There is some ambiguity here whether this judgment is that which brings about death or alters one's fate after death. That some rabbis argue for the possibility of pardon after death and judgment is especially important in light of how differences between Latin and Greek Christian beliefs took shape during the same centuries.

Describing Gehinnom

In addition to debating the fate of large categories such as intermediate sinners, the rabbis considered a wide range of options from denial of one's portion in the world to come (San. 90) to active punishment (Rosh Hash. 17) for

---

36. Matt. 6:14–15: "If you forgive men their trespasses, your heavenly father will also forgive you, (15) but if you do not forgive men their trespasses, neither will your father forgive your trespasses." "As you judge, so shall you be judged" (Matt 7:2); "Out of thine own mouth will I judge thee" (Luke 19:22); "If we judged ourselves truly, we should not be judged" (1 Cor. 11.31). Jesus counsels prayer for precisely this consideration: "And forgive us our debts as we also have forgiven our debtors" (Matt. 6:12; Luke 11:4).

similar actions. In Tractate Erubin 18a–b there is a prohibition against a man crossing a bridge behind a woman for the purpose of observing her body. The penalty is exclusion from the world to come. Similarly, a man who counts out money into the hand of a woman with the intention of looking at her face "will not be free from the judgment of Gehenna (*Gehinnom*)."[37]

It is also Tractate Erubin that assembles the greatest collection of hell lore in the Talmud. Gehinnom has three gates and seven names. Jeremiah ben Eliezer (A4 P) enumerated the gates. The first gate of Gehinnom is in the wilderness, as is clear from Numbers 16:33, where the earth swallowed Korah, Dathan, and Abiram, the rebels who challenged the authority of Moses and Aaron. The biblical text reads, "So they and all that belonged to them went down alive into Sheol; and the earth closed over them." What the Bible calls Sheol, the Talmud calls Gehinnom, an example of infernalization. The second gate is in the sea, as in the story of Jonah, who praised God for hearing him from within the whale, beneath the sea. The biblical text (Jon. 2:2) reads, "Out of the belly of Sheol I cried, and thou didst hear my voice." Again, the Talmud deduces the location of Gehinnom from a biblical statement about Sheol. The third gate of Gehinnom is in Jerusalem. Here is a specific reference to the original Valley of the Son of Hinnom, Ge-Hinnom, the execrable Valley of Slaughter that gave Gehinnom its name, the ravine below the walls of the city where refuse and, at times, sacrificial victims were cast, as in Jeremiah.[38] In this case the location is derived from Isaiah 31:9, which refers to the Lord, "whose fire is in Zion, and whose furnace is in Jerusalem." Says the Talmud, this furnace refers to "the gate of Gehenna (*Gehinnom*)."[39]

Gehinnom's seven names also show how it has embraced older teaching about Sheol. R. Joshua ben Levi (A1 P) itemizes the names. I. W. Slotki's English translation in the Soncino edition of the Talmud gives these as "Nether-world (*she'ol*), Destruction, Pit, Tumultuous Pit, Miry Clay, Shadow of Death, and the Underworld (*she'ol*)."[40] For "Nether-world" R. Joshua's proof text is Jonah 2:3, where the term is "Sheol." The next terms are found in Psalms (88:12, 16:10, 40:3, 107:10) as allusions to the grave or as synonyms for death or variations to indicate parts of Sheol from which escape is particularly difficult. The last term, "Underworld" (*tachtiyth eretz*), from Ezekiel 31:14, is another synonym for "death." These expressions derive from the concept of neutral death in the Hebrew Bible, where death itself was

---

37. BT Erubin 18a–19b; trans. Israel W. Slotki (1938), 120–33, at 125–26.
38. Throughout, but see esp. Jer. 7:31–32; 19:4–5.
39. Further references to the Valley of Ben Hinnom follow.
40. Slotki, 131.

considered a divine punishment.[41] The significance of these names is that they point to the use of Gehinnom, a punitive place for the wicked dead, preferred by the sages, as a substitute for Sheol and its synonyms, to supplant the biblical concept of neutral death.

Given these focused discussions of postmortem sanctions in three different talmudic tractates, it seems increasingly difficult to maintain that postmortem punishment was not a concern of the sages. Indeed, the list of Gehinnom's seven names continues with further exploration of the name Ge-Hinnom itself. By permutating the consonants that make up the name Hinnom, one arrives at "hearth," which brings up Isaiah 30:33, "For a burning place (or hearth) has long been prepared; . . . the breath of the Lord, like a stream of brimstone, kindles it."[42] Most ominous of all, without citation of an authority, the verse is explained: "That [means] that whosoever is enticed by his evil inclination will fall therein." In rabbinic thought, the "Evil Inclination" personifies inducements to base desires. Thus, yielding to the temptation to evil leads to Gehinnom. There could be no clearer expression of a belief that surrender to sin brings punishment in Gehinnom. Johanan ben Zakkai (T1), receiving the students who came to his deathbed, said to them, "There are two ways before me, one leading to Paradise and the other the Gehinnom, and I do not know by which I shall be taken." He sees a binary opposition between paradise and Gehinnom.[43] A very old layer of the Mishnah contains a passage that says, "The disciples of the wicked Balaam descend into Gehenna (*Gehinnom*); the disciples of our father Abraham possess the garden of Eden."[44] There is the Way of Abraham and the Way of Balaam, or, as Judah ben Tema (T5) put it, "Pride leads to Gehenna (*Gehinnom*) and humility to the Garden of Eden."[45]

Once Tractate Erubin names, locates, and defines Gehinnom as the destination of the proud, it begins to consider in more detail who, precisely, is liable to its torments and on what terms. R. Joshua ben Levi (A1 P) speculates that those in Gehinnom, comprehending their fate and awed by the majesty of divine justice, at last praise God: "Thou has judged well, Thou hast condemned well, and well provided Gehinnom for the wicked and Paradise for the righteous" (Erub. 19a; p. 129). But R. Simeon ben Lakish (A2 P) counters

---

41. Bernstein, *Formation*, 136–46, 162–67.

42. Here I quote the RSV. The Soncino translation of Erubin 19a renders this biblical line as "For a hearth is ordered of old."

43. BT Berakoth 28b; p. 173.

44. Mishnah, Abot 5, 19; cited in Costa, *LADR*, 359.

45. Mishnah, Abot 5, 20; cited in Costa, *LADR*, 359. Cf. BT Hagigah 15a; ed. I. Abrahams (1938), 94–95.

that "the wicked do not repent even at the gate of Gehenna (*Gehinnom*)," and
he cites Isaiah 66:24, which refers to "the men that rebel against me." The
context of this passage in Isaiah separates Jews from non-Jews. Now Resh
Lakish (a nickname for the same rabbi), consistent with the context of Isaiah
66:24, excepts the Jews: "The fire of Gehenna (*Gehinnom*) has no power over
the transgressors in Israel" (Erub. 19a; p. 129). He argues that it is the transgressors in Israel who praise divine justice despite enduring its discipline, but
that transgressors among idol worshippers, unrepentant even at its gates,
continue in their rebellion.

   In addition to the comprehension of divine justice, which dawns as they
approach Gehinnom's gates, Jewish transgressors, whatever their misdeeds,
are "as full of good deeds as a pomegranate [with seed]." And, "our father
Abraham comes, brings them up, and receives them."[46] Thus, it would seem
that a life of discipline in Jewish virtue and ritual practice produces good
deeds that outweigh other lapses. If Jews escape a condemnation to Gehinnom, they constitute an exception among the peoples for Resh Lakish. But
there are also exceptions to the exception. Abraham welcomes the Jews out
of Gehinnom "except such an Israelite as had immoral intercourse with the
daughter of an idolater" (Erub. 19a; p. 130). To achieve his seduction, the
Jewish male would have to conceal his circumcision, thus, as editor I. W.
Slotki observes, Abraham would "mistake him for a heathen."[47] The practice of concealing one's circumcision would presumably also include one in
the category cited in Rosh Hashanah, which condemns "those who abandon
the ways of the community" (Rosh Hash. 17a; p. 65). This is the logic of the
exception to the exception. All the thoroughly wicked or moderately wicked
are sent to Gehinnom. Many are excused after a year for their good deeds or
because of their descent from Abraham, *unless* they have repudiated him by
concealing their circumcision to mate with a pagan woman. Gehinnom is
left with a residue of unpardonable sinners, who will never escape. Eternal
punishment exists in rabbinical Judaism. To deny eternal punishment in Jewish literature is to omit these exceptions.[48]

   The threat of eternal punishment exercised the rabbis sufficiently that
they adduced many other grounds for exemption from the torments of
Gehinnom. As in the case of Rosh Hashanah 17a, where divine mercy lifts
middling sinners out of Gehinnom, except for those in the worst categories,

---

46. Other figures can also redeem Jews from suffering in Gehinnom: Isaac (BT Shabbat 104a; ed.
H. Freedman [1938], 502) and David (BT Sotah 10b; trans. A. Cohen [1936], p. 51).

47. Slotki, 130 n. 7.

48. This consideration recalls the lists of exceptions from Rosh Hashanah 17a and Sanhedrin 90a.

so other passages consider other categories and other rationales for exemption.[49] The case of Korah is a good example. This rebel from Numbers 16:1–40 and 26:9–11 is among the archetypal wicked in Judaism. Along with Dathan, Abiram, and On, Korah opposed the restriction of priestly authority to the progeny of Aaron by claiming, "All the congregation are holy!" To suppress this egalitarian challenge, God caused the earth to open beneath their feet. It is said of Korah and his company that they cook in Gehinnom for thirty days at a time (the Jewish calendar is lunar), but then come up to earth, where an Arab showed them to R. bar Bar Hanah (A3 B).[50] These wicked souls get a monthly reprieve, like the weekly relief granted the damned in the *Apocalypse of Paul* or the weekend reprieve granted to Judas in the *Voyage of St. Brendan*. Even in their punishment, Korah and his company have special privileges: "A special place was assigned to them in Gehinnom and they stood on it."[51] Moreover, according to a later midrash, at the coming of the messiah, Korah and his company will be released from Gehinnom.[52]

The tradition in Judaism of periodic relief from Gehinnom goes farther still. Korah and his followers would escape punishment in recognition of their singing the Shirah (a prayer of thanksgiving attributed to Moses)[53] and believing "The Lord bringeth down to Sheol and lifteth up" (1 Sam. 2:6); Absalom, for being "of the seed of Israel" and for being the son of David; Jeroboam because he studied the Torah; Ahab, Doeg, and Jeroboam (again), for being descendants of those who heard Moses and said, "We will do and harken" (Exod. 24:7).[54] Thus, the effort to diminish the impact of Gehinnom was continuous. Still, these grounds for mitigation would not benefit non-Jews who were idol worshippers or blasphemers.

Analogous to the continuous mitigation of punishment and the invention of privileged categories of exempted sinners is the belief that all hell rests on the Sabbath. Different thinkers added different twists as this tradition

---

49. Samuel J. Fox, *Hell in Jewish Literature* (Northbrook, IL: Merrimack College Press, 1972), 136–37, reviews the many rationales devised over the centuries to remove some sinners from Gehinnom or to mitigate its punishments. See also Raphael, *Jewish Views*, 298–308.

50. BT San. 110a; pp. 756–57; BT Baba Bathra 74a; pp. 293–94.

51. Megillah 14a; p. 82. The relief that this elevated place provides seems an ironic evocation of Gehinnom's origin as the "high place of Topheth" (Jer. 7:31) and the other "high places" where the Canaanites and backsliding kings of Israel and Judah set up deviant altars.

52. Louis Ginzberg, *The Legends of the Jews* (1913; Philadelphia: Jewish Publication Society of America, 1968), 4:234, 6:269 n. 114.

53. Wilhelm Bacher and Judah David Eisenstein, "Shirah, Perek," in *Jewish Encyclopedia* (1906), 11:295b: "the Shira of Moses at the Red Sea"; Cyrus Adler and Francis L. Cohen, "Ashirah," in *Jewish Encyclopedia* (1903), 2:188b; W. Gunther Plaut, ed., *The Torah: A Modern Commentary* (New York: UAHC, 1981), 487–88.

54. Fox, *Hell in Jewish Literature*, 136–37.

developed, but the Talmud includes the idea that on the Sabbath, when God rested from the labor of creation and ordained commemorative peace ever after, there is no punishment in Gehinnom. In Christianity, the *Apocalypse of Paul* and other texts also advanced this belief. Even though Jewish and Christian commentators share this view, Islam does not. Because the Islamic view of God's creative energy requires no day of rest, there is no similar claim for Friday, even though it is a special day of prayer.[55] Nonetheless, other, postqur'ānic traditions adduce instances of mitigation of the punishments in Jahannam, the Muslim hell. In all three of the great monotheistic religions there was a movement toward the mitigation of hell, though to different degrees and expressed differently.

The importance of Sabbath rest in Gehinnom takes on greater resonance in Tractate Sanhedrin 65b, which relates an exchange between the famous R. Akiba (T3) and Tinnius Rufus, the Roman governor of Judea whose misrule partly provoked the Bar Kokhba revolt of 132–135. Scoffing at Jewish belief and practice, the Roman officer challenged Akiba to explain how the Sabbath differs from any other day. In one of literature's great jibes, Akiba replied: "The grave of your father shows [this difference] since it does not raise any smoke on the Sabbath."[56] In one sentence, Akiba defends the Sabbath, vilifies the man's parentage, and evokes postmortem punishment—a threat to scoffers and persecutors of Jews.[57] The doctrinal point of the Tinnius Rufus story is that even his pagan father benefits from Sabbath peace, because on that day there is no punishment in Gehinnom.

The sabbatical exception in Gehinnom is itself subject to an exception: previous observance of the Sabbath is required for this benefit.[58] (Therefore smoke *would* have continued to rise from the grave of Tinnius Rufus's father.) R. Simeon ben Pazi (A3? P) cites two previous rabbis as stating, "He who observes [the practice of] three meals on the Sabbath (stipulated in Tractate Shabbat 117b) is saved from . . . the retribution of Gehinnom" (Shabbat

---

55. Ragnar Eklund, *Life between Death and Resurrection according to Islam*, Inaugural Dissertation (Uppsala: Almqvist & Wiksells, 1941), 59, erroneously claims that there is no fire in Jahannam on Friday.

56. BT Sanhedrin 65b; cited in Fox, *Hell in Jewish Literature*, 119.

57. See also Cohen, *Everyman's Talmud*, 382–83, citing Genesis Rabba 11.5. Batya Kedar observes, citing this passage, "The punishment of the wicked in Gehenna was conceived of as parallel to the procedures for punishment in this world. Just as the lower court does not inflict punishment on the Sabbath, so in Gehenna: "During weekdays they suffer, but on the Sabbath they are given rest." Afonso and Kedar, "Netherworld," in *Encyclopaedia Judaica*, 15:110–12, at 112a.

58. BT Shabbat 118a; pp. 580–81. Observance of the Sabbath in life provides relief from Gehinnom on the Sabbath. The importance of this theme expands in kabbalah literature, particularly the Zohar. See Fox, *Hell in Jewish Literature*, 118–28; Raphael, *Jewish Views*, 307–8.

118a). This statement follows the principle of the exception to the exception because it is taught that sins of a certain sort entail punishment in Gehinnom, whether temporary or eternal, except on the Sabbath, except for those who did not observe the Sabbath. It is possible, therefore, for a person to follow the religious law scrupulously, but still sin seriously enough to be assigned to Gehinnom. Whether temporarily or endlessly, such a person will enjoy Sabbath rest in Gehinnom, provided they had honored the Sabbath in life.

Gehinnom Denied

In another tractate, Resh Lakish (A2 P) went beyond mitigating Gehinnom and its pains. He denied altogether the existence of a special receptacle for the punishment of the wicked: "There is no Gehenna (*Gehinnom*) in the Future world, but the Holy One blessed be He, brings the sun out of its sheath, so that it is fierce: the wicked are punished by it, the righteous are healed by it" ('Abod. Zar. 3b; p. 11).[59] Since the natural world is already provided with a mechanism for the punishment of the wicked and the healing of the righteous, he denies anything further. Quoted twice in the Talmud, this denial of Gehinnom certainly qualifies the notion of eternal punishment in rabbinic belief. It seems to dismiss almost impatiently the debate recorded in Rosh Hashanah 17a about intermediate sinners, their squealing in the fire, or the righteous trampling the ashes of the wicked. Nonetheless, Resh Lakish attributes to the sun the very functions assigned to Gehinnom in Rosh Hashanah 17a: healing and punishment. In this he constructs a power that resembles the fire in the *Vision of Fursey* or the evolution of the Aeolian volcanoes, from container of the damned to refiner of souls. The sun as presented by Resh Lakish also serves a function like that of the punishing fire advanced by Caesarius of Arles and Isidore of Seville. The parallel between the speculations in both the Jewish and Christian communities is very strong. Still, Resh Lakish is the rabbi who distinguished Jews from Gentiles by asserting that Jews would repent at the gate of Gehinnom, whereas Gentiles, in their pride, would march right in (Erub. 19a; p. 129). These positions seem hard to reconcile.

For all the latitude granted rabbis in their individual interpretations, for all the debate over which biblical text best proves various aspects of their own positions on resurrection, judgment, reward, and punishment in the otherworld, it is certain that Gehinnom was a fixed presence for the rabbis.

---

59. Cf. BT Nedarim 8b; p. 19. See Cohen, *Everyman's Talmud*, 383; Costa, *LADR*, 261–85. Costa (*LADR*, 31 n. 88) calls Resh Lakish "an Amora inclined to 'demythification'."

Even if Resh Lakish did not believe in its physical existence, he considered it a majority belief and referred to it when convenient. One way to illustrate the power of Gehinnom in the rabbinic imagination is to cite the lesson in cosmology from Tractate Pesa[c]him (94a; p. 503). Here Egypt is said to occupy one-sixtieth the area of Ethiopia: "Ethiopia one sixtieth of the world, the world one sixtieth of the Garden, the Garden one sixtieth of Eden, Eden one sixtieth of Gehinnom. Thus the whole world is like a pot lid [in relation] to Gehinnom."

Saadia Gaon (882–940): Why There Is a Hell

For all the variety of opinion talmudic exposition offered, it did not provide a logically coherent theology to facilitate comparison or competition with other faiths. Besides, given the condition of the Jewish community as subjects in the Land of Israel and exiles elsewhere, no central authority could determine these points definitively. Ever since the Roman exile after the destruction of the temple and later persecution following the failure of Simon ben Kokhba's revolt, the Babylonian Jewish community had been far more numerous and prosperous than the one in Palestine. Of necessity, the task of doctrinal consolidation gradually shifted to the religious academies of Babylonia. Over the centuries, first under Persian, then Byzantine, and finally under Muslim rule, authority migrated to the heads, or *gaonim*, of the academies of Sura and Pumbedita, each of which later moved, independently, to Baghdad. There, in the tenth century, Saadia Gaon, the head of the Sura academy, provided the first systematic synthesis of Jewish doctrine.

Saadia's career illustrates important aspects of diaspora Judaism. Like many other peoples in exile, the Jews of Babylonia learned the language and culture of their secular lords. For this audience, Saadia translated the Bible into Arabic. He composed a Hebrew grammar. There also lived in Babylonia a community of Karaites, a Jewish sect that insisted on strict fidelity to the written Torah and denied the validity of the Talmud. Saadia seems to have aimed his harshest invective against this group. He continued to write *responsa* (expert opinions) even after being forced from the gaonate by the caliph. He wrote the *Book of Beliefs and Opinions* in Arabic (using Hebrew characters) in 933. Only in 1186 did Ibn Tibbon translate it into Hebrew, in Lunel, Southern France, to aid yet another diasporic, Jewish community.[60]

---

60. Much of this background is derived from http://www.jewishvirtuallibrary.org/jsource/biography/SaadiaGaon.html, accessed May 29, 2007. For an overview of his philosophical views, see Sarah Pessin, "Saadyah [Saadia]," *The Stanford Encyclopedia of Philosophy*, accessed February 27, 2014,

The *Book of Beliefs and Opinions* is considered the first Jewish work of what today is called "systematic theology."[61] One sign of Christian and Muslim theological influence on this work is Saadia's categorical conclusion favoring the eternity of postmortem retribution.[62] In contrast to the scattered eschatological treatments in the Talmud, dispersed in their various orders and tractates, which then constituted the Jewish literature on the subject, Saadia expounds the future chronologically and rearranges the various parallel strands of this tradition into consecutive stages, with Resurrection (Treatise 7), Redemption, and restoration to the homeland (Treatise 8) prior to the world to come and its division into regions of Reward and Punishment (Treatise 9). In its chronological organization, the *Book of Beliefs and Opinions* resembles Augustine of Hippo's *City of God* and Julian of Toledo's *Forecast of the Future World.*

The key to Saadia's discussion of postmortem retribution is his conviction that reason demands it. Early in his book, Saadia asserts axiomatically that the goal of all creation is the good of human beings (180–81). It would be incompatible with this goal if the mixture of pleasure and pain found in this world were the end of human existence (323–24). Since we can conceive of the truth and the justice on behalf of which a just person suffers, it would be unjust for God to allow this suffering on behalf of those goods "were it not for the fact that God intended to give him ample reward in return" (325). Rewards and punishments here serve as "a sign and an example of the total compensation" that will come later (208). The use of this world as a sign for

http://plato.stanford.edu/entries/saadya/#Bib. See also Heim Beinart, *Atlas of Medieval Jewish History* (New York: Simon & Schuster, 1992), 29–32.

61. I use the edition of Samuel Rosenblatt, translated from the Arabic and the Hebrew as *Saadia Gaon: The Book of Belief and Opinions*, Yale Judaica Series 1 (New Haven, CT: Yale University Press, 1948). The work is divided into ten treatises and subdivided into chapters. I cite only page numbers in Rosenblatt's edition. The edition by Alexander Altmann in *Three Jewish Philosophers*, ed. H. Lewy, A. Altmann, and I. Heinemann (New York: Atheneum, 1985), is abridged. For an update from 2002, see Saadya Gaon, *The Book of Doctrines and Beliefs*, abridged edition translated from the Arabic with an introduction and notes by Alexander Altmann and a new introduction by Daniel H. Frank (Indianapolis and Cambridge: Hackett, 2002). Some of Saadia's other works appear in *Saadia Gaon: Selected Essays; An Original Anthology*, ed. Steven Katz, Jewish Philosophy, Mysticism & History of Ideas (New York: Arno Press, 1980).

62. Seymour Feldman calls it "the first significant treatise of philosophical theology in Judaism. [It was] influenced by the Muslim school of rationalist theology, the Mu'taziliya *Kalām*." Feldman, "The End of the Universe in Medieval Jewish Philosophy," *AJS Review* 11.1 (Spring 1986): 53–77, at 56. On Saadia's knowledge of Muslim philosophy, see B. Abrahamov, "al-Kāsim ibn Ibrāhīm's Argument from Design," *Oriens* 29 (1986): 259–85, esp. 267; Herbert A. Davidson "John Philoponus as a Source of Medieval Islamic and Jewish Proof of Creation," *Journal of the American Oriental Society* 89 (1969): 357–91, at 362–70. John Philoponus (ca. 490–ca. 570) was a Christian active in Alexandria and concerned to refute Aristotle's position on the world's eternity, debates in which the Mutazilites joined, as did Saadia. Jews, Christians, and Muslims could make common cause in opposing this thesis.

the next is fundamental to Saadia. In this world, he observes, wicked deeds advance the wicked; thus God must have a "second abode" in which good deeds benefit the good (325). The godless prosper and believers suffer now. Later, the reverse will obtain (326).[63]

The first stage in this reversal is Redemption, but Saadia posits two redemptions. Of the first, the exodus from Egypt, he remarks that the enslavement of Israel in Egypt was lighter than in his own day, "nor were the masses of Israel dispersed in the manner in which they are now scattered" (283). The current situation of the Jews becomes for Saadia an argument for the existence of a better world, a second redemption, which must come after death (291–92). "So far as our present enslavement is concerned, however, our Master, exalted and magnified be He, knew that on account of its arduousness and . . . its duration we would not be able to bear up under it without great promises and many good tidings. That is why He rendered the second redemption superior to the first in several respects, one of them being this one—I mean the resurrection of the dead" (283).

Saadia's concern is to explain the apparent prosperity of the wicked and the suffering of the righteous in this world. Without his theory, he fears, the appearance of divine indifference could lead people astray: "It often happens that a generally virtuous person may be afflicted with many failings, on account of which he deserves to be in torment for the greater part of his life. On the other hand, a generally impious individual may have to his credit many good deeds, for the sake of which he deserves to enjoy well-being for the greater part of his earthly existence" (211). Whereas in the Deuteronomic system, divine sanctions promise prosperity and threaten adversity in this world, for Saadia, as for the sages before him, they apply only to the minority of a person's deeds:[64] "It is . . . a [general] rule laid down in this matter by the All-Wise to requite his servants in this world for the minority of their deeds and leave the majority for the next world" (210–11). Later on, Saadia supplements this doctrine by arguing that minor sins, too, are punished not in the next world, but here and now. Even when not repented, the commission of lesser sins is already a sign of restraint against the graver ones. Augustine of Hippo also presents a theory of divine punishment in life, with consequences for the afterlife based partly on the individual's reactions

---

63. Costa (*LADR*, 99) calls this "the most widespread of the rabbis' doctrines of retribution." He attributes its first expression to Akiba. See also Costa, 126 and n. 168.

64. The core of this discussion appears in BT Kiddushin 39b–40b; trans. H. Freedman (1935), 193–201, where the difference between what Saadia calls the majority and minority of one's deeds and the major and minor actions appears as the difference between principal and interest.

to worldly adversity.[65] Thus, when most of a person's "actions are good, retribution for these relatively minor misdeeds is exacted from him in this world, so that he departs from it cleared of all blemish" (351). The strictures of Deuteronomy count, therefore, only for those deeds that are the least numerous or the least significant!

Central to Saadia's view of the afterlife is his reading of Ezekiel 37:12, which prophesies resurrection in these terms: "And I will cause you to come up out of your graves, O My people" (284). Who are God's people? "The entire Jewish nation, the virtuous thereof as well as whoever died repentant" (284).[66] Repentance can be for any sin, including unbelief: "Anyone that has repented from whatever sin it be, even from that of unbelief, is included in this promise" (284). And conversely: "Only if a person dies without having repented is he one of those who are destined to be punished" (430). Considering how central the fate of the Jewish people is in his view of divine justice, it is crucial for Saadia that repentance outweigh ethnicity or adherence to a religious creed as a criterion for being one of "God's people." Any living person can repent and join the righteous. "Even the soiled souls are capable, so long as they are within the body, of being purified and cleansed again" (247). This idea of a soul rendered turbid rather than bright (cf. 206–7) parallels Plato's *Gorgias* (526) and *Republic* (614) or a later, Neoplatonic source.[67] Nonetheless, the notion of the soul's "visual" appearance and the counting of demerits against merits approximates how judgment might take place. This color coding suggests a method different from the weighing and counting mentioned in Tractate Rosh Hashanah.

Saadia's teaching differs from that of the rabbis cited in Tractate Rosh Hashanah 17a, which seriously considered the possibility that one avoids the harshest punishment by practicing forgiveness, whereas Saadia opts solely for repentance. Even given the power of repentance, Saadia names three types of sin that cannot be absolved: deceiving the people and leading them astray, slandering a believer, and retaining stolen goods (224–25). This list is shorter than that in Tractate Rosh Hashanah.[68] Still, divine mercy prefers to

---

65. *City of God* 21.13–15; 41–47. Cf. BT Yebamoth 102b; trans. I. W. Slotki (1938), 705: "As a reward for his affliction He will deliver him from the judgment of Gehenna (*Gehinnom*)." For Augustine, see Bernstein, *Formation*, 316–17.

66. An alternative version of Treatise 7 phrases this idea more clearly: "Every righteous person and penitent of the Jewish nation" qualifies (430). And, again: "There will be resurrection for every penitent. I will say, furthermore, that, in my opinion, those of our nation that die impenitent are few in number" (431).

67. See Bernstein, *Formation*, 56–58.

68. See BT Baba Metzia 58b; p. 349, for a different list of three exceptions.

save rather than to damn, and Saadia blends this theological precept into his discussion of repentance, the Jewish calendar, and the ten days of atonement that mark the New Year.[69]

In addition to those excluded from the world to come, other groups are destined for Gehinnom because of the gravity of their sins. These are the nonbelievers, polytheists, and impenitent perpetrators of grave sins (350). The first two groups are the rebels mentioned in Isaiah 66:24, whose "worm shall not die" (350–51). As for impenitent perpetrators of grave sins, these are liable to the death penalty in this life, and if they are cut off from this world they will also be cut off "from among the righteous in the world to come by reason of their failure to repent" (351). Should one be allowed to live until dying a natural death, but still without repentance, "then his punishment in the hereafter would be all the more severe and his being cut off from among the righteous all the more compulsory by reason of the fact that, although he had been granted a reprieve [i.e., a longer life, more time for atonement], he did not repent" (351).

After judgment, the wicked endure Gehinnom. In contrast to the Garden of Adam (Gan Eden), a "byword for excellence," Gehinnom is an "example of baseness" or defilement, as in Jeremiah 19:6, 11–13. For Saadia, these "physical" places symbolize locations in the otherworld. Similarly, Saadia uses the sun as a sign of postmortem reward and punishment. His treatment recalls the opinion of Resh Lakish, but the Gaon sees the sun as a complement to, not a replacement for, Gehinnom. For Saadia, the sun provides light for the righteous and burning for the wicked (337)—again, we note, a single source for two functions in the afterlife. A long list of texts testifies to the sun's punishing power. Even though there is no historical example of people existing perpetually in fire, "it is precisely because we do not find any analogue thereto that Scripture emphasizes it and declares explicitly concerning the godless: 'For their worm shall not die, neither shall their fire be quenched (Isa. 66:24)" (339–40). For Saadia, as for the Gospel of Mark (9:43–48), this text of Isaiah is one of the Hebrew Bible's chief testimonies for postmortem punishment.

For Saadia, afterlife reward or punishment awaits the resurrection to affect the body and soul together because life itself treats the soul and the body as a unit. He invokes a midrashic parallel between God and an earthly

---

69. Saadia, *Book of Belief*, Tr. 5, reviews the rules about repentance and how they apply to annual observance of the High Holy Days of Atonement. See Tr. 5, chap. 6, for those whose prayer God does not hear, three sins that cannot be absolved, criteria for ranking the quality of repentance according to the quality of forgiveness sought and proximity, in time, to the offense (223–28).

king to support his reasoning on how the pains of Gehinnom preserve the guilty body-soul unit even as they punish it: "Seest thou not that, when kings make up their minds to inflict punishment on a person for a long period of time, they obligate themselves to provide him with food and drink lest he perish before their punishment has been completely carried out upon him, the reason being that their punitive acts are intended by them to fall within the natural capacity for enduring pain? As for the Creator, . . . whose acts are above nature, He can sustain and preserve without food" (340).

Saadia also defends eternal punishment for its impact on human motivation. Since God made it incumbent upon humans to serve him, he had to use "the best of inducements" to encourage compliance. If he had used a lesser inducement and a person did not obey, that person's sins would reflect on God, since if he had used a stronger one, that person might have served him; "Where, however, the stimulant employed is unlimited, there is no longer any excuse left" (344). The same reasoning applies to threats: "That is why God made the torment of the hereafter limitless, employing the strongest possible deterrent" (345). The use of these sanctions is not cruel. Indeed, it is "an act of kindness on the part of God, since his aim in warning [people] against everlasting punishment is to put them in the proper state of mind for serving Him" (345). "[Therefore,] it is necessary for Him to subject them to perpetual torment" (345).

To recapitulate, the evidence of human history and the nature of our oppressive present make it clear that there is no justice in this world. Yet God has instilled in us the ability to conceive of justice and hope for its achievement. Giving us such an expectation without the reality would make God guilty of fraud. Therefore, the resurrection of all humankind to an eternity of reward or punishment is a rational necessity. Moreover, if punishment after death were not unending, God would be guilty of failing to use the strongest possible deterrent, and he, not humans, would be responsible for their wrongdoing. As a consequence, there is a place of eternal punishment for the wicked.

Midrash: Illustrative Folklore and Exempla

Beyond the strictly authoritative texts that prevailed in rabbinic Judaism—the Bible, the Mishnah and its expanded commentaries, the Jerusalem Talmud and the Babylonian Talmud—there arose a penumbra of secondary but still important texts called midrash (pl. midrashim). The legal branch of midrashic literature is called halakah. The branch of concern here is called aggadah, which includes material such as legends, folklore, parables, and exempla, intended to drive home the moral point of arguments.[70] Whereas the Talmud rehearsed the pros and cons of debated points as they developed over time, and Saadia Gaon systematically expounded Jewish theology by emulating the coherence of late antique philosophy, the point of midrashic aggadah was not the logical consistency between tales, but the clarity of comprehension it could give to legal and religious precepts. The sages and Saadia stop periodically to ask, "By what parable may this point be understood?" Frequently, a tale follows that makes an analogy, for example, between a human king's relationship to his subjects and God's relationship to the Jews, if not to the human race as a whole. Midrashim do not form a distinct category, as they are part and parcel of Jewish reasoning in all genres.

The *Tanna debe Eliyyahu*, or *The Lore of the School of Elijah*, gives special attention to this strategy of teaching by exempla. The work has a complicated history.[71] In addition to the title used here, it is also known as the *Seder Eliyyahu (Work of Elijah)*. The *Tanna* relates a legend according to which the prophet Elijah himself dictated the book to a certain R. Anan, a third-century Babylonian teacher and judge. This operation occurred in two installments, an earlier, longer one, the *Eliyyahu Rabbah*, and a later, shorter one, the *Eliyyahu Zuta*. There has been a tendency supported by the present translators to accept this "frame tale" and regard the text as R. Anan's mystical vision of Elijah.[72] Nonetheless, references in the text to debates and personalities of the ninth century move the text to that later time.[73]

Hence, I have chosen five views of the afterlife as illustrated in the *Tanna debe Eliyyahu* to represent midrashic literature, even though the *Tanna* constitutes only a tiny sample of this literature. Taken together, these tales illustrate the same two points that have informed this chapter as a whole. First, Jewish sources present a variety of beliefs about any given subject, and, second, whatever the variety, Gehinnom was a constant presence in Jewish

---

70. This tendency of Jewish literature can be viewed in the broader perspective outlined by the eye-opening survey of Dan Ben-Amos, "Jewish Folklore Studies," *Modern Judaism* 11.1 (February 1991): 17–66.

71. I have used *Tanna debe Eliyyahu: The Lore of the School of Elijah*, trans. William G. (Gershon Zev) Braude and Israel J. Kapstein (Philadelphia: The Jewish Publication Society of America, 5741/1981). Note that the 1997 paperback has different pagination from the original hardbound edition because of a renumbering of the front matter and introduction; I cite the paperback edition. Raphael (*Jewish Views*, 163–84, 206–18) presents an excellent collection of later medieval midrashic literature, but I have preferred the *Tanna debe Eliyyahu* because of its early date.

72. *Tanna debe Eliyyahu*, trans. Braude and Kapstein, xv–xvi.

73. Jacob Elbaum cites studies indicating that the talmudic references (e.g., Sanhedrin 92b; p. 618; Pesachim 94a; p. 504) to a work of the same title are not to this compilation. "Tanna de-Vei Eliyahu," in *Encyclopaedia Judaica*, 19:508.

thought, according to which the community constructed its view of death and the ethical life. I will treat these five exempla one at a time and then sum up, referring to each one by number and my own short title.

1. Gehinnom's Appetite

A female Gehinnom demands to be fed Jews. A tradition dating back to the apocryphal book of 1 Enoch (ca.. 300 BCE, in its earliest layer) ascribes to women a fatal appeal by which women corrupted the heavenly Watcher Angels. Women lured the angels down to earth and created with them the race of giants that had to be exterminated by the flood. This stigmatization of women also affects the characterization of hell. Gehinnom speaks as a female.[74] This anecdote follows a series of declarations praising divine justice for treating everyone equally. In one dramatic scene, the voracious Gehinnom, functioning here much as Satan is sometimes depicted in Christian literature, accuses God of favoritism, of trying to protect the Jews from "her" maw. The different standards by which Jews and Gentiles are judged is also clear in Tractate Rosh Hashanah, but there, Jews are damned for much slighter offenses. (A Gentile must sin sexually to receive as harsh a punishment as a Jew who errs in ceremonial dress.) In this midrash, God tries to protect the Jews with the pretext that Gehinnom is already full. Gehinnom persists, boiling with anger (236).[75] God must cease protecting wicked Jews; only adding Israel's own transgressors will restore calm:

> The Holy One asked [Gehinnom]: "Why are you seething?" And Gehinnom replied: "Master of the universe, now give me those who know Torah, yet transgress it, [and I will be still]." Thereupon the Holy One tried to argue with Gehinnom, saying to her "Perhaps you do not

---

74. "Sheol is always feminine. . . . It is sometimes personified as a voracious monster with a wide-open mouth e.g. Isa. 5:14; Hab. 2:5; Prov. 1:12." Afonso and Kedar, "Netherworld," in *Encyclopaedia Judaica* 15:110–12, at 111a. In addition, see the mouth of Sheol in Ps. 140:7. The earth swallows Dathan and Abiram, dispatching them to Sheol (Num. 16:30–32). For the voracious mouth of the Christian hell, see Bede, *Historia* 5.12: "os Gehennae"; ed. Charles Plummer (Oxford: Clarendon Press, 1896), 1:512. The Aeolian island of Lipari is called a mouth of hell that "belches forth" flames in Gregory I, *Dialogues* 4.31; ed. and trans. A. de Vogüé (Paris: Éditions du Cerf, 1978–80), 4:104–5. For the voracious Hades/Pluto of antiquity, see Emma Maayan Fanar, "Visiting Hades: A Transformation of the Ancient God in the Ninth-Century Byzantine Psalters," *Byzantinische Zeitschrift* 99.1 (2006): 93–108, with 12 figs. on pls. VII–XII; and Margaret English Frazer, "Hades Stabbed by the Cross of Christ," *Metropolitan Museum Journal* 9 (1974): 153–61. The hellmouth appears in Anglo-Saxon art about 1000, for example, in Oxford, Bodleian Library, MS Junius 11, p. 3. It also appears in a difficult to date ivory now at the Victoria and Albert Museum, VAM 253–1867 on the cover of this book. In the Qur'ān the motif occurs in S67:6–8; S25:12.

75. Cf. BT Shabbat 104a; pp. 501–2.

have enough room for them." [Whereupon] Gehinnom swore an oath declaring that she did have room, as is said, "Therefore, by her soul, said Gehinnom (*Sheol*), she had room." (Isa. 5:14–16; 236; my emphasis)[76]

Claiming divine patronage of the Jewish people to the point of partiality, this tale incorporates important elements of folklore and even a grotesque humor. Similar dialogue between Gehinnom and God occurs also in the Qu'rān, where hell seethes restlessly and then moans in satisfaction when fed additional sinners (67:6–8; cf. 25:12). "She" seems to be a living beast who engulfs those abandoned to her innards.

2. Royal Samples

The frequent midrashic parallel drawn between God's justice and that of the earthly king encouraged an ideal view of providential rule.[77] Illustration of that relationship is the explicit purpose of the *Tanna*'s chapter 22. After discussing the legal obligation of Jews to provide charitable support for criminals who have completed their sentences, the text comforts them for their apparent sacrifice, reminding them that those who care for these outcasts "will . . . be well provided for." There follows the traditional, rhetorical question, "By what parable may the matter be understood?" In this case, the *Tanna* relates the parable of the king who set provisions for his

---

76. I have substituted "Gehinnom" for the translators' "Gehenna" in this passage. A related version of this dialogue occurs in a parallel collection of midrashim, the *Pirke of Rabbi Eliezer*, published along with the *Tanna debe Eliyyahu*, 453–86, at 460. An analogue for this debate occurs in BT Shabbat, 104a; p. 502, which says: "The Gehenna (*Gehinnom*) cried out before the Holy One, blessed be He, 'Sovereign of the Universe! I am faint [with hunger]'. [To which He replied,] 'these are the seed of Isaac: Wait! I have whole companies of heathens whom I will give thee." This difficult passage seems to call Satan the Prince of Gehinnom. If that is right, it would be the first occurrence known to me where Satan is considered lord of hell. But there is some ambiguity whether the person disputing with God is Satan the Prince of Gehinnom or a personification of Gehinnom or a fusion of both. Cf. H. A. Kelly, *Satan: A Biography* (Cambridge: Cambridge University Press, 2006), 237–41.

77. Braude and Kapstein themselves (xxxv) call attention to the frequency of these parallels in the *Tanna*. Outside the *Tanna*, there is an outstanding example cited by C. G. Montefiore and H. Loewe, *A Rabbinic Anthology* (New York: Schocken Books, 1974), no. 1632, which relates a king's banquet at which each guest would sit on the seat he brought: "Walk in the light of your fire. . . . In pain shall ye lie down" (Isa. 50:11). Montefiore and Loewe cite Ecclesiastes Rabba 3.9.1 on Eccl. 3:9, fol. 10a. Eccl. 3:9: "What gain has the worker from his toil?" I have seen no discussion in the scholarly literature of this tendency or (what seems to me) its great significance. The setting of these Jewish tales resembles some parables in Christian Scripture. For the king's marriage feast, see Matt. 22:2–14: "The kingdom of heaven is like a king who prepared a wedding banquet for his son." For a more generic host, see Luke 14:16–24. For the parallel between God and the king in midrashic literature, see Ignaz Ziegler, *Die Königsgleichnisse des Midrasch beleuchtet durch die römische Kaiserzeit* (Breslau: Schottlaender, 1903).

people on shelves outside his palace door. Those who accept his munificence speculate on the fare within the palace itself: "From what comes out of the king's palace, they said, one may learn what is within the palace. By the same token, from the chastisements of the righteous in this world, you may learn the measure of punishment of the wicked in Gehinnom. On the other hand, from the prosperity of the wicked in this world you may learn the reward of the righteous in the world to come" (259–60).

These last two sentences contain a stupendous reversal! From the suffering of the righteous in this world we learn the torments of the wicked in the next, and from the prosperity of the wicked in this world, we learn the reward of the righteous in the next. This idea parallels Saadia's notion that the wicked get their rewards now, the righteous in the world to come. For Saadia, the point is a matter of the necessary inversion of this world and the next to reinforce the rational necessity of an afterlife, but in the *Tanna debe Eliyyahu*, the point is the moral of a parable. It nonetheless has a strong doctrinal connection.

3. Prayers for the Damned

A midrashic tradition asserts that prayers on behalf of the dead can liberate them from postmortem punishment. Christians had a similar belief. An important tale in the *Tanna* recounts the fate of a sinner who can still be released from Gehinnom should his son "read and recite Torah." The following story, ascribed in this account to R. Johanan ben Zakkai (T1), a student of Hillel, thus active in the first decades of the Common Era, shows this principle at work:

Once, as I was walking along a road, I came upon a man who was gathering logs. When I spoke to him, he did not reply, but then he came over to me and said, "I am not alive—I am dead." When I asked, "If you are dead, what need have you of logs?" he replied: "Master, listen to me while I tell you my story. When I was alive, my friend and I engaged in sodomy, so when we were sentenced to come here [to Gehenna], a penalty of punishment by burning was handed down against both of us. And now when I gather logs, they are used to burn my friend, and when he gathers logs, they are used to burn me." I asked, "How long is your sentence to last?" He replied: "When I came here, I left my wife pregnant, and I know that the child she bears will be a male. And so I beg you, please watch over him from the time of his birth until he reaches the age of five. Then take him to the house of a teacher to learn to read Scripture. For when he learns to say [the prayer that begins], 'Bless ye the Lord, who is to be blessed,' I shall be brought up from the punishment of Gehenna." (448–49)[78]

The most effective prayer for liberating souls from Gehinnom would eventually become the Kaddish, the Jewish prayer for the dead. At this point in the history of these interventions, the identity of the prayer is not certain. The opening words of this prayer are those of the call to the Law on the Sabbath.[79] The implication is that it is not the recitation of the Kaddish, but a son's attainment of the point of religious education at which he can read the Torah in public that effects release from punishment.[80] By bringing a son to the Law, a father can affect his own fate in the otherworld. In this story, the father's ghost begs R. Johanan ben Zakkai to act in his place. Because the man's punishment involved gathering kindling in this world, he was temporarily released from Gehinnom to perform that task, even though his punishment was still hard labor. His commute between the otherworld and this present world also gave him access to the living rabbi, who was able to intercede. More important, the final result was to be a complete release from Gehinnom. This outcome matches the use of prayer to liberate from hell in contemporary Christian sources.

4. Hell Fights the Flesh

The power of Gehinnom allows a woman to confront a great rabbi, defeat the evil inclination, and avert damnation. Though this exemplum would appear to cast a woman in a heroic light, the contempt it shows for the

---

78. I have modified the translation slightly, to avoid some unfortunate double entendres.

79. This is the opening sentence of "the call to worship at the formal beginning of the daily morning and evening services." Herman Kieval, "Barekhu," in *Encyclopaedia Judaica*, 3:149.

80. See Fox, *Hell in Jewish Literature*, 141. Over time, the prayer that obtained this result for the deceased became the memorial prayer for the dead said at the close of holiday services. See http://learn.jtsa.edu/content/commentary/pesah/5773/laws-passover, accessed February 28, 2014. For later versions of this tale, where the rabbi is Akiba, see Moses Gaster, *The Ma'aseh Book: Book of Jewish Tales and Legends*, 2 vols. in 1 (Philadelphia: Jewish Publication Society of America, 1981), no. 146; and Gaster, *The Exempla of the Rabbis* (New York: KTAV, 1968), no. 134, which cites many parallels, including this one. Gaster also cites M. J. Bin Gorion, ed., *Der Born Judas*, 2nd ed. (Leipzig: Insel Verlag, n. d.), who gives three versions under title, "Der wandernde Tote" at vol. 2, no. 348, pp. 154–59, at p. 154. Ben Gorion cites sources for all three at p. 348 and parallels at p. 368, including the early thirteenth-century Christian compiler of exempla, Caesarius of Heisterbach, *Dialogus miraculorum*, ed. J. Strange (Coloniae: Heberle, 1851), vol. 1, Distinction 1, chaps. 31–34; see now the English translation by H. von E. Scott and C. C. Swinton Bland (1929). Leon Wieseltier reviews the history of this liturgy in *Kaddish* (New York: Knopf, 1998).

female body is so great that it only reinforces the negative stereotype of a voracious Gehinnom personified as female.

A certain rabbi, one of Akiba's disciples, arranged an appointment with a prostitute. Before their rendezvous, she saw him teaching his many students and respected his standing in the community. She feared that causing his downfall would cause her own as well. [No repentance is possible for leading another astray.] She said to herself, "Woe unto this woman to whom all kinds of Gehenna's punishments are bound to affix themselves! . . . Shall this woman respond to his desire and, as a result, when she dies and ceases to exist in this world, inherit Gehenna?" When the rabbi arrived for his appointment, the woman reasoned with him. She compared the one-hour appointment to all of eternity. She frightened him with a crude display of what he thought he desired. At that moment a "Divine Voice" was heard stating that those two were destined for life in the world to come (471).

Here the humble woman upbraids the great man. The association of the vagina with hell puts their encounter into an eschatological perspective. Gehinnom is used as the strongest of deterrents. As Saadia said, if God did not use the strongest possible deterrent and sins were committed, he would be responsible, since a stronger deterrent might have been effective. The woman's action is seen to be godly because she devised the symbolic form of communication and so averted sin.

5. The Bridge of Judgment

Jewish sources represent divine judgment by means of various similes. Rosh Hashanah 17 compares it to weighing and counting, Saadia used color coding, but Jews also shared another image with Zoroastrians, Christians, and Muslims: the bridge. At the time of the final judgment, the nations must carry their idols across a bridge suspended over Gehinnom. Midway, the bridge will narrow to a hair's breadth. They will fall into Gehinnom waiting below (464–66). This is the Jewish version of the Cinvat Bridge, though with the interesting twist of making idolaters carry a symbol of their evil.[81] Seeing the well-being of Israel in the world to come, the idol worshippers will be ashamed: "Forthwith Gehenna will open its [her?] mouth, and all the worshipers of idols will come out. . . . The nations will then ask: Master of the universe, wherein is this people different [from us] that You love them

---

81. This motif anticipates the scene in Christian *Vision of Tundal* (twelfth century), where the visionary must carry across the bridge a cow he has stolen. His burden of sin makes the crossing more difficult.

so much?" The answer: the other nations bowed down to idols. "Put thus to shame, the nations will return to Gehenna, as is said 'The wicked shall return to the nether world (*sheol*), even all the nations that forget God'" (Ps. 9.18; p. 466). (This is the verse that R. Eliezer and R. Joshua debated in the matter of the righteous among non-Jews. The *Tanna* implicitly endorses Eliezer's stricter position.)

The Qur'ān also has scenes that stress the embarrassment of the unbelievers who see, from hell, and learn, too late, that the Prophet was right, and that they have irremediably strayed: "The day that their faces will be turned over in the fire they will say: 'Woe to us! Would that we had obeyed Allah and obeyed the Messenger!'" (33:66ya). In this Jewish source, it is the idols of the Gentiles that topple them off the bridge into Gehinnom!

Latitude, Repentance, Forgiveness

As in our examination of the thought of Gregory I, the motif of the bridge may serve to link the three types of literature that ground this chapter. However reluctant Jewish writers may have been to see Gehinnom as the permanent prison of Jews, it remained exactly that for two categories of people: unrepentant Jews and worshippers of false gods. In the Talmud passages examined above, despite the Sabbath rest, Gehinnom is the endless home of "the thoroughly wicked." Moreover, since repentance is a principal way to escape Gehinnom in the Talmud, and for Saadia the best way, Gehinnom would seem to contain unrepentant Jews forever. Indeed, Saadia regarded repentance as so important he classified anyone of any religion who died repentant as one of "God's people" and hence immune to an eternal Gehinnom: "Anyone that has repented from whatever sin it be, even from that of unbelief, is included in this promise" (284). Saadia's inclusiveness on this point deserves emphasis because he argued that Gehinnom—for the unrepentant—lasts eternally. Saadia's position favors that of R. Joshua, that the righteous of all nations have a portion in the world to come. The *Tanna* opens with the contention that God did indeed create Gehinnom, but he will not use it. It is like the whip that a king puts in the corner with which to threaten his children, but which he would never use on them (9–10). This is the spirit of passages cited by scholars who wish to argue that midrashic texts downplay Gehinnom and stress its positive, purgatorial character.

The five stories from the *Tanna debe Eliyyahu* indicate the opposite. In the first example, "Gehinnom's Appetite," the seething, female Gehinnom demands her share of Jewish offenders, which God grants. True, there is hyperbolic stereotyping of the insatiable receptacle in this tale, but the doctrinal point seems clear.

Hell has its own logic and not even its Creator can deny its conclusions. The second example, "Royal Samples," casts that Creator differently. Portraying him as an earthly king, it emphasizes God's justice. His mercy has come earlier. Punishment follows for those who have misread his signs. In the third example, "Prayers for the Damned," the sinner carrying kindling who pleads for the intercession of R. Johanan ben Zakkai repents after death only after learning how horrible his penalty will be. His repentance earns him his reprieve, but absent penance, absent his approach to rabbinical authority, his cycle of forced labor and fire would continue. Eventually, however, his son's prayers will liberate him, an escape already noted in Christian cases from Perpetua to the drowned boy Wiborada prayed into relief. In the fourth example, "Hell Fights the Flesh," when the prostitute presents her "hell" to the unnamed student of Akiba and he is deterred from sin, *that* Gehinnom is not something he thinks he can avoid by being Jewish or by studying Torah or by being a scholar. He is plenty scared! In contrast to this anecdote, the most universal example from the *Tanna* is the fifth, "The Bridge of Judgment." Here the bridge appears precisely at the world's end, when no more repentance is possible. By this time, one has either turned to God or not. If one still bears an idol—or by extension, any sign of falseness—one will plunge into Gehinnom. There is no Jewish category for such a person other than that from Rosh Hashanah 17: "the thoroughly wicked." Their fate is unending punishment. These are the "sons of Gehinnom."

In conclusion, one cannot speak of a unified "Jewish tradition" that transmits a single doctrine on any given point concerning Gehinnom. The sages debated major issues such as its duration, its residents, and how damnation is assigned. They refined distinctions for how those who were almost evenly divided between good and evil should be judged. Though they found repentance to be the most potent arm against damnation, they registered many differences suggesting other ethical paths, such as forgiveness. This latitude, this respect for debate in its own right, seems to be the distinctive mark of the Talmud, and perhaps of Judaism itself. Still, there clearly is a hell in rabbinic Judaism, from which some will never exit. There are still offenses so heinous that they cannot be pardoned. Heresy is damning, as is leading the people astray, informing on Jews, and denying the Talmud. Latitude has its limits.

As important as the variation in Jewish reflection about the afterlife is a further set of conclusions that show its correspondence in several important regards to other sources already examined and to some, still to be presented in the chapters that remain, expressing different faiths. Several examples are illustrative. Like the Gehenna of Christianity and the Jahannam of Islam, Gehinnom is a place of eternal punishment for the thoroughly wicked. On this point, the Schools of Hillel and Shammai agreed. They differed, however, on the fate of the intermediate. Hillel argued that because God "inclines towards grace," the intermediate pass directly to everlasting life. It was the School of Shammai that insisted on a temporary punishment for the intermediate in Gehinnom. Within that strand of the tradition, therefore, Gehinnom is the site of both temporary purification for the intermediate, similar to the purgatorial fire in Christian documents, and eternal punishment for the thoroughly wicked. Gehinnom's double function in rabbinic Judaism almost certainly precedes its appearance in Christian sources. To be sure, both functions, eternal punishment and purification over time, appear separately in the New Testament, but it was Caesarius of Arles (d. 542) who first saw a single fire punishing mere sinners for a time and the wicked damned forever. Julian of Toledo (d. 690) was of the same opinion. The *Vision of Fursey* (ca. 656–57) and the *Vision of the Monk of Wenlock* (mid-eighth century) also present a single fire that can torture some forever and purify others after a time.

Whatever the duration of postmortem punishment, in Jewish sources there is a pronounced conviction that the Sabbath brings weekly relief to many of those who endure it (if they observed the Sabbath themselves). That idea is much less confidently asserted in Christian writings, because the *Apocalypse of Paul* and the *Apocalypse of Mary* do not have the standing within Christianity that the Talmud has in Judaism. The idea of prayers for the dead and the intercession of the blessed for those on the way to God's presence or in the right group is a steady presence in rabbinic thought, but it was not as established in Jewish institutions as in Christian. The ability of the log carrier's son to liberate his father from hell by initiating Torah reading when he came of age developed into the consistent recitation of the Kaddish in memory of the deceased, a staple of Jewish worship. One persistent theme in rabbinic thought concerns the difference between Jews and non-Jews. There are axiomatic statements such as "All Israel have a portion in the world to come" and "The righteous of all nations have a portion in the world to come." Still, the distinction between Jews and Gentiles and the status of the Noachide laws made this a lively subject of debate in the rabbinic period and beyond. Whatever the intellectual rivalry and its consequences in social conflict, the common features of Jewish, Islamic, and Christian eschatology are many. Whatever the power of hell in the three Abrahamic religions and whatever means were found to alleviate the fear it inspired, the three communities followed parallel paths deriving from a common source in the Hebrew Bible, the cosmopolitan Neoplatonic tradition of Alexandria, and the widespread folklore and mythology of the Mediterranean basin, consistently interacting from the time of Alexander the Great to the fading of Roman imperial power and, in fact, never fully ending.

CHAPTER 8

Byzantine Universalism

The Path Not Taken

> When evil shall have been some day annihilated in the long revolutions of the ages, nothing shall be left outside the world of goodness. . . . Even from those evil spirits shall rise in harmony the confession of Christ's Lordship.
>
> —"Macrina," in Gregory of Nyssa, *On the Soul and Resurrection*

> The fire you threaten me with burns merely for a time and is soon extinguished. It is clear you are ignorant of the fire of everlasting punishment and of the judgement that is to come, which awaits the impious.
>
> —*Martyrdom of Polycarp* 11

In the Greek-speaking Eastern portions of the Roman Empire, Christians of the first centuries CE inherited an approach to eschatology with overtones of classical literature, where Hades was the neutral land of all the dead. The Septuagint, a translation of the Hebrew Bible into Greek, rendered Sheol, the grave or the underworld, as Hades. The Greek New Testament also adopted the term Hades for the netherworld. The spirits in Sheol/Hades suffer after death as lifeless shades but are not punished. The durability of Hades projected the tradition of neutral death into Greek Christianity. Even where death is porous, the supposedly far removed land of the dead is morally neutral. The mythical or heroic figures such as Dionysus, Herakles, and Odysseus who returned from the underworld in ancient Greek literature blended with passages in the Hebrew Bible such as that relating King Saul's evocation of his predecessor in 1 Samuel 28 or Psalms 6:5, and 88:10–11 and Isaiah 38:17–19, which reflected neutral views of death. The tenacity of the ancient, neutral netherworld also affected the way Greek-speaking Christians viewed moral death.

Universalism and Its Theorists

The continuity of the classical Greek Hades shaped a linguistic environment in the Greek community that favored universalism far more than in the Latin one. Partly for that reason, Hades was infernalized less completely, and several centuries later, in Greek lands than in Latin. Universalism is the belief that all are saved. If all are saved, there is no hell. This idea contrasts with the "dual issue" eschatology, in which, after divine judgment, there are two possibilities, heaven and hell.[1] Universalism is a type of moral death because it posits judgment and possibly punishment for some after death, but that punishment is not eternal. Rather, it is therapeutic, healing, medicinal, purgatorial—it leads to salvation. The universalist belief that all are saved includes wicked angels as well as wicked humans.[2] Like neutral death, universalism teaches that all the dead arrive in one place. Unlike neutral death, that place is not the dark underworld, but paradise.

In general, the reasoning behind universalism runs like this.[3] By definition, the Savior saves. He is omnipotent, his actions are effective: his discipline corrects, his preaching converts. He is Lord of all including Sheol/Hades. Psalm 139 celebrates the omnipresence of God and verse 8 states, "If I make my bed in Sheol, thou are there!" One of the earliest texts of the New Testament, Paul's discussion of resurrection (1 Cor. 15:24–28), combines an argument from divine omnipotence with an argument from the precedent of Jesus' own resurrection: he is the first fruit, humans are the harvest, with the result that "God may be everything to everyone" or, as it is sometimes translated, so that "God may be all in all." This vision of a mystical unity returning creation to its Creator assumes that the power to create includes the power to re-create, resurrect, restore. This idea recurs slightly modified in John 17, where Jesus prays for a human unity parallel to the unity between him and his Father, "that they may be one even as we are one, I in them and thou in me" (John 17:22–23), or, excepting only the devil: "None of them is lost but the son of perdition, that the scripture might be fulfilled" (John 17:12). Again: "I, when

---

1. "Dual issue" is superior to "double issue" or "symmetrical" eschatology because it avoids the implication that the number of saved and damned may be equal. See Eugene TeSelle and Daniel Patte, "Universalism," *Cambridge Dictionary of Christianity*, 1278. For "symmetrical," see Alan E. Bernstein, *The Formation of Hell: Death and Retribution in the Ancient and Early Christian Worlds* (Ithaca, NY: Cornell University Press, 1993), 260–62.

2. See the bibliography in C. A. Patrides, "'The Salvation of Satan," *Journal of the History of Ideas* 28.4 (1967): 467–478, at 467 n. 1; for a more comprehensive survey, see Wolf-Friedrich Schäufele, "Die Höllen der Alexandriner: Negative Jenseitsvorstellungen im frühchristlichen Ägypten," *Zeitschrift für Kirchengeschichte* 117.2–3 (2006): 197–210.

3. Bernstein, *Formation*, 205–27 and 305–13.

I am lifted up from the earth, will draw all men to myself" (John 12:32). This notion also finds expression in the declaration that God "desires all men to be saved and to come to the knowledge of the truth" (1 Tim. 2:4). Biblical testimony to this aspiration for universal salvation conflicts with contervailing endorsements of eternal damnation. Still, the fact that proof texts favoring universal salvation have been advanced from Paul, whose letters date from the fifties of the first century to John, whose Gospel probably dates from the nineties, shows how rich these implications were and in fact still are.

Clement of Alexandria and Salvation in Hades

Clement of Alexandria (d. ca. 215) voices the central premise of universalism when he states, "The Saviour also exerts His might because it is His work to save." Clement combines Christian ideas of salvation through Christ with statements from the Hebrew Bible combining divine power and loving kindness—for example, "I have no pleasure in the death of the wicked, but that the wicked turn from his way and live" (Ezek. 33:11);[4] and, like Paul in Acts 2:31, Clement quotes Psalm 16:9–11: "Thou dost not give me up to Sheol, or let thy godly one see the Pit." Christ saves by nature, everywhere, and at all times. "It is not here alone [among the living] that the active power of God is beforehand, but it is everywhere and is always at work." "What then? Did not the same dispensation obtain in Hades?" Thus, Christ can also save the dead. Narratives of the Descent show how this salvific principle also applies in the land of the dead:

> If, then, the Lord descended to Hades for no other end but to preach the Gospel, as He did descend; it was either to preach the Gospel to all or to the Hebrews only. If, accordingly, to all, then all who believe shall be saved, although they may be of the Gentiles, on making their profession there; since God's punishments are saving and disciplinary, leading to conversion, and choosing rather the repentance [than] the death of a sinner; and especially since souls, although darkened by passions, when released from their bodies, are able to perceive more clearly, because of their being no longer obstructed by the paltry flesh.[5]

---

4. Cf. similar statements: "Have I any pleasure in the death of the wicked, says the Lord God, and not rather that he should turn from his way and live?" (Ezek. 18:23); "For I have no pleasure in the death of any one, says the Lord God; so turn, and live" (Ezek. 18: 32); "If my people who are called by my name humble themselves, and pray and seek my face, and turn from their wicked ways, then I will hear from heaven, and will forgive their sin and heal their land" (2 Chron. 7:14).

5. *Strom.* 6. 6; *ANF* 2:490–91; Clément d'Alexandrie, *Les stromates: Stromate VI*, ed. and trans. Patrick Descourtieux, SC 446 (1999), p. 155.

Adversity is therefore divine chastisement; it improves those who experience it. This is certainly true on earth, but even among the dead; in Hades during the interim, where souls are unburdened of the flesh, they are more likely to receive the spiritual truth than they were in life. Thus, they may be converted and saved after death.[6] Because universalism responds to anxieties concerning the dead, and eventually concerning oneself, Orthodox Christianity considers the interim period that follows an individual's death less as the time before the Last Judgment than as a condition of spiritual openness. It interprets Resurrection less as the summons to judgment than as a movement toward eternal life. Thus Greek Orthodox thinkers refer to the interim as the "Middle State of Souls."[7]

Origen and the Personal Fire

Clement's student Origen of Alexandria (ca. 185–ca. 254) applies these principles not only to the dead in Hades during the interim, but also to the fate of those judged. In *On First Principles*, a major exposition of Christian thought along the lines of Neoplatonic philosophy, Origen argued that postmortem chastisement would lead to the amendment of souls and their eventual removal from punishment; indeed, it would effect their restoration to pristine unity with God. Like his teacher, Clement, Origen made 1 Corinthians 15:24–28 central to his thinking: "that blessedness . . . to which even God's enemies are said to be subjected, in which end God is said to be 'all things' and 'in all things'." This perfect fusion of all wills with the divine is not subjection to an impersonal, external fire like that in Matthew 25:41 (the eternal fire prepared for Satan and his angels). Rather, as Origen specifically states, "One is not sunk into some pre-existing fire or one that has been kindled before by another." Individual, inner purification precedes one's ultimate restoration to primal communion. Citing Isaiah 50:11, "Walk by the light of your fire and by the brands which you have kindled," Origen states, "The fire by which each person is punished is proper to that person."

In Origen's theory, this process of punishment and re-formation, suffering and amendment, can require many lifetimes, with progress measured in states of greater or lesser devotion to God. At the end, the soul necessarily

---

6. Martin F. Connell correctly explains the implications of conversion in the land of the dead and whether one should call the place Christ visited "the underworld" (the *inferi*) or "hell" (*infernus*); see Connell, "*Descensus Christi ad Inferos*: Christ's Descent to the Dead," *Theological Studies* 62 (2001): 262–82, at 266–67.

7. See Nicholas Constas, "'To Sleep, Perchance to Dream': The Middle State of Souls in Patristic and Byzantine Literature," *Dumbarton Oaks Papers* 55 (2001): 91–124.

recovers its original likeness to God, at which point it achieves *apokatastasis*, or restoration. (No other result would be possible from divine chastisement.) In the end, all rational beings attain complete conformity to the maker; God is all in all, and the end resembles the beginning. Origen himself expressed doubts about extending his theory this way in all its implications.[8] Admitting uncertainty about the full implications of his effort to blend Scripture with philosophy, he warned, "We speak on these subjects with great fear and caution, discussing and investigating rather than laying down fixed and certain conclusions."[9] That "Origenism" was considered, fairly or unfairly, as radical as stated here is clear from the controversies that surrounded it and the condemnations it attracted. The emperor Justinian condemned Origen's theories in 543 and 553.[10]

Gregory of Nyssa and Macrina: Divine Attraction Annihilates Evil

Over a century intervenes between Origen and the next major advocate of universal salvation, Gregory of Nyssa. Born around 330, he was made bishop of Nyssa, in the province of Cappadocia (in present-day Turkey), in 371. Gregory's older brother was Basil the Great, and Gregory Nazianzen was a companion of both. These three men are called "the Cappadocian Fathers," famous for their defense of the Trinitarian definition of the Council of Nicaea of 325, against Arianism. Omitted from the traditional designation is Macrina, Basil and Gregory of Nyssa's older sister. In his dialogue "On the Soul and Resurrection," Gregory celebrates his sister as his interlocutor,

---

8. For further detail on Origen's own doubts, see Jeffrey A. Trumbower, *Rescue for the Dead: The Posthumous Salvation of Non-Christians in Early Christianity* (Oxford: Oxford University Press, 2001), 115–16. It is not enough to say that Origen expressed doubts. Henri Crouzel overcompensates when he says: "It would . . . be false to say that Origen teaches the non-eternity of the pains of hell." Crouzel, "L'Hadès et la Géhenne selon Origène," *Gregorianum* 59 (1978): 291–331, at 329. There can be no doubt that Origen articulated a theory of final restoration in *On First Principles* and that this is the germ of what history would call Origenism. Even if he expressed doubts and contradicted himself elsewhere, his theory of *apokatastasis* is not just a smear attached to his name by slanderous opponents.

9. Origen, *On First Principles* 1.6.1, trans. G. W. Butterworth (New York: Harper and Row, 1966), 52.

10. D-S nos. 403–11 (in 543), pp. 140–42, and no. 433 (in 553), p. 149. The importance of these condemnations cannot be minimized by observing that the edict of 543 does not mentioned Origen by name and that his mention in canon 11 of Constantinople II may be an interpolation. More plausible is the view that Origen's Neoplatonic and allegorizing approach to Scripture, intellect, and the afterlife were central to the Christological and related issues debated there. See John Meyendorff, "Justinian, the Empire, and the Church," *Dumbarton Oaks Papers* 22 (1968): 43–60, at 56; Meyendorff, *Byzantine Theology* (New York: Fordham University Press, 1974), 25–27; and Frederick W. Norris, "Greek Christianities," in *The Cambridge History of Christianity* (Cambridge: Cambridge University Press, 2007), 2:117, at 102–6.

calling her "the teacher" and casting himself as the questioner.[11] In this work, the longer explanations are attributed to her.

This dialogue is remarkable for the comprehensive way in which it treats a series of questions concerning the fate of the soul after death. As in Origen, much depends on the great importance these universalist thinkers give to the phrase "all in all" (*ta panta en pasin*, 1 Cor. 15:28). This passage of Scripture suggests a Christian context for the central premise in Neoplatonic philosophy that the end of the world will resemble its beginning. Substituting God for the Neoplatonic "One" or "Cause," this reasoning suggests that all of history, after many cycles of gradual progress and despite individual reverses, will recapitulate itself. All emanations from the One (God) will finally return to an original purity (or union with him), thus completing a perfect recycling of all being from perfect beginning to perfect end. The Bible's statement that God will eventually become "all in all" suggests a similar recapitulation, beckoning both mystically and logically as both a premise and a conclusion.

Macrina put it approximately like this. What God made he loves and draws to himself. The process of drawing begins at death when the body is wracked with pain as the soul begins to separate itself from its physical inclinations. It is as if pain results from the soul being freed from the hooks that attached it to the body (if one was hooked on love of the flesh): "When the change is made into the impalpable Unseen, not even then will it be possible for the lovers of the flesh to avoid dragging away with them under any circumstances some fleshly foulness; and thereby their torment will be intensified, their soul having been materialized by such surroundings."[12] Increasingly freed from the flesh, wills correspondingly cleave to God, and evil disappears. As this process continues in soul after soul, a unity of wills develops, and God becomes "all in all." The second death is therefore not eternal punishment, but the pain of postmortem purification: "Not in hatred or revenge for a wicked life, to my thinking [says Macrina], does God bring upon sinners those painful dispensations; He is only claiming and drawing to Himself whatever, to please Him, came into existence."[13]

The experience of the rich man in the Hades of Luke 16 shows how this happens. Macrina interprets this drama figuratively: "This, in my opinion, is the 'gulf'; which is not made by the parting of the earth, but by those

---

11. Translated by William Moore and Henry Austin Wilson in *NPNF-2*, 5:798–872.The Greek, with facing Latin translation, in PG 46:12–161. For *NPNF* online, where the pagination differs, see http://www.ccel.org/ccel/schaff/npnf205.x.iii.ii.html, pp. 429–67.

12. Greg. Nyss. *De Anima*, Moore and Wilson, 835, online 447; PG 46:87–88B.

13. Ibid., 840, online 450; PG 46:97–98D.

decisions in this life which result in a separation into opposite characters. The man who has once chosen pleasure in this life, and has not cured his inconsiderateness by repentance, places the land of the good beyond his own reach; for he has dug against himself the yawning impassable abyss of a necessity that nothing can break through."[14]

Thus, the abyss between the rich man and Lazarus is not a physical one, but the moral one between those who choose to have their pleasures in the present, fleeting world, and those who choose to have their good in the future, eternal kingdom. The fire that torments the rich man comes not from searing flame but from his unquenchable craving and envy. "Meanwhile the denial of [the] blessings which [Abraham and Lazarus] witness becomes in the [wicked] a flame, which burns the soul and causes the craving for the refreshment of one drop out of that ocean of blessings wherein the saints are affluent; which nevertheless *they*—the wicked—do not get."[15] In this psychological Hades, the wicked suffer from seeing the comfort of the saints, which comes from an absence of longing, for in their bliss, the saved realize their long-cultivated desire for God's favor. Both the rich man's pain in the fire of Hades and the satisfaction of Lazarus in the Bosom of Abraham are psychological, not physical, conditions! Moreover, even the rich man's suffering will end, because God's power eventually annihilates evil: "When evil shall have been some day annihilated in the long revolutions of the ages, nothing shall be left outside the world of goodness, but . . . even from those evil spirits shall rise in harmony the confession of Christ's Lordship (*kyriótētos*)."[16]

The Open Hades

Some forms of reflection on the middle state, the soul's experience in the interim, took the shape of interpreting Christ's action during his Descent in a certain way. According to this interpretation, already visible in Clement of Alexandria, during his descent into Hades, Christ preached to the dead and won the conversion of many. Advocates of this interpretation refer principally to two biblical passages: 1 Peter 3:19, Christ "preached to the spirits in prison," and 1 Peter 4:6, "The Gospel was preached even to the dead." Since "in prison" functions in parallel with "the dead," it is clear that the prison in question is Hades, the old term designating the land of the dead in neutral death.

---

14. Ibid., 833, online 446; PG 46:83–84B.
15. Ibid., 835, online 446–47; PG 46:83–84D.
16. Ibid., 828, online 443; PG 46:71–72B.

It is probable that the founder of this tradition was Origen. Henri Crouzel attributes to him the "positive" contribution of opening up Hades. From this open Hades, paradise would still be accessible not only to martyrs, as Tertullian insisted, but to the righteous of the New Testament between death and resurrection.[17] In this theory, souls in the underworld prior to their resurrection use their time free of the flesh to benefit from Christ's preaching there. Under these conditions, they come to a correct view of the cosmos, repentance, and early salvation. This view of Hades became all the more important as a refuge for those sympathetic to universalism after Justinian's condemnations of Origenism in 543 and 553. Jeffrey Trumbower argues that "universal salvation was placed outside the bounds of orthodox Catholic teaching. For some Eastern Orthodox theologians, these rulings have not taken away the possibility of posthumous salvation for at least some sinners and unbaptized persons. By the sixth century in the Latin West, however, Augustine's views denying all forms of posthumous salvation, including universalism, had taken hold."[18] For Trumbower, both universalism and this related idea of an open Hades were characteristic of Orthodox Christianity. In the East, there was no single doctrinal authority like a pope, and no dominant theologian on the scale of an Augustine.[19] Consequently, in Eastern theology, there was more latitude for individual theologians than in the Latin church. Trumbower exaggerates the decisiveness in the West of Augustine's pronouncements on the finality of death as the time for an individual judgment, as the previous examination of exceptions to hell and the many escapes from its clutches has shown. Still, the contrast in tenor between the two linguistic and cultural regions remains valid. For Trumbower, then, the idea of a Hades open for repentance and conversion until the Resurrection remained from a universalist tradition that had, since the days of Augustine, met with increasing resistance culminating in Justinian's condemnations.[20] The tradition of an open Hades, one allowing liberating prayer for the dead, can be seen full force in *Concerning Those Who Have Fallen Asleep in the Faith*, an anonymous treatise ascribed to John of Damascus (ca. 655–ca. 750), but probably written only in the mid-ninth century. (For convenience, I refer to this treatise as *Sleep in the Faith*.) I postpone discussion of a genuine work of John of Damascus until later, because the logic of beginning with universalism requires treating the later author first.

---

17. Crouzel, "L'Hades," 329, with examples at 322–24.
18. Trumbower, *Rescue*, 124.
19. Ibid., 150.
20. See Augustine's Letter 146, to Evodius, CSEL 44 (1904): 521–41; Bernstein, *Formation*, 321.

Sleep in the Faith: Pseudo-John of Damascus

For the anonymous author known as pseudo-John of Damascus, Christ's Descent opened Hades permanently. This is the conquest of death. The newly opened territory is the Sheol/Hades of the Septuagint, not the *infernus*-hell of the Latin sources. It is not even the isolated, punitive Hades of Luke 16:23–24. Only the devil, says pseudo-John of Damascus, emphasizes fear of God and his justice and denies progress after death. Christ's power extends beyond the moment of his Descent; it will indeed prevail forever, until the final reckoning (*eis aei nikhēsei mekhri tēs eskhatēs antapodoseōs*).[21] The anonymous author cites other familiar examples of how prayer affects the otherworld: the Maccabees, Thecla's prayer for Falconilla, Gregory I's prayer for Trajan, and, in a story to be discussed below, the skull that reported to Macarius.

Someone could object, pseudo-John of Damascus observes, betraying an environment critical of universalist aspirations as the context for his composition, that anyone who argues that postmortem repentance or conversion can lead to salvation is essentially arguing for the salvation of everyone. No matter how wickedly a person has lived, according to this criticism, they could enjoy a lifetime of self-indulgence and postpone repentance to the grave, meanwhile ridiculing all who live righteously. But no: God is not swayed by prayers on behalf of such people, whether offered by a spouse, children, siblings, relatives, or friends.[22] As John Chrysostom says, God assures that charity after death depends on charity before.[23] Since prayer is an act of charity, only those who lived charitably can benefit from prayers after they have died, that is, while in Hades. The converse is also true. Just as the charitable recognize and help one another, so the wicked are not recognized and do not help one another, as, in the past, they never did.[24] Thus, the wicked end up in the company of others like themselves. In their moment of supreme need they receive no help and remain isolated. This motif also occurs in Islamic sources.[25] It dramatizes the idea of oblivion. Still, *Sleep in the Faith* insists that such prayer is effective.

---

21. §14; PG 95:262B.
22. §21; PG 95:267B–C.
23. §22; PG 95:267D.
24. §31; PG 95:277A.
25. See Sura 69:35, "So no friend hath he here this day"; 70:10–11, "And no friend will ask after a friend, though they will be put in sight of each other"; and 70:15–17, "The Blazing Fire—Inviting (all) such as turn their backs and turn way their faces (From the Right)." Yusuf Ali translation; see below, chapter 9, note 1. For more detail, see Al-Ghazali, *The Remembrance of Death and the Afterlife*, trans. T. J. Winter (London: Islamic Texts Society, 1989), 198. At the moment of judgment, the resurrected wicked find no beneficiaries to testify on their behalf.

The treatise's extension of hope for prayerful intervention into the postmortem world may help identify its pseudonymous author. It is possible that
the piece was composed in connection with important historical events. This
is not the place for an account of the dramatic and formative controversy over
icons that raged in the Orthodox and Western churches for approximately a
century. These developments may nonetheless have given additional ammu-
nition to the belief in rescue from postmortem punishment. The iconoclast
emperor Theophilus (829–42) supported a politically significant protest
movement that denounced images of Christ, Mary, and the saints as remnants of pagan idolatry and prohibited the use of icons in worship. After
his death, his wife, Theodora, governed as empress-regent until 856. This
same Theodora instituted a new feast, the Triumph of Orthodoxy, that annually celebrated the return of images, implicitly condemning her iconoclast
husband anew. Despite her action against his beliefs, Theodora is said to
have prayed Theophilus out of hell—another escape like those identified in
chapter 4, above. In the midst of these events was Michael Synkellos, who
might plausibly be suggested as the author of *Sleep in the Faith*, since its main
themes—particularly the effectiveness of prayers for the dead—coincide
with the situation of the empress-regent in her relationship with her husband and predecessor.[26]

Sleep in the Faith synthesizes important strands from the universalist tradition even while denying the connection. The widespread liturgy of prayers
for the dead and the sense of community of a church united in commem-
orating those who died in harmony with its faith promoted hope for an
active underworld. It was in Hades that, according to Scripture, Christ had
appeared, preached, and won converts. Thus, the ferment of resurrection
and hope for it in the future extended the "jurisdiction," the field of play,
of the prayerful, charitable community into a new zone, Hades, and into a
new time, the interim period until the General Resurrection.[27] This extension would seem to come at the cost of hell.

---

26. J. M. Hoeck, "Stand und Aufgaben der Damaskenos-Forschung," *Orientalia Christiana Periodica* 17.1–2 (1951): 5–60, at 39 n. 3 (continues on 40). See also Judith Herrin, *The Formation of Christendom* (Princeton, NJ: Princeton University Press, 1989), 468–69, 473–75; Martin Jugie, "La doctrine
des fins dernières dans l'église gréco-russe," *Échos d'Orient* 17 (1914): 7–9; Trumbower, *Rescue*, 150.
For more detail on these circumstances, see S. Vaihlé, "Michel le Sincelle," *Revue de l'Orient Chrétien*
6 (1901): 313–32 and 610–42, at 628–32 and 632 n. 1. According to a story that circulated concerning
these events under the title "On the Absolution of the Emperor Theophilos," both Theodora and
Methodius, the patriarch of Constantinople she had just named, experienced visions assuring them
of the absolution of the late ruler, despite his iconclasm.

27. The real John of Damacus rejects the idea of postmortem conversion, repentance, or
improvement. Leo Allatius, "De S. Damasceni Prolegomena," in PG 94:118–92, at 146 n. 33.

Theophylact of Ochrid and Divine Restraint

At the turn of the twelfth century, the tradition of effective prayers for exceptional sinners received an additional impetus from a one-line remark by an important theologian, Theophylact of Ochrid or of Bulgaria. Theophylact lived from ca. 1050 or 1060 until after 1125. He authored sermons on the Gospels that became authoritative commentaries in their own right. Like the author of *Sleep in the Faith*, Theophylact distanced himself from universalism. In commenting on the parable of the rich man and Lazarus he said the chasm in Hades reflects the moral difference between them in life. "Mark here a conclusion to be drawn against the Origenists," he notes, "who say that there will be a time when there is an end to hell, that the sinners will be united with the righteous and with God, and thus that God will become all in all."[28] However impossible it is to cross the chasm in the divided, punitive Hades of Luke 16, Theophylact seems to retain some of the classical Greek Hades by distinguishing two possibilities. He turns to Luke 12:5: "But I warn you whom to fear: fear him who, after he has killed, has power to cast into Gehenna." Thus, Theophylact returns to the more open Hades:

> Note that Jesus Christ did not say "Fear him who, after he has killed, casts into Gehenna" but instead "has the power to cast into Gehenna." For sinners, after death, are not necessarily thrown into Gehenna, but that depends on God, who is equally able to pardon them. I say this because of the offerings and alms that are made for the dead and that are greatly profitable even to those who die with great sins (*hamartiais bareiais*). . . . Let us not cease, therefore, to appease by alms and prayers the one who has the power to cast into Gehenna, but who does not always make use of this power and who is able to pardon.[29]

Although repudiating universalism Theophylact of Ochrid protects those for whom the pious pray, even if they are guilty of "great sins." Taken together, the Greek sympathy for universalism and the desire to retain an open, fermenting, active Hades where repentance and conversion could occur dramatize the Greek fidelity to the Hades of antiquity and classical literature. This is why believers in the Greek-speaking territories resisted both infernalization and purgatory. Given the durability of Hades, there was no need to open a separate space for purification. For them that space already

---

28. http://www.chrysostompress.org/gospel-commentary-pentecost22, accessed May 15, 2008.

29. Trumbower, *Rescue*, 150, citing Jugie, "Doctrine," 7; and PG 123:880. See also Crouzel, "L'Hadès et la Géhenne," 311. Note that this (unused) power would resemble the idea of Gehinnom as the unused whip in the Jewish midrash mentioned in chapter 7, p. 279.

existed and follows logically from the Descent narratives, 1 Peter 3:19 and 4:6. This determination manifested itself when negotiations, focused primarily on other (Trinitarian) issues, broke down, thus occasioning the schism between the churches in 1054, against initiatives by Pope Innocent IV in 1254, and as late as 1439, at the Council of Ferrara-Florence, when Latin efforts to impose uniformity on the Orthodox led again to extended negotiations and debate. Conversely, the Greek embrace of the active Hades and clarity among Greek speakers about its difference from Gehenna and Tartarus might have influenced reflection during late antiquity and the early Middle Ages and delayed assigning the purgatorial fires the name *purgatory* even in the West. It is also the case that rabbinic consensus included the possibility that those who practice forgiveness in life might receive it from God even as they stand in Gehinnom.

Against Universalism

In contrast to universalism and the retention of an open Hades, a contradictory trend found utility and comfort in a hell that begins immediately at death and lasts forever. "Comfort" may seem a strange word to use in connection with hell, but the sources that demonstrate how this worked come from a very specific context in the history of Christianity—the texts, called "passions," that narrate the deaths of the martyrs at the hands of Roman persecutors. For them, or the narrators, the contrast between the willing victim, eager to seize the palm of martyrdom and the retaliation God would inflict on the torturers, and their superiors was, indeed, a comfort. Here, the notion of "sublimated vengeance" as a function of hell belief comes back into play. (Not since the days of the Hebrew prophets had the contrast between victims and their oppressors, about differing fates in the otherworld, been so prominent in discourse about hell.[30]) A particularly dramatic instance of the reality of this comfort in the form of imagined vengeance comes in the presentation of "fire" in the passion literature.

When their persecutors threatened to kill them with the worst of physical pains, the martyrs retorted that these death-dealing but momentary torments gave access to an endless paradise and hardly compared to the eternal wracking the Roman officials would endure under the jurisdiction of a king of unimaginable majesty. The physical reality of hell is therefore a threat to the persecutors and a consolation to the martyrs. The threat of hell also deterred the martyrs from compromising to save their lives. If they should

---

30. Bernstein, *Formation*, 152–53, 201–2.

sacrifice to false gods or the genius of the emperor, hell would be their end. Given the power of hell to these men and women on the verge of torture and death, it is churlish to ask whether their idea was literal or allegorical, whether they referred to physical or psychological pain. With fires burning, nails and hooks glistening in the sun, wild animals pawing the arena floor, the prospect of hell as an alternative or a point of reference was real in the extreme, however it was understood.[31]

Hell as a Comfort to Martyrs

This pairing of heaven and hell in the martyrs' retorts magnifies the force of dual issue eschatology. One account that illustrates this double-sided aspect of hell is the *Martyrdom of Polycarp*. When threatened by the Roman governor, Polycarp replied, "The fire you threaten me with burns merely for a time and is soon extinguished. It is clear you are ignorant of the fire of everlasting punishment and of the judgement that is to come, which awaits the impious."[32] The "fire of everlasting punishment" combines Matthew 25:41 and 46 with Mark 9:46 and Isaiah 66:24. The idea here is that, in contrast to the context in John Chrysostom's letter to Theodore (to be examined below), where the fire is a threat to a backsliding student, in the mouth of Polycarp, addressed to the governor, it is a comfort to the persevering martyr.

In the *Martyrdom of Conon*, the martyr uses Mark's description of Gehenna to taunt his executioner with the threat of Tartarus, a horrible fate compared to the innocuous fires at the stake. "Beware lest the Judge sentence you to a [Tartarus] that is unsurpassed, a fire unquenchable for ever, where the worm does not die and the fire is not quenched. For the tortures with which you threaten me cannot harm me; I have a God who gives me strength."[33]

Similarly, when the proconsul commands Carpus to venerate the gods in accordance with imperial orders, Carpus explains, "True worshippers . . . take on the image of God's glory and become immortal with him, sharing in eternal life through the Word. So too those who worship *these* gods take on the image of the demons' folly and perish along with them

---

31. Carole Straw, "Settling Scores: Eschatology in the Church of the Martyrs," in *The Last Things: Death and the Apocalypse in the Middle Ages*, ed. Caroline Walker Bynum and Paul Freedman (Philadelphia: University of Pennsylvania Press, 2000), 21–40.

32. *Martyrdom of Polycarp* §11; Musurillo, pp. 10–11. The translation is Musurillo's.

33. *Martyrdom of Conon* §5; Musurillo, pp. 190–91. Musurillo erroneously gives "Hades" as a translation for "Tartarus" (7). *Blepe de mē de ho kritēs tartarōi paradōsēi anupethetōi, puri asbestōi eis aiōnas, hopou ho skōleks ou teleutai kai to pur ou sbennutai*. In fact, the Greek nearly quotes Mark 9:48, where this phrase defines Gehenna. Musurillo, pp. 190–91. The translation is Musurillo's except for "Tartarus/Hades."

in Gehenna."[34] If the Christian yields and sacrifices, that surrender damns. If the Christian perseveres, death is the pathway to heaven, but the unjust execution of the innocent means hell for the persecutor. What is transitory and life-giving to the martyr is eternal and deadly for the executioner.

Chrysostom's Letter to Theodore: Hell Fights the Flesh

Hell comforted the martyrs, as they died thinking it the certain fate of their persecutors. John Chrysostom (d. 407), who was long active in Antioch before becoming the patriarch of Constantinople, transferred the martyrs' target to the Jews, who, he said, should be similarly blamed for the crucifixion of Jesus. In eight sermons preached in Antioch he sought to restrain Christians from easy fellowship with their Jewish neighbors, from sharing in their festivals (the Sabbath, the Passover), consulting their physicians, attending their synagogues. To this end he stigmatized them in the most derogatory terms. In the particularly harsh Sixth Sermon, he characterizes Jews as the prophets had scolded wrongdoers in the Jewish population of their day. God favored you even then, when you sacrificed your own children to idols, he claims, when you persecuted your own prophets. But now, in Christian times, he extrapolates, you are driven from your temple and your land. What is the difference? he asks rhetorically. "Are you not subject to this punishment because you committed atrocity against the world's Savior and ruler (*prostatēn*)?" Exile is not the only consequence of this action, the preacher claimed. You have killed the Savior, therefore you will endure endless servitude (*douleia*).[35] Enslavement is the torment of hell.

From its use to stigmatize religious rivals, eternal punishment had yet another resonance when evoked as a deterrent, as it is in one of John Chrysostom's personal letters. Damnation can be real even when none of its details are considered physical or material. Chrysostom's letter employs vividly specific physical details and pointedly stresses physical pain, but it also retains divine openness to atonement. John Chrysostom writes to express regret that Theodore, his student and friend, has taken up with the beautiful Hermione. As John's student, Theodore can hardly be unaware what his "fall" will

---

34. *Martyrdom of Carpus* §8; Musurillo, p. 23; my emphasis.

35. John Chrysostom, *Adversus Judaeos orationes* 6.1–3; PG 48:843–942, at 905–7; John Chrysostom, *Discourses against Judaizing Christians*, trans. Paul W. Harkins, Fathers of the Church 68 (Washington, D.C.: Catholic University of America Press, 1979), 149–55. Paul Halsall has captured the debate on his website, http://www.fordham.edu/halsall/source/chrysostom-jews6.asp. For the broader context, see Paula Fredrickson and Oded Irshai, "Christian Anti-Judaism: Polemics and Policies," in *The Cambridge History of Judaism* (Cambridge: Cambridge University Press, 2008), 4:977–1034.

cost him. As John put it, Theodore's sins have deformed the image of the divine king he bears in his soul (§13), something more beautiful than Hermione's body (§14). The damnation to which Theodore is headed God did not design as our fate. It is the result only of human indolence (*rhaithumia*) and diabolical or demonic despair. In Theodore's case, the flames of desire compound his wantonness and the despair the devil has implanted. "Extinguish [the fire of lust] *here* or know it will burn even more vehemently *there*" (§9).[36] This life is only a dream; eternity is the reality. The time when repentence is possible and its instantaneous benefits can be gained passes quickly. If late recognition of that lost opportunity were its only torment, hell would still be intolerable (§10). Here, John directly opposes the possibility of reform in Hades. Repent before dying. Death is the deadline.

John Chrysostom presents two possible eternities: the joys of heaven and, at the other extreme, two paired conditions, consciousness of missing that desirable end and the positive pains of hell. Considering the nature of heaven, John asks what price one would not pay for such blessings. But the lack of heaven is hardly the only penalty; there are also hell's own punishments. "Now I pray add the punishment also to the scene, and imagine men not only covered with shame, and veiling their heads, and bending them low, but also being dragged along the road to the fire, and hauled away to the instruments of torture and delivered over to the cruel powers, and suffering these things just at the time when all they who have practised what is good, and wrought deeds worthy of eternal life, are being crowned, and proclaimed conquerors, and presented before the royal throne" (§12). Having surveyed this terrifying prospect, John again urges Theodore to take the slightest of first steps to restore God's image in his soul. There can be incurable diseases of the body, but there are none of the soul. "If God had made us in order to punish us, you might well have despaired, . . . but [since] He created us for no reason [other] than His own good will, and with a view to our enjoying everlasting blessings," there is no excuse for inaction. "To sin may be a merely human failing, but to continue in the same sin ceases to be human, and becomes altogether devilish" (§15).

In sum, John Chrysostom cajoles Theodore with stimuli to action and sanctions against sloth. John evokes the fire of Gehenna as physical, threatening the same body now enmeshed in sensual pleasure. This hell is also psychological because one of its torments consists of the consciousness of others who resisted momentary pleasures but now possess celestial joys

---

36. Quotations from W. R. W. Stephens, in *NPNF-1*, 9:123–67; my emphasis. The Greek appears, with a Latin translation, in PG 47:271–316.

eternally. How one will suffer from the knowledge that one step in the right direction, back toward his mentor and friend and the church, would have loosened the devil's hold on his soul! Thus, arguing for the reality of hell does not, in John Chrysostom's view, exclude the possibility of horrible psychological torments for the damned. Its physicality works in tandem with its prisoners' mental anguish.

The *Vitae Patrum*: Folklore in the Service of Faith

In addition to defenses of eternal punishment, such as John Crysostom's, based on theological principles and the rhetoric of sermons, there were also sources that supported unending penalties very differently. Rather than offering theological reasons explicitly related to particular passages of Scripture or fitting tightly into logical arguments, these present the threat of damnation in vivid terms. Here is a shift in levels of discourse from theology to exemplum, from authority to anecdote. With these tales, we come much closer to religion as it was preached to the people or taught to beginners in religious training. The perception of hell as a physical reality that these stories offer was an integral part of the lore that adorned the reputations of the champions of rigorous, self-denying endurance, the Desert Fathers.[37] These ascetics, both men and women, lived in isolation as hermits, subsisting on only the barest necessities. Athanasius traces such a career in his famous *Life of Anthony*, and Jerome lived as a hermit for part of his life, but far more numerous were the fourth-century hermits of Egypt and Palestine, such as Pachomius and the two Macarii, Macarius the Egyptian (the Elder, the Great) and Macarius of Alexandria.[38] Another figure of particular interest is Evagrius of Pontus (d. 399), who played a significant role in propagating Origen's ideas within this circle.

These exemplary ascetics were central figures in tales that circulated of their lives and their sayings; other edifying stories were attributed to them and circulated under the generic title *Sayings of the Desert Fathers*.[39] Collections of

---

37. Although referred to as "the Fathers," the sayings of three women, Theodora, Sara, and Syncletica, have also been preserved in the Alphabetical Collection: Benedicta Ward, ed., *Sayings of the Desert Fathers: The Alphabetical Collection*, Cistercian Studies 59 (Oxford: Mowbrays, 1975). Facing Greek and Latin texts can be found in PG 65:70–440.

38. For the early growth of Christian monasticism, consult Derwas J. Chitty, *The Desert a City: An Introduction to the Study of Egyptian and Palestinian Monasticism under the Christian Empire* (1966; Crestwood, NY: St. Vladimir's Seminary Press, 1977); Susanna Elm, *"Virgins of God": The Making of Asceticism in Late Antiquity*, Oxford Classical Monographs (1994; Oxford: Clarendon Paperbacks, 1996).

39. Johannes Quasten reviews the different textual traditions of the *Sayings of the Desert Fathers*. Quasten, *Patrology* (Westminster, MD: Christian Classics, 1986), 3:187–89.

the sayings existed by the end of the fifth century in many languages: Coptic, Syriac, Greek, Latin. Some were organized alphabetically by the author to whom each saying is attributed, others topically under headings like "Spiritual Advancement," "Compunction," "Self-Mastery." The *Lausiac History*, by Pachomius, retraces the itinerary he took on his voyage to gather tales of these spiritual battles. Compilers of the various manuscripts sometimes changed attributions, made different decisions about fragmentary texts, or did not always know the most complete version, which itself might conceal interpolations. These anecdotes circulated for centuries as illustrations or condensations of spiritual truth and formed a type of literary expression known as the exemplum.[40] They resemble the sayings of venerated leaders in many religious traditions, such as the wisdom of the Buddha, the midrashim of the great teachers of the postbiblical period in rabbinic Judaism, and the "traditions" or hadith of Islam. Within the Christian tradition, they bear a special relationship to the teachings of Jesus via parables, and so, for tellers and hearers, they constitute a quasi-ritual experience: the storyteller imitating Jesus, the listeners emulating his early followers.[41] Because of their numinous associations, the textual history of these collections—their versions, translations, and fortune in later literature—is extremely complex. From this literature, three narratives will illustrate the directness and power of the image of hell these exempla convey. For convenience, I give each one a short title of its own.

1. MACARIUS AND THE SKULL

This anecdote shows judgment immediately following death, but with consignment to a physically painful place still accessible to the living, and reachable by prayer—namely, the open Hades. Perhaps the most famous of the tales from the *Sayings of the Desert Fathers*, this story features a dialogue between Abbot Macarius the Great (d. ca. 390) and the skull of a pagan priest.[42] In the middle of the tale, the narrative switches from the first to the third person, a complication worth preserving.

---

40. John Whortley, "Death, Judgment, Heaven, and Hell in Byzantine 'Beneficial Tales'," *Dumbarton Oaks Papers* 55 (2001): 53–69; C. Bremond, J. Le Goff, and J.-C. Schmitt, *L'exemplum*, Typologie des Sources du Moyen Âge Occidental 40 (Turnhout, Belgium: Brepols, 1982).

41. See Alan Bernstein, "The *Exemplum* as 'Incorporation' of Abstract Truth in the Thought of Humbert of Romans and Stephen of Bourbon," in *The Two Laws: Studies in Medieval Legal History Dedicated to Stephan Kuttner*, ed. L. Mayali and S. Jefferis-Tibbetts (Washington, D.C.: Catholic University of America Press, 1990), 82–96; Markus Schürer, "Das Beispiel im Begriff: Aspekte einer begriffsgeschichtlichen Erschliessung exemplarischen Erzählens im Mittelalter," *Mittellateinisches Jahrbuch* 38.1 (2003): 199–237.

42. M-38 in the Alphabetical Collection, PG 65:279–80; Ward, *Sayings*, 136–37; Guy, *Les Apophtègmes des Pères: Collection systématique* 3.19; SC 387:158–61.

Once, while walking in the desert, I found the skull of a dead man on the ground and when I touched it with my walking stick, it spoke. I say to it: "you, who are you?" And the skull answered me: "I used to be the priest of the idols and Gentiles who lived on this spot; and you, indeed are Macarius, who bears the Spirit of God. Whenever you are moved by some mercy towards those who are stuck in the punishments (*en kolasei* = the wrath) and pray for them, they feel a slight relief." The old man said: "What is the relief and what is the torment?" [And the skull answered:] "As far as the earth lies beneath the heaven, so far is the fire beneath us, and we stand in the middle of the fire from tip to toe, nor are we permitted to see anyone face to face, for the front of each adheres to the back of the other. But when you pray for us, one is partly able to see the face of another. That is the relief." Weeping, the old man said: "Woe the day that man was born!" And he added: "Is there another, heavier punishment?" The skull replied, "There is a greater punishment beneath us." Then the old man: "What goes on there?" And the skull took up, "We, [pagans] because we did not know God, obtain some mercy, but those who knew God and denied him are beneath us." Then the old man picked up the skull and buried it beneath the earth.

Here is a physical hell indeed, divided into two layers, the higher one for pagans, who never knew God, the lower hell for those who learned the faith but scorned it. Hell's depth can be measured in terms of the distance between heaven and earth. When requested by spiritually qualified specialists, mitigation of its punishments occurs, at least for pagans in its upper level. The anonymous treatise *Sleep in the Faith*, wrongly attributed to John of Damascus, refers to this tale of the skull as evidence for the effectiveness of prayers for the dead.[43] Macarius's encounter with the pagan priest is also the basis of Thomas Aquinas's grudging concession that those condemned to hell immediately at their death can be aided by suffrages, but only during the time that someone actively prays for them.[44] Here, suffrages aid only residents of the upper level, who still will never escape; those below are already beyond reach.

2. WRONGS "THERE," PAINS "HERE," SAY THE DEVILS

Harsher than the story of Macarius's interview with the skull is one that offers no hope of intercession!

---

43. *Sleep in the Faith* §10; PG 95:255.
44. Thomas Aquinas, *Summa Theologiae* III, Supp., q. 71, a. 5; ed. Peter Caramello (Turin: Marietti, 1948–50), 4:257–58.

One of the fathers related the following tale. A priest of our region had a sister who, one day, falls into a trance. Two men dressed in white conduct her to heaven. Accompanied by angels, she sees an elevated throne and an inner, higher rank of angels. Her guides are commanded to show her everything so that she may communicate what she sees to the living. She sees buildings in which are honored bishops who governed well, lower clerics and laypeople who lived honorably according to their rank, and many virgins, widows, and spouses—people who lived in chaste marriages. Among the women, some lived in ascetic communities, others, in solitary retreat. Some were widows who had long lived in poverty and affliction. Some of these had erred, but recovered their honorable status after penance and many tears.

Then her guides take her to a region for the godless and criminals (*asebesi xai paranomois*). Lamentations and groans fill the place. There is a fiery furnace prepared "for those who even though they were of the clergy, outraged the Church of God by their avarice and injustice and led a shameful life without remorse. Many of these were people she recognized from her church and her neighborhood." From there, beyond a river of fire, her guides took her to a place of great darkness where she heard groans and gnashing teeth. Here she saw virgins and widows who concealed their secret liaisons, even aborting children to conceal their sins. Others were bad influences on their ascetic communities. The angels explain, "Their origins are all different, but since they fell into the same faults, they endure the same punishments."[45] Within this darkness she espies two virgins who were her close friends, women whom her brother, the priest, had counseled carefully. But when she questions them about why they were being punished, the women become ashamed. The inmates explain that the punishments "here" (*entautha*) correspond to what they did "there" (*ekei*). They beg her to intervene with the guardians of the place to lighten their punishments, grant them a respite, or even release them. Placing her arms around the guards' knees, she implores mercy for her friends. The refusal is severe. This is no time for repentance or confession. These women regarded the benefits of heaven as fables, how can they ask now to share in them? "It is just that, having committed such acts 'there' (*ekei-then*), they receive the fruits 'here' (*entautha*)." Had they repented there, things would be different here. The punishment they scorned before

45. Guy, *Les Apophtègmes des Pères* 18.49, lines 122–24; pp. 126–27.

cannot end now. "Since they gave their bodies no respite in committing evil, how can they obtain a respite here?"[46]

Seeing their friend's petition rejected, the two false women beg her to carry news of their fate to a friend who practiced the same vice in secret along with them. At least she might repent, as they, in their scorn and pride, did not.[47]

This story echoes Luke 16 (the rich man and Lazarus), since the sinners in their punishment beg to send warnings to a living companion. It occurs in a physically removed place but during the time we are living in now, that is, before the Resurrection and Last Judgment. Like the setting in Luke 16, it occurs at the punitive extreme of Hades, with many themes relating to the Last Judgment, such as the river of fire and the gnashing teeth. Unlike the encounter between Macarius and the pagan priest's skull, this example denies any basis whatever for intercession in the interim. According to the punishing attendants, these false virgins deserve no let up from their suffering because they never let up from their sinning. This interpretation is far from the open Hades of the figures cited favorably by pseudo-John of Damascus in *Concerning Those Who Have Fallen Asleep in the Faith* and from the implications drawn from 1 Peter 3:19 and 4:6, where the netherworld is accessible until the Resurrection to the preaching of Christ, the teaching of the apostles, or the prayers of relatives.

3. The Licentious Mother

The deterrent power of the fate of the two secret sinners in the previous tale is matched in this tale, but again it presents the need to make even the punitive Hades of Luke 16 accessible occasionally to visionaries so that the world may be warned of its dire conditions. Although the closed Hades of Luke 16 offers no escape (and in this account, it is even called Gehenna), the woman's daughter can visit and return so that we may know the tale. Once, an aged ascetic whose name has been lost to us questioned a virgin of advanced age who had pursued a life of chaste retirement. He asked how she had chosen that lifestyle. Her dramatic tale contrasts the conduct of her righteous father and her wanton mother. Her father was a modest, mild man, but all his life he suffered from illness. Her mother was a notorious bawd, conducted herself as a prostitute (*pornē*), even in the home, but enjoyed perfect health.

---

46. Ibid., lines 197–200, pp. 130–31. This statement parallels Gregory I's declaration, "No one whose mind ever wished to lack sin in this life should ever lack punishment." Greg. *Mor.* 34.19.36, lines 46–47; p. 1759.

47. Guy, *Les Apophtègmes des Pères* 18.49; SC 498:114–33.

After they both died, the daughter had to decide which model to follow. Just as she was about to conclude that her mother's health was more important than her way of life, a grand and awe-inspiring figure appeared, who led her to see each of her parents in their postmortem condition. They first met her father in a pleasant meadow. The daughter wished to stay with him, but she also had to visit her mother. Horribly, her mother was confined in a revolting building, resounding with gnashing teeth, moans, and shrieks. It reeked of smoke and crawled with vermin. Below was her mother in a furnace, which she called "the Gehenna of fire" (cf. Matt. 5:22, 18:19; Mark 9:43–47). The mother begged her child to remove her from these torments, but the guards prevented that. Once at home, as the daughter recovered from this vision, those around her asked why she was upset, thus interrupting the momentary pity she experienced for her mother. From this incident, the daughter learned that the visible consequences of one's life's behavior are deceptive and that instead of judging by appearances in this world, one must instead live with an eye to the afterlife. Hence, she became an ascetic.[48]

The deterrent hell shapes the daughter's choice in life. Though clearly prior to the Last Judgment, her parents have already been judged, the father rewarded in a meadow like that in the vision of Drythelm, the mother punished in a furnace explicitly called Gehenna. The interim has collapsed in this tale, at least for the two archetypal figures at the extremes of reward and punishment. The difference between them recalls that between Lazarus and the rich man in Luke 16, where contrasting fates appear immediately after death. Here is an example of Hades as a place of punishment.[49]

The variety in the eschatological views of the Fathers' sayings demands a summary and articulation of categories. In universalism the final destiny can only be the kingdom of God. Whether those still owing some retribution for misdeeds wait in Hades or Tartarus (consider 1 Peter 2:4, where all depends on "judgment"), the goal remains reunion with God. Conversely, in dual issue eschatology, where hell exists opposite heaven, Hades emerges as more punitive, more like the fiery version of Luke 16, separated from the blessed by a great chasm, and in this scenario one's condition is sealed at death.

---

48. Ibid., 18.45; SC 498:96–105.

49. A group of sayings emphasizes the common exhortation to contemplate hell. Unfortunately, the textual tradition is confusing. Attributions differ, as does the terminology. One version emphasizes the middle or interim condition of the soul and locates the punishments in Hades; another refers to Tartarus following the Last Judgment. As given in the Alphabetical Collection, a statement attributed to Evagrius (Letter E, 31) combines two statements in the Topical Collection, 3.2 attributed to Anthony, and 3.5 attributed to Theodore. Based on their unity in the Alphabetical Collection, Jean-Claude Guy ascribes 3.2 and 3.5 to Evagrius. The Greek and Latin texts are in PG 65:175 A-C; and Guy, Les Apophtègmes des Pères, pp. 149–53; trans. in Ward, Sayings, 63.

Beginning immediately, Hades is a place of punishment rather than purification and certainly not a place of preaching, comprehension of the Gospel, and conversion. Even in dual issue eschatology, though, options remain open for exploration. Within what might be called the purgatorial option, the interim may be a time of great drama: (a) souls may be tried after death to determine where they belong after resurrection, and (b) if the character of the soul becomes clear, that soul may be saved even before then. Alternatively, death may itself be decisive. The interim may not constitute a trial. A soul may be judged as saved but still be required to endure the cleansing of slight or confessed sins before eventual salvation.[50] Further, widespread sentiment in favor of hell's physical reality, though not unanimous, was a constant: visible at the literary level of John Chrysostom's letter to Theodore, in the martyrs' visceral reactions to the threats against them, and in the pastoral examples circulated by the Desert Fathers. As it happened, not even this broadly disseminated belief in the physical hell prevented Origen's universalist ideas from attracting continued attention in Eastern Christianity.

Justinian Condemns Origenism Twice

Under the emperor Justinian I (527–565), Origen's system aroused concern among conservative monks at the imperial palace. It was always clear that Origen's premises rested on his understanding of Neoplatonic philosophy. At times tension arises between the conclusions of sophisticated theological systems and the more direct, vivid ideas effective among religious professionals with less specialized training or the dramatic examples presented from the pulpit for pastoral ends.[51] Thus one may understand Justinian's decision in 529 to close the Platonic Academy in Athens, a bastion of pagan or "Hellenizing" philosophy and increasingly anomalous in a political and religious world dominated, in the Greek-speaking area at least, by Constantinople.[52] Such a conflict appears to have arisen also among monks in the Judean desert where some followers of Origen were expelled from their monasteries and denounced for "assuming" a certain Christian faith but actually professing "Greek" or "gnostic" ideas and forming an "intelligentsia."

By this time, opponents of "Origenism" had associated with their rivals theories nowhere to be found in Origen's surviving texts or in those of Evagrius,

---

50. Note the review of three different eschatologies, or approaches to eschatology, in Caroline Walker Bynum and Paul Freedman's introduction to their edited volume, *Last Things*, 5–10.

51. Schäufele, "Die Höllen der Alexandriner," p. 210, item 3.

52. Herrin, *Formation*, 77–79; Etienne Gilson, *History of Christian Philosophy in the Middle Ages* (London: Sheed and Ward, 1955), 181.

a writer deeply influenced by him, such as the notion that the risen body will be "ethereal and spherical."[53] Aided in part by these inaccurate representations, partisans from some Palestinian monasteries secured the support of the emperor Justinian, who criticized Origen's ideas in 543. Notwithstanding these distortions, canons 1 (souls preexist before descending into bodies) and 9 (restoration) of 543 and, at the Second Council of Constantinople in 553, canons 1 (preexistence of souls and restoration) and 2 (turning of minds from contemplation of God to what is worse, the production of bodies) convey key elements of Origenism.[54] Moreover, Constantinople II included Origen on a list of heretics whose ideas all must reject.[55] These condemnations had a dampening effect on Byzantine universalism.[56] It is no surprise that political power wielded by an outstanding ruler should fundamentally influence the ideas of those who witnessed its exercise. Taken together, the letter of 543 and the Second Council of Constantinople spelled the end of any but concealed sympathy for a universalist eschatology that might include a restoration of all to an original, pristine union with God. Imperial authority imposed what must be considered a defeat for universalism, even though that defeat permeated the community only slowly and incompletely.

The Decline of Universalism after Justinian

The interaction between these varying eschatological interpretations by no means disappeared in the centuries after Justinian. In general, theologians continued to stress mercy as a divine attribute and to extend its application as long into the afterlife as they could, but they increasingly made hell eternal and, as compared to the earlier fathers, reduced the options for postmortem pardon in Hades, though they did not altogether eliminate them. The open-door theme allowing rescue observed by Trumbower remains, but it is more and more evidently a minority position overshadowed by a growing

---

53. Brian E. Daley, *The Hope of the Early Church: A Handbook of Patristic Eschatology* (Cambridge: Cambridge University Press, 1991), 189–90; Richard Price, trans., *The Acts of the Council of Constantinople of 553*, Translated Texts for Historians 51 (Liverpool: Liverpool University Press, 2009), 2:281–86. The letter, with a brief introduction, in D-S nos. 403–11, pp. 140–42.

54. Price, *Acts*, 2:281–86. Canon 1 of the letter of 543 says, "If anyone says or holds that the souls of human beings pre-exist . . . and were made to descend into bodies as a punishment, let him be anathema." Canon 9 of the letter of 543 says, "If anyone says or thinks that the suffering of demons and wicked men is temporary and that they will ever come to an end or that there will be a restitution or reintegration of demons or wicked men, let that one be anathema." Original language in D-S nos. 403 and 411, pp. 140–43.

55. D-S no. 223, pp. 148–49.

56. Meyendorff, *Byzantine Theology*, 72–73.

consensus that repentance should be done in life. Prayers on behalf of the dead are effective for both those who pray and those in Hades (not purgatory) to whom the prayers are dedicated. However allegorical its vivid representation, thinkers increasingly stress hell's eternity.

John of Damascus and the Eternal Hell

A good example of one who combines allegorical images of the torments with a strict insistence on their eternity is John of Damascus (ca. 655–ca. 750). Whereas John Chrysostom, in his letter to Theodore, subtracted nothing from the wracking of the soul or the body in hell's eternity, John of Damascus is highly sympathetic to a figurative view of the torments of the damned, but still opts explictly for an eternal hell and death as the deadline for repentance, that is, with no possibility of conversion in Hades. This crucial difference helps distinguish him from the anonymous pseudo-John of Damascus.[57]

Like the Last Judgment scene in Matthew 25:31–46, John's position on hell fits carefully within a chronology involving the devil and his angels and the fire prepared for them. In his *Exposition of the Orthodox Faith* he explains the creation so as to exculpate God from any blame for the existence of evil.[58] He insists that the fallen angels do not spring from something that is itself evil. Their evil has no deeper origin than their own free will. In his rebellion, Satan drew along in his fall those angels who willingly subjected themselves to him, thus moving from good to evil, from light to darkness, their choice being a free operation of the mind. Humans are subject to attack by these evil angels, but are not helpless. The human choice of evil is also a free operation of the mind. Because the devil and his retinue of angels freely chose their rebellion in one, single, decisive moment, there is no return; angels have no ability to repent. By contrast, however often they lapse, humans may repent until they die. John sums up the contrast dramatically: their fall was to the angels what death is for humans, the point beyond which no repentance is possible.[59] Therefore, John of Damascus rejects the idea of postmortem conversion, repentance, or improvement.

---

57. See Allatius in his introduction to the works of John of Damascus, PG 94:146 n. 33.

58. *The Exposition of the Orthodox Faith* 4.19. I have used the translation of S. D. F. Salmond, in *NPNF-2*, 9:1–101; and the Greek edition in PG 94:790–1228. Note also that John quotes from this work in his *Dialogue against the Manichaeans*, in PG 94:1503–4. See also Hoeck, "Stand und Aufgaben," 39 n. 3.

59. *The Exposition of the Orthodox Faith* 2.4; PG 94:878. "Death is to man what their fall was to the angels"; quoted by Thomas Aquinas, *ST* III, Supp., q. 98, a. 2, ad. 3; cf. *ST* I, q. 63, a. 6, ad. 3; and elsewhere.

It is characteristic of the positive tone of Byzantine eschatology that John's last chapter emphasizes, not judgment, heaven, or hell, but the General Resurrection. If there were no resurrection, things would merely follow their natural course, bodies would decompose, and life would lead to no sanctions. Since it is not the soul alone that pursues virtue and resists vice, but the soul together with the body, both receive judgment and retribution. In a manner reminiscent of Plato, John argues that a life without resurrection (and postmortem sanctions) is incompatible with divine justice.[60] After trial, the just will shine like the sun and join the angels forever. The devil, his demons, the Antichrist, the impious (*asebeis*) and the sinful (*hamartōlo*) from Psalm 1:1, will be sent to the "everlasting fire" (*pyr aiōnion*), from Matthew 25:41. Everlasting fire differs by definition from the fire of this world. It is not material, like that on earth, but a fire known only to God (*an eideiē ho theos*). Here is the consequence of John's connecting the immaterial fire to the faults of the mind, the source of evil choice, not the body. Therefore hell's fire, the consequence of evil choice, is, like the mind, immaterial. The resurrected body that suffers in it is also incorruptible and, like the fire, different from what we know in this world.[61]

The *Apocalypse of Mary*: Who Obtains Relief?

Like the *Apocalypse of Paul*, from which it derives, the eleventh-century text known as the *Apocalypse of Mary* emphasizes the physicality of hell.[62] We have considered this text before because it includes a suspension of punishment within hell for the fifty days of Pentecost, but only for some of the Christian damned. Mary's dramatic appearance before the divine throne and her bargaining to obtain mercy for Christian sinners are certainly important aspects of this complex work, but there is more to be learned. The grouping of sinners yields a sociology of hell; the matching of punishments to sins yields a psychology of sin and retribution. Unlike many apocalypses that categorize sinners with the expression "those who," this one also refers to offenders by their gender, and specifies, of adulterers, for example, whether it is the man or woman who has violated the marriage. Moreover, the *Apocalypse of Mary*

---

60. Plato, *Phaedo* 107c; and discussion in Bernstein, *Formation*, 52–61, at 54.

61. *De fide orthodoxa* 4.27; PG 94:1219–28.

62. For the *Apocalypse of Mary*, see Jane Baun, *Tales from Another Byzantium: Celestial Journey and Local Community in the Medieval Greek Apocrypha* (Cambridge: Cambridge University Press, 2007), 386–400. The *Apocalypse of Mary* also receives careful analysis in Martha Himmelfarb, *Tours of Hell: An Apocalyptic Form in Jewish and Christian Literature* (1983; Philadelphia: Fortress Press, 1985), 100–104, 119–26, 178–79, and passim.

frequently names particular body parts. The specification of gender and the anatomical precision manifest the relationship between sin and punishment and heighten the text's theodicial significance. Named regions appear, but some sins and some punishments occur in more than one. Thus, in areas to both the south and west there are sinners who burn and sinners who hang. Those in the south are not identified by religion, whereas those in the west offended against due reverence in church. Similarly, the lake of molten pitch in the west contains non-Christians, specifically Jews, but also other unbelievers, whereas those in the lake of fire are identified as Christians in name only: although baptized, they actually serve the devil.

In prayer on the Mount of Olives, Mary asks for the Archangel Michael to guide her through Hades (ho haides) and finds in it "men and women" who did not worship the Holy Trinity (§3). Nearby, there is a river of pitch symbolizing the darkness that blinds those who have never recognized Mary as the mother who acted in the incarnation. This is a new embarrassment for these souls, for, as they declare, she is the only one to attend to them. "Your blessed Son came upon the earth and did not ask at all about us, nor Abraham the forefather, nor John the Baptist, nor Moses the great prophet, nor the apostle Paul." Once Mary learns from Michael that these had denied her role in the birth of Jesus, she leaves them in their punishment (§4). The pattern of considering some offenses too grave to be lessened is characteristic of both this text and the imperial experiments with the Easter amnesty which, as we shall see, distinguished between those who might benefit from pardon, and those who would not.

Michael now guides Mary "to the south," where, as in the Apocalypse of Paul, there is a river of fire, in which different types of sinners are immersed to different heights according to their sins. Steeped up to their breasts are men who abandoned marriage for adultery (§6). Immersed up to their necks are "whosoever ate people's flesh," such as women who bore children but then abandoned them as food for dogs, and men who "gave up their brothers before kings and archons [governors]." So, figuratively, those who consumed their own kind are consumed by fire (§7). Covered with fire to the top of their heads are those who perjured themselves by swearing on the cross (§8). Next come punishments by hanging: a man hanging by his feet is devoured by worms; the breasts of a woman hanging by her ears are devoured by beasts who exit from her mouth. The man was guilty of usury, the woman of causing strife by gossip (§§9–10). These souls are identified by gender and sin.

Considering the gravity of these sins and the punishments they bring on, Mary observes that it might be better had they never been born, but Michael replies that these are not even the great punishments, which lie to the west (§11). As in the *Apocalypse of Paul*, where a distinction is made between an upper and a lower level seven times worse, the great punishments of the *Apocalypse of Mary* are for offenses against the church and the Christian religion. These torments seem no more severe than those to the south, the principal difference being that they penalize different types of sins. Fire again features prominently. A cloud of fire burns those who sleep rather than attend church on Sunday (§12). Those in church who do not rise when the presbyter (priest) enters are stuck to benches of fire (§13). In this case, the punishment explains the offense with a grotesque humor. As in the southern region, the punishments now shift to hanging: from the iron branches of an iron tree, men and women perjurors, blasphemers, and slanderers hang by their tongues.[63] She saw "a man hanging from all fours, and from his nails blood gushed out violently, and his tongue was tied in a flame of fire, and he was unable to groan or say" a prayer for mercy. This person, a steward in a church, consumes the things of the church. He offers the cynical excuse that "the one who serves the temple from the temple shall be nourished" (§15). There, blood beneath the offender's nails may be a clue about the offense (abuse of the Eucharist), but it may also refer to a more generic sin of skimming ecclesiastical revenues or gifts in kind for one's own use. (In the pre-Constantinian church, when followers celebrated the Eucharist, they brought offerings of food for the poor.[64]) Having seen the punishment and heard the offense, Mary orders the man returned to his fate (§15). Priests with secret sins, whose offenses cause heaven and earth to shake if they stand beside the altar and speak of Christ, hang by their twenty nails, and fire exits their mouths (§16). A three-headed bird pecks the eyes and mouth of a reader (*lector*), whose life contradicts the lessons of the Gospel he represents. The connection between the punished organs and act of reading aloud is obvious (§ 17). Close by, the biblical fire (unquenchable) and worm (deathless) of Gehenna combine to shape the punishment of patriarchs and bishops whose life is the opposite of angelic, even though they pray, "Bless ye holy ones" (§18). "And she saw women hanging by their [nails], and a flame of fire came out from their mouth and burned them up: and all the beasts coming out

---

63. Baun, *Tales*, §14; p. 295 n. 3, specifies that a fifteenth-century manuscript places in this part of Hades the named sinner Herodias, the mother of Salome, a historical figure much elaborated by legend, sometimes considered a leader of witches. See Carlo Ginzburg, *Ecstasies: Deciphering the Witches Sabbath* (New York: Pantheon Books, 1991), 89–104 and passim. In the *Apocalypse of Mary* she appears as an individual. That her name is only interpolated later suggests some hesitation about how well she fits her companions in this western part of Hades.

64. A. Hamman, "Agapè," in *EEC*, 1:16.

from the fire gnawed them in pieces." These women showed disrespect for their first husbands, presbyters, by consummating a second marriage. They complain that their torments are disproportionately horrible (§19). Among other hanging women was a deaconess who fornicated and now hangs from a crag, victim of a specialized two-headed beast that devours her breasts (§20). The sexual partners of the deaconess do not appear here. The type of retribution that fits specially designed beasts to specific body parts belongs in a category that occurs also in the Apocalypse of Peter and the Vision of the Pious Viraf (the Zoroastrian Ardā Virāz Nāmeh).

The text shifts to another part of "the great punishments." Again (§22, as in §11) Mary wishes to see all the torments. Michael takes her to "the left parts of Paradise," a surprising term, since one hardly expects punishments in any part of paradise, but perhaps the sinister connotations of the left resolve that scruple.[65] This area is a sea of boiling pitch that covers sinners beneath its surface. When Mary arrives, the tormenting angels, who clearly are those who fell from heaven and have been living in darkness ever since, give thanks that she has brought "the light." At Mary's request, the river and its darkness recede, exposing numerous, tiny sinners within. Michael calls this ocean of molten pitch "the outer fire," and, he explains, it tortures the Jews, who refused baptism, and whom he also calls "crucifiers of Christ." Despite this portrayal of Jewish rejection, others share the same boiling pitch. They include those who commit fornication, those who debauch mother and daughter, poisoners, those who are violent with the sword, and women who strangle their offspring. Their torments cause even the punishing angels to grieve. After learning the nature of those within, Mary observes that they will be there forever and expresses her sorrow. Mary's concern brings respite for the sinners for this one time in all history, but once she sees them again, she confirms their fate and leaves them as they were: "According to their faith so be it unto them." (§23). The association of Jews purportedly because of their descent from those described in the Gospels with offenders who committed actual wrongs involving sexual abuse or violence is an example of stigmatization. In this text, unlike many other detailed accounts of hell, such as the Apocalypse of Peter and the Apocalypse of Paul, there seems to be a correspondence between explicit mention of Jews and a particularly vivid, material presentation of hell's tortures. A similar correlation exists between John Chrysostom's Sermons against the Jews and his letter to Theodore.

---

65. Similar divisions of the cosmos may be found in 1 Enoch 77, an ancient Jewish apocryphal text. See James H. Charlesworth, ed., The Old Testament Pseudepigrapha (Garden City, NY: Doubleday, 1983), 1:56.

From the boiling sea of pitch and darkness, Michael guides Mary to the lake of fire, a place in its own right, apparently requiring no other name. Here is the punishment of Christians who were baptized but nonetheless performed the work of the devil and did not repent (§24). The difference between the left parts of paradise (the sea of pitch) and the lake of fire appears to be the difference between the godless, impious (the *asebōn, r'shaim, impii*), and the Christian sinners (the *hamartōlōn, hatayim, peccatores*, the contrasts of Psalm 1). Despite their sins, Mary regards these as "the children of her Son" and intercedes on their behalf before the throne of the Father. The reprieve she wins has been discussed before.

In sum, despite the geographical divisions of this very punitive Hades, the names of the areas seem less important than the distinction between the impious—explicitly, here, including Jews, who do not recognize Christ—and Christians who offend by violating their own divine law. The punishments in the *Apocalypse of Mary* are not allegorical. In most cases, they do not appear to symbolize the offense that produced them. Sometimes physical punishments aim specifically at persons of a particular sex and at the body parts peculiar to them and their sins. This pronounced materiality links this text to other apocalypses, such as those of Peter and Paul, and others discussed with an emphasis on their vivid representation of physical punishment, such as the Zoroastrian *Ardā Wirāz Nāmeh* and the Muslim *Miraj Nameh*.

Despite the annual relief Mary obtains for the Christian sinners, her apocalypse illustrates the trend away from universalism. This Greek text insistently calls the scene of the action Hades, but it is the punitive Hades of Luke 16. If there is any reminiscence of the open Hades that derives from 1 Peter 3:19 and 4:6, it is simply the fact that the Archangel Michael can guide her through this horrible underworld, and, based on her perceptions, she can petition for its prisoners. There is room for both the fallen angels and some of the damned to benefit from the insight that there is such a person as Mary, who brings them light and who, alone of all the heavenly figures they name, cares to visit them. Here is a shift in the representation of the motif of a heavenly visit to the underworld in which the protagonist is not Jesus, as in the Descent literature, but Mary. Speculation on the introduction of this gendered factor in Byzantine piety would be out of place here, but it certainly deserves note. Perhaps the introduction of Mary into the punitive Hades is a partial compensation for the gradual retreat from the universalism and the open Hades of earlier centuries. In comparison to the role of Christ in the *Apocalypse of Paul*, who provides relief for all those in the lowest compartment, in the apocalypse named after her, Mary refuses her aid to many when she hears how serious their sins are. This narrows the theme of relief within hell to a considerable extent; it parallels restrictions on the open Hades.

Theodoret of Cyrrhus: A Mystical Transcendence

Having considered this spectrum in the theological, pastoral, and hagiographical texts that range from Origen's universalism to the harsh materiality of the *Apocalypse of Mary* (which nonetheless has its annual reprieve), I wish to return briefly to the patristic period to consider a remarkable text in isolation to provide some perspective on the range of opinions just reviewed. Beside the mysticism of Theodoret of Cyrrhus, even Origen's concern with postmortem punishment appears a crass fixation on fear and pain. Theodoret was born around 393 and became bishop of Cyrrhus near Antioch in 423. He died around 466.[66] Theodoret of Cyrrhus wrote a *History of the Monks of Syria* (also called the *Philotheos*, *The Religious History*, and *Manners of Ascetic Life*) and a series of sermons on the providence of God. Traditionally published at the end of the *Philotheos* is a "Letter on Charity," which, in one passage, puts the desire for heaven and the fear of hell in a radically different perspective: "Reflecting on these and similar sayings, I would not accept the kingdom of heaven without the love relating to them: I would not flee retribution in hell, if it was reasonable for one who has this love to undergo punishment."[67] In this view, one should not desire heaven without possessing the charity that alone attains it and characterizes it, and certainly not from fear of hell. Indeed, for one so motivated, even the punishments of hell would be acceptable provided they could be endured in charity. Here is an elegant expression of the mystical desire for a union with God so intense that it transcends mere theological categories like heaven and hell. The female Muslim mystic Rābiᶜa of Basra would express a similar sentiment.

Political Theology of Hell in Byzantium

Justinian's prohibition of Origenism deeply affected reflection on postmortem punishment in the Byzantine world. It is important to ask why the emperor should legislate concerning the afterlife when it is outside his jurisdiction. The answer is that, like many other rulers, Justinian saw an affinity

---

66. E. Cavalcanti, "Theodoret of Cyrrhus," in *EEC*, 2:827.

67. Theodoret of Cyrrhus, *A History of the Monks of Syria*, trans. Richard M. Price (Kalamazoo, MI: Cistercian Publications, 1985), 190–205, at 195.

between a God who could damn and his own power to condemn.[68] From Augustus to Constantine to Justinian, the primary perception the Roman emperors spread about themselves was that the care or "providence" (*providentia*) they extended over their subjects resembled the rule of the gods. As the dispenser of justice the emperor animates the law (*lex animata*). But, in accord with the reasonableness (*epieikeia*) of his rule, this justice is tempered with clemency. Once the emperors adopted Christianity, they claimed to imitate Christ, whose divine attributes of justice and mercy they assumed for themselves. Balanced by the rule of law, the emperor's administration mirrors creation's own perfection. The ruler is "the human exponent of natural law, and his role is to imitate God's rule of the universe."[69] Consequently, the ideas of order, justice, and law that Byzantine rulers promulgated left little room for debate over postmortem punishment. Just as some criminals were beyond pardon, some sinners should suffer eternally.

The parallel between monotheism and monarchy is also manifest in Scripture, where God is described as a king, and together with his people, the community is a kingdom. God's kingdom appears in Psalms 21:29 (22:28); 102 (103):19; and 144 (145):13. Wisdom 6:21 refers to the eternal kingdom. In midrashic literature there are exempla in which kings parallel God, and his palace doubles as the world.[70] This trend continues in the Christian Scriptures, where for example, Matthew 22:2 relates, "The kingdom of Heaven may be compared to a king who gave a marriage feast for his son." The Lord's Prayer (Matt 6:10) urges, "Thy kingdom come," and suggests that

---

68. Impetus for the assertion of a reciprocal relationship between monarchy and monotheism in medieval sources comes from Ernst Kantorowicz, *The King's Two Bodies: A Study in Mediaeval Political Theology* (Princeton, NJ: Princeton University Press, 1957). For an important collection of articles on the religious nature of monarchical government, see Aziz Al-Azmeh and János M. Bak, eds., *Monotheistic Kingship: The Medieval Variants* (Budapest and New York: Central European University, Department of Medieval Studies, 2004). The lead essay by Al-Azmeh (9–29) vigorously sets out the arguments for "sacral kingship," which incorporates the ideologies not only of monotheistic communities, but also of regimes that practice polytheism. See also Gerhard Podskalsky, "Politische Theologie in Byzanz zwischen Reichseschatolotogie und Reichsideologie," in *Cristianità d'occidente e cristianità d'oriente (secoli vi–xi)*, Settimane di Studio della Fondazione Centro Italiano di Studi sull'Alto Medioevo 51 (Spoleto: Presso la sede della Fondazione, 2004), 1421–33. Although the phrase "political theology" is provocative (how can religion be political?), it seems less objectionable to me than overlooking use of religious terminology to express political ideology. The Hebrew, Christian, and Muslim Scriptures use so many political images, and royal-imperial statements use so many religious images, that it seems impossible to deprive ourselves of such a tool.

69. This statement concludes the excellent overview on this point by John Procopé, "Greek and Roman Political Theory," in *The Cambridge History of Medieval Political Thought* (Cambridge: Cambridge University Press, 1988), 21–36, at 27.

70. See the *Tanna debe Eliyyahu* discussed in chapter 7. Ignaz Ziegler, *Die Königsgleichnisse des Midrasch beleuchtet durch die römische Kaiserzeit* (Breslau: Schottlaender, 1903).

earth should be *ruled* like heaven. In Matthew 16:19 Jesus offers Peter the keys to the kingdom of heaven. Matthew 25:34 invites the charitable: "Come blessed of my father, possess the kingdom prepared for you."[71] Pope Gregory I understood the utility of these metaphors as he defended his levels of discourse. The monarchy as a visible institution was indispensable to communicating the idea of God.

Conversely, Roman political rhetoric played on similar devices to project imperial majesty. In the days of persecution, Christians were executed for failing to honor the divinity claimed by the emperor. The persecutor Diocletian bluntly called himself "god and lord" (*dominus et deus*).[72] Although the living emperors did not consistently claim to be gods, after they died, deceased emperors received the title *divus* (divine). The new interpretation Christians gave to the world included a different view of the emperor and the empire. In literary depictions of Christ's Descent, drawing on Psalm 24 (23)'s image of the King of Glory, Melito, bishop of Sardis, who died in 190 CE, interpreted Christ's mission with images of a triumph that extended even to Hades, where the Resurrection constituted a defeat of death itself. In rhetoric derived from the formal, ritual acclamation of rulers and triumphal processions, he casts the victor recounting his achievement in these terms: "I am the one who destroyed death, and triumphed over the enemy, and trampled Hades under foot, and bound the strong one [Satan], and carried off man to the heights of heaven."[73] Images of the Anastasis, the Resurrection, take up this theme. They show Christ conquering in the underworld, trampling the prostrate personification of Hades, the iconographic successor to the Greek god, while he leads Adam and his progeny to his kingdom.[74]

---

71. Other examples include Matt. 3:2, 4:17, 25:34; Rev. 21:5.

72. Al-Azmeh, *Monotheistic Kingship*, 16.

73. Trans. Gerald Hawthorne, in "A New English Translation of Melito's Pascal Homily," in *Current Issues in Biblical and Patristic Interpretation* (Grand Rapids, MI: William B. Eerdmans, 1975), 147–75, at 173; quoted in Kevin Roddy, "Politics and Religion in Late Antiquity: The Roman Imperial *Adventus* Ceremony and the Christian Myth of the Harrowing of Hell," *Apocrypha* 11 (2000): 147–79, at 150; Greek from Méliton de Sardes, *Sur la Pâque* 101, line 775; ed. Othmar Perler, SC 123 (Paris: Éditions du Cerf, 1966), p. 120.

74. Johannes G. Deckers, "Gnade für Hades? Beobachtungen am Bild der Anastasis," *Jahrbuch für Antike und Christentum* 50 (2007): 123–39. To the linguistic data, Deckers adds (127) numismatic evidence of triumphant Roman commanders posing with fallen barbarian enemies pinned to the ground by the standard of the legion. This tradition enters Christian iconography in a solidus by Emperor Valens of 364–67 CE, where the "standard" has become the labarum, the monogram of Christ, surmounting a staff (Deckers, pl. 8e). For this iconography, see Anna Kartsonis, *Anastasis: The Making of an Image* (Princeton, NJ: Princeton University Press, 1986), 64–81, 147, and pls. 14a, 17b, 44a, 57, 62, etc.

It may be objected that Christianity has nothing to do with governing empires. "My kingdom is not of this world," says Jesus in John 18:36. Earthly application of political theology would therefore seem to distort faith.[75] But, after the end of persecution in 313 and beginning with Constantine's patronage of the church, it became much easier to apply the biblical counsels that endorsed the authority of legitimate government: "Render to Caesar the things that are Caesar's" (Mark 12:17; Luke 20:25; Matt. 22:21); "Let every person be subject to the governing authorities" (Rom. 13:1). Thereafter, many Christian writers (Augustine is an exception) embraced the assimilation between divine rule and imperial power that pagan rulers had used before. Lactantius understood that Christian prayers formerly offered for the stability of the state now seek the "lasting tranquility of the flourishing *church.*"[76] Where one might previously have expected a reference to "the world," Lactantius hopefully, expectantly, almost apocalyptically substitutes "the church."

If God legislates and judges, so, like a commander, he conquers. A Byzantine slogan engraved on the Host as early as the fifth century is *Jesus Christus nika* (conquers). Gradually the expression migrated onto coinage under Constantine V (741–775), an iconoclast emperor.[77] Whether the lord in question is human or divine, the verbs for rulership remain the same. Thus, at a council in Constantinople in 536, the bishops acclaimed the emperor saying, "The orthodox faith of the emperor conquers, reigns," and, of the emperor Justin himself, "Justin Augustus, you conquer, Justin reigns."[78] Other examples occur in the liturgy of Easter, where Christ's approach to Jerusalem assimilated the acclamations used in imperial ceremonies called the *adventus,* to mark the emperor's approach to a subject city.[79]

---

75. Thus Podskalsky, "Politische Theologie in Byzanz." Thomas F. Mathews argues that key visual images represent Christ not as emperor, but rather as God. Mathews, *The Clash of Gods: A Reinterpretation of Early Christian Art,* revised and expanded ed. (1993; Princeton, NJ: Princeton University Press, 1999), 3–22. J.-M. Spieser offers a moderate approach to the points Mathews raises. Spieser, "The Representation of Christ in the Apses of Early Christian Churches," *Gesta* 37.1 (1998): 63–73, at 65–66. As for the problems associated with the scholarship of Ernst Kantorowicz, and particularly *The King's Two Bodies,* emphasized by Mathews, see the evaluative discussions collected by Lorna Hutson in *Representations* 106 (Spring 2009). The relevant Byzantine data are well surveyed in Al-Azmeh, *Monotheistic Kingship,* 19–21.

76. "Florescentis ecclesiae perpetuam quietem." Lactantius, *De mortibus persecutorum* 52.5; ed. and trans. J. L. Creed, Oxford Early Christian Texts (Oxford and New York: Clarendon Press, 1984), 76 (my emphasis); quoted in Adolph Martin Ritter, "Church and State up to c. 300 CE," in *The Cambridge History of Christianity* (Cambridge: Cambridge University Press, 2007), 1:536 and n. 68.

77. Ernst Kantorowicz, *Laudes Regiae: A Study in Liturgical Acclamations and Mediaeval Ruler Worship* (Berkeley and Los Angeles: University of California Press, 1958), 8.

78. Ibid., 26.

79. Roddy, "Politics and Religion in Late Antiquity," *Apocrypha* 11 (2000): 147–79, at 178. Roddy unfortunately refers to hell as the place where souls await the coming of Christ, when it is clearly

There were important consequences to the interaction between the ideological needs of the empire and the theological views of divinity. As Mark Edwards puts it, "The monarchy of Constantine could not tolerate a fragmented church."[80] To assure unity, emperors imposed restrictions on deviant ideas. Condemnations of thought are evident in councils from Nicaea on. A glance at Title XVI of the Theodosian Code will support this thesis for the period from Constantine to Theodosius II (312–438).[81] This record shows how the emperors first allowed Christianity to take root alongside the state religion and the many other cults that varied from region to region and were administered by heads of households. Gradually, they imposed penalties on non-Christian beliefs and practices. Finally, they made Christianity the sole legal religion.

Two aspects of this development stand out. First, there is the generic representation of imperial sanctions: the emperors' disciplinary action strikes [heretics] "first by divine vengeance and then by the punishment of our [imperial] action inspired by the celestial will.[82] The emperors claim their measures reinforce God's. Second, there is the determined pursuit of uniformity in religion. Penalties established against heretics or those who sacrificed in depraved cults are dropped for those who confess "the faith of the one religion" (simplicis fidem religionis).[83] Religio simplex is a crucial phrase. It suggests the emperors' goal in repressing the multitude of sects and faiths in the empire: uniformity of creed for uniformity of behavior and loyalty. Taking the root of "religion" (lex = law) literally, the program becomes "one faith, one law"—all to facilitate loyalty to one emperor who claims to model his rule on that of the one God. Thus the emperor Justinian could claim:

> The greatest gifts of God that in his heavenly clemency he has bestowed on the human race are the priesthood and the imperial command, the one serving what concerns divine things, the other providing care and supervision of human affairs. Both, however, proceed from *one and the same* origin and embellish human life.[84]

Hades. More important is his understanding of the similarity between liturgical acclamations from the late imperial Adventus and sermons preaching the Descent and liberation of the dead from Hades as an "accommodation" and an "appropriation of Roman imperial political language."

80. Mark Edwards, "The First Council of Nicaea," in *Cambridge History of Christianity*, 1:552–67, at 552.

81. See *Les lois religieuses des empereurs romains de Constantin à Théodose II (312–438)*, vol. 1, *Code Théodosien, Livre XVI*, ed. Theodor Mommsen, trans. Jean Rougé, with Roland Delmaire and François Richard, SC 497 (Paris: Cerf, 2005); henceforth CTh.

82. CTh 16.1.2; pp. 114–15.

83. CTh 16.5.41 (407); pp. 290–91.

84. Justinian, *Novellae*, 6, preface; *Corpus Iuris Civilis*, vol. 3, *Novellae*, ed. R. Schoell and G. Kroll, 6th ed. (Berlin: Weidmann, 1954), 35–36 (my emphasis); cited in D. M. Nicol, "Byzantine

The view that divine and human jurisdictions reinforced one another moved not only westward from Constantinople under Justinian, but also eastward from Rome under Pope Gregory I. (Just as Justinian directed military operations in western North Africa and Italy, so, before becoming pope, Gregory had served as a diplomat in Constantinople.) Political utility and religious security seemed to necessitate a theology supportive of the parallel officially asserted, in church and state, in papal and imperial administrations, between divine and human rule.

Clemency Granted and Withheld

The parallels reciprocally claimed for divine and monarchical justice lie at the heart of important reflections on the converse of this model, clemency. Peter Brown has examined precisely this more lenient side of Roman justice.[85] Brown observes the Easter amnesties some emperors granted in the late fourth century were modeled on Christ's own mercy, which the emperors put at the center of their style of government. The imperial amnesty to which Brown alludes took the form of a grace granted every Easter to "release from confinement all those persons who are bound by criminal charges or who are confined in prison."[86] "God's amnesty would wipe clean the slate of human sins, much as an emperor on earth was known to pardon criminals and remit arrears in taxes."[87] Again, "God's supreme power assumed, on an imperial model, an uncircumscribed reserve of mercy that overshadowed the strict implementation of his justice."[88] In this theory, the image of God rises from social institutions.

The pardon, however, had its limitations. In the amnesty issued in 381 or soon after, the emperors prefaced their decree with the usual introductory language that invoked both the feast of Easter and the drama of the Descent: "The day of Easter joy permits not even those persons that have committed crimes to be afraid. The terrible prison shall at that time be open to the unaccustomed light."[89] Thus, Easter provided an exception to the regular admin-

---

Political Thought," in *The Cambridge History of Medieval Political Thought, c. 350–c. 1450*, ed. J. H. Burns (Cambridge: Cambridge University Press, 1988), 51–91, at 68; and quoted in Meyendorff, *Byzantine Theology*, 213.

85. Peter Brown, "The Decline of the Empire of God: Amnesty, Penance, and the Afterlife from Late Antiquity to the Middle Ages," in Bynum and Freedman, *Last Things*, 41–59.

86. CTh 9.38.3 (of 367 or 369); trans. C. Pharr, p. 253a; *Theodosiani Libri XVI*, ed. T. Mommsen, p. 496. See above, chapter 3.

87. Brown, "Decline," 46.

88. Ibid., 48.

89. CTh 9.38.6; Pharr, p. 254b; *Theodosiani Libri XVI*, ed. T. Mommsen, p. 497.

istration of justice, but there were exceptions to the exception. Excluded from this grant of pardon are those guilty of treason, parricide (in the broad sense of killing any relative), murder, adultery, rape, incest, poisoning, use of magic, and counterfeiting. In addition to adding more crimes to the list, this pardon also excludes repeat offenders. The emperors add this restriction so that "the kindness of our august generosity (*liberalitatis augustae . . . humanitas*) may not be extended again to those persons who have used their impunity for an old crime—not for the purpose of reformation (*emendatio*), but for the purpose of habitual criminality."[90] The Easter amnesty could not apply to capital punishments, but only to various forms of exile, labor in the mines, and forced labor in less onerous conditions, such as imperial factories or civic bakeries. The post-Constantinian penal system, therefore, employed graded punishments matched to the severity of the crime. The Easter amnesty, like the later theology and vision literature about the purgatorial fire, limited itself to those considered able to benefit from the grace extended. Those guilty of unpardonable offenses suffered irreversible condemnation to death. Thus the pardon continues: "The person guilty of sacrilege against the Imperial Majesty, the person guilty of crimes against the dead, the sorcerer, or magician, the adulterer, ravisher, or homicide shall be excluded from participation in that boon." Thus, each in their own way, both imperial and divine mercy employed a notion of calibrated punishment and created a conceptual background for the eventual emergence of purgatory as an alternative to hell within the political and social contexts of the late empire and the early Middle Ages.

Even if the emperors thought that by releasing prisoners at Eastertide they might encourage the criminals' improvement, they indicate no expectation that the convicts have made any inner effort to anticipate, to participate, to "merit," the release. The contrary holds for the penitential system built on Paul's fire, which tests the sort of work each one has done (from 1 Corinthians 3:13). A similar inner disposition applies for Jews in the rabbinic interpretation of atonement that begins the New Year. Like Gregory I's theological principles, the Irish penitential system also calibrated degrees of guilt and prescribed exercises, penances, aimed at eradicating the stain.[91] Imperial

---

90. Ibid. The related Sirmondian Constitutions 7 and 8 provide further detail; see CTh, Pharr, pp. 480–81; *Theodosiani Libri XVI*, ed. T. Mommsen, pp. 913–14. The list or description of unpardonable crimes varies from act to act. Michael Hendy lists "the five classic capital crimes of treason, sorcery, murder, adultery, or rape," with counterfeiters added after 381. Hendy, *Studies in the Byzantine Monetary Economy: c. 300–1450* (New York: Cambridge University Press, 1985), 323.

91. "The two systems were drawn together by a fundamental homology. . . . The two traditions collapsed in on one another." Brown, "Decline," 55.

amnesty was a sudden release, but it applied only to noncapital offenses. In Origen's system neglect of God leads to postmortem cycles of suffering and progressive amendment. Gregory of Nyssa has Macrina refer to a gradual dematerialization that overcomes one's love of the flesh. Universalism did not exempt sinners from punishment all in one stroke. It involved a struggle to recover the divine image in the soul. The rescues from Hades catalogued by Trumbower involved temporary pain and implied an ability on the part of the beneficiary to comprehend the divine message or recover a focus on divine help. These concurrent efforts to deal with less than absolute guilt, pardonable offenses committed by those who can benefit from mercy and correction, that is, the system that would become purgatory, developed side by side with a theology that insisted, with imperial support, that complete sovereignty demands the power to punish with finality, the power to punish absolutely—that is, hell.

Byzantium's universalist theologians devised a Christian system in which all postmortem punishment might be temporary. But emperors deliberately assimilated their own sovereignty to God's and assumed, as a vital corollary, the possibility of absolute sanctions: to pardon, but also to kill. Justinian in particular, in 543, and in 553 at the Second Council of Constantinople, took calculated steps to assure the unrestricted continuation of this parallel. Abetted by advisers to be sure, his condemnation of Origenism effectively ended open debate of the question. To this end, he acted to defend that very hell. Peter Brown has summed up the situation. "*Clementia* was an all-important imperial prerogative because the act of forgiveness was a stunning suspension on the part of a Roman emperor of an untrammeled power to harm. It was the same with God."[92] The power to pardon depends on the power to condemn. In order to preserve that power Justinian, like Gregory I, protected the concept and propagated the fear of hell as an aspect of his own monarchical position.

---

92. Brown, "Decline," 47.

CHAPTER 9

Islam

The Mockers Mocked

> That which they mocked at hemmed them in.
>
> —Sura 6:10

> We shall leave him in the path he has chosen, and land him in hell,—What an evil refuge!
>
> —Sura 4:115

> Not one of you but will pass over it [hell].
>
> —Sura 19:71

> O my Lord, if I worship Thee from fear of Hell, burn me in Hell; and if I worship Thee from hope of Paradise, exclude me thence; but if I worship Thee for Thine own sake, then withhold not from me Thine Eternal Beauty.
>
> —Rābiʿa of Basra

As a monotheistic religion that shares a legacy with Judaism and Christianity, Islam has many beliefs with counterparts in the other faiths. Eschatology is one area where these similarities are particularly strong. Some of these common features come from this shared heritage, but Islamic eschatology's particular characteristics derive from the special historical background out of which Islam grew. Pre-Muslim Arabia was polytheistic, but its inhabitants had some familiarity with the principal tenets of Judaism, Christianity, and Zoroastrianism. In his presentation of a universal monotheism, Muhammad therefore emerged between two different rivalries. There were the older, indigenous, regional divinities and the "foreign" monotheisms. Against polytheism, the Qur'ān scorns the earlier gods as merely "associates" or "partners" with God, who, in their base mimicry, offend the deity (6:20). Loyalty to these lesser powers is damning (10:66, 28:61–64, 28:68, 30:40, 42:21). "Soon shall we cast terror into the hearts of the unbelievers, for that they joined partners with God, for which he had sent no authority: their abode will be the Fire: and evil is the home of the wrong-doers!" (3:151). The old gods of Arabian polytheism figure as prominent antagonists in the new Scripture because both Muhammad's own tribe, the Quraysh, and other, rival tribes, resisted the revelation he recited to them. The Qur'ān accuses these tribal elders of leading the people astray. They are not leaders, but, as rendered by Abdullah Yusuf Ali, the translator of the Qur'ān whose English I quote, "misleaders" (38:60).[1]

Knowledge of Judaism and Christianity from its inception suggests ideas common to the three religions, but crucial differences remain. One of the most important concerns the genealogy of the Muslim community as compared to the Jews. In Genesis 22, when God tests the faith of Abraham, the son he is to sacrifice is the younger Isaac, borne to him by his wife Sarah. Abraham's nation is then said to descend from Isaac, the son of a free woman. In Sura 37:100–113, the Qur'ān covers this material differently. The victim to be sacrificed is Ishmael, Abraham's elder son by Hagar, a servant woman. In return for the exemplary submission of both Abraham and Ishmael, Abraham is granted Isaac, a son by Sarah, but his descendants are reckoned through Ishmael, the elder son.[2]

The written evidence for the revelation enshrined in the Qur'ān results from an oral tradition and a long process of editing. Islamic tradition holds that Uthman, the third caliph (644–56), canonized the Qur'ān in its present form.[3] Recent scholarship, however, proposes an examination based on the same source-critical techniques that have benefited understanding of

---

1. The renderings of qur'ānic passages are based on Abdullah Yusuf Ali, *The Holy Qur'ān: English Translation of the Meanings and Commentary* (Mushaf Al-Madinah an-Nabawiyah, Saudi Arabia, 1410/1990), a gift of my friend Said Haimor in Oakland, California. In quoting Yusuf Ali, I have changed "Allah" to "God" and some instances of capitalization. This Saudi edition takes some liberties with Yusuf Ali's original translation, available online. When necessary for clarity, I compare Yusuf Ali's translation to that of A. J. Arberry, *The Koran Interpreted* (New York: Macmillan, 1955). Note, for example, that Yusuf Ali translates "Jahannam" as "Hell," but Arberry renders it as "Gehenna." This alone might recommend Arberry over Yusuf Ali, but, alas, for all his poetry, Arberry's translation is too elusive for those approaching the Qur'ān for the first time. Moreover, words that Arberry regards as implicit, and suppresses, Yusuf Ali displays in parentheses. He also matches his lines of English one for one with the Arabic, as Arberry does not. When I feel Arberry's language is clearer, I append the abbreviation "ar" after the reference to sura and verse. This chapter was mostly written before Oxford University Press published M. A. S. Abdel Haleem's very readable translation in 2004.

2. Shosh Ben-Ari, "Stories about Abraham in Islam: A Geographical Approach," *Arabica* 54.4 (2007): 526–53, at 548–50.

3. Gerhard Endress, *An Introduction to Islam*, trans. Carole Hillenbrand (New York: Columbia University Press, 1988), 23.

the Hebrew Bible and the New Testament.[4] Specialists in this method have extended the period of qur'ānic composition considerably.

The Qur'ān presents models such as Noah, Abraham, Moses, John the Baptist, Jesus, and others as indications of how humans should live and worship (40:78). Muhammad is also called a "warner," in that he has warned humanity of the penalty for not accepting the New Dispensation (35:23–24). Just as creation and resurrection celebrate God's creative (and re-creative) power, so divine judgment guarantees a fair assignment to heaven as reward and hell as punishment (22:5). Sura 98, entitled "The Clear Evidence," sums up. There was a time when Jews, Christians, and Zoroastrians coexisted with polytheists among the local tribes. Then God revealed the Qur'ān to Muhammad, but some refused to obey despite the fact that the demands were simple: believe, pray, give alms. Finally, according to their acceptance of the new revelation, God will assign all people to an eternity full of either pleasure or pain. Hell is therefore an integral part of Islam.[5] It is vividly and symbolically expressed by synecdoche: individual aspects represent the whole concept. Thus Jannah (the Garden) stands for paradise, and Nar (the Fire) or Tannur (the Oven) for hell, which also has the technical name, Jahannam, a transliteration of the Hebrew, Gehinnom, parallel to the Greek transliteration, Gehenna.

Hell in the Qur'ān

For the damned, intimations of the truths taught by Islam emerge as one enters the grave. Hell suddenly appears in the distance, and unbelievers begin to realize that the teachings of the Qur'ān are true (77:29; also 83:14–18). These dead will wish to return to life to amend their ways and affirm the new faith, but they will be prevented by a barrier called the Barzakh (23:100).[6]

---

4. See, for example, John Wansbrough, *Quranic Studies: Sources and Methods of Scriptural Interpretation*, London Oriental Studies 31 (Oxford: Oxford University Press, 1977); Estelle Whelan, "Forgotten Witness: Evidence for the Early Codification of the Qur'ān," *Journal of the American Oriental Society* 118.1 (1998); 1–14; and the essays collected in Andrew Rippin, ed., *The Qur'ān: Formative Interpretation* (Brookfield, VT: Ashgate, 1999), especially the first chapter, by Claude Gilliot, "The Beginnings of Qur'ānic Exegesis," 1–28; Brannon M. Wheeler, *Prophets in the Quran: An Introduction to the Quran and Muslim Exegesis*, Comparative Islamic Studies (London: Continuum, 2002).

5. Nerina Rustomji, *The Garden and the Fire: Heaven and Hell in Islamic Culture* (New York: Columbia University Press, 2008), 20.

6. For the Barzakh, see Ragnar Eklund, *Life between Death and Resurrection according to Islam*, Inaugural Dissertation (Uppsala: Almqvist & Wiksells, 1941); Jane Idleman Smith and Yvonne Yazbeck Haddad, *Islamic Understanding of Death and Resurrection* (Albany: SUNY Press, 1981), 31–61 and 121–26; Mohammad Hassan Khalil, *Islam and the Fate of Others: The Salvation Question* (Oxford: Oxford University Press, 2012), 18 and 158 n. 73.

Here, those who denied resurrection nevertheless find themselves resurrected and facing divine scrutiny. The character of hell will then be apparent.[7] Those who scoffed at reports of hell's existence will run in desperation, but in vain, to locate intercessors. That sense of late recognition of the truth, which now penetrates the sinners' innards, is crucial to the Qur'ān's account of damnation. So, too, are the taunts of the saved and even those of the divine judge.

The Qur'ānic Hellscape

The damned begin to suffer immediately at the Resurrection, since this very event proves the prophecies they rejected to be true. This is the "Sorting," the "Day," or the "Hour" when the risen undergo a separation of the good from the wicked. The wicked receive their sentence: "God will collect the hypocrites and those who defy faith—all in hell" (4:140). This fate follows from ignoring the guidance of Muhammad and the Qur'ān: "We shall leave him in the path he has chosen, and land him in hell,—What an evil refuge! (4:115). Here is the oral quality of the Qur'ān. It demands an inflection to express scorn for the wicked. Thus, frequently, after hell or the Fire is mentioned, the text adds a taunt: "an evil bed indeed (to lie on)!" (e.g., at 2:206; 3:12, 197; 18:29; 38:56).

The Day comes, "and Hell-fire shall be placed in full view for him who sees. Then, for such as had transgressed all bounds, and had preferred the life of this world, the Abode will be Hell-fire" (79:36–38). So clear is fire's primacy as a torment, that the Arabic *nār* (fire) outnumbers the occurrences of Jahannam (Gehenna, Hell). The *Concordance of the Qur'an* by Hanna Kassis gives 106 instances for *nār* (not counting common "fire") to 68 for Jahannam and 8 for the expression "fire of Gehenna."[8] "Your abode is the Fire, and no helpers have ye!" (45:33–34). The inmates of hell are "hemmed in" (40:83) by their fate, as a voice commands, "Embrace ye the Fire" (36:63).

The hellscape also presents other features, but the other terms for hell can barely compete with fire. It can be the Oven, the Burning (38:55), the Blaze, which casts off sparks the size of forts (77:32–33). It is also referred to as the Darkness (80:40) and the "bottomless Pit" (101:9). The damned wander in boiling water (55:43–44). From the fire, three columns of smoke

    7. Einar Thomassen, "Islamic Hell," *Numen* 56 (2009): 401–16; Ludwig Hagemann, "Die 'letzten Dinge' in der Sicht des Korans: Sterben und Weiterleben in islamischer Deutung," in *Unsterblichkeit und Eschatologie im Denken des Nikolaus von Kues*, ed. K. Kremer and K. Reinhardt, Mitteilungen und Forschungsbeiträge der Cusanus-Gesellschaft 23 (Trier: Paulinus-Verlag, 1996), 119–38.
    8. Hanna E. Kassis, *A Concordance of the Qur'an* (Berkeley: University of California Press, 1983), 589–90, 856–68.

rise up, casting shadows, which, however, provide no relief; they are useless against the Blaze (70:30–31). Normally a tree would provide shade, but not Zaqqum, the "tree that springs out of the bottom of Hell-fire" (37:62–64), whose fruit resembles the heads of Satans (35:65–66) and, once eaten, will rake the insides of all who ingest it (56:52–53).[9] Prominent also in the landscape is Barzakh, the barrier that prevents the dead from returning to life before the Resurrection (23:100) and prevents the wicked in hell from polluting the joys of the Garden (23:101).

Beyond hell's physical environment there is its eternity: "From the fire there is no escape" (4:121) and "from it there is no appeal" (41:24). It is unending, but not unvarying. Its temperature may decline, but fresh stoking returns it to full heat (17:97). There is thus a vicious cycle. Burnt skin is restored so the punishment may endure (4:56). The result is a paradox: though the fire and the bodies it burns are cyclically consumed and restored, the punishment itself destroys the person and deserves the nickname "That Which Breaks to Pieces" or, as A. J. Arberry translates it, "The Crusher" (104:4–6). Despite its cyclical variations (fire cools, then is stoked; skin burns, then is restored), the overall pattern is endless. "And when they are cast, bound together, into a constricted place therein, they will plead for destruction there and then!" (25:11–13). But hell's ecology averts annihilation: "This day plead not for a single destruction: Plead for destruction oft-repeated!" (25:14). The irony here is palpable and fatal because the extinction the sinners desire only recycles them for more pain.[10]

Because the Blaze transcends the individual sinner to embrace all the wicked, this fire of God resembles an overarching vault (104:7–8). The vault can also appear as a monstrous gullet or paunch, whose gluttonous heaving the wicked hear (25:12) as it breathes in new arrivals (67:7). The unbelievers are the fire's fuel, the gullet's fodder (21:96, 66:6–7). Nineteen (74:30–31) attendant angels (not, as in Christian literature, demons) cast them in (26:94). As in the Talmud's Ge-Hinnom, Jahannam is once considered female: "One day we shall ask hell, 'Are you full?' and she will say, 'Are there more?'" (50:30).[11]

---

9. See David M. Freidenreich, "The Food of the Damned," in *Between Heaven and Hell: Islam, Salvation, and the Fate of Others*, ed. Mohammad Hassan Khalil (Oxford: Oxford University Press, 2013), 255–72.

10. Cf. "Soon he will cry for perdition" (84:10–12); "[In hell] shall he neither die nor live" (20:74).

11. Cited by Rosalind W. Gwynne, "Hell and Hellfire," in *Encyclopaedia of the Qur'ān*, ed. Jane Dammen McAuliffe (Leiden: Brill, 2001–6), 2:414, col. 1. Both Yusuf Ali and Arberry refer to hell (Gehenna) in this passage as "it."

As the fire destroys and restores its victims, angels preside over every aspect of the proceedings. They dialogue with the dead, they surround the throne of God (39:75), they prepare the heavens for the Sorting, then they gently remove the souls of the blessed but violently extract those of the wicked (79:1–2); they guide the damned into hell, stoke the flames, and administer the punishments. They are the chief officials of hell, its keepers, its wardens, who taunt the damned as they approach its gates (39:71). At their head is Mālik (43:77), whose name is also the Arabic word for "king."[12] Though the Qur'ān names him only once, this overlap implies a potential monarchical, hierarchical arrangement for hell.

Physical Torments

As much as fire pervades hell's overall environment, the Qur'ān details its many effects on the damned. They are heaped up in hell (8:37); herded: "And we shall drive the sinner to hell (like thirsty cattle driven down to water)" (19:86); "marched in ranks to the Fire" (41:19); "led there in groups" (39:71); bound together (25:13). These piles group like with like (81:7). At the moment of the Sorting, God "will parade them about Gehenna hobbling on their knees" (19:69ar), humiliated in terror and confusion. In dread, they bite their hands (25:27). Then, seized by their forelocks and their feet (55:41), they are dragged "prone on their faces" (17:95, 25:34) to spend eternity in the Fire.

Their bodies indicate their individual character in this moment that recapitulates their moral history: "Their hands will speak to us and their feet bear witness, to all that they did" (36:65). They will be "known by their marks" (55:41). The distinctiveness of some punishments serves to identify the individual enduring them. In one dramatic case, an unnamed woman is sentenced eternally to carry the fuel needed to torture her husband. A noose around her neck binds her to her task and to her husband (111:5). This notorious man nicknamed Abū Lahab, or "Father of Flames," was an uncle of the Prophet. He is the only individual named in the Qur'ān as a resident of hell. Although a kinsman, he opposed Muhammad's message, cursed the new religion, and remained loyal to a tribal goddess named al-'Uzzā.[13] Despite obvious differences, the punishment of Abū Lahab's wife recalls the tale in

---

12. Kassis, *Concordance*, 765–68. The reference is to the root *M L K. Associated meanings are the following: dominion, the functions of ownership, rule, mastery (as over a slave), and the titles King, Prince, Master. The noun MALAK is an angel, and in the passage referred to here, 43:77, it is the proper name of Mālik, Prince or King of the Angels.

13. Uri Rubin, "Abū Lahab and Sūra CXI," *Bulletin of the School of Oriental and African Studies* 42.1 (1979): 13–28.

which Rabbi Johanan sees the dead man bearing wood for his own punishment. Another figure in hell is one 'Amr ibn Lu'ayy, who is identified and
described not in the Qur'ān, but in later, oral tradition. This second exception underlines the rarity of specifying the names of sinners, rather than
the categories of the damned.[14] According to this tradition reported by Ibn
Ishaq in his biography of Muhammad, the Prophet said, "I saw 'Amr ibn
Luḥayy dragging his intestines in hell." His sin was to deviate from strict
monotheism. "He was the first to change the religion of [Abraham and] Ishmael, to set up idols, and institute" customs that honored false gods. In sum,
"he introduced idol worship into Arabia." Since his deviation would have
occurred before the introduction of Islam, this idea presupposes an original
Arabian monotheism abandoned prior to Muhammad's restoration.[15] Both
these men and Abū Lahab's wife fit the category of sinners identifiable by
their punishments and visibly distinct in hell.

Once the Sorting is complete, the angels charged with the torments apply
specialized equipment. To herd the wicked, they apply yokes (13:5; cf. 76:4);
to confine them, fetters (14:49); to drag them, chains (40:71) precisely seventy cubits long (69:32). These assaults on the body affect the physical person
entirely, rendering them blind, dumb, and deaf (17:97), thirsty and hungry
(7:50). The hunger and thirst explain the need for food and drink in hell.
The Tree of Zaqqum, rooted in hellfire, plays a particular role here. Like
the pillars of smoke and the cloud, this tree provides no shade, no comfort.
Indeed, it yields a crop of devils' heads (37:58–62), the food of the damned,
whose insides become filled with its fruit (56:52). When consumed, the pulp
of Zaqqum boils inside like scalding water (44:43–46). Then, on top of this
Zaqqum mush, Gehenna's administrators force-feed their prisoners boiling
water (56:54) that cuts up their bowels (47:15).[16] As repelled as they are by
these refreshments, the damned will "drink like fevered, thirsty camels" (56:5).

Psychological Torments

Hell's psychological torments begin at the Resurrection and the Sorting,
when late recognition that the prophecy of resurrection was correct instills

---

14. For 'Amr b. Lu'ayy, see Ibn Ishaq, *The Life of Muhammad: A Translation of Ibn Ishaq's Sirat Rasul
Allah*, trans. A. Guillaume (Karachi: Oxford University Press, 1967), 35.

15. Uri Rubin, *Encyclopaedia of Islam, THREE*, Brill Online, accessed May 22, 2010, http://www.
brillonline.nl/subscriber/entry?entry=ei3_SIM-0327.

16. A related punishment existed in ancient Egypt. *The Book of Gates*, second division, mentions a
water that refreshes worshippers of the true god, but, when fraudulently imbibed by worshippers of
false gods, turns to fire and consumes them. E. A. Wallis Budge, *The Egyptian Heaven and Hell* (1905;
La Salle, IL: Open Court, 1974), 118–19.

dread in the scoffers. At that moment, a chorus of jibes confronts them and becomes a part of their damnation. "(A voice will say,) 'this is the Day of sorting out, whose truth ye (once) denied!'" (37:20). The Qur'ān describes a pain analogous to what Augustine called "fruitless repentance": "The day that their faces will be turned over in the fire they will say: 'Woe to us! Would that we had obeyed God and obeyed the Messenger!'" (33:66). This principle also applies to the denial of hell. "[Scoffers] will be completely encircled by that which they used to mock at!" (45:33; cf. 6:10). There is also the consciousness that these torments will never end. Hell's inmates would prefer not to exist. To the chief angel of hell, they call, "O Mālik! Would that thy Lord put an end to us!" (43:74). To themselves, they moan, "O would that I were dust!" (78:40). The idea of wishing to die, but not being able to, is Pope Gregory the Great's living death, dying life, endless dying, life despite death. In the Qur'ān, one's immediate recognition of hell's eternity and the eternal continuation of that recognition are the worst of its psychological torments. The damned will seek a lightening of their pain, even for a day. It will be denied (40:49–50). God replies: "Did we not give you long enough life so that he that would should receive admonition? And (moreover) the Warner came to you. So taste ye (the fruits of your deeds): For the Wrong-doers there is no helper" (35:37).

Qur'ānic Theodicy

In the Qur'ān, hell's physical and psychological torments fit within a judicial framework that makes them the outcome of errors either of faith or of behavior in life. The justice of these eternal fates emerges even more clearly from its portrayal of the final, divine judgment. The Qur'ān illustrates the justice of the Splitting (82) by a series of mechanisms drawn from human institutions and useful for rendering financial accounts or keeping records. Thus there is a scale or a balance of deeds (7:8–9), and those whose good deeds are heavy "are the prosperers," and those whose good deeds are light "have lost their souls; in hell they will abide" (23:102–3).[17] Sura 83 discusses swindlers and implicitly contrasts them to the divine accounting while simultaneously threatening them with it. There is a book for good deeds called *Illiyin*, and a book for evil deeds called *Sijjin* (83:7–9), but the Reckoning is not a purely mechanical exercise. It illustrates to the sinners the source of their own guilt. It is the culmination of self-knowledge. Individuals now see that the smallest of their thoughts or deeds might determine their fate. The

---

17. Sura 101:6–11 contains an equally explicit use of the metaphor of the balance.

atom's weight of good or evil, already known to God, will now be visible to the accused! (99:7–8). The dialogues with the Voice that sounds at the time of the Resurrection further dramatize the justice of the judgment: "You are requited naught save what you did" (37:39). Wages provide another prominent metaphor. One "earns" one's punishment: "To every soul will be paid in full (the fruit) of its deeds" (39:70); "That Day will every soul be requited for what it earned" (40:17). The term "requital" (ya) or "recompense" (ar) recurs frequently in Suras 39–41. This quantitative or even commercial image is fundamental to the Qur'ān's theodicy.

The payback is not only equal in quantity to the guilt, but also similar in character to the fault: "Whosoever does an evil deed shall be recompensed only with the like of it" (40:40ar). The Arabic term for "like" as a noun is *mithl*. In Arberry's translation and the concordance by Kassis, the term also appears in this sense at 5:95, 6:160, 10:27, 16:126, 22:60, and 42:40. This principle is also true in worldly matters. An example of correct self-restraint is one who "chastises after the manner that he was chastised" (22:60ar). "Do you commit aggression against him the like as he has committed against you" (2:194ar) is a rationale given for jihad.[18] Punishment for a wrong with its like is the essence of retaliation.

Various types of retribution emerge. In *continuity* the punishment consists of some imposition in the future world of the very fault or passion indulged in this world. Thus, "those who were blind in this world will be blind in the Hereafter" (17:72). The continuity may also come from the lack of measure in both worlds, this one and the next. Those who thought their deeds would not be measured will find that in hell, too, their torments will not be measured (78:26–30). There is also the possibility of *contrast*. What one does to another during one's lifetime is done in return to the offender. I call this contrast "subject-object reverse," since the object of the verb in the first clause becomes the subject of the verb in the second or vice versa. Thus: " 'O my Lord, why hast thou raised me blind, and I was wont to see?' God shall say, 'Even so it is. Our signs came unto thee, and thou didst forget them; and so today thou are forgotten' " (20:125–26). Thus the sinner moves from not seeing God (or his signs) to being placed out of sight. Another type of contrast I call "reverse of action," when the subject remains the same in both clauses, but the verb changes into its opposite. Thus, those who followed other gods

---

18. The likeness of the penalty to the misdeed can be questioned, as this is also the reasoning behind the injunction to punish the thief by amputating the offending hands. "As to the thief, male or female, cut off his or her hands: a retribution for their deed and exemplary punishment from God" (5:38). For more on jihad, see Alfred Morabia, *Le Gihad dans l'islam médiéval: Le "combat sacré" des origines au XIIe siècle* (Paris: Albin Michel, 1993), esp. 293–97. I thank Megan Reid for this reference.

will be driven like cattle into hell (19:83–86). In this example, the sinners go from a life of choosing evil to an afterlife enduring evil. The clearest example of reverse of action is this: "those who wax too proud to do Me service shall enter Gehenna utterly abject" (40:60ar). Those who puffed themselves up find themselves pressed down. The use of syntax to dramatize the fit between the sin and the penalty highlights the punishment's justness. This clarity in the use of syntax to present the theodicial relationship of punishment to sin is similar to that in Dante's *Inferno*, where the poet expresses it with the term "contrapasso."

If retaliation matches the punishment to the crime, it is important to see which faults are specifically named as warranting postmortem requital. The most important of these is ingratitude, the failure to recognize God as benefactor of humankind and oneself. This vice denies the fundamental reason for Islam, submission to God. The Creator's munificence may be the most pervasive theme of the Qur'ān. His generosity flows from creation of the universe to conception of individuals to loving chastisement through the flood and other signs: sending the Messenger, dictating a Book of Warning in a readily accessible Arabic form. Therefore, anyone who fails in gratefulness opposes nature and history.[19] "If you are unthankful, God is independent of you" (39:7). There are other terms closely linked to this attitude. Thus Gehenna is the "abode of the arrogant" (16:29, 39:72, 40:76, and others) and of the haughty (39:60). The self-centeredness of the arrogant is clear from an eloquent example. In making sacrifices, these people throw into the fire the parts they themselves like the least: "Without any doubt theirs shall be the Fire and they are hastened in" (16:62).[20]

Beyond character flaws are the conscious decisions made in life by which people devote themselves to one cause, one leader, or another. The most dramatic example is the company of those who rejected God in order to follow the misleader Satan (Iblis). When the envious Iblis refused to prostrate himself before the newly created Adam, God said to Iblis, "I will certainly fill Hell with thee and those that follow thee, every one" (38:85). Thereafter, Satan has been free to lead humans astray. In life he appears as counselor or patron of his followers, but he will abandon them on the Day of Judgment, after which their punishment is grievous (16:63). Thus, all who follow Satan (17:61), all the hosts of Iblis (25:93), such as the ancestral misleaders and

---

19. Ingratitude: 7:8–10, 14:7, 14:28, 16:55 (see also 16:58, ingratitude for birth of a female child), 17:99, 22:38, 30:34, 39:7 (and, for the concept, not the term 39:49).

20. On sacrifice in Islam, see Maulana Muhammad Ali, *The Religion of Islam* (Lahore, Pakistan: The Ahmadiyya Anjuman Isha'at Islam, 1983), 427–30.

those who remained faithful to the old religion, are damned, but so, also, are those who imitate them by violating the Qur'ān and its precepts.

The confessions and laments uttered by the damned and the bite of words addressed to them give the representation of hell in the Qur'ān a special tone. They have many sources. Some come from "a voice." Some taunts upbraid the damned for their unbelief and evil deeds. Thus, at the time of the Sorting "(It will be said:) 'Depart ye to that which ye used to reject as false" (77:29). In Sura 44, the same Voice that orders the Keepers of Hell addresses the damned: "'Truly this is what ye used to doubt!'" (44:49–50). Some taunts come from hell's guardians. When the wicked arrive in hell, "its Keepers will say, 'Did not messengers come to you from among yourselves, rehearsing to you the signs of your Lord, and warning you of the Meeting of this Day of yours?'" (39:71; see also 67:5–14, an extended example).

As the damned recognize what is happening to them, they begin to quarrel among themselves and blame the people who misled them into the Fire. "(The followers shall cry to the misleaders:) 'Nay, ye (too)! No welcome for you! It is ye who have brought this upon us'!" (38:60). But being misled is no excuse. Following the ways of ancestors is another way of ignoring the New Dispensation: "And they would say: 'Our Lord! We obeyed our chiefs and our great ones, and they misled us as to the (right) path'" (33:67). Perhaps God will compensate by punishing the ancestors even more: "Our Lord! Give them double Chastisement and curse them with a very great Curse!" (33:68; cf. 41:25, 29; 38:61). Neither their ancient family gods nor their venerated ancestors will avail them (74:48). Indeed, depending on them instead of God is what led them astray. Thus the damned will heap abuse on their deceivers; they will ask God to punish them even more for deluding others. They will ask God for permission to take out their resentment on those they chose as models. Leading others away from true religion is also condemned strongly in the Talmud. Those of mixed virtues and vices who might otherwise escape postmortem punishment after a time are denied this benefit if one of their sins was leading the masses into sin.[21]

In contrast is the conduct of God's own tribunal (14:14). Just as no evil would remain unknown to him or unpunished, so no good could fail to count in a person's favor. His compassion shapes his justice. Two rhetorical questions suggest the necessity of this arrangement: "Shall we treat those who believe and work deeds of righteousness the same as those who do mischief on earth? Shall we treat those who guard against evil the same as those who turn aside from the right?" (38:28). Expressed in declarative terms, Sura

---

21. Rosh Hash. 17a; trans. Simon, p. 65; and 2 Kings 21:11, discussed above, chapter 7.

41:34 presents the axiom "Goodness and Evil [cannot] be equal." This state-ment is the Qur'ān's answer to Job, who questioned why the righteous and the sinners should "lie down alike in the dust" (Job 21:26; cf. 9:22).[22]

The Qur'ān, the Bible, the Talmud

As compared to the Hebrew Bible, where postmortem retribution makes only a late appearance and does not supplant the far older and more deeply held Deuteronomic theory of punishments in this life, or the Christian Scriptures, where eternal damnation occurs with frank poignancy but infrequently, the Qur'ān evokes hell vividly and often. Jahannam, the Fire, the Chastisement, and its many other guises appear at every level of discourse: theologically, it can be the return owed a creative and compassionate God; more viscerally, it can be an almost folkloric, ravenous beast lamenting an empty gullet.

But the Qur'ān's literal hell is not the whole story. Islamic Scripture opens windows to modifications similar to those in rabbinic and patristic sources and in the Christian vision literature. In Sura 19, named "Mary," hell's fire is turned to a potentially merciful purpose—a means of separating, at the last moment, the marginally good from the marginally wicked. At the time of resurrection, all who who did not believe it possible will be brought around hell on their knees. They will be evaluated for the degree of rebellion in each one.

(70.) . . . We know best
Those who are most worthy
Of being burned therein.

(71.) Not one of you but will
Pass over it: this is
With thy Lord, a decree
Which must be accomplished.

(72.) But we shall save those
Who guarded against evil,
And we shall leave
The wrong-doers therein,
(Humbled) to their knees. (19:70–72)

---

22. Alan E. Bernstein, *The Formation of Hell: Death and Retribution in the Ancient and Early Christian Worlds* (Ithaca, NY: Cornell University Press, 1993), 158.

The fire of Jahannam is more than a torment; it is an intelligent, judicious, judging fire. It can separate the completely wicked, whom it imprisons, from the moderately wicked, whom it singes but frees. All will either face it or go in. The passage begins with a reference to faith in the Resurrection; it ends by separating "those who guarded against evil" from "the wrong-doers." It would seem that even in the face of errors in belief, restraint from evil can be saving.

The Qur'ān promises that just as no wicked action will escape review, so no good deed will pass unnoticed: every "atom's weight" of good or evil will be measured (99:7–8). Just as every least good comes into view, so does a person's disposition. "God doth increase in guidance those who seek guidance" (19:76), but for anyone who "rejects our signs" (19:77), "we shall add and add to his punishment" (19:79). The punishment will therefore correspond to the "atom's weight" of evil done. Through this process, if you turn toward him, God guides you.

This doctrine has obvious affinities with the ideas of the calibration of guilt and its purgation in rabbinic, patristic, and early medieval Jewish and Christian thought. There is one fire, and all except those who need not be judged must either face or enter it, either temporarily or forever. In rabbinic thought, intermediate sinners are punished in Gehinnom for no more than a year unless they have committed one of the seven unpardonable sins, in which case they are confined forever.[23] Analogously, in commenting on 1 Corinthians 3:13, Augustine of Hippo stated, "The fire shall try every man's work," so that not even the just are spared this test.[24] Christian thinkers such as Caesarius of Arles, Julian of Toledo, and the visionary literature with its vague references to "the punitive places" or "the punishments" also combine temporary and eternal punishment in one fire.[25] The vagueness of these phrases expresses the double function of a fire that torments both the righteous to be cleansed eventually during the interim and the damned for eternity.

Although most of the Qur'ān's many references to postmortem retribution are to an inescapable hell, there are traces of some hesitation concerning eternal punishment. In particular, divine freedom, the overarching combination of omnipotence and mercy, suggests that God might spare a seemingly wicked person for a kindness, or damn a seemingly righteous one for a secret

---

23. Rosh Hash. 17a; trans. Simon, p. 64. See above, chapter 7.

24. Augustine, *Enchiridion de fide et spe et caritate* 68; CCSL 46, ed. E. Evans (1969), pp. 86–87; *The Enchiridion on Faith, Hope and Love*, trans. J. F. Shaw (South Bend, IN: Regnery/Gateway, 1961), 80–81.

25. See above, chapter 5, for the theologians; and chapter 6, for the visions.

sin. There may therefore be exceptions even for those condemned to the Fire. "He will say, 'The Fire be your dwelling-place: you will dwell therein for ever, except as God willeth' " (6:128).[26] God is free to extract anyone from the Blaze. Escape is theoretically possible.

Intercession

Human agents may appeal to divine mercy on behalf of others or to a limited number of recognized intercessors. In principle, intercession belongs only to God (39:44; 2:255). It seemed necessary to restrict the number of intercessors for various reasons. The danger of *shirk*, allowing lesser beings to seem like gods or to seem to rival God, reduced the number of those to whom intercession might be made because their reputations might be exaggerated. If too many intercessors were accepted, it might encourage complacency. It is significant that one statement inhibiting intercession comes in the Sura named for Mary: "None shall have the power of intercession, but such a one as has received permission from God most gracious" (19:87). Not all intercession is effective. Some angels cannot perform it (53:26), though, by inference, some can. There is good intercession and bad intercession, and one receives good or evil returns for whichever one performs (4:85, 57:28). Intercession is therefore not to be offered lightly. During the Sorting, resurrected humans under scrutiny may testify on each other's behalf (37:24–26) or present their own excuses (40:49–52). There is also a point after which it is no longer possible (2:254, 20:109, 74:48). Only the exceptionally virtuous see neither trial nor punishment.[27]

Though very carefully defined, it seemed necessary to preserve the possibility of appeal. Perhaps, like the considerations that eventually led to the doctrine of purgatory in Christianity, there was simply a reluctance to take hell too literally or to regard damnation too absolutely.[28] The Talmudic sages also preserved God's willingness to hear those who called from Gehinnom. By the same token, acceptance of Muhammad as God's prophet is a great act, and "God did call upon Muhammad to ask forgiveness for living believers (47:19), and this has been taken by many to be the earthly precedent

---

26. On the basis of this passage, Maulana Muhammad Ali claims the Islamic hell is purgatorial, not eternal (*Religion of Islam*, 303–5). See also Marcia Hermansen, "Acts of Salvation: Agency, Others, and Prayer beyond the Grave in Islam," in *Between Heaven and Hell, Islam, Salvation, and the Fate of Others*, ed. Mohammad Hassan Khalil (Oxford: Oxford University Press, 2013), 273–87.

27. This idea derives from 7:46–49. See Khalil, *Islam and the Fate of Others*, 40, 42, 45.

28. The subject of Khalil, *Islam and the Fate of Others*.

for intercession on the day of judgment."[29] The counsel that states, "If they repent it will be best for them" (e.g., 9:74), or "I am (also) he that forgives again and again, to those who repent, believe, and do right" (20:82), assumes a way to perform penance. Later tradition placed increasing emphasis on Muhammad as intercessor especially for the Muslim community, but the Qur'ān mentions yet another candidate.

Sura 16:120–23 points to Abraham as an example of correct faith and declares "he will be, in the hereafter, in the ranks of the righteous" (16:122). Sura 14 is named after him. Sura 11:75 praises Abraham for his compassion because he interceded on behalf of the people of Sodom, as recounted in Genesis 18:16–23. Contrary to the results in Genesis, the next qur'ānic verse has God refuse the petition concerning Sodom: "The decree of thy Lord hath gone forth: for them there cometh a chastisement that cannot be turned back" (11:76). Abraham also prayed for his father, who, in both Jewish and Muslim tradition, was considered an idolater. Abraham's hope was that his faith in the one God might avert disaster for his parent (19:41–50; cf. 37:83–99). The Qur'ān argues against using Abraham's prayer as a precedent, but the story of his filial devotion was too well-known through the three faith communities to be ignored. There apparently was an expectation or hope among Muslims that channels such as intercession might exist for the pious-but-imperfect even if not for the worst unbelievers, such as the residents of Sodom or idolaters like Abraham's father.[30]

Abraham's intercessory role is common to Islamic, Christian, and Jewish belief. He appears not only in Genesis 18, but also in the Christian Scriptures.[31] His availability is not to be taken for granted, as the rich man did in Luke 16:19–31. Paul and the evangelists warn of counting too heavily on Abraham's reputation. In Matthew 3:9 (Luke 3:8), John the Baptist warns the Sadducees and the Pharisees who sought baptism that empty gestures would avail them nothing. They should not presume to claim, "We have Abraham as our father." Paul varied this teaching when he argued that only those who conform to him in faith, as Abraham believed God, can truly be called children of Abraham (Gal. 3:7).

Theodicial reflection goes beyond emphasizing the fairness of judicial procedures in the Reckoning or the potential effectiveness of intercession. Nor does it limit itself to the figurative rereading of hell's grimmest

---

29. Smith and Haddad, *Islamic Understanding*, 26, cite Sura 47:19 as implying Muhammad as intercessor, though he is not named.

30. John W. Bowker, "Intercession in the Qur'an and the Jewish Tradition," *Journal of Semitic Studies* 11.1 (Spring 1966): 69–82.

31. Ibid., 78 n. 2.

features. Indeed, two countercurrents challenge the idea of the punitive afterlife so widespread in Islam. First is a strand of universalist interpretation, preserved in early oral tradition, claiming that once Jahannam has done its work its inmates will be freed.[32] One comment notes that ʿAbdullāh ibn Masʿūd (d. 32/652) recalled a saying to the effect that "ultimately Hell will be empty of its dwellers."[33] There is also a reference from ʿAbd ibn Ḥamīd (d. 249/863) to the effect that ʿUmar ibn al-Khaṭṭāb, a Companion of the Prophet and the second Sunnī caliph, stated that even if the ages of hell's duration were as numerous as the grains of sand in a large desert, there would be a time when "the People of the Fire" would come out.[34] Orthodox authorities such as al-Ṭabarī (d. 310/923) modified these views to suggest that only Muslims would eventually exit hell; polytheists are doomed to remain there forever.[35] Later still, Ibn Ḥazm (d. 456/1064) claimed authoritative consensus to assert the eternity of the fire.[36] In the early fourteenth century, the tradition arguing for the extinction of hell's fire and the exit of its prisoners resurfaced. Ibn Taymiyya (d. 728/1328) observed that in passages such as "Behold, Gehenna has become an ambush, for the insolent a resort, therein to tarry for ages" (78:21–23ar), "ages" signifies a very long time, but not necessarily eternity.[37] Ibn Taymiyya's student, Ibn Qayyim (d. 751/1350), went farther and argued that God has the eternal, essential attribute of mercy, and wrath is a lesser attribute. Since his wrath's purpose is to purify, it diminishes as it fulfills its objective. Thus hell will perish.[38] The debate over the meaning of "an age" or "ages of ages" also occurred in the Christian patristic period.[39] Origen of Alexandria had also argued that purification allows discipline to end.[40] Among the Talmudic rabbis, the School of Shammai argued that suffering in Gehinnom would cause the

---

32. On the tensions between inclusivists and exclusivists (that is, from paradise) and pluralists, with extreme and moderate participants in each camp, see Khalil, *Islam and the Fate of Others*, 20–25, 141–44.

33. Binyamin Abrahamov, "The Creation and Duration of Paradise and Hell in Islamic Theology," *Der Islam* 79.1 (2002): 87–102, at 95.

34. Jon Hoover, "Islamic Universalism: Ibn Qayyim al-Jawziyya's Salafī Deliberations on the Duration of Hell-Fire," *The Muslim World* 99.1 (2009): 181–201, at 182–83, 186.

35. Abrahamov, "Creation and Duration," 94.

36. Hoover, "Islamic Universalism," 188.

37. Abrahamov, "Creation and Duration," 95; Khalil, *Islam and the Fate of Others*, 74–109.

38. Abrahamov, "Creation and Duration," 97. In "Islamic Universalism," 196, Jon Hoover uses additional evidence, including a contemporary epitome of a late work by Ibn Qayyim, to conclude: "He coaxes and even dares his reader to believe firmly that all chastisement will come to an end." Contra, see Freidenreich, "Food," 265–66.

39. Bernstein, *Formation*, 319–20.

40. See above, chapter 8; and Bernstein, *Formation*, 305–13.

intermediate category of sinners to call to God, who would remove them after no more than a year.[41]

The second important departure from the main presentation of Islamic eschatology is that of the Sufi tradition. Representing a unique fusion of mystical themes from late antique Mediterranean traditions such as Gnosticism and Neoplatonism, Sufism focuses the attention of the devout so intently on God alone that other, doctrinal and ritual aspects of the religion become peripheral. Sufi poetry is allegorical in the sense that it often expresses desire for God in language reminiscent of human love poetry, but God is the sole object of the contemplative's devotion. Using the contemplative techniques of mysticism, the Sufi sought to experience an ascent to the divine, indeed, a union with God, in this life. Beside this all-encompassing focus, ideas of heaven and hell become irrelevant. A dramatic and direct illustration of the Sufi attitude to heaven and hell appears in an anecdote associated with Rābiʿa, a woman poet of Basra, who died in 801. Rābiʿa is said to have been kidnapped as a child and sold into slavery, but eventually liberated by her owner when he recognized her potential. Seen carrying fire in one hand and water in the other, she was asked the reason. "I am going to light a fire in Paradise and pour water on to Hell, so that both veils [i.e., hindrances to the true vision of God] may completely disappear from the pilgrims, and their purpose may be sure, and the servants of God may see Him without any object of hope or motive of fear." Another text, preserved apparently as a prayer, reads, "O my Lord, if I worship Thee from fear of Hell, burn me in Hell; and if I worship Thee from hope of Paradise, exclude me thence; but if I worship Thee for Thine own sake, then withhold not from me Thine Eternal Beauty."[42] This perspective makes purity of focus the sole criterion in the moral life.

Extraqur'ānic Views of Hell

Beyond the Qur'ān itself, over the centuries, compilers called "traditionalists" recorded and codified sayings attributed to the Prophet but not included in Scripture. The "sayings" or "traditions," called hadith, received a "genealogy" or isnād citing each person responsible for preserving the report. Some attributions to Muhammad himself were remembered and later dictated by his Companions, the earliest converts, and then by other authorities, "the Followers," of the next generation. In some ways, the hadith function like the parables of Jesus in the New Testament or like Jewish midrash. Religious

---

41. Rosh Hash. 17a; Simon, p. 64. See above, chapter 7.
42. Margaret Smith, *Readings from the Mystics of Islam* (London: Luzac, 1972), 10–11.

scholars began to compile and organize the sayings into collections that became standardized in the early centuries of Islam, though other hadith continued to circulate outside the officially sanctioned compilations.[43] The four earliest major collections were those of Malik (d. 179/801), al-Bukhari (d. 256/870), Muslim (d. 261/875), and Abu-Dawud (d. 275/888).[44] (With the exception of Malik, who was earlier and whose collection was based on different principles, these scholars were contemporaries of the late Carolingian figure John the Scot Erigena and a generation earlier than Saadia Gaon.)

Hadith, via al-Ghazali

The variations between these authoritative hadith collections attracted the attention of the philosopher and theologian al-Ghazali (d. 1111). Having attained great renown as an academic theologian in Baghdad and Nishapur, al-Ghazali initiated a spiritual retreat around 1095 and moved toward the Sufi tradition represented by Rābiᶜa. He died in a Sufi monastery of his own founding.[45] Al-Ghazali arranged each hadith according to the moment in sacred time to which it applied, from the death of an individual through the body's experience in the grave to the resurrection, judgment, and assignment to heaven or hell. He ends with an account of hell itself, of the Beatific Vision (seeing God face-to-face), and a final reflection on divine mercy.[46]

Al-Ghazali observes that death is only apparent: the spirit lives on and remains conscious after death (126). The trial of the dead person's soul begins in the grave.[47] The person's own deeds appear as personifications to praise or threaten the deceased: "I am your righteous deeds"; "I am your foul deeds" (136–37). They appear as attractive or hideous, as the case may be, and confront the dead person with a visual representation of their life, summed up in a single image. The grave of a believer widens into a verdant

43. Michael Cook, "Eschatology and the Dating of Traditions," in *Princeton Papers in Near Eastern Studies*, ed. Charles Issawi and Bernard Lewis (Princeton, NJ: Darwin Press, 1992), 23–47.

44. The collections of these four are now available online. See http://www.searchtruth.com/searchHadith.php.

45. Khalil, *Islam and the Fate of Others*, 26; Frank Griffel, *Al-Ghazali's Philosophical Theology* (New York: Oxford University Press, 2009), 43; Ignaz Goldhizer, *Introduction to Islamic Theology and Law*, trans. Andras Hamori and Ruth Hamori (1910; Princeton, NJ: Princeton University Press, 1981), 39, 158–60.

46. For this analysis, I use al-Ghazali, *The Remembrance of Death and the Afterlife: Book XL of the Revival of the Religious Sciences*, trans. and intro. T. J. Winter (Cambridge, MA: The Islamic Texts Society, 1989). References in parentheses are to page numbers in this volume. For additional perspective, see Sherman A. Jackson, *On the Boundaries of Theological Tolerance in Islam* (Oxford: Oxford University Press, 2002).

47. Smith and Haddad, *Islamic Understanding*, 31–61.

meadow, but the grave of an unbeliever imprisons the body with ninety-nine dragons (138). Two angels, Munkar and Nakīr, specialized in this task, question the body about its faith and, depending on the answers, make the grave wide like a wedding bed or so tight one's ribs pierce its walls (144–45).

These statements immediately bring up the issue of figurative speech and its ability to represent religious truth. Like Gregory the Great's ideas on the levels of discourse in his *Letter to Leander*, al-Ghazali considers the scorpions, vermin, and snakes said to torment the wicked in these traditions. There are, he says "three degrees of belief." The first is simple acceptance. Second is understanding that the pain the guilty party experiences is real, whether there are objective tormentors or not. This is empathy with the sinner's guilty conscience or consciousness of pain. The third level moves beyond the sensation of pain to an appreciation of the actual damage done, wrong for its own sake. In these matters, the love of anything besides God is a distraction that causes delay in experiencing God, a delay understood as pain, but which is, in fact, the absence of that supreme good (138–41). These levels express in different ways literal detail, figurative representations, and the highest spiritual truth. The dragons and the hooks can all serve an appropriate purpose.

Having provided this perspective, al-Ghazali proceeds with his chronological presentation. The sound of the trumpet at the "moment" of resurrection and the raising of the dead is a time of great anxiety that Islamic lore extends, for the wicked, into a tremendous ordeal of 50,000 years. So great is their trepidation that they will exclaim, "O my Lord! Grant me release from this suffering and this anticipation, even should it be to Hell!" (181). During this time, each guilty person, terrified, searches for intercessors. The pious pass through this process in less time than it took to say any prayer when alive; it is torture only for the wicked (183). The essential investigation spares no one. Jesus, too, receives hard questions: "Did you say to people: Take me and my mother as two gods besides God?" He wrestles with this question for many years. "O, the majesty of that Day, when the Prophets themselves are submitted to judgment by questions such as these!" (190).

The time of the Resurrection and Trial will be the opportunity for one's adversaries to bring their complaints against one, and for one's good deeds to be made over to those whom one has wronged. If you must pay out all your good deeds in this way and are left with nothing, hell is your fate—potentially forever unless some shred of faith mitigates your punishment. The idea is not simply to imagine the frenzy one would experience in this circumstance, but to erect upon that perception a guiding principle for an ethical life. A tradition ascribes to Umar the saying, "Call yourselves to account before you yourselves are called to account" (198). Al-Ghazali explains that this internal self-evaluation requires repenting of every sin, righting all the offenses against God and against one's neighbor, "grain by grain." "He should set their hearts at rest so that when he dies not a single injustice or obligation will remain to his discredit" (198). The psychological consequences of such an ethical imperative resemble the idea of inner death. Only those who mentally balance the books of their good and evil deeds will be able to amend their wrongs in time. Others will pay after death.

The Qur'ān teaches that every grain of evidence is weighed in the judgment (99:7–8; cf. 4:40; 21:47), and if one combines the minuteness of this scrutiny with God's mercy, no aspect of faith will be neglected. In one hadith, only the least degree (*dharrah*), a mustard seed, an ant, or an atom of virtue or of faith is required to gain the Prophet's intercession.[48] Just as the Talmud teaches that "all Israel have a portion in the world to come," and some Christians taught that Christ could convert the dead even in hell, as the collections of hadith accumulated, it seems, greater emphasis was placed on the intercessory powers of Muhammad, particularly in favor of his own people. He appeals to God, who gives him the ability to bring in those of his nation, "for whom there need be no reckoning, by the right-hand Gate of Heaven"; all other nations must pass through the other gates (212–14). The special treatment of Muslims because of Muhammad's advocacy is tempered by another qur'ānic line also brought up by al-Ghazali. In a description of the Reckoning, God interviews Jesus. In deference to God's perfection as judge and punisher, Jesus says, "If Thou chastiseth them, they are Thy servants" (Sura 5:118; al-Ghazali, 211). This statement confirms others that declare God the only judge. Here Jesus is seen to understand chastisement as a loving, paternal, providential concern that benefits its recipient, provided the recipient sees it as loving discipline. If so, the benefits of chastisement need not be limited to Muslims. Since even an iota of faith can save, this approach to intercession could benefit many peoples. Not only can the entrance to heaven be made easier by intercession: so can exit from hell. A powerful corroboration of the responsibility the Prophet assumes for his own people comes in a tradition that says the Prophet's own place in heaven will remain empty until he shall have drawn the last of his nation from hell. The Prophet's rescue of Muslims will leave Mālik, the king of hell, unfathomably frustrated. Muslims may go briefly to hell, but Muhammad's intercession rescues them quickly (212).

---

48. Bukhari 2.21; 76.565; 93.601; accessed Dec. 20, 2016, http://bit.ly/2i897j9. For the least degree of saving faith, Khalil, *Islam and the Fate of Others*, 61, cf. 40–46, 102–6.

Two principles, therefore, can mitigate the fate of the wicked after death. First is the idea that every deed counts, whether good deeds done by the wicked or evil deeds by otherwise good people. Second is the idea that a good deed can gain intercession on behalf of the damned. There is a tradition in which a person in hell calls out for help and reminds someone in paradise that once, when requested, he had given him water to drink. The resident of the Garden then goes to his Lord and begs permission to intercede on behalf of his former benefactor. "And God gives him [permission] to intercede for him, and the order is issued for him to be removed from Hell" (215).

A second example involves the story of Abū Lahab, Muhammad's uncle who refused to convert to Islam and so is named in the Qur'ān as damned (Sura 111). A tradition relates, however, that after prayers from a friend for news of his condition, AbūLahab appeared in a dream and revealed to him that despite his infernal fate, God lessened his punishment with water to drink every Sunday night. Since Muhammad was born on a Sunday night, this concession honors the Prophet's birth and rewards this opponent of Islam for granting freedom to a slave woman, here named Thuwayba (also Thuwaiba), who had been or would become Muhammad's wet nurse (157).[49] This tradition recalls the Christian idea, seen in the *Vision of Paul*, whereby Christ stops punishment of the damned on Sundays (or on Easter), and in the *Voyage of St. Brendan*, which extends the time of relief for Judas from Saturday evening until Monday morning.[50] Similarly, the rabbis argued that God does not punish the residents of Gehinnom on the Sabbath, as it is a day of rest. Although the tradition concerning Abū Lahab is much reduced in scale because it seems to apply only to him, the logic of periodic relief constitutes another theme that the three religions share.[51]

These two hadith exemplify in concrete terms the doctrine of the atom's worth of virtue. The power of good deeds done while alive to affect souls after they have died appears also in Christian sources, by ca. 700 at least, in the tale told by the missionary Boniface. In the *Vision of the Monk of Wenlock*, the airborne monk experiences a balancing of his vices and virtues and

---

49. See Uri Rubin, "Abū Lahab and Sūra CXI," 16 n. 21.

50. *Vita et navigatio Sancti Brendani* §43, p. 73.

51. Ragnar Eklund states in error that Islam grants rest to the damned on Fridays. Eklund, *Life between Death and Resurrection*, 59. On Friday in Islam, see Ignaz Goldhizer, "The Sabbath Institution in Islam," in *The Development of Islamic Ritual*, ed. Gerald Hawting (1900; Burlington, VT: Ashgate/Variorum, 2006), 33–47. G. E. von Grunebaum states, "Friday is not to be a day of rest, and business is to be suspended only during the noon service itself." Von Grunebaum, *Muhammadan Festivals* (London: Curzon Press, 1988), 11.

understands that now, after death, his good deeds have an even greater effect than when performed in life.[52] The monk of Wenlock also saw the soul of a fellow monk who regretted that his brother had not granted freedom to a female serf they jointly controlled. His grief stems from the belief that so great an act of charity would have improved his condition in the afterlife.[53]

Even though an atom's worth of good can be critical, some good deeds are worth more than others. There is a tradition attributed to Anas ibn Malik, a contemporary of the Prophet, who reports that Muhammad questioned one to whom he permitted a glimpse of heaven. When the one who had briefly seen these blessings begged to enter immediately, he was told the price of admission is "your forgiveness of your brother." This saying illustrates the qur'ānic verse "Fear God and make reconciliation amongst yourselves" (8:1). This follows, comments al-Ghazali, because "God reconciles the believers with one another" (203–4). The idea that forgiveness of one's brother is the key to heaven in Islam recalls Micah 7:18 and the story of Rabbi Huna in Talmud Tractate Rosh Hashanah 17a, which states that humans earn divine forgiveness for themselves by forgiving the offenses of others. The Christian Scriptures also teach that God forgives as we forgive.[54] The power of forgiveness to alleviate postmortem discipline is a theme common to all three Abrahamic religions.

Noting these apparently unrelated motifs is worthwhile because, in fact, they are not unrelated. They testify to a broad Mediterranean conversation that endured for centuries, a consequence of the long periods of military, political, and economic interaction imposed on territories under Alexander and his successor regimes or under the Roman Empire.[55] Whatever specific religion invoked these tales, whether called midrashim, exempla, or hadith, they came from a mostly common fund of lore that circulated by word of mouth during these periods and remained as part of the cultural legacy in these areas.[56]

---

52. *Wenlock*, ed. Tangl, p. 10, line 35–p. 11, line 2.

53. *Wenlock*, p. 13, lines 28–36.

54. Rosh Hash. 17a; p. 67. See also Mark 11:25–26; Matt. 6:14–15.

55. Peregrine Horden and Nicholas Purcell, *The Corrupting Sea: A Study of Mediterranean History* (Oxford: Blackwell, 2000); and David Abulafia, *The Great Sea: A Human History of the Mediterranean* (New York: Oxford University Press, 2011).

56. Stith Thompson and Antti Aarne, *Motif-Index of Folk Literature: A Classification of Narrative Elements in Folktales, Ballads, Myths*. 6 vols. (Bloomington: Indiana University Press, 1955–58); David S. Azzolina, *Tale Type- and Motif- Indexes: An Annotated Bibliography* (New York: Garland, 1987). See now Hans-Jörg Uther, *The Types of International Folktales: A Classification and Bibliography, Based on the System of Antti Aarne and Stith Thompson* (Helsinki: Suomalainen Tiedeakatemia, Academia Scientiarum Fennica; 2004).

Abū Lahab and the motif of water as relief for hell's fire suggest another parallel in the story of the rich man and Lazarus in Luke 16:19–31, where the rich man thinks one drop of water is not too much to ask. In Luke, however, the result of the entreaty is negative. Abraham denied the petition on the grounds that the man had not done one drop of good, had let not one crumb fall to benefit the needy. The details vary, but the same structure underlies the different stories. The hadith that relate the exchange of these tokens (drops of water, acts of forgiveness as in the Talmud, a stone such as the one Judas put in the Roman road as recounted in the *Voyage of St. Brendan*) between the good and the wicked recall similar tales in other religious traditions.

Another example of structural similarities that persist despite differences in detail is the weighing of souls. At this time, there are those who go immediately to heaven, those who go immediately to hell, and those in the middle. The books containing the good and evil deeds of those in the middle are placed in the pans of a balance. As the needle moves from side to side, there is no consciousness of anyone but oneself. If the pan of good deeds is light, "the Guardians of hell approach bearing 'hooked rods of iron' (22:21) and attired in garments of fire, and take Hell's lot to Hell" (196). Of 1,000 souls so weighed, hell's portion is 999 (197). This weighing recalls the divisions sketched in Rosh Hashanah 16b and Augustine's *Enchiridion*. More exactly, it fits Gregory I's analysis based on John 3:18, where some need no judgment because they are so good, others are so wicked they are "condemned already," but a middling group requires further deliberation. Here, they are weighed.

Another metaphor for judgment is the test bridge, like that in Gregory I's *Dialogues*. There is qur'ānic authority for the bridge: "Guide them to the Traverse of the Blaze. And stay them for they shall be questioned" (37:23–24). In the collections of hadith, this ordeal receives considerable development. "Mankind . . . shall be driven to the Traverse, which is a bridge stretched over the gulf of Hell, sharper than a sword and thinner than a hair" (206). One's good works provide momentum or light to aid in the crossing, whereas a history of evil deeds is a burden that slows the step, darkens the vision, and tumbles one to where the angels of hell can attach their "hooks and grapples" to pull one in (206).

Countering the demonic forces with hooks is the intercessory power of the Prophet, who wishes to extract them all from pain, but al-Ghazali excludes those who merely assume an outward allegiance to God as not really of Muhammad's nation. These hypocrites go to the hell of hell, that part that sickens hell itself. Its residents are so disgusting that even the gluttonous Jahannam cannot stomach them. This tradition derives from Ali, who said that hell itself has a Chasm or Vale of Grief "in the Inferno from which the Inferno itself seeks God's protection seventy times each day, which God (Exalted is He!) has prepared for the ostentatious reciters of the Qur'an" (222).

Hell's own Vale of Grief, a hell within hell, employs hyperbole, a major figure of speech here, but even more important in the next document to be considered. Predicates for the unspeakable, hyperboles are exaggerations understood in folkloric terms. The image of the hell within hell, the pit of hell that sickens even hell, might be taken as an exponential extension of hell. It is the hell of hell, or "hell squared." Another type of hyperbole draws on numerology and assigns symbolic significance to certain numbers, especially three, seven, ten, and their multiples to exaggerate by symbolic or numinous factors that give the inexpressible a superficial comprehensibility even while keeping it out of reach. In our contemporary language, "I wouldn't do that for a million dollars" doesn't mean that I would do it for a million dollars plus one. It means there is no relationship between my refusal and any sum of money. From this perspective, hyperbole is well suited to approach the undescribable.[57]

Hyperbole might appear antithetical to theological reasoning, but it is necessary to remember al-Ghazali's theory of the degrees of faith and the filters he places between literal statements and their actual meaning. Besides, al-Ghazali offers clues to his figurative approach. Not everyone experiences every punishment. The variety and extent of torments are proportioned to each one's "rebelliousness and sin" (223). Further, he measures his discussion of hell with an analogy showing that, at the literal or apparent level, his statements are false, because the terms he compares are beyond proportion to one another, like time to eternity, man to God, earthly to infernal fire. "There is no correspondence between the fire of this world and that of the Inferno" (223). Still, without the term "fire" we could not understand hell. Yet, if we enter this figure of speech, it becomes clear that "were Hell's inhabitants to come across fire such as ours they would plunge into it submissively in order to flee from their condition" (223). The difficulty is the limit of language in comparison to the heat, voraciousness, and eternity of hell and, for those who direct their lives toward God, the immeasurable bliss of divine love. Adepts in all three Abrahamic religions would make similar statements, indeed homologous statements, because derived from a similar

---

57. See Olivier Reboul, *La rhétorique*, 3rd ed., Que sais-je? 2133 (Paris: Presses universitaires de France, 1990), 48–51.

source: awe at the same divine justice. Qur'ānic authority for this reasoning appears in Sura 3:179: "If you believe and do right, you have a great reward without measure."

The mental framework in which these details are expressed prepares one to examine the literal statements whose exactitude al-Ghazali has just undermined. Hell is so deep, it takes a rock seventy years to reach bottom (222). Those suffering the least of hell's punishments wear sandals of fire that burn out their brains (223). An inversion of exponential hyperbole applies it to distinctions within ideas. Thus, hell is divided into seven parts, its "ramifying valleys" (222). Its duration can be broken down into thousand-year cycles. Its fire is stoked for a thousand years, to make it red, another thousand to make it white, and another thousand to make it black (223).[58] There are paradoxical antitheses: so great is one's pleasure in heaven, if the most miserable man on earth were to receive one drop of it, he would forget ever having experienced misery; so great is the misery of hell, if the most fortunate man on earth were to receive one drop of it, he would forget ever experiencing pleasure (224). Of the food and the drink for the inmates of hell and the pus from their infected wounds: if one drop were to reach the earth it would ruin the lives of its inhabitants. Think what it does for those who regularly ingest or emit such fare! (224–25). The snakes that entwine themselves around the sinners' necks are the wealth on which they paid no tax. The snake addresses the sinner, "I am your wealth! I am your treasure!" This tradition interprets Sura 3:180ar, which includes the statement, "That which they hoard will be their collar on the Day of Arising" (226–27). Thus tradition amplifies a qur'ānic expression, turning an inert weight into a living serpent that taunts its host. Moreover, the body adapts to preserve itself. The torments will never wear it out. Building on Sura 4:56, a tradition states that these enlarged bodies will suffer annihilation and yet be renewed 70,000 times each day, so that the pain of destruction is continuous (227).

There is a point after which the pleas of the damned will not even be heard. Building on Sura 23:108, a tradition rejects their appeals, first to Mālik, chief guardian of hell, and then to God. It takes a thousand years until Mālik brings back the rejection (220; cf. 226). We have noted the possibility that even all Muslims must be tested, however briefly, by hell itself before Muhammad's intercession begins (19:68, 71–72: "Not one of you but will pass over it"). Conversely, "on the Day of Arising," wicked people will be taken from hell to heaven to see its delights before "a voice" rejects them.

---

58. This hadith is also found in Muhammad's *Night Journey, Liber Scale*, d. 11, §24, pp. 58–61. See below, note 66.

Afterward, from hell, they will lament: "Had You put us in Hell without revealing to us the reward which You did show us, and that which You have prepared for those who aided Your cause, the matter would have been easier for us" (230). Though heaven has no further awareness of those in oblivion, the wicked there know the lack their misdeeds and faithlessness now cause them (230).

Miraj Nameh: Muhammad's Night Journey

If the religious utility of hyperbole aids in understanding al-Ghazali's review of the end time it is indispensable to one of Islam's fundamental narratives. The *Night Journey* is the story of how Gabriel guided Muhammad through the cosmos providing views of both paradise and hell. There is only indirect reference to the ascent (*miʿrāj*) in the Qurʾān. However, Sura 17 begins, "Glory to [God] who did take his servant for a journey by night from the sacred mosque to the farthest mosque . . . in order that we might show him some of our signs."[59] As a later complement to the Qurʾān, which tells what he has heard, the *Night Journey* tells what he has seen.[60] In the first extant biography of the Prophet, Ibn Ishaq (b. 55/674, d. 150–52/767–69) states that the alternative to raising Muhammad up would have been to send an angel down. That strategy would have made Muhammad just another inspired man, but his ascension emphasizes his superior status among prophets.[61] This story exists in several versions. Some, such as the one commented by Ibn Arabi, omit the tour of hell, but it is stipulated in Islamic creeds from the tenth century on.[62]

In his *Life of Muhammad*, Ibn Ishaq first acknowledges that what he has of this narrative comes from eight different sources. He provides their names as if this were a typical *isnād*, that is, the usual genealogy of a hadith preserved from the Companions of the Prophet. From the eighth century, therefore, this narrative is understood as oral tradition, though derived from the highest authorities. In brief, Gabriel comes to Muhammad with the wondrous beast Buraq, whose every stride covers all the distance one can see. They journeyed

---

59. Michael Sells, "Ascension," in *Encyclopaedia of the Qurʾān*, ed. Jane Dammen McAuliffe (Leiden: Brill, 2001), 1:176, col. 2.

60. B. Schrieke and J. Horovitz, "Miʿrādj," In *Encyclopaedia of Islam*, ed. P. Bearman et al., 2nd ed. (Leiden: Brill, 2003), 7:97, col. 2.

61. Ibn Ishaq, *Life of Muhammad*, 181. Page numbers given in parentheses are to Guillaume's translation, cited above, note 14.

62. Three references to the ascension appear in William Montgomery Watt, *Islamic Creeds: A Selection* (Edinburgh: Edinburgh University Press, 1994), 50 (that of al-Tawahi, d. 933), 67 (a later Hanafite creed), and 83 (that of al-Nasafi, d. 1142).

to see the "wonders between heaven and earth," until he came to Jerusalem (182). There Muhammad acted as imam and led Abraham, Moses, and Jesus in prayer. Then, climbing the ladder "to which the dying man looks when death approaches," Gabriel and Muhammad ascended to the Gate of the Watchers, the lowest gate of heaven, where they meet the angel Ishmael. They ascend through the eight other heavens, meeting as they go Jesus, John the Baptist, Joseph, Idris (Enoch), Aaron, Moses, and Abraham. Muhammad comments on his own remarkable resemblance to "my father Abraham," and follows him into paradise (186).

During his time with Gabriel in the heavens, Muhammad sees many joyful angels, who wish him success in his tour of the cosmos and his mission. One, however, remains taciturn. This is Mālik, the Keeper of Hell. At the Prophet's request, Gabriel orders Mālik to show him hell, so the gloomy angel opens the lid of a well and out leaps Alfalak, hell's own special fire with flames so fierce Muhammad feared a general conflagration. Ibn Ishaq's different sources relate different aspects of what is to be seen in hell. Men with lips like camels eat stones of fire that exit from their posteriors; these are those who devour the wealth of orphans. As if maddened by thirst, camels trample the engorged stomachs of men rendered immobile by all they had consumed; these are the usurers. Men who choose lean putrid meat and leave aside good, marbled, fat meat are those who "forsake the women which God has permitted and go after those he has forbidden." Women who pursued mates forbidden to them hang by their breasts. When Muhammad returned from his night voyage and related these experiences to the Quraysh they doubted him. If it takes a month for a caravan to travel from Mecca to Syria (or Jerusalem, depending on the account), how could you make it there and back in one night? Muhammad overcomes many doubts by revealing the contents of a caravan about to arrive that day (183–84).

The *Book of the Ladder*

Ibn Ishaq had already drawn on many sources to compile his account of Muhammad's *Night Journey*, but the narrative received further elaboration over the centuries. The account that furnishes the best point of comparison with hell belief in Western Europe was recorded in thirteenth-century Spain. Its title, the *Book of the Ladder* (*Liber Scale*), refers to the ladder Ibn Ishaq said Muhammad used to ascend from Jerusalem after his prayer session with Abraham, Moses, and Jesus. The *Book of the Ladder* survives in two parallel translations, one Latin, one French, that a certain Bonaventure of Siena based on a prior translation from Arabic into Castilian by "Abraham the Physician" on the order of King Alfonso the Wise (r. 1252–84).[63] It will be clear, in considering this thirteenth-century version, that the structure of the journey derives from the versions collected by Ibn Ishaq, and that many of the earlier rhetorical strategies and theodicial convictions remain intact. What differs most is a leap in the number of details provided, the extent of subdivision as an aid to exposition and analysis, and the flair for exponential hyperbole. Structurally, the most important difference, and one that betrays the migration of this text to a place where Latin Christianity is the majority religion, is the fact that now the devil, rather than Mālik, rules in hell.[64]

On his way to heaven, the Prophet encounters and interviews other-world figures. The Angel of Death describes the books that list each person's good and bad deeds (§§15–18). Further on, Muhammad meets the Treasurer of Hell, who develops the hadith about the heating of hell, turning it red, then white, then black. In this version, hell was first made red for 70,000 years, then white for an equal period, then after 70,000 more years, with one fire on top of another, it became totally black.[65] Because of its darkness, hell's fire gives off much heat, but no light. The angels who operate there live in the fire as fish in water. They are thus in their element when they torture and afflict sinners.[66] Gabriel and Muhammad continue their tour and ascend through the eight heavens with side trips through a series of paradises.[67] Finally, Muhammad converses directly with God and receives the Qur'ān and his direct commission as prophet (§§124–25). Then Muhammad hears God order Gabriel to guide him through hell. The resultant account of the infernal regions shows that, like Ibn Ishaq's strategy, the compiler of the *Book of the Ladder* preferred to honor his early sources rather than to trim inconsistencies. *Ladder* is a compilation of traditions unified as a narrative, not a treatise in systematic theology. Visions follow

---

63. I have used *Il "Libro della Scala" e la questione delle fonti arabo-spagnole della divina commedia*, ed. E. Cerulli, Studi e Testi 150 (Vatican City: Biblioteca Apostolica Vaticana, 1949), 11–12; henceforth *Liber Scale* or *Ladder*. Passages in quotation marks are my translations from the Latin, checked against the French and aided by Cerulli's excellent notes.

64. For a study comparing the diabolical figures (and other points) in the *Book of the Ladder* and Dante's *Inferno*, see Massimiliano Chiamenti, "Intertestualità *Liber Scale Machometi—Commedia?*," in *Dante e il locus inferni*, ed. Simone Foà and Sonia Gentile (Rome: Bulzoni, 2000), 45–51, at 49–50. Chiamenti provides excellent arguments that the two texts are related through their common sources rather than by the direct influence of one on the other.

65. Many traditions report these details according to al-Ghazali, 223 and 271 n. 18, though he gives the time for each stage as a thousand years.

66. *Liber Scale*, d. 10, §24, p. 59. The text is divided into 85 distinctions (chapters) and 216 sections. I cite both and the page numbers of Cerulli's edition.

67. For a sensitive, modern overview of the heaven and its gardens, see Rustomji, *Garden and the Fire*, 115–17; 98–100, for the medieval treatises on which her study is based.

their own conventions. Like the text itself, we follow each perspective as Muhammad related it.

The view of hell is complicated by the interweaving of competing conceptual models. In particular, there is an intersection between a vertical model dividing hell in layers and a horizontal model spreading it out into seven lands. Thus, beyond this earth where people live, there is another earth made of fire, inhabited by people "similar to those that are here," and this land is surrounded by a sea of fire, inhabited by fiery fish. Connected to this double land are other lands and peoples and seas and fish of fire, making a total of seven. Beneath them is a great stone that sustains the lands, and beneath that stone is a fish that forms a supportive circle by holding its tail in its mouth. Only darkness lies beneath the fish, and whatever lies beneath the darkness only God knows (§135). The fish is Leviathan (§154; cf. Job 41). The descriptions of these places fit the pattern of exponential exaggeration that reaches a point where, in another hyperbolic trope, the mind can no longer comprehend them. The scorpions of the second land illustrate the technique. They "are the size of mules and their tails are long like the blade of a lance or longer, and in each of the tails there are 360 knots and each of the knots has 360 horns and in each of the horns there are 360 vials, which are all full of poison" (§139). These scorpions strip the sinners in hell of their skin and bones and nerves and pour the poison from the vials into the exposed anatomy. Once their bodies have been destroyed, God restores them so that they may be tortured repeatedly (§140).

The seventh land is the fortress from which the devil rules all hell. Though he commands his armies and his subjects, he is himself bound in iron chains. He is so large his horns reach from his land into ours. This account includes considerable apocalyptic anxiety: "And the time will come in which he will be released and they will send him forth into this world. Then, truly, many of the other devils will come with him. And he will lead with him all the pride and all the fury of hell; and similarly all the sinning souls of the infidels."[68] To this overlay of horizontal and vertical elements in the description of hell, it is necessary also to add a temporal dimension. When God wishes to bring the current world to its end, he will open up the well near hell and loose Alfalak, a fire so strong it burns the fire of hell as easily as fire in this world burns a wad of cotton. Once released, it will dry up all the seas and all the seven lands at once (§151; cf. §§170–71).

---

68. Belief in an eventual "loosing of Satan" as a sign of the end time finds a parallel in Rev. 20:7–8. Perhaps this Christian belief has influenced the work of the thirteenth-century translator, Bonaventure of Siena.

There is a loose correspondence between the lands of hell and the distribution of evil in the world. This "world" includes legendary peoples as well as those with true geographical homes. Thus God gave most foolishness to the people of Gog and Magog, most envy to the people of Arabia, most lust to the people of India, most falsity to the Jews, most arrogance to the Christians and the Persians, ignorance to the Ethiopians, pride to the Berbers, "and the remainder [of vices] he divided among the whole rest of the world" (§175). This stereotypical scheme does not stop there, for God then created delights and gave most of them to women. "And after this he similarly created Paradise, out of which he made ten parts. And from those ten he gave nine to those of your Law [Muslims] and the tenth part that remained, he divided among all the others" (§175). The principle of the worldwide distribution of the remainder means that no one group has a monopoly on any one trait. Very importantly, it also means that paradise is not reserved exclusively for Muslims. This idea matches the rabbinic belief that "the righteous of all nations have a portion in the world to come."

Another interpretive model turns the blessings of heaven into the torments of hell. When Muhammad asks Gabriel whether hell consists of walls and gates and palaces such as those in paradise, the archangel shows him the layout of Hell City. The division of hell into sectors defined by its gates and their names combines evils that vary from wrong belief to wrong observance in religion to unethical business practices and pride. The gates in the wall are so far apart it would take a man 70,000 years to walk from one to the other. The doors (that close the sinners in) are so hot "that if the least hot among them were in the east and a man in the west looked at it, his brain would exit his head through his nose" (§176). The wicked men and devils must gather daily at the gates and "look at the good who are in Paradise and even in this world. And thus by looking at the good, the punishments are doubled for these people" (§176). Beyond this sense of loss, Gabriel reveals to Muhammad in hell a certain satirical inversion of paradise where virgins on couches await the saved (§42).[69] Attached to each of hell's gates are fortifications that contain rooms where "fire ladies" on couches embrace the damned with a deadly fire. "And this seems to them to be such a great torment that they would more willingly die 70,000 times a day if possible, than to undergo that, because each of these ladies applies torments of 70,000 types" (§178).

---

69. For greater detail, see the traditions compiled in al-Ghazali, *Remembrance*, 244–46. This description interprets the qur'ānic lines about the maidens on the couches in the gardens through which rivers flow, such as Sura 55:46–76, 78:33, or 98:8; *Liber Scale*, dd. 35 and 44, §§86–89 and 111; pp. 113–15 and 133–35.

More importantly, the allegory of the gates becomes an analytical principle, as each leads into a population or neighborhood containing a particular type of sinner. The first gate, called "Gehenna," enfolds the idolaters; the second is for believers who turn away from God (apostates); the third is for Gog and Magog and for "those who gathered riches illicitly." The fourth is for those who play "taxillos" (sic), probably gamblers, whose pastime occasions blasphemy. The fifth gate, called "Zakar" (a distortion of "Zakat," or charity), is for those who pray improperly and do not give charity. Sixth is the gate for scoffers, those who denied the prophets and messengers of God. The seventh is for falsifiers of weights and measures, dishonest merchants.[70] The remainder of hell is divided into seven parts, out of which six are prepared for those who accept God, but wrongly associate other beings with him (Christians) or will not make sacrifices on his behalf, but always prefer their own will to his (unrighteous Muslims). All these people are deleted from the Book of Life (§§179–81).

After the immobility of a town's walls and the image of an immense fortress comes a far more aggressive metaphor: hell as the beast that appears at the moment of judgment ready to devour or carry into hell those who fail (§§182–85). This figure resembles Ammit, the crocodile-headed hippopotamus-leopard, who awaits the trial of the heart against the feather of Maat in the Egyptian Book of the Dead. A similar beast attracts the worship of all those not inscribed in the Book of Life in the Christian book of Revelation (13:2, 8). All the text's powers of hyperbole come to play in describing this monster: "The beast has 30,000 mouths, each with 30,000 teeth, each one sharper than any sword."[71] God assigns the beast to duty in hell, but the animal fears suffering there herself. God assures her that the only reason for sending her there is "to destroy those who, not believing in me, have deprived me of my unity especially by dividing me into many parts." (This characterization usually refers to Christians and the doctrine of the Trinity.) On hearing that she will not suffer the punishments of hell, the beast sighs with relief. That sigh alone is so loud that any living person who hears it would die "of a fright beyond fear." It is extremely significant that the pronouns referring to the beast in this Latin adaptation are all female. It preserves the gender identification of the personified Gehinnom in the Jewish sources and fits with the ancient and unfortunate stereotype

---

70. These descriptions of classes of sinners differ from those in the classic Arabic tradition. For these Cerulli, pp. 243–44 n. 286, cites Sura 15:44 and Asín Palacios, La escatología musulmana en la Divina Comedia, 4th ed. (Madrid: Hiperión, 1984), 138–39.

71. Liber Scale, d. 73, §182; 194–95. Cf. al-Ghazali, Remembrance, 228.

of the insatiable female reinforced by the avidity, rapacity, and voraciousness of hell.[72]

One image treated with considerable economy in this text as compared to
others is the procedure by which God prepares the scales with which he will
weigh the deeds of human beings. At first the weighing seems straightfor-
ward, as the heavier pan determines the person's fate. But Gabriel reveals to
Muhammad that if anyone should place a written statement of the Muslim
declaration of faith in the pan, that alone tips the balance toward salvation
(§§187–88). It may not be the case that all non-Muslims are damned, but this
passage makes the Muslim profession of faith decisive in a believer's favor.

The *Book of the Ladder* (§§172, 192–98) develops the metaphor of the
Judgment Bridge far beyond the one in Gregory the Great or the Qur'ān or
al-Ghazali. This account piles horrors on horrors. The bridge is divided into
seven parts (like the lands of hell itself or its gates). Beginning with a span
that takes tens of thousands of years to cross, each section of the bridge
extends itself incrementally. At the entrance to each segment souls must tell
whether they have met different requirements of the religion. "Those who
were of good and strong faith, will go across. Those who were not will fall on
the blades and the hooks of iron [that impede progress across the bridge] and
will fall into the torments of fire in hell" below the bridge, which is thinner
than a hair and sharper than a sword. Beneath are rivers of fire whose flames
leap over the span. Inside the river are dragons and scorpions, each with
70,000 tails, and each tail has 70,000 knots, and each knot has 10,000 horns of
poison used to annihilate the sinners. God does not permit the sinners to die,
however, so they are recreated with 70 skins, the better to withstand these
torments, but still they suffer a cyclical dissolution and reconstitution (§196).

The bridge itself prevents the wicked from crossing, even Muslims. It
impedes the saved but still indicates the path to safety. For his part, Muhammad will station himself at the far end of the bridge, where he will intercede: "O Lord, help, help my people." And the Muslims will then begin to
rush across the bridge at speeds corresponding to their virtue. Meanwhile,
Gabriel, at the near end of the bridge will call, "Save, Savior, Save!" (These
imprecations recall those in the *Vision of Barontus*.) Some will cross quick as
a flash, others with the speed of a strong wind; those with more faults will
go no faster than a child can crawl, exposed to the flames below. Some will
only reach paradise with faces blackened from the fire (§198). The bridge,

---

72. See, for example, Sandra R. Joshel, "Female Desire and the Discourse of Empire: Tacitus's
Messalina," *Signs* 21.1 (Autumn 1995): 50–82, esp. 59 n. 10.

then, divides the damned from the saved; it measures, punishes, and purifies, leading, eventually, for the blessed, to salvation.

As Gabriel guides Muhammad back to the threshold of the temple in Jerusalem at the site that later became the al-Aqsa Mosque, he repeats the charge that he is to relate what he has learned to all peoples so that they might understand the right way and keep themselves from evil. To his wives and his daughter he sums up his experience: "God has shown me his power and his glory and all the heavens and the worlds, the paradises and the hells" (§205). When he explains these things to his people, the Quraysh, all but Abu Bakr remain skeptical. Here the *Book of the Ladder* repeats the "caravan proof" found in Ibn Ishaq. Since no merchant could go from Mecca to Jerusalem and back in one day and one night, Muhammad could not possibly have toured the entire cosmos in the same period of time. The scoffers challenged him to tell the arrival time and the contents of one of their caravans about to arive from Jerusalem. When he successfully explains these things, many believe, but, as Ibn Ishaq related, many do not. Those who accepted Muhammad's words wrote down word for word what he said to them in a book called *al-Miraj* [*Nameh*] about his night journey (§215). Thus, the *Book of the Ladder* is a transcription of Muhammad's account of his voyage. He concluded: "This book has thus been written in the eighth year after the Spirit of God arose in me and I began to prophesy" (§215).

Caravans and the Spread of Ideas

The story of the caravan deserves further reflection. Caravans provide a structural underpinning to this book's multicultural approach. Already, throughout this chapter, and as a recapitulation of part III, I have inserted comparative observations, linking themes found in the Qur'an, the hadith, and the *Night Journey* to similar ones found in Jewish and Christian literature. The contacts between the peoples who transmitted these motifs were numerous. Far from depending on abstractions, travelers—real people: merchants, pilgrims, students—transmitted these stories. To be sure, eschatology, theodicy, soteriological aspirations, messianic hopes, are abstractions, but the parables and other narratives, the artworks, and ritual practices that disseminate them are much less so. In these more concrete forms, they travel routes that also carry commerce.

Representing the role of trade in Arabian life, the caravan that figures in these two versions of the *Night Journey* bears out this contention. The Indian Ocean connected the Arabian Peninsula with South Asia to the east and with the eastern coast of Africa to the west. Similarly, the Mediterranean offered a sea-based web of ports, like Valencia, Syracuse, Alexandria, Tripoli, Antioch, Tyre, and Constantinople, which doubled as endpoints for sea trade and starting points for overland commerce with the interior.[73] The Tigris and Euphrates were navigable only by rafts and shallow boats. Goods arriving from the Persian Gulf could be transported along the banks of the rivers by donkey caravans.[74] Elsewhere, the roads the Romans paved could accommodate wagons drawn by horses, mules, or donkeys. Pack-asses carried goods through the mountains. In desert regions, south across the Sahara and east across Syria and Persia, camels could proceed without paved roads.

Another institution rarely mentioned in the history of ideas or in studies of comparative religion, the hostel or inn, further facilitated the great Mediterranean conversation about death. On the sea, a ship goes for days or months without stopping. Neither passengers nor crews were ethnically homogeneous. On long sea voyages, these people surely exchanged ideas, tales, and behavioral practices whether religious or not. Over land, travelers needed to stop each night. At their watering holes (the colloquial term has a literal sense in late antiquity and the early Middle Ages) there were many hours between sunset and sunrise when travelers arriving from all directions met and mixed in markets, houses of worship, courts and courthouses, baths, brothels, and taverns. Inns were frequently constructed around courtyards with habitation for animals and storage for goods on the ground floor and dwellings for humans a flight above.[75] There would be space for dining, bathing, and other recreation, certainly including the exchange of ideas, whether comparisons of commercial law from country to country, religion to religion, or indeed, comparisons of the religious laws themselves.

In her monograph devoted to the institution of the hostel, Olivia Remie Constable sums up its importance as a node of communication: "As the institution shifted from one realm of political, religious, and linguistic dominance

---

73. Janet L. Abu-Lughod sketches the overall picture in *Before European Hegemony: The World System, A.D. 1250–1350* (New York: Oxford University Press, 1989), 175–78. For Western Europe in an earlier age, see the contrasts between sea and land travel in Michael McCormick, *Origins of the European Economy: Communications and Commerce, AD 300–900* (Cambridge: Cambridge University Press, 2003), 393–430.

74. Guillermo Algaze, "Habuba on the Tigris: Archaic Nineveh Reconsidered," *Journal of Near Eastern Studies* 45.2 (April 1986): 125–37.

75. Olivia Remie Constable, *Housing the Stranger in the Mediterranean World: Lodging, Trade, and Travel in Late Antiquity and the Middle Ages* (Cambridge: Cambridge University Press, 2003), 272–73. See also Deborah Howard, *Venice & the East: The Impact of the Islamic World on Venetian Architecture, 1100–1500* (New Haven, CT: Yale University Press, 2000); Michael Rostovtzeff, *Caravan Cities* (New York: AMS Press, 1971).

to another—from the pagan, Jewish, and early Christian milieu of the late Roman period, into an Islamic context, then later into the Latin Christian sphere of southern Europe—it was both a point of common understanding across cultures and mediation between them."[76] The terms that designate the various establishments changed from cultural zone to cultural zone and language to language—pandocheion, funduq, fondaco, khan, caravanserai—all translated with due respect for differences over time and regional custom as our "inn" or "hostel." In short, the institution was "ubiquitous."[77] The ancient Greek term for an "inn"—*pandocheion*—"means 'accepting all comers'."[78] How common storytelling must have been under these roofs! In such establishments, the motifs of eschatological thought could cross-pollinate and bear fruit. In this way, the wondrous tale of Muhammad predicting a caravan's contents and arrival time, a story itself rooted in everyday life, would have brought his prophetic powers down to earth.

The same is true of the damned and their punishments. The infernal tortures also migrated from culture to culture through institutional, religious, and literary channels. At the conclusion of the Prophet's report on the Bridge of Trial, after the explanation of its purgatorial function, there is an especially poignant moment. From the bridge or its vicinity, Muhammad has glimpsed individual sinners actually in hell. He experiences pangs of pity "beyond anguish" as he considers their fate in the many tortuous lands, amid monstrous beings and overwhelming natural threats from fire and insects, serpents, and other vicious fauna. These torments envelop huge populations of souls, but generally there is no explanation of how they suit the offenders' sins. In one section of the text, however, in answer to the Prophet's questions, Gabriel pairs the torments with the wrongs they requite. At this point, the dialogue begins to resemble the *Apocalypse of Peter* and the *Apocalypse of Paul*. There were some he saw "who had their lips cut off by forceps burning with fire" (*Ladder* §199). Gabriel explained "these were those who sowed words in order to cause discord among peoples." Perjurers have their tongues cut out (*Ladder* §199). The earlier apocalypses reveal similar penalties inflicted on the lips and tongues of sinners. In *Peter*, blasphemers hang by their tongues (§§7, 22; H-S 2:672), and false witnesses or slanderers have their lips cut off (§§9, 29; H-S 2:676). In *Paul*, a red-hot razor cuts out the tongue and removes the lips of a hypocritical prayer leader [reader] (§36b;

---

76. Constable, *Housing*, 3.
77. Ibid.
78. Ibid., 7.

H-S 2:781). In the *Apocalypse of Mary*, men and women perjurers, blasphemers, and slanderers hang by their tongues (§14; Baun, 395).[79]

These punishments cross even more geographical and linguistic boundaries as tongues receive punishment frequently in the Zoroastrian *Ardā Wirāz Nāmag*, where male and female liars have the offending organ cut out (fol. 53; p. 217), as did a corrupt judge "who received bribes and gave devious judgments" (fol. 47; p. 214).[80] A second major example of these motifs' widespread dissemination is the pain directed at sinners' genitals. At the end of burning chains, women are hung by hooks attached to the middle of their "natures," and these were prostitutes (*Ladder* §200). In *Peter* it is male adulterers who merit this particular torment: "And the men who lay with them in fornication are hung by their thighs in that burning place" (§7; H-S 2:673). The details migrate in *Paul*: the fire moves from the razors to the chains, which are attached not to the loins but to the necks of girls being drawn into the darkness for giving up their virginity without their parents' knowledge (*Paul* §39a; H-S 2:782). In the *Ardā Wirāz Nāmag*, snakes bite the penis of a man guilty of adultery and sodomy (fol. 44; p. 213); reptiles enter and exit all the bodily orifices of women hanging by one leg who "defiled their husbands' beds and injured their bodies" (fol. 43; p. 212). Beyond these details is an even more significant, structural motif common to Zoroastrian, Jewish, Christian, and Muslim sources, namely, the Test Bridge or Bridge of Judgment that appears in the Yasnas (46:11), the *Ardā Wirāz Nāmag* (beginning at fol. 8; p. 194), the *Tanna debe Eliyyahu* (464–66), Gregory the Great's *Dialogues* (4.36.7), and the *Book of the Ladder* (§§172, 192–98), which develops mentions in Sura 37:23–24 and al-Ghazali (206). In sum, the seaways of the Mediterranean and the overland routes from its ports were channels for commercial goods and the raw material of afterlife lore, archetypal images of eternal torture—based, as we have already seen, in the equally widespread practice of slavery and its accompanying discipline.

---

79. Jane Baun, *Tales from Another Byzantium: Celestial Journey and Local Community in the Medieval Greek Apocrypha* (Cambridge: Cambridge University Press, 2007).

80. *Ardā Wirāz Nāmag: The Iranian "Divina Commedia,"* ed. and trans. Fereydun Vahman, Scandinavian Institute of Asian Studies Monograph Series 53 (London and Malmo: Curzon, 1986). The first numeral refers to the folio number of the Pahlavi manuscript; the second is the page number of Vahman's edition. For a more thorough list of tongue tortures, see Bruce Lincoln, *Religion, Empire, and Torture* (Chicago: University of Chicago Press, 2010), 139n.

Conclusion

All three Abrahamic religions professed a belief in hell, whether they called it Gehinnom, Gehenna, or Jahannam, and all three successfully resisted similar objections to it within their own communities. To counter these challenges, religious specialists posited purgatorial fringes that offered lesser sinners temporary discipline outside the core of hell, thus sparing them damnation. Despite these threats to hell's essence, authoritative pronouncements succeeded in reasserting eternal punishment as the consensus or orthodox position in the three religions, as typified in Christian thought by Justinian's condemnation of Origenism, in Jewish thought by the rabbis' naming seven types of unforgivable offenses, and in Islam by the Qur'ān's retention of its deniers in Jahannam. Exceptions to these blanket statements exist on the theological level but, as appears in succeeding centuries, stigmatization, the presumption of damnation for non-believers, increasingly took hold and became a practical reality. Belief in hell is self-reinforcing. As the Talmud declares that Gehinnom is for those who deny the Resurrection, hell is for those who deny hell. The Qur'ān threatens hell for those who deny the Hour of final reckoning (83:10–11, 25:11, 74:43–46), and the Fire contains those who reject it (83:16–17). "What they scoff at hems them in" (6:10). Denial of hell is damning.

Judaism, Christianity, and Islam therefore agree on the existence of an eternal hell for incorrigible sinners. Still, it became necessary to reconcile such a dramatic and apparently cruel fate with the mercy of God. In a centuries-long process, hell and its rivals created an ambiguous afterlife territory contemporaries called "the places of punishment." Around the core idea of hell, specialists and visionaries perceived alternatives to hell in the form of escape, periodic relief, and purification. To understand hell's survival despite the resistance it occasioned in the religious sphere, it is important to understand how it fit society's needs. The efforts to balance justice and leniency had major political ramifications.

When they outlawed all religions except Christianity in 407, the coemperors Honorius and Theodosius II proposed to cleanse the empire not only of "crimes," but also of "depraved intentions," thus combining their civil and religious functions. Government theorists consequently articulated a reciprocal relationship between the theological explanations of divine justice and the political premises of imperial administration. For example, the emperors of the late fourth century could portray themselves as following divine example by providing amnesty to lesser criminals each Easter. In parallel with religious debates among their bishops and the contemporary rabbis, the emperors distinguished between minor offenders and perpetrators of the worst crimes. Clemency has its limits, even as the severest penalties enhance the authority of those who would issue pardons. Thus, at the Second Council of Constantinople (553), Justinian anathematized a list of heretics, condemning them to the very hell whose existence he upheld by including Origen. After Justinian defended hell in this way, Greek-language theologians refocused on the need to repent in this life and on the holding power of Gehenna. In the West, Charlemagne would later act similarly.

With loyalty or its opposite involving both earthly and heavenly rulers together, all opponents, whether political or religious, could be stigmatized as subverting cosmic and political order. Here is one danger of hell belief. When the premises in play are based on such absolute authority as that claimed for the emperor and the divinity purportedly working in concert, it could seem that no sanction for disloyalty or infidelity, that is, for challenging the religious justification of the social order, could be too severe. The more the idea of hell connected to social deviance, the more those being threatened came to be stigmatized. Whether named as individuals or, increasingly, named as groups (Muslims, Jews), they were scorned as hell-bound, outcasts, worthy of mistreatment in society because doomed to receive worse in hell.

Just as "the powers that be" found hell useful in advancing their authority, so penitents found hell a guide in atonement. Inner death proposed that infernal punishments invade the conscience and thus uncover offenses. Although related to hell's deterrent function, inner death only serves after deterrence has failed and the guilty conscience requires repair. Given this psychological dynamic, individuals in monastic settings could imagine themselves within range of the afterlife, able to see it and report back on its nature. Whether or not monasticism was a prerequisite to the vision, monastic literacy was required to provide a written record of visions. Visionary literature became its own genre, hell's tortures its clichés. Consistent reiteration made hell more real. However ambiguous the geography of the punitive places, one constant was physical pain and dread of liability to it.

The pains of the damned, including darkness, chains, dismemberment, and torture, were very similar to those imposed on slaves. The rhetoric of religious devotion as slavery to God and sin as slavery to the devil perpetuated this arrangement. Although the distinction between a noble slavery and a base slavery would seem to alleviate this parallel, the fact that slavery was familiar enough to serve as a metaphor assured hell a constant resonance with real-world experience. Propagation of belief in hell reinforced and prolonged slavery. Slavery made hell plausible.

Hell's social utility may have aided its survival, but it does not account for the innovations and shifts in emphasis that occurred over the sweep of these centuries. The spread of monastic institutions fostered penitential introspection and the rise of inner death, a new idea in postmortem punishment. In this contemplative environment, penitential self-examination exposed distinctions within sin itself: not all wrongs deserve eternal punishment. Penance has its rewards, and those who engaged it classified themselves above the impenitent. This distinction produced a calibration of suffering in the penal places where some punishments that varied in time spent yielded eventual release and others, with no release, varied in kind.

As deceased sinners suffered in the interim, the question of whether the living could help them arose. Offerings for the dead exist in many faiths, but in Latin, Christian Europe of the early Middle Ages, suffrages assumed a particular form. They appear prominently in vision literature: the shades benefit from them but do not request them. The reader or hearer of the vision must infer their utility, and if so moved, provide charitable actions on behalf of the soul in the punishments. In the next centuries, the shades will impose particular actions on the percipient, through the agency, and to the profit, of the church.

The history of hell is distinct from its definition by any particular religion, and belief in hell derives from no single biblical authority or even from biblical statements alone. Nor are all biblical statements on the fate of the wicked after death unanimous. Moreover, the term "biblical" unnecessarily restricts the history of hell because the idea of eternal punishment occurs in many

other belief systems, from ancient Persian Zoroastrianism to intertestamental apocalyptic to Greek philosophy, the Talmud, the Qur'ān, and Pahlavi
Zoroastrianism. Postbiblical developments in the interpretation of hell were
crucial to its survival.

The idea of hell, therefore, was available for application in many varied
circumstances and environments. Those in pagan Rome were very different
from those of the Christian emperors who offered Easter amnesties or the
imperial court of Justinian or the monasteries known to Bede. Religious specialists from monastic theorists to popes to imperial counselors could apply
the concept according to the particular needs of their time and place. Hell
survives because it is socially useful. But the passage of time will present
other circumstances, and the combination of hell's functions will change
accordingly—not rigidly or mechanically, but in accord with social, psychological, economic, and other factors that affect the human mind. From the
period examined here, where inner death is perhaps the most characteristic
aspect of hell belief, Western Europe moved in the next centuries to a phase
when hell's function as an impetus to vengeance took over. Those doomed
to hell in the judgment of the politically powerful increasingly became their
targets on earth.

It is my hope to continue this analysis by examining the history of belief
in hell in the next centuries, from the time of Charlemagne to the First Crusade. The nature of visions, the use of suffrages, political theology, all shift in
that period. In later visions and other literature about the afterlife, Jews, Muslims, heretics and schismatics, conspicuously absent as named groups so far,
make their appearance. Propagation of the punitive underworld breaks beyond
linguistic sources to emerge in the visual arts. Manuscript illuminations make
hell visual and therefore more vivid. For all the adventures of its already
centuries-long tradition, even in 800, hell has a future.

Bibliography

Primary Sources

Acts of Thomas. Trans. G. Bornkamm. In H-S 2:425–531.

Alcuin. *De fide sanctae et individuae Trinitatis . . . Libri tres.* PL 101:9–58.

Al-Ghazali. *The Remembrance of Death and the Afterlife: Book XL of the Revival of the Religious Sciences.* Trans. and intro. T. J. Winter. Cambridge, MA: The Islamic Texts Society, 1989.

Ali, Abdullah Yusuf, trans. *The Holy Qur-ān: English Translation of the Meanings and Commentary.* Mushaf Al-Madinah an-Nabawiyah, Saudi Arabia, 1410/1990.

Ambrose. *De paradiso.* Ed. C. Schenkl. CSEL 32, pt. 1, 263–336. Vienna: Tempsky, 1896.

Anglo-Saxon Chronicle. Ed. and trans. M. J. Swanton. New York: Routledge, 1998.

Apocalypse of Mary. In Jane Baun, *Tales from Another Byzantium: Celestial Journey and Local Community in the Medieval Greek Apocrypha,* 386–400. Cambridge: Cambridge University Press, 2007.

Apocalypse of Paul. Trans. Hugo Duensing. In H-S 2:755–98.

———. Trans. M. R. James. In *ANT,* pp. 525–55.

Apocalypse of Peter. Trans. C. Maurer. In H-S 2:663–83.

Apocalypsis Mariae Virginis. Ed. M. R. James. In *AA,* pp. 109–26.

Apocalypsis seu Visio Mariae Virginis. Trans. Marius Chaîne. In *Apocrypha de B. Maria Virgine,* 43–68. Corpus Scriptorum Christianorum Orientalium: Scriptores Aethiopici, 1.7. Rome: Karolus de Luisi, 1909.

Arberry, A. J., trans. *The Koran Interpreted.* New York: Macmillan, 1955.

Ardā Wirāz Nāmag: The Iranian "Divina Commedia." Ed. Fereydun Vahman. Scandinavian Institute of Asian Studies Monograph Series 53. London and Malmo: Curzon Press, 1986.

Augustine. *The City of God.* Trans. Marcus Dods. New York: The Modern Library, 1950.

——. *Contra adversarium legis et prophetarum.* Ed. Klaus D. Daur. CCSL 49. 1985.

——. *De civitate Dei.* Ed. Bernard Dombart and Alphonse Kalb. CCSL 47–48. 1955.

——. *De peccatorum meritis et remissione, et de baptismo parvulorum.* Ed. Karl Franz Urba and Joseph Zycha. CSEL 60. Vienna: Tempsky, 1913.

——. *Enarrationes in Psalmos.* Ed. E. Dekkers and J. Fraipont. CCSL 38, 39, 40. 1956–.

——. *Enchiridion.* Trans. J. F. Shaw. Ed. H. Paolucci. South Bend, IN: Regnery/Gateway, 1961.

——. *Enchiridion de fide et spe et caritate.* Ed. E. Evans. CCSL 46. 1969.

——. *Epistulae.* Ed. Alois Goldbacher. CSEL 57. Vienna: Tempsky; Leipzig: Freytag, 1911.

——. *In Iohannis euangelium tractatus.* Ed. R. Willems. CCSL 36. 1954.

Aulus Gellius. *Noctes Atticae.* Ed. Peter K. Marshall. Oxford: Clarendon Press, 1968.

Bede. *Historia ecclesiastica gentis Anglorum.* Ed. Charles Plummer. 2 vols. Oxford: Clarendon Press, 1896.

——. *A History of the English Church and People.* Trans. Leo Shirley-Price, rev. R. E. Latham. Harmondsworth, UK: Penguin, 1955.

——. *Homeliarum evangelii libri II.* Ed. D. Hurst. CCSL 122. 1955.

——. *In Lucae Euangelium expositio.* Ed. D. Hurst. CCSL 120. 1960.

——. *In prouerbia Salomonis libri iii.* Ed. D. Hurst. CCSL 119B. 1983.

Biblia sacra iuxta Vulgatam versionem. Ed. R. Weber. 4th ed. R. Gryson. Stuttgart: Deutsche Bibelgesellschaft, 1994.

Bibliorum Sacrorum Latinae versiones antiquae: seu vetus Italica, et caeterae quaecunque in codicibus mss. & antiquorum libris reperiri potuerunt quae cum Vulgata Latina & cum textu Graeco comparantur. Ed. P. Sabatier. 1751. Turnhout, Belgium: Brepols, 1981.

Boniface. *Letters.* Trans. Ephraim Emerton. Columbia University Records of Civilization. 1940. New York: Norton, 1976.

Bonifatius et Lullus. *Epistolae.* Ed. Michael Tangl. MGH, Epistolae Selectae 1. Berlin: Weidmann, 1916.

Caesarius Arelatensis. *Opera.* Pt. 1, *Sermones.* Ed. G. Morin. CCSL 103–4. 1953.

Cerulli, E., ed. *Il "Libro della Scala" e la questione delle fonti arabo-spagnole della divina commedia.* Studi e Testi 150. Vatican City: Biblioteca Apostolica Vaticana, 1949.

Charlesworth, James H., ed. *The Old Testament Pseudepigrapha.* 2 vols. Garden City, NY: Doubleday, 1983.

Clément d'Alexandrie. *Les stromates: Stromate VI.* Ed. and trans. Patrick Descourtieux. SC 446. 1999.

Code of Hammurabi. In *The Babylonian Laws,* ed. and trans. D. R. Driver and John C. Miles, vol. 2. Oxford: Clarendon Press, 1955.

Corpus Juris Civilis. Ed. Theodor Mommsen and Paul Krueger. 2 vols. Berlin: Weidmann, 1872–77.

Cyprianus Carthaginensis. *Ad Demetrianum.* Ed. M. Simonetti. CCSL 3A. 1976.

De vera et falsa poenitentia. PL 40:1113–30.

The Earliest Life of Gregory the Great by an Anonymous Monk of Whitby. Ed. and trans. Bertram Colgrave. Lawrence: University of Kansas Press, 1968.

Epstein, Isidore, ed. *The Babylonian Talmud*. 35 vols. London: The Soncino Press, 1935–52.

The Exposition of the Orthodox Faith. Trans. S. D. F. Salmond. In *NPNF-2*. 1899.

Florence of Worcester. *The Chronicle of Florence of Worcester*. London: H. G. Bohn, 1854.

Fry, Timothy, ed. *The Rule of St. Benedict in Latin and English with Notes*. Collegeville, MN: The Liturgical Press, 1980.

Gardiner, Eileen. *Visions of Heaven and Hell before Dante*. New York: Italica, 1989.

Gaster, Moses, ed. *The Exempla of the Rabbis*. New York: KTAV, 1968.

——, ed. *The Ma'aseh Book: Book of Jewish Tales and Legends*. 2 vols in 1. Philadelphia: Jewish Publication Society of America, 1981.

The Gāthās of Zarathustra. Trans. S. Insler. Acta Iranica 8. Leiden: Brill, 1975.

Gesta Dagoberti I regis Francorum. Ed. Bruno Krusch. MGH, SS RR MM 2 (1885): 416–19.

The Gospel of Nicodemus, or Acts of Pilate. Trans. Montague Rhodes James. In *ANT*, pp. 117–46.

Gregorius Turonensis. *Libri historiarum decem*. Ed. W. Arndt and Bruno Krusch. MGH, SS RR MM 1. 1885.

Gregory the Great. *Dialogues*. Ed. and trans. A. de Vogüé. 3 vols. Paris: Éditions du Cerf, 1978–80.

——. *Dialogues*. Trans. Myra L. Uhlfelder. The Library of Liberal Arts. Indianapolis: Bobbs-Merrill, 1967.

——. *Homiliae in euangelia*. Ed. Raymond Etaix. CCSL 141. 1999.

——. *Moralia in Job*. Ed. Marc Adriaen. CCSL 143, 143a, 143b. 1979–85.

Gregory of Nyssa. *De anima et resurrectione dialogus*. PG 46:12–161.

——. *On the Soul and Resurrection*. Trans. William Moore and Henry Austin Wilson. In *NPNF-2*, 5:798–872. 1893.

Gregory of Tours. *Glory of the Confessors*. Trans. Raymond van Dam. Liverpool: Liverpool University Press, 1988.

——. *The History of the Franks*. Trans. Lewis Thorpe. Harmondsworth, UK: Penguin, 1974.

Guy, Jean-Claude, ed. and trans. *Les Apophtègmes des Pères: Collection systématique*. 3 vols. SC 387, 474, 498. 1993–2005.

Hepidannus. *Vita Wiboradae martyris*. In *Acta Sanctorum*, May 2, vol. 1, cols. 301–8. Antwerp, 1680.

Hesiod, the Homeric Hymns, and Homerica. Trans. H. G. Evelyn-White. LCL. 1982.

Hieronymus. *Commentarii in Ezechielem*. Ed. F. Glorie. CCSL 75. 1964.

——. *Commentarii in prophetas minores*. Ed. M. Adriaen. CCSL 76A. 1969–70.

——. *Epistolae*. Ed. I. Hilberg. CSEL 54–56. Vienna: Tempsky, 1910/1918.

——. [Jerome.] *Expositio Evangelii secundum Marcum*. Ed. Michael Cahill. CCSL 82. 1997.

——. *Tractatus lix in Psalmos*. Ed. G. Morin. CCSL 78. 1958.

Hildemar. *Expositio regulae ab Hildemaro tradita*. Ed. P. Rupertus Mittermüller. Ratisbon, NY, and Cincinnati: Frederick Pustet, 1880.

Hincmar Remensis. *Vita Remigii Episcopi Remensis*. Ed. Bruno Krusch. MGH, SS RR MM 3: 239–349. [1896] 1977.

Historia Lausiaca (*Apophthegmata Patrum*). PG 65:72–440.

Hugo Archidiaconus. "Dialogus ad Fulbertum amicum suum de quodam miraculo, quod contigit in translatione Sancti Martini." In Jean Mabillon, *Vetera analecta*, vol. 1 (1675–1676), 349–74; and the nova editio (Paris: Montalant, 1723), 213–17.

Ibn Ishaq, Muhammad. *The Life of Muhammad: A Translation of Ibn Ishaq's Sirat Rasul Allah*. Trans. A. Guillaume. Karachi: Oxford University Press, 1967.

Isidorus Hispalensis. *De differentiis rerum siue Differentiae theologicae uel spiritales*. PL 83:9–98.

——. *Etymologiarum sive Originum libri XX*. Ed. W. M. Lindsay. 2 vols. 1911. Oxford: Clarendon Press, 1971.

——. *Sententiae*. Ed. Pierre Cazier. CCSL 111. 1998.

——. *Synonyma*. Ed. Jacques Elfassi. CCSL 111B. 2009.

Itala: Das Neue Testament in altlateinischer Überlieferung. 4 vols. Berlin: Walter de Gruyter, 1938.

Jироušková, Lenka. *Die Visio Pauli: Wege und Wandlungen einer orientalischen Apokryphe im lateinischen Mittelalter*. Leiden: Brill, 2006.

Joannes Diaconus. *Vita Gregorii Magni*. PL 75:61–240.

John Cassian. *Conlationes xxiiii*. Ed. Michael Petschenig. CSEL 13. Vienna: Gerold, 1886.

——. *Institutions cénobitiques*. Ed. and trans. Jean-Claude Guy. SC 109. 1965.

John Chrysostom. *Adversus Judaeos orationes*. PG 48:843–942.

——. *Discourses against Judaizing Christians*. Trans. Paul W. Harkins. Fathers of the Church 68. Washington, DC: Catholic University of America Press, 1979.

——. *Epistola ad Theodorum Lapsum*. PG 47:271–316.

——. *An Exhortation to Theodore after His Fall*. Trans. W. R. W. Stephens. In *NPNF-1*, 9:123–67. 1889.

John of Damascus. *Expositio fidei orthodoxae*. PG 94:790–1228.

John of Damascus [pseud.]. *Oratio de his qui in fide dormierunt*. PG 95:250–83.

John the Scot Erigena. *De divisione naturae, Liber quintus*. PL 122:859–1022.

——. *Periphyseon (De diuisione naturae)*. Ed. E. A. Jeauneau. CCCM 161–65. 1996–2003.

——. *Periphyseon (On the Division of Nature)*. Ed. and trans. Myra L. Uhlfelder, with summaries by Jean A. Potter. Library of Liberal Arts 157. Indianapolis: Bobbs-Merrill, 1976.

Julianus Toletani. *Prognosticon futuri saeculi*. Ed. Joscelin Hillgarth. CCSL 115. 1976.

Justinian. *Corpus Iuris Civilis*. Vol. 3, *Novellae*. Ed. R. Schoell and G. Kroll. 6th ed. Berlin: Weidmann, 1954.

Lactantius. *De mortibus persecutorum*. Ed. and trans. J. L. Creed. Oxford Early Christian Texts. Oxford and New York: Clarendon Press, 1984.

La Règle de Saint Benoît. Ed. Adalbert de Vogüé and Jean Neufville. 7 vols. SC 181–86 [vol. 7 published independently]. 1971–72.

La Règle du Maître. Ed. Adalbert de Vogüé. SC 105. 1964.

Les lois religieuses des empereurs romains de Constantin à Théodose II (312–438). Vol. 1, *Code Théodosien, Livre XVI*, ed. Theodor Mommsen, trans. Jean Rougé, with Roland Delmaire and François Richard. SC 497. 2005. Vol. 2, *Code Théodosien, Livres I–XV*, ed. Theodor Mommsen, trans. Jean Rougé. SC 531. 2009.

Lysias. *On the Murder of Eratosthenes*. Ed. and trans. W. R. M. Lamb. LCL. 1930.

Martyrdom of Carpus. In *The Acts of the Christian Martyrs*, ed. and trans. H. Musurillo, 22–37. Oxford: Clarendon Press, 1972.

Martyrdom of Conon. In *The Acts of the Christian Martyrs*, ed. and trans. H. Musurillo, 187–93. Oxford: Clarendon Press, 1972.

Martyrdom of Polycarp. In *The Acts of the Christian Martyrs*, ed. and trans. H. Musurillo, 2–21. Oxford: Clarendon Press, 1972.

Méliton de Sardes. *Sur la Pâque.* Ed. Othmar Perler. SC 123. 1966.

Minucius Felix. *Octavius.* Trans. Gerald H. Rendall. LCL. 1931.

Montefiore, C. G., and H. Loewe, *A Rabbinic Anthology.* New York: Schocken Books, 1974.

Musurillo, Herbert, ed. *The Acts of the Christian Martyrs.* Oxford: Clarendon Press, 1972.

Origen. *De principiis.* Ed. Paul Koetschau. Vol. 5 of *Origenes Werke.* Die griechischen christlichen Schriftsteller der ersten drei Jahrhunderte 22. Leipzig: Hinrichs, 1913.

——. *On First Principles.* Trans. G. W. Butterworth. New York: Harper and Row, 1966.

Passion of Ss. Perpetua and Felicitas. In *Medieval Women's Visonary Literature*, ed. Elizabeth Alvida Petroff, 70–77. New York and Oxford: Oxford University Press, 1986.

Passio Perpetuae. In *The Acts of the Christian Martyrs*, ed. and trans. H. Musurillo, 106–30. Oxford: Clarendon Press, 1972.

Paulus Orosius. *Historiae adversum paganos.* Ed. C. Zangemeister. CSEL 5. Vienna: Gerold, 1889.

Petrus Damiani. *Epistolae: Die Briefe des Petrus Damiani.* Ed. Kurt Reindel. 4 vols. Munich: MGH, 1983–93.

Plato. *The Collected Dialogues.* Ed. Edith Hamilton and Huntington Cairns. Bollingen Series 71. Princeton, NJ: Princeton University Press, 1961.

Pliny. *Letters.* Trans. Betty Radice. LCL. 1969.

Plutarch. *On the Delays of the Divine Vengeance.* Trans. Phillip H. De Lacy and Benedict Einarson. In *Moralia.* LCL. 1959.

——. *Plutarch's Lives.* Ed. and trans. Bernadotte Perrin. 11 vols. LCL. 1959.

Polybius. *The Histories.* Trans. W. R. Paton. 3 vols. LCL. 1922–27.

Prudentius. *Carmina.* Ed. Mauricius Cunningham. CCSL 126. 1966.

Rippin, Andrew, ed. *The Qur'ān: Formative Interpretation.* Brookfield, VT: Ashgate, 1999.

Rodulfus Glaber Opera. Ed. John France, Neithard Bulst, and Paul Reynolds. Oxford Medieval Texts. Oxford: Clarendon Press, 1989.

Saadia Gaon. *The Book of Belief and Opinions.* Trans. Samuel Rosenblatt. Yale Judaica Series 1. New Haven, CT: Yale University Press, 1948.

——. *The Book of Doctrines and Beliefs.* An abridged edition translated from the Arabic with an introduction and notes by Alexander Altmann and a new introduction by Daniel H. Frank. Indianapolis and Cambridge: Hackett, 2002.

Seneca. *Ad Lucilium epistulae morales.* Ed. and trans. Richard M. Gummere. 3 vols. LCL. 1917–25.

Silverstein, Theodore. *Visio Sancti Pauli: The History of the Apocalypse in Latin, together with Nine Texts.* Studies and Documents 4. 1935. London: Christophers, 1955.

Silverstein, Theodore, and Anthony Hilhorst, eds. *Apocalypse of Paul: A New Critical Edition of Three Long Latin Versions with 54 plates.* Geneva: Cramer, 1997.

Smaragdus. *Commentary on the Rule of Saint Benedict*. Trans. David Barry. Cistercian Studies Series 212. Kalamazoo, MI: Cistercian Publications, 2007.

——. *Expositio in Regulam S. Benedicti*. PL 102:689–932.

——. *Expositio in Regulam S. Benedicti*. Ed. A. Spannagel and P. Engelbert. Corpus Consuetudinum Monasticarum 8. Siegeburg, Germany: F. Schmitt, 1974.

Taio Caesaraugustanus [of Zaragossa]. *Sententiarum libri quinque*. PL 80:727–990.

Tanna debe Eliyyahu: The Lore of the School of Elijah. Trans. William G. (Gershon Zev) Braude and Israel J. Kapstein. Philadelphia: The Jewish Publication Society of America, 5741/1981.

Tertullian. *De spectaculis*. Trans. T. R. Glover. LCL. 1931.

Theodoret of Cyrrhus. *A History of the Monks of Syria*. Trans. Richard M. Price. Kalamazoo, MI: Cistercian Publications, 1985.

The Theodosian Code and Novels, and the Sirmondian Constitutions. Trans. Clyde Pharr. Princeton, NJ: Princeton University Press, 1952.

Theodosiani Libri XVI. Ed. Theodor Mommsen, Paul M. Meyer, and Jacques Sirmond. Berlin: Weidmann, 1905.

Theophylact of Ochrid. *Enarratio in Evangelium Lucae*. PG 123:683–1127.

Thomas Aquinas. *Summa Theologiae*. Ed. Peter Caramello. 4 vols. Turin: Marietti, 1948–50.

Tischendorf, Constantinus de. *Evangelia Apocrypha*. Leipzig: Mendelssohn, 1876. Reprint, Hildesheim: G. Olms, 1966.

[Titus.] *Epistle*. Trans. A. de Dantos Otero. In H-S 2:141–66.

Tractate Sanhedrin: Mishnah and Tosefta. Trans. Herbert Danby. London and New York: Macmillan, 1919.

Urkundenbuch der Abtei Sanct Gallen. Pt. I, *700–840*. Ed. Hermann Wartmann. Zurich: S. Höhr, 1863.

Venantius Fortunatus [pseud.]. *Vita Remedii [i.e., Remigii]*. Ed. Bruno Krusch. MGH AA 4.2:xxii-xxiv, 64–67. Berlin: Weidmann, 1885.

Vetus latina: Die Reste der altlateinischen Bibel nach Petrus Sabatier neu gesammelt und herausgegeben von der Erzabtei Beuron. Freiburg: Herder, 1956–2000.

Visio Baronti Monachi Longoretensis. Ed. W. Levison. MGH, SS RR MM 5:368–94. Hannover: Hahn, 1910.

Vision of Barontus. Trans. Jocelyn Hillgarth. In *Christianity and Paganism, 350–750*, 195–204. Philadelphia: University of Pennsylvania Press, 1986.

Vision of a Monk of Wenlock. Ed. Michael Tangl. In *S. Bonifatii et Lulli epistolae*, 8–15. MGH, Epistolae Selectae 1. Berlin: Weidmann, [1916].

Vision of the Monk of Wenlock. Trans. Ephraim Emerton. In *The Letters of Saint Boniface*, 25–31. Columbia Records of Civilization. New York: Norton, 1976.

Visio Pauli. Ed. Montague Rhodes James, In *Texts and Studies*, ed. J. Armitage Robinson, vol. 2, no. 3. *AA*, 1–42. Cambridge: Cambridge University Press, 1893.

Visio Sancti Fursei. In Claude Carozzi, *Le voyage de l'âme dans l'au delà d'après la littérature latine (Vᵉ–XIIIᵉ siècle)*, 677–92. Collection de l'École Française de Rome 189. Rome: École française de Rome, 1994.

Visio Tnugdali. Ed. Albrecht Wagner. Erlangen: Deichert, 1882.

Vita et miracula S. Fursei. Ed. W. W. Heist. In *Vitae Sanctorum Hiberniae*, 37–55. Subsidia Hagiographica 28. Brussels: Société des Bollandistes, 1965.

Vita et navigatio Sancti Brendani. Ed. W. W. Heist. In *Vitae Sanctorum Hiberniae*, 56–78. Subsidia Hagiographia 28. Brussels: Société des Bollandistes, 1965.

Zeno Veronensis. *Tractatus*. Ed. B. Löfstedt. CCSL 22. 1971.

Secondary Sources

Abels, Richard. "What Has Weland to Do with Christ? The Franks Casket and the Acculturation of Christianity in Early Anglo-Saxon England." *Speculum* 84.3 (July 2009): 549–81.

Abrahamov, Binyamin. "Al-Kāsim ibn Ibrāhīm's Argument from Design." *Oriens* 29 (1986): 259–85.

———. "The Creation and Duration of Paradise and Hell in Islamic Theology." *Der Islam* 79.1 (2002): 87–102.

Abulafia, David. *The Great Sea: A Human History of the Mediterranean*. New York: Oxford University Press, 2011.

Abu-Lughod, Janet L. *Before European Hegemony: The World System, A.D. 1250–1350*. New York: Oxford University Press, 1989.

Adler, Cyrus, and Francis L. Cohen. "Ashirah." In *Jewish Encyclopedia*, 2:188–90. New York and London: Funk & Wagnalls. 1903.

Afonso, Laurentino Jose, and Batya Kedar. "Netherworld." In *Encyclopaedia Judaica*, 15:110–12. 2nd ed. Detroit: Macmillan, 2007.

Al-Azmeh, Aziz, and János M. Bak, eds. *Monotheistic Kingship: The Medieval Variants*. Budapest and New York: Central European University, Department of Medieval Studies, 2004.

Algaze, Guillermo. "Habuba on the Tigris: Archaic Nineveh Reconsidered." *Journal of Near Eastern Studies* 45.2 (April 1986): 125–37.

Ali, Maulana Muhammad. *The Religion of Islam*. Lahore, Pakistan: The Ahmadiyya Anjuman Isha'at Islam, 1983.

Allatius, Leo. "De S. Damasceni Prolegomena." PG 94:118–92.

Allen, Danielle S. *World of Prometheus: The Politics of Punishing in Democratic Athens*. Princeton, NJ: Princeton University Press, 2000.

Amat, Jacqueline. *Songes et visions: L'au-delà dans la littérature latine tardive*. Paris: Éditions augustiniennes, 1985.

Aubrun, Michel. "Caractères et portée religieuse et sociale des 'Visiones'." *Cahiers de Civilisation Médiévale* 23.2 (1980): 109–30.

Austin, R. G. P. *Vergili Maronis Aeneidos Liber Sextus, Commentary*. Oxford: Clarendon Press, 1977.

Azzolina, David S. *Tale Type- and Motif-Indexes: An Annotated Bibliography*. New York: Garland, 1987.

Bacher, Wilhelm, and Judah David Eisenstein. "Shirah, Perek." In *The Jewish Encyclopedia*, 11:294–96. New York: Funk & Wagnalls, 1906.

Bacher, Wilhelm, Jacob Zallel Lauterbach, Joseph Jacobs, and Louis Ginzberg. "Tannaim and Amoraim." In *The Jewish Encyclopedia*, 12:49–54. New York: Funk and Wagnalls, 1906.

Baker, H. D. "Degrees of Freedom: Slavery in Mid-First Millennium BC Babylonia." *World Archaeology* 33.1 (June, 2001): 18–26.

Baschet, Jérôme. *Le sein du père: Abraham et la paternité dans l'Occident médiéval*. Paris: Gallimard, 2000.

——. *Les justices de l'au-delà: Les representations de l'enfer en France et en Italie (XIIᵉ–XVᵉ siècles)*. Bibliothèque des Écoles Françaises d'Athènes et de Rome 279. Rome: École française de Rome, 1993.

Bauckham, Richard. "The Rich Man and Lazarus: The Parable and the Parallels." *New Testament Studies* 37 (1991): 225–46.

Baun, Jane. *Tales from Another Byzantium: Celestial Journey and Local Community in the Medieval Greek Apocrypha*. Cambridge: Cambridge University Press, 2007.

Beck, Henry G. J. "A Ninth-Century Canonist on Purgatory." *American Ecclesiastical Review* 111.4 (1944): 250–56.

Beinart, Heim. *Atlas of Medieval Jewish History*. New York: Simon & Schuster, 1992.

Ben-Amos, Dan. "Jewish Folklore Studies." *Modern Judaism* 11.1 (February 1991): 17–66.

Ben-Ari, Shosh. "Stories about Abraham in Islam: A Geographical Approach." *Arabica* 54.4 (2007): 526–53.

Bennett, Harold. "Sacer Esto." *Transactions and Proceedings of the American Philological Association* 61 (1930): 5–18.

Bernstein, Alan E. "The *Exemplum* as 'Incorporation' of Abstract Truth in the Thought of Humbert of Romans and Stephen of Bourbon." In *The Two Laws: Studies in Medieval Legal History Dedicated to Stephan Kuttner*, ed. L. Mayali and S. Jefferis-Tibbetts, 82–96. Washington, DC: Catholic University of America Press, 1990.

——. *The Formation of Hell: Death and Retribution in the Ancient and Early Christian Worlds*. Ithaca, NY: Cornell University Press, 1993.

——. "Named Others and Named Places: Stigmatization in the Early Medieval Afterlife." In *Hell and Its Afterlife: Historical and Contemporary Perspectives*, ed. Isabel Moreira and Margaret Toscano, 53–71. Farnham, UK., and Burlington, VT: Ashgate, 2010.

——. Review of *La naissance du purgatoire*, by Jacques Le Goff. *Speculum* 59 (1984): 179–83.

——. "*Tristitia* and the Fear of Hell in Monastic Reflection from John Cassian to Hildemar of Corbie." In *Continuity and Change: The Harvest of Late-Medieval and Reformation History: Essays Presented to Heiko A. Oberman on His 70th Birthday*, ed. Robert J. Bast and Andrew C. Gow, 183–205. Leiden: Brill, 2000.

Bernt, G. "Hildemar v. Corbie." *Lexikon des Mittelalters* 5 (1990): 15–16.

Bin Gorion, M. J., ed. *Der Born Judas: Legenden, Märchen und Erzählungen*. 2nd ed. 6 vols. Leipzig: Insel Verlag, n.d.

Blenkinsopp, Joseph. "Deuteronomy." In *The New Jerome Biblical Commentary*, 94–109. London: Prentice-Hall, 1990.

Borst, Arno. "Three Studies of Death in the Middle Ages." In *Medieval Worlds: Barbarians, Heretics, and Artists in the Middle Ages*, trans. Eric Hansen, 215–43. Chicago: University of Chicago Press, 1992.

Bougerol, Jacques-Guy. "Autour de 'la Naissance du Purgatoire'." *Archives d'Histoire Doctrinale et Littéraire du Moyen Âge* 50 (1983): 7–59.

Bowker, John W. "Intercession in the Qur'an and the Jewish Tradition." *Journal of Semitic Studies* 11.1 (Spring 1966): 69–82.

Boyce, Mary. *A History of Zoroastrianism*. 2 vols. Leiden: Brill, 1975, 1982.

——. *Zoroastrians: Their Religious Beliefs and Practices*. London and Boston: Routledge & Kegan Paul, 1985.

Bradley, Keith, and Paul Cartledge, eds. *The Cambridge World History of Slavery*. Vol. 1, *The Ancient Mediterranean World*. Cambridge: Cambridge University Press, 2011.

——. *Slavery and Society at Rome*. Cambridge: Cambridge University Press, 1994.

Braet, Herman. "La réception médiévale de l'Apocalypse paulinienne: Une réécriture de l'au-delà." In *Miscellanea di studi romanzi offerta a G. Gasca Quierazza*, 75–89. Alexandria: Edizioni dell'Orso, 1988.

Braude, Benjamin, and Marie-Pierre Gaviano. "Race, esclavage et exégèse entre islam, judaïsme et christianisme." *Annales: Histoire, Sciences Sociales* 57.1 (2002): 93–125.

Bremmer, Jan. "Christian Hell: From the *Apocalypse of Peter* to the *Apocalypse of Paul*." *Numen* 56 (2009): 298–325.

Bremond, C., J. Le Goff, and J.-C. Schmitt. *L'exemplum*. Typologie des Sources du Moyen Âge Occidental 40. Turnhout, Belgium: Brepols, 1982.

Briquel, Dominique. "Formes de mise à mort dans la Rome primitive: Quelques remarques sur une approche comparative du problème." In *Du châtiment dans la cité: Supplices corporels et peine de mort dans le monde antique*, ed. Yan Thomas, 225–40. Collection de l'École Française de Rome 79. Rome: École française de Rome, 1984.

Brockopp, Jonathan E. "Slaves and Slavery." In *Encyclopaedia of the Qur'ān*, ed. Jane Dammen McAuliffe, 5: 56b-60b. Leiden and Boston: Brill, 2001-6.

Bronner, Dagmar. "Codeswitching in Medieval Ireland: The Case of the *Vita Tripartita Sancti Patricii*." *Journal of Celtic Linguistics* 9 (2005): 1–12.

Brook, Timothy, Jérôme Bourgon, and Gregory Blue. *Death by a Thousand Cuts*. Cambridge, MA, and London: Harvard University Press, 2008.

Brown, Peter. "The Decline of the Empire of God: Amnesty, Penance, and the Afterlife from Late Antiquity to the Middle Ages." In *The Last Things: Death and the Apocalypse in the Middle Ages*, ed. Caroline Walker Bynum and Paul Freedman, 41–59. Philadelphia: University of Pennsylvania Press, 2000.

——. "The End of the Ancient Other World." Lecture I, "Gloriosus Obitus: Death and Afterlife, 400–700 A.D." In *The Tanner Lectures on Human Values*, 20:21–50. Salt Lake City: University of Utah Press, 1999.

——. "The End of the Ancient Other World." Lecture II, "The Decline of the Empire of God: From Amnesty to Purgatory." In *The Tanner Lectures on Human Values*, 20:51–85. Salt Lake City: University of Utah Press, 1999.

——. *The Rise of Western Christendom*. 2nd ed. Oxford: Blackwell, 2003.

——. "Saint Augustine's Attitude to Religious Coercion." *Journal of Roman Studies* 54.1–2 (1964): 107–16.

Bruyne, Donatien de. "Epistula Titi, Discipuli Pauli, De dispositione sanctimonii." *Revue Bénédictine* 37 (1925): 47–72.

Budge, E. A. Wallis. *The Egyptian Heaven and Hell*. 1905. La Salle, IL: Open Court, 1974.

Bullough, Donald A. *Alcuin: Achievement and Reputation*. Leiden and Boston: Brill, 2004.

Bynum, Caroline Walker, and Paul Freedman. Introduction to *Last Things: Death and the Apocalypse in the Middle Ages*, ed. Caroline Walker Bynum and Paul Freedman, 1–17. Philadelphia: University of Pennsylvania Press, 2000.

Cabassut, A. "La mitigation des peines de l'enfer d'après les livres liturgiques." *Revue d'Histoire Ecclésiastique* 33 (1927): 65–70.

Callon, Callie. "Sorcery, Wheels, and Mirror Punishment in the *Apocalypse of Peter*." *Journal of Early Christian Studies* 18.1 (2010): 29–49.

Cantarella, Eva. *I supplizi capitali in Graecia e a Roma*. Milan: Rizzoli, 1991.

Carozzi, Claude. *Eschatologie et au-delà: Recherches sur l'Apocalypse de Paul*. Aix-en-Provence: Publications de l'Université de Provence, 1994.

———. *Le voyage de l'âme dans l'au delà d'après la littérature latine (V^e–XIIIe siècle)*. Collection de l'École Française de Rome 189. Rome: École française de Rome; Paris: Boccard, 1994.

Carroll, M. "Thomas Aquinas: An Eighth-Century Exegete on Purgatory." *American Ecclesiastical Review* 112.1 (1945): 261–63.

Casey, R. P. "The *Apocalypse of Paul*." *Journal of Theological Studies* 34 (1933): 1–32.

Castelli, David. "The Future Life in Rabbinical Literature." *Jewish Quarterly Review* 1.4 (July 1889): 314–52.

Cavalcanti, E. "Theodoret of Cyrrhus." In *EEC*, 2:827.

Cavanaugh, Alix. "The Abominable Fancy." *Venia Legendi* (blog). Accessed January 8, 2008. http://venialegendi.blogspot.com/2007/08/abominable-fancy.html.

Chiamenti, Massimiliano. "Intertestualità *Liber Scale Machometi—Commedia?*" In *Dante e il locus inferni*, ed. Simone Foà and Sonia Gentile, 45–51. Rome: Bulzoni, 2000.

Chitty, Derwas J. *The Desert a City: An Introduction to the Study of Egyptian and Palestinian Monasticism under the Christian Empire*. 1966. Crestwood, NY: St. Vladimir's Seminary Press, 1977.

Ciccarese, Maria Pia. "Le più antiche rappresentazioni del purgatorio, dalla *Passio Perpetuae* alla fine del IX sec." *Romanobarbarica* 7 (1982–83): 33–76.

Clark, Francis. *The Pseudo-Gregorian Dialogues*. 2 vols. Leiden: Brill, 1987.

Cohen, A[braham]. *Everyman's Talmud*. 1949. New York: Schocken, 1975.

Cohn, Haim Hermann. "Confession." In *Encyclopaedia Judaica*, 5:147. 2nd ed. Detroit: Macmillan, 2007.

———. "Slavery." In *Encyclopaedia Judaica*, 18:667–70. 2nd ed. Detroit: Macmillan, 2007.

Cohn, Haim Hermann, Louis Isaac Rabinowitz, and Menachem Elon. "Capital Punishment." In *Encyclopaedia Judaica*, 4:445–51. 2nd ed. Detroit: Macmillan, 2007.

Cohn-Sherbok, Dan. "The Jewish Doctrine of Hell." *Religion* 8 (1978): 196–209.

Cohn-Sherbok, Lavinia, and Dan Cohn-Sherbok. *Judaism: A Short Introduction*. Oxford: Oneworld Press, 1999.

Colish, Marcia. "The Virtuous Pagan: Dante and the Christian Tradition." In *The Unbounded Community: Conversations across Times and Disciplines*, ed. Duncan Fisher and William Caferro, 43–91. New York: Garland, 1996.

Collins, John J. "The Development of the Sibylline Tradition." *Aufstieg und Niedergang der römischen Welt* 2.20.1 (1987): 421–59.

Connell, Martin F. "*Descensus Christi ad Inferos*: Christ's Descent to the Dead." *Theological Studies* 62 (2001): 262–82.

Constable, Olivia Remie. *Housing the Stranger in the Mediterranean World: Lodging, Trade, and Travel in Late Antiquity and the Middle Ages*. Cambridge: Cambridge University Press, 2003.

Constas, Nicholas. "'To Sleep, Perchance to Dream': The Middle State of Souls in Patristic and Byzantine Literature." *Dumbarton Oaks Papers* 55 (2001): 91–124.

Cook, Michael. "Eschatology and the Dating of Traditions." In *Princeton Papers in Near Eastern Studies*, ed. Charles Issawi and Bernard Lewis, 23–47. Princeton, NJ: Darwin Press, 1992.

Costa, José. *L'au-delà et la résurrection dans la littérature rabbinique ancienne*. Paris and Louvain: Peeters, 2004.

Coupland, Simon. "The Early Coinage of Charles the Bald." *Numismatic Chronicle* 151 (1991): 121–58 and pls. 21–24.

Cracco, Giorgio. "Gregorio e l'oltretomba." In *Grégoire le Grand*, 255–266. Colloques Internationaux du CNRS. Paris: Éditions du CNRS, 1986.

——. "Uomini di Dio e uomini di Chiesa nell'Alto Medioevo (per una reinterpretazione dei *Dialogi* di Gregorio Magno." *Ricerche di Storia Sociale e Religiosa*, n.s. 12 (1977): 163–202.

Crouzel, Henri. "L'Hadès et la Géhenne selon Origène." *Gregorianum* 59 (1978): 291–331.

Czachesz, Istvan. "The Grotesque Body in the *Apocalypse of Peter*." In *The Apocalypse of Peter*, ed. Jan N. Bremmer and István Czachesz, 108–26. Studies on Early Christian Apocrypha 7. Leuven: Peeters, 2003.

Daley, Brian E. *The Hope of the Early Church: A Handbook of Patristic Eschatology*. Cambridge: Cambridge University Press, 1991.

Damon, John. *Soldier Saints and Holy Warriors: Warfare and Sanctity in the Literature of Early England*. Burlington, VT: Ashgate, 2003.

David, Jean-Michel. "Du Comitium à la roche Tarpéienne." *Du châtiment dans la cité: Supplices corporels et peine de mort dans le monde antique*, ed. Yan Thomas, 131–75. Collection de l'École Française de Rome 79. Rome: École française de Rome, 1984.

Davidson, Herbert A. "John Philoponus as a Source of Medieval Islamic and Jewish Proof of Creation." *Journal of the American Oriental Society* 89 (1969): 357–91.

Deckers, Johannes G. "Gnade für Hades? Beobachtungen am Bild der Anastasis." *Jahrbuch für Antike und Christentum* 50 (2007): 123–39.

Deleeuw, Patricia. "Gregory the Great's 'Homilies on the Gospels' in the Early Middle Ages." *Studi Mediaevali*, ser. 3, 26.1 (1986): 855–69.

Devroey, Jean-Pierre. "Men and Women in Early Medieval Serfdom: The Ninth-Century North Frankish Evidence." *Past & Present* 166 (February 2000): 3–30.

Diaz y Diaz, M. "Julian of Toledo." In *Encyclopedia of the Early Church*, 1:458–59. New York: Oxford University Press, 1992.

Dieterich, Albrecht. *Nekyia: Beiträge zur Erklärung der neuentdeckten Petrusapokalypse*. Leipzig: Teubner, 1893.

Dinzelbacher, Peter. *Vision und Visionsliteratur im Mittelalter*. Stuttgart: Anton Hiersemann, 1981.

Duft, Johannes, ed. *Die Abtei St. Gallen*. Vol. 2, *Beiträge zur Kenntnis ihrer Persönlichkeiten*. Sigmaringen: Jan Thorbecke, 1991.

Dunn, Marilyn. "Gregory the Great, the Vision of Fursey, and the Origins of Purgatory." *Peritia* 14 (2000): 238–54.

Dyer, George J. *Limbo: Unsettled Question*. New York: Sheed and Ward, 1964.

Edwards, Mark. "The First Council of Nicaea." In *The Cambridge History of Christianity*, 1:552–67. Cambridge: Cambridge University Press, 2006.

Eklund, Ragnar. *Life between Death and Resurrection according to Islam*. Inaugural Dissertation. Uppsala: Almqvist & Wiksells, 1941.

Elfassi, Jacques. "Genèse et originalité du style synonymique dans les *Synonyma* d'Isidore de Séville." *Revue des Études Latines* 83 (2006): 226–45.

——. "Les deux recensions des *Synonyma*." In *L'édition critique des oeuvres d'Isidore de Séville*, ed. Maria Adelaida Andrés Sanz, Jacques Elfassi, and José Carlos Martín, 153–84. Paris: Institut d'Études Augustiniennes, 2008.

——. "Les *Synonyma* d'Isidore de Séville: Un manuel de grammaire ou de morale?" *Revue d'Études Augustiniennes et Patristiques* 52 (2006): 167–98.

——. "Los dentones de los *Synonyma* de Isidoro de Sevilla." In *IV Congresso Internacional de Latín Medieval Hispânico*, ed. Aires A. Nascimeto and Paulo F. Alberto, 393–401. Lisbon: Centro de Estudos Clássicos, 2006.

Elm, Susanna. *"Virgins of God": The Making of Ascetisicm in Late Antiquity*. Oxford Classical Monographs. 1994. Oxford: Clarendon Paperbacks, 1996.

The Encyclopedia of Judaism. Ed. Geoffrey Wigoder. New York: Macmillan, 1989.

Endress, Gerhard. *An Introduction to Islam*. Trans. Carole Hillenbrand. New York: Columbia University Press, 1988.

Erdmann, Carl. *The Origin of the Idea of Crusade*. Trans. Marshall W. Baldwin and Walter Goffart. 1935. Princeton, NJ: Princeton University Press, 1977.

Fanar, Emma Maayan. "Visiting Hades: A Transformation of the Ancient God in the Ninth-Century Byzantine Psalters." *Byzantinische Zeitschrift* 99.1 (2006): 93–108, with 12 figs. on pls. VII–XII.

Farrar, F. W. *Eternal Hope: Five Sermons Preached in Westminster Abbey, November and December, 1877*. New York: E.P. Dutton, 1878.

Fattal, Antoine. *Le statut légal des non-musulmans en pays d'Islam*. Beirut: Imprimerie Catholique, 1958.

Feldman, Seymour. "The End of the Universe in Medieval Jewish Philosophy." *AJS Review* 11.1 (Spring 1986): 53–77.

Felton, D. *Haunted Greece and Rome: Ghost Stories from Classical Antiquity*. Austin: University of Texas Press, 1999.

Finucane, R. C. *Appearances of the Dead: A Cultural History of Ghosts*. Buffalo, NY: Prometheus Books, 1984.

Fitzgerald, William. *Slavery and the Roman Literary Imagination*. Cambridge: Cambridge University Press, 2000.

Fouracre, Paul. *The Age of Charles Martel*. Harlow, Eng.: Longman, 2000.

Fouracre, Paul, and Richard Gerberding. *Late Merovingian France*. Manchester, UK, and New York: Manchester University Press, 1996.

Fox, Samuel J. *Hell in Jewish Literature*. Northbrook, IL: Merrimack College Press, 1972.

Frazer, Margaret English. "Hades Stabbed by the Cross of Christ." *Metropolitan Museum Journal* 9 (1974): 153–61.

Fredrickson, Paula, and Oded Irshai. "Christian Anti-Judaism: Polemics and Policies." In *The Cambridge History of Judaism*, 4:977–1034. Cambridge: Cambridge University Press, 2008.

Freidenreich, David M. "The Food of the Damned." In *Between Heaven and Hell: Islam, Salvation, and the Fate of Others*, ed. Mohammad Hassan Khalil, 255–72. Oxford: Oxford University Press, 2013.

Friedmann, Richard Elliott. *Who Wrote the Bible?* Englewood Cliffs, NJ: Prentice Hall, 1987.

Friedmann, Yohanan. "Classification of Unbelievers in Sunnī Muslim Law and Tradition." *Jerusalem Studies in Arabic and Islam* 22 (1998): 163–95.

Gagarin, Michael. "The Torture of Slaves in Athenian Law." *Classical Philology* 91.1 (January 1996): 1–18.

Gaillard, Louis. "Hildemar." *Dictionnaire de spiritualité*, vol. 7, pt. 1 (1969): 521–22.

Gaudel, A. "Les limbes." *Dictionnaire de théologie catholique 9* (Paris, 1926): 760–71.

Geary, Patrick J. *Before France and Germany.* New York: Oxford University Press, 1988.

——. "Exchange and Interaction between the Living and the Dead in Early Medieval Society." In *Living with the Dead in the Middle Ages*, 77–92. Ithaca, NY: Cornell University Press, 1994.

Gernet, Louis. "Sur l'exécution capitale." In *Droit et institutions en Grèce antique*, 174–211. Paris: Flammarion, 1983.

Gersh, Harry. *The Sacred Books of the Jews.* New York: Stein & Day, 1972.

Gilliot, Claude. "The Beginnings of Qur'ānic Exegesis." In *The Qur'ān: Formative Interpretation*, ed. Andrew Rippin, 1–28. Brookfield, VT: Ashgate, 1999.

Gilson, Etienne. *History of Christian Philosophy in the Middle Ages.* London: Sheed and Ward, 1955.

Ginzberg, Louis. *The Legends of the Jews.* 7 vols. 1913. Philadelphia: Jewish Publication Society of America, 1968.

Ginzburg, Carlo. *Ecstasies: Deciphering the Witches' Sabbath.* New York: Pantheon Books, 1991.

Glancy, Jennifer A. *Slavery in Early Christianity.* Oxford: Oxford University Press, 2002.

——. "Slaves and Slavery in the Matthean Parables." *Journal of Biblical Literature* 119.1 (Spring 2000): 67–90.

Glorieux, P. "Pour revaloriser Migne." *Mélanges de Science Religieuse 9* (1952), cahier supplémentaire.

Goldhizer, Ignaz. *Introduction to Islamic Theology and Law.* Trans. Andras Hamori and Ruth Hamori. 1910. Princeton, NJ: Princeton University Press, 1981.

——. "The Sabbath Institution in Islam." In *The Development of Islamic Ritual*, ed. Gerald Hawting, 33–47. 1900. Burlington, VT: Ashgate/Variorum, 2006.

Gounelle, Rémi. "L'enfer selon l'évangile de Nicodème." *Revue d'Histoire et de Philosophie Religieuses* 86.3 (July–September 2006): 313–33.

Graf, Arturo. *Miti, leggende e superstizioni del medio evo.* 1892–93. Milan: Mondadori, 1984.

Gray, Alyssa M. "Amoraim." In *Encyclopaedia Judaica*, 2:89a–95b. 2nd ed. Detroit: Macmillan, 2007.

Grierson, Philip. "Coinage in the Feudal Era." In *Il feudalesimo nell'alto medioevo*, 949–63. Settimane di Studio 47. Spoleto: Centro italiano di studi sull'alto Medioevo, 2000.

Griffel, Frank. *Al-Ghazali's Philosophical Theology.* New York: Oxford University Press, 2009.

Griffiths, J. Gwynn. *The Divine Verdict: A Study of Divine Judgement in the Ancient Religions.* Studies in the History of Religions (Supplements to *Numen*) 52. Leiden: Brill, 1991.

Gurevich, Aron. "The 'Divine Comedy,' before Dante." In *Medieval Popular Culture*, trans. by János Bak and Paul A. Hollingsworth, 104–52. Cambridge and Paris: Cambridge University Press and Maison des sciences de l'homme, 1988.

——. "The Individual and the Hereafter." In *Historical Anthropology of the Middle Ages*, 65–89. Chicago: University of Chicago Press, 1992.

——. *Medieval Popular Culture: Problems of Belief and Perception.* Trans. János Bak and Paul A. Hollingsworth. Cambridge and Paris: Cambridge University Press and Maison des Sciences de l'Homme, 1988.

Gwynne, Rosalind W. "Hell and Hellfire." In *Encyclopaedia of the Qur'ān*, ed. Jane Dammen McAuliffe, 2:214. Leiden: Brill, 2001–6.

Hafner, Wolfgang. *Der Basiliuskommentar zur "Regula S. Benedicti": ein Beitrag zur Autorenfrage karolingischer Regelkommentare.* Beiträge zur Geschichte des alten Mönchtums und des Benediktinerordens 23. Münster: Aschendorf, 1959.

Hagemann, Ludwig. "Die 'letzten Dinge' in der Sicht des Korans: Sterben und Weiterleben in islamischer Deutung." In *Unsterblichkeit und Eschatologie im Denken des Nikolaus von Kues*, ed. K. Kremer and K. Reinhardt, 119–38. Mitteilungen und Forschungsbeiträge der Cusanus-Gesellschaft 23. Trier: Paulinus-Verlag, 1996.

Halivni, David Weiss. *The Formation of the Babylonian Talmud.* Oxford: Oxford University Press, 2014.

Hamman, A. "Agapè." In *EEC*, 1:16.

Harries, Jill. *Law and Empire in Late Antiquity.* Cambridge: Cambridge University Press, 1999.

Hawthorne, Gerald. "A New English Translation of Melito's Pascal Homily." In *Current Issues in Biblical and Patristic Interpretation*, 145–75. Grand Rapids, MI: William B. Eerdmans, 1975.

Hendy, Michael F. *Studies in the Byzantine Monetary Economy, c. 300–1450.* Cambridge: Cambridge University Press, 1985.

Henrichs, Albert. "Hades." *OCD*, 661–62.

Herlihy, David. *Medieval Households.* Cambridge, MA: Harvard University Press, 1985.

Hermansen, Marcia. "Acts of Salvation: Agency, Others, and Prayer beyond the Grave in Islam." In *Between Heaven and Hell, Islam, Salvation, and the Fate of Others*, ed. Mohammad Hassan Khalil, 273–87. Oxford: Oxford University Press, 2013.

Herrin, Judith. *The Formation of Christendom.* Princeton, NJ: Princeton University Press, 1989.

Hezser, Catherine. *Jewish Slavery in Antiquity.* Oxford: Oxford University Press, 2006.

Hillgarth, Joscelin. "St. Julian of Toledo in the Middle Ages." *Journal of the Warburg and Courtauld Institutes* 21.1–2 (1958): 7–26.

Himmelfarb, Martha. *Tours of Hell: An Apocalyptic Form in Jewish and Christian Literature.* 1983. Philadelphia: Fortress Press, 1985.

Hoeck, J. M. "Stand und Aufgaben der Damaskenos-Forschung." *Orientalia Christiana Periodica* 17.1–2 (1951): 5–60.

Hoover, Jon. "Islamic Universalism: Ibn Qayyim al-Jawziyya's Salafī Deliberations on the Duration of Hell-Fire." *The Muslim World* 99.1 (2009): 181–201.

Horden, Peregrine, and Nicholas Purcell. *The Corrupting Sea: A Study of Mediterranean History.* Oxford: Blackwell, 2000.

Howard, Deborah. *Venice & the East: The Impact of the Islamic World on Venetian Architecture, 1100–1500.* New Haven, CT: Yale University Press, 2000.

Hudson, Benjamin. "Time Is Short: The Eschatology of the Early Gaelic Church." In *Last Things: Death and the Apocalypse in the Middle Ages*, ed. Caroline Walker Bynum and Paul Freedman, 101–23 and 301–30. Philadelphia: University of Pennsylvania Press, 2000.

Humbert, Michel. "La peine en droit romain." In *La peine/Punishment*, pt. 1, *Antiquity*, 133–83. Transactions of the Jean Bodin Society for Comparative Institutional History 55. Brussels: DeBoeck Université, 1991.

Hunter, Virginia J. *Policing Athens: Social Control in the Attic Lawsuits, 420–320 B.C.* Princeton, NJ: Princeton University Press, 1994.

Hutson, Lorna, ed. "Special Forum: Fifty Years of *The King's Two Bodies*." *Representations* 106 (Spring 2009): 63–142.

Izydorczyk, Zbigniew, ed. *The Medieval Gospel of Nicodemus: Texts, Intertexts, and Contexts in Western Europe*. Tempe, AZ: MRTS, 1997.

Jackson, Kenneth. "The Date of the Tripartite Life of St. Patrick." *Zeitschrift für celtische Philologie* 41 (1986): 5–45.

Jackson, Sherman A. *On the Boundaries of Theological Tolerance in Islam*. Oxford: Oxford University Press, 2002.

James, M. R. "The Rainer Fragment of the *Apocalypse of Peter*." *Journal of Theological Studies* 32 (1931): 270–79.

Jasnow, Richard. "New Kingdom." In *History of Ancient Near Eastern Law*, ed. Raymond Westbrook, 289–360. Boston: Brill, 2003.

Jeremias, Joachim. "Gehenna." *Theological Dictionary of the New Testament*, ed. Gerhard Kittel, 1:657–58. Grand Rapids, MI: Eerdmans, 1964.

——. "Hades." *Theological Dictionary of the New Testament*, ed. Gerhard Kittel, 1:146–49. Grand Rapids, MI: Eerdmans, 1964.

Johnston, Philip S. *Shades of Sheol: Death and Afterlife in the Old Testament*. Downers Grove, IL: InterVarsity Press, 2002.

Jones, A. H. M. *The Later Roman Empire*. 2 vols. Baltimore: Johns Hopkins University Press, 1986.

Jong, Mayke de. "Growing Up in a Carolingian Monastery: Magister Hildemar and His Oblates." *Journal of Medieval History* 9 (1983): 99–128.

Joseph, Morris. *Judaism as Creed and Life*. London: Macmillan, 1903.

Joshel, Sandra R. "Female Desire and the Discourse of Empire: Tacitus's Messalina." *Signs* 21.1 (Autumn 1995): 50–82.

——. *Slavery in the Roman World*. Cambridge: Cambridge University Press, 2010.

Jugie, Martin. "La doctrine des fins dernières dans l'église gréco-russe." *Échos d'Orient* 17 (1914): 5–22.

Kantorowicz, Ernst. *The King's Two Bodies: A Study in Mediaeval Political Theology*. Princeton, NJ: Princeton University Press, 1957.

——. *Laudes Regiae: A Study in Liturgical Acclamations and Mediaeval Ruler Worship*. Berkeley and Los Angeles: University of California Press, 1958.

Kartsonis, Anna. *Anastasis: The Making of an Image*. Princeton, NJ: Princeton University Press, 1986.

Kassis, Hanna E. *A Concordance of the Qur'an*. Berkeley: University of California Press, 1983.

Kelly, H. A. *Satan: A Biography*. Cambridge: Cambridge University Press, 2006.

Khalil, Mohammad Hassan. *Islam and the Fate of Others: The Salvation Question*. Oxford: Oxford University Press, 2012.

Khoury, Adel. *Toleranz im Islam.* Kaiser: Grünewald, 1980.

Kieval, Herman. "Barekhu." In *Encyclopaedia Judaica,* 3:149. 2nd ed. Detroit: Macmillan, 2007.

King, Charles. "The Living and the Dead: Ancient Roman Conceptions of the Afterlife." PhD diss., University of Chicago, 1998.

——. "The Organization of Roman Religious Beliefs." *Classical Antiquity* 22.2 (2003): 275–312.

——. "The Roman Manes: The Dead as Gods." In *Rethinking Ghosts in World Religions,* ed. MuChou Poo, 95–114. Leiden: Brill, 2009.

Kingsley, Peter. "The Greek Origin of the Sixth-Century Dating of Zoroaster." *Bulletin of the School of Oriental and African Studies, University of London* 53.2 (1990): 245–65.

Korn, Eugene. "Gentiles, the World to Come, and Judaism: The Odyssey of a Rabbinic Text." *Modern Judaism* 14 (1994): 265–87.

Koziol, Geoffrey. *Begging Pardon and Favor.* Ithaca, NY: Cornell University Press, 1992.

——. *The Politics of Memory and Identity in Carolingian Royal Diplomas.* Utrecht Studies in Medieval Literacy 28. Turnhout, Belgium: Brepols, 2011.

Kreiner, Jamie. *The Social Life of Hagiography in the Merovingian Kingdom,* Cambridge Studies in Medieval Life and Thought. Cambridge: Cambridge University Press, 2014.

Kyrtatas, Dimitris J. "The Origins of Christian Hell." *Numen* 56.2–3 (2009): 282–97.

Larmann, Marian. "*Contristare* and *Tristitia* in the RB: Indications of Community and Morale." *American Benedictine Review* 30 (1979): 159–74.

Lawrence, C. H. *Medieval Monasticism.* 2nd ed. 1984. London and New York: Longman, 1989.

Le Goff, Jacques. *The Birth of Purgatory.* Trans. Arthur Goldhammer. Chicago: University of Chicago Press, 1984.

——. *La naissance du purgatoire.* Paris: Gallimard. 1981.

——. "Les limbes." *Nouvelle Revue de Psychanalyse* 34 (1986): 151–73.

Le Jan, Régine. "La sacralité de la royauté mérovingienne." *Annales: Histoire, Sciences Sociales* 58 (2003): 1217–41.

Lincoln, Bruce. *Religion, Empire, and Torture.* Chicago: University of Chicago Press, 2010.

Loeb, Isidore. "La controverse de 1240 sur le Talmud." *Revue des Études Juives* 1 (1880): 247–61; 2 (1881): 248–70; 3 (1882): 39–57.

Loraux, Nicole. "Le corps étranglé." In *Du châtiment dans la cité: Supplices corporels et peine de mort dans le monde antique,* ed. Yan Thomas, 195–224. Collection de l'École Française de Rome 79. Rome: École française de Rome, 1984.

Lorton, David. "The Treatment of Criminals in Ancient Egypt: Through the New Kingdom." *Journal of the Economic and Social History of the Orient* 20.1 (1977): 2–64.

MacMullen, Ramsay. "Judicial Savagery in the Roman Empire." *Chiron* 16 (1986): 147–66.

Magdalino, Paul. "Court Society and Aristocracy." In *A Social History of Byzantium,* ed. John Haldon, 212–32. Oxford: Blackwell, 2009.

Martin, Dale B. *Slavery as Salvation: The Metaphor of Slavery in Pauline Christianity.* New Haven, CT, and London: Yale University Press, 1990.

Mathews, Thomas F. *The Clash of Gods: A Reinterpretation of Early Christian Art.* Revised and expanded ed. 1993. Princeton, NJ: Princeton University Press, 1999.

McCormick, Michael. *Origins of the European Economy: Communications and Commerce, AD 300–900.* Cambridge: Cambridge University Press, 2001.

McEleney, Neil J. "1–2 Maccabees." In *The New Jerome Bible Commentary,* 421–46. Englewood Cliffs, NJ: Prentice-Hall, 1990.

McKitterick, Rosamond. *The Frankish Kingdoms under the Carolingians.* London and New York: Longman, 1983.

Mégier, Elisabeth. "Deux exemples de 'prépurgatoire' chez les historiens." *Cahiers de Civilisation Médiévale* 28.1 (1985): 45–62.

Meyendorff, John. *Byzantine Theology.* New York: Fordham University Press, 1974.

——. "Justinian, the Empire and the Church." *Dumbarton Oaks Papers* 22 (1968): 43–60.

Miller, William Ian. *Eye for an Eye.* Cambridge: Cambridge University Press, 2006.

Moore, George Foot. *Judaism.* 2 vols. Cambridge, MA: Harvard University Press, 1950.

Morabia, Alfred. *Le gihad dans l'islam médiéval: Le 'combat sacré' des origines au XIIe siècle.* Paris: Albin Michel, 1993.

Moreira, Isabel. *Dreams, Visions, and Spiritual Authority in Merovingian Gaul.* Ithaca, NY, and London: Cornell University Press, 2000.

——. *Heaven's Purge: Purgatory in Late Antiquity.* Oxford: Oxford University Press, 2010.

Morelle, Laurent. "La mise en oeuvre des actes diplomatiques: L'*auctoritas* des chartes chez quelques historiographes monastiques (IXe–XIe siècle)." In *Auctor et auctoritas: Invention et conformisme dans l'écriture médiévale,* ed. Michel Zimmermann, 73–96. Paris: École des chartes, 2001.

Mortanges, Elke Pahud de. "Der versperrte Himmel: Das Phänomen der *sanctuaires à répit* aus theologiegeschichtlicher Perspektive." *Schweizerische Zeitschrift für Religions- und Kulturgeschichte* 98 (2004): 31–48.

Neusner, Jacob. "Response to Evan M. Zuesse." *Review of Rabbinic Judaism* 7 (2004): 230–46.

Newman, Barbara. "Hildegard of Bingen and the 'Birth of Purgatory'." *Mystics Quarterly* 19.3 (1993): 90–97.

Nicol, D. M. "Byzantine Political Thought." In *The Cambridge History of Medieval Political Thought, c. 350–c. 1450,* ed. J. H. Burns, 51–91. Cambridge: Cambridge University Press, 1988.

Noonan, John T. *Bribes.* New York: Macmillan, 1984.

Norris, Frederick W. "Greek Christianities." In *The Cambridge History of Christianity,* 2:70–117. Cambridge: Cambridge University Press, 2007.

Oelsner, Toni, and Henry Wasserman. "Slave Trade." In *Enyclopaedia Judaica,* 18:670–71. 2nd ed. Detroit: Macmillan, 2007.

Opitz, Hans-Georg. *Urkunden zur Geschichte des arianischen Streites.* In *Athanasius Werke,* 3.1, no. 33, pp. 66–68. Berlin: De Gruyter, 1935.

Owen, D. D. R. *The Vision of Hell.* Edinburgh & London: Scottish Academic Press, 1970.

Palacios, Asín. *La escatología musulmana en la Divina Comedia.* 4th ed. Madrid: Hiperión, 1984.

Patch, H. R. *The Other World, According to Descriptions in Medieval Literature.* Cambridge, MA: Harvard University Press, 1950.

Patrides, C. A. "The Salvation of Satan." *Journal of the History of Ideas* 28.4 (1967): 467–78.

Patterson, Orlando. *Slavery and Social Death*. Cambridge, MA: Harvard University Press, 1982.

Paxton, Frederick S. *Christianizing Death: The Creation of a Ritual Process in Early Medieval Europe*. Ithaca, NY: Cornell University Press, 1990.

Pazdernik, Charles. "'The Trembling of Cain': Religious Power and Institutional Culture in Justinianic Oath-Making." In *The Power of Religion in Late Antiquity*, ed. Andrew Cain and Noel Lenski, 143–54. Farnham, UK: Ashgate, 2009.

Pernot, Hubert. "La Descente de la Vierge aux enfers d'après les manuscrits grecs de Paris." *Revue des Études Grecques* 13 (1900): 233–57.

Pessin, Sarah. "Saadyah [Saadia]." In *The Stanford Encyclopedia of Philosophy*. Accessed February 27, 2014. http://plato.stanford.edu/entries/saadya/.

Pietrzik, Dominik. *Die Brandan-Legende*. Bremmer Beiträge zur Literatur- und Ideengeschichte 26. Frankfurt: Peter Lang, 1999.

Piovanelli, Pierluigi. "Les origines de l'*Apocalypse de Paul* reconsidérées." *Apocrypha* 4 (1993): 25–64.

——. "Le texte originel de l'*Apocalypse de Paul*: Problèmes de datation." *Bulletin de l'AELAC (Association pour l'Étude de la Littérature Apocryphe Chrétienne)* 3 (1993): 25–27.

Plaut, W. Gunther, ed. *The Torah: A Modern Commentary*. New York: UAHC, 1981.

Podskalsky, Gerhard. "Politische Theologie in Byzanz zwischen Reichseschatolotogie und Reichsideologie." In *Cristianità d'occidente e cristianità d'oriente (secoli vi–xi)*, 1421–33. Settimane di Studio della Fondazione Centro Italiano di Studi sull'Alto Medioevo 51. Spoleto: Presso la sede della Fondazione, 2004.

Poo, MuChou, ed. *Rethinking Ghosts in World Religions*. Leiden: Brill, 2009.

Price, Richard, trans. *Acts of the Council of Constantinople of 553*. 2 vols. Translated Texts for Historians 51. Liverpool: Liverpool University Press, 2009.

Prinz, Friedrich. *Frühes Mönchtum im Frankenreich*. Vienna: Oldenberg, 1965.

Procopé, John. "Greek and Roman Political Theory." In *The Cambridge History of Medieval Political Thought*, 21–36. Cambridge: Cambridge University Press, 1988.

Quasten, Johannes. *Patrology*. 4 vols. 1950–60. Westminster, MD: Christian Classics, 1986.

Rankin, Oliver Shaw. *Israel's Wisdom Literature*. 1936. New York: Schocken, 1969.

Raphael, Simcha Paull. *Jewish Views of the Afterlife*. 1994. Lanham, MD: Rowman & Littlefield, 2004.

Rebillard, Éric. *In Hora Mortis: Évolution de la pastorale chrétienne de la mort aux IVᵉ et Vᵉ siècles*. Bibliothèque des Écoles Françaises d'Athènes et de Rome 283. Paris: Boccard, 1994.

Reboul, Olivier. *La rhétorique*. 3rd ed. Que sais-je? 2133. Paris: Presses universitaires de France, 1990.

Ritter, Adolf Martin. "Church and State up to c. 300 CE." In *The Cambridge History of Christianity*, 1:524–37. Cambridge: Cambridge University Press, 2006.

Roddy, Kevin. "Politics and Religion in Late Antiquity: The Roman Imperial *Adventus* Ceremony and the Christian Myth of the Harrowing of Hell." *Apocrypha* 11 (2000): 147–79.

Rose, Herbert Jennings, and Karim W. Arafat. "Laocoön." *OCD*, 814b.

Rosenthal, Judah M. "The Talmud on Trial: The Disputation at Paris in the Year 1240." *Jewish Quarterly Review* 47 (1956–57): 58–76, 145–69.

Rostovtzeff, Michael. *Caravan Cities*. New York: AMS Press, 1971.

Rubenstein, Jeffrey L. Introduction to David Weiss Halivni, *The Formation of the Babylonian Talmud*, xvii-xxx. Oxford: Oxford University Press, 2014.

Rubin, Uri. "Abū Lahab and Sūra CXI." *Bulletin of the School of Oriental and African Studies* 42.1 (1979): 13–28.

Rüpke, Jörg. "You Shall Not Kill: Hierarchies of Norms in Ancient Rome." *Numen* 39.1 (1992): 58–79.

Rustomji, Nerina. *The Garden and the Fire: Heaven and Hell in Islamic Culture*. New York: Columbia University Press, 2008.

Sarris, Peter. "Social Relations and the Land: The Early Period." In *The Social History of Byzantium*, ed. John Haldon, 92–111. Chichester, UK: Wiley-Blackwell, 2009.

Savage, Elizabeth. *A Gateway to Hell, a Gateway to Paradise: The North African Response to the Arab Conquest*. Studies in Late Antiquity and Early Islam 7. Princeton, NJ: Darwin Press, 1997.

Schäufele, Wolf-Friedrich. "Die Höllen der Alexandriner: Negative Jenseitsvorstellungen im frühchristlichen Ägypten." *Zeitschrift für Kirchengeschichte* 117.2–3 (2006): 197–210.

Schneider, Irene "Freedom and Slavery in Early Islamic Times (1st/7th and 2nd/8th Centuries)." *Al-Qanṭara* 28.2 (July–December 2007): 353–82.

Schrieke, B., and J. Horovitz. "Mi'rādj." In *Encyclopaedia of Islam*, ed. P. Bearman, T. Bianquis, C. E. Bosworth, E. van Donzel, and W. P. Heinrichs, 7:97, col 2. 2nd ed. Leiden: Brill, 2003.

Schumacher, Leonhard. *Sklaverei in der Antike: Alltag und Schicksal der Unfreien*. Munich: Beck, 2001.

Schürer, Markus. "Das Beispiel im Begriff. Aspekte einer begriffsgeschichtlichen Erschliessung exemplarischen Erzählens im Mittelalter." *Mittellateinisches Jahrbuch* 38.1 (2003): 199–237.

Seeburger, Francis F. "Humility, Maturity, and the Fear of God: Reflections on RB 7." *American Benedictine Review* 46.2 (1995): 149–68.

Sells, Michael. "Ascension." In *Encyclopaedia of the Qur'ān*, ed. Jane Dammen McAuliffe, 1:176. Leiden: Brill, 2001.

Shaked, Shaul. *Dualism in Transformation: Varieties of Religion in Sasanian Iran*. Jordan Lectures 1991. University of London: School of Oriental and African Studies, 1994.

——. "Iranian Influence on Judaism." In *The Cambridge History of Judaism*, 1:308–25. Cambridge: Cambridge University Press, 1984.

Shanzer, Danuta. Review of *Heaven's Purge*, by Isabel Moreira. *History of Religions* 53.4 (May 2014): 401–5.

——. "Voices and Bodies: The Afterlife of the Unborn." *Numen* 56 (2009): 326–65.

Shemesh, Yael. "Punishment of the Offending Organ." *Novum Testamentum* 55.3 (July 2005): 343–65.

Sherwin-White. A. N., and A. H. M. Jones. "Decuriones." *OCD*, 437–38.

Silverstein, Theodore. "The Date of the 'Apocalypse of Paul'." *Mediaeval Studies* 24 (1962): 335–48.

——. "The Vision of Saint Paul: New Links and Patterns in the Western Traditions." *Archives d'Histoire Doctrinale et Littéraire du Moyen Age* 26 (1959): 199–248.

Smith, Jane Idleman, and Yvonne Yazbeck Haddad. *Islamic Understanding of Death and Resurrection*. Albany: SUNY Press, 1981.

Smith, Katherine Allen. *War and the Making of Medieval Monastic Culture*. Woodbridge, UK: Boydell Press, 2011.

Smith, Margaret. *Readings from the Mystics of Islam*. London: Luzac, 1972.

Smyth, Marina. "The Origins of Purgatory through the Lens of Seventh-Century Irish Eschatology." *Traditio* 58 (2003): 91–132.

Southern, Richard W. "Between Heaven and Hell." *Times Literary Supplement*, no. 4133 (June 18, 1982): 651–52.

Sperber, Daniel. "Tanna, Tannaim." In *Encyclopaedia Judaica*, 19:505a–507b. 2nd ed. Detroit: Macmillan, 2007.

Spieser, J.-M. "The Representation of Christ in the Apses of Early Christian Churches." *Gesta* 37.1 (1998): 63–73.

Stausberg, Michael. "Hell in Zoroastrian History." *Numen* 56 (2009): 217–53.

Steinsaltz, Adin. *The Essential Talmud*. New York: Bantam Books, 1976.

Straw, Carole. Review of *The Pseudo-Gregorian Dialogues*, by Francis Clark. *Speculum* 64 (1989): 397–99.

——. "Settling Scores: Eschatology in the Church of the Martyrs." In *Last Things: Death and the Apocalypse in the Middle Ages*, ed. Caroline Walker Bynum and Paul Freedman, 21–40. Philadelphia: University of Pennsylvania Press, 2000.

TeSelle, Eugene, and Daniel Patte. "Universalism." *Cambridge Dictionary of Christianity*, ed. Daniel Patte, 1278. Cambridge: Cambridge University Press, 2010.

Theis, Laurent. *Dagobert: Un roi pour un peuple*. Paris: Fayard, 1982.

Thomas, Yan. "Citoyens et résidents dans les cités de l'Empire romain: Essai sur le droit d'origine." In *Identité et droit de l'autre*, ed. Laurent Mayali, 1–56. Studies in Comparative Legal History. Berkeley: The Robbins Religious and Civil Law Collection, 1994.

——. "The Division of the Sexes in Roman Law." In *A History of Women in the West*, 1:83–137. Cambridge, MA, and London: The Belknap Press of Harvard University Press, 1992.

Thomassen, Einar. "Islamic Hell." *Numen* 56 (2009): 401–16.

Thompson, Stith, and Antti Aarne. *Motif-Index of Folk-Literature: A Classification of Narrative Elements in Folktales, Ballads, Myths*. Revised and enlarged ed. 6 vols. Bloomington: Indiana University Press, 1955–58.

Thür, Gerhard. "Reply to D. C. Mirhady: Torture and Rhetoric in Athens." *Journal of Hellenic Studies* 116 (1996): 132–43.

Tkacz, Catherine Brown. "*Labor Tam Utilis*: The Creation of the Vulgate." *Vigiliae Christianae* 50 (1996): 42–72.

Townsend, John T. "1 Corinthians 3:15 and the School of Shammai." *Harvard Theological Review* 61.3 (July 1968): 500–504.

Trumbower, Jeffrey A. *Rescue for the Dead: The Posthumous Salvation of Non-Christians in Early Christianity*. Oxford Studies in Historical Theology. Oxford: Oxford University Press, 2001.

Turner, Alice K., and Anne L. Stainton. "The Golden Age of Hell." *Art & Antiques*, January 1991, 46–57.

Uther, Hans-Jörg. *The Types of International Folktales: A Classification and Bibliography, Based on the System of Antti Aarne and Stith Thompson.* Helsinki: Suomalainen Tiedeakatemia, Academia Scientiarum Fennica, 2004.

Vaihlé, Simone. "Michel le Sincelle." *Revue de l'Orient Chrétien* 6 (1901): 313–32 and 610–42.

Verhulst, Adriaan. *The Carolingian Economy.* Cambridge: Cambridge University Press, 2002.

VerSteeg, Russ. *Early Mesopotamian Law.* Durham, NC: Carolina Academic Press, 2000.

Vetus Latina Database. Turnhout, Belgium: Brepols.

von Grunebaum, G. E. *Muhammadan Festivals.* London: Curzon Press, 1988.

Vorgrimler, Herbert. *Geschichte der Hölle.* Munich: Wilhelm Fink, 1993.

Vriezen, T. C., and A. S. van der Woude. *Ancient Israelite and Early Jewish Literature.* Trans. Brian Doyle. 2000. Leiden: Brill, 2005.

Walker, D. P. *The Decline of Hell: Seventeenth-Century Discussions of Eternal Torment.* Chicago: University of Chicago Press, 1964.

Wansbrough, John. *Quranic Studies: Sources and Methods of Scriptural Interpretation.* London Oriental Studies 31. Oxford: Oxford University Press, 1977.

Ward, Benedicta, ed. *Sayings of the Desert Fathers: The Alphabetical Collection.* Cistercian Studies 59. Oxford: Mowbrays, 1975.

Watson, Alan. *Roman Slave Law.* Baltimore: Johns Hopkins University Press, 1987.

Watt, William Montgomery. *Islamic Creeds: A Selection.* Edinburgh: Edinburgh University Press, 1994.

Wemple, Suzanne Fonay. *Women in Frankish Society: Marriage and the Cloister, 500–900.* Philadelphia: University of Pennsylvania Press, 1981.

Westbrook, Raymond. *A History of Ancient Near Eastern Law.* Leiden: Brill, 2003.

———. "What Is the Covenant Code?" In *Theory and Method in Biblical and Cuneiform Law,* ed. Bernard M. Levinson, 15–36. Sheffield, UK: Sheffield Academic Press, 1994.

Whatley, Gordon. "The Uses of Hagiography: The Legend of Pope Gregory and the Emperor Trajan in the Middle Ages." *Viator* 15 (1984): 25–63.

Wheeler, Brannon M. *Prophets in the Quran: An Introduction to the Quran and Muslim Exegesis.* Comparative Islamic Studies. London: Continuum, 2002.

Whelan, Estelle. "Forgotten Witness: Evidence for the Early Codification of the Qur'ān." *Journal of the American Oriental Society* 118.1 (1998): 1–14.

Whortley, John. "Death, Judgment, Heaven, and Hell in Byzantine 'Beneficial Tales'." *Dumbarton Oaks Papers* 55 (2001): 53–69.

Wiedemann, Thomas. *Greek and Roman Slavery.* London: Taylor and Francis, 1981.

Wittenberg, Gunther H. "Legislating for Justice: The Social Legislation of the Covenant Code and Deuteronomy." *Scriptura* 54 (1995): 215–28.

Witthöft, Harald. "Die Rechnung und Zahlung mit Gold und Silber nach Zeugnissen des 6. bis 9. und 13./14. Jahrhunderts." *Hamburger Beiträge zur Numismatik* 32 (1978): 9–36.

Zaleski, Carol. *Otherworld Journeys: Accounts of Near-Death Experience in Medieval and Modern Times.* New York: Oxford University Press, 1987.

Zeitlin, Solomon. "The Origin of the Pharisees Reaffirmed." *Jewish Quarterly Review,* n.s., 59 (April 1969): 255–67.

Zelzer, Klaus. "Überlegungen zu einer Gesamtedition des frühnachkarolingischen Kommentars zur Regula S. Benedicti aus der Tradition des Hildemar von Corbie." *Revue Bénédictine* 91.3–4 (1981): 373–82.

———. "Von Benedikt zu Hildemar: Die Regula Benedicti auf dem Weg zur Alleingeltung im Blickfeld der Textgeschichte." *Regulae Benedicti Studia* 16 (1987): 1–22.

———. "Von Benedikt zu Hildemar: Zu Textgestalt und Textgeschichte der Regula Benedicti auf ihrem Weg zur Alleingeltung." *Frühmittelalterliche Studien* 23 (1989): 112–30.

Ziegler, Ignaz. *Die Königsgleichnisse des Midrasch beleuchtet durch die römische Kaiserzeit*. Breslau: Schottlaender, 1903.

Zuesse, Evan M. "Jacob Neusner and the Rabbinic Treatment of the 'Other'." *Review of Rabbinic Judaism* 7 (2004): 191–229.

INDEX

abortion, postmortem punishment for, 102, 104, 108, 300

Abraham: Bosom of, 21, 50, 51, 52, 164, 228; descent from, 263, 320; intercession by, *333*; in visions, 209

Abrahamic religions: idea of hell in, vii, 1–3, 27–28, 319–20, 355; mitigation of hell in, movement toward, 251, 265; shared aspects of eschatology in, 1–3, 4, 29, 280–81, 330, 341, 353–54; shared cultural legacies of, 11–12, 281, 340–41; slavery in, 130–32

Abū Lahab, 324, 339

acedia (listlessness), 76–77, 83, 92

adultery: postmortem punishment of, 102, 306, 307, 354; Roman law on, 317

Aethelbald (King of Murcia), 225–26, 228

Akiba, Rabbi, 244, 265

Alcuin of York, 185, 188–92

Aldfrid (King of Northumbria), 212, 216, 227

Alfalak (fire of hell), 345, 347

al-Ghazali, 336–44

amaritudo (bitterness), 83–84, 87–88, 92

amnesty. *See* Easter amnesty

angels: fallen, punishment of, 60, 112; guardian, in visions, 201, 202, 203, 205; in Qur'ānic hell, 323, 324, 325, 346; rebel, biblical texts on, 26, 224; rebellion of, archetypal theme of, 11–12; sinning, in Christian Bible, 26; tormenting, in hell, 103, 109, 110, 237, 309; in visions, 202, 204, 205, 206, 207–9, 212, 221–24

Ansellus Scholasticus, 160

Apocalypse of Mary, 144–46, 306–11, 354; on relief in hell, 144–46, 306, 310; on torments of hell, 145, 306–10

Apocalypse of Paul, 101, 105–11, 207, 353; and *Apocalypse of Mary,* 146, 234, 306, 307, 308, 310; lower hell in, 107, 109, 115–16, 139; on relief in hell, 139–41, 166, 218, 238–39, 264, 265, 339; Roman justice system as model for, 115–16, 130; on torments of hell, 107–11, 115–16, 173–74, 233, 236–38, 309, 354

Apocalypse of Peter, 101–5, 353; *Apocalypse of Paul* and, 107–8, 109, 110; on escape from hell, 149–50, 152, 158, 166; model for, 130; on torments of hell, 102–4, 236, 237, 354

Arberry, A. J., 320n1, 323, 327

Ardā Wirāz Nāmag, 7, 225, 309, 310, 354

Athens, penal system of, 112–14, 116

Augustine of Hippo, 27, 63, 68, 116, 128, 179, 189, 217; *City of God,* 137, 173, 174, 177, 189, 268; on conscience, suffering of, 69; on constructive fear, 88; on damnation as exile from God, 116, 194; on damnation of unbaptized infants, 157; on divine punishment in life, 269–70; on division of Hades, 27, 50; *Enchiridion,* 18–19, 42, 131, 142, 174, 175, 177, 183, 189, 213, 229; on human institutions and postmortem punishment, 134; on inner death, 83, 97; on interim, 18–19; against Origen, 106; on probative fire, 331; on purgatorial punishments, 174–75; on relief in hell, 138, 139; on second death, 70; on trial of the heart, 174; visions' departure from, 212, 213, 229; on wicked people vs. sinners, 183

Babylonia: capital punishment in, 111; Jewish community in, 267

Babylonian Talmud, 246–67, 255; functions of Gehinnom in, 231; on world to come, exclusion from, 249

Basil the Great, 234, 286

beast(s): biblical worm as, 74–75; in Egyptian view of afterlife, 5; hell as, 143, 274–75, 349; postmortem punishments by, 103, 104, 108, 109–10, 307, 308–9; in Roman justice, 124, 149

Bede: Advent sermon of, 181–82, 185, 191, 217; Alcuin of York and, 185, 188, 190; *Commentary on the Book of Proverbs,* 182–83, 191, 217; on Fursey, 202, 204; on gradation of sins/punishments, 182–86,

www.ingramcontent.com/pod-product-compliance
Lightning Source LLC
Chambersburg PA
CBHW021153160426

42812CB00082B/2887/J